About TechComm Web
<bedfordstmartins.com/techcomm>

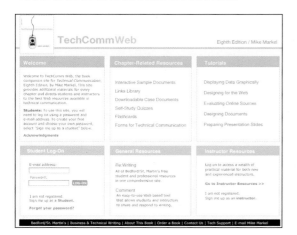

Technical Communication, Eighth Edition, and its companion Web site, TechComm Web <bedfordstmartins.com/techcomm>, are designed to work together. *On TechComm Web* labels in the margins of the book direct you to a variety of useful resources on the site:

Interactive Sample Documents. Students can type in their responses, e-mail their responses to themselves and their instructor, and get instant feedback in the form of suggested answers.

Links Library. This annotated list contains hundreds of links to samples in the text showing models in their original context, additional sample documents online, and other Web sources for every chapter.

Downloadable Case Docs. Students can download and modify documents for the new cases in the text.

Self-Study Quizzes and **Flashcards.** These tools provide immediate feedback that can help students reinforce and test their understanding of the material covered in each chapter.

Forms for Technical Communication. Students can download the forms for collaboration covered in Chapter 4, along with forms for analyzing an audience and evaluating oral presentations, and adapt them to fit their individual needs.

Tutorials. Online tutorials on preparing effective charts and graphs, evaluating electronic sources, creating presentation graphics, using basic document design functions, and designing Web sites provide guidance for dealing with common technical-communication challenges.

To learn more about Re:Writing, Comment, and the instructor resources available on this site, visit <bedfordstmartins.com/techcomm>.

EIGHTH EDITION

Technical Communication

Mike Markel

Boise State University

Bedford/St. Martin's   Boston ◆ New York

For Bedford/St. Martin's

Developmental Editor: Sara Eaton Gaunt
Editorial Assistant: Joanna Lee
Production Supervisor: Jennifer Wetzel
Marketing Manager: Karita dos Santos
Text Design: Claire Seng-Niemoeller/Anna Palchik
Project Management: Books By Design, Inc.
Cover Design: Donna L. Dennison
Cover Art: *X-ray of a Computer Mouse.* Stockbyte/Getty Images.
Composition: Techbooks/GTS Educational Publishing Group
Printing and Binding: RR Donnelley & Sons, Inc.

President: Joan E. Feinberg
Editorial Director: Denise B. Wydra
Editor in Chief: Karen S. Henry
Director of Marketing: Karen Melton Soeltz
Director of Editing, Design, and Production: Marcia Cohen
Manager, Publishing Services: Emily Berleth

Library of Congress Control Number: 2005935043

Manufactured in the United States of America.

2   1   0   9   8   7
f   e   d   c   b   a

For information, write: Bedford/St. Martin's, 75 Arlington Street, Boston, MA 02116   (617-399-4000)

ISBN-10: 0-312-44197-5
ISBN-13: 978-0-312-44197-5

Acknowledgments

Page 8: Courtesy of Xerox Corporation.

Figure 1.1: Reprinted with the permission of Netflix, Inc. All rights reserved.

Page 12: Copyright © 2005 by Dell, Inc. All Rights Reserved.

Figure 2.1: Reprinted with the permission of NSI International, Inc.

Figure 2.2: Reprinted by permission of Texas Instruments Inc.

Page 25: Reprinted with the permission of the Institute for Electronics and Electrical Engineering, Inc.

Acknowledgments and copyrights are continued at the back of the book on pages 681–82, which constitute an extension of the copyright page.

Preface for Instructors

The principles of good technical communication do not change, and *Technical Communication* remains a thorough, accessible introduction to planning, drafting, and designing technical documents. This text continues to offer well-designed, student-friendly coverage of rhetorical, visual, and cross-cultural concerns. I have tried to make this new edition reflect the many exciting developments that have occurred in technical communication—and in ways to teach it—in the past few years. Most prominent among these developments are the greatly expanded importance of electronic communication tools and the increased emphasis on ethics. The eighth edition takes a multidisciplinary approach, keeping pace with current technologies and the realities of technical communication today. It also makes more explicit connections between technical communication in the academy and technical communication in the workplace.

New Features

The eighth edition introduces several new features that show the effects of new technologies on the way people produce technical communication and communicate with one another.

- **Tech Comm at Work** discussions in every chapter introduce students to the real-world applications of technical communication in a wide variety of professions.
- **Ethics Notes**—on issues such as writing honest job-application materials, protecting readers' safety, and presenting honest recommendations—bring increased attention to the ethical considerations and implications of technical communication.
- **Tech Tips** for using basic software tools give students step-by-step, illustrated instructions on topics such as tracking changes, creating graphics, and modifying templates.
- **All new interactive cases** present real-world writing scenarios—such as designing a report template, identifying transferable skills for a career change, and revising an injury report form—and are built around common workplace documents that students can critique, download, and revise in context.

Expanded Coverage

While developing the eighth edition, I reexamined every chapter and relied on the input of fellow technical-communication instructors to inform my decisions about revising the text. Thus, in addition to new features, the book's coverage has been expanded in the following key areas to reflect a wider range of technical documents and new methods of developing them.

Chapter	What's new
Chapter 1: Introduction to Technical Communication	an expanded discussion of the collaboration between technical communicators and technical professionals
Chapter 2: Understanding Ethical and Legal Considerations	an expanded discussion of the relationship between the legal issue of copyright violation and the academic issue of plagiarism
Chapter 3: Understanding the Writing Process	an explanation of the differences between revising and editing
Chapter 4: Writing Collaboratively	a new discussion to help students understand the differences between how academic and workplace writers collaborate new advice on listening effectively
Chapter 5: Analyzing Your Audience and Purpose	a new discussion of repurposing text for a new audience and purpose
Chapter 6: Researching Your Subject	a new discussion to help students understand the differences between how academic and workplace writers conduct research new guidelines for choosing a research method, presenting questionnaire data, and conducting observations and demonstrations
Chapter 7: Organizing Your Information	a new discussion of how to select an appropriate organizational pattern for the kind of argument you wish to present
Chapter 8: Communicating Persuasively	a new discussion of appealing to emotions and a sample white paper
Chapter 10: Writing Coherent Documents	a new discussion of using design elements to enhance the coherence of a document
Chapter 13: Creating Graphics	a new discussion of deployment flowcharts
Chapter 14: Writing Letters, Memos, and E-mails	a discussion of considering the desired level of formality in selecting the type of business correspondence to write
Chapter 15: Preparing Job-Application Materials	a new discussion of the "summary of qualifications"

Chapter 16: Writing Proposals	a new sample proposal
Chapter 17: Writing Informal Reports	a new sample progress report
Chapter 18: Writing Formal Reports	a new sample formal report
	the discussions of front and back matter now in this chapter
Chapter 19: Writing Instructions and Manuals	new discussions of designing, revising, editing, proofreading, and drafting titles for instructions
	the discussion of usability now in this chapter
Chapter 20: Designing Web Sites	new discussions of how to chunk text in Web pages and the ethics of copying site designs
Chapter 21: Making Oral Presentations	new discussions of organizing information for a presentation and introducing and concluding the presentation
Appendix: Reference Handbook	more documentation models and visual documentation guidelines for extra help with identifying and citing information
	a discussion, addressed to nonnative speakers of English in the United States, about cultural and stylistic issues
	expanded style and grammar guidelines for ESL students

Enhanced Companion Web Site

The TechComm Web site at <bedfordstmartins.com/techcomm> offers numerous comprehensive resources for students and instructors. These resources are fully integrated into the text via cross-references in the margins of the book. Interactive Sample Documents, links to additional resources, flashcards, and revised self-study quizzes reinforce students' understanding of the chapters. Online tutorials on evaluating online sources, creating presentation graphics, using basic document design functions, designing Web sites, and creating effective graphs and charts guide students through some of their most common communication challenges. Instructors can find everything from additional exercises and cases to sample syllabi, in-class activities, PowerPoint slides that can be adapted for classroom use, and password-protected reading quizzes to download and distribute to students. In addition, TechComm Web offers teaching topics: "Making the Transition from Composition to Technical Communication," "Integrating Technology," "Using *Technical Communication* in Distance Courses," "Addressing Plagiarism," and "Including Service Learning in the Tech-Comm Course." The *Instructor's Resource Manual*, which includes a chapter-by-chapter teaching guide and advice for using the text and its companion Web site together, can be downloaded from TechComm Web.

Acknowledgments

All the examples in the book—from single sentences to complete documents—are real. Some were written by my students at Boise State University. Some were written by engineers, scientists, health-care providers, and businesspersons with whom I have worked as a consultant for more than 30 years. Because much of the information in these documents is proprietary, I have silently changed brand names and other identifying information. I thank the dozens of individuals—students and professionals alike—who have graciously allowed me to reprint their writing. They have been my best teachers.

The eighth edition of *Technical Communication* has benefited greatly from the perceptive observations and helpful suggestions of my fellow instructors throughout the country. Some completed extensive questionnaires about the previous edition; others reviewed the current edition in its draft form. I thank Teresa Aggen, Pikes Peak Community College; Russell Barrett, Blinn College; LynnDianne Beene, University of New Mexico; Joey R. Brown, Missouri Southern State University; Marcy Carbajal, Santa Fe Community College; Leena Chakrabarti, Kansas State University; Mark Crane, Utah Valley State College; Rosemary Day, Albuquerque Technical Vocational Institute; Sheri Ann Denison, University of Alaska Anchorage; Gene Doty, University of Missouri–Rolla; Douglas Downs, Utah Valley State College; Elizabeth A. Frick, Washington University; Mary H. Garbacz, University of Nebraska–Lincoln; Clark Germann, Metropolitan State College of Denver; Angela M. Gulick, Parkland College; Lisa C. Hastings, Delaware Technical & Community College; Amanda E. Himes, Texas A&M University; Jonathan Himes, John Brown University; Trena Houp, University of Florida; Karen E. Kasonic, University of Washington; Vikki L. Kestell, University of New Mexico; Miles A. Kimball, Texas Tech University; Liz Kleinfeld, Red Rocks Community College; Michael Knievel, University of Wyoming; Barbara L'Eplattenier, University of Arkansas at Little Rock; Paul Madachy, University of Maryland College Park; Andrew J. McCann, Drexel University; Becky Jo McShane, Weber State University; Denise Nemec, Northwest Arkansas Community College; Kathryn E. O'Donnell, Metropolitan State College of Denver; Neil Plakcy, Broward Community College; Marcella Parry Reekie, Kansas State University; Jane M. Schreck, Bismarck State College; Jennifer Sutter, Pikes Peak Community College; Debbie Sydow, Syracuse University; Alexander Thayer, University of Washington; Anthea Tillyer, City College of New York; Janice R. Walker, Georgia Southern University; Scott Warnock, Drexel University; Maria W. Warren, University of West Florida.

I also thank the following instructors who contributed their insights and suggestions for the TechComm Web site: Janice Cooke, University of New Orleans; Dawn L. Elmore-McCrary, San Antonio College; Sandi J. Hubnik, University of Texas at Arlington; Michael Knievel, University of Wyoming; Thomas Long, Thomas Nelson Community College; John Rothfork, North

Arizona University; Alan Sevison, Brigham Young University; Kristi Siegel, Mount Mary College; Clay Kinchen Smith, Santa Fe Community College.

I would like to acknowledge three colleagues from Boise State University. Kevin Wilson wrote many of the questions used in the self-study quizzes, as well as many of the classroom activities. John Battalio contributed many new questions for the self-study quizzes, as well as several of the teaching topics and tutorials. Roger Munger has made many excellent contributions. Roger contributed self-study quiz questions, teaching topics, tutorials, the Tech Tips, and the new end-of-chapter cases. In addition, he wrote additional Interactive Sample Documents for TechComm Web. Kevin, John, and Roger have made the book and the companion Web site much stronger, and I greatly appreciate their expertise and hard work.

I have been fortunate, too, to work with a terrific team at Bedford/St. Martin's, led by Sara Eaton Gaunt, an editor of remarkable intelligence and energy. Sara has helped me better the text in many big and small ways. She is responsible for the book's much-improved treatment of intercultural communication, ethics, and the writing process. She is also responsible for many improvements in the organization and development of the chapters.

I also want to express my appreciation to Joan Feinberg, Denise Wydra, Karen Henry, and Leasa Burton for assembling the first-class team that has worked so hard on this edition, including Emily Berleth, Caroline Thompson, Joanna Lee, Tari Fanderclai, and Nancy Benjamin of Books By Design. For me, Bedford/St. Martin's continues to exemplify the highest standards of professionalism in publishing. They have been endlessly encouraging and helpful. I hope they realize the value of their contributions to this book.

My greatest debt, however, is, as always, to my wife, Rita, who over the course of many months and, now, eight editions, has helped me say what I mean.

A Final Word

I am more aware than ever before of how much I learn from my students, my fellow instructors, and my colleagues in industry and academia. If you have comments or suggestions for making this a better book, please get in touch with me at the Department of English at Boise State University, Boise, ID 83725. My phone number is (208) 426-3088, or you can send me an e-mail from the companion Web site: <bedfordstmartins.com/techcomm>. I hope to hear from you.

Mike Markel

Introduction for Writers

The eighth edition is organized into six parts, highlighting the importance of the writing process in technical communication and giving equal weight to the development of text and graphics in a document.

Part	Coverage
Part One: The Technical-Communication Environment	provides a basic understanding of important topics in technical communication, including ethical and legal considerations, the role of the writing process in planning and developing technical documents, and the practice of collaborating on documents
Part Two: Planning the Document	focuses on rhetorical concerns, such as considering audience and purpose, gathering information through primary and secondary research, and planning the organization of documents
Part Three: Developing the Textual Elements	encompasses both drafting and revising text in a document
	describes communicating persuasively, writing definitions and descriptions, improving the coherence of text, and improving sentence style
Part Four: Developing the Visual Elements	addresses the fundamentals of designing the whole document as well as the individual page
	includes advice on creating graphics for both print and online documents
Part Five: Applications	covers a wide range of types of technical communication: letters, memos, and e-mails; job-application materials, including print and electronic résumés; proposals; informal reports, such as progress and status reports, incident reports, and meeting minutes; formal reports, including informational, analytical, and recommendation reports; instructions and manuals; Web sites; and oral presentations
Appendix: Reference Handbook	offers additional help with skimming sources and taking notes; documenting sources using APA, CSE, and MLA styles; and editing and proofreading documents
	provides multilingual writers with advice on cultural, stylistic, and sentence-level communication issues

Technical Communication offers a wealth of support to help you complete your technical-communication projects:

Tech Comm at Work boxes at the beginning of every chapter introduce you to the real-world applications of technical communication in a wide variety of professions.

TECH COMM AT WORK

In its most recent standards, ABET, the engineering accreditation organization, states that engineering programs must show that their students master the "ability to function on multidisciplinary teams" (ABET, 2003). Engineers aren't the only professionals who collaborate. Teachers collaborate with other teachers, administrators, and the government to develop curricula. Broadcast journalists collaborate with other journalists, editors, photographers, and producers to generate a story. In fact, in every field, from architecture to zoology, professionals need to be able to work effectively with others.

Annotated Examples make it easier for you to learn from the many model documents, illustrations, and screen shots throughout the text.

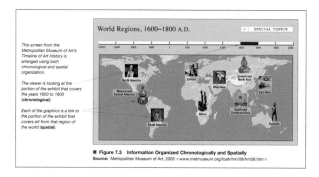

This screen from the Metropolitan Museum of Art's Timeline of Art History is arranged using both chronological and spatial organization.

The viewer is looking at the portion of the exhibit that covers the years 1600 to 1800 (**chronological**).

Each of the graphics is a link to the portion of the exhibit that covers art from that region of the world (**spatial**).

■ **Figure 7.3   Information Organized Chronologically and Spatially**
Source: Metropolitan Museum of Art, 2005 <www.metmuseum.org/toah/hm/09/hm09.htm>.

Guidelines boxes throughout the book summarize crucial information and provide strategies on key topics.

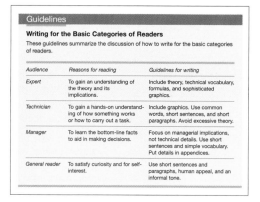

Guidelines

Writing for the Basic Categories of Readers
These guidelines summarize the discussion of how to write for the basic categories of readers.

Audience	Reasons for reading	Guidelines for writing
Expert	To gain an understanding of the theory and its implications.	Include theory, technical vocabulary, formulas, and sophisticated graphics.
Technician	To gain a hands-on understanding of how something works or how to carry out a task.	Include graphics. Use common words, short sentences, and short paragraphs. Avoid excessive theory.
Manager	To learn the bottom-line facts to aid in making decisions.	Focus on managerial implications, not technical details. Use short sentences and simple vocabulary. Put details in appendices.
General reader	To satisfy curiosity and for self-interest.	Use short sentences and paragraphs, human appeal, and an informal tone.

Ethics Notes remind you to think about the ethical considerations and implications of your writing and oral presentations.

Ethics Note

Reporting and Analyzing Data Honestly
When you put a lot of time and effort into a research project, it's frustrating when you can't find the information you need, or when the information you find doesn't help you say what you want to say. As discussed in Chapter 2, your challenge as a professional is to tell the truth.

If the evidence suggests that the course of action you propose won't work, don't omit that evidence or change it. Rather, try to figure out the discrepancy between the evidence and your proposal. Present your explanation honestly.

If you can't find reputable evidence to support your claim, don't just keep silent and hope your readers don't notice. Explain why you think the evidence is missing and how you propose to follow up by continuing your research.

If you make an honest mistake, you are a person. If you cover up a mistake, you're a dishonest person. If you get caught fudging the data, you could become an unemployed dishonest person. If you don't get caught, you're still a smaller person.

Strategies for Intercultural Communication boxes give attention to the realities of the global workplace and help you meet the needs of diverse audiences.

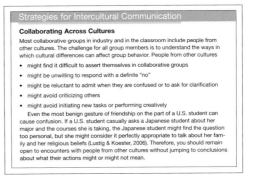

Interactive Sample Documents allow you to apply what you have just read as you analyze a real business or technical document.

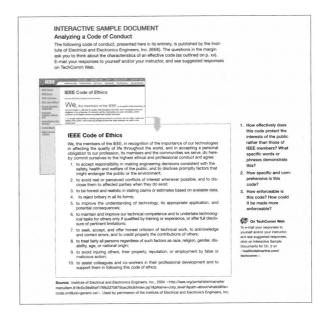

Tech Tips for using basic software tools give you step-by-step, illustrated instructions on topics such as tracking changes, creating graphics, and modifying templates.

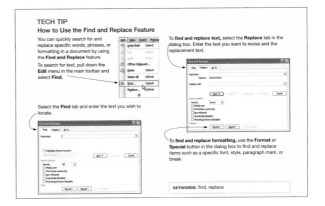

Cross-references in the margins of the text direct you to related materials elsewhere in the book and on the TechComm Web site at <bedfordstmartins .com/techcomm>.

In This Book
For more about copyright issues and the Web, see Ch. 20, p. 538.

On TechComm Web
For more about trademarks, see the U.S. Patent and Trademark Office Web site. Click on Links Library for Ch. 2 on <bedfordstmartins.com/ techcomm>.

Writer's Checklists summarize important concepts and act as handy reminders as you draft and revise your work.

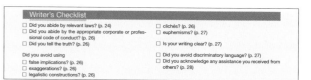

Writer's Checklist

☐ Did you abide by relevant laws? (p. 24)
☐ Did you abide by the appropriate corporate or professional code of conduct? (p. 26)
☐ Did you tell the truth? (p. 26)

Did you avoid using
☐ false implications? (p. 26)
☐ exaggerations? (p. 26)
☐ legalistic constructions? (p. 26)

☐ clichés? (p. 26)
☐ euphemisms? (p. 27)
☐ Is your writing clear? (p. 27)

☐ Did you avoid discriminatory language? (p. 27)
☐ Did you acknowledge any assistance you received from others? (p. 28)

Cases in every chapter present real-world writing scenarios built around common workplace documents that you can critique, download, and revise.

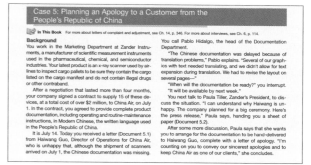

Case 5: Planning an Apology to a Customer from the People's Republic of China

In This Book For more about letters of complaint and adjustment, see Ch. 14, p. 346. For more about interviews, see Ch. 6, p. 114.

Background
You work in the Marketing Department at Zander Instruments, a manufacturer of scientific measurement instruments used in the pharmaceutical, chemical, and semiconductor industries. Your latest product is an x-ray scanner used by airlines to inspect cargo pallets to be sure they contain the cargo listed on the cargo manifest and do not contain illegal drugs or other contraband.

After a negotiation that lasted more than four months, your company signed a contract to supply 15 of these devices, at a total cost of over $2 million, to China Air, on July 1. In the contract, you agreed to provide complete product documentation, including operating and routine-maintenance instructions, in Modern Chinese, the written language used in the People's Republic of China.

It is July 14. Today you received a letter (Document 5.1) from Haiwang Guo, Director of Operations for China Air, who is unhappy that, although the shipment of scanners arrived on July 1, the Chinese documentation was missing.

You call Pablo Hidalgo, the head of the Documentation Department.

"The Chinese documentation was delayed because of translation problems," Pablo explains. "Several of our graphics with text needed translating, and we didn't allow for text expansion during translation. We had to revise the layout on several pages—"

"When will the documentation be ready?" you interrupt.

"It will be available by next week."

You next talk to Paula Tiller, Zander's President, to discuss the situation. "I can understand why Haiwang is unhappy. The company planned for a big ceremony. Here's the press release," Paula says, handing you a sheet of paper (Document 5.2).

After some more discussion, Paula says that she wants you to arrange for the documentation to be hand-delivered to Haiwang Guo, complete with a letter of apology. "I'm counting on you to convey our sincerest apologies and to keep China Air as one of our clients," she concludes.

■ **Document 5.1 Letter from China Air's Director of Operations**

On TechComm Web
For digital versions of case documents, click on Downloadable Case Documents on <bedfordstmartins.com/techcomm>.

■ **Document 5.2 China Air Press Release**

Your Assignment
1. You decide that the first step is to interview a knowledgeable person from the People's Republic of China to learn what you can about how formal apologies are handled there. A friend of yours, Jun Xiaoyan, in Zander's Research and Development Department, is from the People's Republic. You think he might be willing to sit down with you for 15 or 20 minutes. Write a set of questions you would like to ask your friend before apologizing to Haiwang Guo. For each question, write a brief paragraph explaining how the answer to the question might help you

complete an appropriate letter of apology to China Air. For example, you might want to know whether the letter should be highly formal in its vocabulary.

2. Jun Xiaoyan contacts you before your meeting and suggests that you bring along a rough draft of your apology letter. "It will give us something specific to work with," he says. Based on what you already know about intercultural communication, draft a letter of apology to China Air. Include in the margins any specific questions you want to ask Jun about your letter.

For quick reference, many of these features are indexed on the inside back cover of this book. For an overview of the numerous resources available to you on the TechComm Web site, see the inside front cover of this book.

Brief Contents

Contents

PART TWO

Planning the Document   65

PART THREE
Developing the Textual Elements   153

PART FOUR

Developing the Visual Elements   255

12 Designing Documents   256

PART FIVE

Applications   335

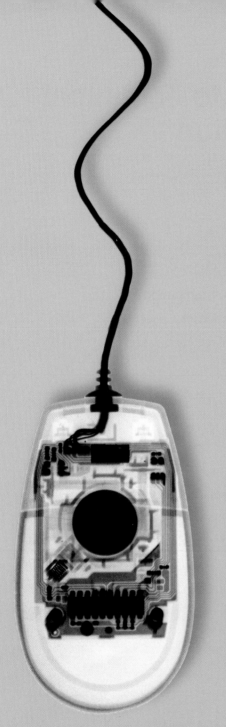

PART ONE

The Technical-Communication Environment

1

Introduction to Technical Communication

TECH COMM AT WORK

Technical communication is workplace communication. Regardless of what field you enter, your success will depend, to a large degree, on how well you can write and speak to co-workers, supervisors, clients, suppliers, and the general public. Think of it this way: a professional is a person who communicates with others about a technical subject. An engineer is a person who communicates about engineering. An architect is a person who communicates about architecture. A historian is a person who communicates about history. The purpose of this book is to help you improve your workplace communication skills, no matter what your field.

According to the Center for Plain Language (2005), up to 40 percent of the cost of managing business and government transactions is due to poor communication. For this reason, employees who communicate well are rewarded. A survey by the Plain English Network (2002) found that 96 percent of the nation's 1,000 largest employers say that employees must have good communication skills to get ahead. Almost 90 percent of more than over 800 business school graduates say that their writing skills help them advance more quickly. More than 80 percent of Fortune 400 companies have identified writing skills as their organizations' greatest weakness. And in a recent survey, eight major companies, including Nike, put communication skills at the top of the list of traits they look for in employees.

The working world depends on written communication. Within most modern organizations, almost every action is documented in writing, whether on paper or online. Here are a few examples:

- a memo or an e-mail to request information or identify a problem
- a set of instructions to introduce and explain a new process or procedure
- a proposal to persuade management to authorize a project
- a report to document a completed project
- an oral presentation to explain a new policy to employees

Every organization also communicates with other organizations and often with the public, using materials such as these:

- inquiry letters, sales letters, goodwill letters, and claim and adjustment letters to customers, clients, and suppliers
- Web sites to describe and sell products and to solicit job applications
- research reports for external organizations
- articles for trade and professional journals

WHAT IS TECHNICAL COMMUNICATION?

When you create technical documents, you are writing, designing, and transmitting technical information so that people can understand it easily and use it safely, effectively, and efficiently.

Much of what you read every day—textbooks, phone books, procedures manuals, journal articles, Web sites, owner's manuals—is technical communication. The words and graphics in these documents are meant to help you understand a subject or carry out a task.

WHO PRODUCES TECHNICAL COMMUNICATION?

Most technical communication is produced by one of two different categories of people:

 **On TechComm Web**

For more on what technical communicators do, see Saul Carliner's *Information Designer's Toolkit.* Click on Links Library for Ch. 1 on <bedfordstmartins.com/ techcomm>.

- *Technical professionals.* Technically trained individuals, such as engineers and accountants, do a lot of writing, including e-mails, letters, proposals, and reports.
- *Technical communicators.* Technical communicators create manuals, proposals, reports, sales literature, Web sites, letters, journal articles, and speeches. Many technical communicators still call themselves technical writers (or tech writers) even though the term *technical communicator* better reflects the increasing importance of graphics and the use of other media, such as online documentation.

Often technical professionals and technical communicators work together. For instance, a computer engineer designing a new microchip will draft the specifications for that chip. The technical communicator will study the draft, interview the engineer to resolve any technical questions, and then revise the specifications. Those specifications will be included in the company's printed product catalog and Web-based marketing material.

TECHNICAL COMMUNICATION AND YOUR CAREER

The course you are taking now will help you meet the demands of the working world. In fact, your first step in obtaining a professional position is to write two technical documents—an application letter and a résumé—that help an organization decide whether to interview you. And once you start work, your supervisors will be looking at your communication skills as well as your technical abilities.

Job ads in newspapers and professional journals suggest that the working world values good communication skills. The following ad from an organization that manufactures medical instruments is typical:

Design Assurance Engineer. Duties include performing electronic/mechanical product, component, and material qualifications. Requires spreadsheet/word-processing abilities and excellent written/oral communication skills. BSEE or biology degree preferred.

This job ad mentions not only computer skills but also communication skills.

More than 60 percent of companies offer regularly scheduled training courses in communication skills; another 35 percent offer that training as needed. Only 4 percent of companies report that they do not offer any training in communication skills (Galvin, 2001). The facts of corporate life today are simple: if you cannot communicate well, you are less valuable; if you can, you are more valuable.

 In This Book

For more about job-application materials, see Ch. 15.

CHARACTERISTICS OF TECHNICAL COMMUNICATION

Technical communication has six major characteristics.

Technical communication has six major characteristics:

Addresses particular readers

Helps readers solve problems

Reflects an organization's goals and culture

Is produced collaboratively

Uses design to increase readability

Consists of words or graphics or both

Addresses Particular Readers

Technical communication addresses particular readers. For instance, if you are planning to write a proposal for your supervisor, you think about that person's job responsibilities, the level of detail he or she would be interested in reading, and personal factors such as history with the organization and attitudes toward your ideas. These factors can help you decide what kind of document to write, how to structure it, how much detail to include, and what sentence style and vocabulary to use.

 In This Book

For more about addressing a particular audience, see Ch. 5, p. 68.

Even if you do not know your readers personally, you should try to create a profile of them. For example, if readers of your brochure are police officers responsible for purchases, you don't know their gender, age, or other personal characteristics, but you do know that they share a police background and a common responsibility for approving expenditures.

Your writing might also be read by people you never intended as your audience, such as managers and executives in your organization, the public, or the media. Avoid writing anything that will embarrass you or your organization.

Helps Readers Solve Problems

Technical communication helps readers learn something or carry out a task. For instance, you read your company's employee-benefits manual to help you decide which benefits package you should select. In other words, you read it because you need information to help you analyze a situation and solve a problem.

Strategies for Intercultural Communication

Communicating Across Cultures

Often you will write for people from different cultures or whose native language is different from yours. These readers will react differently to the design, organization, and writing style of documents than will people from your own culture. Therefore, you will need to consider these cultural differences as you write.

A good first step is to read a full-length discussion of the topic, such as one or more of the following respected resources:

- Hofstede, G. H. (2001). *Culture's consequences: Comparing values, behaviors, institutions and organizations across nations.* Thousand Oaks, CA: Sage.

- Intercultural Communication Institute <www.intercultural.org>. This nonprofit organization offers articles, training, and resource lists.

- Klyukanov, Igor. (2005). *Principles of intercultural communication.* Upper Saddle River, NJ: Allyn & Bacon.

- Neuliep, J. W. (2003). *Intercultural communication: A contextual approach* (2nd ed.). Boston: Houghton Mifflin.

- Trompernaars, F., & Hampden-Turner, C. (1997). *Riding the waves of culture: Understanding diversity in global business* (2nd ed.). New York: McGraw-Hill.

Reflects an Organization's Goals and Culture

Technical communication furthers an organization's goals. For example, a state government department that oversees vocational-education programs submits an annual report to the state legislature, as well as a lot of technical information for the public: flyers, brochures, pamphlets, radio and television ads, and course materials. These documents help the department secure its funding and reach its audience.

Technical communication also reflects an organization's culture. Some organizations expect employees to format their documents in a particular way and to write only to their immediate supervisors and to others on their own level. In other organizations, the culture permits or even encourages employees to make their own decisions on these questions.

Is Produced Collaboratively

In This Book

For more about collaboration, see Ch. 4.

In This Book

For more about design, see Ch. 12.

In This Book

For more about graphics, see Ch. 13.

Although you will often work alone in writing short documents, you will probably work as part of a team in producing more-complicated documents. Collaboration can range from having a colleague review your two-page memo to working with a team of a dozen technical professionals and technical communicators on a 200-page catalog.

Collaboration is common in technical communication because no one person has enough time or all the information or skills to create a large document. Writers, editors, designers, and production specialists work with subject-matter experts—the various technical professionals—to create a better document than any one of them could have made working alone.

Successful collaboration requires interpersonal skills. You have to listen to people with other views and from other business and ethnic cultures, express yourself clearly and diplomatically, and compromise.

Uses Design to Increase Readability

Technical communicators use design features—typography, spacing, color, special paper, and so forth—to accomplish three basic purposes:

- *To make the document look attractive and professional.* If it is attractive and creates a positive impression, you are more likely to accomplish your goal.
- *To help the reader navigate the document.* Because a technical document can be long and complicated and most readers want to read only parts of it, design features, such as headings, color, or highlighting, help readers see where they are and get where they want to be.
- *To help the reader understand the document.* If all the safety warnings in a manual appear in a color and size different from the rest of the text, readers will be better able to recognize the importance of the information.

Consists of Words or Graphics or Both

Most technical documents include words and graphics. Graphics help the writer perform five main functions:

- make the document more interesting and appealing to readers
- communicate and reinforce difficult concepts
- communicate instructions and descriptions of objects and processes
- communicate large amounts of quantifiable data
- communicate with nonnative speakers

Technical professionals and technical communicators alike use high-tech tools to produce documents. Although you are unlikely to need to become an expert user of these tools, some of them, such as word processors and

TECH TIP

How to Use Help

All professional software includes online help. You can also access online resources such as how-to articles, tips, and training courses. In Microsoft Word, you can access help in three ways:

1. By typing a question or phrase in the **Type a question for help** box in the main toolbar at the top of the screen. Use keywords, such as "index" or "template."

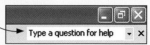

2. By pulling down the **Help** menu in the main toolbar at the top of the screen.

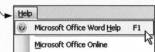

Once you have selected Microsoft Office Word Help, you can locate help topics by typing keywords in the **Search for** box or by using the **Table of Contents**.

3. If you have access to the Internet, you can find resources by selecting **Microsoft Office Online**.

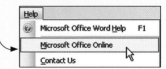

KEYWORDS: help, Microsoft Office Online

Each Tech Tip in this book concludes with a list of keywords that you can enter in the program's Online help to learn more about the topic.

INTERACTIVE SAMPLE DOCUMENT
Studying How Technical Communication Combines Words and Graphics

This is a cover from an eight-page quick-start brochure that accompanies a photo-copier. The questions in the margin ask you to consider how technical communication combines words and graphics. E-mail responses to yourself and/or your instructor, and see suggested responses on TechComm Web.

1. How have the writers used graphic elements in the sentence below the title to emphasize the message in that sentence?

2. In what other ways have the writers used words and graphics to make the document more interesting and appealing to readers?

3. How have the writers used text and graphics to present the tasks that people can accomplish with this machine?

On TechComm Web

To e-mail your responses to yourself and/or your instructor and to see suggested responses, click on Interactive Sample Documents for Ch. 1 on <bedfordstmartins.com/techcomm>.

Source: Xerox Corporation, 2000.

spreadsheets, are fundamentally important. You can make the most of these tools by taking advantage of the help they offer.

A LOOK AT A SAMPLE DOCUMENT

The home page from the Netflix Web site (2005) in Figure 1.1 is an excellent example of technical communication. It illustrates a number of the characteristics of technical communication discussed in this chapter.

MEASURES OF EXCELLENCE IN TECHNICAL COMMUNICATION

Eight measures of excellence characterize all technical communication.

Characteristics of technical communication:

- **addresses particular readers.** *Is targeted to people who like to watch movies at home*
- **helps readers solve problems.** *Provides information about the services offered by Netflix*
- **reflects an organization's goals and culture.** *Focuses on young adults*
- **is produced collaboratively.** *Was created by technical communicators, graphic artists, Web authors, and others*
- **uses design to increase readability.** *Is neatly organized into four sections: links at the top, textual information on the left, photograph on the right, and more links at the bottom*
- **consists of both words and graphics.** *The words explain how the service works. The photograph contains the persuasive message*

■ **Figure 1.1   A Web Page That Shows the Characteristics of Technical Communication**
Source: Netflix.com, 2005 <www.netflix.com/Default/>.

Measures of excellence in technical communication:

| Honesty
| Clarity
| Accuracy
| Comprehensiveness
| Accessibility
| Conciseness
| Professional appearance
| Correctness

 In This Book

For more about the ethical and legal aspects of technical communication, see Ch. 2.

Honesty

The most important measure of excellence in technical communication is honesty. For three reasons, you have to tell the truth and not mislead the reader:

- *It is the right thing to do.* Technical communication is meant to help people make wise choices as they use the information available in a high-tech culture.
- *If you are dishonest, readers can get hurt.* Misinforming your readers or deliberately omitting important information can injure or kill people.
- *If you are dishonest, you and your organization could face serious legal charges.* If a court finds that your document's failure to provide honest, appropriate information caused a substantial injury or loss, your organization might have to pay millions of dollars.

Ethics Note

You will find Ethics Notes throughout this book. These notes describe typical ethical problems involved in technical communication and suggest ways to think about them.

Clarity

Your goal is to produce a document that conveys a single meaning the reader can understand easily. The following directive, written by the British navy (*Technical Communication,* 1990), is an example of what to avoid:

> It is necessary for technical reasons that these warheads should be stored upside down, that is, with the top at the bottom and the bottom at the top. In order that there may be no doubt as to which is the top and which is the bottom, for storage purposes, it will be seen that the bottom of each warhead has been labeled with the word TOP.

Technical communication must be clear for two reasons:

- *Unclear technical communication can be dangerous.* A carelessly drafted building code, for example, could tempt contractors to use inferior materials or techniques.
- *Unclear technical communication is expensive.* The average cost of a telephone call to a customer-support center is more than $20 (Michaels, 2003). Clear technical communication in the product's documentation—its instructions—can greatly reduce the number and length of such calls.

Accuracy

You need to get your facts straight. A slight inaccuracy can confuse and annoy your readers; a major inaccuracy can be dangerous and expensive. In another sense, accuracy is a question of ethics. Technical communication must be as objective and unbiased as you can make it. If readers suspect that you are slanting information by overstating or omitting facts, they will doubt the validity of the entire document.

Comprehensiveness

A good technical document provides all the information readers need. It describes the background so that readers who are unfamiliar with the subject can understand it. It contains sufficient detail so that readers can follow the discussion and carry out any required tasks. It refers to supporting materials clearly or includes them as attachments.

　　Comprehensiveness is crucial because readers need a complete, self-contained discussion in order to use the information safely, effectively, and efficiently. A document also often serves as the official company record of a project, from its inception to its completion.

Accessibility

Most technical documents, both in print and online, are made up of small, independent sections. Because few people will read a document from beginning to end, your job is to make its various parts accessible. That is, readers should not be forced to flip through the pages or click links unnecessarily to find the appropriate section.

 In This Book
For more about making documents accessible, see Chs. 10 and 12.

Conciseness

A document must be concise enough to be useful to a busy reader. You can shorten most writing by 10 to 20 percent simply by eliminating unnecessary phrases, choosing short words rather than long ones, and using economical grammatical forms. Your job is to figure out how to convey a lot of information economically.

 In This Book
For more about writing concisely, see Ch. 11.

Professional Appearance

You start to communicate before anyone reads the first word of the document. If the document looks neat and professional, readers will form a positive impression of it and its authors. Your documents should adhere to the format standards of your organization or your professional field, and they should be well designed and neatly printed. For example, a letter should follow one of the traditional letter formats and have generous margins.

Correctness

A correct document is one that adheres to the conventions of grammar, punctuation, spelling, and usage. Sometimes, incorrect writing can confuse readers or even make your document inaccurate. The biggest problem, however, is that incorrect writing makes you look unprofessional. If your writing is full of errors, readers will wonder if you were also careless in gathering, analyzing, and presenting the technical information. If readers doubt your professionalism, they will be less likely to accept your conclusions or follow your recommendations.

Technical communication is meant to fulfill a mission: to convey information to a particular audience so that they understand something or carry out a task. To accomplish these goals, it must be honest, clear, accurate, comprehensive, accessible, concise, professional in appearance, and correct.

Exercises

 In This Book　For more about memos, see Ch. 14, p. 352.

1. **INTERNET EXERCISE**　Form small groups to study the following Web page from Dell (2005). Meet to discuss which characteristics of technical communication you see in this Web page. How effective is this page? What changes would you make to improve it? Present your ideas in a brief memo to your instructor.

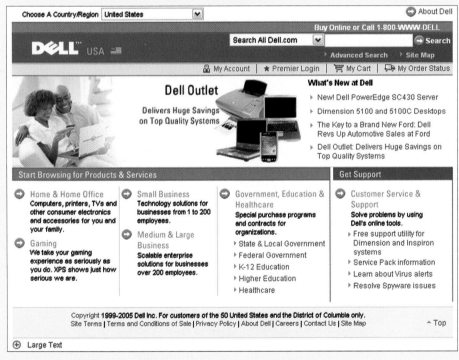

Source: Dell Inc., 2005 <www.dell.com>.

2. Locate an owner's manual for a consumer product, such as a coffeemaker, bicycle, or hair dryer. In a memo to your instructor, describe and evaluate the manual. To what extent does it meet the measures of excellence discussed in this chapter? In what ways does it fall short? Submit a photocopy of the document (or a representative portion of it) with your memo.

3. **INTERNET EXERCISE** Locate a document on the Web that you believe to be an example of technical communication. Describe the aspects of the document that illustrate the characteristics of technical communication discussed in this chapter. Then evaluate the effectiveness of the document. Write your response in a memo to your instructor. Submit a printout of the document (or a representative portion of it) with your assignment.

Case 1: Judging Entries in a Technical-Communication Competition

 In This Book For more about memos, see Ch. 14, p. 352.

Background

The English department at Bonita Vista High School decided to sponsor a technical-communication competition open to all students. The teachers expect the competition to help promote student awareness of the technical-communication profession and encourage students to develop and showcase their technical-communication skills. The teachers encouraged students to submit original papers, essays, lab reports, instructions, presentation slides, illustrations, Web sites, and the like on a technical subject of their choice. Students also were asked to include a brief description of the assignment.

You are one of three judges selected from the community to evaluate entries. The other two judges are named Cheryl and Pat. Cheryl has a bachelor of science degree in Forest Management and works as a natural-resource specialist for the state's department of forestry. Pat works as a freelance animator and has 3-D modeling/animation skills. Both have experience creating technical documents or illustrations. You were asked to join the judging panel because you are taking a technical-communication course in college. The panel's task is to evaluate the quality of each submission and to reach a consensus on first-, second-, and third-place winners. A new English teacher, Mr. Insko, is coordinating the competition. He has left the details of how to judge the entries up to the panel.

At your first meeting, Cheryl confesses, "I'm not sure where to begin. The entries are all so different. How are we going to evaluate each entry on its own merits?" She points to three entries spread out on the table (see Documents 1.1–1.3).

Pat admits that she has never served as a judge of a competition. "Look at this entry," she says, pointing to Document 1.1. "The student has a spelling mistake in the first line. Should this entry win an award?"

"Maybe," Cheryl explains. "This entry demonstrates that the student understands the concept of chunking."

"What do you mean by chunking?" Pat asks.

You realize that you all seem to have different ideas of how to define a good technical document. You propose that the panel start by agreeing on some type of scoring or rating sheet with several criteria by which you could judge each entry.

"I agree," Cheryl says. "Each criterion could be worth up to a certain number of points. By totaling the points for each entry, we could determine the awards."

"I like this approach," Pat says. "However, in art school I learned the most from people's comments, not some numeric score. I think it's important that we comment on all the entries. Let's make this a learning experience for the students and not just a 'Who's the Best' contest."

You volunteer to put together a scoring guide that incorporates all of these elements. You explain that you will e-mail your sample scoring guide and a brief explanation of your approach to Cheryl and Pat. You also suggest that the three of you use your scoring guide to judge just these three entries. Based on how well that goes, you'll revise the guide, if necessary, before the panel tackles the two boxes of entries sitting on Mr. Insko's desk.

Your Assignment

1. Create a scoring guide to evaluate the entries. Write a brief memo to the other judges explaining why you think your approach is effective and fair.

2. Using this scoring guide, evaluate Documents 1.1–1.3. Include a one-paragraph comment on each entry.

■ **Document 1.1   Entry 001**

Student's statement: "For health class, Ms. Ransberg gave us an assignment to create a flyer on a health issue of interest to students. My flyer is on high blood pressure and teenagers."

 On TechComm Web

For digital versions of case documents, click on Downloadable Case Documents on <bedfordstmartins.com/techcomm>.

Under Too Much Pressure?

What is it?

High blood pressure, or hypertension, is when your blood pressure stays too high all the time. Doctors define high blood pressure as 140/90. However, doctors think an adult's blood pressure should be lower than 120/80. The first number (140), or systolic pressure, is your blood pressure when your heart beats. The bottom number (90), or diastolic pressure, is your blood pressure when your heart is at rest.

Am I at risk?

1 in 3 adults have high blood pressure. If you're overweight you are at risk for high blood pressure. Most of us will eventually get high blood pressure or die from heart disease. It's not too early to start worrying. Doctors say that kids as young as 18 are having heart attacks. If your under 18, your blood pressure should be lower than what the table says below.

BOYS	
Age	Blood Pressure
15	131/83
16	134/84
17	136/87

GIRLS	
Age	Blood Pressure
15	127/83
16	128/84
17	129/84

(National Heart, Lung, and Blood Institute)

What are the symptoms?

There are no symptoms so that is why its called the "silent killer."

How do I prevent it?

✓ Get your blood pressure checked regularly
✓ Exercise
✓ Avoid fast food
✓ Lose weight
✓ You shouldn't smoke (or drink☺)
✓ Don't get stressed

Allison Sullivan
Health, per. 5

Alexander Luthor
Computer Science, period 2

Java assignment to calculate an integer to an inputted power.

In order to write a program to calculate an integer to an inputted power, I had to figure out how the math is done. Raising an integer to a power is just multiplying that number by itself a certain number of times. In the program, I have the user enter the number and the power. Then the computer has to multiply it out. I did this using a *while loop* so it would be easy to count the number of times the multiplication happened.

```
public class        //starts program – introduces it to compiler
{       /*everything until matching bracket at the end belongs to this
class*/
        public static void main(string[]args)
/*describes particular program information. Void – not returning value
to anything. Using strings and arguments in the program.*/
        {       //everything until matching closing belongs to this main
        int x,y;            //introduce variables that are integers
        int i=1;            //introduce and make value equal 1
        int power=1;
        x=inInt("Enter base as an integer: ");
/*output " " text and then take value typed on keyboard. Assigns
value to variable x and y*/
        y=inInt("Enter exponent as an integer: ");

        while(i<=y)        /*do the following until i value is more
than y value*/
                {
                        power=power*x;  /*assign a value of power to
be itself times x (the number we entered on the keyboard)*/
                        i++;            //increase our counter by 1
                }

        system.out.println(+ power);  /*print the final value of
power to the computer screen*/
        }
}
```

■ **Document 1.2   Entry 002**

Student's statement: "This assignment was to write a program to calculate the power of a number. We had to have the number and power entered from the keyboard and then have the program do the math."

■ **Document 1.3   Entry 003**

Student's statement: "The assignment was to explain how to use a feature of Microsoft Word that many students wouldn't already know how to use but would like to. We had to include at least one graphic."

Jonathan O'Toole
English, period 4

Equation Editor in Microsoft Word

The **Equation Editor** in Microsoft Word is an excellent tool to use if a student wants to use his computer for taking notes for math class. A student can take notes on his computer when studying math at home or recopy his handwritten notes from class. If he's a geek, he can bring his computer to class. He can even do his homework on the computer. The **Equation Editor** has hundreds of mathematical symbols and dozens of equation templates for Algebra, Geometry, and Calculus. All a student needs is Microsoft Word.

When a student wants to write an equation, he should pick **Object** from the **Insert** menu. Next, the student should choose the **Create New** tab. Next, he should scroll down the list and select **Microsoft Equation Editor 3.0**. After that, hit **OK**. Now the student is ready to write the equation by picking the symbols he needs for the equation.

This is an **algebra** class example. $x \geq 6$

This is a **geometry** class example (quadratic formula). $x = \dfrac{-b \pm \sqrt{b^2 - 4ac}}{2a}$

This is a **calculus** class example (I think). $\int_{-\pi/2}^{\pi/2} (1 + \cos \chi) d\chi$

When the student is finished with the equation, he should click somewhere in his Word document.

2 Understanding Ethical and Legal Considerations

TECH COMM AT WORK

In the workplace, you are likely to encounter situations that force you to think about your values and make some hard decisions. For instance, when an accountant writes an e-mail message in her work at an accounting firm, is she protected by privacy laws? Is a technical writer allowed to use words and graphics from an existing manual in writing a new manual? If a company manufactures fire-protection equipment, what is the company's responsibility if a customer gets hurt while using one of its products? Although some of these questions have clear-cut, simple answers based on settled law, others are far more complicated. One thing is certain: employees at all levels are expected to understand the basics of workplace ethics.

As a technical professional or technical communicator, you need a basic understanding of ethical principles, if only because you are likely to confront ethical dilemmas on the job. Technical communicators and technical professionals also need to understand several areas of the law related to communication.

Ethical and legal pitfalls can lurk within the words and graphics of many kinds of documents. For example, in writing a proposal, you might be asked to exaggerate or lie about your organization's past accomplishments, pad the résumés of the project personnel, list as project personnel some workers who will not be contributing to the project, or present an unrealistically short work schedule. In drafting product information, you might be asked to exaggerate the quality of products shown in catalogs or manuals or to downplay the hazards of using these products. In creating graphics, you might be asked to hide an item's weaknesses in a photograph by manipulating the photo electronically.

A BRIEF INTRODUCTION TO ETHICS

Ethics is the study of the principles of conduct that apply to an individual or a group. For some people, ethics is a matter of intuition—what their gut feelings tell them about the rightness or wrongness of an act. Others see ethics in terms of the Golden Rule: treat others as you would like them to treat you.

YOUR LEGAL OBLIGATIONS

Although most people believe that ethical obligations are more comprehensive and more important than legal obligations, the two sets of obligations are closely related. Our ethical values have shaped many of our laws. For this reason, professionals should know the basics of four different bodies of law.

Bodies of law relevant to technical communication:

Copyright law

Trademark law

Contract law

Liability law

Ethics Note

Understanding Ethical Standards

The ethicist Manuel G. Velasquez (2002) outlines four moral standards that are useful in thinking about ethical dilemmas:

- **Rights.** This standard concerns individuals' basic needs and welfare. Everyone agrees, for example, that people have a right to a reasonably safe workplace. When we buy a product, we have a right to expect that the information that accompanies it is honest and clear.

- **Justice.** This standard concerns how the costs and benefits of an action or a policy can be distributed fairly among a group. For example, the cost of maintaining a highway should be borne, in part, by people who use that highway. However, because everyone benefits from the highway, it is just that general funds also be used.

- **Utility.** This standard concerns the positive and negative effects that an action or a policy has, will have, or might have on others. For example, if a company is considering closing a plant, the company's leaders should consider not only the money they would save but also the financial hardship of laid-off workers and the economic effects of the closing on the community. The tricky part in thinking about utility is figuring out the time frame to examine. An action can have one effect in the short run—laying off employees can help a company's quarterly balance sheet—and a very different effect in the long run—hurting the company's productivity or the quality of its products.

- **Care.** This standard concerns the relationships we have with other individuals. We owe care and consideration to all people, but we have greater responsibilities to people in our families, our workplaces, and our communities.

These standards often conflict. For instance, according to the care standard, you might wish to promote a friend of yours in the company, even though he is not the most deserving candidate. According to the justice standard, promoting the friend would be unfair to other candidates. In terms of utility, the promotion would probably not be in the best interests of the organization, although it might be in the best interests of your friend.

Ethical problems are difficult to resolve because no rules exist to determine when one standard outweighs another. If your family relies on you for the health insurance that your employer provides, you will find it more difficult to put your job (and your benefits) at risk by taking a principled stand against deliberately communicating inaccurate information to customers. In this case, your obligation to your family (the standard of care) is likely to outweigh the customers' right to receive honest information.

On TechComm Web

For more about copyright law, see the U.S. Copyright Office Web site. Click on Links Library for Ch. 2 on <bedfordstmartins.com/ techcomm>.

Copyright Law

As a student, you are constantly reminded to avoid *plagiarism*—intentionally or unintentionally copying someone else's work without properly acknowledging where the ideas or information came from. If a student is caught plagiarizing, she might fail the course or even be expelled from school. If a medical researcher or reporter writing in a journal or newspaper is caught plagiarizing, he would likely be fired or at least find it difficult to publish in the future. But plagiarism is an ethical, not a legal, issue. Although a plagiarist might be expelled from a community, he or she will not be fined or sent to prison.

By contrast, copyright is a legal issue. *Copyright law* is the body of law that relates to the appropriate use of a person's intellectual property: written documents, pictures, musical compositions, and the like. Copyright literally refers to a person's *right* to *copy* the work that he or she has created. The copyright holder is entitled to profit from the sale and distribution of that work.

The most important concept in copyright law is that only the copyright holder—the person or organization that owns the work—can copy it. For instance, if you work for IBM, you can legally copy information from the IBM Web site and use it in other IBM documents. In fact, this reuse of information is routine in business, industry, and government. The same description of a company might appear in its press releases, its marketing brochures, its proposals, and many other kinds of documents. Information that is meant to be reused is often called *boilerplate*. Using boilerplate information is efficient and helps ensure that the information a company distributes is both consistent and accurate.

However, if you work for IBM, you cannot simply copy information that you find on the Dell Web site and put it on the IBM site. Unless you obtain written permission from Dell to use its intellectual property, you will be infringing on Dell's copyright.

You might wonder why the individual who wrote the information for Dell doesn't own the copyright to that information. The answer lies in a legal concept known as *work made for hire*. Anything written or revised by an employee on the job is the company's property, not the employee's.

Although copyright gives the owner of the intellectual property some rights, it doesn't give the owner all rights. You can place small portions of copyrighted text in your own document without getting formal permission from the copyright holder. When you quote a few lines from an article, for example, you are taking advantage of an aspect of copyright law called *fair use*. Under fair-use guidelines, you have the right to use material, without getting permission, for purposes such as criticism, commentary, news reporting, teaching, scholarship, or research. Unfortunately, *fair use* is based on a set of general guidelines that are meant to be interpreted on a case-by-case basis. Keep in mind that you should still cite the source accurately to avoid plagiarism.

 On TechComm Web

The U.S. Copyright Office Web site describes work made for hire. Click on Links Library for Ch. 2 on <bedfordstmartins.com/techcomm>.

Guidelines

Determining Fair Use

Courts consider four factors in disputes over fair use:

▶ **The purpose and character of the use, especially whether the use is for profit.** Profit-making organizations are scrutinized more carefully than nonprofits.

On TechComm Web

The U.S. Copyright Office Web site describes fair use. Click on Links Library for Ch. 2 on <bedfordstmartins.com/techcomm>.

▶ **The nature and purpose of the copyrighted work.** When the information is essential to the public—for example, medical information—fair use is applied more liberally.

▶ **The amount and substantiality of the portion of the work used.** A 200-word passage would be a small portion of a book but a large portion of a 500-word brochure.

▶ **The effect of the use on the potential market for the copyrighted work.** Any use of the work that is likely to hurt the author's potential to profit from the original work will probably not be considered fair use.

Fair use does not apply to graphics: you must obtain written permission to use any graphics.

In This Book

For more about documenting your sources, see Appendix, Part B.

In This Book

For more about copyright issues and the Web, see Ch. 20, p. 536.

Guidelines

Dealing with Copyright Questions

Consider the following advice when using material from another source:

▶ **Abide by the fair-use concept.** Do not rely on excessive amounts of another source's work (unless the information is company-approved boilerplate).

▶ **Seek permission.** Write to the source, stating what portion of the work you wish to use and the publication you wish to use it in. The source is likely to charge you for permission.

▶ **Cite your sources accurately.** Citing sources fulfills your ethical obligation and strengthens your writing by showing the reader the range of your research.

▶ **Consult legal counsel if you have questions.** Copyright law is complex. Don't rely on instinct or common sense.

On TechComm Web

For more about trademarks, see the U.S. Patent and Trademark Office Web site. Click on Links Library for Ch. 2 on <bedfordstmartins.com/techcomm>.

Trademark Law

Companies use *trademarks* and *registered trademarks* to ensure that the public recognizes the name or logo of a product.

- A *trademark* is a word, phrase, name, or symbol that is identified with a company. The company uses the ™ symbol after the product name to claim the design or device as a trademark. For instance, Adobe Systems Incorporated claims Streamline™ as a trademark. Claiming a trademark permits a company to go to state court to try to prevent other companies from using the trademarked item for their own products.

- A *registered trademark* is a word, phrase, name, or symbol that the company has registered with the U.S. Patent and Trademark Office. The company can then use the ® symbol after the product name. Registering a trademark, a process that can take years, ensures much more legal protection throughout the United States, as well as in other nations.

Communicators are responsible for using the trademark and registered trademark symbols accurately when referring to a company's products.

Guidelines

Protecting Trademarks

Use the following techniques to protect your client's or employer's trademark:

▶ **Distinguish trademarks from other material.** Use boldface, italics, a different typeface or size, or a different color to distinguish the trademarked item.

▶ **Use the trademark symbol.** At least once in each document—preferably the first time—use the appropriate symbol after the name or logo, followed by an asterisk. At the bottom of the page, include a statement such as the following: "*COKE is a registered trademark of The Coca-Cola Company."

▶ **Use the trademarked item as an adjective, not as a noun or verb.** Trademarks can become confused with the generic term they refer to. Use the trademarked item along with the generic term, as in Xerox® photocopier or LaserJet® printer.

▶ **Do not use the plural form or the possessive form of the term.** Doing so reduces the uniqueness of the item and encourages the public to think of the term as generic.

DOES NOT PROTECT TRADEMARK	take some Kodacolors®
PROTECTS TRADEMARK	take some photographs using Kodacolor® film
DOES NOT PROTECT TRADEMARK	Kodacolor's® fine quality
PROTECTS TRADEMARK	the fine quality of Kodacolor® film

Contract Law

Contract law deals with agreements between two parties. In most cases, disputes concern whether a product lives up to the manufacturer's claims. These claims are communicated as express warranties or implied warranties.

An *express warranty* is a written or oral statement that the product has a particular feature or can perform a particular function. For example, a statement in a printer manual that the printer produces 17 pages per minute is an express warranty. An *implied warranty* is a warranty that is not written or spoken explicitly but inferred by the purchaser. Implied warranties also occur in more-casual communications, such as letters to customers or conversations between salespeople and customers. Figure 2.1 illustrates an implied warranty.

Liability Law

A product-liability action is "a lawsuit for personal injury, death, property damage, or financial loss caused by a defective product" (Helyar, 1992, p. 126). Liability is an important concern for communicators because courts frequently rule that manufacturers are responsible for providing adequate operating instructions and for warning consumers about the risks of using their products.

■ **Figure 2.1   An Implied Warranty**

This photograph of a child operating a particular rock polisher is an implied warranty that children can operate it safely.

Source: Amazon.com, 2005 <http://images .amazon.com/images/P/B00000ISUU.01 ._SCLZZZZZZZ_.jpg>.

Guidelines

Abiding by Liability Laws

Helyar (1992) summarizes the communicator's obligations and offers ten guidelines for abiding by liability laws.

▶ **Understand the product and its likely users.** Learn everything you can about the product and its users.

▶ **Describe the product's functions and limitations.** Help people determine whether it is the right product to buy. In one case, the manufacturer was found liable for not stating that its electric smoke alarm does not work during a power outage.

▶ **Instruct users on all aspects of ownership.** Include assembly, installation, use and storage, testing, maintenance, first aid and emergencies, and disposal.

▶ **Use appropriate words and graphics.** Use common terms, simple sentences, and brief paragraphs. Structure the document logically and include specific directions. Make graphics clear and easy to understand; where necessary, show people performing tasks. Make the words and graphics appropriate to the education, mechanical ability, manual dexterity, and intelligence of intended users. For products that will be used by children or nonnative speakers of your language, include graphics illustrating important information.

In This Book

For a discussion of danger, warning, and caution, see Ch. 19, p. 504.

▶ **Warn users about the risks of using or misusing the product.** Warn users about the dangers of using the product, such as chemical poisoning. Describe the cause, extent, and seriousness of the danger. A car manufacturer was found liable for not having warned consumers that parking a car on grass, leaves, or other combustible material could cause a fire. For particularly dangerous products, explain the danger and how to avoid it, then describe how to use the product safely. Use *mandatory language*, such as *must* and *shall*, rather than *might*, *could*, or *should*. Use the words *warning* and *caution* appropriately.

▶ **Include warnings along with assertions of safety.** When product information says that a product is safe, readers tend to pay less attention to warnings. Therefore, include detailed warnings to balance the safety claims.

▶ **Make directions and warnings conspicuous.** Safety information must be in large type and easily visible, appear in an appropriate location, and be durable enough to withstand ordinary use of the product.

▶ **Make sure that the instructions comply with applicable company standards and local, state, or federal statutes.**

In This Book

For a discussion of usability testing, see Ch. 19, p. 521.

▶ **Perform usability testing on the product (to make sure it is safe and easy to use) and on the instructions (to make sure they are accurate and easy to understand).**

▶ **Make sure users receive the information.** If you discover a problem after the product has been shipped to the retailer, tell users by direct mail or e-mail if possible or newspaper advertising if not. Automobile-recall notices are one example of how manufacturers contact their users.

CODES OF CONDUCT AND WHISTLEBLOWING

Between 70 and 90 percent of large corporations have codes of conduct (Murphy, 1995), as do almost all professional societies. Codes of conduct vary greatly from organization to organization. Many are a few paragraphs long; some are several volumes.

An effective code has three major characteristics:

- *It protects the public rather than members of the organization or profession.* For instance, the code should condemn unsafe building practices but not advertising, which increases competition and thus lowers prices.

- *It is specific and comprehensive.* A code is ineffective if it merely states that people must not steal, or if it does not address typical ethical offenses such as bribery in companies that do business in other countries.

- *It is enforceable.* A code is ineffective if it does not stipulate penalties, up to and including dismissal from the company or expulsion from the profession.

Although many codes are too vague to be useful in determining whether a person has violated one of their principles, writing and implementing a code can be valuable because it forces an organization to clarify its own values and can foster an increased awareness of ethical issues. Texas Instruments, like many organizations, encourages employees to report ethical problems to a committee or a person—sometimes called an *ethics officer* or an *ombudsperson*—who investigates and reaches an impartial decision.

Figure 2.2 on page 24 shows Texas Instruments' TI Ethics Quick Test and the links to the company's other ethics resources and policies.

If you think there is a serious ethical problem in your organization, find out what resources your organization has to deal with it. If there are no resources, work with your supervisor to solve the problem.

What do you do if you have exhausted all the resources at your organization and, if appropriate, the professional organization in your field? The next step will likely involve *whistleblowing*—the practice of going public with information about serious unethical conduct within an organization. For example, an engineer is blowing the whistle when she tells a regulatory agency or a newspaper that quality-control tests on a company product were faked.

Ethicists such as Manuel Velasquez (2002) argue that whistleblowing is justified if you have tried to resolve the problem through internal channels, if you have strong evidence that the problem is hurting or will hurt other parties, and if the whistleblowing is reasonably certain to prevent or stop the wrongdoing. But Velasquez also points out that whistleblowing is likely to hurt the employee, his or her family, and any other parties. Whistleblowers

On TechComm Web

For a detailed code from the Institute of Scientific and Technical Communicators, click on Links Library for Ch. 2 on <bedfordstmartins.com/techcomm>.

On TechComm Web

For links to codes of conduct from around the world, see Codes of Conduct/Practice/Ethics from Around the World. Click on Links Library for Ch. 2 on <bedfordstmartins.com/techcomm>.

The additional documents linked here help the company communicate its ethics policies in more detail.

The company provides an easy way for employees to contact the TI Ethics Office.

■ **Figure 2.2   Texas Instruments' Ethics Quick Test**
Source: Texas Instruments, 2005 <www.ti.com/corp/docs/company/citizen/ethics/quicktest.shtml>.

can be penalized through negative performance appraisals, transfers to undesirable locations, or isolation within the company.

PRINCIPLES FOR ETHICAL COMMUNICATION

As an employee, you are obligated to further your employer's legitimate aims and to refrain from any activities that run counter to them. You need to be honest, to present information accurately, and to avoid conflicts of interest that pit your own personal goals against those of the organization. You are also obligated to help your organization treat its customers fairly by providing safe and effective products or services. The seven principles for ethical communication can help you fulfill these obligations.

Abide by Relevant Laws

You must adhere to the laws governing intellectual property. Here are some examples:

- *Do not plagiarize.* When you want to publish someone else's copyrighted material, such as graphics you find on the Web, get written permission from the copyright owner.

Principles for ethical communication:

Abide by relevant laws.

Abide by the appropriate corporate or professional code of conduct.

Tell the truth.

Don't mislead your readers.

Be clear.

Avoid discriminatory language.

Acknowledge assistance from others.

INTERACTIVE SAMPLE DOCUMENT
Analyzing a Code of Conduct

The following code of conduct, presented here in its entirety, is published by the Institute of Electrical and Electronics Engineers, Inc. (IEEE). The questions in the margin ask you to think about the characteristics of an effective code (as outlined on page 23). E-mail your responses to yourself and/or your instructor, and see suggested responses on TechComm Web.

IEEE Code of Ethics

We, the members of the IEEE, in recognition of the importance of our technologies in affecting the quality of life throughout the world, and in accepting a personal obligation to our profession, its members and the communities we serve, do hereby commit ourselves to the highest ethical and professional conduct and agree:

1. to accept responsibility in making engineering decisions consistent with the safety, health and welfare of the public, and to disclose promptly factors that might endanger the public or the environment;

2. to avoid real or perceived conflicts of interest whenever possible, and to disclose them to affected parties when they do exist;

3. to be honest and realistic in stating claims or estimates based on available data;

4. to reject bribery in all its forms;

5. to improve the understanding of technology, its appropriate application, and potential consequences;

6. to maintain and improve our technical competence and to undertake technological tasks for others only if qualified by training or experience, or after full disclosure of pertinent limitations;

7. to seek, accept, and offer honest criticism of technical work, to acknowledge and correct errors, and to credit properly the contributions of others;

8. to treat fairly all persons regardless of such factors as race, religion, gender, disability, age, or national origin;

9. to avoid injuring others, their property, reputation, or employment by false or malicious action;

10. to assist colleagues and co-workers in their professional development and to support them in following this code of ethics.

Source: Institute of Electrical and Electronics Engineers, Inc., 2004 <http://ieee.org/portal/site/mainsite/menuitem.818c0c39e85ef176fb2275875bac26c8/index.jsp?&pName=corp_level1&path=about/whatis&file=code.xml&xsl=generic.xsl>. Used by permission of the Institute of Electrical and Electronics Engineers, Inc.

1. How effectively does this code protect the interests of the public rather than those of IEEE members? What specific words or phrases demonstrate this?

2. How specific and comprehensive is this code?

3. How enforceable is this code? How could it be made more enforceable?

 On TechComm Web

To e-mail your responses to yourself and/or your instructor and to see suggested responses, click on Interactive Sample Documents for Ch. 2 on <bedfordstmartins.com/techcomm>.

- *Honor the laws regarding trademarks.* For instance, use the trademark symbol (™) and the registered trademark symbol (®) properly.
- *Live up to the express and implied warranties on your company's products.*
- *Abide by all laws governing product liability.* Helyar's (1992) guidelines, presented in this chapter on page 22, are a good introduction.

Abide by the Appropriate Corporate or Professional Code of Conduct

Find out what codes apply and abide by them. Your company or the professional organization in your industry is likely to have a code that goes beyond legal issues to express ethical principles, such as telling the truth, reporting information accurately, respecting the privacy of others, and avoiding conflicts of interest.

Tell the Truth

Sometimes, employees are asked to lie about their own company's products or about those of their competitors. Obviously, lying—knowingly providing inaccurate information—is unethical. Your responsibility is to resist this pressure, even by going over the supervisor's head, if necessary. Telling the truth also means not covering up negative information. If the package for a portable compact-disc player suggests that it can be used by joggers but does not mention that the bouncing will probably make it skip, that statement is misleading.

Don't Mislead Your Readers

In This Book

For a more detailed discussion of misleading writing, see Ch. 11. For a discussion of avoiding misleading graphics, see Ch. 13.

A misleading statement—one that invites or even encourages the reader to reach a false conclusion—is ethically no better than lying. Avoid these four common kinds of misleading technical communication:

- *False implications.* If you work for SuperBright and write "Use only SuperBright batteries in your new flashlight," you imply that only that brand will work. If that is untrue, the statement is misleading. Communicators sometimes use clichés such as *user-friendly, ergonomic,* and *state of the art* to make the product sound better than it is. Use specific, accurate information to back up your claims about a product.
- *Exaggerations.* If you say "Our new Operating System 2500 makes system crashes a thing of the past," but the product only makes them less likely, you are exaggerating. Provide the specific technical information on the reduction of crashes. Do not write "We carried out extensive market research" if all you did was make a few phone calls.
- *Legalistic constructions.* It is unethical to write "The 3000X was designed to operate in extreme temperatures, from −40 degrees to 120 degrees

Fahrenheit" if the product cannot operate reliably in those temperatures. Although the statement might technically be accurate—the product was *designed* to operate in those temperatures—it is misleading.

- *Euphemisms.* If you refer to someone's being fired, say *fired* or *released*, not *granted permanent leave* or *offered an alternative career opportunity*.

Be Clear

Clear writing helps your readers understand your message easily. Your responsibility is to write as clearly as you can to help your audience understand what you are saying. For instance, if you are writing a product warranty, make it as simple and straightforward as possible. Don't hide behind big words and complicated sentences. Design your documents so that readers can easily find the information they seek. Use tables of contents, indexes, and other accessing devices to help your readers find what they need.

 In This Book

For techniques for writing clearly, including avoiding discriminatory language, see Ch. 11.

Avoid Discriminatory Language

Don't use language that discriminates against people because of their sex, religion, ethnicity, race, sexual orientation, or physical or mental abilities. Employees have been disciplined or fired for sending inappropriate jokes on the company e-mail system. In some cases, employees have even been fired

---

Strategies for Intercultural Communication

Communicating Ethically Across Cultures

Companies face special challenges when they market their products and services to people in other countries and to people in their home countries who come from other cultures:

- **Companies have to make their communications understandable and clear to their target audiences.** Otherwise, they risk offending their audiences.

- **Companies are ethically obligated not to reinforce patterns of discrimination in product information.** It would be wrong, for example, to include a photograph of a workplace setting that excludes women. This principle is what Donaldson (1991) calls the *moral minimum*.

- **Companies are not obligated to challenge the prevailing prejudice directly.** A company is not obligated to include a photograph that shows women performing roles they do not normally perform within that culture, nor is it obligated to portray women wearing clothing, makeup, or jewelry that is likely to offend local standards. But there is nothing to prevent an organization from adopting a more activist stance. Organizations that actively oppose discrimination are acting admirably.

In This Book

For a discussion of sexist writing, see Ch. 11, p. 243.

for information posted on their private blogs when that information reflects negatively on the company.

 In This Book
For more about citing sources, see Appendix, Parts A and B.

Acknowledge Assistance from Others

Don't suggest that you did all the work yourself if you didn't. Cite your sources and your collaborators accurately and graciously.

Writer's Checklist

- ☐ Did you abide by relevant laws? (p. 24)
- ☐ Did you abide by the appropriate corporate or professional code of conduct? (p. 26)
- ☐ Did you tell the truth? (p. 26)

Did you avoid using
- ☐ false implications? (p. 26)
- ☐ exaggerations? (p. 26)
- ☐ legalistic constructions? (p. 26)

- ☐ clichés? (p. 26)
- ☐ euphemisms? (p. 27)

- ☐ Is your writing clear? (p. 27)

- ☐ Did you avoid discriminatory language? (p. 27)
- ☐ Did you acknowledge any assistance you received from others? (p. 28)

Exercises

 In This Book For more about memos, see Ch. 14, p. 352.

1. It is late April, and you need a summer job. In a local newspaper, you see an ad for a potential job. The only problem is that the ad specifically mentions that it is "a continuing, full-time position." You know that you will be returning to college in the fall. Is it ethical for you to apply for the job without mentioning this fact? Why or why not? If you feel it is unethical to withhold the information that you plan to return to college in the fall, is there any way you can ethically apply? Be prepared to share your ideas with the class.

2. **INTERNET EXERCISE** Find an article or advertisement in a newspaper or magazine or on the Web that you feel contains untrue or misleading information. Write a memo to your instructor describing the ad and analyzing the unethical techniques. How might the information have been presented more honestly? Submit a photocopy or a printout of the ad with your memo.

3. **GROUP EXERCISE** Study your college or university's code of conduct for students. Then write a memo to your instructor describing and evaluating it. Consider questions such as the following: How long is the code? How comprehensive is it? Does it provide detailed guidelines or merely make general statements? Where does the code appear? From your experience, does it appear to be widely publicized, enforced, and adhered to? Are there sources on campus that could provide information on how the code is applied?

4. **GROUP EXERCISE** Form small groups. Study the code of conduct of a company or organization in your community. (Many companies and other organizations post their codes on their Web sites.)

   • One group member could study the code to analyze how effectively it states the ideals of the organization, describes proper and improper behavior and practices for employees, and spells out penalties.

   • Another group member could interview the officer who oversees the use of the code in the organization. Who wrote the code? What were the circumstances that led the organization to write it? Is it based on another organization's code? Does this officer of the organization believe the code is effective? Why or why not?

   • A third group member could secure the code of one of the professional groups in the organization's field (search for the code on the Web). For example, if the local organization produces electronic equipment, one professional group would be the Institute of Electrical and Electronics Engineers. To what extent does the code of the local organization reflect the principles and ideals of the professional group's code?

- As a team, write a memo to your instructor presenting your findings. Attach the local organization's code to your memo.

Case 2: Playing the Name Game

 In This Book   For more about memos, see Ch. 14, p. 352.

Background

Crescent Petroleum, an oil-refining corporation based in Riyadh, Saudi Arabia, has issued a request for proposals for constructing an intranet that will link its headquarters with its three facilities in the United States and Europe. McNeil Informatics, a networking consulting company, is considering responding with a proposal. Most of the work will be performed at the company headquarters in Riyadh.

Crescent Petroleum was established 40 years ago by family members who are related by marriage to the Saudi royal family. At the company headquarters, the support staff and clerical staff include women, most of whom are related to the owners of the company. The professional, managerial, and executive staff is all male, which is traditional in Saudi corporations. Crescent is a large company, with revenues in the billions of dollars.

McNeil Informatics is a small firm (12 employees) established two years ago by Denise McNeil, a 29-year-old computer scientist with a master's degree in computer engineering. She divides her time between working on her MBA and getting her company off the ground. As a result, the company is struggling financially, and she realizes that it must get the Crescent contract to meet its current financial obligations. Her employees include both men and women at all levels. The chief financial officer is a woman, as are several of the professional staff. The technical writer is a man.

Denise traveled to New York from her headquarters in Pittsburgh to attend a briefing by Crescent. All the representatives from Crescent were middle-aged Saudi men; Denise was the only woman among the representatives of the seven companies that attended the briefing. When Denise shook hands with Mr. Fayed, the team leader, he smiled slightly as he mentioned that he did not realize that McNeil Informatics was run by a woman. Denise did not know what to make of his comment, but she got a strong impression that the Crescent representatives felt uncomfortable in her presence. During the break, they drifted off to speak with the men from the other six vendors, leaving Denise to stand awkwardly by herself.

Once back in her hotel room, Denise was still bothered by the Crescent representatives' behavior at the meeting. She thought about the possibility of gender discrimination but decided to bid for the project anyway, because she believed that her company could write a persuasive proposal. McNeil Informatics had done several projects of this type in the past year.

She phoned Josh Lipton, the technical writer, to get him started on the proposal. "When you put in the boilerplate about the company, I'd like you to delete the stuff about my founding the company. Don't say that a woman is the president, okay? And when you assemble the résumés of the project team, I'd like you to use just the first initials, not the first names."

"I don't understand, Denise. What's going on?" Josh asked.

"Well, Crescent looks like an all-male club, very traditional. I'm not sure they would want to hire us if they knew we have a lot of women at the top."

"You know, Denise, there's another problem."

"Which is?"

"I'm thinking of the lead engineer we used in the other networking projects this year."

"Mark Steinberg," she said, sighing. "Do you think this will be a problem?"

"I don't know," Josh said. "I guess we could use another person. Or kind of change his name on the résumé."

"Before we commit more resources to this project, we need to find out if Crescent would act prejudicially. We need more information. Do you have any ideas?"

"Let me think about this a little bit. I'll e-mail you tomorrow morning."

After hanging up with Josh, Denise decided to phone her mentor, Jane Adams. Denise explained what had happened at the meeting with the Crescent representatives and asked, "If I conceal the gender and ethnicity of my employees and never mention I am the company's founder, am I condoning the same types of prejudice that led me to start my own company in the first place, or am I just being a practical businesswoman?"

Jane avoided responding immediately to Denise's question and instead asked for more information: "Besides what happened today, do you have any other evidence that suggests Crescent won't do business with you if you disclose such information in your proposal?"

"I don't know yet. I've asked one of my employees to come up with a research plan. But what if we find out they do business only within the Saudi version of the good-old-boy network?"

"What if you find no signs of antiwomen or ethnic prejudices?" Jane countered.

After a long pause, Denise said, "Either way, I'm not sure what to do."

Your Assignment

1. How should Denise research the situation? In an e-mail to Denise, outline a research strategy to find out more about Crescent's business relationships with non-Arab and female-run vendors.

2. What should Denise do about the fact that the person she wishes to designate as the principal investigator has an ethnic last name that might elicit a prejudiced reaction from Crescent officials? Is Denise's decision to disguise the sex of her employees and to cover up her own role in founding her company justified by common sense, or is it giving in to what she perceives as prejudice? Should she assign someone other than Mark Steinberg to run the project? Should she tailor his name to disguise his ethnicity? If you were Denise's mentor, what advice would you give her? Respond in a 500-word memo to your instructor.

A version of this case first appeared in *Ethics in Technical Communication: A Critique and Synthesis* (Westport, CT: Greenwood, 2001), by Mike Markel.

Understanding the Writing Process

3

TECH COMM AT WORK

A mathematician doesn't solve a differential equation by closing her eyes and hoping for inspiration to strike. She uses a process. The same is true for technical communication. A city planner uses the writing process to complete an application for a government grant. A social worker uses the writing process to compile a report on his client's needs. Understanding the writing tools and techniques used by experienced writers will help you write more effectively—and more efficiently.

Why should you worry about the writing process? Understanding the tools and techniques used by experienced writers can help you write faster and help your readers use your documents more effectively.

UNDERSTANDING THE WRITING PROCESS

Everybody's approach to the writing process—planning, drafting, revising, editing, and proofreading—is somewhat different. And every document you write poses special challenges. Still, every experienced writer plans, drafts, and revises. This process is summarized in Figure 3.1.

USING SPECIAL TECHNIQUES FOR REVISING TECHNICAL DOCUMENTS

For technical communication, it's best to turn to two kinds of people for help in revising documents:

In This Book
For more about critiquing another person's draft, see Ch. 4, p. 55.

- *Subject-matter experts.* If, for instance, you have written about alternative technologies for automobiles, you could ask an automotive expert to review your document. Important documents are routinely reviewed by technical experts before being released to the public.
- *People who are like those in the targeted audience.* People who fit the profile of the eventual readers can help you see problems that you or other knowledgeable readers don't notice. Knowledgeable readers might not be sufficiently critical because they will understand the technical aspects of the document even if the writing isn't clear.

When you ask someone for help, provide specific instructions. Tell the person as much as you can about your audience and purpose and about

Planning

- **Analyze your audience.** What do they know about your subject, what do they want to know, and how are they going to read the document? See Ch. 5, page 68.
- **Analyze your purpose.** What do you want your readers to know, believe, or do after they have read your document? See Ch. 5, page 88.
- **Generate ideas about your topic.** Ask journalistic questions (*who, what, when, where, why,* and *how*), brainstorm, freewrite, talk with someone, and create cluster diagrams or branching diagrams.
- **Research additional information.** Once you know what questions remain to be answered, conduct primary and secondary research. See Ch. 6.
- **Organize and outline your document.** Group items into categories, then sequence the categories. Choose an appropriate format for the outline.
- **Devise a schedule and a budget.** Figure out when you will write each element of the document and what resources you will need.

Drafting

Get comfortable, then write quickly, without stopping to get more information or to revise. If you find yourself stopping, turn down the contrast on the monitor. Write for an hour, then stop in the middle of a section, so that when you resume writing, you'll be able to pick up where you left off.

Revising

- **Reconsider your audience.** Is your understanding of the audience's needs still accurate?
- **Reconsider your purpose.** Are you still satisfied that you have accurately identified what you want to accomplish?
- **Reconsider your organization and development.** Is the document organized effectively, so that it flows logically from one point to the next, or should you reorder the points? Is each point developed sufficiently, or do you need more support for some points? See Ch. 7.

Editing and Proofreading

- **Let the document sit, overnight if possible.** Return to the document after a break, when you are fresh.
- **Edit the document carefully.** Check for grammar, punctuation, style, and diction errors. Use the spell checker, the grammar checker, and the thesaurus. Check for problems with mechanics, such as capitalization and the correct use of numbers. (See Appendix, Part C, in this book.) Also refer to checklists, such as those in this book.
- **Format the document carefully.** Use the appropriate organization and design for the document.
- **Proofread the document carefully.** If possible, have another person proofread it, too.

■ **Figure 3.1**
An Overview of the Writing Process

The writing process is not linear. At any step, you might double back to do more planning, drafting, or revising.

 On TechComm Web

For more about analyzing an audience, see Writing Guidelines for Engineering and Science Students. Click on Links Library for Ch. 3 on <bedfordstmartins.com/techcomm>.

 On TechComm Web

For more about outlining, see Paradigm Online Writing Assistant. Click on Links Library for Ch. 3 on <bedfordstmartins.com/techcomm>.

On TechComm Web

For more about revising, see Robin A. Cormier's excellent essay (1997). Click on Links Library for Ch. 3 on <bedfordstmartins.com/techcomm>.

the tasks you still need to complete. Then tell the person what kinds of problems you want him or her to look for; better yet, write them down. Here's an example:

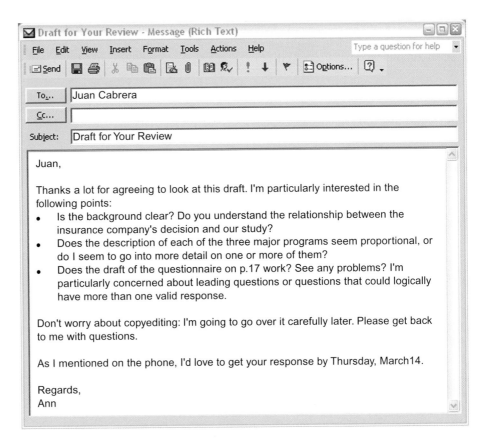

Strategies for Intercultural Communication

Having Your Draft Reviewed by a Person from the Target Culture

Sometimes people in the United States incorrectly assume that their own cultural values are shared by everyone. If your readers come from another culture, try to have your draft reviewed by someone from that culture. That person can help you answer questions such as the following:

- **Have you made correct assumptions about how readers will react to your ideas?** As discussed in Chapter 5, people from some cultures would likely consider a company-sponsored health-promotion program perfectly appropriate and would likely feel obligated to participate. By contrast, people from other cultures would consider it an unreasonable intrusion into employees' private lives.

- **Have you chosen appropriate kinds of evidence?** As discussed in Chapter 8, some cultures favor hard evidence, such as test results and statistical data. Other cultures favor traditional ideas and testimonials from authorities.

- **Have you organized the draft effectively?** As discussed in Chapter 7, in most Western cultures, documents move from general information to specific information. In many other cultures, the sequence is reversed.

- **Have you designed the document and crafted the sentences appropriately?** As discussed in Chapter 11, most nonnative speakers benefit from the use of short sentences and simple vocabulary. As discussed in Chapter 12, people from other cultures might be surprised by some design elements used in reports, such as marginal comments.

Writing a note such as this increases the chances that your colleagues will be able to point out your document's strengths and weaknesses (sections that need to be expanded, deleted, or revised). The note also reduces the chance that your readers will waste time working on something you don't need.

In addition to showing a document to others, technical communicators use a more formal kind of review called usability testing. *Usability testing* is the process of performing experiments with people who represent real users to see how well they understand a document and how easily they can use it. Instructions and manuals are the types of documents that most often undergo usability testing. See Chapter 19, page 521, for a discussion of usability testing.

USING WORD-PROCESSING TOOLS IN THE WRITING PROCESS

A word processor includes a number of tools—some more useful than others—that can help you write more quickly and more effectively.

Using a word processor involves:

Using the outline view

Using templates

Using styles

Using the spell checker

Using the grammar checker

Using the thesaurus

Using the find and replace feature

TECH TIP

How to Use the Outline View

When organizing your document, you can use the **Outline** view to examine and revise the structure of your document. For you to view the structure of your document in the outline view, your document must be formatted with Word's built-in heading styles or outline levels.

To view the structure of your document, select **Outline** from the **View** menu.

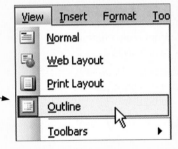

A plus or minus sign indicates whether a heading has any subheadings or text associated with it.

Headings are indented to show subordinate levels.

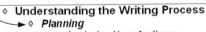

Use the **Outlining** toolbar to **promote** or **demote** headings or body text, **move, expand,** or **collapse** sections, and to **show levels.** Choose **Show All Levels** to see the sentences that make up the paragraphs.

KEYWORDS: outline view, create a document outline, outline levels

Using the Outline View

Most of the time, you use the normal view or the page layout view when you write. When you outline, use the outline view.

Using Templates

Templates are preformatted designs for different types of documents, such as letters, memos, newsletters, and reports. Templates incorporate the design specifications for the document, including typeface, type size, margins, and spacing. Organizations create their own templates to standardize the look of their documents. Company-designed templates also prompt writers for the information that readers expect in the document. For instance, if the first heading in a trip-report template is "Date of Trip," the writer doesn't have to remember to provide that information.

Although company-designed templates can be helpful, templates that come with commercial software such as word processors can lead to three problems:

- *They do not always reflect the best design principles.* For instance, most letter and memo templates default to 10-point rather than 12-point type, even though 12-point type is easier to read.

- *They bore readers.* Readers get tired of seeing the same designs.

- *They cannot help you answer important questions about your document.* Commercial templates cannot help you determine how to organize and write a document. Sometimes templates can even send you the wrong message. For example, résumé templates in word processors present a set of headings that might work better for some job applicants than for others.

Using Styles

Styles are like small templates in that they apply to the design of smaller elements, such as headings. Like templates, styles can save you time. For

TECH TIP
How to Modify Templates

You can modify an existing document **template** to address your specfic writing situation. You can then save this modified document as a template and use it again in similar writing situations.

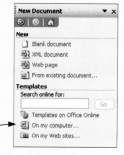

1. Open an existing template on your computer by selecting **New** on the **File** menu and then clicking **On my computer.**

2. Use **tabs** in the **Templates** window to find an appropriate template.

3. Select **Document** in the **Create New** box.

4. After making changes to the design of the document, click **Save As** on the **File** menu.

5. In the **Save As** dialog box, type a file name and select **Document Template** in the **Save as type** menu.

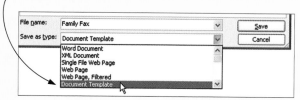

Your saved template will now appear as an icon you can select on the **General** tab of the **Templates** dialog box.

KEYWORDS: templates, about templates, modify a template

---

example, as you draft your document, you don't need to add all the formatting each time you want to designate an item as a first-level heading. You simply put your cursor in the text you want to be a first-level heading and use a pull-down menu to select that style. The text automatically incorporates all the specifications of the style. Styles also help ensure consistency, because you don't have to change four or five technical specifications every time you want to change an item's style.

If you decide to modify a style—by adding italics to a heading, for instance—you change it only once; the software automatically changes every instance of that style in the document. As you create collaborative documents, styles make it easier to achieve a consistent look.

Using the Spell Checker

A *spell checker* alerts you when it sees a word that isn't in its dictionary. Although that word might be misspelled, it might be correctly spelled but

 In This Book

For more about design, see Ch. 12. For more about graphics, see Ch. 13.

 In This Book

For an explanation of how to use styles to set up a table of contents, see Ch. 18, p. 470.

INTERACTIVE SAMPLE DOCUMENT

Identifying the Strengths and Weaknesses of a Commercial Template

The following template from Microsoft Word (Microsoft, 2004) presents one style of writing a memo. The questions in the margin ask you to think about the assumptions underlying this memo. E-mail your responses to yourself and/or your instructor, and see suggested responses on TechComm Web.

1. How well does the explanation of how to use the template help you understand how to write an effective memo?

2. How well does the template help you understand how to reformat the elements, such as the date?

 On TechComm Web

To e-mail your responses to yourself and/or your instructor and to see suggested responses, click on Interactive Sample Documents for Ch. 3 on <bedfordstmartins.com/techcomm>.

Company Name Here

Memo

To:	[Click **here** and type name]
From:	[Click **here** and type name]
CC:	[Click **here** and type name]
Date:	8/16/2005
Re:	[Click **here** and type subject]

How to Use This Memo Template

Select text you would like to replace, and type your memo. Use styles such as Heading 1-3 and Body Text in the Style control on the Formatting toolbar. To save changes to this template for future use, choose Save As from the File menu. In the Save As Type box, choose Document Template. Next time you want to use it, choose New from the File menu, and then double-click your template.

Source: Microsoft, 2004 <http://office.microsoft.com/en-us/templates/TC010129271033.aspx?CategoryID=CT011389821033>.

TECH TIP
How to Use Styles

As you draft your document, you can use the **Styles and Formatting** feature to apply styles to such elements as headings, lists, and body text.

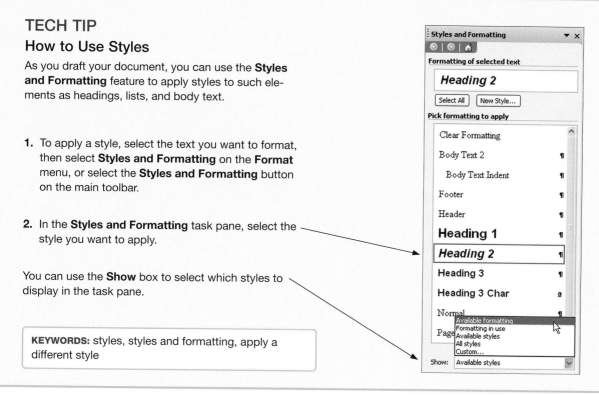

1. To apply a style, select the text you want to format, then select **Styles and Formatting** on the **Format** menu, or select the **Styles and Formatting** button on the main toolbar.

2. In the **Styles and Formatting** task pane, select the style you want to apply.

You can use the **Show** box to select which styles to display in the task pane.

> **KEYWORDS:** styles, styles and formatting, apply a different style

not in the spell checker's dictionary. You can add the word so that the spell checker will recognize it in the future. If your spell checker is set to alert you as soon as you have typed a word that is not in the dictionary, such as by highlighting the word, consider turning off this function so that you can concentrate on drafting. Run the spell checker later, as you edit. And don't forget to proofread your draft carefully for spelling errors. A spell checker cannot tell whether you have used the correct word. If you have typed "We need too dozen test tubes," the spell checker won't see a problem.

Using the Grammar Checker

A *grammar checker* can help you identify and fix potential grammatical and stylistic problems, such as wordiness, subject-verb disagreement, and double negatives. Many grammar checkers identify abstract words and suggest more-specific ones, or point out sexist terms and provide nonsexist alternatives.

Grammar checkers can identify "errors" that aren't errors at all. For this reason, many writing teachers advise that, unless you are a capable and

TECH TIP

How to Use Spelling and Grammar Checkers

When revising your document, you can use the **Spelling and Grammar** feature to check for misspelled words and to identify and fix potential grammatical and stylistic problems. You can check spelling and grammar as you write or all at once after you have finished writing.

To check spelling and grammar as you write, select **Options** on the **Tools** menu.

Select **Check spelling as you type** and **Check grammar as you type** boxes on the **Spelling & Grammar** tab.

You can also use this window to change how the software checks spelling and grammar.

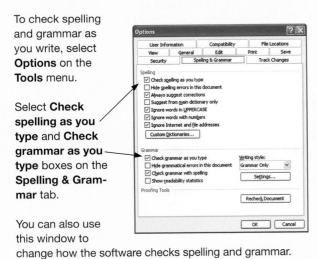

Wavy red underlines indicate potential spelling errors, and **wavy green underlines** indicate potential grammar problems.

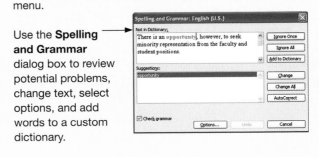

By **right-clicking** an underlined word, you can select an alternative or choose how to treat the potential problem.

To check spelling and grammar after you have finished writing, select **Spelling and Grammar** on the **Tools** menu.

Use the **Spelling and Grammar** dialog box to review potential problems, change text, select options, and add words to a custom dictionary.

KEYWORDS: spelling, grammar, automatic spelling and grammar checking

---

experienced writer who knows when to ignore bad advice, you shouldn't use a grammar checker.

Using the Thesaurus

A *thesaurus* lists synonyms or related words. An electronic thesaurus has the same strengths and weaknesses as a printed one: if you can't quite think of the word you are looking for, it can help you remember it. But the listed terms might not be related to the key term closely enough to function as synonyms. Unless you know the shades of meaning, you might substitute an inappropriate word. For example, one electronic thesaurus includes *infamous* and *notorious* as synonyms for *famous*. If you use either, you could embarrass yourself.

Using the Find and Replace Feature

One of the most useful features of a word processor is the find and replace feature. This feature lets you find, or find and replace, text you have written

TECH TIP
How to Use the Find and Replace Feature

You can quickly search for and replace specific words, phrases, or formatting in a document by using the **Find and Replace** feature.

To search for text, pull down the **Edit** menu in the main toolbar and select **Find.**

To **find and replace text,** select the **Replace** tab in the dialog box. Enter the text you want to revise and the replacement text.

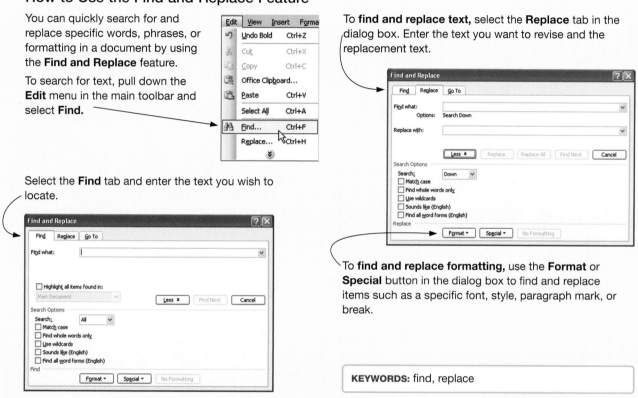

Select the **Find** tab and enter the text you wish to locate.

To **find and replace formatting,** use the **Format** or **Special** button in the dialog box to find and replace items such as a specific font, style, paragraph mark, or break.

KEYWORDS: find, replace

or styles you have used. When you revise and edit documents, use this feature to change a specific style, to locate information quickly, or to correct a recurring mistake, such as a misspelling. For example, if you often mistype *they're* or *there* for *their*, your spelling and grammar checker won't catch it. However, you can use the find feature to search for the mistyped word and replace it with the correct word.

The tools discussed in this section cannot replace a careful reading by you and by other people. These tools don't understand your subject, your audience, and your purpose. They cannot identify unclear explanations, contradictions, inaccurate data, inappropriate tone, and so forth. Use the tools, but don't rely on them. Revise, edit, and proofread your document yourself, then get help from someone you trust.

Writer's Checklist

In revising, editing, and proofreading the document, did you

☐ use the spell checker and proofread for spelling errors? (p. 37)

☐ use the grammar checker carefully? (p. 39)

☐ use the thesaurus carefully? (p. 40)

Did you revise the document by obtaining help from

☐ appropriate subject-matter experts? (p. 32)

☐ people similar to the eventual readers? (p. 32)

Exercises

1. Read the online help about using the outline view in your word processor. Make a file with five headings, each of which has a sentence of body text. Practice using the outline feature to do the following tasks:

    a. change a level-one heading to a level-two heading

    b. move the first heading to the end of the document

    c. hide the body text that goes with one of the headings

2. Your word processor probably contains a number of templates for documents such as letters, memos, faxes, and résumés. Evaluate one of these templates. Is it clear and professional-looking? Does it present an effective design for all users or only for some? What changes would you make to the template to improve it? Write a memo to your instructor presenting your findings.

Case 3: Using Revision Software Effectively

 In This Book   For more about memos, see Ch. 14, p. 352.

Background

Six months ago, Jim Williams joined the state Department of Environmental Quality (DEQ) as an environmental hydrogeologist. The DEQ enforces various state and federal environmental regulations and laws designed to ensure clean air, water, and land in the state. It is also responsible for protecting the state's citizens from the adverse health effects of pollution, cleaning up spills and releases of hazardous materials, and managing the proper disposal of hazardous and solid wastes.

Since being hired, Jim has focused on groundwater issues in the state. His fieldwork includes drilling and testing wells and collecting water samples. He also writes numerous reports. Unfortunately, Jim has never considered himself a strong writer. For him, the first draft of a report is the final draft. He would much rather be in the field collecting data than completing reports in the office.

Jim's lack of enthusiasm for writing reports is reflected in the poor quality of his reports and, much to Jim's annoyance, his recent performance review. While going over his latest performance review, Jim's supervisor, Charles Molder, told him, "Writing good, clean, concise reports is a main part of a hydrogeologist's job." He then commented specifically on Jim's poor writing skills and told him that unless his reports improved, he would be let go. Charles told Jim to spend time revising, editing, and proofreading his reports and to ask another hydrogeologist to review his drafts before he submits his final reports. "At the very least," Charles advised, "use the spelling and grammar checkers on your computer." Jim left the meeting worried about his job but committed to doing better on his next report.

After drafting a section of a report (Document 3.1), Jim used his word processor's tools to make some revisions (Document 3.2). Then he stopped by your office and asked if you would be willing to take a look at this passage and give him some advice on how to improve it.

Although hydrogeology is not your area of expertise, you agree to review the revised passage. After a quick read-through, you tell Jim, "This passage doesn't sound like you. The language is awkward, and I noticed several careless mistakes."

"I don't understand," Jim replies in frustration. "I used the spelling, grammar, *and* thesaurus tools. I followed all of the advice. Now you're telling me that it *still* has errors?"

"I think I understand what happened. Let me borrow both drafts, and I'll get back to you tomorrow. I'd like to show you some of the limitations of the software."

■ **Document 3.1**
Original Draft of Passage

 On TechComm Web

For digital versions of case documents, click on Downloadable Case Documents on <bedfordstmartins.com/techcomm>.

Yearly water quality testing is increasingly popular however less DEQ staff are currently qualified to conduct water quality sampling efforts resulting in a crunch at the years' dead line. In this study, Jim Williams, the principle investigator, collected and reported the data to Walt Shapiro, and he analyzed the data. The water quality sampling schedule took place for a full year to encompass the high flow and base flow for each stream. Its commonly assmed that during a streams high flow it's banks are inaccessible due to safety concerns thus no samples were collected. In one case, the river was not to high to safely access for only too months in the studies time period. The scientists sampling on most of the streams began early May 2004 and continued too late April 2005. Some of the stream's that are impacted and will have state and federal cost share programs on it, will have monitorring continued through an additional year. Samples were collected bi-weekly from April through September, then once a month from October through March, then back to bi-weekly for the remainder of the sampling period. Scientists should analyze samples for total suspended solids, total volatile solids, nitrate + nitrite, ammonia, total nitrogen, total phosphorus, fecal coliform and *E. coli if* you want to cover the major water quality measures. In addition to these analytical tests, on-site field parameters for disolved oxygen, temperature, conductivity total dissolved solids, PH, and discharge are measured, when possible, during each sampling event.

■ **Document 3.2**
Revised Draft of Passage

Yearly water quality testing is increasingly popular however; less DEQ staff is currently qualified to conduct water quality sampling efforts resulting in a crunch at the years' dead line. In this study, Jim Williams, the principle investigator, accumulated and accounted the data to Walt Shapiro, and he analyzed the data. The water quality-sampling schedule took place for a full year to encompass the high flow and base flow for each stream. A scientist commonly assumes that during a streams high flow its banks are inaccessible due to safety concerns thus he collects no samples. In one case, the waterway was not too high to safely access for very months in the studies time. The scientists sampling on most of the streams began early May 2004 and continued too late April 2005. Some of the stream's that are impacted and will have state and federal cost share programs on it, will have monitoring continued through an additional year. A scientist collected samples bi-weekly from April through September, then once a month from October through March, then back to bi-weekly for the remainder of the sampling period. Scientists should analyze samples for total suspended solids, total volatile solids, nitrate + nitrite, ammonia, total nitrogen, total phosphorus, fecal coli form and *E. coli if* you want to cover the major water quality measures. In addition to these analytical tests, a scientist measured on-site field parameters for dissolved oxygen, temperature, conductivity total dissolved solids, PH, and discharge, when possible, during each sampling incident.

Your Assignment

1. Download the Microsoft Word file of Document 3.1 from <bedfordstmartins.com/techcomm> or type the passage in a Word document. Using Word's tools, do the following:

   a. Run the passage through the spell checker. Note the limitations of the spell checker.

   b. Run the passage through the grammar checker. Note the limitations of the grammar checker.

   c. Compare the original passage to the revised passage (Document 3.2). Identify places where Jim used an inappropriate word likely suggested by the thesaurus. Note the limitations of the thesaurus.

   Write Jim a short memo in which you explain the limitations of the tools and suggest how he could use them more effectively.

2. Revise Jim's original passage (Document 3.1) to create a more effective report. Send your revision to Jim, along with a brief memo explaining your changes.

Writing Collaboratively

4

People collaborate in writing everything from memos to books. Longer, more complex, or more important documents—such as proposals, reports, manuals, corporate annual reports, and Web sites—are more likely to be written collaboratively.

Figure 4.1 shows three basic patterns of collaboration.

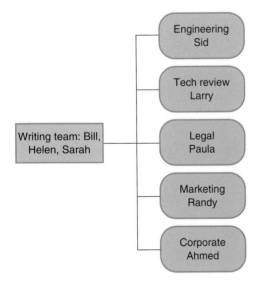

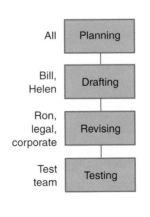

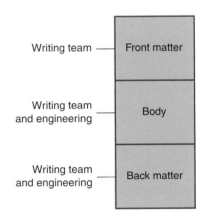

Collaboration based on job specialty. On this team, an engineer is the subject-matter expert, the person in charge of contributing all the technical information; other professionals are in charge of their own specialties. The writing team writes, edits, and designs the document.

Collaboration based on the stages of the writing process. Group members collaborate during the planning stage by sharing ideas about the document's content, organization, and style, then establish a production schedule and an evaluation program. They collaborate less during the drafting stage, because drafting collaboratively is much more time-consuming than drafting individually. During the revising phase, they return to collaboration.

Collaboration based on the section of the document. One person takes responsibility for one section of the document, another person does another section, and so forth. This pattern is common for large projects with separate sections, such as proposals.

■ **Figure 4.1   Patterns of Collaboration**

ADVANTAGES AND DISADVANTAGES OF COLLABORATION

As a student, you might have already worked collaboratively on course projects. As a professional, you will work on many more. And in the workplace, the stakes might be higher. Effective collaboration can make you look like a star, but ineffective collaboration can ruin an important project—and hurt group members' reputations.

The best way to start thinking about collaboration is to understand its main advantages and disadvantages.

Advantages of Collaboration

Writers who collaborate can create a better document and improve the way an organization functions:

- *Collaboration draws on a greater knowledge base.* Therefore, it can be more comprehensive and more accurate than a single-author document.

- *Collaboration draws on a greater skills base.* No one person can be an expert manager, writer, editor, graphic artist, and production person.

- *Collaboration provides a better idea of how the audience will read the document.* Each group member acts as an audience, offering more questions and suggestions than one person could while writing alone.

- *Collaboration improves communication among employees.* Because group members share a goal, they learn about each other's jobs, responsibilities, and frustrations.

- *Collaboration helps acclimate new employees to an organization.* New employees learn how things work—which people to see, what forms to fill out, and so forth—as well as what the organization values, such as the importance of ethical conduct and the willingness to work hard and sacrifice for an important initiative.

Disadvantages of Collaboration

Collaboration can also have important disadvantages:

- *Collaboration takes more time than individual writing.* It takes longer because of the time needed for the collaborators to communicate.

- *Collaboration can lead to groupthink.* When group members value getting along more than thinking critically about the project, they are prone to *groupthink*. Groupthink, which promotes conformity, can result in an inferior document, because no one wants to cause a scene by asking tough questions.

- *Collaboration can yield a disjointed document.* Sections can contradict or repeat each other or be written in different styles. To prevent these problems, writers need to plan and edit the document carefully.

- *Collaboration can lead to inequitable workloads.* Despite the project leader's best efforts, some people will end up doing more work than others.
- *Collaboration can reduce collaborators' motivation to work hard on the document.* The smaller the role a person plays in the project, the less motivated he or she is to make the extra effort.
- *Collaboration can lead to interpersonal conflict.* People can disagree about the best way to create the document or about the document itself. Such disagreements can hurt working relationships during the project and long after.

CONDUCTING MEETINGS

Collaboration involves conducting meetings. The following discussion covers five aspects of meetings.

Conducting meetings involves:

| Listening effectively |
| Setting your group's agenda |
| Conducting efficient face-to-face meetings |
| Communicating diplomatically |
| Critiquing a group member's work |

Listening Effectively

Participating in a meeting involves listening and speaking. If you listen effectively to the other people, you will understand what they are thinking, and you will be able to speak knowledgeably and constructively.

Listening is more than just hearing (receiving and processing sound waves). Listening involves understanding what the speaker is saying and interpreting the information.

Guidelines

Listening Effectively

Follow these five steps to improve your effectiveness as a listener.

▶ **Pay attention to the speaker.** Look at the speaker, and don't let your mind wander. If you're counting the number of times the speaker says "you know," you're not paying attention to what the person is saying.

▶ **Listen for main ideas.** Pay attention to phrases that signal important information, such as "What I'm saying is . . ." or "The point I'm trying to make is . . . ."

▶ **Don't get emotionally involved with the speaker's ideas.** Even if you disagree, keep listening. Keep an open mind. Don't stop listening so that you can plan what you are going to say next.

▶ **Ask questions to clarify what the speaker said.** After the speaker finishes, ask questions to make sure you understand. For instance, you might ask, "When you said that each journal recommends different printers, did you mean that each journal recommends several printers or that each journal recommends a different printer?"

▶ **Provide appropriate feedback.** The most important feedback is to look into the speaker's eyes. You can nod your approval to signal that you understand what he or she is saying. Appropriate feedback helps assure the speaker that he or she is communicating. That assurance improves the communication.

Setting Your Group's Agenda

It's important to get your group off to a smooth start. In the first meeting, start to define your group's agenda.

Guidelines

Setting Your Agenda

▶ **Define the group's task.** What document, or "deliverable," will your group submit? Every group member has to agree, for example, that your task is to revise the employee manual by April 10 and that the revision must be no longer than 200 pages. You also need to agree on more-conceptual aspects of the task, including the audience, purpose, and scope of the document.

▶ **Choose a group leader.** This person serves as the link between the group and management. (In a school setting, the group leader represents the group in communicating with the instructor.) The group leader also keeps the group on track, leads the meetings, and coordinates communication among group members.

▶ **Define tasks for each group member.** As Figure 4.1 on page 46 shows, there are three main ways to divide the tasks. All group members will participate in each phase of the project, and each group member will review the document at every stage. However, each member will have chief responsibility for a task to which he or she is best suited. Group members will likely assume informal roles, too. One person might be good at clarifying what others have said, another at preventing unnecessary arguments, and another at asking questions that force the group to reevaluate its decisions.

▶ **Establish working procedures.** Before starting to work, members need answers—in writing, if possible—to the following questions:

— When and where will we meet?

— What procedures will we follow in the meetings?

— How, and how often, are we to communicate with other group members, including the leader?

▶ **Establish a procedure for resolving conflict productively.** Disagreements about the project can lead to a better product. Give members a chance to express ideas fully and find areas of agreement, then resolve the conflict by a vote.

▶ **Create a style sheet.** If all group members draft using a similar writing style, the document will need less revision. Discuss as many style questions as you can: use of headings and lists, paragraph style and length, level of formality, and so forth. And be sure to use styles, as discussed in Chapter 3.

▶ **Establish a work schedule.** For example, to submit a proposal on February 10, you must complete an outline by January 25, a draft by February 1, and a revision by February 8. These dates are called *milestones*.

▶ **Create evaluation materials.** Group members have a right to know how their work will be evaluated. In schools, students often evaluate themselves and other group members. But in the working world, managers are more likely to do the evaluations.

In This Book

For more about style, see Chs. 10 and 11.

In This Book

Fig. 4.2 on page 50 shows a work schedule form. Fig. 4.3 on page 51 shows a form that group members can use to evaluate other group members. Fig. 4.4 on page 52 shows a self-evaluation form.

■ **Figure 4.2**
Work-Schedule Form

*Notice that milestones some-
times are presented in reverse
chronological order; the
delivery-date milestone, for
instance, comes first. On other
forms, items are presented in
normal chronological order.*

*The form includes spaces for
listing the person responsible for
each milestone and progress
report and for stating the
progress toward each milestone
and progress report.*

 On TechComm Web

For printable versions of Figures
4.2, 4.3, and 4.4, click on Forms
for Technical Communication on
<bedfordstmartins.com/
techcomm>.

WORK-SCHEDULE FORM

Name of Project: *VoIP feasibility study*

Principal Reader: *Joan*

Other Readers: *Carlton, Wendy*

Group Members: *Saada, Larry, Randy, Ahmed*

Type of Document Required: *recommendation report*

Milestones	Responsible Member	Status	Date
Deliver Document	*Saada*		*May 19*
Proofread Document	*all*		*May 18*
Send Document to Print Shop	*n/a*		*n/a*
Complete Revision	*Randy*		*May 17*
Review Draft Elements	*all*	*Done*	*May 16*
Assemble Draft	*Ahmed*	*Done*	*May 13*
Establish Tasks	*Larry*	*Done*	*May 9*

Progress Reports	Responsible Member	Status	Date
Progress Report 3	*n/a*		
Progress Report 2	*n/a*		
Progress Report 1	*Randy*	*Done*	*May 15*

Meetings	Agenda	Location	Date	Time
Meeting 3	*Review final draft*	*Room C*	*May 18*	*3:30*
Meeting 2	*Review draft elements*	*Room B*	*May 16*	*2:00*
Meeting 1	*Kickoff meeting*	*Room C*	*May 9*	*3:00*

Notes

■ Figure 4.3
Group-Members
Evaluation Form

GROUP-MEMBERS EVALUATION FORM

Your name: _____ *Mackenzie Hopkins* _____

Title of the project: _____ *4-wheel drive feasibility report* _____

Date: _____ *October 14, 2006* _____

Instructions

Use this form to evaluate the other members of your group. Write the name of each group member other than yourself in one of the columns, then assign a score of 0 to 10 (0 being the lowest grade, 10 the highest) to each group member for each criterion. Then total the scores for each member. Because each group member has different strengths and weaknesses, the scores you assign will differ. On the back of this sheet, write any comments you wish to make.

Criteria	Group Members			
	Kurt	*Amber*	*Bob* ◄	
1. Regularly attends meetings	1. *10*	1. *9*	1. *6*	1. ____
2. Is prepared at the meetings	2. *9*	2. *8*	2. *5*	2. ____
3. Meets deadlines	3. *9*	3. *9*	3. *2*	3. ____
4. Contributes good ideas in meetings	4. *9*	4. *10*	4. *9*	4. ____
5. Contributes ideas diplomatically	5. *8*	5. *9*	5. *9*	5. ____
6. Submits high-quality work	6. *9*	6. *9*	6. *7*	6. ____
7. Listens to other members	7. *8*	7. *10*	7. *6*	7. ____
8. Shows respect for other members	8. *9*	8. *10*	8. *6*	8. ____
9. Helps to reduce conflict	9. *9*	9. *10*	9. *5*	9. ____
10. Your overall assessment of this person's contribution	10. *9*	10. *9*	10. *7*	10. ____
Total Points	*89*	*93*	*62*	____

Mackenzie gives high grades to Kurt and Amber but low grades to Bob. If Kurt and Amber agree with Mackenzie's assessment of Bob's participation, the three of them should meet with Bob to discuss why his participation has been weak and to consider ways for him to improve.

■ Figure 4.4
Self-Evaluation Form

SELF-EVALUATION FORM

Your name: _Lucas Barnes_   Date: _April 12, 2006_

Title of the project: _digital-camera study progress report_

Instructions

On this form, record and evaluate your own involvement in this project. In the Log section, record the activities you performed as an individual and those you performed as part of the group. For all activities, record the date and the number of hours you spent. In the Evaluation section, write two brief statements, one about aspects of your contribution you think were successful and one about the aspects you want to improve.

Log Individual Activities	Date	Number of Hours
Reviewed proposal and analyzed the Simmons article	April 9	1.5
Wrote a draft of the progress report	April 10	2.5
Revised a draft of the progress report	April 11	1

Activities as Part of Group	Date	Number of Hours
Met to discuss test research	April 10	1
E-mailed group and replied to questions about draft	April 11	2.5
Met to discuss revision of progress report	April 11	1.5

Evaluation
Aspects of My Participation That Were Successful

I think I did a good job in reviewing the proposal and critiquing the research. I had the draft ready on time, although there were some rough parts in it. I participated effectively in the group meeting about the revision. I think I'm getting a little better about being less sensitive when the group suggests revisions.

Aspects of My Participation That I Want to Improve in the Future

I still need to get better at completing my work early enough so I can set it aside before getting it out to the other group members. I get embarrassed when they point out superficial mistakes that I should have caught. I need to practice using styles so that my drafts are easier to incorporate into the group's draft. The other members remembered to use them. I didn't.

The evaluation section of the form is difficult to fill out, but it can be the most valuable section for you in assessing your skills in collaborating. When you get to the second question, be thoughtful and constructive. Don't merely say that you want to improve your skills in using the software. Don't just write "None."

Conducting Efficient Face-to-Face Meetings

Human communication is largely nonverbal. That is, people communicate through words but also through the tone, rate, and volume of their speech. They communicate, too, through body language. For this reason, face-to-face discussions provide the most information about what a person is thinking and feeling—and the best opportunity for group members to understand one another.

Guidelines

Conducting Efficient Meetings

▶ **Arrive on time.** If you know you will have to miss a meeting, notify the group leader as soon as possible.

▶ **Stick to an agenda.** Create the agenda beforehand so that everyone can come prepared. Don't stray too far from the agenda. If you need to discuss a point that isn't on the agenda, schedule another meeting.

▶ **Record the important decisions made at the meeting.** One group member should serve as secretary by making a record of the meeting focusing on decisions the group makes and tasks to be carried out next.

▶ **Summarize your accomplishments and make sure every member understands his or her assignment.** The group leader should formally close the meeting by summarizing the progress the group has made and stating the tasks each group member is to perform before the next meeting. If possible, the secretary should give each group member this informal set of meeting minutes.

 On TechComm Web

For an excellent discussion of how to conduct meetings, see Matson (1996). Click on Links Library for Ch. 4 on <bedfordstmartins.com/techcomm>.

 In This Book

For a discussion of meeting minutes, see Ch. 17, p. 447.

Communicating Diplomatically

Because collaborating can be stressful, it can lead to interpersonal conflict. People can become frustrated and angry with one another because of personality clashes or because of disputes about the project. If the project is to succeed, however, group members have to work together productively. When you speak in a group meeting, you want to appear helpful, not critical or overbearing.

Guidelines

Communicating Diplomatically

▶ **Listen carefully, without interrupting.** See the Guidelines box on page 48.

▶ **Give everyone a chance to speak.** Don't dominate the discussion.

▶ **Avoid personal remarks and insults.** Be tolerant and respectful of other people's views and working methods. Doing so is right—and smart: if you anger people, they will go out of their way to oppose you.

▶ **Don't overstate your position.** A modest qualifier such as "I think" or "it seems to me" is an effective signal to your listeners that you realize that everyone may not share your views.

OVERBEARING	My plan is a sure thing; there's no way we're not going to kill Allied next quarter.
DIPLOMATIC	I think this plan has a good chance of success: we're playing off our strengths and Allied's weaknesses.

In the diplomatic version, the speaker calls it "this plan," not "my plan."

▶ **Don't get emotionally attached to your own ideas.** When people oppose you, try to understand why. Digging in is usually unwise—unless it's a matter of principle. Although you may be right and everyone else wrong, that's not likely.

▶ **Ask pertinent questions.** Bright people ask questions to understand what they hear, to connect it to other ideas, and to encourage other group members to examine what they hear.

▶ **Pay attention to nonverbal communication.** Bob might *say* that he understands a point, but his facial expression might show that he doesn't. If a group member looks confused, ask him or her about it. A direct question is likely to elicit a statement that will help the group clarify its discussion.

Critiquing a Group Member's Work

In collaborating, group members often critique notes and drafts written by other group members. Knowing how to do this without offending the writer is a valuable skill.

Guidelines

Critiquing a Colleague's Work

▶ **Start with a positive comment.** Even if the work is weak, say "You've obviously put a lot of work into this, Joanne. Thanks." Or, "This is a really good start. Thanks, Joanne."

▶ **Discuss the larger issues first.** Begin with the big issues, such as organization, development, logic, design, and graphics. Then work on the smaller issues, such as paragraph development, sentence-level matters, and word choice. Leave editing and proofreading until the end of the process.

▶ **Talk about the document, not the writer.**

RUDE	You don't explain clearly why this criterion is relevant.
BETTER	I'm having trouble understanding how this criterion relates to the topic.

Your goal is to improve the quality of the document you will submit, not to evaluate the writer or the draft. Offer constructive suggestions.

RUDE	Why didn't you include the price comparisons here, as you said you would?
BETTER	I wonder if the report would be stronger if we included the price comparisons here.

In the better version, the speaker focuses on the goal—to create an effective report—rather than on the writer's draft. Also, the speaker qualifies his recommendation by saying "I wonder if . . . ." This approach sounds constructive rather than boastful or annoyed.

USING ELECTRONIC TOOLS IN COLLABORATION

Electronic media are useful collaborative tools for two reasons:

- *Face-to-face meetings are not always possible or convenient.* Most electronic media enable people to communicate *asynchronously.* That is, a person can read an e-mail when it is convenient, not when the writer sent it.

- *Electronic communication is digital.* Group members can store and revise comments and drafts, incorporating them as the document develops.

> **Communicating electronically may call for:**
>
> Using the comment, revision, and highlighting features of a word processor
>
> Using e-mail to send files
>
> Using groupware

Using the Comment, Revision, and Highlighting Features of a Word Processor

Word processors offer three powerful features you will find useful in collaborative work:

- The *comment feature* lets a reader add electronic comments to a writer's file.

TECH TIP

How to Use the Comment, Revision, and Highlighting Features

When collaborating with others, you can distribute your document to readers electronically so that they can add comments, revise text, and highlight text. You can then review their comments, keep track of who suggested which changes, and decide whether to accept or decline their changes without ever having to print your document. You can use the **Reviewing** toolbar to electronically review a document or to revise a document that has already been commented on by readers.

On the **View** menu, open the **Reviewing** toolbar.

To **electronically review** a document, highlight relevant text and do the following:

 Select the **Insert Comment** button to write comments in a cartoon bubble in the margin.

 Select the **Highlight** button to emphasize a particular passage.

 Select the **Track Changes** button to turn on change tracking so that a writer can distinguish revised text from original text.

To **change the color or design** of comment bubbles or markup, use the **Track Changes** tab in the **Options** dialog box.

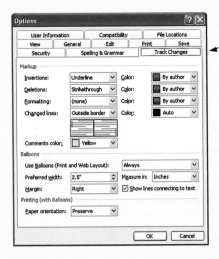

To **revise a document** that has already been commented on by reviewers, do the following:

Use the menu on the **Reviewing** toolbar to change **displays** of the document.

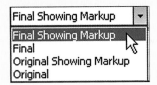

Select buttons on the **Reviewing** toolbar to see **previous** or **next** comment and to **accept** or **decline** markup.

 Select the **Reviewing Pane** button to review all comments and changes.

KEYWORDS: reviewing toolbar, comments, reviewing pane, track changes

- The *revision feature* lets readers mark up the text by deleting, revising, and adding words while allowing the writer to keep track of who made which changes.
- The *highlighting feature* lets a reader use one of about a dozen "highlighting pens" to call the writer's attention to a particular passage.

Using E-mail to Send Files

Most e-mail software lets you attach a file to an e-mail message. This means that you can easily send a file, such as a document written in WordPerfect or a spreadsheet prepared in Excel. A recipient who has the software in which the document was saved can open it.

Using Groupware

Groupware is software that lets people at the same or different locations plan, draft, revise, and track a document. You may already be familiar with groupware programs such as Lotus Notes or Microsoft NetMeeting. Manufacturers of office suites such as Microsoft and Corel are putting more and more collaboration features in their products.

    Team members at different locations can perform six important collaborative activities:

- *Share files.* Team members can post files to a document library, enabling other team members to view them or download them.
- *Carry out asynchronous discussions.* Team members can carry out discussions by posting comments to a discussion list. All team members can read and download the comments at their convenience.
- *Carry out synchronous discussions.* Using instant messaging, team members can trade text messages in real time.
- *Comment on documents.* Team members can attach comments to files without actually changing the text.
- *Distribute announcements.* Team members can post announcements, such as reminders about deadlines or schedule revisions.
- *Create automated change notifications.* Team members can sign up to be notified by e-mail when a document has been changed.

Many groupware programs also offer two additional tools:

- *Whiteboards.* Whiteboard software lets people at different locations draw on the screen as if they were all in a room with a whiteboard. Anything drawn on one screen is displayed immediately on every screen. The image can be printed or saved as a file. Figure 4.5 on page 58 shows the whiteboard screen from Microsoft's NetMeeting.

 On TechComm Web

For a tutorial on NetMeeting's collaborative tools, see Microsoft's Web site. Click on Links Library for Ch. 4 on <bedfordstmartins.com/techcomm>.

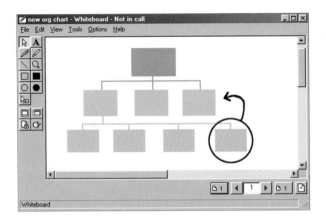

■ Figure 4.5 A Whiteboard Screen

All the people participating in the whiteboard session see the same screen. Whenever anyone changes anything on his or her screen, all participants see the change on their screens.

■ Figure 4.6 A Videoconference

A camera mounted on top of the monitor or installed on the ceiling sends a video image to the other group of participants. Most videoconferencing systems let participants display additional "windows" on a monitor.
Source: Aethra, 2005 <www.aethra.com/worldwide/proddoc.asp ?IDProd=74&IDT=10&M=150>.

- *Videoconferencing.* Standard video cameras can be connected to computers, enabling people to see one another as they talk. Figure 4.6 shows a
  videoconference.

GENDER AND COLLABORATION

Effective collaboration involves two related challenges: maintaining the group as a productive, friendly working unit and accomplishing the task. Scholars of gender and collaboration see these two challenges as representing the feminine and the masculine perspectives.

This discussion should begin with a qualifier: in discussing gender, we are generalizing; we are not talking about particular people. In other words, the differences in behavior between any two individual men or two individual women are likely to be greater than the differences between men and women in general.

The differences in how the sexes communicate and work in groups have been traced to every culture's traditional family structure. As the primary caregivers, women have learned to value nurturing, connection, growth, and cooperation. As the primary breadwinners, men have learned to value separateness, competition, debate, and even conflict (Chodorow, 1978).

For decades, scholars have studied the speech differences between women and men. Women tend to use more qualifiers and "tag" questions, such as "Don't you think?" (Tannen, 1990). Some scholars, however, suggest

INTERACTIVE SAMPLE DOCUMENT
Critiquing a Draft Clearly and Diplomatically

This is an excerpt from the methods section of a report about computer servers. In this section, the writer is explaining the tasks he performed in analyzing different servers. In a later section, he explains what he learned from the analysis. The comments in the balloons were inserted into the document by the author's colleague.

The questions in the margin ask you to think about techniques for critiquing (as outlined on page 55). E-mail your responses to yourself and/or your instructor, and see suggested responses on TechComm Web.

The first task of the on-site evaluations was to set up and configure each server. We noted the relative complexity of setting up each system to our network.

Comment: Huh? What exactly does this mean?

After we had the system configured, we performed a set of routine maintenance tasks: Add a new memory module, swap a hard-drive, swap a power supply and perform system diagnostics.

Comment: Okay, good. Maybe we should explain why we chose these tests.

We recorded the time and relative difficulty of each task. Also, we tried to gather a qualitative feeling for how much effort would be involved in the day-to-day maintenance of the systems.

Comment: What kind of scale are you using? If we don't explain it, it's basically useless.

Comment: Same question as above.

After each system was set up, we completed the maintenance evaluations and began the benchmark testing. We ran the complete WinBench and NetBench test suites on each system. We chose several of the key factors from these tests for comparison.

Comment: Will readers know these are the right tests? Should we explain?

1. What is the tone of the comments? How can they be improved?

2. How well does the collaborator address the larger issues?

3. How well does the collaborator address the writing, not the writer?

4. How well do the collaborator's comments focus on the goal of the document, rather than judge the quality of the writing?

 On TechComm Web

To e-mail your responses to yourself and/or your instructor and to see suggested responses, click on Interactive Sample Documents for Ch. 4 on <bedfordstmartins.com/techcomm>.

that women might be using these patterns because it is expected of them and that they use them mainly in groups that include men (McMillan, Clifton, McGrath, & Gale, 1977). Many experts caution against using qualifiers and tag questions, which can suggest subservience and powerlessness.

In collaborative groups, women appear to value consensus and relationships, to show more empathy, and to demonstrate superior listening skills (Borisoff & Merrill, 1987). Women talk more about topics unrelated to the task (Duin, Jorn, & DeBower, 1991), but this talk is central to maintaining group coherence. Men appear to be more competitive and more likely to assume leadership roles. Scholars of gender recommend that all professionals strive to achieve an androgynous mix of the skills and aptitudes commonly associated with both women and men.

CULTURE AND COLLABORATION

Gender is just one of many aspects of collaboration that differ from one culture to another. In some cultures, oral and written communication follow strict conventions related to the gender, age, and professional seniority of the people involved.

Strategies for Intercultural Communication

Collaborating Across Cultures

Most collaborative groups in industry and in the classroom include people from other cultures. The challenge for all group members is to understand the ways in which cultural differences can affect group behavior. People from other cultures

- might find it difficult to assert themselves in collaborative groups
- might be unwilling to respond with a definite "no"
- might be reluctant to admit when they are confused or to ask for clarification
- might avoid criticizing others
- might avoid initiating new tasks or performing creatively

Even the most benign gesture of friendship on the part of a U.S. student can cause confusion. If a U.S. student casually asks a Japanese student about her major and the courses she is taking, the Japanese student might find the question too personal, but she might consider it perfectly appropriate to talk about her family and her religious beliefs (Lustig & Koester, 2006). Therefore, you should remain open to encounters with people from other cultures without jumping to conclusions about what their actions might or might not mean.

In This Book

For more about multicultural issues, see Ch. 5, p. 83.

Collaborator's Checklist

In your first group meeting, did you
- [ ] define the group's task? (p. 49)
- [ ] choose a group leader? (p. 49)
- [ ] define tasks for each group member? (p. 49)
- [ ] establish working procedures? (p. 49)
- [ ] establish a procedure for resolving conflict? (p. 49)
- [ ] create a style sheet? (p. 49)
- [ ] establish a work schedule? (p. 49)
- [ ] create evaluation materials? (p. 49)

To conduct efficient face-to-face meetings, do you
- [ ] arrive on time? (p. 53)
- [ ] stick to an agenda? (p. 53)
- [ ] make sure that a group member records important decisions made at the meeting? (p. 53)

- [ ] make sure that a group member summarizes your accomplishments and that every member understands what his or her assignment is? (p. 53)

To communicate diplomatically, do you
- [ ] listen carefully? (p. 54)
- [ ] let others talk? (p. 54)
- [ ] avoid personal remarks and insults? (p. 54)
- [ ] avoid overstating your position? (p. 54)
- [ ] avoid getting emotionally attached to your own ideas? (p. 54)
- [ ] ask pertinent questions? (p. 54)
- [ ] pay attention to body language? (p. 54)

In critiquing a group member's draft, do you

- ☐ start with a positive comment? (p. 55)
- ☐ discuss the larger issues first? (p. 55)
- ☐ talk about the writing, not the writer? (p. 55)
- ☐ focus on the group's document, not on the group member's draft? (p. 55)

If appropriate, do you

- ☐ use the comment, revision, and highlighting features of a word processor? (p. 55)
- ☐ use e-mail to send files? (p. 57)
- ☐ use groupware? (p. 57)

Exercises

1. Experiment with the comment, revision, and highlighting features of your word processor. Using online help if necessary, learn how to make, revise, and delete comments; make, undo, and accept revisions; and add and delete highlights.

2. **INTERNET EXERCISE** Using a search engine, find e-mail shareware or freeware on the Internet. Download the software and install it on your computer at home. Learn how to use the feature that lets you send attached files.

3. You have probably had a lot of experience working in collaborative teams in previous courses or on the job. Brainstorm for five minutes, listing some of your best and worst experiences participating in collaborative teams. Choose one positive experience and one negative experience. Think about why the positive experience went well. Was there a technique that a team member used that accounted for the positive experience? Think about why the negative experience went wrong. Was there a technique or action that accounted for the negative experience? How might the negative experience have been prevented or fixed? Be prepared to share your responses with the rest of the class.

4. **INTERNET EXERCISE** Your college or university wishes to update its Web site to include a section called "For

Prospective International Students." Along with members of your group, first determine whether your school's Web site already has information of particular interest to prospective international students. If it does, write a memo to your instructor describing and evaluating the information. Is it accurate? Comprehensive? Clear? Useful? What kinds of information should be added to the site to make it more effective?

If the school's site does not have this information, perform the following tasks:

- *Plan.* What kind of information should it include? Does some of this information already exist, or does it all have to be created from scratch? For example, can you create a link to information on how to obtain a student visa, or does this information not exist on the Web? Write an outline of the main topics that should be covered.

- *Draft.* Write the following sections: "Where to Live on or Near Campus," "Social Activities on or Near Campus," and "If English Is Not Your Native Language." What graphics could you include? Are they already available? What other sites should you link to for these three sections?

In a memo, present your suggestions to your instructor.

Case 4: Handling Interpersonal Conflict

 In This Book   For more about claims and persuasion, see Ch. 8. For more about memos, see Ch. 14, p. 352.

Background

Your company, Green Flag Solutions, provides a wide range of e-commerce and Web site-development solutions to the motor-sports industry. Brooks, a company offering specialized automotive parts to racing teams, has sent out a request for proposals to develop an e-catalog of its products. Colby Larson, Green Flag Solutions' Vice President of Development, has assigned you to an interdisciplinary

team responsible for responding to this request. The other members of the team are Allison and Ken. Allison is a software engineer; Ken is a customer sales representative; you are a Web designer.

At your first meeting, you choose Allison as the team leader. As the company's top software engineer, she has had a lot of experience working collaboratively and is happy to take on the task of supervising your team's work.

The first meeting to discuss the proposal is scheduled for 11 A.M. Monday in the company's conference room.

It is 11:15 Monday, and Ken has not arrived for the meeting. Neither Allison nor you have heard from him. At 11:30, you and Allison decide to call Ken on his cell phone. There is no answer.

You and Allison are angry that Ken hasn't arrived or left a message. The two of you are unwilling to start work on the project without him. You decide to cancel the meeting. Allison says that she will call him later that afternoon.

At about 3 P.M., you get a call from Allison. She received a phone message from Ken (Document 4.1) sent to her at 10:50 A.M. She just spoke with Ken, who has agreed to meet the next day at 3 P.M. in the conference room. Is that okay with you? Allison says that Ken has agreed to bring to the meeting marketing information on companies that might be bidding against Green Flag Solutions. She asks you to bring a summary of the e-catalog requirements the team's proposal must address. You agree and write the time in your appointment book.

The next day, at 3:15 P.M., Ken rushes into the conference room. "Sorry I'm late," he says with a smile. You and Allison give him a cold look. Allison begins the discussion.

"Okay, we each agreed to bring information to the meeting today. Ken, what have you got?"

"That was for today? I'm really sorry. I just didn't get to it. Don't we already have something similar from the, um, Lindt Motors proposal we sent off earlier this year?"

Allison stares at Ken for a second or two and turns to you. You read your summary of e-catalog requirements. Then Allison outlines a possible strategy for meeting the client's needs. You and Allison agree that the team needs some rough cost estimates for the proposed solution. Allison asks Ken to bring the cost estimates to the next meeting. While the group sets a time for the next meeting and decides on an agenda, Ken answers two calls on his cell phone. When the meeting concludes, Ken quickly leaves with his cell phone to his ear. At 5:15, Allison sends an e-mail reminder (Document 4.2) to both of you.

At the next meeting, you and Allison are left waiting for Ken again. After 15 minutes, Allison decides to check her e-mail. She finds that Ken sent her an e-mail message (Document 4.3) just before midnight the previous night.

"I'm not happy with what I see developing with Ken," she says. "We're going to be slowed down if he doesn't come to the meetings or prepare. I'm tempted to send him an e-mail message right now telling him to get with the program. Do you think we should?"

"Let's take a few hours to cool down and think about what's happening before we do anything. I'll send you an e-mail message when I get back from lunch."

Your Assignment

1. How should you respond to Allison? Should you merely hope that Ken will start to participate more responsibly? Is there some way to delegate tasks that will motivate Ken to participate more actively? Should you and Allison go ahead with the project, letting Ken participate when he chooses to? Should Allison talk with him? Should both of you talk with him together? Write Allison an e-mail message suggesting how to address the conflict.

2. Ken doesn't respond well to your latest communication, and you and Allison decide to discuss the matter with Colby Larson. What should you say to her? How should you prepare, and what sort of documentation should you collect? How will you support your claims? In a memo to Colby, explain the situation and request her advice in resolving the team's conflict.

"Hey, Allison, I'm busy with Michael Glenn at Racing Solutions. He seems real interested in talking about our e-commerce services, especially our work for Blanchard Custom Wheels. Sorry I can't make it today. Talk to you when I'm back in the office."

■ **Document 4.1**
Message Left by Ken

 On TechComm Web

For digital versions of case documents, click on Downloadable Case Documents on <bedfordstmartins.com/techcomm>.

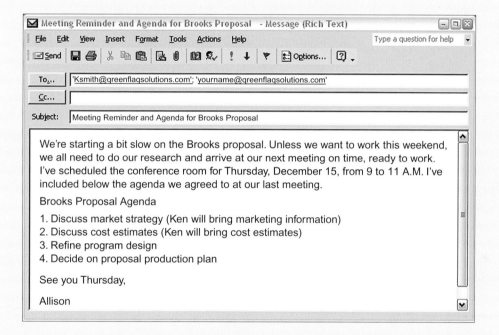

■ **Document 4.2**
Allison's E-mail Reminder

Meeting Reminder and Agenda for Brooks Proposal — Message (Rich Text)

File Edit View Insert Format Tools Actions Help   Type a question for help

Send

To... 'Ksmith@greenflagsolutions.com'; 'yourname@greenflagsolutions.com'

Cc...

Subject: Meeting Reminder and Agenda for Brooks Proposal

We're starting a bit slow on the Brooks proposal. Unless we want to work this weekend, we all need to do our research and arrive at our next meeting on time, ready to work. I've scheduled the conference room for Thursday, December 15, from 9 to 11 A.M. I've included below the agenda we agreed to at our last meeting.

Brooks Proposal Agenda

1. Discuss market strategy (Ken will bring marketing information)
2. Discuss cost estimates (Ken will bring cost estimates)
3. Refine program design
4. Decide on proposal production plan

See you Thursday,

Allison

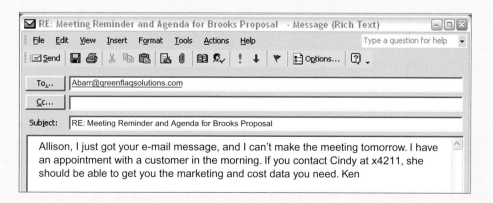

■ **Document 4.3**
Ken's E-mail Reply

RE: Meeting Reminder and Agenda for Brooks Proposal — Message (Rich Text)

File Edit View Insert Format Tools Actions Help   Type a question for help

Send

To... Abarr@greenflagsolutions.com

Cc...

Subject: RE: Meeting Reminder and Agenda for Brooks Proposal

Allison, I just got your e-mail message, and I can't make the meeting tomorrow. I have an appointment with a customer in the morning. If you contact Cindy at x4211, she should be able to get you the marketing and cost data you need. Ken

PART TWO

Planning the Document

5

Analyzing Your Audience and Purpose

McDonald's made a mistake when it printed take-out bags decorated with flags from around the world. Among the flags was that of Saudi Arabia, which contains excerpts from the Koran. This was extremely offensive to the Saudis, who considered it sacrilegious to throw out the bags because they contained these excerpts. How are technical professionals and technical communicators to know when they write something that could offend an audience? The answer is that the content and form of every technical document you write are determined by the writing situation: your audience and your purpose.

Understanding the writing situation helps you meet your readers' needs—and your own. Audience and purpose are not unique to technical communication. When a classified ad describes a job, for example, the writing situation is clear:

AUDIENCE   prospective applicants

PURPOSE   to describe the job opening and motivate qualified persons to apply

Once you have identified the two basic elements of your writing situation, you must analyze them before deciding what to say and how to say it.

Ethics Note

Meeting Your Readers' Needs Responsibly

A major theme of this chapter is that effective technical communication meets your readers' needs. What this theme means is that as you plan, draft, revise, and edit, you should always be thinking of who your readers are, why they are reading your document, and the context of use: how they will be reading the document. For example, if your readers include many nonnative speakers of English, you will adjust your vocabulary, sentence structure, and other textual elements so that they can understand your document easily. If your readers will be sitting at computer terminals as they use your document, you will choose a page size that lets your readers place the document next to their terminals.

Meeting your readers' needs does *not* mean writing a misleading or inaccurate document. If your readers want you to slant the information, omit crucial data, or downplay bad news, they are asking you to act unethically. You are under no obligation to do so. For more information on ethics, see Chapter 2.

 **On TechComm Web**

For more about audience analysis, see Writing Guidelines for Engineering and Science Students. Click on Links Library for Ch. 5 on <bedfordstmartins .com/techcomm>.

ANALYZING AN AUDIENCE

There are three steps in analyzing an audience:

- *Identifying primary and secondary audiences.* The primary audience will study your document and take some action in response to it. The secondary audience will read your document to keep abreast of what you are saying.
- *Identifying basic categories of readers.* Different categories of readers—experts, technicians, managers, and general readers—need different kinds of information, presented in different ways.
- *Identifying individual characteristics of readers.* The more you know about your readers—their needs, their preferences, and the uses to which they will put the information—the more effectively you can present the information to them.

To carry out these steps, you need to think, interview people, and read documents they have written.

Identifying Primary and Secondary Audiences

Start by classifying your readers into two categories:

- A *primary audience* of people who use your document in carrying out their jobs. This audience might include an executive who reads your document while deciding whether to authorize building a new facility and a treasurer who reads it while calculating whether the organization can pay for the building.
- A *secondary audience* of people who need to stay aware of developments in the organization but who will not directly act on or respond to your document. An example is a manager who wants to know where her company's new facility will be located.

The needs of your primary audience are more central than those of your secondary audience. For example, if members of your primary audience need to know a project's financial details, provide that information prominently. But if only members of a secondary audience will need that information, put it in a less prominent part of the document.

Categories of readers:
The expert
The technician
The manager
The general reader

Identifying Basic Categories of Readers

You can classify your readers according to their knowledge of your subject. Most readers can be classified into one or two of four categories: the expert, the technician, the manager, and the general reader. Ellen DeSalvo, for example, a PhD in materials engineering, would be an expert in that particular field; she might also be the manager of the materials group at her company.

The Expert   The expert is a highly trained individual with an extensive theoretical and practical understanding of the subject. Often an expert carries out basic or applied research and communicates his or her research findings. One example would be a physician trying to understand the AIDS virus who delivers papers at professional conferences and writes research articles for scholarly journals. Another example would be an engineer trying to devise a simpler, less expensive test for structural flaws in composite materials.

In short, almost everyone with a postgraduate degree, and many people with undergraduate degrees in technical fields, is an expert in one area.

Figure 5.1 on page 70 illustrates the needs and interests of the expert reader.

The Technician   The technician takes the expert's ideas and turns them into real products and procedures. The technician builds, operates, maintains, and repairs mechanisms, and sometimes teaches other people how to operate them. An engineer having a problem with an industrial laser will talk with a technician. After they agree on a possible cause of the problem and a way to fix it, the technician will get to work.

Figure 5.2 on page 71 illustrates the needs and interests of the technician.

The Manager   A manager makes sure an organization operates smoothly and efficiently. For instance, the manager of the procurement department at a manufacturing plant sees that raw materials are purchased and delivered on time so that production continues. Upper-level managers, known as executives, address longer-range concerns. They foresee problems years ahead by considering questions such as the following:

- Is current technology at the company becoming obsolete?
- How expensive are the newest technologies?
- How much would they disrupt operations if they were adopted?
- What other plans would have to be postponed or dropped altogether?
- When would the new technologies start to pay for themselves?
- What has been the experience of other companies that have adopted these new technologies?

Executives are concerned with these and dozens of other broad questions that go beyond day-to-day managerial concerns.

Managers want to know the bottom line. They have to get a job done on schedule; they don't have time to consider theory in the way an expert does. Rather, managers must juggle constraints—financial, personnel, time,

The two-digit numbers (such as 61) refer to components shown in the block diagram below.

Writing addressed to experts often includes high-level theoretical discussions. Here the writers are describing the mathematical algorithm used to balance the Segway.

Notice, too, that the passage uses technical vocabulary and relatively long sentences. Expert readers generally are comfortable with this style.

A simplified control algorithm for achieving balance in the embodiment of the invention according to FIG. 1 when the wheels are active for locomotion is shown in the block diagram of FIG. 6. The plant 61 is equivalent to the equations of motion of a system with a ground contacting module driven by a single motor, before the control loop is applied. T identifies the wheel torque. The character theta identifies the fore-aft inclination (the pitch angle of the vehicle with respect to gravity, i.e., the vertical), X identifies the fore-aft displacement along the surface relative to the reference point, and the dot over a character denotes a variable differentiated with respect to time. The remaining portion of the figure is the control used to achieve balance. The boxes 62 and 63 indicate differentiation. To achieve dynamic control to insure stability of the system, and to keep the system in the neighborhood of a reference point on the surface, the wheel torque T in this embodiment is set to satisfy the following equation:

$$T = K.sub.1 \ .theta. + K.sub.2 \ .theta. + K.sub.3 \ x + K.sub.4 \ x$$

The gains K.sub.1, K.sub.2, K.sub.3, and K.sub.4 are dependent upon the physical parameters of the system and other effects such as gravity. The simplified control algorithm of FIG. 6 maintains balance and also proximity to the reference point on the surface in the presence of disturbances such as changes to the system's center of mass with respect to the reference point on the surface due to body motion of the subject or contact with other persons or objects.

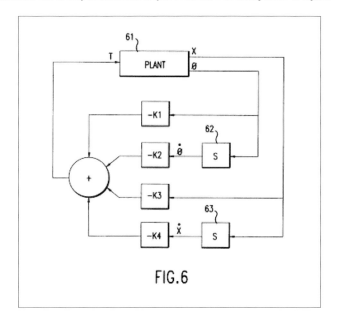

FIG.6

■ **Figure 5.1 Writing Addressed to an Expert Audience**

This passage, from the patent application for the Segway personal-transportation device, discusses advanced concepts of interest to engineers and physicists.
Source: Kamen et al., 1999 <www.uspto.gov>.

and informational—and make decisions quickly. And they have to communicate with their own supervisors.

If you know that your reader will take your information and use it in a document addressed to executives, make your reader's job easier. Include an

FIG. 29 is a block diagram providing detail of the driver interface assembly 273 of FIG. 27. A peripheral microcomputer board 291 receives an input from joystick 292 as well as from inclinometer 293. The inclinometer provides information signals as to pitch and pitch rate. (The term "inclinometer" as used in this context throughout this description and in the accompanying claims means any device providing an output indicative of pitch or pitch rate, regardless of the arrangement used to achieve the output; if only one of the pitch and pitch rate variables is provided as an output, the other variable can be obtained by suitable differentiation or integration with respect to time.) To permit controlled banking into turns by the vehicle (thereby to increase stability while turning) it is also feasible to utilize a second inclinometer to provide information as to roll and roll rate or, alternatively, the resultant of system weight and centrifugal force. Other inputs 294 may also be desirably provided as an input to the peripheral micro controller board 291. Such other inputs may include signals gated by switches (knobs and buttons) for chair adjustment and for determining the mode of operation (such as lean mode or balance mode described below). The peripheral micro controller board 291 also has inputs for receiving signals from the battery stack 271 as to battery voltage, battery current, and battery temperature. The peripheral micro controller board 291 is in communication over bus 279 with the central micro controller board 272.

The three-digit numbers (such as 273) refer to components shown in the block diagram below.

The writers assume that technicians are comfortable with the concepts and vocabulary related to the microprocessor and that they can interpret the block diagram without assistance.

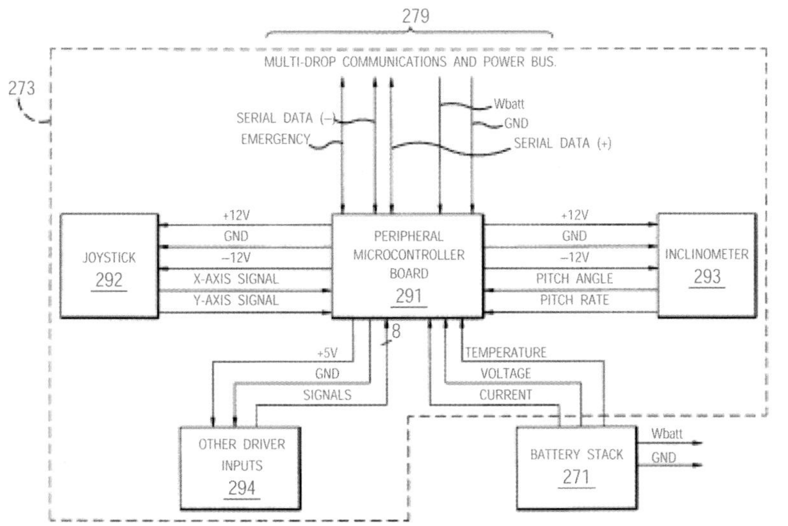

FIG.29

■ **Figure 5.2   Writing Addressed to Technicians**
Source: Kamen et al., 1999
<www.uspto.gov>.

executive summary (see Chapter 18, page 470) and use frequent headings (Chapter 10, page 206 to highlight your major points. Ask your reader if there is an organizational pattern, a format, or a strategy for writing the document that will help him or her use your document as source material.

Figure 5.3 on page 72 illustrates the interests and needs of the manager.

In writing to a manager, try to determine his or her technical background and then choose appropriate vocabulary and sentence length. Focus on practical information. For example, if you are a police officer describing a new product to the police chief, you might begin with some theoretical background but then concentrate on the product's capabilities and its advantages over competing products.

Segway's business plan calls for selling the device first to large corporate customers, such as the U.S. Postal Service and police departments. After the public becomes accustomed to seeing the device, the company will sell it to individuals.

This passage explains how Segway's business plan will work. Rather than focus on technical information about the device, the passage concentrates on issues that a manager needs to understand: efficiency and safety.

FOR IMMEDIATE RELEASE.

Tampa Post Office to test Segway™ Human Transporter

Five city letter carrier routes will be first in the nation to begin feasibility tests

TAMPA, FL, January 14, 2002—Tampa Postmaster Rich Rome today announced that the Tampa Post Office is the first United States Postal Service site to test feasibility of the Segway™ Human Transporter (HT), a self-balancing, electric-powered transportation device, for use in mail delivery.

"The United States Postal Service has a long history of testing innovative modes of transportation," said Postmaster Rome. "As an organization dedicated to deploying technology that drives efficiency, we are proud to be selected as a test site and look forward to giving the Segway HT a thorough evaluation."

The Segway HT will be used on five "park and loop" residential delivery routes where a portion of deliveries are made by a letter carrier on foot. Each route has approximately 500 delivery addresses.

The Postal Service will be evaluating whether use of the Segway HT results in greater delivery efficiency. "To determine the potential for cost savings and increased efficiency, we'll be evaluating delivery time using the Segway HT compared to straight walking time, as well as safety and ergonomics," said Rome. With the Segway HT, up to 35 pounds of mail normally carried by the letter carrier can be transferred to satchels mounted on the human transporter.

"We believe the Segway HT will provide the U.S. Postal Service with a meaningful solution that enables letter carriers to do their job more efficiently and with less physical demand," said Dean Kamen, Segway LLC's chairman and CEO.

■ **Figure 5.3   Writing Addressed to a Manager**
Source: Norton, 2002 <www.segway.com/consumer/team/press_releases/pr_011402.html>.

The General Reader   Often your writing will address the general reader, sometimes called the *layperson*. A nuclear scientist reading about economics is a general reader, as is a historian reading about astronomy.

The layperson reads out of curiosity or self-interest. An article in the magazine supplement of the Sunday paper—on ways to increase the populations of endangered species in zoos, for example—will attract the general reader's attention if it seems interesting and well written. The general reader may also seek specific information that will bring direct benefits: someone interested in buying a house might read articles on new alternative-financing methods.

Figure 5.4 on page 74 illustrates the interests and needs of the general reader.

Guidelines

Writing for the Basic Categories of Readers

These guidelines summarize the discussion of how to write for the basic categories of readers.

Audience	Reasons for reading	Guidelines for writing
Expert	To gain an understanding of the theory and its implications.	Include theory, technical vocabulary, formulas, and sophisticated graphics.
Technician	To gain a hands-on understanding of how something works or how to carry out a task.	Include graphics. Use common words, short sentences, and short paragraphs. Avoid excessive theory.
Manager	To learn the bottom-line facts to aid in making decisions.	Focus on managerial implications, not technical details. Use short sentences and simple vocabulary. Put details in appendices.
General reader	To satisfy curiosity and for self-interest.	Use short sentences and paragraphs, human appeal, and an informal tone.

Identifying Individual Characteristics of Readers

Knowing that a reader is, for example, a manager can tell you something about what that person might want to see in a communication. But it doesn't tell you whether that person is a native speaker of English, whether she is receptive or hostile to your message, or whether she needs to use information from your document in a document she is writing. In other words, placing a reader into a category doesn't tell you anything about that reader as an individual. Try to find out as much as you can about your reader's individual characteristics.

Determine individual characteristics by asking:

Who is your reader?

What are your reader's attitudes and expectations?

Why and how will your reader use your document?

Who Is Your Reader?   In thinking about who your reader is, consider six specific factors:

• *The reader's education.* Think not only about the person's degree but also about when the person earned the degree. A civil engineer who earned a BS in 1986 has a much different background from a person who earned the same degree in 2006. Also consider formal and informal course work the person has completed while on the job.

■ **Figure 5.4   Writing Addressed to the General Reader**
Source: Heilemann, 2001 <www.time.com/time/business/ article/0,8599,186660,00.html>.

GREGORY HEISLER FOR TIME

This photograph shows a person on a Segway, surrounded by pedestrians and a bicyclist on a crowded sidewalk. It shows the general reader what the Segway looks like and reinforces the theme of the article: that the Segway is intended to be a personal-transportation device. As such, the Segway will be competing with pedestrians and bicyclists, not automobiles.

In writing to a general audience, use simple vocabulary and relatively short sentences. Translate jargon into standard English and use analogies and examples to clarify your discussion. Include the human angle: how the situation affects people. Present historical or ethical background, for example, so that your reader can follow the discussion easily. Concentrate on the implications of this information for the reader.

Because writing addressed to the general reader must be interesting, this passage begins with the writer's report of his test drive of the Segway. The purpose of this passage is to give the reader a sense of what it was like to ride the Segway, not to explain how it works or whether it will succeed in the marketplace.

"Come to me!"

On a quiet Sunday morning in Silicon Valley, I am standing atop a machine code-named Ginger—a machine that may be the most eagerly awaited and wildly, if inadvertently, hyped high-tech product since the Apple Macintosh. Fifty feet away, Ginger's diminutive inventor, Dean Kamen, is offering instruction on how to use it, which in this case means waving his hands and barking out orders.

"Just lean forward," Kamen commands, so I do, and instantly I start rolling across the concrete right at him.

"Now, stop," Kamen says. How? This thing has no brakes. "Just think about stopping." Staring into the middle distance, I conjure an image of a red stop sign—and just like that, Ginger and I come to a halt.

"Now think about backing up." Once again, I follow instructions, and soon I glide in reverse to where I started. With a twist of the wrist, I pirouette in place, and no matter which way I lean or how hard, Ginger refuses to let me fall over. What's going on here is all perfectly explicable—the machine is sensing and reacting to subtle shifts in my balance—but for the moment I am slack-jawed, baffled. It was Arthur C. Clarke who famously observed that "any sufficiently advanced technology is indistinguishable from magic." By that standard, Ginger is advanced indeed.

SEGWAY'S SPECS

COST: About $8,000 for industrial models; consumer versions may cost $3,000.

MAXIMUM SPEED: 5 m.p.h to 17 m.p.h., depending on settings

RANGE: About 17 miles per battery charge on level ground; decelerating or going downhill generates electricity, extending its range

RECHARGE TIME: One hour of charge for two hours of operation

PAYLOAD: Passenger ◆ 250 lbs. Cargo ◆ 75 lbs.

WEIGHT: 65 or 80 lbs., depending on the model

Knowing your reader's educational background helps you determine how much supporting material to provide, what level of vocabulary to use, what kind of sentence structure and length to use, what types of graphics to include, and whether to provide such formal elements as a glossary or an executive summary.

Discovering your reader's educational background can be difficult. You cannot ask people to send you a current résumé. But you can try to learn as much as possible in conversations with your colleagues.

- *The reader's professional experience.* A nurse with a decade of experience might have represented her hospital on a community committee to encourage citizens to give blood and might have contributed to the planning for the hospital's new delivery room. In short, her range of experience might have provided several areas of competence or expertise that you need to consider as you plan the document's content and style.

- *The reader's job responsibility.* Consider the major job responsibility of your primary reader and how your document will help that person accomplish it. For example, if you are writing a feasibility study on ways to cool the air for a new office building and you know that your reader, an upper-level manager, has to worry about utility costs, you should explain how you are estimating future utility costs.

- *The reader's personal characteristics.* The reader's age might suggest how he or she will read and interpret your document. A senior manager at age 60 is probably less interested in tomorrow's technology than a 30-year-old manager is. Does your reader have any other personal characteristics you should consider, such as impaired vision, that would affect the way you write and design your document?

- *The reader's personal preferences.* One person might hate to see the first-person pronoun *I* in technical documents. Another might find the word *interface* distracting when the writer isn't discussing computers. A good way to learn a person's preferences is to read that person's own documents. Try to accommodate as many of your reader's preferences as you can.

- *The reader's cultural characteristics.* Knowing your reader's cultural characteristics can help you appeal to his or her interests and avoid being confusing or offensive. As discussed later in this chapter (page 78), cultural characteristics can affect virtually every aspect of a reader's comprehension of a document and perception of the writer.

What Are Your Reader's Attitudes and Expectations?   In thinking about your reader's attitudes and expectations, consider these three factors:

- *Your reader's attitude toward you.* Most people will like you because you are hardworking, intelligent, and cooperative. Some won't. If a reader's animosity toward you is irrational or unrelated to the current project, try to earn that person's respect and trust by meeting him or her on some neutral ground, perhaps by discussing other, less volatile projects or some shared interest, such as gardening, skiing, or science-fiction novels.

- *Your reader's attitude toward the subject.* If possible, discuss the subject thoroughly with your primary reader to determine whether he or she is positive, neutral, or negative toward it. Here are some basic strategies for responding to different attitudes.

If . . .	Try this . . .
Your reader is neutral or positively inclined toward your subject	Write the document so that it responds to the reader's needs; make sure that vocabulary, level of detail, organization, and style are appropriate.
Your reader is hostile to the subject or your approach to it	• Find out what the objections are, then answer them directly. Explain why the objections are not valid or are less important than the benefits. • Organize the document so that your recommendation follows your explanation of the benefits. This strategy encourages the hostile reader to understand your argument rather than to reject it out of hand. • Avoid describing the subject as a dispute. Seek areas of agreement and concede points. Avoid trying to persuade the reader overtly. People don't like to be persuaded, because it threatens their egos. Instead, suggest that some new facts need to be considered. People are more likely to change their minds when they realize this.
Your reader was instrumental in creating the policy or procedure that you are arguing is ineffective	In discussing the present system's shortcomings, be especially careful if you risk offending your reader. When you address such an audience, don't write "The present system for logging customer orders is completely ineffective." Instead, write "While the present system has worked well for many years, new developments in electronic processing of orders might enable us to improve logging speed and reduce errors substantially."

- *Your reader's expectations about the document.* Think about how your reader expects to see the information treated in terms of scope, organizational pattern, and amount of detail. Consider, too, the type of document. If your reader expects to see the information presented as a memo, use a memo unless some other format would clearly work better.

Why and How Will Your Reader Use Your Document? In thinking about how your reader will use your document, consider the following four factors:

- *Your reader's reasons for reading your document.* Does the reader need to use the document to carry out a task? To learn the answer to a specific question? To understand the broad outlines of the subject? The more specifically you can answer such questions, the more likely it is that your document will meet your reader's needs.

- *The way your reader will read your document.* Will he or she
  - — file it?
  - — skim it?
  - — read only a portion of it?
  - — study it carefully?
  - — modify it and submit it to another reader?
  - — try to implement recommendations?
  - — use it to perform a test or carry out a procedure?
  - — use it as a source document for another document?

  If only 1 of your 15 readers will study the document for detailed information, you don't want the other 14 people to have to wade through it. Therefore, put this information in an appendix. If you know that your reader wants to use your status report as raw material for a report to a higher-level reader, try to write it so that it requires little rewriting. Use the reader's own writing style and give the reader the electronic file so that your report can be merged with the new document without requiring retyping.

- *Your reader's reading skill.* Consider whether you should be writing at all, or whether it would be better to do an oral presentation or use computer-based training. If you decide to write, consider whether your reader can understand how to use the type of document you have selected, handle the level of detail you will present, and understand your graphics, sentence structure, and vocabulary.

In This Book

For more about designing a document for use in different environments, see Ch. 12, p. 261.

- *The physical environment in which your reader will read your document.* Often, technical documents are formatted in a special way or constructed of special materials to improve their effectiveness. Documents used in poorly lit places might be printed in larger-than-normal type. Some documents might be used on ships, on aircraft, or in garages, where they might be exposed to wind, water, and grease. You might have to use special waterproof bindings, oil-resistant or laminated paper, coded colors, and unusual-size paper.

Guidelines

Identifying Individual Characteristics of Readers

Use the specific questions in the following table to identify your reader's individual characteristics.

General questions	Specific questions
Who is your reader?	• What is the reader's education? • What is the reader's professional experience? • What is the reader's job responsibility? • What are the reader's personal characteristics? • What are the reader's personal preferences? • What are the reader's cultural characteristics?

General questions	Specific questions
What are your reader's attitudes and expectations?	• What is the reader's attitude toward you? • What is the reader's attitude toward the subject? • What are the reader's expectations about the document?
Why and how will your reader use your document?	• Why is the reader reading your document? • How will the reader read your document? • What is the reader's reading skill? • What is the physical environment in which the reader will read your document?

COMMUNICATING ACROSS CULTURES

Our society and our workforce are becoming increasingly diverse, both culturally and linguistically, and businesses are exporting more and more goods and services. As a result, technical communicators and technical professionals often communicate with nonnative speakers of English in the United States and abroad and with speakers of other languages who read texts translated from English into their own languages.

The economy of the United States depends on international trade. In 2003, the United States exported more than $1.3 trillion worth of goods and services (U.S. Census, 2004, p. 799). In 2002, direct investment abroad by U.S. companies totaled more than $1.8 trillion (U.S. Census, 2004, p. 805). Exports are responsible for four of five new jobs created in the United States (Lustig & Koester, 2006). In addition, the population of the United States itself is truly multicultural. Each year, the United States admits more than a million immigrants (U.S. Census, 2004, p. 11). In 2002, more than 1 in 10 U.S. residents was foreign-born (U.S. Census, 2004, p. 50).

Effective communication requires an understanding of culture: the beliefs, attitudes, and values that motivate people's behavior.

Understanding the Cultural Variables "on the Surface"

Communicating effectively with people from another culture requires understanding a set of cultural variables that lies on the surface. You need to know, first, what language or languages to use. You also need to be aware of political, social, religious, and economic factors that can affect how readers will interpret your documents. Understanding these factors is not an exact science, but it does require that you learn as much as you can about the culture of those you are addressing.

A brief example: An American manufacturer of deodorant launched an advertising campaign in Japan in which a cute octopus applied the firm's product under each of its eight arms. But the campaign failed because in Japan, an octopus has eight *legs*, not eight arms (Bathon, 1999).

In *International Technical Communication*, Nancy L. Hoft (1995) describes seven major categories of cultural variables that lie on the surface:

- *Political.* This category includes trade issues and legal issues (for example, some countries forbid imports of certain foods or chemicals) and laws about intellectual property, product safety, and liability.

- *Economic.* In many developing countries, most people cannot afford personal computers.

- *Social.* This category covers many issues, including gender and business customs. In most Western cultures, women play a much greater role in the workplace than they do in many Middle Eastern and Asian cultures. Business customs—including forms of greeting, business dress, and gift giving—also vary from culture to culture.

- *Religious.* Religious differences can affect diet, attitudes toward individual colors, styles of dress, holidays, and hours of business.

- *Educational.* In the United States, 40 million people are only marginally literate. In other cultures, that rate can be much higher or much lower. In some cultures, classroom learning with a teacher is considered the most acceptable way to study. In others, people tend to study on their own.

- *Technological.* If you sell high-tech products, you need to know whether your readers have the hardware, software, and technological infrastructure to use them.

- *Linguistic.* In some countries, English is taught to all children starting in grade school. In other countries, English is seen as a threat to the national language. In many cultures, the orientation of text on a page and in a book is not from left to right.

In addition to these basic differences, you need to understand dozens of other factors. For instance, the United States is the only major country that has not adopted the metric system. In addition, Americans use periods to separate whole numbers from decimals and commas to separate thousands from hundreds. Much of the rest of the world reverses this usage.

United States:	3,425.6
Europe:	3.425,6

In the United States, the format for writing out and abbreviating dates is different from that of most other cultures:

United States:	March 2, 2006	3/2/06
Europe:	2 March 2006	2/3/06
Japan:	2006 March 2	06/3/2

These cultural variables are important in an obvious way: you can't send a fax to a person who doesn't have a fax machine. However, there is another set of cultural characteristics—those beneath the surface—that you also need to understand.

Understanding the Cultural Variables "Beneath the Surface"

Scholars of multicultural communication have identified a set of cultural variables that is less obvious than that discussed in the previous section but just as important. Table 5.1, based on an excellent article by Tebeaux and Driskill (1999), explains six key variables and how they are reflected in technical communication.

As you consider this set of cultural variables, keep four points in mind:

- *Each variable represents a spectrum of attitudes.* Terms such as *high context* and *low context*, for instance, represent the two endpoints on a scale. Many cultures occupy a middle ground.

- *The six variables do not line up in a clear pattern.* Although Table 5.1 suggests that several of the variables correlate—for example, individualistic cultures tend to see a great distance between business and personal lives—in any one culture, the six variables do not form a consistent pattern. For example, the dominant culture in the United States is highly individualistic rather than group oriented but only about midway along the scale of attitudes toward accepting uncertainty.

- *Different organizations within the same culture can vary greatly.* For example, one software company in Germany might have a management style that does not tolerate uncertainty, whereas another software company in Germany might have a management style that tolerates a lot of uncertainty.

- *An organization's cultural attitudes are fluid, not static.* How an organization operates is determined not only by the dominant culture but also by its own people. As new people join an organization, its culture changes. The IBM of 1986 is not the IBM of 2006.

For you as a communicator, this set of variables offers no answers. Instead, it offers a set of questions. You cannot know in advance the attitudes of the people in an organization. You have to interact with them for a long time before you can reach even tentative conclusions. The value of being aware of the variables is that they can help you study the communications from people in that organization and become more aware of underlying values that affect how they will interpret your documents.

Considering Cultural Variables as You Write

The challenge of communicating effectively with a person from another culture is that you are communicating with a person, not a culture. You cannot be sure which cultures have influenced that person (Lovitt, 1999). For example, a 50-year-old Japanese-born manager for the computer manufacturer

■ **Table 5.1 Cultural Variables "Beneath the Surface"**

Variable	Explanation	How this variable is reflected in technical communication
Focus on individuals or groups	Some cultures, especially in the West, value individuals more than groups. The typical employee doesn't see his or her identity as being defined by the organization. Other cultures, particularly in Asia, value groups more than individuals. The typical employee sees himself or herself first as a member of the organization rather than an individual who works there.	Communication addressed to people from individualistic cultures focuses on the writer's and reader's needs rather than on those of the two organizations. Writers use the pronoun *I* rather than *we*. Letters are addressed to the principal reader and signed by the writer. Communication addressed to people from group-oriented cultures focuses on the organization's needs by emphasizing the benefits to be gained by the two organizations through a cooperative relationship. Writers emphasize the relationship between the writer and reader rather than the specific technical details of the message. Writers use *we* rather than *I*. They might address letters "Dear Sir" and use the organization's name, not their own, in the complimentary close.
Distance between business life and private life	In some cultures, especially in the West, people separate their business lives from their private lives. When the workday ends, they are free to go home and spend their time as they wish. In other cultures, particularly in Asia, people see a much smaller distance between their business lives and their private lives. Even after the day ends, they still see themselves as employees of the organization. Cultures that value individualism tend to see a great distance between business and personal lives. Cultures that are group oriented tend to see a smaller distance between business life and private life.	Communication addressed to people from cultures that see a great distance between business lives and private lives focuses on the technical details of the communication, with relatively little reference to personal information about the writer or the reader. Communication addressed to people from cultures that see a smaller distance between business lives and personal lives contains much more personal information—about the reader's family and health—and more information about, for example, the weather and the seasons. The goal is to build a formal relationship between the two organizations. Both the writer and the reader are, in effect, on call after business hours and are likely to transact business during long social activities, such as elaborate dinners or golf games.
Distance between ranks	In some cultures, the distance in power and authority between workers within an organization is small. This small distance is reflected in a close working relationship between supervisors and their subordinates. In other cultures, the distance in power and authority between workers within an organization is great. Supervisors do not consult with their subordinates. Subordinates use formal names and titles—"Mr. Smith," "Dr. Jones"—when addressing higher-ranking people.	In cultures with a small distance between ranks, communication is generally less formal. Informal documents (e-mails and memos) are appropriate, and writers often sign their documents with their first names only. Keep in mind, however, that many people in these cultures resent inappropriate informality, such as receiving letters or e-mails addressed "Dear Jim" if they have never met the writer. In cultures with a great distance between ranks, communication is generally formal. Writers tend to use their full professional titles and to prefer formal

⬇

■ **Table 5.1** *(continued)*

Variable	Explanation	How this variable is reflected in technical communication
Distance between ranks *(continued)*	Cultures that focus on individualism and that separate business and private lives tend to have a smaller distance between ranks.	documents (such as letters) to informal ones (such as memos and e-mails). Writers make sure their documents are addressed to the appropriate person and contain the formal design elements (such as title pages and letters of transmittal) that signal their respect for their readers.
Nature of truth	Some cultures feel that truth is a universal concept. An action is either wrong or right. There are no exceptions. If facts are presented clearly and comprehensively, all reasonable readers will understand them in the same way. Other cultures think that truth is a more complex and relative concept, and that reasonable people can have different perspectives on complex ethical issues.	In cultures that take a universal approach to truth, such as the United States, documents tend to be comprehensive and detailed. They spell out the details of the communication, leaving nothing to interpretation. In cultures that take a relative view of truth, documents tend to be less detailed and less conclusive. Discussions might seem vague, as if the writer is unwilling to reach a clear conclusion.
Need to spell out details	Some cultures value full, complete communication. The written text must be comprehensive, containing all the information a reader needs to understand it. These cultures are called *low context.* Other cultures value documents in which some of the details are merely implied. This implicit information is communicated through other forms of communication that draw upon the personal relationship between the reader and the writer, as well as social and business norms that prevail in the culture. These cultures are called *high context.* Low-context cultures tend to be individualistic; high-context cultures tend to be group oriented.	In low-context cultures, writers spell out all the details. Documents are like contracts in that they provide the specific information that indicates the rights and responsibilities of both the writer and the reader and explain procedures in great detail. In high-context cultures, writers tend to omit information that they consider obvious because they don't want to insult the reader. For example, a manual written for people in a high-context culture might not mention that a remote control for a television set requires batteries, because everyone knows that a remote control needs a power source.
Attitudes toward uncertainty	In some cultures, people are comfortable with uncertainty. They communicate less formally and rely less on written policies. In many cases, they rely more on a clear set of guiding principles, as communicated in a code of conduct or a mission statement. In other cultures, people are uncomfortable with uncertainty. Businesses are structured formally, and they use written procedures for communicating.	In cultures that tolerate uncertainty, written communication tends to be less detailed. Oral communication is used to convey more of the information that is vital to the relationship between the writer and the reader. In cultures that value certainty, communication tends to be detailed. Policies are lengthy and specific, and forms are used extensively. Everyone knows what he or she is supposed to do, and there is a wide distance between ranks.

Fujitsu in Japan has been shaped by the Japanese culture, but he also has been influenced by the culture of his company and of the Japanese computer industry in general. It is also likely that he has worked outside of Japan for several years and has absorbed influences from another culture.

A further complication is that when you communicate with a person from another culture, to that person *you* are from another culture, and you cannot know how much that person is trying to accommodate your cultural patterns. As Bell (1992) points out, the communication between the two of you is carried out in a third, hybrid culture. When you write to a large audience, the complications increase. A group of managers for Fujitsu represents a far more complex mix of cultural influences than one manager for Fujitsu.

No brief discussion of cultural variables can answer questions about how to write for a particular multicultural audience. You need to study your readers' culture and, as you plan the document, seek assistance from someone native to the culture who can help you avoid blunders that might confuse or offend your readers.

Start by reading some of the basic guides to communicating with people from other cultures, and then study guides to the particular culture you are investigating. In addition, numerous sites on the Internet provide useful guidelines that can help you write to people from other cultures. Here, for instance, is an excerpt from a guide to writing letters to Japanese recipients (Anderson School, 2002):

> A Japanese letter is the reverse of one in the West, in the sense that you proceed first from the general to the specific. You need to begin with the social niceties, with small talk about the weather, the holidays, or some seasonal reference. Include at least a paragraph of such material before getting to the heart of the correspondence. You may begin the business section with a phrase such as: "We are so happy that your business is becoming even more prosperous," and then state your business in a "soft" manner. Even then, do not be overly direct or assertive. Use phrases like: "I am not sure…"; "I wonder if…"; "I hope this is not too bold a request but…." Also include some sort of reference to the personal, trusting relationship you have both put so much effort into, and how you desire its continuance. Your letter should end with a closing general phrase at the bottom, followed by the date. The date is given in the reverse order of dates in the West: the year, the month, and then the day.

 On TechComm Web

For a discussion of communication practices in China, see Coggin, Coggin, and Li's "Living and Working in China: Understanding Communication Requirements." Click on Links Library for Ch. 5 on <bedfordstmartins.com/techcomm>.

If possible, study documents written by people in your audience. If you don't have access to them, try to locate documents written in English by people from that culture. Figure 5.5 on page 84 shows several excerpts from documents on the Internet that provide useful glimpses into cultural variables.

Using Graphics and Design for Multicultural Readers

One of the challenges in writing for people from another culture is that they are likely to be nonnative speakers of English. One way to overcome the language barrier is to use effective graphics and design the document effectively.

Excerpt	Commentary
From a Japanese electronics company (Sugimoto, 2004)	
We FDK group are considered as the comprehensive electronic-component manufacturer. We supply from electronic materials to hybrid electronic components to achieve our aim at the realization of comfortable society.	Notice how the writer links his corporation with the goal of realizing a "comfortable society."
Our corporate message says that we are "A Key Device Supplier in Broadband Internet Fields" and thus we have been rapidly shifting our concentration of supply to the key-devices area preparing for the coming Ubiquitous Computing Society where all electrical and electric equipments are connected via networks. . . .	Again he speaks of the broader goal of contributing to the creation of the "Ubiquitous Computing Society."
Based on the materials technologies, circuit technologies, high-density technologies and mounting technologies cultivated and accumulated by manufacturing of electronic products and batteries over a half-century, FDK group will continue to supply highly innovated quality products to result in our customer satisfaction.	Notice the direct statement about the importance of satisfying the customer's needs. The Japanese culture stresses building a strong business relationship for the benefit of both parties.
Recognizing the importance of the global environment, FDK group will continue to contribute our society as the best supplier of the key devices.	Although this document provides some information about the company, the focus is on how the company will satisfy the customer's needs and, in so doing, contribute to the growth of an advanced high-tech culture.
From an administrator for India's railway network (Jain, 2002)	
Indian Railways, the single largest infrastructural organisation under a single management, have evolved highly responsive and effective systems of disaster management of various kinds particularly attributable to a sacred continuing mission of ensuring safety and continuity of rail traffic under all circumstances. Over 150 years of its existence, the Railways have nurtured and perfected an organisational temperament in which every threat to the continuity of the traffic is dealt with in the same manner as if an accident has occurred. Such perceptions are deeply ingrained into the temperament of the Railway personnel cutting across the hierarchical positions and, therefore, each impending disaster is preceded by meticulous planning, mobilization and strategy formulation even before the disaster actually occurs.	The cultural value of service to other people is communicated as early as the first sentence, with its reference to "a sacred continuing mission of ensuring safety and continuity of rail traffic under all circumstances." The writer refers to the railway's long history of excellent service to the people of India. To someone from the United States, references to the employees' "deeply ingrained" attitudes and "meticulous planning" might sound insincere and self-serving. To an Indian audience, these phrases sound perfectly appropriate.
From the head of the Patent Office in Finland (Enäjärvi, 2004)	
The productivity of work in the National Board of Patents and Registration grew by 3.1 per cent, which clearly exceeded the targets set. The highlight of our busy operating year was the appointment of the National Board of Patents and Registration as a PCT Authority. Finland was the 11th country to obtain these rights. The body granting them is a specialised agency of the United Nations, the World Intellectual Property WIPO, its PCT Union to be precise. A description of the PCT system is given elsewhere in this Report. We are especially satisfied with the significant fact-based support which WIPO's Director General Kamil Idris and Secretariat gave Finland in this matter.	Although this Finnish manager's use of English does not sound exactly like a native speaker's, his strategy sounds very much like that used in the United States. He reports the productivity growth in percent, and he highlights WIPO's recognition of his organization. Notice the gracious tone of his final sentence.

■ **Figure 5.5** **Passages Reflecting Cultural Variables**

Strategies for Intercultural Communication

Writing for Readers from Other Cultures

The following eight guidelines will help you communicate more effectively with multicultural readers:

- **Limit your vocabulary.** Every word should have only one meaning, as called for in Simplified English and in other basic-English languages.

- **Keep sentences short.** There is no magic number, but try for an average length of no more than 20 words.

- **Define abbreviations and acronyms in a glossary.** Don't assume that your readers know what a GFI (ground fault interrupter) is, because the abbreviation is derived from English vocabulary and word order.

- **Avoid jargon unless you know your readers are familiar with it.** For instance, your readers might not know what a *graphical user interface* is.

- **Avoid idioms and slang.** These terms are culture specific. If you tell your Japanese readers that your company plans to put on a *full-court press*, most likely they will be confused.

- **Use the active voice whenever possible.** It is easier for nonnative speakers of English to understand the active voice than the passive voice.

- **Be careful with graphics.** The garbage-can icon on the Macintosh computer does not translate well, because garbage cans have different shapes and might be made of different materials in other countries.

- **Be sure someone from the culture reviews your document.** Even if you have had help in planning the document, have it reviewed before you publish and distribute it.

 In This Book
For a discussion of Simplified English, see Ch. 11, p. 246.

 In This Book
For more about voice, see Ch. 11, p. 236.

 In This Book
For more about graphics, see Ch. 13.

 In This Book
For more about design for multicultural readers, see Ch. 12, p. 261. For more about graphics for multicultural readers, see Ch. 13, p. 329.

However, the use of graphics and design can differ from culture to culture. A business letter written in Australia uses different-size paper and a different format than a similar letter in the United States. An icon for a file folder in a software program made in the United States could confuse European readers, who use a different size and shape for file folders in offices (Bosley, 1999). A series of graphics arranged left to right could confuse readers from the Middle East, who read from right to left. For this reason, you should study samples of documents written by people from the culture you are addressing to learn the important differences.

WRITING FOR MULTIPLE AUDIENCES

Many documents of more than a few pages are addressed to more than one reader. Often, multiple audiences consist of people with widely different backgrounds. Some might be experts or technicians, others might be managers, and still others might be general readers.

INTERACTIVE SAMPLE DOCUMENT
Examining Cultural Variables in a Business Letter

These two versions of the same business letter were written by a sales manager for an American computer company. The first letter was addressed to a potential customer in the United States; the second version was addressed to a potential customer in Japan. The questions in the margin ask you to think about how the cultural variables affect the nature of the evidence, the structure of the letters, and their tone (see pages 80–83). E-mail your responses to yourself and/or your instructor, and see suggested responses on TechComm Web.

Server Solutions
Cincinnati, OH 46539
Nadine Meyer
Director of Marketing

July 3, 2006

Mr. Philip Henryson, Director of Purchasing
Allied Manufacturing
1321 Industrial Boulevard
Boise, ID 83756

Dear Mr. Henryson:

Thank you for your inquiry about our PowerServer servers. I'm happy to answer your questions.

The most popular configuration is our PowerServer 3000. This model is based on the Intel® Xeon processor, ServerSure High-End UltraLite chipset with quad-peer PCI architecture, and embedded RAID. The system comes with our InstallIt system-management CD, which lets you install the server and monitor and manage your network with a simple graphical interface. With six PCI slots, the PowerServer 3000 is equipped with redundant cooling as well as redundant power, and storage expandability to 950 GB. I'm taking the liberty of enclosing the brochure for this system to fill you in on the technical details.

The PowerServer 3000 has performed extremely well on a number of industry benchmark tests. I'm including with this letter copies of feature articles on the system from *PC World, InternetWeek,* and *Windows 2000 Magazine.*

It would be a pleasure for me to arrange for an on-site demo at your convenience. I'll give you a call on Monday to see what dates would be best for you. In the meantime, please do not hesitate to get in touch with me directly if you have any questions about the PowerServer line.

I look forward to talking with you next week.

Sincerely,

Nadine Meyer

Nadine Meyer
Director of Marketing

Attachments:
   "PowerServer 3000 Facts at a Glance"
   "Another Winner from ServerSolutions"
   "Mid-Range Servers for 2006"
   "Four New Dual-Processor Workhorses"

Server Solutions
Cincinnati, OH 46539
Nadine Meyer
Director of Marketing

Mr. Kato Kirisawa, Director of Purchasing
Allied Manufacturing
3-7-32 Kita Urawa
Saitama City
Saitama Pref. 336-0002
Japan

Dear Sir:

It is my sincere hope that you and your loved ones are healthy and enjoying the pleasures of summer. Here in the American Midwest, the warm rays of the summer sun are accompanied by the sounds of happy children playing in the neighborhood swimming pools. I trust that the same pleasant sounds greet you in Saitama City.

Your inquiry about our PowerServer 3000 suggests that your company is growing. Allied Manufacturing has earned a reputation in Japan and all of Asia for a wide range of products manufactured to the most demanding standards of quality. We are not surprised that your company requires new servers that can be expanded to provide fast service for more and more clients.

For more than 15 years, Server Solutions has had the great honor of manufacturing the finest computer servers to meet the needs of our valued customers all over the world. We use only the finest materials and most innovative techniques to ensure that our customers receive the highest-quality, uninterrupted service that they have come to expect from us.

One of my great pleasures is to talk with esteemed representatives such as yourself about how Server Solutions can help them meet their needs for the most advanced servers. I would be most gratified if our two companies could enter into an agreement that would be of mutual benefit.

Sincerely,

Nadine Meyer

Nadine Meyer
Director of Marketing

Attachments:
"PowerServer 3000 Facts at a Glance"
"Another Winner from ServerSolutions"
"Mid-Range Servers for 2006"
"Four New Dual-Processor Workhorses"

2006 July 3

1. How does the difference in the salutation (the "Dear . . ." part of the letter) reflect a cultural difference?

2. Does the first paragraph have any function beyond delaying the discussion of business?

3. What is the function of telling Mr. Kirisawa about his own company? How does this paragraph help the writer introduce her own company's products?

4. To a reader from the United States, the third paragraph would probably seem thin. What aspect of Japanese culture makes it effective in the context of this letter?

5. Why doesn't the writer make a more explicit sales pitch at the end of the letter?

 On TechComm Web

To e-mail your responses to yourself and/or your instructor and to see suggested responses, click on Interactive Sample Documents for Ch. 5 on <bedfordstmartins.com/techcomm>.

If you think your document will have a number of readers, consider making it *modular*: break it up into components addressed to different kinds of readers. A modular report might contain an executive summary for managers who don't have the time, knowledge, or desire to read the whole report. It might also contain a full technical discussion for expert readers, an implementation schedule for technicians, and a financial plan in an appendix for budget officers.

THE AUDIENCE PROFILE SHEET

To help you analyze your audience, fill out an audience profile sheet for each primary and secondary reader (assuming, of course, that there are just a few). See Figure 5.6 for a sample audience profile sheet.

DETERMINING YOUR PURPOSE

Once you have identified and analyzed your audience, it's time to examine your purpose. Ask yourself this: "What do I want this document to accomplish?" When your readers have finished reading what you have written, what do you want them to *know* or *believe*? What do you want them to *do*? Your writing should help your readers carry out a task, understand a concept, or hold a particular belief.

In defining your purpose, think of a verb that represents it. (Sometimes, of course, you have several purposes.) The following list presents verbs in two categories: those used to communicate information to your readers and those used to convince them to accept a particular point of view.

Communicating Verbs

describe	explain	inform	illustrate
review	outline	authorize	describe
define	summarize		

Convincing Verbs

assess	request	propose
recommend	forecast	evaluate

This classification is not absolute. For example, *review* could in some cases be a *convincing verb* rather than a *communicating verb*: one writer's review of a complicated situation might be very different from another's.

Here are a few examples of how you can use these verbs to clarify the purpose of your document (the verbs are italicized).

- This report *describes* the research project intended to determine the effectiveness of the new waste-treatment filter.
- This letter *authorizes* the purchase of six new PCs for the Jenkintown facility.
- This memo *recommends* that we revise the Web site as soon as possible.

AUDIENCE PROFILE SHEET

Reader's Name: Harry Becker

Reader's Job Title: Manager, Drafting and Design Department

Kind of Reader: Primary _X_ Secondary ___

Education: BS, Architectural Engineering, Northwestern, 1989. CAD/CAM Short Course, 1989; Motivating Your Employees Seminar, 1991; Writing on the Job Short Course, 1994

Professional Experience: Worked for two years in a small architecture firm. Started here 16 years ago as a draftsperson. Worked his way up to Assistant Manager, then Manager. Instrumental in the Wilson project, particularly in coordinating personnel and equipment.

Job Responsibilities: Supervises a staff of 12 draftspersons. Approves or denies all requests for capital expenditures over $2,000 coming from his department. Works with employees to help them make the best case for the purchase. After approving or denying the request, forwards it to Tina Buterbaugh, Manager, Finance Dept., who maintains all capital expenditure records.

Personal Characteristics: N/A

Personal Preferences: Likes straightforward documents, lots of evidence, clear structure. Dislikes complicated documents full of jargon.

Cultural Characteristics: Nothing of note.

Attitude Toward the Writer: No problems.

Attitude Toward the Subject: He understands and approves of my argument.

Expectations about the Subject: Expects to see a clear argument with financial data and detailed comparisons of available systems.

Expectations about the Document: Expects to see a report, with an executive summary, of about 10 pages.

Reasons for Reading the Document: To offer suggestions and eventually approve or deny the request.

Way of Reading the Document:
Skim it ___   Study it _X_ Read a portion of it ___   Which portion?
Modify it and submit it to another reader ___
Attempt to implement recommendations ___
Use it to perform a task or carry out a procedure ___
Use it to create another document ___
Other ___   Explain.

Reading Skill: Excellent

Reader's Physical Environment: N/A

■ **Figure 5.6**
An Audience Profile Sheet

Assume that you work in the drafting department of an architectural engineering firm. You know that the company's computer-assisted design (CAD) software is out-of-date and that recent CAD technology would make it easier and faster for the draftspersons to do their work. You want to persuade your company to authorize buying a CAD workstation that costs about $4,000. To do so, you fill out an audience profile sheet for your primary reader, Harry Becker, the manager of your company's Drafting and Design Department.

 On TechComm Web

You should modify this form to meet your own needs and those of your organization. For a down-loadable version of Fig. 5.6, click on Forms for Technical Communication on <bedfordstmartins.com/techcomm>.

Sometimes your real purpose differs from your expressed purpose. For instance, if you want to persuade your reader to lease a new computer system rather than purchase it, you might phrase the purpose this way: *to explain the advantages of leasing over purchasing.* As mentioned earlier, many readers don't want to be *persuaded* but are willing to learn new facts or ideas.

GAINING MANAGEMENT'S APPROVAL

After you have analyzed your audience and purpose, consider gaining the approval of management before you proceed. The larger and more complex the project and the document, the more sense it makes to be sure that you are on the right track before you invest too much time and effort.

For example, you are planning the CAD equipment project. You already know your audience and purpose, and you are drafting a general outline in your mind. But before you actually start to write an outline or gather the information you will need, spend another 10 or 15 minutes making sure your primary reader agrees with your thinking. You don't want to waste days or even weeks working on a document that won't fulfill its purpose. If you have misunderstood what your supervisor wants, it is far easier to fix the problem at this early stage.

Your statement to the manager can also serve another purpose: if you want your reader's views on which of two strategies to pursue, you can describe each one and ask your reader to state a preference.

What should this statement look like? It doesn't matter. You can write an e-mail or a memo, as long as you clearly and briefly state what you are trying to do. Here is an example of a statement you might submit to your boss about the CAD equipment.

Juan:

The purpose of the memo

Please tell me if you think this is a good approach for the proposal on CAD equipment.

A statement of the audience for the proposal

A statement of the purpose, followed by early statements of the scope of the document

Outright purchase of the complete system will cost more than $1,000, so you would have to approve it and send it on for Tina's approval. (I'll provide leasing costs as well.) I want to show that our CAD hardware and software are badly out-of-date and need to be replaced. I'll be thorough in recommending new equipment, with independent evaluations in the literature as well as product demonstrations. The proposal should specify what the current equipment is costing us and show how much we can save by buying the recommended system.

A statement of how the writer intends to follow up on this memo

I'll call you later today to get your reaction before I begin researching what's available.

Renu

Once you have received your reader's approval, you can feel confident about starting to gather information.

REVISING INFORMATION FOR A NEW AUDIENCE AND PURPOSE

Chapter 2 introduced the concept of boilerplate information: standard text or graphics that are plugged into various documents (see page 19). But not all information can be standardized and distributed in one form. In other

FOR IMMEDIATE RELEASE.

Contact information:
Carla Vallone or Eric Fleming
Phone: 866-473-4929
media@segway.com

Segway LLC Introduces 2005 Product Line with More Power, More Attitude and More Options

New Lithium-Ion Batteries Extend Riding Range and Support New Product Categories

New Colors and Features Give Customers Freedom to Customize Segway® HT

BEDFORD, N.H.—March 1, 2005—Today Segway LLC introduced its 2005 product line featuring three new models and lithium-ion batteries that double the range of the Segway® Human Transporter (HT). The line includes the new Segway HT i180 in Midnight Blue, Midnight Blue/Solar Yellow and Midnight Blue/Sport Red color combinations; the Segway Cross-Terrain Transporter (XT); and the Segway Golf Transporter (GT).

"We are proud to introduce such a robust product line in 2005. We're giving our customers what they've been asking for: more range, more customization options and more riding opportunities," said Klee Kleber, Segway LLC's vice president of marketing. "The new colorful i180 models are the most striking Segway HTs we've ever released—and they're available with batteries that deliver incredible range. The Segway XT and Segway GT will enable riders to enjoy the outdoors like never before."

"The original Segway HT product line has established itself as being technologically innovative, as well as amazingly reliable and useful," said Doug Field, Segway LLC's vice president of design and engineering. "We are very proud of the Segway HT's track record of customer satisfaction. Our new products build on this reputation, with range improvements, new riding opportunities and bold new designs."

A press release is a statement distributed by a company to the news media to promote a new development at the company. The company hopes the news media will print the release, thereby publicizing the development. Notice the marketing spin in the title and subtitle of the press release. The writer is trying to attract potential customers, especially young people. Segway wants young people to see the product as edgy, not geeky.

The first paragraph introduces the major sections of the release: the new batteries, colors, and models.

Press releases usually include quotations from company officials. These quotations are meant to suggest a groundswell of enthusiasm for the product, as well as the company's enthusiasm for responding to its customers' needs. In marketing documents, the news is always good.

■ **Figure 5.7   Press Release**

Source: Segway, 2005 <www.segway.com/aboutus/press_releases/pr_030105c.html>.

words, one size doesn't necessarily fit all. Most of the time, you need to revise information to accommodate a new audience and purpose.

Figure 5.7 shows the first three paragraphs of a press release from Segway LLC (2005). The press release continues with more details about the new batteries, colors, and accessories; technical specifications; company information; and information about how to contact a dealer.

This information is based on Segway's own product information and press release. Writers may not plagiarize, but they may use the facts from a company's product information.

Here the writer presents information that is not found in the press release. Because this writer's audience consists of the general public, he presents a more balanced description of the Segway rollout. Financial analysts are skeptical about the long-term success of the company.

In the final paragraph, the writer points out that readers cannot know for sure how many machines the company has sold or will sell, because the company is not required to publish financial information. The writer uses the word claimed *not* to suggest that Segway is lying, but to clarify that consumers cannot verify the company's sales figures.

Segway Rolling Out Three New Models
Segway Rolling Out Three New Models; All Feature Better Batteries for Longer Travel

BEDFORD, N.H. Mar. 3, 2005 — Segway LLC is rolling out three new models of its self-balancing, two-wheeled machines.

A rack transforms one version into a single-person golf cart, and wide tires outfit another for off-road riding. The final model looks more like previous versions, but comes in sportier colors like red and yellow.

Each new Segway also features better batteries for longer ranges. They can travel twice as far, up to 24 miles in some cases.

But suggested retail prices aren't coming down. Each one costs at least $5,000 with the new batteries.

Analysts have been skeptical about the company's future, arguing that prices must drop sharply for Segways to be mass-market successes. The machines were unveiled in December 2001. A September 2003 recall revealed only about 6,000 had sold.

Company officials claimed U.S. sales doubled last year in a 10-week period starting on Oct. 25, but the privately held company doesn't release financial figures.

■ **Figure 5.8   Article Based on a Press Release**
Source: Stetson, 2005 <http://abcnews.go.com/Technology/wireStory?id=547289>.

Figure 5.8 is a brief article (Stetson, 2005) about the Segway announcement. The writer works for the Associated Press, a syndicate that provides news stories for print and broadcast media. His purpose is not to advertise the product, but to present a more objective analysis of what the development means.

Writer's Checklist

Following is a checklist for analyzing your audience and purpose. Remember that your document might be read by one person, several people, a large group, or several groups with various needs.

In analyzing your audience, did you consider the following questions about each of your most important readers?

☐ What is your reader's educational background? (p. 73)
☐ What is your reader's professional experience? (p. 75)
☐ What is your reader's job responsibility? (p. 75)
☐ What are your reader's personal characteristics? (p. 75)
☐ What are your reader's personal preferences? (p. 75)
☐ What are your reader's cultural characteristics? (p. 75)
☐ What is your reader's attitude toward you? (p. 75)
☐ What is your reader's attitude toward the subject? (p. 76)
☐ What are your reader's expectations about the subject? (p. 76)
☐ What are your reader's expectations about the document? (p. 76)
☐ Why is your reader reading your document? (p. 76)
☐ How will your reader read your document? (p. 77)
☐ What is your reader's reading skill? (p. 77)
☐ What is the physical environment in which your reader will read your document? (p. 77)

In planning to write for an audience from another culture, did you consider the following cultural variables:

☐ political? (p. 79)
☐ economic? (p. 79)
☐ social? (p. 79)
☐ religious? (p. 79)
☐ educational? (p. 79)
☐ technological? (p. 79)
☐ linguistic? (p. 79)

In planning to write for an audience from another culture, did you consider the other set of cultural variables:

☐ focus on individuals or groups? (p. 81)
☐ distance between business life and private life? (p. 81)
☐ distance between ranks? (p. 81)
☐ nature of truth? (p. 82)
☐ need to spell out details? (p. 82)
☐ attitudes toward uncertainty? (p. 82)

In writing for a multicultural audience, did you

☐ limit your vocabulary? (p. 85)
☐ keep sentences short? (p. 85)
☐ define abbreviations and acronyms in a glossary? (p. 85)
☐ avoid jargon unless you know that your readers are familiar with it? (p. 85)
☐ avoid idioms and slang? (p. 85)
☐ use the active voice whenever possible? (p. 85)
☐ use graphics carefully? (p. 85)
☐ have the document reviewed by someone from the reader's culture? (p. 85)

☐ Did you consider your purpose in writing and express it in the form of a verb or verbs? (p. 88)
☐ Did you fill out an audience profile sheet for your primary and secondary audiences (p. 88)

Exercises

1. **INTERNET EXERCISE** Choose a 200-word passage from a technical article addressed to an expert audience, one related to your major course of study. (You can find a technical article on the Web by using a directory search engine such as Yahoo!, selecting a subject area such as "science," and then selecting "journals." In addition, many federal government agencies publish technical articles and reports on the Web.) Rewrite the passage so that it is clear and interesting to the general reader. Submit the original passage to your instructor along with your revision.

2. The following passage is an advertisement from a translation service. Revise the passage to make it more appropriate for a multicultural audience. Submit the revision to your instructor.

   If your technical documents have to meet the needs of a global market but you find that most translation houses are swamped by the huge volume, fail to accommodate the various languages you require, or make your deadlines, where do you turn?

   Well, your search is over. Translations, Inc., provides comprehensive translations in addition to full-service documentation publishing.

   We utilize ultrasophisticated translation programs that can translate a page in the blink of an eye. Then our crack linguists comb each document to give it that personalized touch.

No job too large! No schedule too tight! Give us a call today!

3. **INTERNET EXERCISE** Audience is your primary consideration in many types of nontechnical writing. Choose a one- or two-page magazine advertisement or Web site for an economy car, such as a Kia, and one for a luxury car, such as a Mercedes. In a memo to your instructor, contrast the audiences for the two ads according to age, sex, economic means, hobbies, interests, and leisure activities. In contrasting the two audiences, consider the explicit information in the ads—the writing—as well as the implicit information—hidden persuaders such as background scenery, color, lighting, angles, and the situation portrayed by any people photographed. Keep in mind that your purpose is to contrast the two audiences, not merely to describe the content of the ad or its design. Submit color photocopies or the original ads from the magazines or sites along with your memo.

4. **GROUP EXERCISE** Form small groups and study two Web sites that advertise competing products. For instance, you might choose the Web sites of two car manufacturers, two television shows, or two music publishers. Have each person in the group, working *alone*, compare and contrast the two sites according to these three criteria:

a. the kind of information they provide: hard, technical information or more emotional information

b. the use of multimedia, such as animation, sound, or video

c. the amount of interactivity they invite—that is, the extent to which you can participate in activities while you visit the site

After each person has separately studied the sites and taken notes about the three points, come together as a group. Each person should share his or her findings and then discuss the differences as a group. Which aspects of these sites cause the most differences in group members' reactions? Which aspects seemed to elicit the most consistent reactions? In a brief memo to your instructor, describe and analyze how the two sites were perceived by the different members of the group.

Case 5: Planning an Apology to a Customer from the People's Republic of China

 In This Book   For more about letters of complaint and adjustment, see Ch. 14, p. 346. For more about interviews, see Ch. 6, p. 114.

Background

You work in the Marketing Department at Zander Instruments, a manufacturer of scientific measurement instruments used in the pharmaceutical, chemical, and semiconductor industries. Your latest product is an x-ray scanner used by airlines to inspect cargo pallets to be sure they contain the cargo listed on the cargo manifest and do not contain illegal drugs or other contraband.

After a negotiation that lasted more than four months, your company signed a contract to supply 15 of these devices, at a total cost of over $2 million, to China Air, on July 1. In the contract, you agreed to provide complete product documentation, including operating and routine-maintenance instructions, in Modern Chinese, the written language used in the People's Republic of China.

It is July 14. Today you received a letter (Document 5.1) from Haiwang Guo, Director of Operations for China Air, who is unhappy that, although the shipment of scanners arrived on July 1, the Chinese documentation was missing.

You call Pablo Hidalgo, the head of the Documentation Department.

"The Chinese documentation was delayed because of translation problems," Pablo explains. "Several of our graphics with text needed translating, and we didn't allow for text expansion during translation. We had to revise the layout on several pages—"

"When will the documentation be ready?" you interrupt.

"It will be available by next week."

You next talk to Paula Tiller, Zander's President, to discuss the situation. "I can understand why Haiwang is unhappy. The company planned for a big ceremony. Here's the press release," Paula says, handing you a sheet of paper (Document 5.2).

After some more discussion, Paula says that she wants you to arrange for the documentation to be hand-delivered to Haiwang Guo, complete with a letter of apology. "I'm counting on you to convey our sincerest apologies and to keep China Air as one of our clients," she concludes.

**17th floor, United Centre, No. 93
Queensway, Hong Kong**

*Haiwang Guo
Director of Operations, China Air*

[your name]
Director of Far East Marketing
Zander Instruments
9500 Zelzah Avenue
Northridge, CA 91324

Dear [your name]:

I hope that cool ocean breezes greet your summer season and your family enjoys health and happiness. The new cooperation between Zander Instruments and China Air will be a major boost to our cargo network and improve our distribution ability as we move into the future.

China Air wishes to thank you for your role in establishing a prosperous relationship between our companies. I appreciate the management of your company seeing the value of our two organizations working together and I recommit to you my desire on behalf of my company.

In January 2005, your company contracted to supply China Air 15 x-ray scanners on July 1, 2005. The scanners arrived on July 1 with only English documentation. China Air had been very much busy planning a ceremony at its Hong Kong headquarters in preparation for the installation of the scanners at five major airports. The missing documentation resulted in China Air canceling the ceremony on July 3.

It is hoped that Zander Instruments understands the urgency in the request by China Air to supply the Chinese documentation for the scanners and looks forward to providing China Air with an answer just as soon as possible.

May you be lucky, safe, and sound this season, and may our goodwill reach everyone.

Sincerely,

Haiwang Guo

Haiwang Guo
Director of Operations, China Air

2005 July 10

■ **Document 5.1 Letter from China Air's Director of Operations**

 On TechComm Web

For digital versions of case documents, click on Downloadable Case Documents on
<bedfordstmartins.com/techcomm>.

FOR IMMEDIATE RELEASE

CHINA AIR ANNOUNCES JOINT VENTURE
WITH ZANDER INSTRUMENTS

HONG KONG, June 1, 2005 /XFNHK-ChinaNet/ —

China Air today announced that it will install state-of-the-art cargo scanners at the five major airports the airline serves. Supplied by Zander Instruments (United States), the new scanners will allow the airline to more efficiently inspect cargo pallets. To celebrate this new business relationship between China Air and Zander Instruments, China Air's Director of Operations, Haiwang Guo, announced today that the company will hold a ceremony at its Hong Kong headquarters to celebrate the purchase and installation of the new scanners. The ceremony will illustrate China Air's management spirit of "safety first and customers highest."

About China Air:

China Air, formally known as China Northern, was founded in 1995. It is one of only six airlines in mainland China not directly controlled by the Civil Aviation Administration of China (CAAC). China Air began its operations with one Boeing jet. Since then, China Air has grown gradually. In the end of 2003, it offered its quality services with 4 aircrafts to 5 destinations with a total of 150 skillful employees. Following the successful expansion of its domestic cargo service in 2004, China Air is now ready to spread its wings into domestic skies as a new alternative cargo carrier.

For more information, contact:

Haiwang Guo, Director of Operations, China Air
E-mail: hw@china-air.com
Web: www.china-air.com

# # #

■ **Document 5.2　China Air Press Release**

Your Assignment

1. You decide that the first step is to interview a knowledgeable person from the People's Republic of China to learn what you can about how formal apologies are handled there. A friend of yours, Jun Xiaoyan, in Zander's Research and Development Department, is from the People's Republic. You think he might be willing to sit down with you for 15 or 20 minutes. Write a set of questions you would like to ask your friend before apologizing to Haiwang Guo. For each question, write a brief paragraph explaining how the answer to the question might help you complete an appropriate letter of apology to China Air. For example, you might want to know whether the letter should be highly formal in its vocabulary.

2. Jun Xiaoyan contacts you before your meeting and suggests that you bring along a rough draft of your apology letter. "It will give us something specific to work with," he says. Based on what you already know about intercultural communication, draft a letter of apology to China Air. Include in the margins any specific questions you want to ask Jun about your letter.

Researching Your Subject

6

This chapter focuses on conducting *primary research* and *secondary research* to find information to use as evidence and help you answer questions. Primary research involves creating technical information yourself. Secondary research involves collecting information that other people have already discovered or created.

This chapter presents secondary research first. Only rarely would you do primary research before doing secondary research. To design the experiments or the field research that goes into primary research, you need a thorough understanding of the information that already exists about your subject.

UNDERSTANDING THE DIFFERENCES BETWEEN ACADEMIC AND WORKPLACE RESEARCH

Although academic research and workplace research can overlap, in most cases they differ in their goals and their methods.

In *academic research*, your goal is to find information that will help you answer a scholarly question: "What would be the effect on the balance of trade between the United States and China if China lowered the value of its currency?" "What effects will global warming have on agriculture in the United States in the year 2050?" "At what age do babies learn to focus on people's eyes?" Academic research questions are often more abstract than applied. That is, they get at the underlying principles of a phenomenon. Academic research usually requires extensive secondary research: reading scholarly literature in academic journals and books. If you do primary research, as scientists in labs do, you begin this research only after you have conducted extensive secondary research.

In *workplace research*, your goal is to find information to help you answer a practical question, usually one that involves the organization you work for: "Should we stay with our distributed printing configuration or adopt a centralized configuration?" "What would be the advantages and disadvantages if our company adopted a European-style privacy policy for customer information?" Because workplace research is often focused on improving a situation at a particular company, it calls for much more primary research.

You need to learn about your own company's processes and how the people in your company will probably respond to your ideas.

Regardless of whether you are conducting academic or workplace research, the basic research methods are fundamentally the same, as is the basic goal: to answer questions.

UNDERSTANDING THE RESEARCH PROCESS

When you need to perform research, you want the process to be effective and efficient. That is, you want the information you find to answer the questions you need to answer. And you don't want to spend any more time than is necessary getting that information. To meet these goals, you have to think about how the research relates to the other aspects of the overall project. Figure 6.1 provides an overview of the research process.

■ Figure 6.1   An Overview of the Research Process

Analyze Your Audience

Are your most important readers experts, technicians, managers, or general readers? What are their personal characteristics, their attitudes toward your subject, and their motivations for reading? If you are writing to an expert audience that might be skeptical about your message, you need to do a lot of research to gather the evidence for a convincing argument. See Ch. 5.

Analyze Your Purpose

Why are you writing? Understanding your purpose helps you understand the types of information readers will expect. Think in terms of what you want your readers to know, believe, or do after they finish reading your document. See Ch. 5.

Analyze Your Subject

What do you already know about your subject? What do you still need to find out? Using techniques such as freewriting and brainstorming, you can determine those aspects of the subject you need to investigate. See Ch. 3.

Work Out a Schedule and a Budget for the Project

When is the deliverable — the document or the presentation — due? Do you have a budget for phone calls, database searches, or travel to libraries or other sites? See Ch. 5.

Visualize the Deliverable

What kind of document will you need to deliver: a proposal, a report, a Web site? What kind of oral presentation will you need to deliver?

■ **Figure 6.1**   *(continued)*

Determine What Information Will Need to Be Part of That Deliverable

Draft an outline of the contents, focusing on the kinds of information that readers will expect to see in each part. See Ch. 3.

Determine What Information You Still Need to Acquire

Make a list of the pieces of information you don't have.

Create Questions You Need to Answer in Your Deliverable

Writing a list of questions forces you to think carefully about your topic. One question suggests another, and soon you have a lengthy list of questions that you need to answer.

Conduct Secondary Research

Study journal articles and Web-based sources such as online journals, discussion groups, and bulletin boards.

Conduct Primary Research

You can answer some of your questions by consulting company records, interviewing experts in your organization, distributing questionnaires, and interviewing other people in your company.

Evaluate Your Information

Once you have your information, you need to evaluate its quality: is it accurate, comprehensive, unbiased, and current?

Do More Research

If the information you have acquired doesn't sufficiently answer your questions, do more research. If you have thought of additional questions that need to be answered, do more research. When do you stop doing research? Only when you think you have enough high-quality information to create the deliverable.

CHOOSING APPROPRIATE RESEARCH METHODS

Once you have determined the questions you need to answer in your document, think about the various research techniques you can use to answer them. Different research questions require different research methods.

For example, your research methods for finding out how a current situation is expected to change would be different from your research methods for finding out how well a product might work for your organization. That is, if you want to know how outsourcing will change the computer-support industry over the next 10 to 20 years, you might search for long-range predictions in journal and magazine articles and on reputable Web sites. You also might check whether experts have made forecasts on blogs. By contrast, if you want to figure out whether a specific scanner will produce the quality of scan that you need and function reliably, you might read product reviews on reputable Web sites and study discussion lists, observe the use of the product or service at a vendor's site, schedule product demos at your site, follow up by interviewing others in your company, and perform an experiment in which you try two different scanners and then analyze the results.

Choosing research methods means choosing the ways in which you will conduct your research. Start by thinking about the questions you need to answer:

- *What types of research media might you use?* Should you look for information in books, journals, and reports, or online in Web sites, discussion boards, and blogs?

- *What types of research tools might you use?* Are these media best accessed via online catalogs, reference works, indexes, or abstract services?

- *What types of primary research might you conduct?* Should you conduct field research such as observations, demonstrations, inspections, experiments, interviews, and questionnaires?

You are likely to find that your research plan changes as you conduct your research. You might find, for instance, that you need more than one method to get the information you need, or that the one method you thought would work doesn't. Still, having a plan can help you discover the most appropriate methods more quickly and efficiently. The advice in Figure 6.2 on page 102 provides a good starting point.

In addition to planning, researching a subject requires perseverance, organization, and judgment.

Guidelines

Researching a Topic

Follow these three guidelines as you gather information to use in your document.

▶ **Be persistent.** Don't be discouraged if a research method doesn't yield useful information. Even experienced researchers fail as often as they succeed. Be prepared to rethink how you might find the information. Don't hesitate to ask a reference librarian for help or post questions to online discussion groups.

▶ **Record your data carefully.** Prepare the materials you will need. Write information down, on paper or online. Record interviews (with the interviewee's permission). Cut and paste the URLs of the sites you visit into your notes. Bookmark sites so you can return to them easily.

▶ **Triangulate your research methods.** *Triangulating* means using more than one or two sources. If a manufacturer's Web site says a printer produces 17 pages per minute, an independent review in a reputable journal agrees, and you get 17 pages per minute in a demo at your office with your own documents, the printer will probably produce 17 pages per minute.

■ **Figure 6.2   Research Questions and Research Media**

Type of question	Example of question	Appropriate research media
What is the theory behind this process or technique?	How do greenhouse gases contribute to global warming?	**Encyclopedias, handbooks,** and **journal articles** present theory. You can also find theoretical information on the **Web sites** of reputable professional organizations and universities. Search using keywords such as "greenhouse gases" and "global warming."
What is the history of this phenomenon?	When and how did engineers first try to extract shale oil?	**Encyclopedias** and **handbooks** present history. You can also find historical information on the **Web sites** of reputable professional organizations and universities. Search using keywords such as "shale oil" and "petroleum history."
What techniques are being used now to solve this problem?	How are companies responding to the federal government's new laws on health-insurance portability?	If the topic is recent, you will have better luck with digital media such as **Web sites** than with traditional print media. Search using keywords such as "health-insurance portability." Your search will be most effective if you use "official" terminology in your search, such as "HIPAA" for the health-insurance law.
How is a current situation expected to change?	What changes will outsourcing cause in the computer-support industry over the next 10 to 20 years?	For long-range predictions, you can find information in **journal articles** and **magazine articles** and on reputable **Web sites.** Experts might even write forecasts in **blogs.**
What products are available to perform a task or provide a service?	How can we maintain our company's Web site?	For current products and services, search **Web sites**. Reputable manufacturers and service providers will have sites describing their offerings. But be careful not to accept vendors' claims on face value. Even the specifications they provide might be exaggerated.
What are the strengths and weaknesses of competing products and services?	Which portable GPS product is the lightest?	Search for articles by experts in the field, such as a **journal article**—either in print or on the Web—about camping and outfitting that compares the available GPS products according to reasonable criteria. Also check **online discussion groups** for reviews. If appropriate, do **field research** to answer your questions.
Which product or service do experts recommend?	Which four-wheel-drive SUV offers the best combination of features and quality for our needs?	Experts write **journal articles, magazine articles,** and sometimes **blogs.** Often they participate in **online discussion groups.** Sometimes you can **interview** them, in person or on the phone, or you can write **inquiry letters.**
What are the facts about how we do our jobs at this company?	Do our chemists use gas chromatography in their analyses?	Sometimes you can **interview** an expert, in person or on the phone, to answer a simple question. To find out if our chemists use chromatography, contact the head of the department in which the chemist works.

⬇

■ **Figure 6.2**   *(continued)*

Type of question	Example of question	Appropriate research media
What can we learn about what caused a problem in our organization?	What caused the contamination in the clean room?	You can **interview** personnel who were closest to the problem and **inspect** the scene to determine the cause of the problem.
What do our personnel think we should do about a situation?	Do our quality-control analysts think we need to revise our sampling quotient?	If there are only a few analysts, **interview** them. If there are many, use a **questionnaire** to get the information more quickly.
How well would this product or service work in our organization?	Would this scanner produce the quality of scan that we need and interface well with our computer equipment?	Read product reviews on reputable **Web sites**. Study **discussion lists**. **Observe** the use of the product or service at a vendor's location. Schedule product **demos** at your office. Follow up by **interviewing** others in your company to get their thinking. Do an **experiment** in which you try two different solutions to a problem, then analyze the results.

Strategies for Intercultural Communication

Planning a Research Strategy for Multicultural Audiences

As discussed in Chapter 5, readers bring their cultural values to the documents they read. When you plan a research strategy, think about what kinds of evidence your readers will consider appropriate. In many non-Western cultures, tradition or the authority of the person making the claim can be extremely important—more important than scientific evidence, which is often favored in Western cultures.

Don't forget that people pay particular attention to information that comes from their own culture. If you are writing to European readers about telemedicine, for instance, try to find information from European authorities about European telemedicine. This information will interest your readers and will likely reflect their cultural values and expectations.

CONDUCTING SECONDARY RESEARCH

Even though workplace research focuses on primary research, you will almost always need to do secondary research as well. Some subjects call for research in a library. You might need specialized handbooks or access to online subscription services that are not freely available on the Internet. As a college student, you probably do most of this research in one of the libraries on campus. As a working professional, you might find most of the information in your organization's information center. An *information center* is the organization's library, a resource that collects different kinds of information critical to the organization's operations. Large organizations have specialists who can answer research questions or get articles or other kinds of data to you. Often, however, you can do much or even most of your research on the Internet.

Understanding the Research Media

Today, most technical information is being distributed not only in print but also through digital media accessible on the Internet. For your research, you will probably use information published in five major media, as described in Figure 6.3.

Basic research tools:

Online catalogs

Reference works

Periodical indexes

Newspaper indexes

Abstract services

Using Basic Research Tools

There is a tremendous amount of information in the different media. The trick is to learn how to find what you want. This section discusses five basic research tools.

Online Catalogs   An online catalog is a database of books, microforms, films, compact discs, phonograph records, tapes, and other materials. In most cases, an online catalog lists and describes the holdings at one particular library or group of libraries. Your college library has an online catalog of its holdings. To search for an item, consult the instructions for searching, which are almost always located right next to the search window. These instructions explain how to limit your search by characteristics such as the type of media, date of publication, and language. The instructions also explain how to use punctuation and words such as *and*, *or*, and *not* to focus your search effectively.

Reference Works   Reference works include general dictionaries and encyclopedias, biographical dictionaries, almanacs, atlases, and dozens of other general research tools. These print and online works are especially useful when you begin a research project because they provide an overview of the subject and often list the major works in the field.

How do you know if there is a dictionary of the terms used in a given field? The following reference books—the guides-to-the-guides—list the many resources available:

- Mullay, M., & Schlicke, P. (Eds.). (1998–2000). *Walford's guide to reference material* (8th ed., Vols. 1–3). London: Library Association.
- Rasmussen, K. G. (2003). *A writer's guide to research and documentation* (5th ed.). East Rutherford, NJ: Prentice Hall.
- Hacker, D. *Research and documentation online* <dianahacker.com/resdoc>.
- Palmquist, M. *The Bedford researcher* <bedfordresearcher.com/links/>.

To find information on the Web, use a library Web site or search engine and go to its "reference" section. There you will find numerous sites that contain links to excellent collections of reference works online, such as the Best Information on the Net, CyberStacks^{SM}, and the Internet Public Library.

 On TechComm Web

For links to these and other reference sources, click on Links Library for Ch. 6 on <bedfordstmartins.com/techcomm>.

Print

Books, journals, reports, and other documents will continue to be produced in print because printed information is portable and you can write on it. For documents that do not need to be updated periodically, print remains a useful and popular medium. To find it, you will continue to use online catalogs, as you do now.

Online Databases

Most libraries—even many public libraries—subscribe to services, such as Lexis-Nexis, ProQuest, InfoTrac, and EBSCOhost, that provide access to large databases of journal articles, conference proceedings, newspapers, and other documents.

Web Sites

Because there are billions of pages of information on the Web, searching for information can be a challenge. There are three basic ways to locate Web sites: enter the URL of the site you wish to visit, enter a keyword or phrase in a search engine, or use a directory search engine to do a subject search.

Online Discussion Groups

There are two major forums for online discussions: Usenet newsgroups and electronic mailing lists.

- *Usenet newsgroups*, sometimes called *bulletin boards*, publish e-mail messages sent by group members. Newsgroups give participants an opportunity to discuss issues, ask questions, and get answers. Usenet consists of thousands of newsgroups organized according to 10 basic categories, including computer science, science, recreation, and business. In a Usenet newsgroup, mail is not sent to individual computers, but is stored on databases, which you then access.
- *Electronic mailing lists* are like newsgroups in that they publish e-mail messages sent by members. The basic difference is that mailing lists send e-mail messages to every person who subscribes. The mail comes to you; you don't go to it, as you do with a newsgroup.

Personal Publications Such as Blogs and Podcasts

Although many *blogs*—Web logs—are personal diaries that are of little or no value to a researcher, many others are useful. Scientists, engineers, journalists, and other professionals now publish blogs that can help you understand topics being discussed by professionals in your field. *Podcasts*—downloadable audio files playable on Apple iPods and similar audio players—are another increasingly popular means of disseminating information. When you use blogs and podcasts, be sure to verify the authority of the information source, and search for more formal versions of the information presented in edited media such as reputable newspapers and journals.

■ **Figure 6.3   Five Major Information Media**

 On TechComm Web

The Internet Public Library Reference Center is an excellent resource for all aspects of Internet research. Click on Links Library for Ch. 6 on <bedfordstmartins.com/techcomm>.

On TechComm Web

For sites that list newsgroups and listservs, click on Links Library for Ch. 6 on <bedfordstmartins.com/techcomm>.

Periodical Indexes Periodicals are an excellent source of information for most research projects because they offer recent, authoritative discussions of limited subjects. The biggest challenge in using periodicals is identifying and locating the dozens of relevant articles that are published each month. Although only half a dozen major journals may concentrate on your field, a useful article might appear in one of hundreds of other publications. A periodical index, which is simply a list of articles classified according to title, subject, and author, can help you determine which journals you want to locate.

There are periodical indexes in all fields. The following brief list gives you a sense of the diversity of titles:

- *Applied Science & Technology Index*
- *Business Periodicals Index*
- *Readers' Guide to Periodical Literature*
- *Engineering Index*

You can also use a directory search engine. Many directory categories include a subcategory called "journals" or "periodicals" listing online and printed sources.

Once you have created a bibliography of printed articles you want to study, you have to find them. Check your library's online catalog, which includes all the journals your library receives. If your library does not have an article you want, you can use one of two techniques for securing it:

- *Interlibrary loan.* Your library uses an online directory to learn which nearby library has the article. That library photocopies the article and sends it to your library. Although this service is free or very inexpensive, it can take more than a week for the article to arrive at your library.
- *Document-delivery services.* If you are in a hurry, you can log on to a document-delivery service, such as Ingenta, which searches a database of 17 million articles in 28,000 periodicals. If the service has the article, it faxes it to you or makes an electronic copy available.

Newspaper Indexes Many major newspapers around the world are indexed by subject. The three most important indexed U.S. newspapers are the following:

- *The New York Times.* Perhaps the most reputable U.S. newspaper for national and international news.
- *The Christian Science Monitor.* Another highly regarded general newspaper.
- *The Wall Street Journal.* The most authoritative news source on business, finance, and the economy.

 **On TechComm Web**

For links to online newspapers, click on Links Library for Ch. 6 on <bedfordstmartins.com/ techcomm>.

Many newspapers are now available on the Web and can be searched electronically, although sometimes they charge for archived articles. Keep in mind that the print version and the electronic version of a newspaper can vary greatly. If you wish to cite a quotation from an article in a newspaper, the print version is the preferred one.

TI: Title: Reflections on a Greeting: The History of Ciao

OT: Other Title: Riflessioni intorno a un saluto: la storia di "ciao"

AU: Author: De Boer, Minne-Gerben

AF: Author Affiliation: Dipt Lingue Straniere, Utrecht, Netherlands
        [mailto:m.g.deboer@let.uu.nl]

SO: Source: Lingua e Stile, 1999, 34, 3, Sept, 431-448

IS: ISSN 0024-385X

CD: Coden: LGSTB7

AB: Abstract: Mario Alinei's (1991) observations on the history of the Italian greeting
        ciao are reviewed, with the addition of numerous examples from the period be-
        tween the end of the 18th century & the aftermath of WWII. It is argued that, in
        Contemporary Italian, the words slavo, schiavo & ciao are distinct lexical items;
        from a phonological point of view, ciao is a kind of interjection & semantically it
        represents the generic informal greeting both for meeting & leaving people. It is
        supposed to have originated in the second half of the 18th century. Its diffusion
        over the whole of Italy occurred in three stages: first from the Veneto-region to
        northern Italy, then to Rome & Sicily, & finally to the other regions as well. 16 Ref-
        erences. Adapted from the source document

LA: Language: Italian

PY: Publication Year: 1999

PT: Publication Type: Abstract of Journal Article (aja)

CP: Country of Publication: Italy

DE: Descriptors: *Etymology (23250); *Word Meaning (97700); *Speech Acts
        (82400); *Italian (38950); *Conversation (15600); *Semantic Change (76600)

CL: Classification: 5211 lexicography/lexicology; lexicology. 5111 descriptive linguis-
        tics; diachronic linguistics

UD: Update: 200008

AN: Accession Number: 200002972

■ **Figure 6.4   An Abstract**
Source: CSA Illumina, 2005 <www.csa.com/factsheets/llba-set-c.php>.

Abstract Services   Abstract services are like indexes but also provide abstracts: brief technical summaries of articles. In most cases, reading an abstract will enable you to decide whether to seek out the full article. The title
of an article alone is often a misleading indicator of its contents.

Some abstract services, such as *Chemical Abstracts*, cover a broad field,
but many are specialized rather than general. *Adverse Reaction Titles*, for instance, covers research on the subject of adverse reactions to drugs. Figure 6.4
shows an abstract from *Linguistics and Language Behavior Abstracts*.

 In This Book
For more about abstracts, see
Ch. 18, p. 467.

Researching Government Information

The U.S. government is the world's biggest publisher. In researching any field of science, engineering, or business, you are likely to find that a government agency or department has produced a relevant brochure, report, or book.

 **On TechComm Web**

For links to the *Monthly Catalog*, to FirstGov, and to other government information, click on Links Library for Ch. 6 on <bedfordstmartins.com/techcomm>.

Government publications are not usually listed in the indexes and abstract journals. The *Monthly Catalog of United States Government Publications*, available on paper, on CD, and on the Web, provides extensive access to these materials.

Printed government publications are usually cataloged and shelved separately from other kinds of materials. They are classified according to the Superintendent of Documents system, not the Library of Congress system. A reference librarian or a government documents specialist at your library can help you use government publications.

You can also access many government sites and databases on the Internet. The major entry point for federal government sites is FirstGov, which links to more than 180 million pages of government information and services. It also features a topical index, online transactions, and links to state and local governments.

 On TechComm Web

For an excellent guide to using government information, see Patricia Cruse and Sherry DeDecker's "How to Effectively Locate Federal Government Information on the Web." Click on Links Library for Ch. 6 on <bedfordstmartins.com/techcomm>.

For additional information on government publications, consult these two printed guides:

- Garvin, P. (2003). *Government information on the Internet* (6th ed.). Lanham, MD: Bernan Associates.
- Morehead, J. (1999). *Introduction to United States government information sources* (6th ed.). Englewood, CO: Libraries Unlimited.

Evaluating the Information

In This Book

For more about taking notes, paraphrasing, and quoting, see Appendix, Part A.

You've taken notes, paraphrased, and quoted material from your secondary research. Now, with more information than you can possibly use, you try to figure out what it all means. You realize that you still have some questions—that some of the information is incomplete, some contradictory, and some just unclear. There is no shortage of information; the challenge is to find the right information. Look for information that has these six characteristics:

- *Accurate.* You are researching whether your company should consider flextime scheduling. You start by determining the number of employees who might be interested in flextime. If you estimate that number to be 500 but it is in fact closer to 50, you will waste time doing an unnecessary study.
- *Unbiased.* You want sources that have no financial stake in the project. A private company that transports workers in vans is likely to be a biased source because of an interest in contracting with your company.
- *Comprehensive.* You want to hear from different kinds of people—in terms of gender, cultural characteristics, and age—and from people representing all views of the topic.
- *Appropriately technical.* Good information is sufficiently detailed to respond to the needs of your readers, but not so detailed that they cannot

understand it. For the study of flextime, you need to find out whether opening your building an hour earlier and closing it an hour later will significantly affect your utility costs. You can get this information by interviewing people in operations. You will not need to do a detailed inspection of all the utility records of the company.

- *Current.* If your information is 10 years old, it might not accurately reflect today's situation.
- *Clear.* You want information that is easy to understand. Otherwise, you'll waste time trying to figure it out, and you might misinterpret it.

The most difficult kind of material to evaluate is information from the Internet, because it often appears on the Internet without passing through the formal review procedure used for books and professional journals.

 On TechComm Web

For links to sources on finding and evaluating Internet information, click on Links Library for Ch. 6 on <bedfordstmartins.com/ techcomm>.

Guidelines

Evaluating Print and Online Sources

Criteria	For printed sources	For online sources
Authorship	Do you recognize the name of the author? Can you learn about the author's credentials and current position from a biographical note? If this information is not included in the document itself, can you find it in a who's who or by searching for other books or other journal articles by the author?	If you do not recognize the name, did you find the site by linking from another reputable site? Does the site contain links to other reputable sites? Does the site contain biographical information — the author's current position and credentials? Can you use a search engine to find other references to the author's credentials or other documents by the author?
Publishing body	What is the publisher's reputation? To be reliable, a book should be published by a reputable trade, academic, or scholarly publisher; a journal should be sponsored by a professional association or university. Are the editorial board members well-known names in the field? Trade publications — magazines about a particular industry or group — often promote the interests of that industry or	Can you determine the publishing body's identity from headers or footers? Is the publishing body reputable in the field? If the site comes from a personal account on an Internet service provider, the author might be writing outside his or her field of expertise. Many Internet sites exist largely for public relations or advertising. For instance, the home page for the White House is not going to provide information critical of the administration.

On TechComm Web

Evaluating sources is easier if you start searching from a reputable list of links, such as that of the WWW Virtual Library, sponsored by the World Wide Web Consortium. Click on Links Library for Ch. 6 on <bedfordstmartins.com/ techcomm>.

Criteria	For printed sources	For online sources
	group. For example, don't automatically assume the accuracy of information in trade publications for loggers or environmentalists. If you doubt the authority of a book or journal, ask the reference librarian or a professor.	Likewise, the Web sites of corporations and other organizations are unlikely to contain information critical of those corporations or organizations.
Knowledge of the literature	Does the author appear to be knowledgeable about the major literature in the field? Is there a bibliography? Are there notes throughout the document?	Analyze the Internet source as you would any other source. Often references to other sources will take the form of links.
Accuracy and verifiability of the information	Is the information based on reasonable assumptions? Does the author clearly describe the methods and theories used in producing the information, and are they appropriate to the subject? Has the author used sound reasoning? Has the author explained the limitations of the information?	Is the site well constructed? Is the information well written? Is the information based on reasonable assumptions? Are the claims supported by appropriate evidence? Has the author used sound reasoning? Has the author explained the limitations of the information? Are sources cited?
Timeliness	Does the document rely on recent data? Was the document published recently?	Was the document created recently? Was it updated recently? If a site is not yet complete, be wary.

On TechComm Web

For more help with evaluating online sources, click on Tutorials on <bedfordstmartins.com/techcomm>.

Types of primary research:

Observations and demonstrations

Inspections

Experiments

Field research

Interviews

Inquiry letters or e-mails

Questionnaires

CONDUCTING PRIMARY RESEARCH

Although the library and the Internet offer a wealth of secondary sources, in the workplace you will often need to conduct primary research to acquire new information. There are seven major categories of primary research.

Observations and Demonstrations

Observations and demonstrations are two common forms of primary research. When you *observe*, you simply watch some activity to understand some aspect of it. For instance, if you are trying to determine whether the location of the break room on a factory floor is interfering with the work on the floor, you could observe the situation, preferably at different times of the day and on different days of the week. If you saw workers distracted by people

INTERACTIVE SAMPLE DOCUMENT
Evaluating Information from Internet Sources

This image is an excerpt from a Web page about teenage deaths in motor vehicles. The questions in the margin ask you to consider the guidelines for evaluating Internet sources (on pages 109–10). E-mail your responses to yourself and/or your instructor, and see suggested responses on TechComm Web.

4. How do crashes involving teenagers differ from those of other drivers? Teenagers not only have higher crash rates than other age groups, their crashes are different. Analyses of fatal crash data indicate that teenage drivers are more likely to be at fault in their crashes.[3] Teenagers' crashes and violations are more likely to involve speeding than those of older drivers, and teenagers are more likely than drivers of other ages to be in single-vehicle fatal crashes. Plus, teenagers do more of their driving at night, and in small and older cars[3] compared with adults. About 40% of teenagers' fatalities occur at night, especially weekend nights.[4]

And for 16 year-olds, all these problems are heightened. The combination of inexperience behind the wheel and immaturity produces a pattern of fatal crashes among 16 year-olds that includes the highest percentage of crashes involving speeding, the highest percentage of single-vehicle crashes, the highest percentage of crashes with driver error, and the highest vehicle occupancy.[3]

References

[1]Mayhew, D.R.; Simpson, H.M.; and Pak, A. 2003. Changes in collision rates among novice drivers during the first months of driving. *Accident Analysis and Prevention* 35: 683-691.

[2]Highway Loss Data Institute. 1999. Insurance special report (A-56): rated driver insurance losses by age and gender. Arlington, VA.

[3]Cammisa, M.X.; Williams, A.F.; and Leaf, W.A. 1999. Vehicles driven by teenagers in four states. *Journal of Safety Research* 30(1): 25-30.

[4]Williams, A.F.; Preusser, D.F.; Ulmer, R.G.; and Weinstein, H.B. 1995. Characteristics of fatal crashes of 16-year-old drivers: Implications for licensure policies. *Journal of Public Health Policy* 16(3): 347-360.

Source: Insurance Institute for Highway Safety, Highway Loss Data Institute, 2005 <www.hwysafety.org/research/qanda/teens.html>.

1. What is the publishing body for this site? Is it reputable? Is the information within the realm of the publishing body's expertise?

2. How can the information be verified?

3. How timely is the information?

 **On TechComm Web**

To e-mail your responses to yourself and/or your instructor and to see suggested responses, click on Interactive Sample Documents for Ch. 6 on TechComm Web <bedfordstmartins.com/techcomm>.

moving in and out of the room or by sounds made in the room, you would record your observations by taking notes, taking still pictures, or videotaping the events. An observation might lead to other forms of primary research. You might, for example, follow up by interviewing some employees who might help you understand what you have observed.

When you witness a *demonstration*, or *demo*, you are watching someone carry out a process. For instance, if your company is considering purchasing a mail-sorting machine, you could arrange to visit a manufacturer's facility, where technicians would show you how the various machines work. If your company is looking at a portable machine, such as a laptop computer, the manufacturer or dealer could bring its products to your facility.

When you plan to observe a situation or witness a demo, prepare beforehand. Write down the questions you need answered or the points you want to investigate. Prepare interview questions in case you have the opportunity to speak with someone. Think about how you are going to incorporate the information you acquire into the document you will write. Finally, make sure to bring whatever equipment you will need (pen and paper, computer, camera, audio recorder, etc.) to the site of the observation or demo.

Inspections

Inspections are like observations, but you participate more actively. For example, a civil engineer can determine what caused the crack in a foundation by inspecting the site: walking around, looking at the crack, photographing it and the surrounding scene, picking up the soil. An accountant can determine the financial health of an organization by inspecting its financial records, perhaps performing calculations and comparing the data she finds with other data.

These professionals are applying their knowledge and professional judgment as they inspect a site, an object, or a document. Sometimes inspection techniques are more complicated. A civil engineer inspecting a crack in the foundation might want to test his hunches by taking soil samples back to the lab and studying them.

When you carry out an inspection, make sure to do your homework beforehand. Think about how you will use the information in your document: will you need photographs, video files, or computer data? Then prepare the materials and equipment you'll need to capture the data.

Experiments

Learning to conduct the many kinds of experiments used in a particular field can take months or even years. This discussion is a brief introduction.

In many cases, conducting an experiment involves four phases.

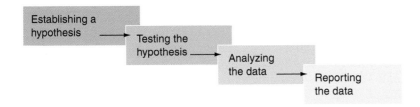

- *Establishing a hypothesis.* A hypothesis is an informed guess about the re-lationship between two factors. In a study relating gasoline octane and miles per gallon, a hypothesis might be that a car will get 10 percent bet-ter mileage with 89 octane gas than with 87 octane.
- *Testing the hypothesis.* Usually, you need an experimental group and a control group. These two groups are identical except for the condition you are studying: in the above example, the gasoline. The control group would be a car running on 87 octane. The experimental group would be an identical car running on 89 octane. The experiment would consist of driving the two cars over an identical course at the same speed—prefer-ably in some sort of controlled environment—over a given distance, such as 1,000 miles. Then you would calculate the miles per gallon. The re-sults would either support or refute your original hypothesis.
- *Analyzing the data.* Do your data show a correlation—one factor changing along with another—or a causal relationship? For example, we know that sports cars are involved in more fatal accidents than sedans, but we don't know whether the car or the way it is driven is the important factor.
- *Reporting the data.* When researchers report their findings, they explain what they did, why they did it, what they saw, what it means, and what ought to be done next.

📖 **In This Book**

For more about reports, see Chs. 17 and 18.

Field Research

Whereas an experiment yields quantitative data that can be measured, most field research is qualitative. It yields data that cannot be measured or, at least, cannot be measured as precisely as experimental data. Often in field research, you seek to understand the quality of an experience. For instance, you might want to understand how a new seating arrangement might affect group dynamics in a classroom. You could design a study in which you ob-served and recorded the classes and interviewed the students and the in-structor about their reactions. Then you could do the same in a traditional classroom and compare the results.

Some kinds of studies have both quantitative and qualitative elements. In the case of classroom seating arrangements, you could include some quantitative measures, such as the number of times students talked with each other. You could also distribute questionnaires to elicit the opinions of the students and the instructor. If you used these same quantitative measures on enough classrooms, you could gather valid quantitative information.

When you are doing quantitative or qualitative studies on the behavior of animals—from rats to monkeys to people—try to minimize two common problems:

- *The effect of the experiment on the behavior you are studying.* In studying the effects of the classroom seating arrangement, minimize the effects of your own presence. For instance, make sure that the camera is placed unobtrusively and that it is set up before the students arrive, so they don't see the process. Still, any time you bring in a camera, you can never be sure that what you witness is typical.

- *Bias in the recording and analysis of the data.* Bias can occur because researchers want to confirm their hypotheses. In an experiment to determine whether word processors help students write better, the researcher might see improvement where other people don't. For this reason, the experiment should be designed so that it is *double-blind.* That is, the students doing the writing shouldn't know what the experiment is about so they won't change their behavior to support or negate the hypothesis. And the data being analyzed should be disguised so that researchers don't know whether they are examining the results from the control group or the experimental group. If the control group wrote in ink and the experimental group used word processors, for example, the control group's papers should be formatted on a word processor so that all the papers look identical.

Conducting an experiment or field research is relatively simple; the hard part is designing your study so that it accurately measures what you want it to measure.

Interviews

Interviews are extremely useful when you need information on subjects that are too new to have been discussed in the professional literature or are inappropriate for widespread publication (such as local political questions).

In choosing a respondent—a person to interview—answer three questions:

- *What questions do you want answered?* Only after you answer this question can you begin to search for a person who can provide the information.

- *Who could provide this information?* The ideal respondent is an expert willing to talk. Unless the respondent is an obvious choice, such as the professor carrying out the research you are studying, use directories, such as local industrial guides, to locate potential respondents.

- *Is the person willing to be interviewed?* On the phone or in writing, state what you want to ask about. The person might not be able to help you but might be willing to refer you to someone who can. Explain why you have decided to ask him or her. (A compliment works better than admitting that the person you really wanted to interview is out of town.) Explain what you plan to do with the information, such as write a report or give a talk. If the person is willing to be interviewed, set up an appointment at his or her convenience.

Guidelines

Conducting an Interview

Preparing for the interview

▶ **Do your homework.** If you ask questions that are already answered in the professional literature, the respondent might become annoyed and uncooperative.

▶ **Prepare good questions.** Good questions are clear, focused, and open.

—Be clear. The respondent should be able to understand what you are asking.

UNCLEAR	Why do you sell Trane products?
CLEAR	What are the characteristics of Trane products that led you to include them in your product line?

The unclear question can be answered in a number of unhelpful ways: "Because they're too expensive to give away" or "Because I'm a Trane dealer."

—Be focused. The question must be narrow enough to be answered briefly. If you want more information, you can ask a follow-up question.

UNFOCUSED	What is the future of the computer industry?
FOCUSED	What will the American chip industry look like in 10 years?

—Ask open questions. Your purpose is to get the respondent to talk. Don't ask a lot of questions that have yes or no answers.

CLOSED	Do you think the federal government should create industrial partnerships?
OPEN	What are the advantages and disadvantages of the federal government's creating industrial partnerships?

▶ **Check your equipment.** If you will be taping the interview, test your tape recorder or video camera to make sure it is operating properly.

 On TechComm Web

For an excellent discussion of interview questions, see Joel Bowman's *Business Communication: Managing Information and Relationships*. Click on Links Library for Ch. 6 on <bedfordstmartins.com/ techcomm>.

Beginning the interview	▶ **Arrive on time.**
	▶ **Thank the respondent for taking the time to talk with you.**
	▶ **State the subject and purpose of the interview and what you plan to do with the information.**
	▶ **If you wish to tape the interview, ask permission.**
Conducting the interview	▶ **Take notes.** Write down important concepts, facts, and numbers, but don't take such copious notes that you are still writing when the respondent finishes an answer.
	▶ **Start with prepared questions.** Because you are likely to be nervous at the start, you might forget important questions. Have your first few questions ready.
	▶ **Be prepared to ask follow-up questions.** Listen carefully to the respondent's answer and be ready to ask a follow-up question or request a clarification. Have your other prepared questions ready, but be willing to deviate from them if the respondent leads you in unexpected directions.
	▶ **Be prepared to get the interview back on track.** Gently return to the point if the respondent begins straying unproductively, but don't interrupt rudely or show annoyance. Do not say, "Whoa! I asked about layoffs in this company, not in the whole industry." Rather, say "On the question of layoffs at this company, do you anticipate...?"
Concluding the interview	▶ **Thank the respondent.**
	▶ **Ask for a follow-up interview.** If a second meeting would be useful, ask to arrange it.
	▶ **Ask for permission to quote the respondent.** If you think you might want to quote the respondent by name, ask for permission now.
After the interview	▶ **Write down the important information while the interview is fresh in your mind.** (This step is unnecessary, of course, if you have recorded the interview.) If you will be printing a transcript of the interview, make the transcript now.
	▶ **Send a brief thank-you note.** Within a day or two, send a note that shows you appreciate the courtesy and that you value what you have learned. In the letter, confirm any previous offers you have made, such as sending the respondent a copy of your final document.

When you wish to present the data from an interview in a document you are preparing, include a transcript of the entire interview or an excerpt from it. It is generally best to present an entire transcript in an appendix so that readers can refer to it but are not slowed down when reading the body of the document. You might decide to present brief excerpts from the interview in the body of the document as evidence for points you make.

Figure 6.5 is from a transcript of an interview with an attorney specializing in information technology. The interviewer is a student who is writing about legal aspects of software ownership.

Interview Transcript, Page 1

Q. Why is copyright ownership important in marketing software?

A. If you own the copyright, you can license and market the product and keep other people from doing so. It could be a matter of millions of dollars if the software is popular.

Q. Shouldn't the programmer automatically own the copyright?

A. If the programmer wrote the program on personal time, he or she should and does own the copyright.

Q. So "personal time" is the critical concept?

A. That's right. We're talking about the "work-made-for-hire" doctrine of copyright law. If I am working for you, anything I make under the terms of my employment is owned by you.

Q. What is the complication, then? If I make the software on my machine at home, I own it; if I'm working for someone, my employer owns it.

A. Well, the devil is in the details. Often the terms of employment are casual, or there is no written job description or contract for the particular piece of software.

Q. Can you give me an example of that?

A. Sure. There was a 1992 case, *Aymes v. Bonelli*. Bonelli owned a swimming pool and hired Aymes to write software to handle record keeping on the pool. This was not part of Bonelli's regular business; he just wanted a piece of software written. The terms of the employment were casual. Bonelli paid no health benefits, Aymes worked irregular hours, usually unsupervised—Bonelli wasn't a programmer. When the case was heard, the court ruled that even though Bonelli was paying Aymes, Aymes owned the copyright because of the lack of involvement and participation by Bonelli. The court found that the degree of skill required by Aymes to do the job was so great that, in effect, he was creating the software by himself, even though he was receiving compensation for it.

Q. How can such disagreements be prevented? By working out the details ahead of time?

A. Exactly. The employer should have the employee sign a statement that the project is being carried out as work-made-for-hire and should register the copyright with the U.S. Copyright Office in Washington. Conversely, employees should try to have the employer sign a statement that the project is not work made-for-hire and should try to register the copyright themselves.

Q. And if agreement can't be reached ahead of time?

A. Then stop right there. Don't do any work.

Notice how the student prompts the attorney to expand her answers.

Notice how the student responds to the attorney's answers, making the interview more of a discussion.

Inquiry Letters or E-mails

A useful alternative to a personal interview is an inquiry letter or e-mail. Most large organizations make it more convenient for you to e-mail than to send a letter (look for the Contact Us link on the site). Many people prefer to receive e-mail inquiries because it is easier to hit the Reply button than to create a

In This Book

For more about inquiry letters, see Ch. 14, p. 346.

letter. However, letters are more formal than e-mail messages and therefore might be more appropriate if the topic is important (concerning personnel layoffs, for instance) or related to safety.

If you are lucky, your respondent will provide detailed and helpful answers. However, the respondent might not clearly understand what you want to know or might choose not to help you. Although the strategy of the inquiry letter is essentially that of a personal interview, inquiry letters can be less successful, because the recipient has not already agreed to provide information and might not respond. Also, a written inquiry, unlike an interview, gives you little opportunity to follow up by asking for clarification.

Keep a copy of the e-mail message or letter that you send. You might need to include it as an appendix item if you include the recipient's reply in your document.

Questionnaires

Questionnaires enable you to solicit information from a large group of people. You can send questionnaires through the mail, e-mail them, or present them as forms on a Web site.

Unfortunately, questionnaires rarely yield completely satisfactory results, for three reasons:

- *Some of the questions will misfire.* Some respondents will misinterpret some of your questions or supply useless answers.

- *You won't obtain as many responses as you want.* The response rate will almost never exceed 50 percent. In most cases, it will be closer to 10 to 20 percent.

- *You cannot be sure the respondents are representative.* People who feel strongly about an issue are much more likely to respond than are those who do not. For this reason, you need to be careful in drawing conclusions based on a small number of responses to a questionnaire.

When you send a questionnaire, you are asking the recipient to do you a favor. Your goal should be to construct questions that will elicit the information you need as simply and efficiently as possible.

Asking Effective Questions   To ask effective questions, keep two points in mind:

- *Use unbiased language.* Don't ask, "Should U.S. clothing manufacturers protect themselves from unfair foreign competition?" Instead, ask, "Are you in favor of imposing tariffs on men's clothing?"

- *Be specific.* If you ask, "Do you favor improving the safety of automobiles?" only an eccentric would answer no. Instead, ask, "Do you favor requiring automobile manufacturers to equip new cars with side-impact air bags, which would raise the price by an average of $300 per car?"

Table 6.1 explains common types of questions used in questionnaires.

■ **Table 6.1 Common Types of Questions Used in Questionnaires**

Type of question	Example	Comments
Multiple choice	Would you consider joining a company-sponsored sports team? Yes_____ No_____	The respondent selects one of the alternatives.
Likert scale	The flextime program has been a success in its first year. strongly disagree __ __ __ __ __ __ strongly agree	The respondent ranks the degree to which he or she agrees or disagrees with the statement. Using an even number of possible responses (six, in this case) increases your chances of obtaining useful data. With an odd number, many respondents choose the middle response.
Semantic differentials	simple __ __ __ __ __ __ difficult interesting __ __ __ __ __ __ boring	The respondent registers a response along a continuum between a pair of opposing adjectives. Usually, these questions measure a person's feelings about a task, an experience, or an object. As with Likert scales, an even number of possible responses yields better data.
Ranking	Please rank the following work schedules in order of preference. Put a 1 next to the schedule you would most like to have, a 2 next to your second choice, and so on. 8:00–4:30 _____ 9:00–5:30 _____ 8:30–5:00 _____ flexible _____	The respondent indicates a priority among a number of alternatives.
Short answer	What do you feel are the major advantages of the new parts-requisitioning policy? 1. _____ 2. _____ 3. _____	The respondent writes a brief answer using phrases or sentences.
Short essay	The new parts-requisitioning policy has been in effect for a year. How well do you think it is working? _____ _____ _____ _____ _____ _____ _____	Although an essay question can yield information you never would have found using closed-ended questions, you will receive fewer responses because they require more effort. Also, essays cannot be quantified precisely, as the data from the other types of questions can.

Include an introductory explanation with the questionnaire. This explanation should clearly indicate who you are, why you are writing, what you plan to do with the information, and when you will need it.

In This Book

For more about testing documents, see Ch. 19, p. 521.

Testing the Questionnaire   Before you send out *any* questionnaire, show it and the accompanying letter or memo to a few people who can help you identify any problems. After you have revised the materials, test them on people whose backgrounds are similar to those of your real respondents. Revise the materials a second time and, if possible, test them again. Once you have sent the questionnaire, you cannot revise it and resend it to the same people.

Administering the Questionnaire   Determining who should receive the questionnaire can be simple or difficult. If you want to know what the residents of a particular street think about a proposed construction project, your job is easy. But if you want to know what mechanical-engineering students in colleges across the country think about their curricula, you will need background in sampling techniques to isolate a representative sample.

Make it easy for respondents to present their information. For mailed questionnaires, include a self-addressed, stamped envelope.

Figure 6.6 shows a sample questionnaire.

Presenting Questionnaire Data in Your Document   To decide where and how to present the data that you acquire from your questionnaire, think about your audience and purpose. Start with this principle: important information is presented and analyzed in the body of a document, whereas less-important information is presented in an appendix (a section at the end of the document that only some of your audience will read). Most often, some version of the information appears in both places, but in different ways.

If you think your questionnaire data are relatively unimportant, present the questionnaire in an appendix. If you can, present the respondents' data—the answers they provided—in the questionnaire itself, as shown here.

If you think your reader will benefit from statistical analyses of the data, present them. For instance, you could calculate the percentages of each response. (For question 1, 12 people—17 percent—say they do not eat in the cafeteria at all.) You could present the percentages within parentheses after each number. For example: 12 (17%).

1. Approximately how many days per week do you eat lunch in the cafeteria?
   0 <u>12</u> 1 <u>16</u> 2 <u>18</u> 3 <u>12</u> 4 <u>9</u> 5 <u>4</u>

2. At approximately what time do you eat in the cafeteria?
   11:30–12:30 <u>3</u> 12:00–1:00 <u>26</u> 12:30–1:30 <u>7</u> varies <u>23</u>

If you think your questionnaire data are relatively important, present the full data in an appendix and interpret selected data in the body of the document. For instance, you might want to devote a few sentences or paragraphs to the data for one of the questions. The following example shows how one writer might discuss the data from question 2.

Question 2 shows that 26 people say that they use the cafeteria between noon and 1:00. Only 10 people selected the two other times, 11:30–12:30 and

September 6, 2006

To: All employees
From: William Bonoff, Vice President of Operations
Subject: Evaluation of the Lunches Unlimited food service

As you may know, every two years we evaluate the quality and cost of the food service that caters our cafeteria. We would like you to help in our evaluation by sharing your opinions about the food service. Please note that your responses will remain anonymous. Please drop the completed questionnaires in the marked boxes near the main entrance to the cafeteria.

1. Approximately how many days per week do you eat lunch in the cafeteria?
    0 _____   1 _____   2 _____   3 _____   4 _____   5 _____

2. At approximately what time do you eat in the cafeteria?
    11:30–12:30 _____   12:00–1:00 _____   12:30–1:30 _____   varies _____

3. A clean table is usually available.
    Strongly Disagree _____ _____ _____ _____ _____ _____ Strongly Agree

4. The Lunches Unlimited personnel are polite and helpful.
    Strongly Disagree _____ _____ _____ _____ _____ _____ Strongly Agree

5. Please comment on the quality of the different kinds of food you have eaten in the cafeteria.
    a. Daily specials
        excellent _____   good _____   satisfactory _____   poor _____

    b. Hot dogs and hamburgers
        excellent _____   good _____   satisfactory _____   poor _____

    c. etc.

6. What *foods* would you like to see served that are not served now?
    _____

7. What *beverages* would you like to see served that are not served now?
    _____

8. Please comment on the prices of the foods and beverages served.
    a. Hot meals (daily specials)
        too high _____   fair _____   a bargain _____

    b. Hot dogs and hamburgers
        too high _____   fair _____   a bargain _____

    c. etc.

9. Would you be willing to spend more money for a better-quality lunch if you thought the price was reasonable?
    yes, often _____   sometimes _____   not likely _____

10. On the other side of this sheet, please provide whatever comments you think will help us evaluate the catering service.

Thank you for your assistance.

Likert-scale questions 3 and 4 make it easy for the writer to quantify data about subjective impressions.

Short-answer questions 6 and 7 are best for soliciting ideas from respondents.

12:30–1:30. Of the 23 people who said that they use the cafeteria at various times, we can conclude that at least a third—some 8 people—use it between noon and 1:00. If this assumption is correct, some 34 people (26 + 8) use the cafeteria between noon and 1:00. This would explain why people routinely cannot find a table during the noon hour, especially between 12:15 and 12:30. To alleviate this

Ethics Note

Reporting and Analyzing Data Honestly

When you put a lot of time and effort into a research project, it's frustrating when you can't find the information you need, or when the information you find doesn't help you say what you want to say. As discussed in Chapter 2, your challenge as a professional is to tell the truth.

If the evidence suggests that the course of action you propose won't work, don't omit that evidence or change it. Rather, try to figure out the discrepancy between the evidence and your proposal. Present your explanation honestly.

If you can't find reputable evidence to support your claim, don't just keep silent and hope your readers don't notice. Explain why you think the evidence is missing and how you propose to follow up by continuing your research.

If you make an honest mistake, you are a person. If you cover up a mistake, you're a dishonest person. If you get caught fudging the data, you could become an unemployed dishonest person. If you don't get caught, you're still a smaller person.

problem, we might consider asking department heads not to schedule meetings between 11:30 and 1:30, which would make it easier for their people to choose one of the less popular times.

The body of a document is also a good place to discuss important non-quantitative data. For example, you might wish to discuss and interpret several representative textual answers to open-ended questions.

Writer's Checklist

Did you

☐ determine the questions you need to answer in your document? (p. 98)

☐ choose appropriate secondary-research methods to answer those questions, including, if appropriate,

  ☐ online catalogs? (p. 104)

  ☐ reference works? (p. 104)

  ☐ periodical indexes? (p. 106)

  ☐ newspaper indexes? (p. 106)

  ☐ abstract services? (p. 107)

☐ choose appropriate primary-research methods to answer those questions, including, if appropriate,

  ☐ observations and demonstrations? (p. 110)

  ☐ inspections? (p. 112)

  ☐ experiments? (p. 112)

  ☐ field research? (p. 113)

  ☐ interviews? (p. 114)

  ☐ inquiry letters or e-mails? (p. 117)

  ☐ questionnaires? (p. 118)

☐ in evaluating information, carefully assess

  ☐ the author's credentials? (p. 109)

  ☐ the publishing body? (p. 109)

  ☐ the author's knowledge of literature in the field? (p. 110)

  ☐ the accuracy and verifiability of the information? (p. 110)

  ☐ the timeliness of the information? (p. 110)

☐ appropriately present and analyze the information you acquired? (p. 122)

Exercises

 In This Book   For more about memos, see Ch. 14, p. 352.

1. **INTERNET EXERCISE** Use a search engine to find at least 10 sites about some key term or concept in your field, such as "genetic engineering," "hospice care," or "fuzzy logic." For each site, write a brief paragraph explaining why it would or would not be a credible source of information for a research report.

2. **INTERNET EXERCISE** Using a search engine, answer the following questions. Provide the URL of each site you mention. If your instructor requests it, submit your answers in an e-mail to him or her.

   a. What are the three largest or most important professional organizations in your field? For example, if you are a construction-management major, your field is construction management, civil engineering, or industrial engineering.

   b. What are three important journals read by people in your field?

   c. What are the three important online discussion lists or bulletin boards read by people in your field?

   d. What are the date and location of an upcoming national or international professional meeting for people in your field?

   e. Name and describe, in one paragraph for each, three major issues being discussed by practitioners or academics in your field. For instance, nurses might be discussing the effect of managed care on the quality of medical care delivered to patients.

3. Revise the following interview questions to make them more effective. In a brief paragraph for each, explain why you have revised it as you have.

   a. What is the role of communication in your daily job?

   b. Do you think it is better to relocate your warehouse or go to just-in-time manufacturing?

   c. Isn't it true that it's almost impossible to train an engineer to write well?

   d. Where are your company's headquarters?

   e. Is there anything else you think I should know?

4. Revise the following questions from questionnaires to make them more effective. In a brief paragraph for each, explain why you have revised it as you have.

   a. Does your company provide tuition reimbursement for its employees? Yes_____ No_____

   b. What do you see as the future of bioengineering?

   c. How satisfied are you with the computer support you receive?

   d. How many employees work at your company? 5–10_____ 10–15_____ 15 or more_____

   e. What kinds of documents do you write most often? memos_____ letters_____ reports_____

5. **GROUP/INTERNET EXERCISE** Form small groups and describe and evaluate your college or university's Web site. A different member of the group might carry out each of the following tasks:

   - In an e-mail to the site's Webmaster, ask questions about the process of creating the site. For example, how involved with the content and design of the site was the Webmaster? What is the Webmaster's role in maintaining the site?

   - Analyze the kinds of information the site contains and determine whether the site is intended primarily for faculty, students, alumni, legislators, or prospective students.

   - Determine the overlap between information on the site and information in printed documents published by the school. In those cases in which they overlap, is the information on the site merely a duplication of the printed information, or has it been revised to take advantage of the unique capabilities of the Web?

   In a memo to your instructor, present your findings and recommend how the site might be improved.

Case 6: Choosing an Appropriate Primary-Research Method

 In This Book For more about memos, see Ch. 14, p. 352.

Background

You are part of a five-person documentation group for In-telliplay, a video game-development company. Intelliplay develops entertainment software for personal computers and advanced game systems. The company's documentation group is responsible for writing the brief player manuals shipped with the games. These player manuals, each about five small pages long, cover topics such as system requirements, installation, game controls, game rules, play options, and technical support.

Intelliplay is developing a game tentatively titled Stomp, Crunch, and Munch, in which players control giant monsters similar to those popularized by Hollywood's B movies of the 1950s and 1960s. The object of the game is for a monster to destroy as much of a city as possible, while avoiding the military forces sent to protect the city. Players can select single-player or multiplayer mode. Multiplayer mode allows each of several players to control a monster or military unit and play on a LAN (local area network) or the Internet. Currently, the documentation team is writing the instructions for multiplayer mode.

A recently hired colleague, David Vidinah, walks into your office and confides, "I can't seem to get much help." He explains that he is writing a section on how to host a multiplayer game over the Internet. He e-mailed a message (Document 6.1) to Intelliplay's president, Erik Warden, and

■ **Document 6.1**
E-mail Message
Requesting Help

 On TechComm Web

For digital versions of case documents, click on Downloadable Case Documents on <bedfordstmartins.com/techcomm>.

the four other game developers. Only Erik and two of the game developers, Sonja Morganfeld and Matt Giller, replied to David. Since being hired, David has had little interaction with Erik and has never spent much time talking with the game developers. David knows that Sonja is a new mother just back from maternity leave and works part-time. He frequently sees Matt shooting baskets or playing game prototypes with other employees, including people from the documentation group.

"I'm confused," David says. "Erik implied I did something wrong, and the game developers basically ignored me. What responses I did get were contradictory or not very helpful. What's going on?"

You offer to take a look at David's message and the replies (Documents 6.2–6.4) and get back to him the next day.

Your Assignment

1. Examine David's request for help (Document 6.1) and the responses he received from the company president (Document 6.2) and the game developers (Documents 6.3 and 6.4). What can you infer about the relationship each wants to have with David? How do you think each wants to communicate with him? Write David an e-mail message explaining why you think he didn't get the help he wanted and what he should do next.

2. Who are the appropriate people for David to contact with his questions, and what is the best way to approach each of them? Write David an e-mail message telling him whom he should contact and how he should approach each of them.

3. Think about what steps David needs to take and what materials he needs to create to get answers to his questions. Create the materials that will enable him to finish the documentation for the game's multiplayer mode.

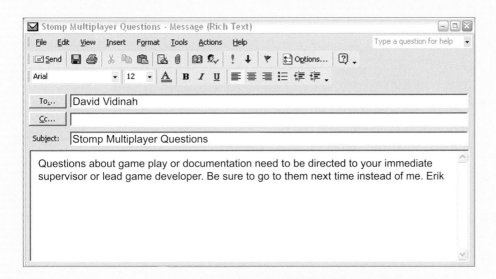

■ **Document 6.2
E-mail Reply from the
Company President**

Stomp Multiplayer Questions - Message (Rich Text)

File   Edit   View   Insert   Format   Tools   Actions   Help   Type a question for help

Send

Arial   12   A   B   I   U

To...   David Vidinah

Cc...

Subject: Stomp Multiplayer Questions

Questions about game play or documentation need to be directed to your immediate supervisor or lead game developer. Be sure to go to them next time instead of me. Erik

**■ Document 6.3
E-mail Reply from Sonja
Morganfeld, Game
Developer**

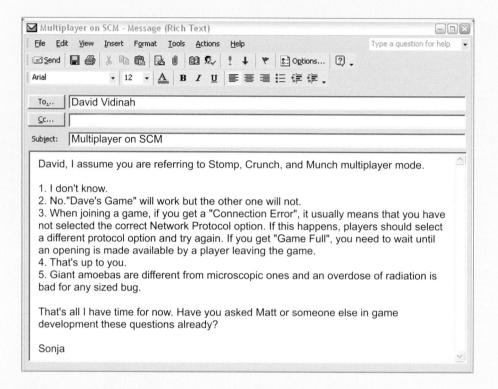

> Multiplayer on SCM - Message (Rich Text)
>
> File   Edit   View   Insert   Format   Tools   Actions   Help   Type a question for help
>
> ⌐Send | 🖫 🖨 | ✂ 🖻 🖺 | 🖺 📎 | 🕮 🕮 | ! ↓ ❦ | ⌐ Options... | ② .
>
> Arial   ▼ 12 ▼ | A | B I U | ▤ ▤ ▤ ⣇ | 🗏 🗏 .
>
> To... | David Vidinah
> Cc... |
> Subject: | Multiplayer on SCM
>
> David, I assume you are referring to Stomp, Crunch, and Munch multiplayer mode.
>
> 1. I don't know.
> 2. No."Dave's Game" will work but the other one will not.
> 3. When joining a game, if you get a "Connection Error", it usually means that you have not selected the correct Network Protocol option. If this happens, players should select a different protocol option and try again. If you get "Game Full", you need to wait until an opening is made available by a player leaving the game.
> 4. That's up to you.
> 5. Giant amoebas are different from microscopic ones and an overdose of radiation is bad for any sized bug.
>
> That's all I have time for now. Have you asked Matt or someone else in game development these questions already?
>
> Sonja

**■ Document 6.4
E-mail Reply from Matt
Giller, Game Developer**

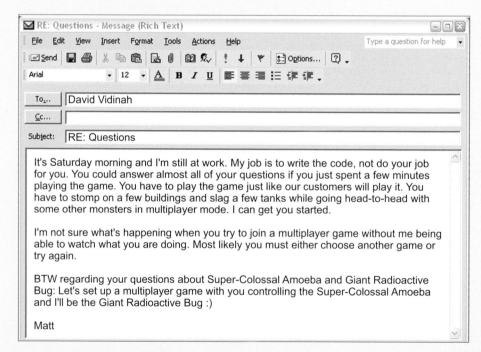

> RE: Questions - Message (Rich Text)
>
> File   Edit   View   Insert   Format   Tools   Actions   Help   Type a question for help
>
> ⌐Send | 🖫 🖨 | ✂ 🖻 🖺 | 🖺 📎 | 🕮 🕮 | ! ↓ ❦ | ⌐ Options... | ② .
>
> Arial   ▼ 12 ▼ | A | B I U | ▤ ▤ ▤ ⣇ | 🗏 🗏 .
>
> To... | David Vidinah
> Cc... |
> Subject: | RE: Questions
>
> It's Saturday morning and I'm still at work. My job is to write the code, not do your job for you. You could answer almost all of your questions if you just spent a few minutes playing the game. You have to play the game just like our customers will play it. You have to stomp on a few buildings and slag a few tanks while going head-to-head with some other monsters in multiplayer mode. I can get you started.
>
> I'm not sure what's happening when you try to join a multiplayer game without me being able to watch what you are doing. Most likely you must either choose another game or try again.
>
> BTW regarding your questions about Super-Colossal Amoeba and Giant Radioactive Bug: Let's set up a multiplayer game with you controlling the Super-Colossal Amoeba and I'll be the Giant Radioactive Bug :)
>
> Matt

Organizing Your Information

7

TECH COMM AT WORK

Before you can draft a document, you need to organize the information that will go into it. If you're a new employee at a publishing company writing your first trip report, how should you organize it? If you're a police officer writing an accident report or a lawyer working on a nondisclosure agreement, how do you find out how to organize that document, and how much freedom do you have to change the organization? In every case, you will want to organize your documents to reflect your audience, purpose, and subject. This chapter presents techniques for organizing technical documents so that they meet your readers' needs.

At this point, you should know for whom you are writing and why, and you should have done most of your research. Now it is time to start organizing the information that will make up the body of your document.

PRINCIPLES FOR ORGANIZING TECHNICAL INFORMATION

Follow these three principles in organizing your information:

- Analyze your audience and purpose.
- Use conventional patterns of organization.
- Display your organizational pattern prominently.

Analyze Your Audience and Purpose

Although you have thought about your audience and purpose as you have planned and researched your subject, your initial analyses of audience and purpose are likely to change as you continue. Therefore, it is useful to review your assessment of audience and purpose before you proceed.

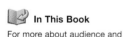

In This Book

For more about audience and purpose, see Ch. 5.

Will your audience like the message you will present? If so, announce your main point early in the document. If not, consider an organizational pattern that presents your important evidence before your main message. Is your audience used to seeing a particular organizational pattern in the kind of document you will be writing? If they are, you will probably want to use that pattern, unless you have a good reason to use a different one.

What is your purpose in writing the document? Do you want your audience to understand a body of information or to accept a point of view and perhaps act on it? One purpose might call for a brief report without any appendices; the other might require a detailed report, complete with appendices.

Strategies for Intercultural Communication

Organizing Documents for Readers from Other Cultures

Organizational patterns can vary from culture to culture. If you can, study documents written by people from the culture you are addressing to see whether they favor an organizational pattern different from the one you are considering.

- **Does the text follow expected organizational patterns?** For example, this chapter discusses the general-to-specific organization. Does the text you are studying present the specific information first?

- **Do the introductions and conclusions present the kind of information you would expect?** In the United States, main findings are often presented in the introduction. In other cultures, the main findings are not presented until late in the document.

- **Is the text organized into paragraphs?**

- **Does the text appear to be organized linearly?** Is the main idea presented first in a topic sentence or thesis statement? Does supporting information follow?

- **Does the text use headings?** If so, does it use more than one level?

If documents from the culture you plan to address are organized very differently from those you're used to seeing, take extra steps to ensure that you don't distract readers by using an unfamiliar organizational pattern.

Use Conventional Patterns of Organization

This chapter presents a number of conventional patterns of organization, such as the chronological pattern and the spatial pattern. You should begin by asking yourself whether a conventional pattern for presenting your information already exists. Using a conventional pattern makes things easier for you as a writer and for your audience.

For you, a conventional pattern serves as a template or checklist, helping you remember which information to include and where to put it. In a proposal, for example, you include a budget, which you put near the end or in an appendix. For your audience, a conventional pattern makes your document easier to read and understand. Readers who are familiar with proposals can find the information they want because you have put it where others have put similar information.

Does this mean that technical communication is merely the process of filling in the blanks? No. You need to assess the writing situation continuously as you work. If you think you could communicate your ideas better by modifying a conventional pattern or by devising a new pattern, do so. However, you gain nothing if an existing pattern would work just as well.

Display Your Organizational Pattern Prominently

Make it easy for your readers to understand the overall arrangement of your information. Displaying your organizational pattern prominently involves three main steps:

- *Creating a detailed table of contents.* If your document has a table of contents, include at least two levels of headings to help readers find the information they seek.
- *Using headings liberally.* Headings break up the text, making your page more interesting visually. They also communicate the subject of the section, improving readers' understanding.
- *Using topic sentences at the beginning of your paragraphs.* The topic sentence announces the main point of a paragraph and helps the reader understand the details that follow.

BASIC PATTERNS OF ORGANIZING INFORMATION

Every argument calls for its own organizational pattern. Figure 7.1 explains the relationship between the organizational pattern and the kind of information you are presenting.

Long, complex arguments often require several organizational patterns. For instance, one part of a document might be a causal analysis of the problem you are writing about, whereas another might be a comparison and

■ Figure 7.1   Organizational Patterns and the Kinds of Information You Want to Present

If you want to...	Consider using this organizational pattern	For example...
Explain events that occurred or might occur or tasks the reader is to carry out	**Chronological** (p. 132). Most of the time, you present information in chronological order. Sometimes, however, you use reverse chronology.	You describe the process you used to diagnose the problem with the accounting software. Or, in a job résumé, you describe your more recent jobs before your less recent ones.
Describe a physical object or scene, such as a device or location	**Spatial** (p. 133). You choose an organizing principle such as top to bottom, east to west, or inside to outside.	You describe the three buildings that will make up the new production facility.
Explain a complex situation, such as the factors that led to a problem or the theory that underlies a process	**General to specific** (p. 133). You present general information first, then specific information. Understanding the big picture helps readers understand the details.	You explain the major changes in, and the details of, the law mandating the use of the new refrigerant in cooling systems.

In This Book

For more about tables of contents, see Ch. 18, p. 468. For more about headings and topic sentences, see Ch. 10, pp. 206 and 210.

On TechComm Web

For a discussion of organizing information, see Paradigm Online Writing Assistant. Click on Links Library for Ch. 7 on <bedfordstmartins.com/techcomm>.

Patterns typically used in organizing information:

Chronological

Spatial

General to specific

More important to less important

Comparison and contrast

Classification and partition

Problem-methods-solution

Cause and effect

■ **Figure 7.1** *(continued)*

If you want to...	Consider using this organizational pattern	For example...
Present a set of factors	**More important to less important** (p. 135). You discuss the most important issue first, then the next most important issue, and so forth. In technical communication, you don't want to create suspense.	When you launch a new product, you discuss market niche, competition, and then pricing.
Present similarities and differences between two or more items	**Comparison and contrast** (p. 136). You choose from one of two patterns: (1) discuss all the factors related to one item, then all the factors related to the next item, and so forth; (2) discuss one factor as it relates to all the items, then another factor as it relates to all the items, and so forth.	You discuss the strengths and weaknesses of three companies bidding on a contract your company is offering.
Assign items to logical categories or discuss the elements that make up a single item	**Classification and partition** (p. 139). Classification involves placing items in categories. Partition involves breaking a single item down into its major elements.	You group the motors your company manufactures according to the fuel they burn: gasoline or diesel. Or you explain how each major component of one of your motors operates.
Discuss a problem you encountered, the steps you took to address the problem, and the outcome or solution	**Problem-methods-solution** (p. 144). You can use this pattern in discussing the past, the present, or the future. Readers understand this organizational pattern because everyone uses it every day in his or her normal routine.	In describing how your company is responding to a new competitor, you discuss the problem (the recent loss in sales), the methods (how you plan to examine your product line and business practices), and the solution (which changes will help your company remain competitive).
Discuss the factors that led to (or will lead to) a given situation or the effects that a situation led to or will lead to	**Cause and effect** (p. 145). You can start from causes and speculate about effects, or start with the effects and work backward to determine the causes.	Sales of one of your products have dipped in the last year. You want to discuss factors that you think contributed to the sales dip.

1. Safety Information	Placing safety information at the start is an example of the **more-important-to-less-important** pattern.
2. Introduction	
2.1 Background	In Section 2, placing background information first is an example of the **general-to-specific** pattern.
2.2 Materials and Tools	
3. Step by Step	In Section 2.2, categorizing items as either materials or tools is an example of **classification.**
3.1 Step 1	
3.2 Step 2	The steps are arranged according to the **chronological** pattern.
3.3 Step 3	
4. Troubleshooting	Section 4 precedes Section 5 according to the **chronological** pattern. After you perform the steps, you check to see if you have followed them correctly. Then you think about the future: performing maintenance tasks.
4.1 Problem 1	
4.2 Problem 2	
4.3 Problem 3	Within Section 4, you might arrange the problems **chronologically** (leading with problems related to starting the device you have just assembled), from **general to specific** (leading with the most basic problems), or from **more important to less important** (leading with problems that affect the greatest number of aspects of operating the device).
5. Maintenance	

■ **Figure 7.2   Using Multiple Organizational Patterns in a Single Document**

contrast of two options for solving that problem. Figure 7.2 shows how different organizational patterns might be used in a single document.

Chronological

The chronological—or time-line—pattern commonly describes events. In an *accident report*, you describe the events in the order in which they occurred. In the background section of a *report*, you describe the events that led to the present situation. In a *reference manual*, you explain how to carry out a task by describing the steps in sequence.

In This Book

For more about transitions, see Ch. 10, p. 214.

Guidelines

Organizing Information Chronologically

▶ **Provide signposts.** If the passage is more than a few hundred words long, use headings. Choose words such as *step*, *phase*, *stage*, and *part*, and consider numbering them. Add descriptive phrases to focus readers' attention on the topic of the section:

    Phase One: Determining Our Objectives

    Step 3: Installing the Lateral Supports

At the paragraph and sentence levels, transitional words such as *then*, *next*, *first*, and *finally* help your readers to follow your discussion.

▶ **Consider using graphics to complement the text.** Flowcharts, in particular, help you emphasize chronological passages for all kinds of readers, from the expert to the general reader.

▶ **Analyze events where appropriate.** When you use chronology, you are explaining what happened in what sequence, but you are not necessarily explaining why or how an event happened or what it means. For instance, the largest section of an accident report is usually devoted to the chronological discussion, but the report is of little value unless it explains what caused the accident, who bears responsibility, and how such accidents can be prevented.

 In This Book
For more about graphics, see Ch. 13.

Spatial

The spatial pattern is commonly used to describe objects and physical sites. In an *accident report*, you describe the physical scene of the accident. In a *feasibility study* about building a facility, you describe the property on which it would be built. In a *proposal* to design a new microchip, you describe the layout of the new chip.

Guidelines

Organizing Information Spatially

▶ **Provide signposts.** Help your readers follow the argument by using words and phrases that indicate location (*to the left*, *above*, *in the center*) in headings, topic sentences, and support sentences.

▶ **Consider using graphics to complement the text.** Diagrams, drawings, photographs, and maps clarify spatial relationships.

▶ **Analyze events where appropriate.** A spatial arrangement doesn't explain itself; you have to do the analysis: a diagram of a floor plan cannot explain why the floor plan is effective or ineffective.

Figure 7.3 on page 134 shows the use of both chronological and spatial organization of information.

 On TechComm Web
To view Fig. 7.3 in context on the Web, click on Links Library for Ch. 7 on <bedfordstmartins.com/techcomm>.

General to Specific

The general-to-specific pattern is used when readers need a general understanding of a subject before they can understand and remember the details. For example, in a *report*, you include an executive summary—an overview for managers—before the body of the report. In a set of *instructions*, you

This screen from the Metropolitan Museum of Art's Timeline of Art History is arranged using both chronological and spatial organization.

*The viewer is looking at the portion of the exhibit that covers the years 1600 to 1800 (**chronological**).*

*Each of the graphics is a link to the portion of the exhibit that covers art from that region of the world (**spatial**).*

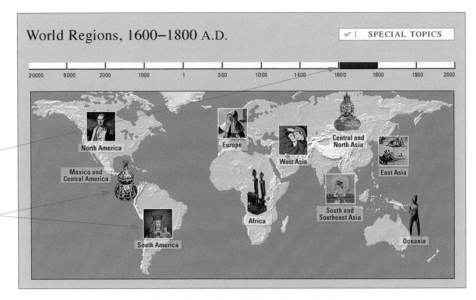

■ **Figure 7.3   Information Organized Chronologically and Spatially**
Source: Metropolitan Museum of Art, 2005 <www.metmuseum.org/toah/hm/09/hm09.htm>.

provide general information about the necessary tools and materials and about safety measures before providing the step-by-step instructions. In a *memo,* you present the background information before going into the details.

Guidelines

Organizing Information from General to Specific

▶ **Provide signposts.** Explain that you will address general issues first and then move on to specific concerns. If appropriate, incorporate the words *general* and *specific* or other relevant terms into the major headings or at the start of the text for each item you are describing.

▶ **Consider using graphics to complement the text.** Diagrams, drawings, photographs, and maps help your readers understand the general or fine points of the information.

Figure 7.4 is an example of how to organize information from general to specific. This passage begins the consumer fact sheet "Compatibility of Cable TV and Digital TV Receivers—'Plug-and-Play,'" from the Federal Communications Commission (FCC).

New Rules Make DTV Transition Easier

The Federal Communications Commission (FCC) has adopted rules that will help smooth the transition to digital television (DTV) for millions of Americans. The FCC's new "plug-and-play" rules will ensure that most cable systems are compatible with DTV receivers and related consumer electronics equipment. This is crucial toward building products and developing services to help spur the digital transition.

Background

Congress has determined that current broadcast television service must eventually convert completely to digital operation. Cable television and other video media are also transitioning to digital operation. Because DTV is delivered digitally, it allows for the delivery of a signal virtually free of interference. DTV broadcasters will be able to offer television with movie-quality pictures and Dolby digital surround sound, along with a variety of other enhancements. DTV technology is more efficient than analog technology and will allow the same number of stations to broadcast using less spectrum.

The FCC's plug-and-play rules are important to the digital transition because they will facilitate the direct connection of digital navigation devices or customer premises equipment, such as television receivers, set-top boxes, and digital recorders that are purchased from retail outlets to cable television systems.

The first paragraph is the most general, explaining the government's decision to help spread the use of digital television and the relationship between plug-and-play and cable systems.

The background section explains more specifically why Congress has mandated the shift from analog to digital television.

Finally, this paragraph presents more specific information on the purpose of plug-and-play rules.

■ **Figure 7.4   Information Organized from General to Specific**
Source: U.S. Federal Communications Commission, 2004
<http://hraunfoss.fcc.gov/edocs_public/attachmatch/DOC-238865A1.pdf>.

More Important to Less Important

The more-important-to-less-important pattern recognizes that readers often want the bottom line—the most important information—first. For example, in an *accident report*, you describe the three most important factors that led to the accident before describing the less-important factors. In a *feasibility study* about building a facility, you present the major reasons that the site is appropriate, then the minor reasons. In a *proposal* to design a new microchip, you describe the major applications for the new chip, then the minor applications.

Although the more-important-to-less-important pattern works well in most documents, sometimes other patterns work better. People who write for readers outside their own company often reverse the more-important-to-less-important pattern because they want to make sure their audience reads the whole discussion. This pattern is also popular with writers who are delivering bad news. For instance, if you want to justify recommending that your organization *not* go ahead with a popular plan, the reverse sequence lets you explain the problems with the popular plan before you present the plan you recommend. Otherwise, readers might start to formulate objections before you have had a chance to explain your position.

In This Book

For more about feasibility reports, see Ch. 18, p. 459.

Guidelines

Organizing Information from More Important to Less Important

▶ **Provide signposts.** Tell your readers how you are organizing the passage. For instance, in the introduction to a proposal to design a new microchip, you might write, "The three applications for the new chip, each of which is discussed below, are arranged from most important to least important."

　In assigning signposts, be straightforward. If you have two very important points and three less-important points, present them that way. Group the two important points and label them, as in "Major Reasons to Retain Our Current Management Structure." Then present the less-important factors as "Other Reasons to Retain Our Current Management Structure." Being straightforward makes the material easier to follow and enhances your credibility.

▶ **Explain why one point is more important than another.** Don't just say that you will be arranging the items from more important to less important. Explain why the more important point is more important.

▶ **Consider using graphics to complement the text.** Diagrams and numbered lists often help to suggest levels of importance.

Figure 7.5 shows the more-important-to-less-important organizational structure.

Comparison and Contrast

Typically, the comparison-and-contrast pattern is used to describe and evaluate two or more items or options. For example, in a *memo*, you compare and contrast the credentials of three finalists for a job. In a *proposal* to design a new microchip, you compare and contrast two different strategies for designing the chip. In a *feasibility report* describing a legal challenge that your company faces, you compare and contrast several options for responding.

　The first step in comparing and contrasting two or more items is to determine the *criteria*: the standards or needs you will use in studying the items. For example, a professional musician who plays a piano in restaurants might be looking to buy a new portable keyboard. She might compare and contrast available instruments using the number of keys as one criterion. For this person, 88 keys would be better than 64. Another criterion might be weight. A keyboard that weighs 25 pounds would be better than one that weighs 46 pounds.

　Almost always, you will need to consider several or even many criteria. Start by deciding whether the criterion represents a necessary quality or merely a desirable one. In studying keyboards, for instance, the number of keys might be a necessary quality. If you need an 88-key instrument to play your music, you are not going to consider any instruments without 88 keys. The same thing might be true of touch-sensitive keys. But a MIDI interface

Infinity Software
3200 Industrial Parkway, Dallas, TX 75201, 972-555-3278

To: **Customer Service Staff**
From: **Larry Jenkins, Director**
Subject: **A Three-Point Program to Improve Service**
Date: **June 19, 2006**

This excerpt is from a memo written by an executive at a company that sells equipment used in manufacturing semiconductors.

In this memo, I want to introduce a new program that I hope will help us improve our customer service.

As you know, our most significant goal for this year has been to improve our customer service. Over the past six weeks, we have attempted to learn what our customers expect—and demand—in the service they receive. Toward that end, we have attended numerous conferences and conducted many focus groups.

What we have learned from recent conferences of semiconductor purchasers and from the focus groups is that customers expect and demand better service than the industry currently provides. By better service I don't mean merely returning phone calls. I mean something much more ambitious and difficult to attain: helping our customers do their jobs by anticipating and addressing their total needs. For this reason, I have formed a Customer Satisfaction Panel, chaired by Maureen Bedrich, whose job will be to develop policies that will enable us to improve the quality of the service we offer our customers.

I have asked the panel, under Maureen Bedrich's direction, to consider three major areas:
• improving the ease of use of our equipment
• improving preventive and corrective maintenance
• improving our compatibility with other vendors' products

Improving the Ease of Use of Our Equipment
User friendliness is the most important area we need to improve, because it affects our customers during the entire lifetime of the product. When we deliver a new product, we have to sit down with the customers and explain how to integrate it into their manufacturing processes. This session is time-consuming and costly for us and for them. Therefore, we must explore the option of automating it.

The writer states his organizational pattern in the topic sentence and explains why this first area is the most important one he will discuss.

Improving Preventive and Corrective Maintenance
The second most important area for study is improving preventive and corrective maintenance. Our customers will no longer tolerate down times approaching 10 percent; they will accept no more than 2 percent to 3 percent. Preventive maintenance is critical in our industry because gases used in vapor-deposition systems periodically have to be removed from the inside of the equipment. Customers want to be able to plan for these stoppages to reduce costs. Currently, we have no means of helping them do so.

The writer again indicates his organizational pattern.

Improving Our Compatibility with Other Vendors' Products
Finally, we have to accept the fact that because no one in our industry is likely to control the market, we have to make our products more compatible with those of other manufacturers. This means that we must be willing to put our people on-site to see what the customers' setup is and help them determine how to modify our product to fit in efficiently. We can no longer offer a "take-it-or-leave-it" product.

I hope you will extend every effort to work constructively with Maureen and her committee over the coming months to ensure that we improve the overall service we offer our customers.

■ **Figure 7.5   Information Organized from More Important to Less Important**

The whole-by-whole pattern provides a coherent picture of each option: the 5L and the 6L. This pattern works best if your readers need an overall assessment of each option, or if each option is roughly equivalent according to the criteria.

Whole by whole	Part by part
Model 5L • price • resolution • print speed	Price • Model 5L • Model 6L
	Resolution • Model 5L • Model 6L
Model 6L • price • resolution • print speed	Print speed • Model 5L • Model 6L

The part-by-part pattern lets you focus your attention on the criteria. If, for instance, Model 5L produces much better resolution than Model 6L, the part-by-part pattern reveals this difference more effectively than the whole-by-whole pattern does. The part-by-part pattern is best for detailed comparisons and contrasts.

might be less important—a merely desirable quality: you would like MIDI capability, but you would not eliminate an instrument from consideration just because it doesn't have MIDI.

Two typical patterns for organizing a comparison-and-contrast discussion are *whole by whole* and *part by part.* The table above illustrates the difference between them. In this table, two printers—Model 5L and Model 6L—are being compared and contrasted according to three criteria: price, resolution, and print speed.

You can have it both ways. If you want to use a part-by-part pattern to emphasize particular aspects, you can begin the discussion with a general description of the various items. Once you have chosen the overall pattern— whole by whole or part by part—you can decide how to organize the second-level items. That is, in a whole-by-whole passage, you have to sequence the "aspects"; in a part-by-part passage, you have to sequence the "options."

Guidelines

Organizing Information by Comparison and Contrast

▶ **Establish criteria for the comparison and contrast.** Choose criteria that are consistent with the needs of your audience.

▶ **Evaluate each item according to the criteria you have established.** Draw your conclusions.

▶ **Organize the discussion.** Choose either the *whole-by-whole* or *part-by-part* pattern, or some combination of the two. Then organize the second-level items.

▶ **Consider using graphics to complement the text.** Graphics can clarify and emphasize comparison-and-contrast passages. Diagrams, drawings, and tables are common ways to provide such clarification and emphasis.

Ethics Note

Comparing and Contrasting Fairly

Because the comparison-and-contrast organizational pattern is used frequently in evaluating items, it appears often in product descriptions as part of the argument that one company's products are better than another's. There is nothing unethical in this. But it is unethical to misrepresent items, such as when a writer portrays his own product as better than it is or a competitor's as worse than it is. Obviously, lying about a product is unethical.

But some practices are not so easy to characterize. For example, your company makes laptop computers. Your chief competitor's model has a longer battery life than yours. In comparing and contrasting the two laptops, are you ethically obligated to mention battery life? No, you are not. If readers are interested in battery life, they are responsible for figuring out what your failure to mention battery life means and for seeking further information from other sources. However, if you do mention battery life, you must do so honestly, using industry-standard techniques for measuring it. You cannot measure your laptop's battery life under one set of conditions and your competitor's under another set.

Figure 7.6 on page 140 shows a comparison-and-contrast passage organized according to the whole-by-whole pattern.

Classification and Partition

Classification is the process of assigning items to categories. For instance, all the students at a university could be classified by sex, age, major, and many other characteristics. You can also create subcategories within categories, such as males and females majoring in business.

Classification is common in technical communication. In a *feasibility study* about building a facility, you classify sites into two categories: domestic and foreign. In a *journal article* about ways to treat a medical condition, you classify the treatments as surgical and nonsurgical. In a description of a major in a *college catalog*, you classify courses as required or elective.

Partition is the process of breaking a unit into its components. For example, a stereo system could be partitioned into the following components: CD player, tuner, amplifier, and speakers. Each component is separate, but together they form a whole stereo system. Each component can, of course, be partitioned further.

Partition is used in descriptions of objects, mechanisms, and processes (see Chapter 9). In an *equipment catalog*, you use partition to describe the major components of one of your products. In a *proposal*, you use partition to present a detailed description of an instrument being proposed for

This passage from BrightPlanet compares and contrasts searching the surface Web and searching the deep Web.

The first paragraph uses a metaphor of dragging a net to introduce the main difference between the surface Web and the deep Web.

The two remaining paragraphs are organized according to the whole-by-whole pattern. The first of the two paragraphs is devoted to traditional search engines that search the surface Web. The second highlights the company's new search engine, which searches the deep Web.

Searching on the Internet today can be compared to dragging a net across the surface of the ocean. While a great deal may be caught in the net, there is still a wealth of information that is deep, and therefore, missed. The reason is simple: Most of the Web's information is buried far down on dynamically generated sites, and standard search engines never find it.

Traditional search engines create their indices by spidering or crawling surface Web pages. To be discovered, the page must be static and linked to other pages. Traditional search engines cannot "see" or retrieve content in the deep Web—those pages do not exist until they are created dynamically as the result of a specific search. Because traditional search engine crawlers cannot probe beneath the surface, the deep Web has heretofore been hidden.

The deep Web is qualitatively different from the surface Web. Deep Web sources store their content in searchable databases that only produce results dynamically in response to a direct request. But a direct query is a "one at a time" laborious way to search. BrightPlanet's search technology automates the process of making dozens of direct queries simultaneously using multiple-thread technology and thus is the only search technology, so far, that is capable of identifying, retrieving, qualifying, classifying, and organizing both "deep" and "surface" content.

■ **Figure 7.6   Information Organized by Comparison and Contrast**
Source: Based on Bergman, 2004 <www.brightplanet.com/technology/deepweb.asp>.

INTERACTIVE SAMPLE DOCUMENT
Comparing and Contrasting Honestly

This comparison-and-contrast table is from the Web site of the manufacturer of an orthodontic product called Invisalign. The questions in the margin ask you to think about the ethics of the table. E-mail your responses to yourself and/or your instructor, and see suggested responses on TechCommWeb.

1. Is it unethical for the company to present the column on its product before the columns on metal braces and veneers?

2. Some of the criteria, such as "removable," are based on factual claims. That is, the three technologies are either removable or not. But some of the other criteria are based on opinions, not facts. Identify one criterion that is based on opinions, then determine whether the use of that criterion is fair.

3. Is the criterion "No metal or brackets to irritate your mouth" a fair criterion to present in this table? Why or why not?

4. The text above the table discusses the average treatment time for Invisalign. Why isn't that criterion included in the table itself? Is it unethical not to include it in the table?

 On TechComm Web

To e-mail your responses to yourself and/or your instructor and to see suggested responses, click on Interactive Sample Documents for Ch. 7 on <bedfordstmartins.com/techcomm>.

Is Invisalign for Me?

» Product Comparison

🖨 Printer Friendly

Find Experienced Invisalign Doctors in Your Area

Learn More »

The Invisalign technology has allowed me to have discreet and effective orthodontic treatment.
-Allison, Ozawkie, KS

Product Comparison Chart

Take a look at the chart below to see how Invisalign compares to other treatment options. Considering that the average treatment time for an Invisalign patient is generaly about a year, the choice is clear—Invisalign.

	Invisalign®	Metal Braces	Veneers
How Does It Work?	Invisalign® uses a series of clear removable aligners to straighten your teeth without metal wires or brackets.	Metal braces use wires and brackets to pressure your teeth into straighter alignment.	Laminates that are bonded to teeth to cover up imperfections.
Invisible	Yes	No	n/a
Removable	Yes	No	n/a
Comfortable	Yes	No	n/a
No metal or brackets to irritate your mouth	Yes	No	n/a
Does not require grinding to remove tooth enamel	Yes	Yes	No
Does not require costly replacement	Yes	n/a	No
Able to brush and floss normally during treatment	Yes	No	n/a

Source: Invisalign, 2005 <www.invisalign.com/generalapp/us/en/for/compare.jsp>.

development. In a *brochure*, you describe how to operate a product by describing each of its features.

Guidelines

Organizing Information by Classification or Partition

▶ **Choose a basis of classification or partition that fits your audience and purpose.** If you are writing a warning about snakes for hikers in a particular state park, your basis of classification will probably be whether the snakes are poisonous. You will describe all the poisonous snakes, then all the nonpoisonous ones.

▶ **Use only one basis of classification or partition at a time.** If you are classifying graphics programs according to their technology—paint programs and draw programs—do not include another basis of classification, such as cost.

▶ **Avoid overlapping.** In classifying, make sure that no single item could logically be placed in more than one category. In partitioning, make sure that no listed component includes another listed component. Overlapping generally occurs when you change the basis of classification or the level at which you are partitioning a unit. In the following classification of bicycles, for instance, the writer introduces a new basis of classification that results in overlapping categories:

—mountain bikes

—racing bikes

—touring bikes

—ten-speed bikes

The first three items share a basis of classification: the general category of bicycle. The fourth item has a different basis of classification: number of speeds. Adding the fourth item is illogical because a particular ten-speed bike could be a mountain bike, a racing bike, or a touring bike.

▶ **Be inclusive.** Include all the categories necessary to complete your basis of classification. For example, a partition of an automobile by major systems would be incomplete if it included the electrical, fuel, and drive systems but not the cooling system. If you decide to omit a category, explain why.

▶ **Arrange the categories in a logical sequence.** Use a reasonable plan: chronology (first to last), spatial development (top to bottom), importance (most important to least important), and so on.

▶ **Consider using graphics to complement the text.** Organization charts are commonly used in classification passages; drawings and diagrams are often used in partition passages.

In Figure 7.7, a discussion of nondestructive testing techniques, the writer uses classification effectively in introducing nondestructive testing to a technical audience.

■ Figure 7.7   Information
Organized by Classification
and Subclassification

*The writer classifies
nondestructive testing into
four categories.*

TYPES OF NONDESTRUCTIVE TESTING

Nondestructive testing of structures permits early detection of stresses that can cause fatigue and ultimately structural damage. The least sensitive tests isolate macrocracks. More sensitive tests identify microcracks. The most sensitive tests identify slight stresses. All sensitivities of testing are useful because some structures can tolerate large amounts of stress — or even cracks — before their structural integrity is threatened.

Currently there are four techniques for nondestructive testing, as shown in Figure 1. These techniques are presented from least sensitive to most sensitive.

*Notice that the writer clearly
explains the sequence of the
document's organization.*

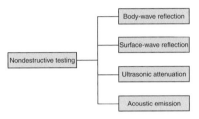

Figure 1. Types of Nondestructive Testing

*This simple block diagram helps
the readers get an overview of
the subject.*

Body-Wave Reflection
In this technique, a transducer sends an ultrasonic pulse through the test material. When the pulse strikes a crack, part of the pulse's energy is reflected back to the transducer. Body-wave reflection cannot isolate stresses: the pulse is sensitive only to relatively large cracks.

Surface-Wave Reflection
The transducer generates an ultrasonic pulse that travels along the surface of the test material. Cracks reflect a portion of the pulse's energy back to the transducer. Like body-wave reflection, surface-wave reflection picks up only macrocracks. Because cracks often begin on interior surfaces of materials, surface-wave reflection is a poor predictor of serious failures.

Ultrasonic Attenuation
The transducer generates an ultrasonic pulse either through or along the surface of the test material. When the pulse strikes cracks or the slight plastic deformations associated with stress, part of the pulse's energy is scattered. Thus, the amount of the pulse's energy decreases. Ultrasonic attenuation is a highly sensitive method of nondestructive acoustic testing.

There are two methods of ultrasonic attenuation. One technique reflects the pulse back to the transducer. The other uses a second transducer to receive the pulses sent through or along the surface of the material.

*Here the writer introduces a
second level of classification.*

Acoustic Emission
When a test specimen is subjected to a great amount of stress, it begins to emit waves; some are in the ultrasonic range. A transducer attached to the surface of the test specimen records these waves. Current technologies make it possible to interpret these waves accurately for impending fatigue and cracks.

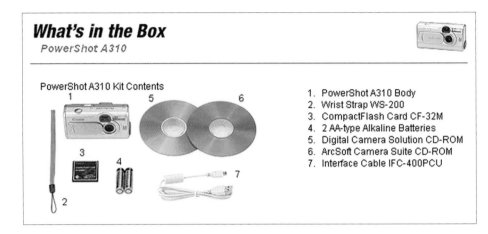

This "kit contents" page from a user's manual for a camera partitions the kit into its components. The manual then discusses each component.

What's in the Box
PowerShot A310

PowerShot A310 Kit Contents

1. PowerShot A310 Body
2. Wrist Strap WS-200
3. CompactFlash Card CF-32M
4. 2 AA-type Alkaline Batteries
5. Digital Camera Solution CD-ROM
6. ArcSoft Camera Suite CD-ROM
7. Interface Cable IFC-400PCU

■ **Figure 7.8   Information Organized by Partition**
Source: Canon, 2005 <http://consumer.usa.canon.com/ir/controller?act=BoxContentsAct&fcategoryid=145&modelid=9829>.

Figure 7.8 is an example of partition. For more examples of partition, see Chapter 9, which includes descriptions of objects, mechanisms, and processes (page 187).

Problem-Methods-Solution

The problem-methods-solution pattern reflects the logic used in carrying out a project. The three components of this pattern are simple to identify:

- *Problem.* A description of what was not working (or not working effectively) or what opportunity exists for improving current processes.
- *Methods.* The procedure performed to confirm the analysis of the problem, solve the problem, or exploit the opportunity.
- *Solution.* The statement of whether the analysis of the problem was correct or what was discovered or devised to solve the problem or capitalize on the opportunity.

The problem-methods-solution pattern is common in technical communication. In a *proposal,* you describe a problem in your business, how you plan to carry out your research, and how your deliverable (an item or a report) can help solve the problem. In a *completion report* about a project to improve a manufacturing process, you describe the problem that motivated the project, the methods you used to carry out the project, and the findings: the results, conclusions, and recommendations.

Guidelines

Organizing Information by Problem-Methods-Solution

▶ **In describing the problem, be clear and specific.** Don't write "Our energy expenditures are getting out of hand." Instead, write "The energy usage has increased 7 percent in the past year, while utility rates have risen 11 percent." Then calculate the total increase in energy costs.

▶ **In describing your methods, help your readers understand what you did and why you did it that way.** You might need to justify your choices. Why, for example, did you use a *t*-test in calculating the statistics in an experiment? If you can't defend your choice, you lose credibility.

▶ **In describing the solution, don't overstate.** Avoid overly optimistic claims, such as "This project will increase our market share from 7 percent to 10 percent within 12 months." Instead, be cautious: "This project could increase our market share from 7 percent to 10 percent." That way, you won't be embarrassed if things don't turn out as well as you had hoped.

▶ **Choose a logical sequence.** The most common sequence is to start with the problem and conclude with the solution. However, different sequences work equally well as long as you provide a preliminary summary to give readers an overview and provide headings or some other design elements (see Chapter 12) to help readers find the information they want. For instance, you might want to put the methods last if you think your readers already know them or are more interested in the solution.

▶ **Consider using graphics to complement the text.** Graphics, such as flow-charts, diagrams, and drawings, can clarify problem-methods-solution passages.

The example of the problem-methods-solution argument in Figure 7.9 on page 146 is based on a discussion about improving child safety in automobiles.

Cause and Effect

Technical communication often involves cause-and-effect discussions. Sometimes you will reason forward, from cause to effect. If we raise the price of a particular product we manufacture (cause), what will happen to our sales (effect)? Sometimes you will reason backward, from effect to cause. Productivity went down by 6 percent in the last quarter (effect); what factors led to this decrease (causes)? Cause-and-effect reasoning, therefore, provides a way to answer the following two questions:

- What will be the effect(s) of X?
- What caused X?

CHILD RESTRAINT LAWS

The Problem

The writer uses statistics and examples to define the problem of child safety in automobiles.

A 1996 Safety Board child-passenger safety study involving more than 180 restrained children showed that the children tended to be restrained in systems too advanced for their physical development. For example, the report showed that 52 children used vehicle seat belts when they should have been placed in child restraint systems or booster seats.

The results can be tragic. In the summer of 1996 in Washington State, a 4-year-old, 45-pound boy was buckled into a lap/shoulder belt by his mother in accordance with State law. When their sport utility vehicle rolled over in a violent crash, the boy's lap/shoulder belt remained buckled, but the young boy was ejected from the restraint and the car, and killed.

The Centers for Disease Control and Prevention (CDC) issued a report in February 1999 indicating that 4- through 8-year-olds are not being protected because of gaps in the State laws that govern child safety seats. As a result, the CDC estimates that almost 500 children die on our highways every year because they are not properly secured in restraint systems — booster seats — that are appropriate for their age, height, and weight.

Twenty-eight States and the District of Columbia require children of all ages (infants through teenagers) to be buckled up, although most permit seat belts to be substituted for child safety seats or booster seats. Only eight States require all children age 4 and under to be in child safety seats.

In addition, 6 out of 10 children killed in traffic crashes are not buckled up at all. The number of children killed each year could be reduced by 50 percent if every child were buckled up. There should be no tolerance for unbuckled children. State child restraint laws should be enforced and supported to reduce the number of children killed and injured in traffic crashes.

What We Are Doing

The writer describes the actions taken by the Safety Board—the methods—to combat the problem described earlier in the discussion.

Although all 50 States and the District of Columbia have child passenger protection laws, in 1996, the Safety Board called on the States to strengthen their child restraint laws to do the following:

- Require all children under 4 years old to be in child safety seats.
- Require that 4- to 8-year-old children use auto safety booster seats.
- Eliminate provisions that permit children under 8 years old to be buckled up in a seat belt.
- Require all children under age 13 to ride in the back seat, if a seat is available.

Safety Improvements

The writer describes the "solution": the results of the efforts made by the Safety Board. Naturally, the solutions do not completely fix the problem, but they represent progress.

We are starting to see States take positive steps to improve child safety in automobiles. As a result of the Safety Board's urging, the following actions were taken:

- Washington State and California enacted laws in 2000 to require children under 6 years of age or 60 pounds to ride in a booster seat.
- Delaware, North Carolina, and Rhode Island now require children to ride in the back seat of air bag–equipped cars. In Louisiana, all children less than 13 years of age must ride in the rear seat when one is available.

The Safety Board recently began an education campaign "Boost 'em before you Buckle 'em" to ensure that 4- to 8-year-olds get buckled up in age-appropriate restraint systems.

Our efforts at educating state legislatures and executives continue, but we are beginning to see real progress in protecting America's most vulnerable automobile passengers.

■ **Figure 7.9   Information Organized by the Problem-Methods-Solution Pattern**
Source: National Transportation Safety Board, 2000 <www.ntsb.gov/Publictn/2000/SR0002.pdf>.

Arguments organized by cause and effect are common in technical communication. In an *environmental impact statement*, you argue that a proposed construction project would have three important effects on the ecosystem. In the recommendation section of a *report*, you argue that a recommended solution would improve operations in two major ways. In a *memo*, you describe a new policy, then explain the effects you anticipate the policy will have.

Cause-and-effect relationships are difficult to describe because there is no scientific way to determine causes or effects. You draw on your common sense and your knowledge of your subject. When you try to determine, for example, why the product you introduced last year failed to sell, you start with the obvious possibilities: the market was saturated, the product was of low quality, the product was poorly marketed, and so forth. The more you know about your subject, the more precise and insightful your analysis will be.

A causal discussion can never be certain. You cannot *prove* why a product failed in the marketplace. But you can explain why you think the causes or effects you are identifying are the most plausible ones. For instance, to make a plausible case that the main reason is that it was poorly marketed, you can show that, in the past, your company's other unsuccessful products were marketed in similar ways and that your company's successful products were marketed in other ways.

Guidelines

Organizing Information by Cause and Effect

▶ **Explain your reasoning.** To support your claim that the product was marketed poorly, use specific facts and figures: the low marketing budget, delays in beginning the marketing campaign, and so forth.

▶ **Avoid overstating your argument.** For instance, if you write that Steve Jobs, the founder of Apple, "created the computer revolution," you are claiming too much. It is better to write that Steve Jobs "was one of the central players in creating the computer revolution."

▶ **Avoid logical fallacies.** Logical fallacies, such as hasty generalizations or *post-hoc* reasoning, can also undermine your discussion.

▶ **Consider using graphics to complement the text.** Graphics, such as flowcharts, organization charts, diagrams, and drawings, can clarify and emphasize cause-and-effect passages.

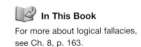
In This Book
For more about logical fallacies, see Ch. 8, p. 163.

Figure 7.10 on page 148 illustrates an effective cause-and-effect argument.

This excerpt from a white paper on energy policy presents two cause-and-effect arguments.

Section 1.7 argues that global warming has already led to the problems cited in the bulleted list.

Section 1.8 argues that if global warming continues, the results could be widespread and costly. Note that the authors make clear that they cannot speak with certainty about the future; they can only speculate based on today's best science.

1.7   The rise in temperatures has been accompanied by changes in the world around us:

- ice caps are retreating from many mountain peaks like Kilimanjaro;
- global mean sea level rose by an average of 1–2mm a year during the 20th century;
- summer and autumn arctic sea ice has thinned by 40% in recent decades;
- global snow cover has decreased by 10% since the 1960s;
- El Nino events have become more frequent and intense during the last 20–30 years;
- usage of the Thames Barrier has increased from once every two years in the 1980s to an average six times a year over the past 5 years; and
- weather-related economic losses to communities and businesses have increased tenfold over the last 40 years.

1.8   In this century, without action to reduce emissions, the earth's temperature is likely to rise at a faster rate than any time in the last 10,000 years or more. In the UK, the risks of droughts and flooding are likely to increase. Sea levels will rise, so that extreme high water levels could be 10 to 20 times more frequent at some parts of the east coast by the end of the century. Worldwide, the consequences could be devastating, especially in the developing world where many millions more people are likely to be exposed to the risk of disease, hunger and flooding. In addition, there is a risk of large scale changes such as the shut-down of the Gulf Stream or melting of the West Antarctic ice sheet, which although they may have a very low probability of occurring, would have dramatic consequences.

■ **Figure 7.10   A Discussion Organized by the Cause-and-Effect Pattern**
Source: United Kingdom Department of Trade and Industry, 2003 <www.dti.gov.uk/energy/whitepaper/wp_text.pdf>.

Writer's Checklist

Did you

☐ analyze your audience and purpose? (p. 128)
☐ consider using a conventional pattern of arrangement? (p. 129)
☐ display your organization prominently by
  ☐ creating a detailed table of contents? (p. 130)
  ☐ using headings liberally? (p. 130)
  ☐ using topic sentences at the beginnings of your paragraphs? (p. 130)

The following checklists cover the eight organizational patterns discussed in this chapter.

Chronological and Spatial

Did you

☐ provide signposts, such as headings or transitional words or phrases? (p. 132)
☐ consider using graphics to complement the text? (p. 133)
☐ analyze events where appropriate? (p. 133)

General to Specific

Did you

☐ provide signposts, such as headings or transitional words or phrases? (p. 134)
☐ consider using graphics to complement the text? (p. 134)

More Important to Less Important

Did you

☐ provide signposts, explaining clearly that you are using this organizational pattern? (p. 136)
☐ make clear why the first point is the most important, the second is the second most important, and so forth? (p. 136)
☐ consider using graphics to complement the text? (p. 136)

Comparison and Contrast

Did you

☐ establish criteria for the comparison and contrast? (p. 136)
☐ choose a structure—whole by whole or part by part—that is most appropriate for your audience and purpose? (p. 138)
☐ choose appropriate organizational patterns for your second-level items? (p. 138)
☐ consider using graphics to complement the text? (p. 138)

Classification and Partition

Did you

☐ choose a basis consistent with the audience and purpose of the document? (p. 142)
☐ use only one basis at a time? (p. 142)
☐ avoid overlapping? (p. 142)
☐ include all the appropriate categories? (p. 142)
☐ arrange the categories in a logical sequence? (p. 142)
☐ consider using graphics to complement the text? (p. 142)

Problem-Methods-Solution

Did you

☐ describe the problem clearly and specifically? (p. 145)
☐ if appropriate, justify your methods? (p. 145)
☐ avoid overstating your solution? (p. 145)
☐ arrange the discussion in a sequence consistent with the audience and purpose of the document? (p. 145)
☐ consider using graphics to complement the text? (p. 145)

Cause and Effect

Did you

☐ explain your reasoning? (p. 147)
☐ avoid overstating your argument? (p. 147)
☐ avoid logical fallacies? (p. 147)
☐ consider using graphics to complement the text? (p. 147)

Exercises

1. **INTERNET EXERCISE** Using a search engine, find the Web site of a company that makes a product used by professionals in your field (personal computers are a safe choice). Locate three discussions on the site. For example, there will probably be the following: a passage devoted to ordering a product from the site (using a chronological pattern), a description of a product (using a partition pattern), and a passage describing why the company's products are superior to those of its competitors (using a comparison-and-contrast argument). Print a copy of the passages you've identified.

2. For each of the lettered topics that follow, identify the best organizational pattern for a discussion of the subject. For example, a discussion of distance education and on-campus courses could be organized using the comparison-and-contrast pattern. Write a brief explanation about why this would be the best organizational pattern to use. (Use each of the organizational patterns discussed in this chapter at least once.)

 a. how to register for courses at your college or university

 b. how you would propose reducing the time required to register for classes or to change your schedule

 c. your car's dashboard

 d. the current price of gasoline

 e. advances in manufacturing technology

 f. the reasons you chose your college or major

 g. a student organization on your campus

 h. the tutorials that come with two different software programs

 i. personal computers

 j. how you would propose increasing the ties between your college or university and local business and industry

 k. college courses

 l. increased security in airports

 m. the room in which you are sitting

 n. the three most important changes you would like to see at your school

 o. a guitar

 p. cooperative education and internships for college students

 q. digital and film photography

 r. how to prepare for a job interview

3. Write a 500-word discussion of one of the lettered topics in Exercise 2. If appropriate, include graphics. Preface your discussion with a sentence explaining the audience and purpose of the discussion.

Case 7: Organizing a Document

 In This Book   For more about memos, see Ch. 14, p. 352. For more about interviews, see Ch. 6, p. 114.

Background

"One of the first items on my agenda is to write an internship handbook," Georgia McCallum told the group seated around the conference table. This was the first meeting of the Internship Working Group. Georgia, the newly hired university internship director, had assembled the group to review current practices for academic internships and to create reasonable, consistent university-wide standards for academic internships. Attending the meeting were Professors Leandra Lucas and Rick Burtt. Leandra Lucas serves as the internship coordinator for the School of Engineering; Rick Burtt coordinates internships for the Department of Kinesiology. You were invited to participate as a student representative.

"One of the things I learned when I interviewed all the internship coordinators this fall was that internship standards tend to be set by individual departments," Georgia explained. "I also learned that new internship coordinators don't have much guidance or resources. They don't know what options they have in regard to working with student interns and the sponsoring organizations. The result is an inconsistent internship experience for students and confused sponsoring organizations."

"I agree," you said. "When I interned at KBCI-TV, I had to write a learning agreement, keep a learning log, submit weekly progress reports, and complete a self-evaluation. I even think my internship coordinator met with my supervisor at KBCI once or twice. Another intern from a different department only had to write a one-page report at the end of the semester."

"My point exactly. Should both students earn the same amount of academic credit?" Georgia asked the group.

"With the number of interns I supervise each semester," Rick said, "I couldn't possibly maintain that level of contact with the interns and their supervisors."

"That's why I think we should establish some basic requirements, such as number of hours worked per credit hour, and leave the details up to the individual internship coordinators," Leandra added.

"Didn't the Office of the Registrar already establish that an intern must work 50 hours per credit hour of the internship?" Rick asked.

"I worked only 45 hours per credit—"

"See," Georgia interrupted. "That's what I see as the role of this internship handbook: to outline the basic requirements for internships offered through the university and then to provide resources for providing high-quality internship experiences for our students."

"I think the handbook also needs to address some of the issues raised by the employers who responded to the internship survey we conducted last summer, especially those responses relating to how we could improve the college internship program," Leandra added. She pointed to a page from the survey report listing some of the employer comments (Document 7.1).

"Absolutely. The employers had some great ideas. I think faculty would be really receptive to their ideas," Georgia agreed.

"So this handbook is for faculty internship coordinators?" Rick asked.

"Yes. I also want to give this handbook to sponsoring organizations. I think it would be great if the handbook was reorganized and made available to students as well."

Georgia paused after looking at the group's concerned faces. "I know this sounds like an ambitious undertaking with only a few weeks left in the semester, but I already have an outline developed for faculty coordinators and sponsoring organizations," she explained as she distributed the outline (Document 7.2).

After a few minutes, Leandra asked Georgia, "How do you want us to help?"

"This is a very rough draft and needs lots of work. It's all subject to change. I was hoping that each of you could take a look at the outline and let me know if the organization makes sense to you and whether I should change or add topics. I'd also like your advice on how to reorganize the material for students."

Your Assignment

1. Download Document 7.2 from <bedfordstmartins.com/techcomm> and study it in Microsoft Word's outline view.

On TechComm Web

For digital versions of case documents, click on Downloadable Case Documents on <bedfordstmartins.com/techcomm>.

Responses to Open-Ended Question Number 3

Question number 3 asked employers, "In what ways could our college internship program be improved?" A total of 213 comments were received. Comments were placed in five categories: collaboration and communication, planning, student expectations, procedures for matching interns with sponsoring organizations, and miscellaneous comments.

Collaboration and Communication

Nearly half of the comments focused on the topic of collaboration and communication (97 of 213). Following are representative examples of comments in this category:

I'm tired of being the one who always comes to campus. I think the professors should visit the employer.

Better supervision by faculty. My intern's faculty supervisor took no interest in her and never tried to contact me.

We offer several internships a semester, and it seems like I'm always filling out something different for each intern. Get your act together and have a single set of internship requirements!

I believe it would be better if the faculty supervisor was available to help the intern if he or she had questions about how to do something.

I want to be able to contact professors if I have questions.

Let employers know what we are expected to do—paperwork, meetings, etc.

Better communication. When we have to hire an intern from among several applicants, I would like the faculty supervisor to provide some input.

The intern supervisor should work more closely with the employer and the intern.

■ **Document 7.1 Employer Responses to Survey Question**

- ✦ **Basic Internship Information**
  - □ *Getting Involved*
  - □ *Department Requirements for Internship Programs*
  - □ *Concluding Thoughts*
- ✦ **The Roles of the Faculty Member and Student Intern**
  - ✦ *The Role of the Student Intern*
    - □ Intern Responsibilities
    - □ The Student Release Form
    - □ Activity Log
    - □ Guidelines for Learning Agreements
  - □ *The Learning Agreement*
  - □ *The Student Release Form*
  - ✦ *Interacting with your Student Interns*
    - ✦ Communicating with Interns
      - □ Phone
      - □ E-mail
      - □ Site visits
  - □ *Placing Students in Internships*
- □ **Site Visits**
- □ **The Learning Agreement**
- ✦ **The Role of the Agency Supervisor**
  - ✦ *Legal Issues Concerning Internships*
    - □ Sponsoring Organization Responsibilities
  - □ *Getting Involved*
  - □ *Interacting with Your Intern*
  - □ *The Learning Agreement*
- ✦ **Evaluation of Interns**
  - ✦ *Evaluation Methods*
    - □ Intern Self-Evaluation
    - □ Reflective Journals
    - □ Agency Supervisor's Evaluation
- ✦ **Legal Matters**
  - □ *The Student Release Form*
- □ **University Policy Statement on Academic Internships and Rationale for Policy**
- □ **Index**

■ **Document 7.2   Outline of Internship Handbook**

Then reorganize the outline to make it more logical based on your study of Chapter 7 and your understanding of the author's purpose and audiences. Create an outline for faculty coordinators and sponsoring organizations, then create a different outline for student interns. Keep in mind that your outlines might incorporate several different patterns of organization. If appropriate, add or delete topics.

2. Write Georgia a memo in which you explain why your approaches are the best ones to use. Attach your revised outlines.

PART THREE

Developing the Textual Elements

8

Communicating Persuasively

In technical communication, often your job is to convince a reader of a viewpoint—about what factors caused a situation, for example, or what a company ought to do to solve a problem. If you are lucky, you will be reinforcing a viewpoint the reader already has. Sometimes, however, you want to change the reader's mind. Regardless, you are presenting an *argument*: an arrangement of facts and judgments about some aspect of the world.

CONSIDERING THE CONTEXT OF YOUR ARGUMENT

An argument can be as short as a sentence or as long as a multivolume report. It can take many forms, including oral communication. And it can discuss almost any kind of issue. Here are some examples:

- *from a description of a construction site:*

    Features A, B, and C characterize the site.

- *from a study of why a competitor is outselling your company:*

    Company X's dominance can be attributed to four major factors: A, B, C, and D.

- *from a feasibility study considering four courses of action:*

    Alternative A is better than alternatives B, C, and D.

- *from a set of instructions for performing a task:*

    The safest way to perform the task is to complete task A, then task B, and so on.

To develop an effective argument, you must understand your audience's broader goals and work within constraints.

Understanding Your Audience's Broader Goals

When you analyze your audience, think about their broader goals. Certainly, most people want their company to prosper, but they are also concerned about their own welfare and interests within the company. Your argument is

 On TechComm Web

For an excellent discussion of persuasion, see Business Communication: Managing Information and Relationships. Click on Links Library for Ch. 8 on <bedfordstmartins.com/techcomm>.

most likely to be effective if it responds to three goals that most people share: security, recognition, and personal and professional growth.

Security   People resist controversial actions that might hurt their own interests. Those who might lose their jobs will likely oppose an argument that their division be eliminated, even if there are many valid reasons to support the argument. Another aspect of security is workload; most people resist an argument that calls for them to work more.

Recognition   People like to be praised for their hard work and their successes. Where appropriate, be generous in your praise. Similarly, people hate being humiliated in public. Therefore, allow people to save face. Avoid criticizing their actions or positions and speculating about their motivations. Instead, present your argument as a response to the company's present and future needs. Look ahead, not back, and be diplomatic.

Personal and Professional Growth   People want to develop and grow on the job and in their personal lives. In an obvious way, this means that they want to learn new skills and assume new duties. This desire is also reflected in efforts to improve how the organization treats its employees and customers, relates to the community, and coexists with the environment. Your argument will be more persuasive if you can show how the recommended action will help your organization become an industry leader, for example, or reduce environmental pollution or help needy people in your city. We want to be associated with, and contribute to, organizations that are good at what they do and that help us become better people.

 **On TechComm Web**

To view Fig. 8.1 in context on the Web, click on Links Library for Ch. 8 on <bedfordstmartins.com/techcomm>.

Figure 8.1, from the employment section on the Microsoft Web site, profiles an employee the company believes reflects the personality and character of those who work at Microsoft.

Working Within Constraints

In planning a persuasive document, you need to work within the constraints that shape your environment on the job. As a student, you routinely work within constraints: the amount of information you can gather for a paper, the required length and format, the due date, and so forth. In business, industry, and government, similar constraints play a role.

 In This Book

For more about ethical and legal constraints, see Ch. 2.

Ethical Constraints   Your greatest responsibility is always to your own sense of what constitutes ethical behavior. Being asked to lie or mislead can directly challenge your ethical standards, but in most cases, you have options. Some organizations and professional communities have a published code of conduct. In addition, many large companies have ombudspersons, who use mediation to help employees resolve ethical conflicts.

By profiling employee Jayendran in the employment section of the Microsoft Web site, the company hopes to encourage like-minded people to apply for positions.

Professional growth is the theme of this passage. Jayendran has the opportunity to grow professionally by taking on new challenges and accepting new responsibilities, and he feels that the company appreciates his efforts.

↓ Employee Profile

"I have been with Microsoft more than five years. I am a developer in the Live Meeting Group"

Jayendran
Software Development Engineer
WA - Redmond

Go Back

Campus Life
"There is a beautiful jogging trail and a mini forest area on campus. My wife and I live nearby, and on weekends we hang out there and enjoy the gardens. It's become an extension of our apartment!"

Fueling the Fire
"The work is very challenging intellectually. Every day I feel empowered to make decisions that help improve the quality of products we ship to the customer. Because the products are used by consumers worldwide, the opportunities seem endless."

Opening Doors
"I learn something new, feel challenged and hone my skills as I solve some of the toughest problems. My managers have always been extremely good in providing me opportunities that help me grow in my career. In short, every single day is a great experience for me at work."

On the Job
"Because of the nature of the industry there are a lot of things to learn. People are often surprised to find everyone at Microsoft is working at their own pace. There is no hand-holding; you have to find your way through your career as soon as you arrive. If you are talented, you plug into that and become a very bright team member."

■ **Figure 8.1 Appealing to an Audience's Broader Goals**
Source: Microsoft, 2005 <www.microsoft.com/careers/epdb/profileDetailPage.aspx?profileID=41>.

Legal Constraints Abide by all applicable laws on labor practices, environmental issues, fair trade, consumer rights, and so forth. If you think the action recommended by your supervisor might be illegal, meet with your organization's legal counsel and, if necessary, attorneys outside the organization.

Political Constraints Don't spend all your energy and credibility on a losing cause. If you know that your proposal would help the company but that management disagrees with you or that the company can't afford to approve it, consider what you might achieve through some other means or scale back the idea. Two big exceptions to this rule are matters of ethics and matters of safety. As discussed in Chapter 2, ethical and legal constraints may mean that compromise is unacceptable.

Informational Constraints The most common informational constraint you might face is that the information you need is not available. You might want your organization to buy a piece of equipment, for example, but you can't find evidence from controlled tests that would convince a skeptical reader.

What do you do? You tell the truth. Explain the situation, weighing the available evidence and carefully noting what is missing. If you unintentionally suggest that your evidence is better than it really is, you will lose your most important credential: your credibility.

Personnel Constraints The most typical personnel constraint you might face is a lack of access to as many collaborators as you need. In such cases, present a persuasive proposal to hire the personnel you need. However, don't be surprised if you have to make do with fewer people than you want.

 In This Book
For more about collaboration, see Ch. 4.

Financial Constraints Financial constraints are related to personnel constraints: if you had unlimited funds, you could hire all the personnel you need. But financial constraints can also affect other kinds of resources: you might not be able to print as many copies of the document as you want, or you might need to settle for black and white instead of full color.

Time Constraints Start by determining the document's deadline. (Sometimes a document will have several intermediate deadlines.) Then create a schedule. Keep in mind that tasks almost always take longer than estimated. And when you collaborate, the number of potential problems increases, because when one person is delayed, others may lack the necessary information to proceed, causing a logjam.

Format and Tone Constraints You will be expected to work within one additional set of constraints:

- *Format.* Format constraints are limitations on the size, shape, or style of a document. For example, all tables and figures must be presented at the end of the report. If you are writing to someone in your own organization, follow the format constraints described in the company style guide, if there is one, or check similar documents to see what other writers have done. Also ask more-experienced co-workers for their advice. If you are writing to someone outside your organization, learn what you can about that organization's preferences.
- *Tone.* When addressing superiors, use a formal, polite tone. When addressing peers or subordinates, use a less formal tone but be equally polite.

To craft a persuasive argument:

Identify the elements of your argument.

Use the right kinds of evidence.

Consider opposing viewpoints.

Appeal to emotions responsibly.

Decide where to present the claim.

CRAFTING A PERSUASIVE ARGUMENT

Persuasion is important, whether you wish to affect a reader's attitude or merely present information clearly.

Identify the Elements of Your Argument

A persuasive argument has three main elements:

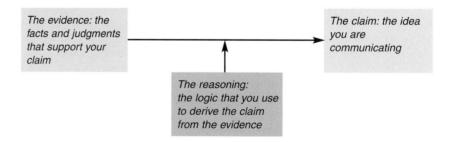

The *claim* is the conclusion you want your readers to accept. For example, your claim might be that your company should institute flextime, a scheduling approach that gives employees some flexibility in when they begin and end their workdays. You want your readers to agree with this idea and to take the next steps toward instituting flextime.

The *evidence* is the information you want your readers to consider. For the argument about flextime, the evidence might include the following:

- The turnover rate of our female employees is double that of our male employees.
- At exit interviews, 40 percent of our female employees under the age of 38 state that they quit so that they can be home for their school-age children.
- Replacing a staff-level employee costs us about one-half the employee's annual salary. Replacing a professional-level employee costs a whole year's salary.
- Other companies have found that flextime significantly decreases turnover among female employees under the age of 38.
- Other companies have found that flextime has additional benefits and introduces no significant problems.

The *reasoning* is the logic you use to connect the evidence to your claim. In the discussion of flextime, the reasoning involves three links:

- Flextime appears to have reduced the turnover problem among younger female employees at other companies.
- Our company is similar to these other companies.
- Flextime, therefore, is likely to prove helpful at our company.

Use the Right Kinds of Evidence

People most often react favorably to four kinds of evidence:

- *"Commonsense" arguments.* Here, *commonsense* means "most people would think that . . . ." The following sentence presents a commonsense argument that flextime is a good idea:

  > Flextime makes sense because it gives people more control over how they plan their schedules.

  A commonsense argument says, "I don't have hard evidence to support my conclusion, but it stands to reason that . . . ." In this case, the argument is that people like to have as much control over their time as possible. If your audience's commonsense arguments match yours, your overall argument is likely to be persuasive.
- *Numerical data.* Numerical data—statistics—are generally more persuasive than commonsense arguments.

  > Statistics drawn from the personnel literature (McClellan, 2005) show that among Fortune 500 companies, flextime decreases turnover by 25 to 35 percent among female employees younger than 38.

Notice that the writer states that the study covered many companies, not just one or a handful. If the sample size were small, the claim would be much less persuasive. (The discussion of logical fallacies later in this chapter explains such *hasty generalizations*.)

- *Examples.* An example makes an abstract point more concrete and therefore more vivid and memorable.

    > Mary Saunders tried for weeks to arrange for child care for her two preschoolers that would enable her to start work at 7 A.M., as required at her workplace. The best she could manage was having her children stay with a non-licensed provider. When conditions at that provider led to ear infections in both her children, Mary decided that she could no longer continue working.

    Examples are often used along with numerical data. The example gives the problem a human dimension, but the argument also requires numerical data to show that the problem is part of a pattern, not a coincidence.

- *Expert testimony.* A message from an expert is more persuasive than the same message from someone without credentials. A well-researched article on flextime written by a respected business scholar in a reputable business journal is likely to be persuasive. When you make arguments, you will often cite expert testimony from published sources or interviews you have conducted.

In This Book

For advice on evaluating information from the Internet, see Ch. 6, p. 109.

Consider Opposing Viewpoints

When you present an argument, you need to address opposing points of view. If you don't, your opponents will simply conclude that your argument is flawed because it doesn't address problems that they think are important. In meeting the skeptical or hostile reader's possible objections to your case, you can use one of several tactics:

- *The opposing argument is based on illogical reasoning or on inaccurate or incomplete facts.* You can counter the argument that flextime increases utility bills by citing unbiased research studies showing that it does not.

- *The opposing argument is valid but less powerful than your own.* If you can show that the opposing argument makes sense but is outweighed by your own argument, you appear to be a fair-minded person who understands that reality is complicated. You can counter the argument that flextime reduces carpooling opportunities by showing that only 3 percent of your employees use carpooling and that three-quarters of these employees favor flextime because of its other advantages.

- *There might be a way to reconcile the two arguments.* If an opposing argument is not invalid or clearly inferior to your own, you can offer to study the situation thoroughly to find a solution that incorporates the best from each argument. For example, if flextime might cause serious problems for your company's many carpoolers, you could propose a trial period during

INTERACTIVE SAMPLE DOCUMENT
Analyzing Evidence in an Argument

In "Piracy Is Progressive Taxation, and Other Thoughts on the Evolution of Online Distribution" (O'Reilly, 2002), Tim O'Reilly argues that file sharing helps creative artists. The excerpt printed here discusses artists such as musicians, authors, and filmmakers. The questions in the margin ask you to consider the evidence O'Reilly uses. E-mail your responses to yourself and/or your instructor, and see suggested responses on TechComm Web.

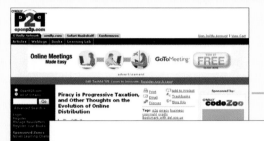

For all of these creative artists, most laboring in obscurity, being well-enough known to be pirated would be a crowning achievement. Piracy is a kind of progressive taxation, which may shave a few percentage points off the sales of well-known artists (and I say "may" because even that point is not proven), in exchange for massive benefits to the far greater number for whom exposure may lead to increased revenues.

Our current distribution systems for books, music, and movies are skewed heavily in favor of the "haves" against the "have nots." A few high-profile products receive the bulk of the promotional budget and are distributed in large quantities; the majority depend, in the words of Tennessee Williams' character Blanche DuBois, "on the kindness of strangers."

Lowering the barriers to entry in distribution, and the continuous availability of the entire catalog rather than just the most popular works, is good for artists, since it gives them a chance to build their own reputation and visibility, working with entrepreneurs of the new medium who will be the publishers and distributors of tomorrow.

I have watched my 19 year-old daughter and her friends sample countless bands on Napster and Kazaa and, enthusiastic for their music, go out to purchase CDs. My daughter now owns more CDs than I have collected in a lifetime of less exploratory listening. What's more, she has introduced me to her favorite music, and I too have bought CDs as a result. And no, she isn't downloading Britney Spears, but forgotten bands from the 60s, 70s, 80s, and 90s, as well as their musical forebears in other genres. This is music that is difficult to find—except online—but, once found, leads to a focused search for CDs, records, and other artifacts. eBay is doing a nice business with much of this material, even if the RIAA [Recording Industry Association of America] fails to see the opportunity.

1. In the second sentence, the writer presents a parenthetical comment questioning whether file sharing costs well-known artists any income. How might the writer make this point more persuasively?

2. In the third paragraph, the writer argues that having artists' works available online helps them build their reputations. Of the four kinds of evidence discussed on pp. 159–60, which kind is the author using here? How effective is it? How might the writer make it more effective?

3. The final paragraph is built around examples. How effective is it? How might the writer make the argument more effective?

 On TechComm Web

To e-mail your responses to yourself and/or your instructor and to see suggested responses, click on Interactive Sample Documents for Ch. 8 on <bedfordstmartins.com/techcomm>.

which you would study several ways to help employees find other carpooling opportunities. If the company cannot solve the problem, or if most of the employees prefer the old system, you will switch back to it. This proposal can remove much of the threat posed by your ideas.

When you address an opposing argument, be gracious and understated. Focus on the argument, not on the people who oppose you. If you embarrass or humiliate them, you undermine your own credibility and motivate your opponents to continue opposing you.

There is no one best place to address opposing arguments. In general, however, if you know that important readers hold opposing views, address those views relatively early. Your goal is to show *all* your readers that you are a fair-minded person who has thought carefully about the subject and that your argument is stronger than the opposing arguments.

Appeal to Emotions Responsibly

Writers sometimes appeal to the emotions of their readers. Writers usually combine emotional appeals with appeals to reason. For example, an argument that we ought to increase foreign aid to drought-stricken African countries might describe (and present images of) the human plight of the victims but also include reason-based arguments about the extent of the problem, the causes, the possible solutions, and the pragmatic reasons we might want to increase foreign aid.

When you use emotional appeals, do not overstate or overdramatize them, or you will risk alienating readers. Try to think of additional kinds of evidence to present that will also help support your claim. Figure 8.2 shows a brief argument that relies on an emotional appeal.

This document from PETA (People for the Ethical Treatment of Animals) relies on emotion in describing the "cruelest practices" of the food company. The bulk of the passage details the physical suffering endured by the chickens. To the extent that readers are moved emotionally by these descriptions, the argument will be persuasive.

The passage also uses another strategy: the celebrity of the people supporting the message. This strategy is a weak form of the argument based on authority (see Table 8.1 on p. 163).

Emmylou Harris Steers Motorists Away from KFC

"BOYCOTT KFC"
—Emmylou Harris

Live Scalding, Painful Debeaking, Crippled Chickens

KentuckyFriedCruelty.com PeTA

Motorists from coast to coast are getting some food for thought from Emmylou, who is urging them to boycott KFC as part of PETA's international campaign to pressure the restaurant chain to eliminate the cruelest practices in the intensive factory farms and slaughterhouses that supply it.

Chickens raised for KFC's restaurants are packed by the tens of thousands into extremely crowded sheds for their entire lives and are never able to do any of the things that come naturally to them. KFC routinely cuts the beaks off baby birds, it breeds and drugs chickens to grow so large, so quickly that the chickens actually become crippled under their own weight and can spend their entire lives in chronic pain. Because KFC refuses to heed the advice of the industry's most respected animal welfare experts, countless chickens have their throats slit and are dunked into tanks of scalding-hot water (for feather removal) while still completely conscious. When you see for yourself the ways in which these chickens are abused, you'll agree that these horrors must be stopped.

When Emmylou learned that millions of chickens are tortured in these horrible ways by KFC each year, she decided to join an ever-growing roster of high-profile PETA pals who are speaking up for these sensitive and intelligent animals. **Sir Paul McCartney, Pamela Anderson, the Dalai Lama,** and former KFC spokesperson **Jason Alexander have all backed PETA's KFC boycott**.

■ **Figure 8.2   An Argument That Uses an Emotional Appeal**
Source: KentuckyFriedCruelty.com, 2005 <www.kentuckyfriedcruelty.com/EmmyLouHarris.asp>.

Decide Where to Present the Claim

In most cases, the best place to state your claim is at the start of the argument. Then provide the evidence and, if appropriate, the reasoning. Sometimes, however, it is more effective to place the claim *after* the evidence and the reasoning. This indirect structure works best if a large number of readers oppose your claim. If you present your claim right away, these readers might become alienated and stop paying attention. You want a chance to present your evidence and your reasoning without causing this kind of undesirable reaction.

AVOIDING LOGICAL FALLACIES

Logical fallacies can undercut the persuasiveness of your writing. Table 8.1 explains some of the most common logical fallacies.

 On TechComm Web

For exercises on logical fallacies, see Writing Guidelines for Engineering and Science Students. Click on Links Library for Ch. 8 on <bedfordstmartins.com/techcom>.

■ **Table 8.1 Common Logical Fallacies**

Fallacy	Explanation	Example and comment
Ad hominem, also called *argument against the speaker*	Argument against the writer, not the writer's argument.	"Of course Matthew favors buying more computers—he's crazy about computers." The fact that Matthew loves computers doesn't necessarily mean that his argument for buying more computers is unwise.
Argument from ignorance	A claim is true because it has never been proven false, or false because it has never been proven true.	"Nobody has ever proven that global warming is occurring. Therefore, global warming is a myth." The fact that a concept has not yet been proven does not necessarily mean that it is false. Perhaps the measurement techniques are insufficiently precise or not yet available.
Appeal to pity	An argument based on emotion, not reason.	"We shouldn't sell the Ridgeway division. It's been part of the company for over 40 years." The fact that the division has long been a part of the company is not in itself a good reason to retain it.
Argument from authority	An argument that a claim is valid because the person making the claim is an authority.	"According to Dr. Smith, global warming is a fact." Even if Dr. Smith is a recognized authority in this field, saying that global warming is a fact is not valid unless you present a valid argument to support it.

⬇

■ **Table 8.1** *(continued)*

Fallacy	Explanation	Example and comment
Circular argument, also called *begging the question*	An argument that assumes what it is attempting to prove.	"Compaq is more successful than its competitors because of its consistently high sales." Because "more successful" means roughly the same thing as achieving "consistently high sales," this statement says only that Compaq outsells its competitors. The writer needs to explain *why* Compaq outsells its competitors and is therefore more successful.
Either-or argument	An argument that poses only two alternatives when in fact there might be more.	"If we don't start selling our products online, we're going to be out of business within a year." This statement does not explain why these are the only two alternatives. The company might improve its sales by taking measures other than selling online.
Ad populum argument, also called the *bandwagon argument*	An argument that a claim is valid because many people think it is or act as if it is.	"Our four major competitors have started selling online. We should, too." The fact that our competitors are selling online is not in itself an argument that we should.
Hasty generalization, sometimes called *inadequate sampling*	An argument that draws conclusions on the basis of an insufficient number of cases.	"The new Gull is an unreliable car. Two of my friends own Gulls, and both have had reliability problems." Before reaching any valid conclusions, you would have to study a much larger sample and compare your findings with those for other cars in the Gull's class.
Post hoc reasoning (the complete phrase is *post hoc, ergo propter hoc*)	An argument that claims that because A preceded B, A caused B.	"There must be something wrong with the new circuit breaker in the office. Ever since we had it installed, the air conditioners haven't worked right." Maybe the air conditioners are malfunctioning because of the circuit breaker, but the malfunctioning might have other causes.
Oversimplifying	An argument that omits important information in establishing a causal link.	"The way to solve the balance-of-trade problem is to improve the quality of the products we produce." Although improving quality is important, international trade balances are determined by many factors, including tariffs and currency rates, and therefore cannot be explained by simple cause-and-effect reasoning.

PRESENTING YOURSELF EFFECTIVELY

A big part of presenting yourself effectively is showing that you know the appropriate information about your subject. However, you also need to come across as a professional.

Guidelines

Creating a Professional Persona

Your *persona* is how you appear to your readers. Demonstrating the following characteristics will help you establish an attractive professional persona.

- **Cooperativeness.** Make clear that your goal is to solve a problem, not advance your own interests.

- **Moderation.** Be moderate in your judgments. The problem you are describing will not likely spell doom for your organization, and the solution you propose will not solve all the company's problems.

- **Fair-mindedness.** Acknowledge the strengths of opposing points of view, even as you offer counterarguments.

- **Modesty.** If you fail to acknowledge that you don't know everything, someone else will be sure to volunteer that insight.

The following paragraph shows how a writer can demonstrate the qualities of cooperativeness, moderation, fair-mindedness, and modesty.

> This plan is certainly not perfect. For one thing, it calls for a greater up-front investment than we had anticipated. And the return on investment through the first three quarters is likely to fall short of our initial goals. However, I think this plan is the best of the three alternatives for the following reasons. . . . Therefore, I recommend that we begin planning immediately to implement the plan. I am confident that this plan will enable us to enter the flat-screen market successfully, building on our fine reputation for high-quality advanced electronics.

In the first three sentences, the writer acknowledges the problems with his recommendation.

The use of "I think" adds an attractive modesty; the recommendation might be unwise.

The recommendation itself is moderate; the writer does not claim that the plan will save the world.

In the last two sentences, the writer shows a spirit of cooperativeness by focusing on the company's goals.

USING GRAPHICS AND DESIGN AS PERSUASIVE ELEMENTS

Graphics and design elements are fundamentally important in communicating persuasively because they help you convey both technical data and nontechnical information. Figure 8.3 on page 166, for example, shows a typical combination of verbal and visual techniques used to make a persuasive argument on a corporate Web page.

Graphics make it easy to tell a story: the woman enjoys using the music player while doing the laundry.

The primary claim is stated: "a DJ saved my night."

A paragraph expands on this claim.

Readers who wish to learn more can follow the link to the technical specifications of the two products. The specs provide the evidence for the claim that "your music goes with you."

NEW DJ 20 and Pocket DJ from Dell
On the road. On the town. On the move. Wherever you go, with a Dell DJ your music goes with you. From the fully functional DJ 20, to the curiously convenient Pocket DJ, you've got tunes at the touch of a button.

GET UP CLOSE - Learn More About Dell **DJs**

■ **Figure 8.3   Verbal and Visual Techniques in Persuasion**
Source: Dell Inc., 2005 <www1.us.dell.com/content/products/category.aspx/dj?c=us&cs=19&l=en&s =dhs&~ck=mn>.

Strategies for Intercultural Communication

Persuading Multicultural Audiences

As discussed in Chapter 5, cultures differ significantly not only in matters such as business customs but also in their most fundamental values. These differences can affect persuasive writing. Culture determines two factors:

- **What makes an argument persuasive.** Statistics and experimental data are fundamental kinds of evidence in the West, but testimony from respected authority figures can be much more persuasive in the East.

- **How to structure an argument.** In a Western culture, the claim is usually presented up front. In an Eastern culture, it is likely to be delayed or to remain unstated but implied.

When you write for an audience from another culture, use two techniques:

- Study that culture and adjust the content, structure, and style of your arguments.

- Include in your budget the cost of having your important documents reviewed and edited by a person from the target culture. Few people are experts on cultures other than their own.

THE ESCAPE SURVEY

Think you've got it tough? Maybe you do. A recent survey found that ... nurses, teachers and homemakers are the three most overworked professions. Many of the situations from which people often wanted to escape involved problems with neighbors and bosses.

ENTER SOMEONE TODAY!

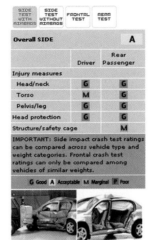

SIDE TEST WITH AIRBAGS	SIDE TEST WITHOUT AIRBAGS	FRONTAL TEST	REAR TEST

Overall SIDE		A
	Driver	Rear Passenger
Injury measures		
Head/neck	G	G
Torso	M	G
Pelvis/leg	G	G
Head protection	G	G
Structure/safety cage		M

IMPORTANT: Side impact crash test ratings can be compared across vehicle type and weight categories. Frontal crash test ratings can only be compared among vehicles of similar weights.

G Good A Acceptable M Marginal P Poor

TOP LEFT: View of the vehicle and barrier just after the crash test Larger photo

TOP RIGHT: View of the vehicle after the crash with doors removed, showing the side airbag and damage to the occupant compartment Larger photo

BOTTOM LEFT: Action shot taken during the side impact crash test showing the driver dummy's head was protected from hitting hard structures by the side curtain airbag Larger photo

BOTTOM RIGHT: Smeared greasepaint shows where the rear passenger dummy's head was protected by the side airbag. Larger photo

This excerpt from the Web site of the Insurance Institute for Highway Safety uses graphics effectively to make information persuasive.

The table with the color-coded grades for the crash test effectively and efficiently communicates the results.

The four photos effectively communicate the nature and extent of the damage that the car and the crash-test dummy sustained. They provide a more vivid sense of the crash test than the table alone would.

■ **Figure 8.4   Graphics and Design Used to Create a Persuasive Message**

In this sample, the words do some of the persuasive work, but the photograph does the real work. The couple pictured are relaxed and smiling—no kids, neighbors, or bosses in sight! **Source:** Princess Cruises, 2005.

■ **Figure 8.5   Photographs Used Effectively in a Persuasive Message**

Source: Insurance Institute for Highway Safety, 2005 <www.hwysafety .org/vehicle_ratings/ce/html/side/s0501.htm>.

Graphics and design can also be used to present evidence in a less technical way. Figure 8.4 shows a portion of a page from a catalog written by a cruise line.

Figure 8.5, an excerpt from the Web site of the Insurance Institute for Highway Safety, uses graphics effectively to make information persuasive.

Ethics Note

Seeming Honest versus *Being* Honest in Persuasive Writing

The young actor asks the old actor, "What's the key to great acting?" The old actor replies, "Sincerity. Once you learn how to fake sincerity. ..." Any discussion of image and persuasion has to address the question at the heart of this old joke: does a writer have to *be* cooperative to *appear* cooperative?

Well, not really. There are tricks for appearing cooperative, and they can work for a while. But the easiest way to appear honest and cooperative is to be honest and cooperative. As suggested in Chapter 2, you need to tell the truth and not mislead your readers. As suggested in Chapter 4, you need to be cooperative, diplomatic, and constructive. And as suggested in this chapter, you need to remember people's broader goals: to protect their own security, to achieve recognition, and to learn and grow in their professional lives.

A LOOK AT SEVERAL PERSUASIVE ARGUMENTS

The following examples of technical communication show how the persuasive elements of an argument differ depending on a writer's purpose.

Figure 8.6 presents two paragraphs from a student's job-application letter.

A student writer uses specific examples to persuade a prospective employer.

Without making her claim explicit, the writer presents evidence that she is hardworking and lets the prospective employer draw his or her own conclusions.

At Western State University, I have earned 87 credits toward a degree in Technical Communication. I have been a full-time student (no fewer than 12 credit hours per semester) while working full-time for the Northwest Watershed Research Center. The four upper-division courses I am taking this semester, including Advanced Technical Communication and Technical Editing, are required for the BA in Technical Communication.

In addition to my formal education, I have completed 34 training courses on the job. These courses have included diverse topics such as financial management, the Fair Labor-Standards Act, the Americans with Disabilities Act, career-development opportunities in public affairs, and software applications such as MS Office, Quark Xpress, and RoboHelp.

In listing some of the training courses she has taken, the writer supports an earlier claim that her broad background might be of use to her next employer.

■ **Figure 8.6   Persuading a Prospective Employer**

Supporting Volunteerism and Civic Engagement

At AT&T, we support and value the volunteer efforts of our own employees, but we also recognize and support the efforts of all volunteers by providing financial support to organizations dedicated to engaging Americans in community service.

AT&T is a leading corporate sponsor of Business Strengthening America (BSA) a peer-to-peer campaign to mobilize the business community to support effective service and civic engagement by every American. AT&T was one of 18 companies that came together to create BSA in 2002. BSA has continued to grow and AT&T is joined by more than 350 companies and business organizations, large and small, representing three million employees across the country and around the world.

AT&T also supports the Points of Light Foundation and its Volunteer Center National Network. As a sponsor of National Volunteer Week and the National Conference on Community Volunteering and National Service, AT&T is proud to support an organization that provides effective leadership and training in the field of volunteerism. We believe in the power of volunteerism and in the importance of involving youth. Through our partnership with the Points of Light, AT&T has also supported Students in Service to America, a USA Freedom Corps initiative. Students in Service to America involves the US Department of Education, the Corporation for National and Community Service, the Points of Light Foundation and the Volunteer Center National Network, to engage America's students in a lifelong habit of service.

Published on AT&T's Web site, this statement aims to persuade readers that AT&T is a socially responsible company.

Notice how the photograph of two people in front of a damaged building gives AT&T a human "face."

The first paragraph contains the claim: AT&T is committed to volunteerism and community service.

The next two paragraphs support the claim by presenting specific evidence.

■ **Figure 8.7   Persuading Employees and Customers**

Source: AT&T Foundation, 2004 <www.att.com/foundation/programs/community.html>.

Figure 8.7, a statement about the AT&T Foundation's disaster-relief program, illustrates an effective use of tone and evidence.

Figure 8.8 on page 170, an excerpt from a white paper, is another example of persuasive writing.

Figure 8.9 on page 171, from the Honeywell Web site, is intended to persuade the public that the new R-410A refrigerant used in home air conditioners is better than the old refrigerant.

■ **Figure 8.8   Persuading Potential Customers**
Source: Hewlett-Packard, 2004 <http://h71028.www7.hp.com/ERC/downloads/HP%20SMB%20WP%20final%20print.pdf>.

A white paper is a document published by a company, a professional organization, or a government agency. The purpose of a white paper might be to inform or persuade readers or to do both. For instance, a U.S. government agency might publish a white paper evaluating the effectiveness of antiterrorism efforts in the nuclear industry.

This excerpt was published by Hewlett-Packard. The argument is that digital color copiers help companies reduce the cost and increase the effectiveness of their marketing campaigns.

In other passages of the white paper, the company presents specific information on its digital color products, including printers, copiers, and cameras. The white paper uses statistics from scholarly reports, testimonials from satisfied customers, and commonsense arguments to support its claims.

 On TechComm Web

For more information on white papers, see WhitePaperSource Forum. Click on Links Library for Ch. 8 on <bedfordstmartins.com/techcomm>.

SECTION 2: DIGITIZING YOUR MARKETING CONTENT FOR GREATER FLEXIBILITY

Managing the cost of publishing isn't the only advantage of digital color. If the content that you plan to use for your marketing materials is in digital format, you can save time, increase productivity and flexibility, and open up new avenues of communications, which can help boost your company's image.

Specifically, you can:

- **Generate materials quicker and retain more control over the end result.** By digitizing the content of the materials you want to create, you can make changes to that content quickly and easily without incurring additional costs. Then, utilizing the wide range of media choices available today, you can create just about any type of customized marketing collateral in house. Finally, you may print only the number of collateral pieces you need, when you need them. This ability to create and print highly customized collateral on demand can help your company increase efficiencies and respond to customer needs quicker.

- **Customize, customize, customize.** Digitized content helps you to use and reuse, edit and re-edit color documents, graphics and photos for many different purposes, easily and inexpensively. This lets you customize and target marketing materials with laser precision to the exact needs of different types of clients and customers at the exact right time, a process known as real-time targeted marketing (RTTM).

- **Extend your customer reach.** Thanks to digital color, you can distribute your color document electronically to a wider range of potential clients and customers. How? Now that just about everyone has a PC and access to a color printer, the practice of printing color materials and distributing them via mail or fax machine is expanded to include the practice of distributing color materials digitally, and letting the receiving parties view or print as they wish.

Honeywell would like people who are building new homes or installing air-conditioning systems in their existing homes to understand the advantages of this refrigerant and buy systems that use it.

This passage uses the more-important-to-less-important organizing principle. Although the environmental factor might not be most important to every reader, Honeywell is trying to persuade readers that it is an environmentally responsible company.

The first argument—that the existing refrigerant is being phased out—directly appeals to the reader's self-interest: repairs will be costly and inconvenient.

The remaining two arguments concern the technical characteristics of the new refrigerant. Notice that the writer skillfully explains that these characteristics help make the new refrigerant a smart choice for the typical consumer, who wants his or her air conditioner to run smoothly and effectively for many years.

What makes R-410A a better refrigerant?

It's Environmentally Friendlier.
If your system ever leaks, the escaping refrigerant won't contribute to ozone depletion!

You avoid the risk that R-22 could become expensive or difficult to get when your system needs to be repaired in a few years.
The old refrigerant R-22 will be phased out along with other ozone depleting chemicals, and both supply and demand of this chemical will be significantly affected by current and upcoming regulations. By selecting an air conditioner or heat pump that uses R-410A, you will avoid the risk associated with purchasing a product that is destined to become obsolete.

R-410A systems can be more reliable than R-22 systems.
R-410A air conditioning and heat pump are today's "state of the art" systems, and utilize the most current technology available for efficient and reliable operation. The heart of every air conditioner or heat pump is the compressor, and newer systems are specifically designed to use R-410A refrigerant. They often incorporate smaller, heavier-duty "scroll-type" compressors that are quieter and operate with less damaging vibration than older compressors that operate on R-22. Since R-410A can absorb and release heat more efficiently than R-22 ever could, compressors with R-410A run cooler than R-22 systems, reducing the risk of burnout due to overheating.

It uses a synthetic lubricant that helps to keep the system operating smoothly.
All air-conditioning systems use an oil that circulates through the inside of the system to keep all of the parts well lubricated, just like the engine of your car. R-22 air conditioners use an oil known as "mineral oil" that has been used for decades. R-410A air conditioners use newer synthetic lubricants that are usually more soluble with the R-410A than the old mineral oils are with the older R-22 refrigerants. This means the synthetic lubricants and R-410A can mix and circulate more efficiently to keep the compressor and other moving parts lubricated, reducing wear and extending their life. Also, just as many new cars use synthetic oils because they are less likely to break down under high stress and heat, the new synthetic oils used in R-410A air conditioners are less likely to break down under extreme conditions.

■ **Figure 8.9 Persuading the Public About a Technological Advance**
Source: Honeywell.com, 2005 <www.410a.com/about/index.html>.

Writer's Checklist

In analyzing your audience, did you consider the broader goals of

☐ maintaining security? (p. 156)
☐ achieving recognition? (p. 156)
☐ growing personally and professionally? (p. 156)

In planning, did you consider the following constraints:

☐ ethical? (p. 156)
☐ legal? (p. 157)
☐ political? (p. 157)
☐ informational? (p. 157)
☐ personnel? (p. 157)
☐ financial? (p. 157)
☐ time? (p. 158)
☐ format and tone? (p. 158)

In crafting a persuasive argument, did you

☐ use the three-part structure of claim, evidence, and reasoning? (p. 158)
☐ choose the appropriate kinds of evidence? (p. 159)
☐ consider opposing viewpoints? (p. 160)
☐ appeal to emotions responsibly? (p. 162)
☐ decide where to present the claim? (p. 163)

In writing the argument, did you avoid the following logical fallacies:

☐ *ad hominem* argument? (p. 163)
☐ argument from ignorance? (p. 163)
☐ appeal to pity? (p. 163)
☐ argument from authority? (p. 163)
☐ circular argument? (p. 164)
☐ either-or argument? (p. 164)
☐ *ad populum* argument? (p. 164)
☐ hasty generalization? (p. 164)
☐ post hoc reasoning? (p. 164)
☐ oversimplifying? (p. 164)

In drafting your argument, did you create a persona that is

☐ cooperative? (p. 165)
☐ moderate? (p. 165)
☐ fair-minded? (p. 165)
☐ modest? (p. 165)

☐ In addressing a multicultural audience, did you consider what types of evidence and what argument structures would be most effective? (p. 166)

Exercises

 In This Book   For more about memos, see Ch. 14, p. 352.

1. **INTERNET EXERCISE** Visit the Web site of a car manufacturer, such as Ford <www.ford.com> or Mercedes-Benz <www.mbusa.com>. Identify the major techniques of persuasion used in the words and graphics on the site. For example, what claims are made? What types of evidence are used? Is the reasoning sound?

2. For each of the following items, write one paragraph identifying the logical flaw:

   a. The election couldn't have been fair—I don't know anyone who voted for the winner.

   b. It would be wrong to prosecute Allied for age discrimination; Allied has always been a great corporate neighbor.

   c. Increased restrictions on smoking in public are responsible for the decrease in smoking.

   d. Bill Jensen's proposal to create an on-site day-care center is just the latest of his harebrained ideas.

   e. Since the introduction of cola drinks at the start of this century, cancer has become the second greatest killer in the United States. Cola drinks should be outlawed.

   f. If mutual-fund guru Peter Lynch recommends this investment, I think we ought to buy it.

   g. We should not go into the DRAM market; we have always been a leading manufacturer of integrated processors.

   h. The other two hospitals in the city have implemented computerized patient record keeping; I think we need to do so, too.

   i. Our Model X500 didn't succeed because we failed to sell a sufficient number of units.

   j. No research has ever established that Internet businesses can earn money; they will never succeed.

3. **GROUP/INTERNET EXERCISE** Form groups of two for this research project on multicultural communication styles.

Each person in the group will secure a document written in English by a person working in a company or government agency outside the United States. Follow these steps:

a. Using a search engine, enter the name of a country and the word "business." For example, enter "Nicaragua business." Find the Web site of a business, then print out the About the Company page or some similar page, such as Mission or Projects. Or enter the name of a country and the word "government," such as "Nicaragua government." Find a government agency that has published a report that is available on the Internet. Print several pages of the report.

b. On your copy of the pages you have printed, disguise the country of origin by blacking out the name of the company or government agency and any other information that would indicate the country of origin.

c. Exchange pages with the other person in your group. Study your partner's pages. Do the pages show a different strategy of persuasion than you would expect from a writer in the United States? For instance, does the writer support his or her claims with the kind of evidence you would expect to see in the United States? Is the organization of the information as you would expect it to be in the United States? Does the writer create a persona as you would expect to see in the United States?

d. Meet with your partner and explain to him or her what you see in the pages that is similar or different from what you would expect if the document came from the United States. Ask your partner whether he or she saw the same things. Present your findings in a memo to your instructor.

Case 8: Being Persuasive About Privacy

 In This Book For more about memos, see Ch. 14, p. 352.

Background

You and the other members of your group are in the Corporate Communications Department at Blanchard Ag-Supply, an agricultural seed company. Your company specializes in developing, breeding, processing, packaging, and distributing a variety of forage and cool-season turfgrass seeds to clients in North America, Australia, and Europe. Forage crops represent a major feed component in the diets of animals that graze or eat hay. Turfgrass seeds are used for home lawns, sports fields, golf courses, and decorative landscaping. Blanchard Ag-Supply relies heavily on its Web site to conduct its global business. This site includes the company's privacy statement (Document 8.1).

Although you knew your company posted a privacy statement on its Web site, you had never taken the time to read it until you received a series of e-mail messages forwarded to you from your supervisor, Andrea Dugan. Earlier today, Andrea stopped you in the hallway and said, "I'm caught in the middle of an argument between Lance Bulos in Marketing and Burt Christensen in Legal. Burt wants us to revise the company's privacy statement; Lance doesn't think the statement needs any revision. With their permission, I

just forwarded you the e-mail messages Burt forwarded to me. I want your help." (See Documents 8.2 and 8.3.)

"Sure, what sort of help do you need?"

"Right from the first paragraph, where it says we want to balance our company's need to be competitive and our customers' right to privacy, something seems off. Would you mind studying the statement and getting back to me on whether it has any problems?" Andrea asks.

"I'll get back to you in a day or two."

Your Assignment

1. Identify those elements of persuasion in Document 8.1 that are used effectively and those that are used ineffectively, then write a memo responding to Andrea's request.

2. Later, Andrea stops by your office. "It looks as if we need to revise the privacy statement," she tells you. "You've read the e-mails from Burt and Lance. I'd like you to recommend an approach to fixing the statement and show me a draft of your revised privacy statement." Write Andrea a memo in which you suggest how to fix the statement. Include a revised privacy statement that reflects your recommendations.

Blanchard Ag-Supply Privacy Statement

At Blanchard Ag-Supply, we want our customers to always be aware of any information we collect, how we use it, and under what circumstances, if any, we release it. Blanchard Ag-Supply's goal is to balance the realities of conducting business in a competitive global market with your right to control how your personal information is used. We want our customers to be offered the products that best meet their needs. As a result, we collect personal information to personalize your visit and to develop and offer competitively priced products and services.

The collection of personal information

We respect each customer's right to personal privacy and online security. We may request such personally identifiable information as first and last name, e-mail address, street address, and phone number from our visitors to process and fulfill orders for products or services. Blanchard Ag-Supply uses this information to make sure you find the right product or service at the right price. Blanchard Ag-Supply may also use this information to provide advertisements about goods and services of value to you.

You may visit our site without divulging any personal information. However, if you choose not to reveal some identifying information, Blanchard Ag-Supply cannot guarantee that we can provide the highest-quality service tailored to your specific needs.

Blanchard Ag-Supply also collects information such as demographic data and browsing patterns automatically each time you visit our site. Such data collection requires no effort on your part and allows Blanchard to better serve you during your current and subsequent visits.

Disclosure to Blanchard Ag-Supply team members

Our goal is satisfied customers. To this end, if Blanchard feels that you would benefit from services or products offered by Blanchard Ag-Supply team members, Blanchard may share information with these third parties. If you receive marketing materials not meeting your current business needs from our team members, please contact them directly.

Blanchard Ag-Supply reserves the right to change the way we use your personal information and to change, modify, or update this privacy statement at any time without notice. Blanchard recommends you read this privacy statement each time you visit our site.

■ **Document 8.1** **Privacy Statement Posted on Blanchard Ag-Supply's Web Site**

 On TechComm Web

For digital versions of case documents, click on Downloadable Case Documents on <bedfordstmartins.com/techcomm>.

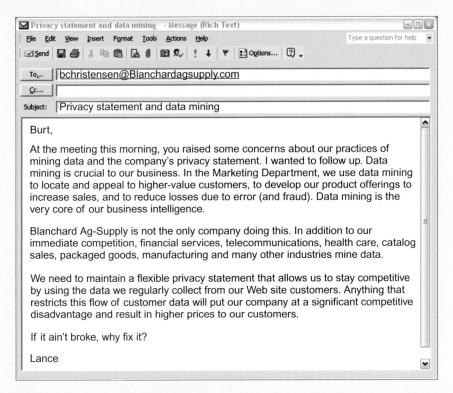

■ **Document 8.2   E-mail from Lance Bulos in the Marketing Department**

Privacy statement and data mining - Message (Rich Text)

File   Edit   View   Insert   Format   Tools   Actions   Help   Type a question for help

Send

To...   bchristensen@Blanchardagsupply.com

Cc...

Subject: Privacy statement and data mining

Burt,

At the meeting this morning, you raised some concerns about our practices of mining data and the company's privacy statement. I wanted to follow up. Data mining is crucial to our business. In the Marketing Department, we use data mining to locate and appeal to higher-value customers, to develop our product offerings to increase sales, and to reduce losses due to error (and fraud). Data mining is the very core of our business intelligence.

Blanchard Ag-Supply is not the only company doing this. In addition to our immediate competition, financial services, telecommunications, health care, catalog sales, packaged goods, manufacturing and many other industries mine data.

We need to maintain a flexible privacy statement that allows us to stay competitive by using the data we regularly collect from our Web site customers. Anything that restricts this flow of customer data will put our company at a significant competitive disadvantage and result in higher prices to our customers.

If it ain't broke, why fix it?

Lance

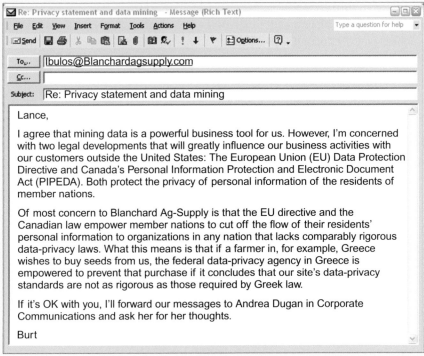

■ **Document 8.3   E-mail from Burt Christensen in the Legal Department**

Re: Privacy statement and data mining - Message (Rich Text)

File   Edit   View   Insert   Format   Tools   Actions   Help   Type a question for help

Send

To...   lbulos@Blanchardagsupply.com

Cc...

Subject: Re: Privacy statement and data mining

Lance,

I agree that mining data is a powerful business tool for us. However, I'm concerned with two legal developments that will greatly influence our business activities with our customers outside the United States: The European Union (EU) Data Protection Directive and Canada's Personal Information Protection and Electronic Document Act (PIPEDA). Both protect the privacy of personal information of the residents of member nations.

Of most concern to Blanchard Ag-Supply is that the EU directive and the Canadian law empower member nations to cut off the flow of their residents' personal information to organizations in any nation that lacks comparably rigorous data-privacy laws. What this means is that if a farmer in, for example, Greece wishes to buy seeds from us, the federal data-privacy agency in Greece is empowered to prevent that purchase if it concludes that our site's data-privacy standards are not as rigorous as those required by Greek law.

If it's OK with you, I'll forward our messages to Andrea Dugan in Corporate Communications and ask her for her thoughts.

Burt

9

Drafting and Revising Definitions and Descriptions

TECH COMM AT WORK

Regardless of your field, you will write definitions and descriptions frequently. A NASA physicist speaking to a congressional hearing about plans to build a *solar-sail-powered spacecraft* might define it, then describe it and its capabilities. An engineer writing a proposal for funding a construction project might describe the need, the proposed activity, and the expected outcome. A career counselor might first define a forensic nurse as a nurse who specializes in treating cases of trauma, acts of violence, sexual assault, and abuse; then the counselor might describe in more detail how forensic nurses collect evidence, document cases, provide follow-up care, and testify in court. Whether you are communicating with the public, with managers, or with other technical professionals, you need to be able to define and describe your topic.

Definitions help readers understand a word or phrase. Descriptions usually provide a more detailed picture of an object, a mechanism, or a process, often explaining the components of the object or the stages of the process.

UNDERSTANDING THE ROLE OF DEFINITIONS

The world of business and industry depends on clear definitions. Suppose you learn at a job interview that the prospective employer pays tuition and expenses for employees' job-related education. You'll need to study the employee-benefits manual to understand just what the company will pay for. Who, for instance, is an *employee*? Is it anyone who works for and is paid by the company, or is it someone who has worked for the company full-time (40 hours per week) for at least six uninterrupted months. What is *tuition*? Does it include incidental laboratory and student fees? What is *job-related education*? Does a course about time management qualify under the company's definition? What, in fact, constitutes *education*?

Definitions are common in communicating policies and standards "for the record." Definitions also have many uses outside legal or contractual contexts. Two such uses occur frequently.

- *Definitions clarify a description of a new development or a new technology in a technical field.* For instance, a zoologist who has discovered a new animal species names and defines it.

- *Definitions help specialists communicate with less knowledgeable readers.* A manual explaining how to tune up a car includes definitions of parts and tools.

Definitions, then, are crucial in many kinds of technical communication, from brief letters and memos to technical reports, manuals, and journal articles. All readers, from the general reader to the expert, need effective definitions to carry out their jobs.

Before you can start to write a definition, you need to analyze the writing situation, determine the kind of definition needed, and decide where to place the definition.

In This Book

For more about audience and purpose, see Ch. 5.

ANALYZING THE WRITING SITUATION FOR DEFINITIONS

The first step in writing effective definitions is to analyze the writing situation: the audience and the purpose of the document.

Unless you know who your readers will be and how much they know about the subject, you cannot determine which terms to define or what kind of definition to write. Physicists wouldn't need a definition of *entropy*, but lawyers might. Builders know what a Molly bolt is, but many insurance agents don't.

Think, too, about your purpose. For readers who need only a basic understanding of a concept—say, time-sharing vacation resorts—a brief, informal definition is usually sufficient. However, readers who need to understand an object, a process, or a concept thoroughly and be able to carry out related tasks need a more formal and elaborate definition. For example, the definition of a "Class 2 Alert" written for operators at a nuclear power plant must be comprehensive, specific, and precise.

Strategies for Intercultural Communication

Defining Terms for Readers from Another Culture

If you are writing to people whose first language is not English, consider the following suggestions:

- **Add a glossary: a list of definitions.** For more on glossaries, see Chapter 18, page 473.

- **Use Simplified English and easily recognizable terms in definitions.** For more on Simplified English, see Chapter 11, page 246.

- **Pay close attention to key terms.** Be sure to carefully define terms that are essential for understanding the document. If, for instance, your document is about angioplasty, you will want to be especially careful when defining it.

- **Use visuals to help readers understand a term or concept.** Graphics are particularly helpful to readers of different languages, and they reduce the cost of translating text from one language to another.

DETERMINING THE KIND OF DEFINITION TO WRITE

Types of definitions:
Parenthetical
Sentence
Extended

Definitions can be short or long, informal or formal. The type of definition you use will depend on your audience and your purpose. There are three basic types.

Writing Parenthetical Definitions

A *parenthetical definition* is a brief clarification within an existing sentence. Sometimes a parenthetical definition is simply a word or phrase that is enclosed in parentheses or commas or introduced by a colon or dash. In the following examples, the term being defined is shown in italics, and the definition is underscored:

> The computers were infected by a *Trojan horse* (<u>a destructive program that appears to be benign</u>).

> Summit Books announced its intention to create a new *colophon* (<u>emblem or trademark</u>).

A parenthetical definition also can take the form of a longer explanatory phrase or clause:

> Motorboating is permitted in the *Jamesport Estuary*, <u>the portion of the bay that meets the mouth of the Jamesport River</u>.

> Before the metal is plated, it is immersed in the *pickle*: <u>an acid bath that removes scales and oxides from the surface</u>.

Parenthetical definitions are not meant to be comprehensive; rather, they serve as quick and convenient ways of introducing terms. When you address general readers especially, make sure that the definition itself is clear. You have gained nothing if readers don't understand it:

> Next, check for blight on the *epicotyl*, <u>the stem portion above the cotyledons</u>.

Although this parenthetical definition of *epicotyl* would be clear to botanists, they probably wouldn't need a definition of that word. General readers, however, would need a definition of *epicotyl* that is free of other specialized terms, such as *cotyledons*.

Writing Sentence Definitions

A *sentence definition*—a one-sentence clarification—is more formal than a parenthetical definition. A sentence definition usually follows a standard pattern: the item to be defined is placed in a category of similar items and then distinguished from them.

Item	=	Category	+	Distinguishing characteristics
Crippleware	is	shareware		in which some features of the program are disabled until the user buys a license to use the program.
Hypnoanalysis	is	a psychoanalytical technique		in which hypnosis is used to elicit information from a patient's unconscious mind.
An electron microscope	is	a microscope		that uses electrons rather than visible light to produce magnified images.

In many cases, a sentence definition also includes a graphic. For example, the definition of an electron microscope would probably include photographs, diagrams, or drawings.

Sentence definitions are more formal or more informative than brief parenthetical definitions. Writers often use sentence definitions to present a working definition for a particular document: "In this report, *electron microscope* refers to any microscope that uses electrons rather than visible light to produce magnified images." Such definitions are sometimes called *stipulative definitions*, because the writer is stipulating how the term will be used in the document.

Guidelines

Writing Effective Sentence Definitions

The following four suggestions can help you write effective sentence definitions:

▶ **Be specific in stating the category and the distinguishing characteristics.** If you write, "A Bunsen burner is a burner that consists of a vertical metal tube connected to a gas source," the imprecise category—"a burner"—ruins the definition: many types of large-scale burners use vertical metal tubes connected to gas sources.

▶ **Don't describe a specific item if you are defining a general class of items.** If you wish to define *catamaran*, don't describe a particular catamaran. The catamaran you see on the beach in front of you might be made by Hobie and have a white hull and blue sails, but those characteristics are not essential to catamarans in general.

▶ **Avoid writing circular definitions—that is, definitions that merely repeat the key words or the distinguishing characteristics of the item being defined in the category.** The definition "A required course is a course that is required" is useless: required of whom or by whom? However, in defining electron microscopes, you can repeat *microscope* because *microscope* is not the difficult part of the term. The purpose of defining *electron microscope* is to clarify *electron* as it applies to a particular type of microscope.

▶ **Be sure the category contains a noun or a noun phrase rather than a phrase beginning with *when, what,* or *where.***

INCORRECT	A brazier is what is used to . . .
CORRECT	A brazier is a metal pan used to . . .
INCORRECT	Hypnoanalysis is when hypnosis is used to . . .
CORRECT	Hypnoanalysis is a psychoanalytical technique in which . . .

Writing Extended Definitions

An *extended definition* is a detailed clarification—usually one or more paragraphs—of an object, a process, or an idea. Often an extended definition begins with a sentence definition, which is then elaborated. For instance, the sentence definition "An electrophorus is a laboratory instrument used to generate static electricity" tells you the basic function of the device, but it doesn't explain how it works, what it is used for, and its strengths and limitations. An extended definition would address these and other topics.

There is no one way to "extend" a definition. Your analysis of the audience and purpose of your communication will help you decide which method to use. In fact, an extended definition sometimes employs several of the following nine techniques.

Techniques used in extended definitions:

- Graphics
- Examples
- Partition
- Principle of operation
- Comparison and contrast
- Analogy
- Negation
- Etymology
- History of the term

Graphics   Perhaps the most common way to present an extended definition in technical communication is to use a graphic, then explain it. Graphics are useful in defining not only physical objects but also concepts and ideas. A definition of *temperature inversion*, for instance, might include a diagram showing the forces that create temperature inversion.

The following passage on additive color shows how graphics can complement words in an extended definition.

> Additive color is the type of color that results from mixing colored light, as opposed to mixing pigments such as dyes or paints. When any two color lights are mixed, they produce a third color that is lighter than either of the two original colors, as shown in this diagram. And when green, red, and blue lights are mixed together in equal parts, they form white light.
>
> We are all familiar with the concept of additive color from watching TV monitors. A TV monitor projects three beams of electrons—one each for red, blue, and green—onto a fluorescent screen. Depending on the combinations of the three colors, we see different colors on the screen.

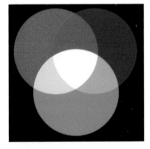

The graphic effectively and economically clarifies the concept of additive color.

Examples   Examples are particularly useful in making an abstract term easier to understand. The following paragraph is an extended definition of *hazing activities* (Fraternity, 2003).

> No chapter, colony, student or alumnus shall conduct nor condone hazing activities. Hazing activities are defined as: "Any action taken or situation created, intentionally,

This extended definition is effective because the writer has presented a clear sentence definition followed by numerous examples.

whether on or off fraternity premises, to produce mental or physical discomfort, embarrassment, harassment, or ridicule. Such activities may include but are not limited to the following: use of alcohol; paddling in any form; creation of excessive fatigue; physical and psychological shocks; quests, treasure hunts, scavenger hunts, road trips or any other such activities carried on outside or inside of the confines of the chapter house; wearing of public apparel which is conspicuous and not normally in good taste; engaging in public stunts and buffoonery; morally degrading or humiliating games and activities; and any other activities which are not consistent with academic achievement, fraternal law, ritual or policy or the regulations and policies of the educational institution or applicable state law."

In This Book

For more about partitioning, see Ch. 7, p. 139.

Partition   Partitioning is the process of dividing a thing or an idea into smaller parts so that the reader can understand it more easily. The following example (Brain, 2005) uses partition to define *computer infection*.

Types of Infection

When you listen to the news, you hear about many different forms of electronic infection. The most common are:

- **Viruses**—A virus is a small piece of software that piggybacks on real programs. For example, a virus might attach itself to a program such as a spreadsheet program. Each time the spreadsheet program runs, the virus runs, too, and it has the chance to reproduce (by attaching to other programs) or wreak havoc.

- **E-mail viruses**—An e-mail virus moves around in e-mail messages, and usually replicates itself by automatically mailing itself to dozens of people in the victim's e-mail address book.

- **Worms**—A worm is a small piece of software that uses computer networks and security holes to replicate itself. A copy of the worm scans the network for another machine that has a specific security hole. It copies itself to the new machine using the security hole, and then starts replicating from there, as well.

- **Trojan horses**—A Trojan horse is simply a computer program. The program claims to do one thing (it may claim to be a game) but instead does damage when you run it (it may erase your hard disk). Trojan horses have no way to replicate automatically.

Principle of Operation   Describing the principle of operation—the way something works—is an effective way to develop an extended definition, especially for an object or a process. The following excerpt from an extended definition of a parabolic-dish solar-energy system (U.S. Department of Energy, 2001) is based on the mechanism's principle of operation.

A Solar Dish-Engine System is an electric generator that "burns" sunlight instead of gas or coal to produce electricity. The figure shows the two major parts of a system—the solar concentrator (or dish) and the power conversion unit (PCU). The dish tracks the sun over the course of a day and reflects concentrated sunlight to a single point, its focus, where it is converted in the PCU into heat to power an engine/generator to produce electricity. These systems are modular, allowing their assembly into plants ranging in size from a few kilowatts to tens of megawatts. They are made from readily available materials (steel, aluminum, and glass) using conventional manufacturing techniques common to the automotive industry.

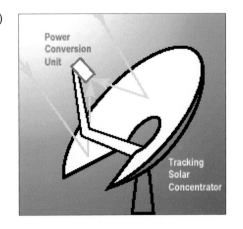

This paragraph describes the principle of operation of the device. This principle is illustrated in the diagram.

Comparison and Contrast   Using comparison and contrast, a writer discusses the similarities or differences between the item being defined and an item with which readers are more familiar. The following definition of VoIP (Voice over Internet Protocol) contrasts this new form of phone service to the form we all know.

 In This Book

For more about comparison and contrast, see Ch. 7, p. 136.

> Voice over Internet Protocol is a form of phone service that lets you connect to the Internet through your cable or DSL modem. VoIP service uses a device called a telephony adapter, which attaches to the broadband modem, transforming phone pulses into IP packets sent over the Internet.
>
>   VoIP is considerably cheaper than traditional phone service: for as little as $20 per month, users get unlimited local and domestic long-distance service. For international calls, VoIP service is only about three cents per minute, about a third the rate of traditional phone service. In addition, any calls from one person to another person with the same VoIP service provider are free.
>
>   However, sound quality in VoIP cannot match that of a traditional land-based phone. On a good day, the sound is fine on VoIP, but frequent users comment on clipping and dropouts that can last up to a second. In addition, sometimes the sound has the distant, tinny quality of some of today's cell phones.

In this excerpt, the second and third paragraphs briefly compare VoIP and traditional phone service.

Notice that this passage is organized according to the part-by-part comparison-and-contrast pattern. For more details, see Ch. 7, p. 136.

Analogy   An *analogy* is a specialized kind of comparison. In a traditional comparison, the writer compares one item to another similar item: an electron microscope to a common microscope, for example. In an analogy, however, the item being defined is compared to an item that is in some ways completely different but that shares some essential characteristic. For instance, the central processing unit of a computer is often compared to a brain. Obviously, these two items are very different, except that the relationship of the central processing unit to the computer is similar to that of the brain to the body.

The following example (Sweetman, 2002), from an explanation of a radar system on a JointSTAR, a U.S. reconnaissance airplane, shows the effective use of an analogy.

The writer of this passage employs the VCR analogy to explain how the operator uses the radar system. Obviously, the radar system differs from a VCR in most ways.

> This radar system acts much like a VCR in the hands of one of 18 operators onboard the plane, who can fast-forward through images recorded during the previous 6 hours or run them backward to show, for example, where a column of vehicles originated. If the targets stop moving, the radar operator can take a high-resolution picture of the area and store it until motion is spied again. Data can be relayed to commanders on the ground, fighters and other planes in the air, and to the Pentagon for analysis and action.

Negation A special kind of contrast is sometimes called *negation* or *negative statement*. Negation clarifies a term by distinguishing it from a different term with which the reader might confuse it. The following example uses negation to distinguish the term *ambulatory* from *ambulance*.

> An ambulatory patient is not a patient who must be moved by ambulance. On the contrary, an ambulatory patient is one who can walk without assistance from another person.

Negation is rarely the only technique used in an extended definition; in fact, it is used most often in a sentence or two at the start. Once you have explained what the item is not, you still have to explain what it is.

Etymology *Etymology*, the derivation of a word, is often a useful and interesting way to develop a definition. The following example uses the etymology of *spam*—unsolicited junk e-mail—to define it.

> For many decades, Hormel Foods has manufactured a luncheon meat called Spam, which stands for "Shoulder Pork and hAM"/"SPiced hAM." Then, in the 1970s, the English comedy team Monty Python's Flying Circus broadcast a skit about a restaurant that served Spam with every dish. In describing each dish, the waitress repeats the word *Spam* over and over, and several Vikings standing in the corner chant the word repeatedly. In the mid-1990s, two businessmen hired a programmer to write a program that would send unsolicited ads to thousands of electronic newsgroups. Just as Monty Python's chanting Vikings drowned out other conversation in the restaurant, the ads began drowning out regular communication online. As a result, people started calling unsolicited junk e-mail *spam*.

Etymology is a popular way to begin definitions of *acronyms,* which are abbreviations pronounced as words, as illustrated in the following examples.

> Scuba stands for self-contained underwater breathing apparatus.

> RAID, which stands for redundant array of independent (or inexpensive) disks, refers to a computer storage system that can withstand a single (or, in some cases, even double) disk failure.

Etymology, like negation, is rarely used alone in technical communication, but it is an effective way to introduce an extended definition.

History of the Term A common way to define a term is to explain its history. Often an extended definition explains the original use of the term and then describes how the meaning has changed in response to historical events or technological advances. The following example (Microsoft, 2005, p. 10) uses the history of the term *burglary* to define it:

> The common law definition of burglary is breaking and entering the dwelling house of another in the nighttime with the intent to commit a felony therein. The requirement of *breaking* is satisfied by forcing open a locked door or window, by opening a closed but unlocked door or window, or even by opening wider a partly closed door or window to obtain entry. If the person had the resident's consent to enter, then the use of force to gain entry is not a breaking. *Entering* is satisfied by a person's passing entirely through the door, window, or other opening by putting any portion of the body through or even by holding a pole or other item through the opening while angling for some property inside. . . .
>
> Modern statutes have enlarged the scope of the common law definition of burglary in various ways. They sometimes eliminate the requirement of a breaking, so that an entry without a breaking may still constitute burglary. Some statutes consider gaining entry by means of fraud, threat, or intimidation to be *constructive breaking*—that is, the legal equivalent of forceful breaking. Modern statutes also typically provide that breaking into certain nonbuildings—such as railroad cars, automobiles, and boats—constitutes burglary. Most modern statutes have abandoned the requirement that the breaking and entering occur at night. Finally, some statutes provide that a person commits burglary if he or she has an intention to commit a misdemeanor—rather than an intention to commit a felony—after breaking and entering.

The first paragraph in this passage presents the traditional definition of *burglary*.

The second paragraph presents the more modern definition of the term.

A Sample Extended Definition Figure 9.1 on page 186 is an example of an extended definition addressed to a general audience.

DECIDING WHERE TO PLACE THE DEFINITION

If you are writing a sentence definition or an extended definition, you need to decide where to put it. A definition is typically placed in one of these six locations:

- *In the text.* The text is an appropriate place for sentence definitions that many or most of your readers will need and for extended definitions of important terms.
- *In a marginal gloss.* Sentence definitions placed in the margin are easy to see, but they don't interrupt readers who don't need them.
- *In a hyperlink.* In a hypertext document such as a Web page, definitions can be put in a separate file, enabling the reader to click on highlighted or underlined words to view the definitions.
- *In a footnote.* A footnote is a logical place for an occasional sentence definition or extended definition. The reader who doesn't need it will ignore it. However, footnotes can slow readers down by interrupting the flow of the discussion. If you think you will need more than one footnote for a definition on every two to three pages, consider including a glossary.

The first paragraph of this extended definition of the greenhouse effect begins with a general description and ends with a sentence that explains the etymology of the term.

The body of this extended definition is a discussion of the factors that have increased the greenhouse effect.

Questions are effective in topic sentences, particularly in discussions aimed at general readers.

This diagram aids the reader by visually summarizing the principle of operation of the greenhouse effect.

 On TechComm Web

To view Fig. 9.1 in context on the Web, click on Links Library for Ch. 9 on <bedfordstmartins.com/techcomm>.

THE GREENHOUSE EFFECT

Energy from the sun drives the earth's weather and climate, and heats the earth's surface; in turn, the earth radiates energy back into space. Atmospheric greenhouse gases (water vapor, carbon dioxide, and other gases) trap some of the outgoing energy, retaining heat somewhat like the glass panels of a greenhouse.

Without this natural "greenhouse effect," temperatures would be much lower than they are now, and life as known today would not be possible. Instead, thanks to greenhouse gases, the earth's average temperature is a more hospitable 60°F. However, problems may arise when the atmospheric concentration of greenhouse gases increases.

Since the beginning of the industrial revolution, atmospheric concentrations of carbon dioxide have increased nearly 30%, methane concentrations have more than doubled, and nitrous oxide concentrations have risen by about 15%. These increases have enhanced the heat-trapping capability of the earth's atmosphere. Sulfate aerosols, a common air pollutant, cool the atmosphere by reflecting light back into space; however, sulfates are short-lived in the atmosphere and vary regionally.

Why are greenhouse gas concentrations increasing? Scientists generally believe that the combustion of fossil fuels and other human activities are the primary reason for the increased concentration of carbon dioxide. Plant respiration and the decomposition of organic matter release more than 10 times the CO_2 released by human activities; but these releases have generally been in balance during the centuries leading up to the industrial revolution with carbon dioxide absorbed by terrestrial vegetation and the oceans.

What has changed in the last few hundred years is the additional release of carbon dioxide by human activities. Fossil fuels burned to run cars and trucks, heat homes and businesses, and power factories are responsible for about 98% of U.S. carbon dioxide emissions, 24% of methane emissions, and 18% of nitrous oxide emissions. Increased agriculture, deforestation, landfills, industrial production, and mining also contribute a significant share of emissions. In 1997, the United States emitted about one-fifth of total global greenhouse gases.

Estimating future emissions is difficult, because it depends on demographic, economic, technological,

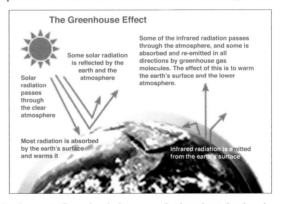

policy, and institutional developments. Several emissions scenarios have been developed based on differing projections of these underlying factors. For example, by 2100, in the absence of emissions control policies, carbon dioxide concentrations are projected to be 30–150% higher than today's levels.

■ **Figure 9.1   An Extended Definition**

Source: U.S. Environmental Protection Agency, 2001 <www.epa.gov/globalwarming/climate/index.html>.

- *In a glossary.* A glossary—an alphabetized list of definitions—can accommodate sentence definitions and extended definitions of fewer than three or four paragraphs in one convenient location. A glossary can be placed at the beginning of a document (for example, after the executive summary in a report) or at the end, preceding the appendices.

- *In an appendix.* An appendix is appropriate for an extended definition of one page or longer, which would be cumbersome in a glossary or in a footnote.

UNDERSTANDING THE ROLE OF DESCRIPTIONS

Technical communication often requires descriptions: verbal and visual representations of objects, mechanisms, and processes.

- *Objects.* An object is anything ranging from a physical site such as a volcano to a synthetic artifact such as a hammer. A tomato plant is an object, as is an automobile tire or a book.

- *Mechanisms.* A mechanism is a synthetic object consisting of a number of identifiable parts that work together. A DVD player is a mechanism, as is a voltmeter, a lawn mower, or a submarine.

- *Processes.* A process is an activity that takes place over time: species evolve; steel is made; plants perform photosynthesis. *Descriptions of processes*, which explain how something happens, differ from *instructions*, which explain how to do something. Readers of a process description want to *understand* the process; readers of instructions want a step-by-step guide to help them *perform* it.

Descriptions of objects, mechanisms, and processes appear in virtually every kind of technical communication. For example, an employee who wants to persuade management to buy some equipment includes a mechanism description of the equipment in the proposal to buy it. A company manufacturing a consumer product provides a description and a graphic on its Web site to attract buyers. A developer who wants to build a housing project includes in his proposal to municipal authorities descriptions of the geographical area and of the process he will use in developing that area.

Notice that a description is usually part of a larger document. For example, a maintenance manual for an air-conditioning system might begin with a description of the system to help the reader understand first how it operates and then how to fix or maintain it.

ANALYZING THE WRITING SITUATION FOR DESCRIPTIONS

Before you begin to write a description, consider carefully how the audience and the purpose of the document will affect what you write.

 In This Book

For more about glossaries and appendices, see Ch. 18, pp. 473 and 474.

 In This Book

For more about instructions, see Ch. 19, p. 497.

 In This Book

For more about audience and purpose, see Ch. 5.

What does the audience already know about the general subject? For example, if you want to describe how the next generation of industrial robots will affect car manufacturing, you first have to know whether your readers understand the current process and whether they understand robotics.

Your sense of your audience will determine not only how technical your vocabulary should be but also how long your sentences and paragraphs should be. Another audience-related factor is your use of graphics. Less knowledgeable readers need simple graphics; they might have trouble understanding sophisticated schematics or decision charts. As you consider your audience, think about whether any of your readers are from other cultures and might therefore expect different topics, organization, or writing style in the description.

Consider, too, your purpose. What are you trying to accomplish with this description? If you want your readers to understand how a personal computer works, write a *general description* that applies to several varieties of computers. If you want your readers to understand how a specific computer works, write a *particular description.* A general description of personal computers might classify them by size, then go on to describe palmtops, laptops, and desktops in general terms. A particular description, however, will describe only one model of personal computer, such as a Millennia 200. Your purpose will determine every aspect of the description, including its length, the amount of detail, and the number and type of graphics.

WRITING THE DESCRIPTION

There is no single structure or format to use in writing descriptions. Because descriptions are written for different audiences and different purposes, they can take many shapes and forms. However, the following four suggestions will guide you in most situations.

Clearly Indicate the Nature and Scope of the Description

If the description is to be a separate document, give it a title. If the description is to be part of a longer document, give it a section heading. In either case, clearly state the subject and indicate whether the description is general or particular. For instance, a general description of an object might be titled "Description of a Minivan," and a particular description might be called "Description of the 2006 Honda Odyssey." A general description of a process might be titled "Description of the Process of Designing a New Production Car," and a particular description might be called "Description of the Process of Designing the Saturn L-Series."

Introduce the Description Clearly

Provide the information that readers need to understand the detailed information that follows. Most introductions to descriptions are general: you want to give readers a broad understanding of the object, mechanism, or

Principles for writing descriptions:

Clearly indicate the nature and scope of the description.

Introduce the description clearly.

Provide appropriate detail.

Conclude the description.

 In This Book

For more about titles, see Ch. 10, p. 205, and Ch. 18, p. 476. For more about headings, see Ch. 10, p. 206.

process. You also might provide a graphic that introduces your readers to the overall concept. For example, in describing a process, you might include a flowchart summarizing the steps in the body of the description; in describing an object, such as a bicycle, you might include a photograph or a drawing showing the major components you will describe in detail in the body.

Table 9.1 shows some of the basic questions you might want to answer in introducing object, mechanism, and process descriptions. If the answer is obvious, simply move on to the next question.

Figure 9.2 on page 190 shows the introductory graphic accompanying a description of a headlamp.

■ **Table 9.1 Questions to Answer in Introducing a Description**

For object and mechanism descriptions	*For process descriptions*
• *What is the item?* You might start with a sentence definition.	• *What is the process?* You might start with a sentence definition.
• *What is the function of the item?* If the function is not implicit in the sentence definition, state it: "Electron microscopes magnify objects that are smaller than the wavelengths of visible light."	• *What is the function of the process?* Unless the function is obvious, state it: "The central purpose of performing a census is to obtain current population figures, which government agencies use to revise legislative districts and determine revenue-sharing."
• *What does the item look like?* Include a photograph or drawing if possible. (See Ch. 13 for more about incorporating graphics with text.) If not, use an analogy or comparison: "The cassette that encloses the tape is a plastic shell, about the size of a deck of cards." Mention the material, texture, color, and the like, if relevant. Sometimes an object is best pictured with both graphics and words.	• *Where and when does the process take place?* "Each year the stream is stocked with hatchery fish in the first week of March." Omit these facts only if your readers already know them.
• *How does the item work?* In a few sentences, define the operating principle. Sometimes objects do not "work"; they merely exist. For instance, a ship model has no operating principle.	• *Who or what performs the process?* If there is any doubt about who or what performs the process, state it.
• *What are the principal parts of the item?* Limit your description to the principal parts. A description of a bicycle, for instance, would not mention the dozens of nuts and bolts that hold the mechanism together; it would focus on the chain, gears, pedals, wheels, and frame.	• *How does the process work?* "The four-treatment lawn-spray plan is based on the theory that the most effective way to promote a healthy lawn is to apply different treatments at crucial times during the growing season. The first two treatments—in spring and early summer—consist of. . . ."
	• *What are the principal steps of the process?* Name the steps in the order in which you will describe them. The principal steps in changing an automobile tire, for instance, include jacking up the car, replacing the old tire with the new one, and lowering the car back to the ground. Changing a tire also includes secondary steps, such as placing chocks against the tires to prevent the car from moving once it is jacked up. Explain or refer to these secondary steps at the appropriate points in the description.

■ **Figure 9.2   Graphic with Enlarged Detailed Graphics**

In this description of a headlamp, the introductory graphic includes five graphics showing different portions or views of the headlamp or additional components. Notice the use of the numbered boxes to help readers link the individual boxes to the main photograph of the headlamp.
Source: Petzl, 2005.

Provide Appropriate Detail

In the body of a description—the part-by-part or step-by-step section—treat each major part or step as a separate item. In describing an object or a mechanism, define each part and then, if applicable, describe its function, operating principle, and appearance. In discussing the appearance, include shape, dimensions, material, and physical details such as texture and color (if essential). Some descriptions might call for other qualities, such as weight or hardness. If a part has important subparts, describe them in the same way.

In describing a process, treat each major step as if it were a separate process. Do not repeat your answer to the question about who or what performs the action unless a new agent performs it, but do answer the other important questions: what the step is, what its function is, and when, where, and how it occurs. If the step has important substeps, explain them, too.

A description resembles a map with a series of detailed insets. A description of a computer system includes a keyboard as one of its parts, and the description of the keyboard includes the numeric keypad as one of its parts. And the description of the numeric keypad includes the arrow keys as one of its parts. The level of detail depends on the complexity of the item and the readers' needs. The same principle applies in describing processes: a step might have substeps. For each substep, you need to describe who or what performs it (if it is not obvious), and you need to describe what the substep is, what its function is, and when, where, and how it occurs.

Guidelines

Providing Appropriate Detail in Descriptions
Use the following techniques to flesh out your descriptions.

For mechanism and object descriptions	*For process descriptions*
• **Choose an appropriate organizing principle.** Two organizational principles are common: —Functional: how the item works or is used. In a radio, for instance, the sound begins at	• **Structure the step-by-step description chronologically.** If the process is a closed system—such as the cycle of evaporation and condensation—and thus has no first step, begin with any principal step.

For mechanism and object descriptions	For process descriptions
the receiver, travels into the amplifier, and then flows out through the speakers. —Spatial: based on the physical structure of the item: from top to bottom, east to west, outside to inside, and so forth. Descriptions can be organized in various ways. For instance, the description of a house could be organized functionally (the different electrical and mechanical systems) or spatially (top to bottom, inside to outside, east to west, and so on). A complex description can use a combination of patterns at different levels in the description. • **Use graphics.** Present a graphic for each major part. Use photographs to show external surfaces, drawings to emphasize particular items on the surface, and cutaways and exploded diagrams to show details beneath the surface. Other kinds of graphics, such as graphs and charts, are often useful supplements (see Ch. 13).	• **Explain causal relationships among steps.** Don't present the steps as if they have nothing to do with one another. In many cases, one step causes another. In the operation of a four-stroke gasoline engine, for instance, each step creates the conditions for the next step. • **Use the present tense.** Discuss steps in the present tense unless you are writing about a process that occurred in the historical past. For example, use the past tense in describing how the Snake River aquifer was formed: "The molten material condensed. . . ." However, use the present tense in describing how steel is made: "The molten material is then poured into. . . ." The present tense helps readers understand that, in general, steel is made this way. • **Use graphics.** Whenever possible, use graphics to clarify each point. Consider additional flowcharts or other kinds of graphics, such as photographs, drawings, and graphs. For example, in a description of how a four-stroke gasoline engine operates, use diagrams to illustrate the positions of the valves and the activity occurring during each step.

Conclude the Description

A description typically has a brief conclusion that summarizes it and prevents readers from overemphasizing the part or step discussed last.

A common technique for concluding descriptions of mechanisms and of some objects is to state briefly how the parts function together. At the end of a description of a telephone, for example, the conclusion might include the following paragraph:

> When you make a phone call, everything that happens depends on the flow of current through the phone lines and on what your phone and the other person's phone do with that current. When the phone is off the hook, a current flows through the carbon granules. The intensity of the speaker's voice causes a greater or lesser movement of the phone's diaphragm and thus a greater or lesser intensity in the

INTERACTIVE SAMPLE DOCUMENT
Introducing a Description

The following introduction to a description of food irradiation (U.S. Department of Agriculture, 2000) is addressed to the general reader. The questions in the margin ask you to think about the discussion of introducing process descriptions in Table 9.1 (page 189). E-mail your responses to yourself and/or your instructor, and see suggested responses on TechComm Web.

Table 9.1 presents six questions that should be answered in an introduction to a process description:

1. What is the process?

2. What is the function of the process?

3. Where and when does the process take place?

4. Who or what performs the process?

5. How does the process work?

6. What are the principal steps of the process?

Determine whether each of these questions is answered and, if so, where.

 On TechComm Web

To e-mail your responses to yourself and/or your instructor and to see suggested responses, click on Interactive Sample Documents for Ch. 9 on <bedfordstmartins.com/techcomm>.

What is food irradiation?
Food irradiation is a process in which products are exposed to radiant energy including gamma rays, electron beams, and x-rays in amounts approved by the Food and Drug Administration (FDA)....

Why is food irradiated? What are the benefits?
Food is irradiated to make it safer. It can reduce the risk of foodborne illness by destroying harmful bacteria, parasites, insects, and fungi.

Irradiation does not destroy all pathogens (very tiny disease-causing organisms) in amounts approved by the FDA for refrigerated or frozen raw meat and poultry sold to consumers, but it does reduce their number. To sterilize food (destroy all pathogens), a higher amount of radiation must be used. Hospitals have used irradiation for many years to sterilize food for cancer patients and others with weakened immune systems. Some perishable food taken into space by astronauts is irradiated because the food must be guaranteed free of disease-causing organisms.

It also reduces spoilage. Like freezing, canning, and drying, irradiation can also extend the shelf life of perishable food products. For example, irradiated strawberries stay unspoiled in the refrigerator up to 3 weeks versus only 3 to 5 days for untreated berries.

How is food irradiated?
At a food irradiation plant that uses gamma radiation, food is irradiated in an area that is surrounded by concrete walls at least 6-feet thick, which keep any rays from escaping. The radiation source, usually Cobalt 60, is held in a resting position in a pool of water. A conveyor system transports the meat or poultry product to the area. The radiation source is then raised out of the water and the food is exposed for a defined period of time. When the source is raised, lights and alarms are sounded to make people aware that the product is being irradiated. Once the food is irradiated, the source automatically returns to the resting position, and the food leaves the area for further processing.

current flowing through the carbon granules. The phone receiving the call converts the electrical waves back into sound waves by means of an electromagnet and a diaphragm. The varying intensity of the current transmitted by the phone lines alters the strength of the current in the electromagnet, which in turn changes the position of the diaphragm. The movement of the diaphragm reproduces the speaker's sound waves.

Like an object or mechanism description, a process description usually has a brief conclusion: a short paragraph summarizing the principal steps. Here, for example, is the concluding section of a description of how a four-stroke gasoline engine operates:

> In the intake stroke, the piston moves down, drawing the air-fuel mixture into the cylinder from the carburetor. As the piston moves up, it compresses this mixture in the compression stroke, creating the conditions necessary for combustion. In the power stroke, a spark from the spark plug ignites the mixture, which burns rapidly, forcing the piston down. In the exhaust stroke, the piston moves up, expelling the burned gases.

For descriptions of more than a few pages, a discussion of the implications of the process might be appropriate. For instance, a description of the big bang might conclude with a discussion of how the theory has been supported and challenged by recent astronomical discoveries and theories.

Ethics Note

Balancing Multiple Purposes

In the working world, when you write definitions and descriptions, often you will have two different purposes: to inform and to persuade. You want to present unbiased information to readers, but you might also want to persuade readers to buy products or services from your company. You can fulfill both functions ethically. Your desire to persuade should not interfere with your desire to inform. For example, if you work for a company that plans events, such as business conferences, and you are describing the process of planning a big conference, don't leave out a step just because your company does not perform that step. Instead, describe the step and explain how the client can hire another contractor to perform that step. Ultimately, being honest is good business because it builds your credibility.

A LOOK AT SEVERAL DESCRIPTIONS

A look at some sample descriptions will give you an idea of how different writers adapt basic approaches for particular audiences and purposes.

Figure 9.3 shows the extent to which a process description can be based on graphics. The topic is drivetrain efficiencies for vehicles powered by internal combustion engines and for vehicles powered by electricity. The audience is the general reader.

Figure 9.4 on page 195 shows two screens from a Web site about the use of biometrics in security systems. The audience is the general reader.

Figures 9.5 and 9.6 on page 196 are excerpts from a description of the Ford Escape Hybrid.

Figure 9.7 on page 197 is a description of autopsies as presented on the Web site of a university college of forensics in Australia.

At each step in the process of turning raw materials into energy to power the vehicles, the efficiency is noted as a percentage.

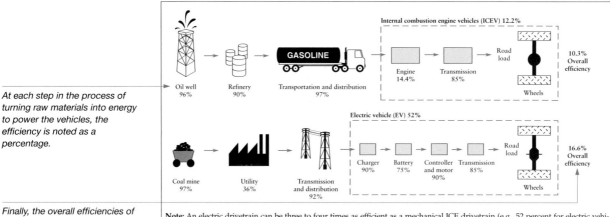

Finally, the overall efficiencies of the two technologies are compared.

Note: An electric drivetrain can be three to four times as efficient as a mechanical ICE drivetrain (e.g., 52 percent for electric vehicles (EVs) versus 12 percent for ICEVs). This efficiency differential drops substantially when the overall fuel chain efficiency for ICEVs and EVs is taken into consideration (16.6 percent for coal-powered EVs versus 10.3 percent for gasoline-powered ICEVs). The fuel chain efficiency for EVs could be much higher if new power generation technologies are deployed. Advanced coal plants might achieve efficiencies close to 50 percent, while efficiencies of 60 percent are possible for advanced natural gas plants. With an advanced natural gas plant the overall fuel chain efficiency for EVs could rise to 27 percent.

Source: John Brogan and S. Venkateswaran, "Diverse Choices for Hybrid and Electric Motor Vehicles, " in *Proceedings of the International Conference on Urban EVs* (Stockholm, Sweden: Organization for Economic Cooperation and Development, May 1992).

■ **Figure 9.3   A Process Description Based on Graphics**

Notice how effectively graphics show the relative efficiencies of an internal combustion engine vehicle (top row) and an electric vehicle (bottom row). The graphics clarify the process and make it interesting.
Source: U.S. Congress, Office of Technology Assessment, 1995b.

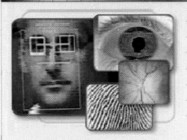

Biometric security systems grant—or deny—access to buildings, information and benefits by automatically verifying the identity of people through their distinctive physical or behavioral traits.

Once "captured," a biometric is translated algorithmically into a complex string of numbers and stored in a database as a template. Later, this template can be compared to any "live" biometric presented as proof of identity.

Click on the categories above to learn how common biometric systems work.

Source: MSNBC Research

This graphic, part of an article about the use of biometrics in security systems, uses the Web to create an interesting, informative description.

The screen shown here is the introduction to biometrics. It presents the principle of operation underlying all biometric systems.

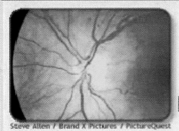

Retinal scanning: The retina at the back of the eye is scanned, revealing a unique pattern of capillaries that can be mapped and encoded.

Source: MSNBC Research

This screen shows the graphic and text that appear when the user clicks on Retinal Scanning. A new graphic and explanation appear, describing this principle.

■ **Figure 9.4 Excerpts from a Web-Based Description**
Source: Masterson, 2001 <www.msnbc.com/news/65478 8.asp?cp1=1>.

This first image from the Ford Web site shows one way to present information about one of the features or components of the car. Each of the red dots expands when the mouse is held over it. Note that the paragraphs about regenerative braking are presented in different typefaces.

The first excerpt explains the operating principle of the feature.

The second excerpt explains the advantage to the owner.

A more traditional explanation of the feature is presented beneath the "x-ray view." It has the same two-part structure: technical explanation on the left, benefits on the right.

■ **Figure 9.5   Excerpt from a Mechanism Description**
Source: Ford, 2004a
<www.fordvehicles.com/escape hybrid/technology/>

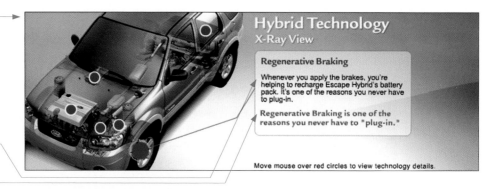

Hybrid Technology
X-Ray View

Regenerative Braking

Whenever you apply the brakes, you're helping to recharge Escape Hybrid's battery pack. It's one of the reasons you never have to plug-in.

Regenerative Braking is one of the reasons you never have to "plug-in."

Move mouse over red circles to view technology details.

Regenerative Braking

In a conventional vehicle when you brake, the energy is lost as heat. During braking in the Escape Hybrid, the electric motor captures this energy that is normally lost and sends it back to the battery pack to be stored for later use.

Regenerative Braking is one of the reasons you never have to "plug-in."

Whenever you apply the brakes, you are, in effect, recharging the battery pack. Engineers call this regenerative braking and it represents a major part of the Escape Hybrid's fuel efficiency advantage over conventional vehicles. Although Escape Hybrid will never make stop and go driving any more enjoyable, that is actually when it is at it's fuel saving best.

An important kind of description is called a specification. A typical specification consists of a graphic and a set of statistics about the device and its performance characteristics. Specifications help readers understand the capabilities of an item. You will see specifications on devices as small as transistors and as large as aircraft carriers.

■ **Figure 9.6   Excerpt from Specifications**
Source: Ford, 2004b
<www.fordvehicles.com/suvs/ escapehybrid/features/specs/>.

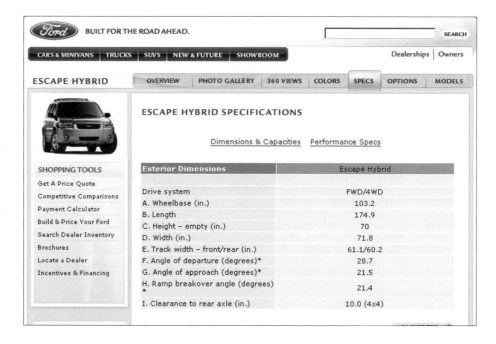

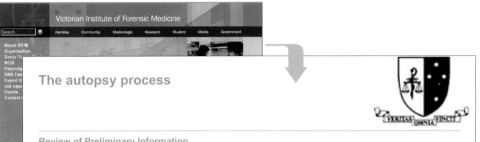

■ **Figure 9.7**
An Effective Process
Description
Source: Victorian Institute,
2005 <www.vifm.org/fp
_autopsyprocess.phtml>.

The autopsy process

Review of Preliminary Information
Prior to conducting a physical examination of the body, the initial stage of an autopsy involves the review of medical records, witness statements and/or circumstantial information and reports surrounding the death. This information allows the pathologist to construct a differential diagnosis as to what underlying pathologies including disease and injuries may be present in the body. This preliminary information allows a pathologist to focus on the important issues that may be in doubt about what happened.

Preliminary Tests
On completion of the review of background information, a number of preliminary examinations may have to take place. These may include: the collection of samples including trace evidence from the surface of the body, removal of clothing and personal possessions for secure storage or examination, and non invasive procedures such as radiographs or xrays. In some cases it may be necessary to undertake specialised imaging procedures including CT scans or MRI scans of the body. Photography, including specialised invisible radiation photography such as infrared or ultraviolet imaging, may also be required in selected cases.

External Examination
The physical examination of the body starts with a detailed external examination of the body, which is very similar to the external examination of a living patient. The eyes, ears, nose and mouth are checked together with the surface of the skin. Scars and artificial marks such as tattoos are described, and these can assist with confirmation of identity. Many internal diseases in the body are associated with changes that can appear in the skin, so that a detailed external examination of the body can be of considerable importance in focusing the subsequent internal examination.

Internal Examination
The internal examination of the body is carried out as an extended surgical technique. The examination takes place in a mortuary environment using instruments that are the same as, or derived from, normal surgical instruments. Occupational health and safety procedures need to be very carefully observed, as the pathologist and forensic scientific and technical staff may in some cases be exposed to considerable infectious hazards.

Specimen Collection
During the course of the autopsy, body fluids and tissues may be collected for specialist chemical or toxicological analysis. This is designed to indicate the presence or absence of particular drugs, poisons or chemicals. This analysis may be very significant in reconstructing how the death occurred, and in many cases, may reveal the cause of death. Depending on the types of drugs or poisons involved, it may take many weeks for the analysis of these fluids and tissues to be completed.

Tissue is also collected for histological analysis to help determine the nature and extent of disease or injury that may be relevant to the cause of death.

The Autopsy Report
On completion of all of the scientific and medical tests an autopsy report is completed which contains the results of the autopsy findings together with the results of any specialist tests that may have been undertaken. In forensic cases, this report is forwarded to the Coroner and together with witness statements, forms the majority of the information the Coroner relies upon in arriving at their legal finding with regards of the death. The Coroner is a magistrate (lawyer), not a medical practitioner, who makes the final determination as to who the deceased person was, where and when they died, how they died, and the cause of their death. The findings of the pathologists form a very important part of the Coroner's investigation of the death and the pathologist is often involved in giving evidence at any subsequent inquest.

Perhaps because visitors to this site do not need a definition of autopsy, the writer begins with the first step.

Notice that the second step is linked to the first step: the first step has to take place before the second step can be carried out. When you write any description, don't forget to explain logical relationships between steps.

Notice that most of this description is written in the passive voice. The writer is emphasizing the activities, not the person performing them. For more about passive voice, see Ch. 11, p. 236.

Note that most of the headings are noun phrases ("Internal Examination") rather than verb phrases ("Performing an Internal Examination"). In Australia, where this document was composed, more-formal noun phrases are used more than in the United States.

Note that this description contains no graphics. Although it would be possible to create a flowchart showing the steps, the writer apparently concluded that this treatment of the subject would not benefit from graphics.

Writer's Checklist

Parenthetical, Sentence, and Extended Definitions

☐ Are all necessary terms defined? (p. 178)

Are the parenthetical definitions

☐ appropriate for the audience? (p. 179)
☐ clear? (p. 179)
☐ smoothly integrated into the sentences? (p. 179)

Does each sentence definition

☐ contain a sufficiently specific category and distinguishing characteristics? (p. 179)
☐ avoid describing one particular item when a general class of items is intended? (p. 180)
☐ avoid circular definition? (p. 180)
☐ contain a noun or a noun phrase in the category? (p. 181)

☐ Are the extended definitions developed logically and clearly? (p. 181)
☐ Are the definitions placed in the location most useful to the readers? (p. 185)

Descriptions of Objects and Mechanisms

☐ Did you clearly indicate the nature and scope of the description? (p. 188)

In introducing the description, did you answer, if appropriate, the following questions:

☐ What is the item? (p. 189)
☐ What does it do? (p. 189)
☐ What is its function? (p. 189)
☐ What does it look like? (p. 189)
☐ What is its principle of operation? (p. 189)
☐ What are its principal parts? (p. 189)

☐ Did you include a graphic identifying all the principal parts? (p. 190)

In providing detailed information, did you

☐ answer, for each of the major components, the questions for introducing the description in Table 9.1? (p. 189)
☐ choose an appropriate organizing principle? (p. 190)
☐ include graphics for each of the components? (p. 191)

In concluding the description, did you

☐ summarize the major points in the part-by-part description? (p. 191)
☐ include (where appropriate) a description of the item performing its function or an attempt to motivate the reader to take action? (p. 191)

Process Descriptions

☐ Did you clearly indicate the nature and scope of the description? (p. 188)

In introducing the description, did you answer, if appropriate, the following questions:

☐ What is the process? (p. 189)
☐ What is its function? (p. 189)
☐ Where and when does the process take place? (p. 189)
☐ Who or what performs it? (p. 189)
☐ How does the process work? (p. 189)
☐ What are its principal steps? (p. 189)

☐ Did you include a graphic identifying all the principal steps? (p. 190)

In providing detailed information, did you

☐ answer, for each of the major steps, the questions for introducing a description in Table 9.1? (p. 189)
☐ discuss the steps in chronological order or other logical sequence? (p. 190)
☐ make clear the causal relationships among the steps? (p. 191)
☐ use the present tense? (p. 191)
☐ include graphics for each of the principal steps? (p. 191)

In concluding the description, did you

☐ summarize the major points in the step-by-step description? (p. 191)
☐ discuss, if appropriate, the importance or implications of the process? (p. 193)
☐ attempt (if appropriate) to motivate the reader to take action? (p. 193)

Exercises

1. Add a parenthetical definition for each italicized term in the following sentences:

   a. Reluctantly, he decided to *drop* the physics course.

   b. Last week the computer was *down*.

   c. The department is using *shareware* in its drafting course.

   d. The tire plant's managers hope they do not have to *lay off* any more employees.

   e. Please submit your assignments *electronically*.

2. Write a sentence definition for each of the following terms:

   a. catalyst

   b. MP3 player

   c. job interview

   d. Web site

   e. automatic teller machine

   f. fax machine

   g. intranet

3. Revise any of the following sentence definitions that need revision:

   a. A thermometer measures temperature.

   b. The spark plugs are the things that ignite the air-gas mixture in a cylinder.

   c. Parallel parking is where you park next to the curb.

   d. A strike is when the employees stop working.

   e. Multitasking is when you do two things at once while you're on the computer.

4. Write a 500- to 1,000-word extended definition of one of the following terms or of a term used in your field of study. If you do secondary research, cite your sources clearly and accurately (see Appendix, Part B, for documentation systems). In addition, check that the graphics are appropriate for your audience and purpose. In a brief note at the start, indicate the audience and purpose for your definition.

   a. flextime

   b. binding arbitration

   c. robotics

   d. an academic major (don't focus on any particular major; instead, define what a major is)

   e. bioengineering

   f. fetal-tissue research

5. Write a 500- to 1,000-word description of one of the following items or of a piece of equipment used in your field. Include appropriate graphics. In a note preceding the description, specify your audience and indicate the type of description (general or particular) you are writing.

   a. locking bicycle rack

   b. dead-bolt lock

   c. photocopy machine

   d. cooling tower at a nuclear power plant

   e. jet engine

   f. ammeter

   g. automobile jack

   h. camera phone

6. Write a 500- to 1,000-word description of one of the following processes or a similar process with which you are familiar. Include appropriate graphics. In a note preceding the description, specify your audience and indicate the type of description (general or particular) you are writing. If you use secondary sources, cite them properly (see Appendix, Part B, for documentation systems).

   a. how a nuclear power plant works

   b. how a food co-op works

   c. how a suspension bridge is constructed

   d. how we see

   e. how a baseball player becomes a free agent

Case 9: Describing Backcountry Touring Gear

 In This Book For more about memos, see Ch. 14, p. 352. For more about Web-site design, see Ch. 20.

Background

You are a student intern working for your Campus Recreation Department's Outdoor Program. The Outdoor Program provides educational seminars, gear rentals, special events, and adventure trips to foster an interest and involvement in outdoor recreational opportunities. Designed to appeal to novice through experienced outdoor enthusiasts, the Outdoor Program offers students a chance to participate in activities such as rock climbing, camping, backpacking, mountaineering, snowshoeing, cross-country skiing, kayaking, rafting, and surfing.

To support such a variety of outdoor activities, the Outdoor Program operates a large, four-season equipment-rental program. With campus enrollment steadily increasing, more and more students are taking advantage of the Outdoor Program's offerings. The program's Web site is currently undergoing a major upgrade to accommodate the large number of students who use the site as their primary method of learning about the program's activities and rental equipment. Your supervisor, Xavier Majic, has asked you to help develop content for the Web site.

"Cross-country skiing has really taken off in terms of popularity among our students," Xavier explains. "Unfortunately, we spend a lot of time on the phone and at the rental office explaining the differences between several types of cross-country skiing equipment. We offer cross-country equipment packages—boots, poles, and skis—for traditional touring, backcountry touring, skate skiing, telemark skiing, and randonnée skiing."

"I didn't know there were so many different types," you admit.

"That's one of the problems we're trying to address on the Outdoor Program's Web site. We're developing basic descriptions of each cross-country skiing style and its equipment. And that's where I need your help. I've created a rough draft of the backcountry touring gear in Microsoft Word. Right now, I want to focus on coming up with an effective approach. Once we decide on that, we can develop descriptions for the other cross-country skiing styles. Later, our Webmaster will create the HTML versions for our site." (See Document 9.1.)

"What would you like me to do?" you ask.

"I'd like you to revise my draft, making sure that my definitions and descriptions are clear and accurate."

"OK."

"I'd also like your recommendations on how to present this material on our Web site. I've sketched rough versions of two different approaches. The first approach is more or less designed around informative paragraphs. The other approach would use a *mouseover* effect to create text boxes that appear when a user holds the mouse cursor over relevant parts of a graphic. I'm not committed to either of them, however." (See Document 9.2.)

"A lot depends on the typical user of the site," you explain.

"I agree," Xavier says. "Our last intern conducted some research on the students who use our Web site. She developed two typical personas of our users. I'd like you to consider her research when making your revisions and recommendations." (See Document 9.3.)

Your Assignment

1. Revise Xavier's backcountry touring information (Document 9.1) so that the document uses effective definitions and descriptions. If necessary, use the Internet to research cross-country skiing vocabulary.

2. Create an effective approach to presenting the backcountry touring information based on the typical users of the Outdoor Program's Web site (Document 9.3). You may recommend one of Xavier's approaches (Document 9.2), a combination of his approaches, or something entirely different. Write Xavier a memo in which you recommend an approach and justify your decision. Attach a rough sketch of your approach.

Backcountry Touring Gear

Originally developed in Nordic countries as a method of transportation, cross-country skiing is now a popular winter recreational activity. *Cross-country* (also referred to as *Nordic*) skiing encompasses a collection of skiing styles using free-heeled (as opposed to fixed-heel boots used in Alpine skiing) ski equipment. Backcountry skiing (or touring) is one such cross-country ski style. Best defined as skiing in terrain that has not been altered by people, backcountry skiers leave the groomed trails in favor of fresh snow.

Backcountry touring gear is different from the gear you would use on trails groomed for skiing. Classic "kick-and-glide" skis designed for groomed trails are narrower, lack metal edges, and use lightweight boots—not the type of gear you would want for backcountry conditions. Below we describe the backcountry touring gear you'll want if you venture off the groomed trails.

Backcountry Skis

When choosing backcountry skis, keep six essential factors in mind: length, width, sidecut, camber, flex, and metal edges. Backcountry skis are generally shorter in length (and thus more maneuverable) than kick-and-glide, or general touring, skis. Backcountry skis are manufactured wider than general touring skis to provide better stability in soft snow. *Sidecut* refers to how much the side of your skis curve inward (thus, a short "waist" in the middle of the ski and wider at either end). A ski's sidecut as well as its metal edges determine how easy it is to "carve," or turn. *Nordic camber* refers to the high arch built into skis to allow better gliding in backcountry skiing. *Flex* determines how stiff your skis feel as you move over different types of snow.

Backcountry Poles

Sturdy, lightweight backcountry poles help you propel yourself up hills and balance while going down hills. Because backcountry skiing is often synonymous with avalanche territory, some backcountry poles convert to avalanche probes. (For more information on avalanche safety, take our Backcountry Avalanche Safety course.)

Backcountry Bindings

Backcountry bindings provide a durable, secure connection to your skis. Our rental shop stocks a binding connection system called "New Nordic Norm Backcountry" (NNN BC). This system replaces the traditional "three-pin" bindings. With NNN BC bindings, you attach your boot to your binding by clipping a short metal rod mounted in the toe of your boot to your matching ski binding (picture a door hinge mechanism).

Backcountry Boots

When skiing on flat, groomed terrain, lightweight boots are sufficient. However, the demands of backcountry skiing require you to use durable boots that provide ankle support and protection from the weather (warmth).

■ **Document 9.1**
Description of Backcountry Touring Gear

 On TechComm Web

For digital versions of case documents, click on Downloadable Case Documents on <bedfordstmartins.com/techcomm>.

■ **Document 9.2
Sketches of Two Different
Web Page Designs**

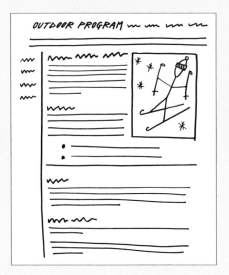 

■ **Document 9.3   Two
Personas for Users of the
Outdoor Program's Web
Site**

Jen

Jen is a 33-year-old legal secretary. She works full-time, while taking one or two evening courses a semester. After being away from school for more than a decade, she is eager to update her skills as well as participate in campus life. Jen is in good health and tries to make it to the gym for a cardio class once a week but has never participated in organized sports. Her outdoor experience is limited to an occasional day hike or an overnight car-camping trip. Jen is very interested in expanding her outdoor recreation skills and escaping the stress of her courses. However, she is intimidated by the variety of outdoor gear available and is afraid she'll embarrass herself if she asks a dumb question. She regularly uses the Web and e-mail at work and for school. Jen occasionally uses the Outdoor Program's Web site to check on upcoming seminars and adventure programs. This persona represents approximately 70 to 80 percent of users of the site.

Dean

Dean is 20 years old and goes to school full-time. He works a part-time job as a waiter at a local restaurant. Dean frequently hangs out in the Student Union, lifts weights at the campus gym, and participates in the intramural sports program with other members of his residence hall. Dean grew up playing sports and lettered in two sports in high school. Dean likes adrenaline sports such as mountain-bike racing, rock climbing, white-water rafting, snowboarding, and mountaineering. His enthusiasm for the outdoors often overshadows good judgment and safety concerns. He spends a great deal of time on the Web for entertainment and school. When looking for information, Dean looks on the Internet first. He doesn't want to deal with paper if he can help it. Dean regularly uses the Outdoor Program's Web site to register for upcoming adventure trips, learn about new programs, and reserve outdoor gear. This persona represents approximately 20 to 30 percent of users of the site.

Writing Coherent Documents

10

TECH COMM AT WORK

A securities analyst preparing a report wants to make sure his headings are clear and logically parallel with one another, so that when they appear in the table of contents, they are easy to understand and look professional. An anthropologist reporting the results of her latest dig for a journal article wants to create clear, concise lists for the methods section of the article. In fact, every writer needs to know the techniques of making documents coherent, from the paragraph level to the whole-document level. You want your technical documents to be easy to read, understand, and remember. That is, you want to make the pieces of the document hang together so that readers can move smoothly from one piece to the next or, if they prefer, find the particular piece they want.

 In This Book

For more about planning, drafting, revising, and editing a document, see Ch. 3.

A coherent document flows smoothly from one part to the next, allowing the reader to concentrate on understanding the information it contains. An incoherent document is harder to read; the reader can easily misunderstand the information or become confused, unable to determine how a particular point relates to one that precedes it.

Should you worry about coherence when you draft or when you revise and edit? Because many writers need to concentrate fully on making the information clear and accurate when they draft, they concentrate on coherence only after they have a complete draft. More-experienced writers automatically incorporate these coherence techniques into the document as they draft it. Whatever process you use, make sure the document is coherent before it gets to the reader.

REVISING THE WHOLE DOCUMENT FOR COHERENCE

In looking for problems that need fixing, most writers look for the largest, most important problems first, then work on the smaller, less important ones. That way, they don't waste time on awkward paragraphs they might eventually decide to throw out. They begin revising by considering the document as a whole (for organization, development, and content), saving the sentence-level concerns (such as grammar, punctuation, and spelling) for later.

 On TechComm Web

For more advice on revising the whole document, see Purdue University's Online Writing Lab handouts on revising. Click on Links Library for Ch. 10 on <bedfordstmartins.com/techcomm>.

Guidelines

Revising the Whole Document for Coherence

After you finish your draft, look through it to make sure the big picture is clear. Answer the following seven questions:

▶ **Have you left out anything in turning your outline into a draft?** Check the outline to make sure all the topics are included in the document itself.

▶ **Have you included all the elements your readers expect to see?** If, for instance, the readers of a report expect a transmittal letter, they might be distracted if it is missing.

▶ **Is the organization logical?** Readers should be able to understand the logical progression from one topic to the next. Check the opening passages of each section to be sure they clearly and logically connect that section to the one that precedes it.

▶ **Is the content strong?** Have you presented your claims clearly and emphatically? Have you provided sufficient—and appropriate—evidence to support them? Is your reasoning valid and persuasive?

▶ **Do you come across as reliable, honest, and helpful?** Check to see that your persona is fully professional.

▶ **Are all the elements presented consistently?** Check to see that parallel items are presented consistently. For example, are all your headings on the same level structured the same way? Also check for grammatical parallelism, particularly in lists.

▶ **Is the emphasis appropriate throughout the document?** If a major point is treated only briefly, mark it for possible expansion. If a minor topic is treated at great length, mark it for possible condensing.

 In This Book

For more about evidence and persona, see Ch. 8, pp. 159 and 165.

Perhaps the best way to check your whole document for coherence is to study the outline view of the document. Figure 10.1 shows how the outline view gives you a bird's-eye view of the text.

In addition to making sure the whole document is coherent, focus on the most important structural components of the document.

⊕ **Executive Summary**
⊕ **Introduction**
⊕ **Methods**
⊕ **Conclusions and Recommendations**
⊕ **Results** ◀
 ⊕ *Analysis of Maintenance Costs*
 ⊕ *Truck Comparisons and Test Drives*
▫ **Work Cited**
▫ **Appendices**
⊕ **Appendix A- Survey Results** ◀
 ▫ *Appendix B-IntelliChoice Side by Side Comparison*

Here the writer has set the outline view to show the first two levels of his report.

Using the outline view, it is easy to identify coherence problems:
• The results section should precede the conclusions and recommendations section.
• Appendix A and Appendix B should both be second-level headings.

■ **Figure 10.1   Studying the Coherence of a Document Using the Outline View**

WRITING COHERENT TITLES

The title is crucial because it is your first chance to define the subject and purpose of the document for your readers. Everything else that follows has to relate clearly to the title.

You might want to put off giving a final title to your document. Until you have completed the document, you cannot be sure that the subject and purpose you established during the planning stages will not change. However, you should jot down a working title before you start drafting to give you a sense of direction, then come back to revise it at the end.

An effective title is precise. For example, if you are writing a feasibility study on the subject of offering free cholesterol screening at your company, the title should contain the terms *cholesterol screening* and *feasibility.* The following title would be effective:

> Offering Free Cholesterol Screening at Thrall Associates: A Feasibility Study

If your document is an internal report discussing company business, you might not need to identify the company. In that case, the following would be clear:

> Offering Free Cholesterol Screening: A Feasibility Study

Or you could present the purpose before the subject:

> A Feasibility Study of Offering Free Cholesterol Screening

Avoid substituting general terms, such as *health screening,* for *cholesterol screening;* the more precise your terms, the more useful your readers will find the title. Readers should be able to paraphrase it in a clear, meaningful sentence. For instance, "A Feasibility Study of Offering Free Cholesterol Screening" could be paraphrased as "This document reports on whether it is feasible to offer free cholesterol screening for our employees." But notice what happens when the title is incomplete: "Free Cholesterol Screening." The reader knows that the document has something to do with free cholesterol screening, but is the writer recommending that it be instituted or discontinued? Or is the writer reporting on how well an existing program is working?

WRITING COHERENT HEADINGS

A heading is a lower-level title inside a document. A clear, informative heading is vital because it announces the subject and purpose of the discussion that follows. This information helps readers understand what they will be reading or, in some cases, whether they need to read it. For the writer, a heading eliminates the need for a sentence such as "Let us now turn to the advantages of the mandatory enrollment process."

Because headings introduce text, you should avoid back-to-back headings. In other words, avoid following one heading directly with another heading:

3. Approaches to Neighborhood Policing
   3.1 Community Policing

Instead, separate the headings with text, as in this example:

3. Approaches to Neighborhood Policing

Over the past decade, the scholarly community has concluded that community policing offers significant advantages over the traditional patrol car–based approach. However, the traditional approach has some distinct strengths. In the following discussion, we define each approach and then explain its advantages and disadvantages. Finally, we profile three departments that have successfully made the transition to community policing while preserving the major strengths of the traditional approach.

3.1 Community Policing

The text after the heading "3. Approaches to Neighborhood Policing," called an *advance organizer,* indicates the background, purpose, scope, and organization of the discussion that follows. Advance organizers improve coherence by giving readers an overview of the discussion before they encounter the details.

Guidelines

Revising Headings

▶ **Avoid long noun strings.** The following example is hard to understand:

> Production Enhancement Proposal Analysis Techniques

Add prepositions to make the title clearer:

> Techniques for Analyzing the Proposal for Enhancing Production

This version says more clearly that the writer is going to describe the techniques.

 In This Book

For more about noun strings, see Ch. 11, p. 239.

▶ **Be informative.** In the preceding example, you could add information about how many techniques will be described:

> Three Techniques for Analyzing the Proposal for Enhancing Production

You can go one step further by indicating what you wish to say about the three techniques:

> Advantages and Disadvantages of the Three Techniques for Analyzing the Proposal for Enhancing Production

Don't worry if the heading seems too long; clarity is more important than conciseness.

▶ **Use a grammatical form appropriate to your audience.** The question form works well for less-knowledgeable readers (Benson, 1985) or for nonnative speakers:

> What Are the Three Techniques for Analyzing the Proposal for Enhancing Production?

The "how-to" form is best for instructional material, such as manuals:

> How to Analyze the Proposal for Enhancing Production

 In This Book

For more about how to format headings, see Ch. 12, p. 276.

The gerund form *(-ing)* works well for processes:

Analyzing the Proposal for Enhancing Production

▶ **Avoid back-to-back headings.** Use advance organizers to separate the headings.

WRITING COHERENT LISTS

Lists add a visual dimension to the text, making it easier for readers to understand the discussion. Lists work especially well for any kind of information that can be itemized or expressed in a sequence.

For readers, the chief advantage of a list is that it makes the information easier to read and remember: the design mirrors the logic of the discussion. The key terms in the list are set off with bullets or numbers, which help readers see them easily. This arrangement enhances coherence: readers see the overall structure before they read the details.

The following discussion covers paragraphs that can be turned into lists. (For a discussion of using lists in individual sentences, see Chapter 11, page 225.)

For you as a writer, turning paragraphs into lists has four advantages:

- *It forces you to look at the big picture.* In drafting a document, it is easy to lose sight of the information outside the paragraph you are working on. By looking for opportunities to create lists as you revise, you focus on the key idea in each paragraph. This practice increases your chances of noticing that an important item is missing or that an item is unclear.

- *It forces you to examine the sequence.* As you turn some of your paragraphs into lists, you get a chance to see whether the sequence of the information is logical.

- *It forces you to create a clear lead-in.* In the lead-in, you can add a number signal that further forecasts the content and organization of the material that follows:

    Auto imports declined last year because of four major factors:

  You can add the same kind of number signal in a traditional paragraph, but you are less likely to think in these terms if you are not focusing on the list.

- *It forces you to tighten and clarify your prose.* When you make a list, look for a word, phrase, or sentence that identifies each item. Your focus shifts from weaving sentences together in a paragraph to highlighting key ideas. And once you have formatted the list, you can look at it critically and revise it until it is clear and concise.

Figure 10.2 shows a passage displayed in a paragraph form and in a list form. The authors are discussing the idea that engineers have a special social responsibility.

Paragraph format	List format
Currently, there are three conceptions of the relation between engineering as a profession and society as a whole.	Currently, there are three conceptions of the relation between engineering as a profession and society as a whole.

Paragraph format

Currently, there are three conceptions of the relation between engineering as a profession and society as a whole.

The first conception is that there is no relation. Engineering's proper regard is properly instrumental, with no constraints at all. Its task is to provide purely technical solutions to problems.

The second conception is that engineering's role is to protect. It must be concerned, as a profession, with minimizing the risk to the public. The profession is to operate on projects as presented to it, as an instrument; but the profession is to operate in accordance with important safety constraints, which are integral to its performing as a profession.

The third conception is that engineering has a positive social responsibility to try to promote the public good, not merely to perform the tasks that are set for it, and not merely to perform those tasks such that risk is minimized or avoided in performing them. Rather, engineering's purpose as a profession is to promote the social good.

List format

Currently, there are three conceptions of the relation between engineering as a profession and society as a whole.

- *There is no relation.* Engineering's proper regard is properly instrumental, with no constraints at all. Its task is to provide purely technical solutions to problems.
- *The engineer's role is to protect society.* Engineering is concerned, as a profession, with minimizing the risk to the public. The profession is to operate on projects as presented to it, as an instrument; but the profession is to operate in accordance with important safety constraints, which are integral to its performing as a profession.
- *The engineer's role is to promote social responsibility.* Engineering has a positive social responsibility to try to promote the public good, not merely to perform the tasks that are set for it, and not merely to perform those tasks such that risk is minimized or avoided in performing them. Rather, engineering's purpose as a profession is to promote the social good.

Turning the paragraph into a list forces the writer to create headings that sharply focus each bulleted entry.

By deleting the wordy topic sentences from the paragraph version, the writer saves space. The list version of the passage is almost the same length as the paragraph version, despite the indentations and extra white space.

■ **Figure 10.2   Paragraph Format and List Format**
Source: Based on Cohen & Grace, 1994.

Strategies for Intercultural Communication

Using Headings and Lists Appropriately for Multicultural Audiences

In the United States and other Western countries, writers use headings and lists frequently. In many other cultures, however, headings and lists are considered too informal for some documents.

Try to find samples written by people from the culture you are addressing to examine their use of headings and lists.

- How does the writer make the information accessible?

- How does the writer show the relationship among units? Are items grouped, highlighted, listed, set off by headings, or set in a different typeface?

- How does the writer communicate to readers the organization of the document?

- How does the writer make transitions from one subject to another?

WRITING COHERENT PARAGRAPHS

 On TechComm Web

For more about paragraphing, see Guide to Grammar and Writing. Click on Links Library for Ch. 10 on <bedfordstmartins.com/ techcomm>.

There are two kinds of paragraphs: body paragraphs and transitional paragraphs.

A *body paragraph*, the basic unit for communicating information, is a group of sentences (or sometimes a single sentence) that is complete and self-sufficient and that contributes to a larger discussion. In an effective paragraph, all the sentences clearly and directly support one main point. In addition, the whole paragraph follows logically from the material that precedes it.

A *transitional paragraph* helps readers move from one major point to another. Usually it summarizes the previous point, introduces the next point, and helps readers understand how the two are related.

The following example of a transitional paragraph appeared in a manual explaining how to write television scripts. The writer has already described six principles of writing for an episodic program, including introducing characters, pursuing the plot, and resolving the action at the end of the episode.

The first sentence contains the word *then* to signal that it introduces a summary.

The six basic principles of writing for episodic television, then, are the following:

- Reintroduce the characters.
- Make the extra characters episode-specific.
- Present that week's plot swiftly.
- Make the characters react according to their personalities.
- Resolve the plot neatly.
- Provide a denouement that hints at further developments.

The final sentence clearly indicates the relationship between what precedes it and what follows it.

But how do you put these six principles into action? The following section provides specific how-to instructions.

Structure Paragraphs Clearly

Most paragraphs consist of a topic sentence and supporting information.

The Topic Sentence   Put the point—the topic sentence—up front. The topic sentence summarizes or forecasts the main point of the paragraph. Technical communication should be clear and easy to read, not full of suspense. If a paragraph describes a test you performed, include the result in your first sentence:

The point-to-point continuity test on Cabinet 3 revealed no problems.

Then go on to explain the details. If the paragraph describes a complicated idea, start with an overview. In other words, put the "bottom line" on top:

Mitosis occurs in four stages: (1) prophase, (2) metaphase, (3) anaphase, and (4) telophase.

Notice how difficult the following paragraph is to read. The writer has structured the discussion in the same order in which she performed her calculations:

DRAFT   Our estimates are based on our generating power during eight months of the year and purchasing it the other four. Based on the 2005 purchased power rate of $0.034/KW (January through April cost data) inflating at 8 percent annually and a constant coal cost of $45 to $50, the projected 2006 savings resulting from a conversion to coal would be $225,000.

Putting the bottom line on top makes the paragraph much easier to read. In the revision, notice that the writer has added a numbered list after the topic sentence:

REVISION   The projected 2006 savings resulting from a conversion to coal are $225,000. This estimate is based on three assumptions: (1) that we will be generating power during eight months of the year and purchasing it the other four, (2) that power rates will inflate at 8 percent from the 2005 figure of $0.034/KW (January through April cost data), and (3) that coal costs will remain constant at $45 to $50.

Make sure each of your topic sentences relates clearly to the organizational pattern you are using. In a discussion of why water consumption in the United States is declining even though the population is increasing, for example, you might use a more-important-to-less-important format and start a paragraph with the following topic sentence:

The most important reason for the decline in water usage is the increasing use of water-saving devices such as low-flow showerheads and toilets.

Your next paragraph should begin with a topic sentence that continues the more-important-to-less-important organization:

Also important in the decline of water usage is the role of increasing utility rates.

The phrase "also important" suggests that increasing utility rates are important, but less important than the water-saving devices discussed in the previous paragraph. Similarly, if your first topic sentence is "First, we need to . . ." your next topic sentence should refer to the chronological pattern: "Second, we should. . . ."

The Support   The supporting information makes the topic sentence clear and convincing. Sometimes a few explanatory details provide all the support needed. At other times, however, this part of the paragraph must clarify a difficult thought or defend a controversial one.

The supporting information usually fulfills one of these five roles:

- It defines a key term or idea included in the topic sentence.
- It provides examples or illustrations of the situation described in the topic sentence.

The writer has buried the bad news in a paragraph that begins with a topic sentence that appears to suggest good news. The last sentence, too, suggests good news.

Ethics Note

Avoiding Burying Bad News in Paragraphs

The most emphatic location in a paragraph is the topic sentence, usually the first sentence in a paragraph. The second most emphatic location is the end of the paragraph. Do not bury bad news in the middle of the paragraph, hoping readers won't see it. It would be misleading to structure a paragraph like this:

> In our proposal, we stated that the project would be completed by May. In making this projection, we used the same algorithms that we have used successfully for more than 14 years. In this case, however, the projection was not realized, due to several factors beyond our control.... We have since completed the project satisfactorily and believe strongly that this missed deadline was an anomaly that is unlikely to be repeated. In fact, we have beaten every other deadline for projects this fiscal year.

A more forthcoming approach would be as follows:

> We missed our May deadline for completing the project. Although we derived this schedule using the same algorithms that we have used successfully for more than 14 years, several factors, including especially bad weather at the site, delayed the construction....
>
> However, we have since completed the project satisfactorily and believe strongly that this missed deadline was an anomaly that is unlikely to be repeated.... In fact, we have beaten every other deadline for projects this fiscal year.

Here the writer forthrightly presents the bad news in a topic sentence. Then he creates a separate paragraph with the good news.

- It identifies causes: factors that led to the situation.
- It defines effects: implications of the situation.
- It supports the claim made in the topic sentence.

Supporting information is most often developed using the basic patterns of organization discussed in Chapter 7.

Paragraph Length   How long should a paragraph be? In general, 75 to 125 words are enough for a topic sentence and four or five supporting sentences. Long paragraphs are more difficult to read than short paragraphs because they require more concentration. They also can intimidate some readers, who then skip over them.

Don't let arbitrary guidelines about length take precedence over your own analysis of the audience and purpose. You might need only one or two sentences to introduce a graphic, for example. Transitional paragraphs are also likely to be quite short. If a brief paragraph fulfills its function, let it be. Do not combine two ideas in one paragraph simply to achieve a minimum word count.

You may need to break up your discussion of one idea into two or more paragraphs. An idea that requires 200 or 300 words to develop should probably not be squeezed into one paragraph.

Guidelines

Dividing Long Paragraphs

Here are three techniques for dividing long paragraphs.

Technique	Example
Break the discussion at a logical place. The most logical place to divide this paragraph is at the introduction of the second factor. Because the paragraphs are still relatively long, this strategy works best for skilled readers.	High-tech companies have been moving their operations to the suburbs for two main reasons: cheaper, more modern space and a better labor pool. A new office complex in the suburbs will charge from one-half to two-thirds of the rent charged for the same square footage in the city. And that money goes a lot further, too. The new office complexes are bright and airy; new office space is already wired for computers; and exercise clubs, shopping centers, and even libraries are often on-site. The second major factor attracting high-tech companies to the suburbs is the availability of experienced labor. Office workers and middle managers are abundant. In addition, the engineers and executives, who tend to live in the suburbs anyway, are happy to forgo the commuting, the city wage taxes, and the noise and stress of city life.

Make the topic sentence a separate paragraph and break up the support.
 	
This revision is easier for all readers to understand because the brief paragraph at the start clearly introduces the information. In addition, each of the two main paragraphs now has a clear topic sentence.
	High-tech companies have been moving their operations to the suburbs for two main reasons: cheaper, more modern space and a better labor pool.
	    First, office space is a bargain in the suburbs. A new office complex will charge from one-half to two-thirds of the rent charged for the same square footage in the city. And that money goes a lot further, too. The new office complexes are bright and airy; new office space is already wired for computers; and exercise clubs, shopping centers, and even libraries are often on-site.
	    Second, experienced labor is plentiful. Office workers and middle managers are abundant. In addition, the engineers and executives, who tend to live in the suburbs anyway, are happy to forgo the commuting, the city wage taxes, and the noise and stress of city life.

Use a list. This is the easiest of the three versions for all readers because of the extra visual cues provided by the list format.	High-tech companies have been moving their operations to the suburbs for two main reasons: • **Cheaper, more modern space.** Office space is a bargain in the suburbs. A new office complex will charge anywhere from one-half to two-thirds of the rent charged for the same square footage in the city. And that money goes a lot further, too. The new office complexes are bright and airy; new office space is already wired for computers; and exercise clubs, shopping centers, and even libraries are often on-site. • **A better labor pool.** Office workers and middle managers are abundant. In addition, the engineers and executives, who tend to live in the suburbs anyway, are happy to forgo the commuting, the city wage taxes, and the noise and stress of city life.

Use Coherence Devices Within and Between Paragraphs

Emphasizing coherence:

Add transitional words and phrases.

Repeat key words.

Use demonstrative pronouns followed by nouns.

In a coherent paragraph, the thoughts are linked together clearly and logically. Parallel ideas are expressed in parallel grammatical constructions. Even if the paragraph already moves smoothly from sentence to sentence, however, you can emphasize the coherence by adding transitional words and phrases, repeating key words, and using demonstrative pronouns followed by nouns.

Add Transitional Words and Phrases   Transitional words and phrases help the reader understand a discussion by explicitly signaling the logical relationship between two ideas. Table 10.1 lists the most common logical relationships between two ideas and some of the common transitions that express those relationships.

In the following examples, the first version contains no transitional words or phrases. Notice how much clearer the second version is.

WEAK	Neurons are not the only kind of cells in the brain. Blood cells supply the brain with oxygen and nutrients.
IMPROVED	Neurons are not the only kind of cells in the brain. *For instance,* blood cells supply the brain with oxygen and nutrients.
WEAK	The project was originally expected to cost $300,000. The final cost was $450,000.
IMPROVED	The project was originally expected to cost $300,000. *However,* the final cost was $450,000.

■ **Table 10.1 Transitional Words and Phrases**

Relationship	*Transition*
addition	also, and, finally, first (second, etc.), furthermore, in addition, likewise, moreover, similarly
comparison	in the same way, likewise, similarly
contrast	although, but, however, in contrast, nevertheless, on the other hand, yet
illustration	for example, for instance, in other words, to illustrate
cause-effect	as a result, because, consequently, hence, so, therefore, thus
time or space	above, around, earlier, later, next, to the right (left, west, etc.), soon, then
summary or conclusion	at last, finally, in conclusion, to conclude, to summarize

WEAK	The manatee population of Florida has been stricken by an unknown disease. Marine biologists from across the nation have come to Florida to assist in manatee-disease research.
IMPROVED	The manatee population of Florida has been stricken by an unknown disease. *As a result*, marine biologists from across the nation have come to Florida to assist in manatee-disease research.

Place transitions as close as possible to the beginning of the second idea. As shown in the examples above, the link between two sentences should be near the start of the second sentence.

You should also use transitional words to maintain coherence *between* paragraphs, just as you use them to maintain coherence *within* paragraphs. The link between two paragraphs should be near the start of the second paragraph.

Repeat Key Words   Repeating key words—usually nouns—helps readers follow the discussion. In the following example, the first version could be confusing:

UNCLEAR	For months, the project leaders carefully planned their research. The cost of the work was estimated to be more than $200,000.
	What is the work: the planning or the research?
CLEAR	For months, the project leaders carefully planned their research. The cost of the research was estimated to be more than $200,000.

From a misguided desire to be interesting, some writers keep changing their important terms. *Plankton* becomes *miniature seaweed,* then *the ocean's fast food.* Avoid this kind of word game; it can confuse readers.

Of course, too much repetition can be boring. You can vary nonessential terms, as long as you don't sacrifice clarity.

SLUGGISH	The purpose of the new plan is to reduce the problems we are seeing in our accounting operations. We hope to see a reduction in the problems by early next quarter.
BETTER	The purpose of the new plan is to reduce the problems we are seeing in our accounting operations. We hope to see an improvement by early next quarter.

Use Demonstrative Pronouns Followed by Nouns   Demonstrative pronouns—*this, that, these,* and *those*—can help you maintain the coherence of a discussion by linking ideas securely. In almost all cases, demonstrative pronouns should be followed by nouns. In the following examples, notice that a demonstrative pronoun by itself can be vague and confusing.

1. In what ways does the topic sentence function as it should?

2. Identify the transitional words or phrases. How are they used effectively?

3. Identify the repeated key words. How effectively does the writer use key words?

4. Identify the demonstrative pronouns followed by nouns. How effectively does the writer use them?

 **On TechComm Web**

To e-mail responses to yourself and/or your instructor and to see suggested responses, click on Interactive Sample Documents for Ch. 10 on <bedfordstmartins .com/techcomm>.

INTERACTIVE SAMPLE DOCUMENT
Identifying the Elements of a Coherent Paragraph

The following paragraph is taken from a report published by a water company. In this paragraph, the writer is describing how he decided on a method for increasing the company's business within his particular branch. (The sentences are numbered.)

The questions in the margin ask you to think about the qualities of coherent paragraphs (as outlined on pages 210–17). E-mail your responses to yourself and/or your instructor, and see suggested responses on TechComm Web.

---

(1) We found that the best way to improve the Montana branch would be to add a storage facility to our existing supply sources. (2) Currently, we can handle the average demand on a maximum day; the storage facility will enable us to meet peaking requirements and fire-protection needs. (3) In conducting our investigation, we considered developing new supply sources with sufficient capacity to meet current and future needs. (4) This alternative was rejected, however, when our consultants (Smith and Jones) did groundwater studies that revealed that insufficient groundwater is available and that the new wells would have to be located too far apart if they were not to interfere with each other.

UNCLEAR	New screening techniques are being developed to combat viral infections. *These* are the subject of a new research effort in California.
	What is being studied in California: new screening techniques or viral infections?
CLEAR	New screening techniques are being developed to combat viral infections. *These techniques* are the subject of a new research effort in California.
UNCLEAR	The task force could not complete its study of the mine accident. *This* was the subject of a scathing editorial in the union newsletter.
	What was the subject of the editorial: the mine accident or the task force's inability to complete its study of the accident?
CLEAR	The task force failed to complete its study of the mine accident. *This failure* was the subject of a scathing editorial in the union newsletter.

Even when the context is clear, a demonstrative pronoun used without a noun might interrupt the readers' progress by referring them back to an earlier idea.

TECH TIP
How to Modify and Create Styles

As you write, you can modify and create styles to address your specific writing situation using the **Styles and Formatting** feature.

1. To modify a style, select **Styles and Formatting** from the **Format** menu or click on the **Styles and Formatting** button in the main toolbar.

   In the **Styles and Formatting** task pane, select the style you want to modify and select **Modify** from the drop-down menu that appears.

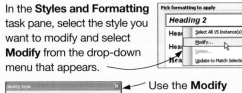

Use the **Modify Style** dialog box to make changes.

Additional formatting options for elements such as font, paragraph, and numbering are available by clicking on the **Format** button.

2. To create a new style, click on the **New Style** button in the **Styles and Formatting** task pane.

Use the **New Style** dialog box to name your new style and apply formatting to the style.

KEYWORDS: styles, create a new style

INTERRUPTIVE	The law firm advised that the company initiate proceedings. This caused the company to search for a second legal opinion.
FLUID	The law firm advised that the company initiate proceedings. *This advice* caused the company to search for a second legal opinion.

CREATING A COHERENT DESIGN

So far, this chapter has focused on making the words in your document coherent. You should also make sure the design of your document is coherent. Focus on the design of headers and footers and on the typefaces used in the document.

Using Headers and Footers to Enhance Coherence

Headers and footers appear at the tops and bottoms of pages and contain information that helps readers navigate the document. This information might include page number, chapter or section title and number, and document

 In This Book

For more about headers and footers, see Ch. 12, p. 265.

PERFORMANCE SECTION • *STRATEGIC GOAL 5: ECONOMIC PROSPERITY AND SECURITY*

FY 2004 PERFORMANCE ACCOUNTABILITY REPORT | **173**

■ **Figure 10.3   Headers and Footers Enhance Coherence**

Headers and footers help make documents coherent. The header on this page contains the appropriate section and subsection titles. The footer contains the document title and appropriate page number.

Source: U.S. Agency for International Development, 2005 <www.usaid.gov/policy/par04/performance.pdf>.

title. You can create headers and footers using your word-processing software. Figure 10.3 shows two headers and a footer in a report.

In This Book

For more about typefaces, see Ch. 12, p. 271.

Using Typefaces to Enhance Coherence

Using consistent typefaces in headings and body text helps make your document coherent. As discussed in Chapter 3, the best way to make sure you use typefaces consistently is to use styles in your word processor. Styles enable you to make the design of various elements consistent.

Styles also help you to distinguish one element from another. For instance, as you revise, you might notice that two levels of headings are not sufficiently distinct. You can easily use the styles function to change the design of one level to prevent confusion.

Writer's Checklist

Did you check the whole document to make sure that

☐ you didn't leave out anything in turning your outline into a draft? (p. 204)

☐ you have included all the elements your readers expect to see? (p. 205)

☐ the organization is logical? (p. 205)

☐ the content is strong? (p. 205)

☐ you come across as reliable, honest, and helpful? (p. 205)

☐ all the elements are presented consistently? (p. 205)

☐ the emphasis is appropriate throughout the document? (p. 205)

Did you revise the title so that it

☐ clearly refers to your audience and the purpose of your document? (p. 205)

☐ is sufficiently precise and informative? (p. 206)

Did you revise the headings to

☐ avoid long noun strings? (p. 207)

☐ be informative? (p. 207)

☐ use the question form for less knowledgeable readers? (p. 207)

☐ use the "how-to" form in instructional materials, such as manuals? (p. 207)

☐ use the gerund form (-*ing*) to suggest a process? (p. 208)
☐ avoid back-to-back headings by including an advance organizer? (p. 208)

☐ Did you look for opportunities to turn traditional paragraphs into lists? (p. 208)

Did you revise your paragraphs so that each one
☐ begins with a clear topic sentence? (p. 210)
☐ has adequate and appropriate support? (p. 211)

☐ is not too long for readers? (p. 212)
☐ uses coherence devices such as transitional words and phrases, repetition of key words, and demonstrative pronouns followed by nouns? (p. 214)

☐ Did you use headers and footers to help enhance coherence? (p. 217)
☐ Did you use consistent typefaces in the body text and headings to enhance coherence? (p. 218)

Exercises

1. Write a one-paragraph evaluation of each of the following titles. How clearly does the title indicate the subject and purpose of the document? On the basis of your analysis, rewrite each title.

   a. Recommended Forecasting Techniques for Haldane Company

   b. A Study of Digital Cameras

   c. Agriculture in the West: A 10-Year View

2. Write a one-paragraph evaluation of each of the following headings. How clearly does the heading indicate the subject of the text that will follow? On the basis of your analysis, rewrite each heading to make it clearer and more informative. Invent any necessary details.

   a. Multigroup Processing Technique Review Board Report Findings

   b. The Great Depression of 1929

   c. Intensive-Care Nursing

3. Revise the following passage (based on Snyder, 1993) using a list format. The subject is *bioremediation*: the process of using microorganisms to restore natural environmental conditions.

   Scientists are now working on several new research areas. One area involves using microorganisms to make some compounds less dangerous to the environment. Although coal may be our most plentiful fossil fuel, most of the nation's vast Eastern reserve cannot meet air-pollution standards because it emits too much sulfur when it is burned. The problem is that the aromatic compound dibenzothiothene (DBT) attaches itself to hydrocarbon molecules, producing sulfur dioxide. But the Chicago-based Institute of Gas Technology last year patented a bacterial strain that consumes the DBT (at least 90 percent, in recent lab trials) while leaving the hydrocarbon molecules intact.

   A second research area is the genetic engineering of microbes in an attempt to reduce the need for toxic chemicals. In 1991, the EPA approved the first genetically engineered pesticide. Called Cellcap, it incorporates a gene from one microbe that produces a toxin deadly to potato beetles and corn borers into a thick-skinned microbe that is hardier. Even then, the engineered bacteria are dead when applied to the crops.

   A third research area is the use of microorganisms to attack stubborn metals and radioactive waste. Microbes have been used for decades to concentrate copper and nickel in low-grade ores. Now researchers are exploiting the fact that if certain bacteria are given special foods, they excrete enzymes that break down metals and minerals. For example, researchers at the U.S. Geological Survey found that two types of bacteria turn uranium from its usual form—one that easily dissolves in water— into another one that turns to a solid that can be easily removed from water. They are now working on doing the same for other radioactive waste.

4. Provide a topic sentence for each of the following paragraphs:

   a. _____. The goal of the Web Privacy Project is to make it simple for users to learn the privacy practices of a Web site and thereby decide whether to visit the site. Site owners will electronically "define" their privacy practices according to a set of specifications. Users will enter their own preferences through settings on their browsers. When a user attempts to visit a site, the browser will read the site's practices. If those practices match the user's preferences, the user will seamlessly enter the site. However, if the site's practices do not match the user's preferences, the user will be asked whether he or she wishes to visit the site.

b. _____. The reason for this difference is that a larger percentage of engineers working in small firms may be expected to hold high-level positions. In firms with fewer than 20 engineers, for example, the median income was $62,200. In firms of 20 to 200 engineers, the median income was $60,345. For the largest firms, the median was $58,600.

5. The following paragraph was written by the contractor for a nuclear power plant. The audience is a regulator at the Nuclear Regulatory Commission (NRC), and the purpose of the paragraph is to convince the regulator to waive one of the regulations. In this paragraph, transitional words and phrases have been removed. Add an appropriate transition in each blank space. Where necessary, add punctuation.

As you know, the current regulation requires the use of conduit for all cable extending more than 18 inches from the cable tray to the piece of equipment. _____ conduit is becoming increasingly expensive: up 17 percent in the last year alone.

_____ we would like to determine whether the NRC would grant us any flexibility in its conduit regulations. Could we _____ run cable without conduit for lengths up to 3 feet in low-risk situations such as wall-mounted cable or low-traffic areas? We realize _____ that conduit will always remain necessary in high-risk situations. The cable specifications for the Unit Two report to the NRC are due in less than two months; _____ we would appreciate a quick reply to our request, because this matter will seriously affect our materials budget.

6. In each of the following exercises, the second sentence begins with a demonstrative pronoun. Add a noun after the demonstrative to enhance coherence.

a. The Zoning Commission has scheduled an open hearing for March 14. This _____ will enable concerned citizens to voice their opinions on the proposed construction.

b. The university has increased the number of parking spaces, instituted a shuttle system, and increased parking fees. These _____ are expected to ease the parking problems.

c. The president's decision to limit federal support for stem-cell research was a shock to the U.S. biomedical research community. This _____ is seen as instrumental in the growth of the European biomedical research community.

Case 10: Writing Guidelines About Coherence

 On TechComm Web   For digital versions of case documents, click on Downloadable Case Documents on <bedfordstmartins.com/techcomm>.

Background
You are a public-information officer recently hired by the Agency for Healthcare Research and Quality (AHRQ). One of your responsibilities is to make sure that your agency's public information on the Web is clear and accurate. Your supervisor, Paloma Martinez, has asked you to write a set of guidelines for physicians and other researchers who write the articles you put on your site. You ask her why she thinks they need guidelines. "Their writing is factually correct," Paloma replies, "but because they are taking excerpts from longer, more scientific studies, their documents can be choppy. They need to be smoothed out."

"Do you have examples, both good and bad?" you ask.

Paloma directs you to two AHRQ Focus on Research fact sheets highlighting AHRQ research projects and findings. "This is a good sample of how to write to the general reader," she tells you, pointing at the HIV Disease fact sheet (Document 10.1). "This other one just doesn't seem to flow smoothly." (See Document 10.2.)

AHRQ Focus on Research: HIV Disease

Scope of the Problem

About 40,000 Americans were infected with HIV in 2000. Despite progress in treating HIV disease, the costs are high—$18,300 per year for each patient—and disparities in mortality and care of HIV patients remain:

- Four of every 10 HIV patients are black. Nearly 1 in 5 is Hispanic.

- Blacks are over 1.5 times more likely than whites to die from HIV/AIDS.

- More than $7 billion is spent each year by Medicaid, Medicare, the Department of Veterans Affairs, and the Ryan White CARE Act to treat people with HIV disease.

- Around 44 percent of HIV patients depend on Medicaid, or Medicaid combined with Medicare, to pay for HIV treatment. Six percent depend on Medicare alone.

- One in 5 HIV patients is uninsured.

Background

The Agency for Healthcare Research and Quality (AHRQ) supports research on improving the quality of health care, reducing cost, enhancing patient safety, and broadening access to and use of essential services. Part of AHRQ's goal in studying HIV is to learn more about access to health care for people living with the disease as well as the benefits and risks of new treatments.

AHRQ's mission in examining what works and what does not work in health care includes not only translating research findings into better patient care but also providing public policymakers and other health care leaders with information needed in making critical health care decisions. By disseminating the results of its research on HIV, AHRQ aims to ensure that health care needs of the diverse populations with HIV are effectively met.

Impact of AHRQ Research

AHRQ research informs the health care system about costs, access, and outcomes of different approaches to HIV care. The contributions of two major research studies, HIV Cost and Services Utilization Study (HCSUS) and Comprehensive Health Enhancement Support System (CHESS), are discussed below.

HIV Cost and Services Utilization Study (HCSUS)

As the first major research effort to collect information on a nationally representative sample of HIV patients, HCSUS examined many aspects of care and quality of life for HIV patients. These aspects include access and costs of care, use of services, unmet needs for medical and nonmedical services, social support, satisfaction with medical care, and knowledge of HIV therapies. The following two findings from HCSUS have informed the health care system:

- People with HIV who have case managers to help them obtain and coordinate care are more likely to be meeting their needs for income assistance, home care, and emotional counseling. HIV patients with case managers are also 1.5 times more likely than those without this support to be following at least two HIV drug regimens.

- Blacks are 65 percent less likely than whites to receive new antiretroviral drug therapies even when severity levels of HIV disease are similar.

Comprehensive Health Enhancement Support System (CHESS)

CHESS is a computer-based system developed with AHRQ support that gives people with HIV access to information, expert advice, and support from other patients. Using CHESS not only helps HIV patients keep track of their condition and alert their doctors when they are having problems, but it also has helped lower their average treatment costs by $400 a month.

Current Projects

AHRQ is currently funding two major projects:

- *HIV Research Network.* AHRQ and three other agencies in the Department of Health and Human Services are sponsors of this network that collects information on persons with HIV disease from providers who specialize in HIV care. The purpose of the data is to provide policymakers and others with timely information about the cost, quality, and access to care for persons with HIV.

- *Medication Errors in HIV Patients.* Researchers at the University of Illinois at Chicago are designing and testing a computerized system that integrates genotype resistance test results with patients' medication data. The goal is to reduce antiretroviral prescribing errors and improve doctors' selection of drugs.

■ **Document 10.1   HIV Disease Fact Sheet**

Source: Based on Agency for Healthcare Research and Quality, March 2002 <www.ahrq.gov/news/focus/fochiv.htm>.

AHRQ Focus on Research: Health Care for Women

In 1900, the leading causes of death among U.S. women included infectious diseases and complications of pregnancy and childbirth. Today, other health problems and chronic conditions face women. Heart disease is the number one killer of women in the United States. Approximately 185,000 new cases of breast cancer are diagnosed among U.S. women each year, and nearly 45,000 women die from the disease. Each year, about 600,000 women have a hysterectomy. By age 60, more than one-third of U.S. women have had a hysterectomy. Costs associated with hysterectomy are estimated at $5 billion per year. An estimated 4 million women a year are victims of domestic violence.

Finally, by age 65, half of all women have two or more chronic diseases. These illnesses occur most often in minority and low-income women.

AHRQ Research

The Agency for Healthcare Research and Quality (AHRQ) supports research on all aspects of women's health care, including quality, access, cost, and outcomes. A priority is given to identify and reduce disparities in the health care of minority women, address the health needs of women living in rural areas, and care for women with chronic illness and disabilities.

This important information is brought to the attention of policymakers, health care providers, and consumers who can make a difference in the quality of health care women receive. This agency serves as a catalyst for change by promoting the results of research findings and incorporating those findings into improvements in the delivery and financing of health care.

Impact

AHRQ funded the development of two software tools, now standard features on hospital electrocardiograph machines, that have improved diagnostic accuracy and dramatically increased the timely use of "clot-busting" medications in women having heart attack. Women treated in emergency rooms (ERs) are less likely to receive life-saving medication for heart attack.

Older black women are least likely to be referred for cardiac catheterization. A survey of physician referral practices found that blacks and women, particularly older black women, were much less likely to be referred for cardiac catheterization than whites and men. This stimulated new research to examine why these disparities in health care occur and to evaluate interventions to reduce them.

Poor and minority women have fewer mammograms than other women. AHRQ-funded researchers have used less traditional approaches, such as providing information through churches, to increase mammography screenings. Over the past two decades, AHRQ has been a co-sponsor of research that supported mobile mammography screening vans. This intervention has also increased access to mammography for poor and minority women.

Outpatient mastectomies have increased over the last decade. Several key factors influence whether a woman gets a complete mastectomy in the hospital or in an outpatient setting: the State where she lives and who is paying for it. According to an AHRQ study, women in New York were more than twice as likely, and in Colorado nearly nine times as likely, as women in New Jersey to have an outpatient complete mastectomy.

Most patients are satisfied with the results of hysterectomy. According to a Maryland study, 96 percent of women interviewed at 1 and 2 years after hysterectomy surgery said the problems or symptoms they experienced before the surgery were completely or mostly resolved.

Fibroid tumors are the most common reason for hysterectomy for women. AHRQ studies have found that black women at any age who have uterine fibroids are more likely to have them surgically removed than are white or Hispanic women with fibroids. To date, only limited evidence shows that drugs and other nonsurgical treatments are effective in avoiding or postponing the need for a hysterectomy.

Initiatives

Clinical preventive services are the focus of the U.S. Preventive Services Task Force (USPSTF), an independent panel of experts in primary care and prevention whose work is supported by AHRQ. They are updating its recommendations for preventive interventions on many conditions affecting women. For example, the USPSTF recently recommended screening mammography, with or without clinical breast examination, every 1 to 2 years for women ages 40 or older. Second, heart disease is the subject of an unprecedented long-term public-private sector collaboration to clarify which diagnostic and therapeutic interventions are most effective for women, as well as evaluate strategies to improve outcomes for older women. Finally, domestic violence is the second leading cause of death among women of child bearing age. A new 5-year effort supported by AHRQ will assess and compare health care intervention models for screening and treatment of domestic violence victims.

■ **Document 10.2   Health Care for Women Fact Sheet**

Source: Based on Agency for Healthcare Research and Quality, March 2002 <www.ahrq.gov/news/focus/focwomen.htm>.

Your Assignment

1. Study the two fact sheets, noting the different techniques the writer used to achieve coherence in Document 10.1 and the areas that could be improved in Document 10.2. Focus on the titles, the headings, and the paragraphs. Write a brief set of guidelines using excerpts from these samples to illustrate your advice.

2. Using your guidelines, revise Document 10.2.

11

Writing Effective Sentences

People read technical communication to learn how to carry out a task, to keep abreast of developments, or to gather information. In other words, they read it to get a job done. To help them, make your sentences clear, concise, and easy to understand.

STRUCTURING EFFECTIVE SENTENCES

Good technical communication consists of clear, correct, and graceful sentences that convey information without calling attention to themselves. This section consists of seven principles for structuring effective sentences.

Use Lists

Many sentences in technical communication are long and complicated:

> We recommend that more work on heat-exchanger performance be done with a larger variety of different fuels at the same temperature, with similar fuels at different temperatures, and with special fuels such as diesel fuel and shale-oil-derived fuels.

Here readers cannot concentrate fully on the information because they are trying to remember all the "with" phrases following "done." If they could *see* how many phrases they had to remember, their job would be easier:

> We recommend that more work on heat-exchanger performance be done
>
> - with a larger variety of different fuels at the same temperature
> - with similar fuels at different temperatures
> - with special fuels such as diesel fuel and shale-oil-derived fuels

In this version, the arrangement of the words on the page reinforces the meaning. The bullets direct the reader's eyes to three items in a series, and the fact that each item begins at the same left margin helps, too.

To structure effective sentences:

- Use lists.
- Emphasize new and important information.
- Choose an appropriate sentence length.
- Focus on the "real" subject.
- Focus on the "real" verb.
- Use parallel structures.
- Use modifiers effectively.

If you don't have enough space to list the items vertically, or if you are not permitted to do so, number the items within the sentence:

> We recommend that more work on heat-exchanger performance be done (1) with a larger variety of different fuels at the same temperature, (2) with similar fuels at different temperatures, and (3) with special fuels such as diesel fuel and shale-oil-derived fuels.

Guidelines

Creating Effective Lists

▶ **Set off each listed item with a number, a letter, or a symbol (usually a bullet).**

— Use numbers to suggest sequence (as in the steps in a set of instructions) or priority (the first item being the most important). Using numbers helps readers see the total number of items in a list (as in the "Seven Warning Signals of Cancer" from the American Cancer Society). For sublists, use lowercase letters:

1. Item
   a. subitem
   b. subitem

2. Item
   a. subitem
   b. subitem

— Use bullets to avoid sequence or priority, such as for lists of people (everyone except number 1 gets offended). For sublists, use dashes.

- Item
  – subitem
  – subitem

— Use an open (unshaded) box (□) for checklists.

 In This Book

For more about designing checklists, see Ch. 13, p. 320.

▶ **Break up long lists.** Most people can remember only 5 to 9 items easily; break up lists of 10 or more items.

Original list	*Revised list*
Tool kit:	*Tool kit:*
• handsaw	• Saws
• coping saw	– handsaw
• hacksaw	– coping saw
• compass saw	– hacksaw
• adjustable wrench	– compass saw
• box wrench	• Wrenches
• Stillson wrench	– adjustable wrench
• socket wrench	– box wrench
• open-end wrench	– Stillson wrench
• Allen wrench	– socket wrench
	– open-end wrench
	– Allen wrench

▶ **Present the items in a parallel structure.** In the parallel list below, each item starts with a verb phrase.

Nonparallel	Parallel
Here is the sequence we plan to follow:	Here is the sequence we plan to follow:
1. construction of the preliminary proposal	1. write the preliminary proposal
2. do library research	2. do library research
3. interview with the Bemco vice president	3. interview the Bemco vice president
4. first draft	4. write the first draft
5. revision of the first draft	5. revise the first draft
6. after we get your approval, preparing the final draft	6. prepare the final draft, after we get your approval

 In This Book

For more about parallelism, see p. 232.

▶ **Structure and punctuate the lead-in correctly.** Although standards vary from organization to organization, the most common lead-in consists of a grammatically complete clause followed by a colon, as shown in the following examples:

Following are the three main assets:

The three main assets are as follows:

The three main assets are the following:

If you cannot use a grammatically complete lead-in, use a dash or no punctuation at all:

The committee found that the employee
- did not cause the accident
- acted properly immediately after the accident
- reported the accident properly

▶ **Punctuate the list correctly.** Because rules for punctuating lists vary, you should find out whether people in your organization have a preference. If not, punctuate lists as follows:

—If the items are phrases, use a lowercase letter at the start. Do not use a period or a comma at the end. The white space beneath the last item indicates the end of the list.

The new facility will offer three advantages:
- lower leasing costs
- shorter commuting distance
- larger pool of potential workers

—If the items are complete sentences, use an uppercase letter at the start and a period at the end.

The new facility will offer three advantages:
- The leasing costs will be lower.
- The commuting distance for most employees will be shorter.
- The pool of potential workers will be larger.

—If the items are phrases followed by complete sentences, use an initial upper-case letter and a final period. Begin the complete sentences with an uppercase letter and end them with a period. Use italics to emphasize the main idea in each bullet point.

The new facility will offer three advantages:
- *Lower leasing costs.* The lease will cost $1,800 per month; currently we pay $2,300.
- *Shorter commuting distance.* Our workers' average commute of 18 minutes would drop to 14 minutes.
- *Larger pool of potential workers.* In the past decade, the population has shifted westward to the area near the new facility. We would increase our potential workforce in both the semiskilled and managerial categories.

—If the list consists of two kinds of items—phrases and complete sentences— punctuate both with uppercase letters and periods.

The new facility will offer three advantages:
- Lower leasing costs.
- Shorter commuting distance. Our workers' average commute of 18 minutes would drop to 14 minutes.
- Larger pool of potential workers. In the last decade, the population has shifted westward to the area near the new facility. We would increase our potential workforce in both the semiskilled and managerial categories.

In most lists, the second and subsequent lines, called *turnovers,* align under the first letter of the first line, highlighting the bullet or number to the left of the text. This *hanging indentation* helps the reader see and understand the organization of the passage.

Emphasize New and Important Information

Sentences are often easier to understand and more emphatic if new information appears at the end. For instance, if your company has labor problems and you want to describe the possible results, structure the sentence like this:

Because of the labor problems, we anticipate a three-week delay.

In this case, the three-week delay *is the new information.*

If your readers already expect a three-week delay but don't know the reason for it, reverse the structure:

We anticipate the three-week delay in production because of labor problems.

Here, labor problems *is the new and important information.*

Try not to end the sentence with qualifying information that blunts the impact of the new information.

| WEAK | The joint could fail under special circumstances. |
| IMPROVED | Under special circumstances, the joint could fail. |

Put new or difficult terms at the end of the sentence.

| WEAK | You use a wired glove to point to objects. |
| IMPROVED | To point to objects, you use a wired glove. |

Choose an Appropriate Sentence Length

Sometimes sentence length affects the quality of the writing. In general, an average of 15 to 20 words is effective for most technical communication. A series of 10-word sentences would be choppy. A series of 35-word sentences would probably be too demanding. And a succession of sentences of approximately the same length would be monotonous.

In revising a draft, use your software to compute the average sentence length of a representative passage.

Avoid Overly Long Sentences   How long is too long? There is no simple answer, because ease of reading depends on the vocabulary, sentence structure, and sentence length; the reader's motivation and knowledge of the topic; and the purpose of the communication.

Often a draft will include sentences such as the following:

> The construction of the new facility is scheduled to begin in March, but it might be delayed by one or even two months by winter weather conditions, which can make it impossible or nearly impossible to begin excavating the foundation.

To make this difficult 40-word sentence easier to read, divide it into two sentences:

> The construction of the new facility is scheduled to begin in March. However, construction might be delayed until April or even May by winter weather conditions, which can make it impossible or nearly impossible to begin excavating the foundation.

As discussed in the Guidelines box on page 226, sometimes an overly long sentence can be fixed by creating a list.

Avoid Overly Short Sentences   Just as sentences can be too long, they can also be too short and choppy, as in the following example:

TECH TIP

How to Create Bulleted and Numbered Lists

To create lists, click on the **Numbering** or **Bullets** button or apply a list style using the **Style and Formatting** task pane.

Highlight the text you wish to include in a list, then click on the **Numbering** or **Bullets** button in the main toolbar.

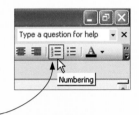

You can modify, format, and customize your list by using the **Bullets and Numbering** dialog box in the **Format** menu.

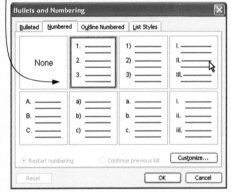

If you wish to apply the same list style consistently throughout your document and make it easy to modify the style, apply a list style to highlighted text by using the **Styles and Formatting** task pane.

KEYWORDS: lists, bullets, numbering

On TechComm Web

For more about varying sentence length, search for "sentence variety" in Guide to Grammar & Writing. Click on Links Library for Ch. 11 on <bedfordstmartins .com/techcomm>.

Customarily, environmental cleanups are conducted on a "time-and-materials" (T&M) basis. Using the T&M basis, the contractor performs the work. Then the contractor bills for the hours worked and the cost of equipment and materials used during the work. With the T&M approach, spending for environmental cleanups by private and government entities has been difficult to contain. Also, actual contamination reduction has been slow.

The problem here is that the sentences are choppy and contain too little information. In cases like this, the best way to revise is to combine sentences:

Customarily, environmental cleanups are conducted on a "time-and-materials" (T&M) basis: the contractor performs the work, then bills for the hours worked and the cost of equipment and materials. With the T&M approach, spending for environmental cleanups by private and government entities has been difficult to contain, and contamination reduction has been slow.

Another problem with excessively short sentences is that they needlessly repeat key terms. Again, consider combining sentences:

SLUGGISH	I have experience working with various microprocessor-based systems. Some of these microprocessor-based systems include the T90, RCA 9600, and AIM 7600.
BETTER	I have experience working with various microprocessor-based systems, including the T90, RCA 9600, and AIM 7600.

Focus on the "Real" Subject

 On TechComm Web

For more about using "real" subjects, see the e-handout on revising prose from the Writing Center @ Rensselaer. Click on Links Library for Ch. 11 on <bedfordsmartins.com/ techcomm>.

The conceptual, or "real," subject of the sentence should also be the grammatical subject. Don't disguise or bury the real subject in a prepositional phrase following a weak grammatical subject. In the following examples, the weak subjects disguise the real subjects (the grammatical subjects are italicized).

WEAK	The *use* of this method would eliminate the problem of motor damage.
STRONG	This *method* would eliminate the problem of motor damage.

WEAK	The *presence* of a six-membered lactone ring was detected.
STRONG	A six-membered lactone *ring* was detected.

Another way to make the subjects of sentences prominent is to reduce the number of grammatical expletives. *Expletives* are words that serve a grammatical function but have no meaning. The most common expletives are *it is*, *there is*, and *there are*, along with related phrases.

WEAK	There is no alternative for us except to withdraw the product.
STRONG	We have no alternative except to withdraw the product.

WEAK	It is hoped that testing the evaluation copies of the software will help us make this decision.
STRONG	We hope that testing the evaluation copies of the software will help us make this decision.

The second example uses the expletive *it is* with the passive voice.

Expletives are not errors. Rather, they are conversational expressions that can clarify meaning by emphasizing the information that follows them.

In This Book

For more about using the passive voice, see p. 236.

WITH THE EXPLETIVE	It is hard to say whether the recession will last more than a few months.
WITHOUT THE EXPLETIVE	Whether the recession will last more than a few months is hard to say.

The second version is harder to understand because the reader has to remember a long subject—"Whether the recession will last more than a few months"—before getting to the verb—"is." However, the sentence could also be revised in other ways to make it easier to understand and to eliminate the expletive.

I don't know whether the recession will last more than a few months.

Nobody knows whether the recession will last more than a few months.

Use the find function of your word processor to locate both weak subjects (usually they precede the word *of*) and expletives (search for *it is, there is,* and *there are*).

In This Book

For more about using the find and replace feature, see p. 41.

Focus on the "Real" Verb

A "real" verb, like a "real" subject, should stand out in every sentence. A common problem in technical communication is the inappropriate use of a *nominalized* verb—a verb that has been changed into a noun, then coupled with a weaker verb. *To install* becomes *to effect an installation; to analyze* becomes *to conduct an analysis.* Notice how nominalizing the verbs make the following sentences both awkward and unnecessarily long (the nominalized verbs are italicized).

WEAK	Each *preparation* of the solution is done twice.
STRONG	Each solution is prepared twice.

WEAK	*Consideration* should be given to an acquisition of the properties.
STRONG	We should consider acquiring the properties.

Like expletives, nominalizations are not errors. In fact, many common nouns are nominalizations—*maintenance, requirement,* and *analysis,* for example. In addition, nominalizations often effectively summarize an idea from a previous sentence (in italics in the following example).

 **On TechComm Web**

For interactive exercises on parallelism and other topics discussed in this chapter, click on Re:Writing, then Exercise Central on <bedfordstmartins.com/techcomm>.

The new *legislation* could delay our *entry* into the HDTV market. This *delay* could cost us millions.

Some software programs search for common nominalizations. With any word processor, however, you can identify most of them by searching for character strings such as *tion, ment, sis, ence, ing,* and *ance,* as well as the word *of.*

Use Parallel Structures

A sentence is parallel if its coordinate elements follow the same grammatical form. For example, all the clauses are either passive or active, all the verbs are either infinitives or participles, and so on. A recognizable pattern makes a sentence easier for the reader to follow. For example, the verbs in the following sentence are nonparallel because they do not use the same verb form.

NONPARALLEL	Our present system is costing us profits and reduces our productivity.
PARALLEL	Our present system is costing us profits and reducing our productivity.
NONPARALLEL	The compositor should follow the printed directions; do not change the originator's work.
PARALLEL	The compositor should follow the printed directions and should not change the originator's work.

When using parallel constructions, make sure that parallel items in a series do not overlap, causing confusion or even changing the meaning of the sentence:

CONFUSING	The speakers will include partners of law firms, businesspeople, and civic leaders.
	"Partners" appears to apply to "businesspeople" and "civic leaders," as well as to law firms. The revision solves the problem by rearranging the items so that "partners" can apply only to "law firms."
CLEAR	The speakers will include businesspeople, civic leaders, and partners of law firms.
CONFUSING	We need to buy more lumber, hardware, tools, and hire the subcontractors.
	The writer has linked two ideas inappropriately. The first idea is that we need to buy three things: lumber, hardware, and tools. The second is that we need to hire the subcontractors. Hiring is not in the same category as the items to buy.
CLEAR	We need to buy more lumber, hardware, and tools, and we need to hire the subcontractors.

Use Modifiers Effectively

Modifiers are words, phrases, and clauses that describe other elements in the sentence. To make your meaning clear, you must indicate whether a modifier provides necessary information about the word or phrase it refers to (its *referent*) or whether it simply provides additional information. You must also clearly identify the referent.

Distinguish Between Restrictive and Nonrestrictive Modifiers   As the term implies, a *restrictive modifier* restricts the meaning of its referent: it provides information that the reader needs to identify the referent and is, therefore, crucial to understanding the sentence. Notice that restrictive modifiers—italicized in the following examples—are not set off by commas:

> The aircraft *used in the exhibitions* are slightly modified.
>
> *The phrase "used in the exhibitions" identifies which aircraft.*
>
> Please disregard the notice *you recently received from us.*
>
> *The phrase "you recently received from us" identifies which notice.*

In most cases, the restrictive modifier doesn't require a relative pronoun, such as *that* or *which*. If you choose to use a pronoun, however, use *that* (*who* or *whom* when referring to a person):

> The aircraft *that* are used in the exhibits are slightly modified.

A *nonrestrictive modifier* does not restrict the meaning of its referent: the reader does not need the information to identify the referent. If you omit the nonrestrictive modifier, the sentence retains its primary meaning.

> The Hubble telescope, *intended to answer fundamental questions about the origin of the universe,* was last repaired in 2002.

If you use a relative pronoun, choose *which* (*who* or *whom* when referring to a person). Be sure to use commas to separate a nonrestrictive modifier from the rest of the sentence.

> When you arrive, go to the Registration Area, *which is located on the second floor.*

Avoid Misplaced Modifiers   The placement of the modifier often determines the meaning of the sentence, as the placement of *only* illustrates in the following sentences.

> *Only* Turner received a cost-of-living increase last year.
>
> *Meaning: Nobody else received one.*
>
> Turner received *only* a cost-of-living increase last year.
>
> *Meaning: He didn't receive a merit increase.*

Turner received a cost-of-living increase *only* last year.

Meaning: He received a cost-of-living increase as recently as last year.

Turner received a cost-of-living increase last year *only*.

Meaning: He received a cost-of-living increase in no other year.

Misplaced modifiers—those that appear to modify the wrong referent—are a common problem. Usually, the best solution is to place the modifier as close as possible to its intended referent.

MISPLACED   The subject of the meeting is the future of geothermal energy *in the downtown Webster Hotel.*

CORRECT   The subject of the meeting *in the downtown Webster Hotel* is the future of geothermal energy.

A *squinting modifier* falls ambiguously between two possible referents, so the reader cannot tell which one is being modified:

UNCLEAR   We decided *immediately* to purchase the new system.

               Did we decide immediately, or did we decide to make the purchase immediately?

CLEAR   We *immediately* decided to purchase the new system.

CLEAR   We decided to purchase the new system *immediately*.

A subtle form of misplaced modification can occur with correlative constructions, such as *either . . . or, neither . . . nor,* and *not only . . . but also.*

NONPARALLEL   The new refrigerant not only decreases energy costs but also spoilage losses.

PARALLEL   The new refrigerant decreases not only energy costs but also spoilage losses.

Here, "decreases" applies to both "energy costs" and "spoilage losses." Therefore, the first half of the correlative construction should follow "decreases." Note that if a sentence contains two different verbs, the first half of the correlative construction should precede the verb:

The new refrigerant not only decreases energy costs but also reduces spoilage losses.

Avoid Dangling Modifiers   A dangling modifier has no referent in the sentence and can therefore be unclear:

DANGLING   Trying to solve the problem, the instructions seemed unclear.

This sentence says that the instructions are trying to solve the problem. To correct the dangling modifier, rewrite the sentence, adding the clarifying information either within the modifier or next to it:

| CORRECT | As I was trying to solve the problem, the instructions seemed unclear. |
| CORRECT | Trying to solve the problem, I thought the instructions seemed unclear. |

Sometimes you can correct a dangling modifier by switching from *the indicative mood* (a statement of fact) to the *imperative mood* (a request or command):

| DANGLING | To initiate the procedure, the Begin button should be pushed. |
| CORRECT | To initiate the procedure, push the Begin button. |

CHOOSING THE RIGHT WORDS AND PHRASES

Choosing the right words and phrases:

Select an appropriate level of formality.

Be clear and specific.

Be concise.

Use inoffensive language.

The following section discusses four principles that will help you use the right words and phrases in the right places.

Select an Appropriate Level of Formality

Although no standard definitions of levels of formality exist, most experts would agree that there are three levels:

INFORMAL	The Acorn 560 is a real screamer. With 3.8GHz of pure computing power, it slashes through even the thickest spreadsheets before you can say 2 + 2 = 4.
MODERATELY FORMAL	With its 3.8GHz microprocessor, the Acorn 560 can handle even the most complicated spreadsheets quickly.
HIGHLY FORMAL	With a 3.8GHz microprocessor, the Acorn 560 is a high-speed personal computer designed for computation-intensive applications such as large spreadsheets.

Technical communication usually requires a moderately or highly formal style.

To achieve the appropriate level and tone, think about your audience, your subject, and your purpose:

- *Audience.* You would write more formally to a group of retired executives than to a group of college students. You would likewise write more formally to the company vice president or to people from most other cultures than to your subordinates.

- *Subject.* You would write more formally about a serious subject—safety regulations or important projects—than about plans for an office party.

- *Purpose.* You would write more formally in a report to shareholders than in a company newsletter. Instructions, however, tend to be relatively informal, often using the second person, contractions, and the imperative mood (see Chapter 19).

 In This Book

For more about writing to a multicultural audience, see Ch. 5, p. 78.

In general, it is better to err on the side of formality. Avoid an informal style in any writing you do at the office for two reasons:

- *Informal writing tends to be imprecise.* In the example "The Acorn 560 is a real screamer," what exactly is a *screamer*?
- *Informal writing can be embarrassing.* If your boss spots your e-mail to a colleague, you might wish it didn't begin, "What up, loser?"

Be Clear and Specific

Follow these seven guidelines to make your writing clear and specific:

- Use the active voice and the passive voice appropriately.
- Be specific.
- Avoid unnecessary jargon.
- Use positive constructions.
- Avoid long noun strings.
- Avoid clichés.
- Avoid euphemisms.

 On TechComm Web

For more about choosing an appropriate voice, see "The Passive Engineer" by Helen Moody. Click on Links Library for Ch. 11 on <bedfordstmartins.com/techcomm>.

Use the Active and Passive Voice Appropriately In a sentence using the active voice, the subject performs the action expressed by the verb: the "doer" of the action is the grammatical subject. In a sentence using the passive voice, the subject receives the action. Compare the following examples (the subjects are italicized):

ACTIVE	*Dave Brushaw* drove the launch vehicle.
PASSIVE	The launch *vehicle* was driven by Dave Brushaw.

In most cases, the active voice works better than the passive voice because it emphasizes the agent. An active-voice sentence also is shorter because it does not require a form of the verb *to be* and the past participle, as a passive-voice sentence does. In the active version of the example sentence, the verb is "drove" rather than "was driven," and "by" is unnecessary.

The passive voice, however, is generally better in these four cases:

- When the agent is clear from the context:

  Students are required to take both writing courses.

  The context makes it clear that the college sets the requirements.

- When the agent is unknown:

  The comet was first referred to in an ancient Egyptian text.

  We don't know who wrote this text.

- When the agent is less important than the action:

  The documents were hand-delivered this morning.

  It doesn't matter who the messenger was.

- When a reference to the agent is embarrassing, dangerous, or in some other way inappropriate:

Incorrect data were recorded for the flow rate.

It might be unwise or tactless to specify who recorded the incorrect data. It is unethical, however, to use the passive voice to avoid responsibility for an action: "Mistakes were made."

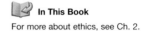

In This Book

For more about ethics, see Ch. 2.

The passive voice also can help you maintain the focus of your paragraph.

LANs have three major advantages. First, they are inexpensive to run. Second, they can be expanded easily....

Some people believe that the active voice is inappropriate because it emphasizes the person who does the work rather than the work itself, making the writing less objective. In many cases, this objection is valid. Why write "I analyzed the sample for traces of iodine" if there is no ambiguity about who did the analysis or no need to identify who did it? The passive focuses on the action, not the actor: "The samples were analyzed for traces of iodine." But if in doubt, use the active voice.

Other people argue that the passive voice produces a double ambiguity. In the sentence "The sample was analyzed for traces of iodine," the reader is not quite sure who did the analysis (the writer or someone else) or when it was done (during the project or sometime previously). Although a passive-voice sentence can indicate the actor, the writer often fails to mention it.

The best approach is to recognize that the two voices differ and to use each one where it is most effective.

Many grammar checkers can help you locate the passive voice. Some will advise you that the passive is undesirable, almost an error, but this advice is misleading. Use the passive voice when it works better than the active voice for your purposes.

In This Book

For more about using a grammar checker, see p. 40. For more about using the find and replace feature, see p. 41.

Any word processor allows you to search for the forms of *to be* used most commonly in passive-voice expressions: *is, are, was,* and *were.* You can also search for *ed* to isolate past participles, which appear in most passive-voice constructions.

Be Specific   Being specific involves using precise words, providing adequate detail, and avoiding ambiguity.

- *Use precise words.* A Ford Focus is an automobile, but it is also a vehicle, a machine, and a thing. In describing the Focus, *automobile* is better than the less specific *vehicle*, because *vehicle* can also refer to pickup trucks, trains, hot-air balloons, and other means of transport. As words become more abstract—from *machine* to *thing*, for instance—chances for misunderstanding increase.

- *Provide adequate detail.* Readers probably know less about your subject than you do. What might be perfectly clear to you might be too vague for them.

VAGUE	An engine on the plane experienced some difficulties.
	Which engine? What plane? What kinds of difficulties?
CLEAR	The left engine on the Martin 411 lost power during flight.

- *Avoid ambiguity.* Don't let readers wonder which of two meanings you are trying to convey.

AMBIGUOUS	After stirring by hand for 10 seconds, add three drops of the iodine mixture to the solution.
	After stirring the iodine mixture or the solution?
CLEAR	Stir the iodine mixture by hand for 10 seconds. Then add three drops to the solution.
CLEAR	Stir the solution by hand for 10 seconds. Then add three drops of the iodine mixture.

If you don't have the specific data, you should approximate—and clearly tell readers you are doing so—or explain why the specific data are unavailable and indicate when they will be available:

> The fuel leakage is much greater than we had anticipated; we estimate it to be at least five gallons per minute, not two.

> The fuel leakage is much greater than we had anticipated; we expect to have specific data by 4 P.M. today.

Avoid Unnecessary Jargon   Jargon is shoptalk. To the general reader, *ATM* means automated (or automatic) teller machine; to an electrical engineer, it means asynchronous transfer mode; to a math teacher, it means Association of Teachers of Mathematics. Although jargon is often ridiculed, it is useful in its proper sphere. However, using unnecessary jargon is inadvisable for four reasons:

- *It can be imprecise.* If you ask a co-worker to review a document and provide *feedback*, are you asking for a facial expression, body language, a phone call, or a written evaluation?
- *It can be confusing.* If you ask a computer novice to *cold swap the drive*, he or she might have no idea what you're talking about.
- *It is often seen as condescending.* Many readers react as if the writer is showing off—displaying a level of expertise that excludes them. If readers are feeling alienated, they will likely miss the message.
- *It is often intimidating.* People might feel inadequate or stupid because they do not know what the writer is talking about. Obviously, this reaction undermines communication.

If you are addressing a technically knowledgeable audience, use jargon recognized in that field.

Use Positive Constructions   The term *positive construction* has nothing to do with being cheerful. It indicates that the writer is describing what something is instead of what it is not. In the sentence "I was sad to see this project completed," "sad" is a positive construction. The negative construction would be "not happy."

On TechComm Web

For advice on positive constructions, see *A Plain English Handbook* by the Securities and Exchange Commission. Click on Links Library for Ch. 11 on <bedfordstmartins.com/techcomm>.

Here are a few more examples of positive and negative constructions:

Positive Construction	Negative Construction	Positive Construction	Negative Construction
most	not all	inefficient	not efficient
few	not many	reject	cannot accept
on time	not late, not delayed	impossible	not possible
positive	not negative		

Readers understand positive constructions more quickly and more easily than negative constructions. Consider the following examples:

DIFFICULT   Because the team did not have sufficient time to complete the project, it was not surprising that it was unable to prepare a satisfactory report.

SIMPLER   Because the team had too little time to complete the project, it produced an unsatisfactory report.

Avoid Long Noun Strings   A noun string contains a series of nouns (or nouns, adjectives, and adverbs), all of which modify the last noun. For example, in the phrase *parking-garage regulations*, the first two words modify *regulations*. Noun strings save time, and if your readers understand them, they are fine. It is easier to write *passive-restraint system* than *restraint system that is passive*.

In This Book

For more about hyphens, see Appendix, Part C, p. 646.

Hyphens can clarify noun strings by linking words that go together. For example, in the phrase *flat-panel monitor*, the hyphen links *flat* and *panel*. Together they modify *monitor*. In other words, it is not a *flat panel* or a *panel monitor*, but a *flat-panel monitor*. However, noun strings are sometimes so long or so complex that hyphens can't ensure clarity. Untangle the phrases and restore prepositions, as in the following example:

UNCLEAR   preregistration procedures instruction sheet update

CLEAR   an update of the instruction sheet for preregistration procedures

An additional danger is that noun strings can sometimes sound pompous. If you are writing about a simple smoke detector, there is no reason to call it a *smoke-detection device*—or worse, a *smoke-detection system*.

Avoid Clichés   Good writing is original and fresh. Rather than use a cliché, say what you want to say in plain English. Instead of "thinking outside the box," write "thinking creatively." Other clichés include *pushing the envelope*; *mission critical*; *paradigm shift*; and *been there, done that.* The best advice is to avoid clichés. If you are used to hearing or reading a phrase, don't use it.

Compare the following cliché-filled sentence and its plain-English translation:

TRITE	Afraid that we were between a rock and a hard place, we decided to throw caution to the wind with a grandstand play that would catch our competition with its pants down.
PLAIN	Afraid that we were in a difficult position, we decided on a risky, aggressive move that would surprise our competition.

Avoid Euphemisms   A euphemism is a polite way of saying something that makes people uncomfortable. A near miss between two airplanes is officially an "air proximity incident." The more uncomfortable the subject, the more often people resort to euphemisms. Dozens of euphemisms deal with drinking, bathrooms, sex, and death. David Lord (as quoted in Fuchsberg, 1990) lists 48 euphemisms for firing someone, including:

personnel surplus reduction	dehiring
workforce imbalance correction	decruiting
degrowing	redundancy elimination
indefinite idling	career-change-opportunity creation
corporate downsizing	

Be Concise

The following five principles promote concise technical communication:

- Avoid obvious statements.
- Avoid filler.

Ethics Note

Truth Telling and Euphemisms

There is nothing wrong with using the euphemism *restroom*, even though most people don't visit one to rest. The British use the phrase *go to the toilet* in polite company, and nobody seems to mind. In this case, if you want to use a euphemism, no harm done.

But it is unethical to use a euphemism to paper over an issue that has important implications for people or the environment. People get uncomfortable when discussing layoffs—and they should; it's an uncomfortable issue. But calling a layoff a *redundancy elimination initiative* ought to make you even more uncomfortable. Don't use language to cloud reality. It's an ethical issue.

- Avoid unnecessary prepositional phrases.
- Avoid wordy phrases.
- Avoid pompous words.

Avoid Obvious Statements   Writing can become sluggish if it overexplains. The italicized words in the following example are sluggish:

SLUGGISH   The market for *the sale of* flash memory chips is dominated by *two chip manufacturers*: Intel and Advanced Micro Systems. These two *chip manufacturers* were responsible for 76 percent of the $1.3 billion market *in flash memory chips* last year.

IMPROVED   The market for flash memory chips is dominated by Intel and Advanced Micro Systems, two companies that claimed 76 percent of the $1.3 billion industry last year.

Avoid Filler   In our writing, we sometimes use filler, much of which is more suited to speech. Consider the following examples:

basically	kind of
certain	sort of
essentially	various

Such words are common in oral communication, when you have to think on your feet, but they are meaningless in writing.

BLOATED   *I think that*, *basically*, the board felt *sort of* betrayed, *in a sense*, by the *kind of* behavior the president displayed.

BETTER   The board felt betrayed by the president's behavior.

But modifiers are not always meaningless. For instance, it might be wise to use *I think* or *it seems to me* to show that you are aware of other views.

BLUNT   Next year we will face unprecedented challenges to our market dominance.

LESS BLUNT   In my view, next year we will face unprecedented challenges to our market dominance.

Of course, a sentence that sounds blunt to one reader can sound self-confident to another. As you write, keep your audience's preferences in mind.

Other fillers include redundant expressions, such as *collaborate together*, *past history, end result, any and all, still remain, completely eliminate*, and *very unique.* Say it once.

REDUNDANT   I would like to welcome each and every one of you to our workshop.

BETTER   I would like to welcome you to our workshop.

Avoid Unnecessary Prepositional Phrases   A prepositional phrase consists of a preposition followed by a noun or a noun equivalent, such as *in the summary*, *on the engine*, and *under the heading*. Unnecessary prepositional phrases, often used along with abstract nouns and nominalizations, can make your writing long and boring.

> LONG   The increase *in* the number *of* students enrolled *in* the materials-engineering program *at* Lehigh University is a testament *to* the regard *in* which that program is held *by* the university's new students.
>
> SHORTER   The growth of Lehigh University's materials-engineering program suggests that the university's new students consider it a good program.

Avoid Wordy Phrases   Wordy phrases also make writing long and boring. For example, some people write *on a daily basis* rather than *daily*. The long phrase appears to carry the weight of scientific truth, but *daily* says the same thing more concisely.

Compare the following wordy sentence and its concise translation:

> WORDY   I am of the opinion that in regard to profit achievement, the statistics pertaining to this month will appear to indicate an upward tendency.
>
> CONCISE   I think this month's statistics will show an increase in profits.

Table 11.1 lists common wordy phrases and their more concise equivalents.

Avoid Pompous Words   Writers sometimes think they will impress their readers by using pompous words—*initiate* for *begin*, *perform* for *do*, and

■ **Table 11.1 Wordy Phrases and Their Concise Equivalents**

Wordy phrase	Concise phrase	Wordy phrase	Concise phrase
a majority of	most	in the event that	if
a number of	some, many	in view of the fact that	because
at an early date	soon	it is often the case that	often
at the conclusion of	after, following	it is our opinion that	we think that
at the present time	now	it is our recommendation that	we recommend that
at this point in time	now	it is our understanding that	we understand that
based on the fact that	because	make reference to	refer to
check out	check	of the opinion that	think that
despite the fact that	although	on a daily basis	daily
due to the fact that	because	on the grounds that	because
during the course of	during	prior to	before
during the time that	during, while	relative to	regarding, about
have the capability to	can	so as to	to
in connection with	about, concerning	subsequent to	after
in order to	to	take into consideration	consider
in regard to	regarding, about	until such time as	until

■ **Table 11.2 Fancy Words and Their Plain-Word Equivalents**

Fancy word	Plain word	Fancy word	Plain word
advise	tell	herein	here
ascertain	learn, find out	impact (verb)	affect
attempt (verb)	try	initiate	begin
commence	start, begin	manifest (verb)	show
demonstrate	show	parameters	variables, conditions
employ (verb)	use	perform	do
endeavor (verb)	try	prioritize	rank
eventuate (verb)	happen	procure	get, buy
evidence (verb)	show	quantify	measure
finalize	end, settle, agree, finish	terminate	end, stop
furnish	provide, give	utilize	use

prioritize for *rank*. In technical communication, plain talk is best. Compare the following pompous sentence with its plain-English version:

POMPOUS   The purchase of a database program will enhance our record-maintenance capabilities.

PLAIN   Buying a database program will help us maintain our records.

Table 11.2 lists commonly used fancy words and their plain equivalents.

Use Inoffensive Language

Writing to avoid offense is not merely a matter of politeness; it also is a matter of perception. Language reflects attitudes, but it also helps to form attitudes. Writing inoffensively is one way to break down stereotypes.

Use Nonsexist Language   Sexist language favors one sex at the expense of the other. Although sexist language can shortchange men—as some writing about nursing and similar female-dominated professions does—in most cases it shortchanges women. Common examples are nouns such as *workman* and *chairman*. In addition, when writers use male pronouns to represent both males and females—"Each worker is responsible for his work area"—they are using sexist language.

 On TechComm Web

For a list of fancy words and redundant expressions, see Pacific Northwest National Laboratory. Click on Links Library for Ch. 11 on <bedfordstmartins.com/techcomm>.

 On TechComm Web

For more about nonsexist language, see Jenny R. Redfern's essay. Click on Links Library for Ch. 11 on <bedfordstmartins.com/techcomm>.

Guidelines

Avoiding Sexist Language

▶ **Replace the male-gender words with non-gender-specific words.** *Chairman*, for instance, can become *chairperson* or *chair*. *Firemen* are *firefighters*, *policemen* are *police officers*.

▶ **Switch to a different form of the verb.**

SEXIST	The operator must pass rigorous tests before he is promoted.
NONSEXIST	The operator must pass rigorous tests before being promoted.

▶ **Switch to the plural.**

NONSEXIST	Operators must pass rigorous tests before they are promoted.

Some organizations accept the use of plural pronouns with singular nouns, particularly in memos and other informal documents:

> If an employee wishes to apply for tuition reimbursement, they should consult Section 14.5 of the Employee Manual.

Careful writers and editors, however, still consider this construction a grammar error because it switches from singular to plural. Sometimes switching to the plural makes the sentence unclear:

UNCLEAR	Operators are responsible for their operating manuals.
	Does each operator have one operating manual or more than one?
CLEAR	Each operator is responsible for his or her operating manual.

▶ **Switch to *he or she, he/she, s/he,* or *his or her.*** *He or she*, *his or her*, and related constructions are awkward, especially if overused, but at least they are clear and inoffensive.

▶ **Address the reader directly.** Use *you* and *your*, or the understood *you*.

▶ **Alternate *he* and *she*.** The language scholar Joseph Williams (2003) and many other language authorities recommend alternating *he* and *she* from one paragraph or section to the next.

In This Book

For books about nonsexist language, see Selected Bibliography, p. 678.

You can use your word processor to search for *he, man,* and *men,* the words and parts of words most often associated with sexist writing. Some grammar checkers identify common sexist terms and suggest alternatives. But use your common sense. You don't want to produce a sentence like this one from a benefits manual: "Every employee is responsible for the cost of his or her gynecological examination."

Use Inoffensive Language When Referring to People with Disabilities   One in five Americans—some 50 million people—has a physical, sensory, emotional, or mental impairment that interferes with daily life (Freedman, Martin, and Schoeni, 2004). In writing about people with disabilities, use the "people-first" approach: treat the person as someone with a disability, not as someone defined by that disability. The disability is a condition the person has, not what the person is.

INTERACTIVE SAMPLE DOCUMENT
Revising for Conciseness

The following passage is from a request for proposals published by the National Science Foundation. (Sentence numbers have been added for convenience.) The questions in the margin ask you to think about conciseness (as discussed on pages 240–43). E-mail your responses to yourself and/or your instructor, and see suggested responses on TechComm Web.

1 Proposals that miss the target date will be handled as time permits. **2** Significant delays in submissions will prohibit inclusion of the proposal within the group reviews for the program as a whole, and this may necessitate postponement of the review process until the following fiscal year. **3** We also ask that you not submit proposals any earlier than one month before the appropriate target date, unless approved by the cognizant Program Director.

4 The above date does not apply to proposals sent to the Physics Division in response to Foundation-wide solicitations, such as the Faculty Early Career Development (CAREER) or Research Experiences for Undergraduates (REU) programs. **5** These programs have specified target or deadline dates contained in their program announcements. **6** Demonstrably multidisciplinary proposals sent to the Physics Division, which are likely to be jointly reviewed with other programs within the Foundation, may be impacted by different target dates for the different programs involved. **7** If you are contemplating submitting such a proposal, you should contact the relevant Program Director in the Physics Division before submission.

Source: National Science Foundation, 2002 <www.nsf.gov/pubs/2002/nsf02139/nsf02139.txt>.

1. These two paragraphs contain many prepositional phrases. Identify two of them. For each one, is its use justified, or would the sentence be easier to understand if the sentence were revised to eliminate it?

2. These two paragraphs contain a number of examples of wordy phrases. Identify two of them. How can they be made into simpler, clearer expressions?

3. These two paragraphs contain a number of examples of pompous words. Identify two of them. How can they be translated into plain English?

 **On TechComm Web**

To e-mail your responses to yourself and/or your instructor and to see suggested responses, click on Interactive Sample Documents for Ch. 11 on <**bedfordstmartins.com/techcomm**>.

Guidelines

Using the People-First Approach

When writing about people with disabilities, follow these guidelines, which are based on Snow (2001).

▶ **Refer to the person first, the disability second.** Write "people with mental retardation," not "the mentally retarded."

▶ **Don't confuse *handicap* with *disability*.** *Disability* refers to the impairment or condition; *handicap* refers to the interaction between the person and his or her environment. A person can have a disability without being handicapped.

▶ **Don't refer to victimization.** Write "a person with AIDS," not "an AIDS victim" or "an AIDS sufferer."

▶ **Don't refer to a person as "wheelchair-bound" or "confined to a wheelchair."** People who use wheelchairs to get around are not confined.

▶ **Don't refer to people with disabilities as abnormal.** They are atypical, not abnormal.

UNDERSTANDING SIMPLIFIED ENGLISH FOR NONNATIVE SPEAKERS

 On TechComm Web

For more about Simplified English, see Userlab's manual on Simplified English. Click on Links Library for Ch. 11 on <bedfordstmartins.com/ techcomm>.

Because English is the language of more than half of the world's scientific and technical communication, millions of nonnative speakers of English read technical communication in English. Many companies and professional associations have created versions of Simplified English. Each version consists of a basic set of grammar rules and a vocabulary of about 1,000 words, each of which has only one meaning: *right* is the opposite of *left*; it does not mean *correct*. Each version of Simplified English is made for a specific discipline. For example, ASD Simplified English is intended for aerospace workers.

Here is a sample of text and its Simplified English version:

ORIGINAL	Before filling the gas tank, it is necessary to turn off the propane line to the refrigerator. Failure to do so significantly increases the risk of explosion.
SIMPLIFIED ENGLISH	Before you pump gasoline into the gas tank, turn off the propane line to the refrigerator. If you do not turn off the propane tank, it could explode.

For more on Simplified English, see Userlab (2004).

PREPARING TEXT FOR TRANSLATION

As discussed in Chapter 5, more and more organizations prepare their documents and Web sites not only in English but also in other languages. Although you won't have to do the translating yourself, you should be aware of some simple steps you can take to make it easier for someone else to translate your writing. Luckily, most of these steps are the same ones you use to make your writing clear and easy to read in English.

Strategies for Intercultural Communication

Making Text Easy to Translate

Use these seven techniques to make it easy to translate your writing into other languages.

- **Use short sentences.** Try for an average of no more than 20 words.
- **Use the active voice.** The active voice ("You should do this procedure after the engine has run for 100 hours") is easier to translate than the passive voice ("This procedure should be done after the engine has run for 100 hours").
- **Use simple words.** Translators will find it easier to translate *do* than *perform*.
- **Include a glossary.** If you need to use technical terms, define them in a glossary.
- **Use words that have only one meaning.** Write "This is the correct valve," not "This is the right valve," because *right* could also mean *the one on the right side*.
- **Use pronouns carefully.** Don't write "Matthews phoned Hawkins to learn whether he was scheduled to speak at the meeting." The translator might not know which person *he* refers to. Instead, write "Matthews phoned Hawkins to learn whether Hawkins was scheduled to speak at the meeting."
- **Avoid jokes, puns, and culture-bound references.** Humor doesn't translate well. If you refer to a box of computer pointing devices as "a box of mice," the translator might translate the words literally because the device is not known by that name everywhere. Also avoid other culture-bound references, such as sports metaphors (*hat trick*) or references to national heroes or holidays.

 On TechComm Web

For more about preparing text for translation, see George Rimalower's essay "Crossing Borders—Tips for Preparing Your Writing for Subsequent Translation." Click on Links Library for Ch. 11 on <bedfordstmartins.com/techcomm>.

 In This Book

For more about glossaries, see Ch. 18, p. 473.

Writer's Checklist

Lists

- ☐ Is each list of the appropriate kind: numbered, lettered, bulleted, or checklist? (p. 226)
- ☐ Does each list contain an appropriate number of items? (p. 226)
- ☐ Are all the items in each list grammatically parallel? (p. 227)
- ☐ Is the lead-in to each list structured and punctuated properly? (p. 227)
- ☐ Are the items in each list punctuated properly? (p. 227)

Sentences

☐ Are the sentences structured with the new or important information near the end? (p. 228)
☐ Are the sentences the appropriate length: neither long and difficult to understand nor short and choppy? (p. 229)
☐ Does each sentence focus on the "real" subject? (p. 230)
☐ Have you reduced the number of expletives used as sentence openers? (p. 230)
☐ Does each sentence focus on the "real" verb, without weak nominalizations? (p. 231)
☐ Have you eliminated nonparallelism from your sentences? (p. 232)
☐ Have you used restrictive and nonrestrictive modifiers appropriately? (p. 233)
☐ Have you eliminated misplaced modifiers, squinting modifiers, and dangling modifiers? (p. 233)

Words and Phrases

Did you
☐ use active and passive voice appropriately? (p. 236)
☐ use precise words? (p. 237)
☐ provide adequate detail? (p. 237)
☐ avoid ambiguity? (p. 238)
☐ avoid unnecessary jargon? (p. 238)
☐ use positive rather than negative constructions? (p. 239)
☐ avoid long noun strings? (p. 239)
☐ avoid clichés? (p. 239)
☐ avoid euphemisms? (p. 240)
☐ use the most concise phrases? (p. 240)
☐ avoid stating the obvious? (p. 241)
☐ avoid filler? (p. 241)
☐ avoid unnecessary prepositional phrases? (p. 242)
☐ avoid redundancy? (p. 241)
☐ avoid pompous words? (p. 242)
☐ use nonsexist language? (p. 243)
☐ use the people-first approach in referring to people with disabilities? (p. 246)
☐ write in such a way that it will be easy to translate? (p. 247)

Exercises

1. Refer to the advice on pages 225–28 and rewrite each of the following sentences in the form of a list.

   a. The causes of burnout can be studied from three perspectives: physiological—the roles of sleep, diet, and physical fatigue; psychological—the roles of guilt, fear, jealousy, and frustration; environmental—the role of the physical surroundings at home and at work.

   b. There are several problems with the online registration system used at Dickerson University. First, lists of closed sections cannot be updated as often as necessary. Second, students who want to register in a closed section must be assigned to a special terminal. Third, the computer staff is not trained to handle student problems. Fourth, the Computer Center's own terminals cannot be used on the system; therefore, the university has to rent 15 extra terminals to handle registration.

2. The following sentences might be too long for some readers. Refer to the advice on page 229 and break each sentence into two or more sentences.

   a. If we get the contract, we must be ready by June 1 with the necessary personnel and equipment to get the job done, so with this in mind a staff meeting, which all group managers are expected to attend, is scheduled for February 12.

   b. Once we get the results of the stress tests on the 125-Z fiberglass mix, we will have a better idea of where we stand in terms of our time constraints, because if the mix isn't suitable we will really have to hurry to find and test a replacement by the Phase 1 deadline.

   c. Although we had a frank discussion with Backer's legal staff, we were unable to get them to discuss specifics on what they would be looking for in an out-of-court settlement, but they gave us a strong impression that they would rather settle out of court.

3. The following examples contain choppy, abrupt sentences. Refer to the advice on pages 229–30 and combine sentences to create a smoother style.

   a. I need a figure on the surrender value of a policy. The number of the policy is A4399827. Can you get me this figure by tomorrow?

b. The program obviously contains an error. We didn't get the results we anticipated. Please ask Paul Davis to test the program.

c. The supervisor is responsible for processing the outgoing mail. He is also responsible for maintaining and operating the equipment.

4. In the following sentences, the "real" subjects are buried in prepositional phrases or obscured by expletives. Refer to the advice on pages 230–31 and revise the sentences so that the real subjects appear prominently.

a. There has been a decrease in the number of students enrolled in our training sessions.

b. It is on the basis of recent research that I recommend the new CAD system.

c. The use of in-store demonstrations has resulted in a dramatic increase in business.

5. In the following sentences, unnecessary nominalization obscures the "real" verbs. Refer to the advice on pages 231–32 and revise the sentences to focus on the real verbs.

a. Pollution constitutes a threat to the Wilson Wildlife Preserve.

b. Evaluation of the gumming tendency of the four tire types will be accomplished by comparing the amount of rubber that can be scraped from the tires.

c. Reduction of the size of the tear-gas generator has already been completed.

6. Refer to the advice on page 232 and revise the following sentences to eliminate nonparallelism.

a. The next two sections of the manual discuss how to analyze the data, the conclusions that can be drawn from your analysis, and how to decide what further steps are needed before establishing a journal list.

b. With our new product line, you would expand your tax practice, your other accounting areas, and improve the company's visibility.

c. Sections 1 and 2 will introduce the entire system, while Sections 3 and 4 describe the automatic application and step-by-step instructions.

7. Refer to the advice on pages 233–34 and revise the following sentences to correct punctuation or pronoun errors related to modifiers.

a. You press the Greeting-Record button to record the greeting which is stored on a microchip inside the machine.

b. This problem that has been traced to manufacturing delays, has resulted in our losing four major contracts.

c. Please get in touch with Tom Harvey who is updating the instructions.

8. Refer to the advice on pages 233–34 and revise the following sentences to eliminate the misplaced modifiers.

a. Over the past three years, we have estimated that an average of eight hours per week are spent on this problem.

b. Information provided by this program is displayed at the close of the business day on the information board.

c. The computer provides a printout for the Director that shows the likely effects of the action.

9. Refer to the advice on pages 234–35 and revise the following sentences to eliminate the dangling modifiers.

a. By following these instructions, your computer should provide good service for many years.

b. To examine the chemical homogeneity of the plaque sample, one plaque was cut into nine sections.

c. The boats in production could be modified in time for the February debut by choosing this method.

10. Refer to the advice on pages 235–36 and revise the following informal sentences to make them moderately formal.

a. The learning modules were put together by a couple of profs in the department.

b. The biggest problem faced by multimedia designers is that users freak if they don't see a button—or, heaven forbid, if they have to make up their own buttons!

c. If the University of Arizona can't figure out where to dump its low-level radioactive waste, Uncle Sam could pull the plug on millions of dollars of research grants.

11. Refer to the advice on pages 236–37 and rewrite the following sentences to remove inappropriate use of the passive voice.

a. Most of the information you need will be gathered as you document the history of the journals.

b. Mistakes were made.

c. Come to the reception desk when you arrive. A packet with your name on it can be picked up there.

12. Refer to the advice on pages 240–43 and revise the following sentences to remove the redundancies.

   a. In grateful appreciation of your patronage, we are pleased to offer you this free gift as a token gesture of our gratitude.

   b. An anticipated major breakthrough in storage technology will allow us to proceed ahead in the continuing evolution of our products.

   c. During the course of the next two hours, you will see a demonstration of our improved speech-recognition software, which will be introduced for the first time in November.

13. Refer to the advice on pages 237–38 and revise the following sentences by replacing the vague elements with specific information. Make up any reasonable details.

   a. The results won't be available for a while.

   b. The fire in the lab caused extensive damage.

   c. A soil analysis of the land beneath the new stadium revealed an interesting fact.

14. Refer to the advice on page 238 and revise the following sentences to remove unnecessary jargon.

   a. Please submit your research assignment in hard-copy mode.

   b. The perpetrator was apprehended and placed under arrest directly adjacent to the scene of the incident.

   c. The new computer lab supports both major platforms.

15. Refer to the advice on page 239 and revise the following sentences to convert the negative constructions to positive constructions.

   a. Williams was accused by management of filing trip reports that were not accurate.

   b. We must make sure that all our representatives do not act unprofessionally to potential clients.

   c. The shipment will not be delayed if Quality Control does not disapprove any of the latest revisions.

16. Refer to the advice on page 239 and rewrite the following sentences to eliminate the long noun strings, which general readers might find awkward or difficult to understand.

   a. The corporate-relations committee meeting location has been changed.

   b. The research team discovered a glycerin-initiated, alkylene-oxide-based, long-chain polyether.

   c. We are considering purchasing a digital-imaging-capable, diffusion-pump-equipped, tungsten-gun SEM.

17. Refer to the advice on pages 239–40 and revise the following sentences to eliminate clichés.

   a. We hope the new program will positively impact all our branches.

   b. If we are to survive this difficult period, we are going to have to keep our ears to the ground and our noses to the grindstone.

   c. If everyone is on the same page and it turns out to be the wrong page, you're really up a creek.

18. Refer to the advice on page 240 and revise the following sentences to eliminate euphemisms.

   a. Downsizing our workforce will enable our division to achieve a more favorable cash-flow profile.

   b. Of course, accident statistics can be expected to show a moderate increase in response to a streamlining of the training schedule.

   c. Unfortunately, the patient failed to fulfill his wellness potential.

19. Refer to the advice on page 241 and revise the following sentences to eliminate the obvious material.

   a. To register to take a course offered by the university, you must first determine whether the university will be offering that course that semester.

   b. The starting date of the project had to be postponed for a certain period of time due to a delay in obtaining the necessary authorization from the Project Oversight Committee.

   c. After you have installed DataQuick, please spend a few minutes responding to the questions about the process, then take the card to a post office and mail it to us.

20. Refer to the advice on page 241 and revise the following sentences to remove meaningless filler.

   a. It would seem to me that the indications are that the project has been essentially unsuccessful.

   b. For all intents and purposes, our company's long-term success depends to a certain degree on various factors that are in general difficult to foresee.

c. The presentation was quite well received overall, despite the fact that we received a rather small number of comment cards.

21. Refer to the advice on page 242 and revise the following sentences to eliminate unnecessary prepositional phrases.

a. The complexity of the module will hamper the ability of the operator in the diagnosis of problems in equipment configuration.

b. The purpose of this test of your aptitudes is to help you with the question of the decision of which major to enroll in.

c. Another advantage of the approach used by the Alpha team is that interfaces of different kinds can be combined.

22. Refer to the advice on pages 240–43 and revise the following sentences to make them more concise.

a. The instruction manual for the new copier is lacking in clarity and completeness.

b. The software packages enable the user to create graphic displays with a minimum of effort.

c. We remain in communication with our sales staff on a daily basis.

23. Refer to the advice on pages 242–43 and revise the following sentences to eliminate the pomposity.

a. This state-of-the-art soda-dispensing module is to be utilized by the personnel associated with the Marketing Department.

b. It is indeed a not insupportable inference that we have been unsuccessful in our attempt to forward the proposal to the proper agency in advance of the mandated date by which such proposals must be in receipt.

c. Deposit your newspapers and other debris in the trash receptacles located on the station platform.

24. Refer to the advice on pages 243–44 and revise the following sentences to eliminate the sexism.

a. Each doctor is asked to make sure he follows the standard procedure for handling Medicare forms.

b. Policemen are required to live in the city in which they work.

c. Professor Harry Larson and Ms. Anita Sebastian — two of the university's distinguished professors — have been elected to the editorial board of *Modern Chemistry.*

25. Refer to the advice on pages 243–46 and revise the following sentences to eliminate the offensive language.

a. This year, the number of female lung-cancer victims is expected to rise because of increased smoking.

b. Mentally retarded people are finding greater opportunities in the service sector of the economy.

c. This bus is specially equipped to accommodate the wheelchair-bound.

26. **GROUP EXERCISE** Form small groups. Have one person in each group distribute a multipage document he or she has written recently, either in this class or in another. Have each group member annotate a copy of this document according to the principles of sentence effectiveness discussed in this chapter. Then have each group member write a summary statement about the document, highlighting its effective techniques of sentence construction and possible improvements. Meet as a group, study these annotated documents, and as a group write a memo to your instructor describing the sentence features cited by more than one group member, as well as those aspects cited by only one group member. Overall, what are the basic differences between the annotations and the summary statement from one group member and those from another? Do you think that, as a general practice, it would be worthwhile to have a draft reviewed and annotated by more than one person? What have you learned about the usefulness of peer review?

Case 11: Preparing Products for the Global Marketplace

 In This Book   For more about memos, see Ch. 14, p. 352.

Background

MetraPark Fitness Solutions is known in the U.S. commercial and corporate fitness industries for producing durable fitness machines based on highly regarded research in biomechanics, physiology, and anatomy. Now the company has decided to market its fitness equipment to commercial gyms in Europe. You were hired two weeks ago to take charge of the company's documentation needs. Up to that time, the design engineers had been responsible for writing the product descriptions.

"Fifteen thousand dollars?" asks Rex Bookwalter, your new boss. You have just shown Rex a translation company's bid to translate your product descriptions into German, Spanish, French, and Italian.

"Yes, that quote is for translating 31 product descriptions into four languages," you answer.

"Why can't we just use our existing English-language descriptions?"

"The first step toward breaking into the European market is translating our promotional literature. Recent e-commerce research suggests that consumers are three times more likely to buy online on a Web site written in their native language."

"What about translating our products into just one other language—say, German?"

"That would certainly save us money in the short term," you explain. "However, we could reach nearly 90 percent of Europe's online population if we went with German, Spanish, French, and Italian. In the long run, reaching a broader customer base might be a better business strategy."

"Okay, but why is it so expensive to translate these product descriptions? They're not that long or complicated."

"Depending on the language, we're paying the translation company 20 to 30 cents per word—"

"*Per word?* Let me take a look at one of those product descriptions."

You hand Rex the product description for the MFS Leg Extension Machine (Document 11.1). After about five minutes, he hands the description back to you and says, "We can do better. Rewrite this description so it's not so long and boring."

Your Assignment

1. Using the techniques explained in this chapter, revise Document 11.1 to make the description more concise and easier to translate.

2. Use the Internet to research strategies for preparing text for translation. Write a memo to company employees in which you provide guidelines for writing documents that will be easy to translate.

■ **Document 11.1 Product Description for MFS Leg Extension Machine**

 On TechComm Web

For digital versions of case documents, click on Downloadable Case Documents on <bedfordstmartins.com/techcomm>.

MFS® Leg

MFS® LEG EXTENSION
Product # : 08281967
Price: $3,999

At MFS, we let a muscle's function dictate the design of our equipment. That's why our machines provide the correct resistance in every position. MFS Leg Extension is no exception. Designed for novice and expert users, the MFS Leg Extension provides both superior biomechanics and greater results than ever before.

Proven Biomechanics

Most conventional exercise machines in addition to free weights provide only linear (or straight up and down) resistance. The problem caused by this fact is that all movement in the human body involves rotation around an axis (or joint). Take, for example, the common biceps curl with free weights (see Figure 1). Although the weight moves in a rotary fashion as a lifter performs a biceps curl, gravity causes the resistance to be linear. The end result is the weight being the heaviest at 90 degrees but almost no effective resistance at the start or end of his motion. The lifter is always limited in his training by how much weight he can lift in the weakest position.

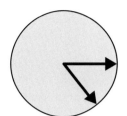
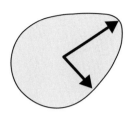

Figure 1.
*Rotary Movement
versus Linear Resistance*

Figure 2.
Traditional Pulley

Figure 3.
MFS Cam

Other types of commercial exercise machines that typically employ round pulleys are not any more efficient. Due to the fact that the strength of your muscle varies as it progresses through its range of motion, it requires variable resistance: lower resistance in weaker positions and higher in your stronger positions. The effective lever arm of round pulleys never changes during the time that the muscle moves through the exercise (see Figure 2). Therefore, the resistance is completely out of whack with the actual strength curve of your muscle, and you waste your time, energy, and money.

The legendary MFS cam, backed by years of research in the fields of biomechanics, physiology, and anatomy, is a proven method of varying resistance during rotary movement around a joint. By varying the radius of the cam, the changes in the effective lever are produced (see Figure 3). The shape of the MFS cam is determined by exacting research on the specific muscle group's strength curve being targeted in the exercise. The end result is that you get the correct resistance in every position. Engineered to be safe, each MFS machine is efficient and functional when utilized.

Superior Features

MFS exercise machines are the only equipment that is designed with the structural functions of the human muscle in mind, as well as a user's comfort and safety. Features include friction-free bearings, easy-to-access weight stacks, quick-set seat adjustments, oversized movement-arm roller pad, detailed instructions on the placard, range-limiting device, and an integrated seat belt for the stability and the safety of handicapped users.

Built-Tough™ Construction

MFS exercise machines feature Built-Tough™ construction features such as rubber footplates and bumpers for quiet operation and wear reduction, bent-steel tubing with exceptional durability, integral bearings and cables, and wear covers that are replaceable.

Product Specs

Weight Stack: 320 lb. (145 kg), **Footprint:** 46" (117 cm) W x 48" (123 cm) L x 58" (147 cm) H, **Weight:** 670 lb. (305 kg)

PART FOUR

Developing the
Visual Elements

12

Designing Documents

The effectiveness of a document largely depends on how well it is designed, because readers see the document before they actually read it. In less than a second, the document has made an impression on them, one that might determine how well they read it—or even whether they read it at all.

 In This Book

To learn about special considerations in designing Web pages, see Ch. 20.

GOALS OF DOCUMENT DESIGN AND PAGE DESIGN

In designing a document and its pages, you have five major goals:

- *To make a good impression on readers.* Your documents should reflect your own professional standards and those of your organization.

- *To help readers understand the structure and hierarchy of the information.* As they navigate a document, readers should know where they are and how to get where they are headed. They should also be able to see the hierarchical relationship between one piece of information and another.

- *To help readers find the information they need.* Usually, people don't read technical documents from cover to cover. Design elements (such as tabs, icons, and color), page design, and typography help readers find the information they need—quickly and easily.

- *To help readers understand the information.* Effective document and page design can clarify information. For instance, designing a set of instructions so that the text describing each step is next to the accompanying graphic makes the instructions easier to understand.

- *To help readers remember the information.* An effective design helps readers create a visual image of the information, making it easier to remember. Text boxes, pull quotes, and similar design elements help readers remember important explanations and passages.

UNDERSTANDING DESIGN PRINCIPLES

To design effective documents and pages, you need to understand a few basic design principles. The following discussion is based on Robin Williams's *The Non-Designer's Design Book*, second edition (Berkeley, CA:

 On TechComm Web

Also see Roger C. Parker's design site. Click on Links Library for Ch. 12 on <bedfordstmartins .com/techcomm>.

Peachpit Press, 2004). Williams explains how you can create effective technical documents if you understand four principles of design:

- proximity
- alignment
- repetition
- contrast

On TechComm Web

See John Magnik's essay "Typography & Page Layout." Click on Links Library for Ch. 12 on <bedfordstmartins.com/techcomm>.

Proximity

The principle of proximity is simple: group related items together. If two items appear close to each other, the reader will interpret them as related to each other. If they are far apart, the reader will interpret them as unrelated. Text describing a graphic should be positioned close to the graphic. Figure 12.1 shows the proximity principle.

Alignment

The principle of alignment is that you should consciously place text and graphics on the page so that the reader can understand the relationships among these elements. Figure 12.2 shows how alignment works to help organize information.

■ **Figure 12.1   Effective Use of Proximity**

Text and graphics are clearly related by the principle of proximity. The fabric options are placed near the car to which they refer.
Source: Nissan, 2004.

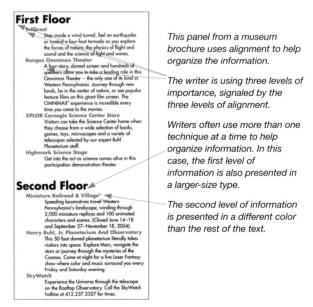

This panel from a museum brochure uses alignment to help organize the information.

The writer is using three levels of importance, signaled by the three levels of alignment.

Writers often use more than one technique at a time to help organize information. In this case, the first level of information is also presented in a larger-size type.

The second level of information is presented in a different color than the rest of the text.

■ **Figure 12.2   Effective Use of Alignment**
Source: Carnegie Science Center, n.d.

Repetition

The principle of repetition is that you should treat the same kind of information in the same way to create consistent patterns. For example, all first-level headings should have the same typeface, size, spacing above and below, and so forth. This repetition signals a connection between headings, making the content easier to understand. Other elements that are used to create consistent visual patterns are colors, icons, rules, and screens. Figure 12.3 shows an effective use of repetition.

Contrast

The principle of contrast works in several different ways in technical documents. For example, black print is easiest to see against a white background; larger letters stand out among smaller ones; information printed in a color,

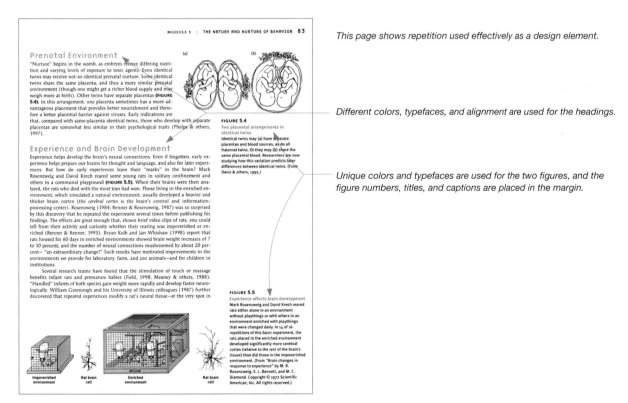

This page shows repetition used effectively as a design element.

Different colors, typefaces, and alignment are used for the headings.

Unique colors and typefaces are used for the two figures, and the figure numbers, titles, and captions are placed in the margin.

■ **Figure 12.3   Effective Use of Repetition**
Source: Myers, 2003, p. 83.

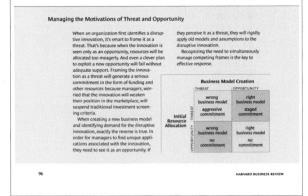

HBR Spotlight: Practical Strategy

the process, uncovered new demand for convenience, storage, and selectivity. These applications drove the development of digital photography. Framing digital technology as a threat helped Kodak free up resources for the new technology, but it seems to have also biased the way those resources were managed.

Now consider a very different, but equally cautionary, story. In 1994, executives at printing giant R.R. Donnelly & Sons believed that digital technology could very well change the economics of book publishing by allowing printers to publish short runs of books on demand. So they established a business unit to pursue the opportunity. Unfortunately, R.R. Donnelly's leading customers showed little interest in the technology. The new business didn't perform as well as expected, and key executives started moving on. Absent a clear threat to the core organization, a commitment to the new business was difficult to sustain, and in just two years, the unit closed.

Although Kodak and R.R. Donnelly took different tacks, their failures had a common cause: Both framed the disruptive technology in singular terms—as either a strong threat or an independent opportunity. That's a natural response, for companies as well as for individuals. But it's usually wrong. It's possible to arrive at an organizational framing that makes good use of the adrenaline that a threat creates as well as the creativity that an opportunity affords. Executives at the most successful organizations we've observed did just that. When money and other re-

sources were being allocated, they treated the disruptive innovation as a threat. But when the hard strategic work of discovering and responding to new markets began, they treated it as an opportunity. (See the exhibit "Managing the Motivations of Threat and Opportunity.") The ability to manage the competing frames of threat and opportunity is not an easy skill to master. In fact, we suspect that it's not even possible without some adjustments to organizational structure and the processes governing new business funding. But it can be done.

Framing the Issue

Because the way a challenge is perceived influences an organization's behavior, framing is a critical responsibility of business leaders. Let's look, first, at the problems that arise when a disruptive innovation is perceived as a threat. Management practices that "create a crisis" exploit the human tendency to respond with greater energy and commitment when we feel threatened than when we feel safe. But when the motivation to change comes from feeling threatened, managers and teams usually respond not just aggressively but also rigidly: They focus on defending the existing business model (as opposed to creating a new one); they commit resources in large lump sums (rather than in staged investments); and they tighten the existing organization's authority (instead of giving the new venture autonomy).

Managing the Motivations of Threat and Opportunity

When an organization first identifies a disruptive innovation, it's smart to frame it as a threat. That's because when the innovation is seen only as an opportunity, resources will be allocated too meagerly. And even a clever plan to exploit a new opportunity will fail without adequate support. Framing the innovation as a threat will generate a serious commitment in the form of funding and other resources because managers, worried that the innovation will weaken their position in the marketplace, will suspend traditional investment screening criteria.

When creating a new business model and identifying demand for the disruptive innovation, exactly the reverse is true. In order for managers to find unique applications associated with the innovation, they need to see it as an opportunity. If

they perceive it as a threat, they will rigidly apply old models and assumptions to the disruptive innovation.

Recognizing the need to simultaneously manage competing frames is the key to effective response.

	Business Model Creation	
	THREAT	OPPORTUNITY
Initial Resource Allocation — THREAT	wrong business model — aggressive commitment	right business model — staged commitment
Initial Resource Allocation — OPPORTUNITY	wrong business model — no commitment	right business model — no commitment

96   HARVARD BUSINESS REVIEW

■ **Figure 12.4   Effective Use of Contrast**

This page clearly consists of two parts: the top and the bottom. The most obvious contrast between the two parts is that the bottom part is printed over a tan screen. But the column width, typeface, type size, alignment, and justification also differ between the two parts. These aspects of design will be discussed in this chapter.
Source: Harvard, 2002, p. 96.

📖 **In This Book**

For more about analyzing your audience, see Ch. 5. For more about tables of contents, see Ch. 18, p. 468.

such as red, grabs attention sooner than information printed in black. Figure 12.4 shows an effective use of contrast.

PLANNING THE DESIGN OF THE DOCUMENT AND THE PAGE

The first step in designing any kind of technical document is planning. Analyze your audience's needs and expectations, and consider your resources.

Analyzing Your Audience's Needs and Expectations

Consider factors such as the audience's knowledge of the subject, their attitudes, their reasons for reading, the way they will be using the document, and the kinds of tasks they will perform. For instance, if you are writing a benefits manual for employees, you know that few people will read it from start to finish but many people will refer to it. Therefore, you should build in accessing tools: table of contents, index, tabs, and so forth.

Think, too, about your audience's expectations. Readers expect to see certain kinds of information presented in certain ways. Try to fulfill those expectations. For instance, tutorial information for complicated software programs is often presented in a small-format book, bound so that it lies flat on the table next to the keyboard.

Considering Your Resources

Think about your resources of time, money, and equipment. Short, informal documents are usually produced in-house. For more-ambitious projects, you might subcontract some of the jobs to professionals. If your organization has a technical-publications department, consult the professionals there about scheduling and budgeting.

- *Time.* What is your schedule? A sophisticated design might require professionals at service bureaus and print shops, and their services can require weeks. Creating even a simple design for a newsletter can take hours.

- *Money.* Can you afford professional designers and print shops? Most managers would budget thousands of dollars to design an annual report but not an in-house newsletter.

Strategies for Intercultural Communication

Designing Documents to Suit Cultural Preferences

Many aspects of design vary from one culture to another. In memos, letters, reports, and manuals, you may see significant differences in design practice. The best advice, therefore, is to study documents from the culture you are addressing. Here are a few design elements to look for:

- **Paper size.** Paper size will dictate some aspects of your page design. If your document will be printed in another country, find out about standard paper sizes in that country.

- **Typeface preferences.** One survey (Ichimura, 2001) found that readers in the Pacific Rim prefer sans-serif typefaces in body text, whereas Western readers prefer serifs. (Typography is discussed later in this chapter.)

- **Color preferences.** In China, for example, red suggests happiness, whereas in Japan it suggests danger.

- **Text direction.** If some members of your audience read right to left and others read left to right, you might arrange your graphics vertically, from top to bottom; everybody reads from top to bottom. Or you might use Arabic numerals to indicate the order in which items are to be read (Horton, 1993).

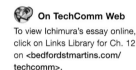 **On TechComm Web**

To view Ichimura's essay online, click on Links Library for Ch. 12 on <bedfordstmartins.com/techcomm>.

- *Equipment.* Complex designs require graphics software and desktop-publishing programs. A basic laser printer can produce attractive documents in black and white, but you need a more expensive printer for high-resolution color.

DESIGNING THE DOCUMENT

Before you design individual pages, design the whole document. You want the different elements to work together to accomplish your objectives. Consider these four elements in designing the whole document: size, paper, bindings, and accessing tools.

Size

Size refers to two aspects of document design: page size and page count.

- *Page size.* Think about the best page size for your information and about how the document will be used. For a procedures manual that will sit on a shelf most of the time, standard 8.5 × 11-inch paper, punched to fit in a three-ring binder, is a good choice. For a software tutorial that will fit easily on a desk while the reader works at the keyboard, consider a 5.5 × 8.5-inch size.

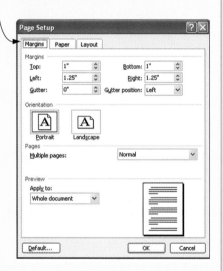
Paper comes precut in a number of standard sizes in addition to 8.5 × 11 inches, such as 4.5 × 6 inches and 6 × 9 inches. Although paper can be cut to any size, nonstandard sizes are more expensive. Check with your technical-publications department or a print shop for prices and availability.

- *Page count.* Because paper is expensive and heavy, you want as few pages as possible, especially if you are printing and mailing many copies. And there is a psychological factor as well: people don't want to spend a lot of time reading technical communication. Therefore, if you can design the document so that it is 15 pages long rather than 30—but still easy to read—your readers will appreciate it.

Paper

Paper is made not only in different standard sizes but also in different weights and with different coatings.

The lowest-quality paper is newsprint. It is extremely porous, allowing ink to bleed through to the other side and picking up smudges and oil. It can also turn yellow in a few weeks. For these reasons, use newsprint only for newspapers, informal newsletters, and other quick, inexpensive bulk publications.

The most widely used paper is the relatively inexpensive stock used in photocopy machines and laser printers. Others include bond (for letters and memos), book paper (a higher grade that permits better print resolution), and text paper (an even higher grade used for more-formal documents, such as announcements and brochures).

Most paper comes coated or uncoated. The coating, which increases strength and durability, provides the best print resolution. However, some glossy papers also produce an annoying glare. To deal with this problem, designers often choose paper with a slight tint.

Work closely with printing professionals. They know, for example, about UV-coated paper, which greatly reduces fading. And they know about recycled paper, which is constantly improving in quality and becoming less expensive.

Bindings

Although documents of a few pages can be attached with a paper clip or a staple, longer documents require more-sophisticated binding techniques. Table 12.1 illustrates and describes the four types of bindings commonly used in technical communication.

Accessing Tools

In a well-designed document, readers can easily find the information they seek. Most accessing tools use the design principles of repetition and contrast to help readers navigate the document. Table 12.2 on page 264 explains six common kinds of accessing aids.

■ **Table 12.1 Common Types of Bindings**

Loose-leaf binders. Loose-leaf binders are convenient when pages must be added and removed frequently. A high-quality binder can cost as much as several dollars.

 On TechComm Web

For more on bindings, see Jacci Howard Bear's Binding Decisions. Click on Links Library for Ch. 12 on <bedfordstmartins.com/techcomm>.

Ring or spiral binders. The wire or plastic coils or combs that hold the pages together let you open the document on a desk or even fold it over so that it takes up the space of only one page. Print shops can bind documents of almost any size in plastic coils or combs for about a dollar each.

Saddle binding. The document is opened to its middle pages, and large staples are inserted from the outside. Saddle binding is impractical for large documents.

Perfect binding. Pages are glued together along the spine edge, and a cover is attached. Perfect binding, used in book publishing, produces the most formal appearance, but it is relatively fragile, and the open document usually does not lie flat.

■ **Table 12.2 Typical Accessing Aids**

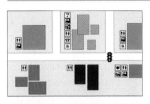

The icons in the legend help readers understand where various resources and facilities are located in the area.
Source: Kittery Outlets, 2005.

Icons. Icons are pictures that symbolize actions or ideas. An hourglass or a clock tells you to wait while the computer performs a task. Perhaps the most important icon is the stop sign, which alerts you to a warning. Icons depend on repetition: every time you see the warning icon, you know what kind of information the writer is presenting.

Don't be too clever in thinking up icons. One computer manual uses a cocktail glass about to fall over to symbolize "tip." This is a bad idea, because the pun is not functional: when you think of a cocktail glass, you don't think of a tip for using computers. Don't use too many different icons, or your readers will forget what each one represents.

 In This Book

For more about using color, see Ch. 13, p. 301.

 On TechComm Web

Color Vision Simulator, from Vischeck, lets you see what graphics look like to people with different color disabilities. Click on Links Library for Ch. 12 on <bedfordstmartins.com/techcomm>.

Here the color red is used to emphasize the title of the feature, the heading for each letter, the erratum box, and the reference to more letters on the journal's Web site.
Source: Discover magazine, 2005.

Color. Perhaps the strongest visual attribute is color (Keyes, 1993). Use color to draw attention to important features of the document, such as warnings, hints, major headings, and section tabs. But use it sparingly, or it will overpower everything else in the document.

Color exploits the principles of repetition (every item in a particular color is logically linked) and contrast (items in one color contrast with items in another color).

Use color logically. Third-level headings should not be in color, for example, if first- and second-level headings are printed in black.

Using different-colored paper for each section of a document is another way to simplify access.

Dividers and tabs. You are already familiar with dividers and tabs from loose-leaf notebooks. A tab provides a place for a label, which enables readers to identify and flip to a particular section. Sometimes dividers and tabs are color-coded. Tabs work according to the design principle of contrast: the tabs literally stick out.

■ **Table 12.2** *(continued)*

Read . . .	To learn to . . .	**Cross-reference tables.** These tables, which exploit the principle of alignment, refer readers to related discussions.
Ch. 1	connect to the Net	
Ch. 2	use e-mail	

Headers and footers. Headers and footers help readers see where they are in the document. In a book, for example, the headers on the left-hand pages might repeat the chapter number and title; those on the right-hand pages might contain the most recent first-level heading. Sometimes writers build other identifying information into the headers. For example, your instructor might ask you to identify your assignments with a header like the following: "Smith, Progress Report, English 302, page 6." Headers and footers work according to the principle of repetition: readers learn where to look on the page to see where they are.

 On TechComm Web

For more about header and footers, see the Document Design Tutorial on <bedfordstmartins.com/techcomm>.

Source: Microsoft, 2001.

Page numbering. For one-sided documents, use Arabic numerals in the upper right corner. (The first page of most documents is unnumbered.) For two-sided documents, put the page numbers near the outside margins.

Complex documents often use two number sequences: lowercase roman numerals (i, ii, and so on) for front matter and Arabic numerals for the body. The title page is unnumbered; the page following it is ii.

Appendices are often paginated with a letter and number combination: Appendix A begins with page A-1, followed by A-2, and so on; Appendix B starts with page B-1 and so on.

Sometimes documents list the total number of pages in the document (so recipients can be sure they have all of them). The second page is "2 of 17," and the third page is "3 of 17."

Documents that will be updated are sometimes numbered by section: Section 3 begins with page 3-1, followed by 3-2; Section 4 begins with 4-1. This way, a complete revision of one section does not affect the page numbering of subsequent sections.

Source: Gibaldi, 1999.

DESIGNING THE PAGE

A page of technical communication is effectively designed if the reader can recognize a pattern—such as where to look for certain kinds of information.

 On TechComm Web

For information on design principles and software, see the discussion about desktop publishing at About.com. Click on Links Library for Ch. 12 on <bedfordstmartins .com/techcomm>.

Guidelines

Understanding Learning Theory and Page Design

In designing the page, create visual patterns that help readers find, understand, and remember information. Three principles, based on research into how people learn, can help you design effective pages: chunking, queuing, and filtering.

- **Chunking.** People understand information best if it is delivered to them in chunks—small units—rather than all at once. For single-spaced type, chunking involves double-spacing between paragraphs, as shown in Figure 12.5.

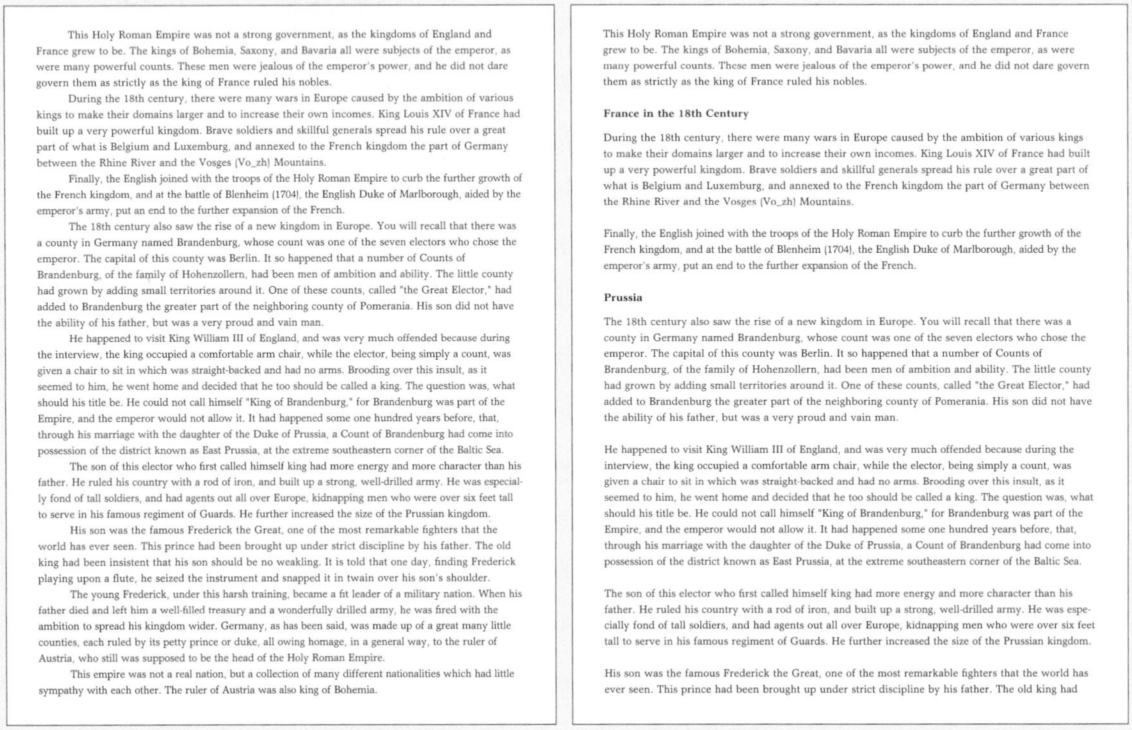

This Holy Roman Empire was not a strong government, as the kingdoms of England and France grew to be. The kings of Bohemia, Saxony, and Bavaria all were subjects of the emperor, as were many powerful counts. These men were jealous of the emperor's power, and he did not dare govern them as strictly as the king of France ruled his nobles.
During the 18th century, there were many wars in Europe caused by the ambition of various kings to make their domains larger and to increase their own incomes. King Louis XIV of France had built up a very powerful kingdom. Brave soldiers and skillful generals spread his rule over a great part of what is Belgium and Luxemburg, and annexed to the French kingdom the part of Germany between the Rhine River and the Vosges (Vo_zh) Mountains.
Finally, the English joined with the troops of the Holy Roman Empire to curb the further growth of the French kingdom, and at the battle of Blenheim (1704), the English Duke of Marlborough, aided by the emperor's army, put an end to the further expansion of the French.
The 18th century also saw the rise of a new kingdom in Europe. You will recall that there was a county in Germany named Brandenburg, whose count was one of the seven electors who chose the emperor. The capital of this county was Berlin. It so happened that a number of Counts of Brandenburg, of the family of Hohenzollern, had been men of ambition and ability. The little county had grown by adding small territories around it. One of these counts, called "the Great Elector," had added to Brandenburg the greater part of the neighboring county of Pomerania. His son did not have the ability of his father, but was a very proud and vain man.
He happened to visit King William III of England, and was very much offended because during the interview, the king occupied a comfortable arm chair, while the elector, being simply a count, was given a chair to sit in which was straight-backed and had no arms. Brooding over this insult, as it seemed to him, he went home and decided that he too should be called a king. The question was, what should his title be. He could not call himself "King of Brandenburg," for Brandenburg was part of the Empire, and the emperor would not allow it. It had happened some one hundred years before, that, through his marriage with the daughter of the Duke of Prussia, a Count of Brandenburg had come into possession of the district known as East Prussia, at the extreme southeastern corner of the Baltic Sea.
The son of this elector who first called himself king had more energy and more character than his father. He ruled his country with a rod of iron, and built up a strong, well-drilled army. He was especially fond of tall soldiers, and had agents out all over Europe, kidnapping men who were over six feet tall to serve in his famous regiment of Guards. He further increased the size of the Prussian kingdom.
His son was the famous Frederick the Great, one of the most remarkable fighters that the world has ever seen. This prince had been brought up under strict discipline by his father. The old king had been insistent that his son should be no weakling. It is told that one day, finding Frederick playing upon a flute, he seized the instrument and snapped it in twain over his son's shoulder.
The young Frederick, under this harsh training, became a fit leader of a military nation. When his father died and left him a well-filled treasury and a wonderfully drilled army, he was fired with the ambition to spread his kingdom wider. Germany, as has been said, was made up of a great many little counties, each ruled by its petty prince or duke, all owing homage, in a general way, to the ruler of Austria, who still was supposed to be the head of the Holy Roman Empire.
This empire was not a real nation, but a collection of many different nationalities which had little sympathy with each other. The ruler of Austria was also king of Bohemia.

This Holy Roman Empire was not a strong government, as the kingdoms of England and France grew to be. The kings of Bohemia, Saxony, and Bavaria all were subjects of the emperor, as were many powerful counts. These men were jealous of the emperor's power, and he did not dare govern them as strictly as the king of France ruled his nobles.

France in the 18th Century

During the 18th century, there were many wars in Europe caused by the ambition of various kings to make their domains larger and to increase their own incomes. King Louis XIV of France had built up a very powerful kingdom. Brave soldiers and skillful generals spread his rule over a great part of what is Belgium and Luxemburg, and annexed to the French kingdom the part of Germany between the Rhine River and the Vosges (Vo_zh) Mountains.

Finally, the English joined with the troops of the Holy Roman Empire to curb the further growth of the French kingdom, and at the battle of Blenheim (1704), the English Duke of Marlborough, aided by the emperor's army, put an end to the further expansion of the French.

Prussia

The 18th century also saw the rise of a new kingdom in Europe. You will recall that there was a county in Germany named Brandenburg, whose count was one of the seven electors who chose the emperor. The capital of this county was Berlin. It so happened that a number of Counts of Brandenburg, of the family of Hohenzollern, had been men of ambition and ability. The little county had grown by adding small territories around it. One of these counts, called "the Great Elector," had added to Brandenburg the greater part of the neighboring county of Pomerania. His son did not have the ability of his father, but was a very proud and vain man.

He happened to visit King William III of England, and was very much offended because during the interview, the king occupied a comfortable arm chair, while the elector, being simply a count, was given a chair to sit in which was straight-backed and had no arms. Brooding over this insult, as it seemed to him, he went home and decided that he too should be called a king. The question was, what should his title be. He could not call himself "King of Brandenburg," for Brandenburg was part of the Empire, and the emperor would not allow it. It had happened some one hundred years before, that, through his marriage with the daughter of the Duke of Prussia, a Count of Brandenburg had come into possession of the district known as East Prussia, at the extreme southeastern corner of the Baltic Sea.

The son of this elector who first called himself king had more energy and more character than his father. He ruled his country with a rod of iron, and built up a strong, well-drilled army. He was especially fond of tall soldiers, and had agents out all over Europe, kidnapping men who were over six feet tall to serve in his famous regiment of Guards. He further increased the size of the Prussian kingdom.

His son was the famous Frederick the Great, one of the most remarkable fighters that the world has ever seen. This prince had been brought up under strict discipline by his father. The old king had

a. Without chunking

b. With chunking

■ Figure 12.5 Chunking

Chunking, on the right, emphasizes units of related information. Note how the use of headings creates clear chunks of information.

- **Queuing.** Queuing refers to creating visual distinctions to indicate levels of importance. In a traditional outline, the Roman numeral "I" heading is more important than the Arabic numeral "1" heading. On a page, more-emphatic elements—those with bigger type or boldfaced type—are more important than less-emphatic ones.

  Another visual element of queuing is alignment. Designers start more-important information closer to the left margin and indent less-important information. (An exception is titles, which are often centered in reports in the United States.) Figure 12.6 shows queuing.

- **Filtering.** Filtering is the use of visual patterns to distinguish various types of information. In a set of instructions, a stop sign, for example, often signals safety information. Introductory material might be displayed in larger type, and notes might appear in italics or another typeface. Figure 12.7 shows filtering.

- *Color.* The more-important heading is presented in a warmer color, the rust, which stands out more than the cooler blue.
- *Size.* The more-important heading is larger than the other headings.
- *The heading's placement on the line.* The more-important heading is on its own line, giving it more emphasis than the run-in headings.
- *Line spacing.* The more-important heading has more space above it.

limits for "hardship" reasons; and the definition of "work" is somewhat flexible, as up to 30% of recipients can count education or job-skills training as work.

Supplemental Security Income (SSI) SSI is a program that provides cash welfare to the aged, blind, and disabled. Essentially, the job of SSI is to fill holes that are left by the incomplete nature of two of our major social insurance programs, Social Security and disability insurance (DI). Some individuals who have not worked enough in the past may not qualify for benefits under either of these social insurance programs, so they qualify for SSI: for example, a young person who has never worked and is disabled in a car accident would not qualify for DI, but he can receive SSI. Indeed, a large share of the SSI caseload is youth, due to a 1990 court decision that qualified youth with learning disabilities as disabled for SSI purposes. This decision led to a rise in the number of youths on the program from under 300,000 in 1990 to over 800,000 in just four years.[9] This rapid rise in enrollment highlights the problems in truly defining disability, particularly in a population such as children. SSI is not very widely known, nor is it debated with the ferocity of TANF, but it is in fact a bigger program, with expenditures of $31.6 billion in 2002.[10]

In-Kind Programs

Along with these two cash programs, there are four major types of in-kind benefits provided to the poor in the United States.

Food Stamps The food stamps program traditionally provided vouchers to individuals that they could use to pay for food at participating retailers. These vouchers have been replaced by debit card–like systems where individuals are issued a card for a certain value of food, which is drawn down as they make purchases.

Food stamps is a national program, with spending of $24.1 billion in 2002.[11] Households composed entirely of TANF, SSI, or other state cash welfare recipients are automatically eligible for food stamps; otherwise, monthly cash income is the primary eligibility determinant. Households without elderly or disabled members must have income below 130% of the poverty line to receive food stamps, and the amount of the food stamp benefit falls as income rises. In addition, able-bodied adults are required to register for work and be willing to take any job offered; if they violate these conditions, the welfare agency may discontinue benefits for one to six months. Finally, many noncitizens are ineligible: permanent residents must have been in the United States for at least five years to receive food stamps.

Medicaid We discussed the Medicaid program extensively in the previous chapter, but it is worth remembering that this is by far the largest categorical welfare program in the United States, with expenditures of $250 billion in 2003.

[9] See Garrett and Glied (2000) for a discussion of this change.
[10] U.S. House of Representatives Committee on Ways and Means (2004), Section 3.
[11] U.S. House of Representatives Committee on Ways and Means (2004), Section 15.

■ **Figure 12.6   Queuing**
Source: Gruber, 2005, p. 461.

Throughout the book from which this page was excerpted, different kinds of information are designed to be easy for the reader to identify.

Figures are presented with a tan screen behind them. The figure title preceded by a red square is set in a different typeface than the body text. The caption is presented against a gray screen.

Definitions appear in the margin, set off with faint red rules.

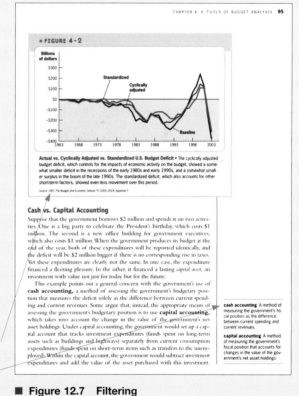

CHAPTER 4 • TOOLS OF BUDGET ANALYSIS   **95**

■ FIGURE 4-2

Actual vs. Cyclically Adjusted vs. Standardized U.S. Budget Deficit • The cyclically adjusted budget deficit, which controls for the impacts of economic activity on the budget, showed a somewhat smaller deficit in the recessions of the early 1980s and early 1990s, and a somewhat smaller surplus in the boom of the late 1990s. The standardized deficit, which also accounts for other short-term factors, showed even less movement over this period.

Source: CBO, The Budget and Economic Outlook: FY 2005-2014, Appendix F.

Cash vs. Capital Accounting

Suppose that the government borrows $2 million and spends it on two activities. One is a big party to celebrate the President's birthday, which costs $1 million. The second is a new office building for government executives, which also costs $1 million. When the government produces its budget at the end of the year, both of these expenditures will be reported identically, and the deficit will be $2 million bigger if there is no corresponding rise in taxes. Yet these expenditures are clearly not the same. In one case, the expenditure financed a fleeting pleasure. In the other, it financed a lasting *capital asset*, an investment with value not just for today but for the future.

This example points out a general concern with the government's use of **cash accounting**, a method of assessing the government's budgetary position that measures the deficit solely as the difference between current spending and current revenues. Some argue that, instead, the appropriate means of assessing the government's budgetary position is to use **capital accounting**, which takes into account the change in the value of the government's net asset holdings. Under capital accounting, the government would set up a capital account that tracks investment expenditures (funds spent on long-term assets such as buildings and highways) separately from current consumption expenditures (funds spent on short-term items such as transfers to the unemployed). Within the capital account, the government would subtract investment expenditures and add the value of the asset purchased with this investment.

cash accounting A method of measuring the government's fiscal position as the difference between current spending and current revenues.

capital accounting A method of measuring the government's fiscal position that accounts for changes in the value of the government's net asset holdings.

■ **Figure 12.7   Filtering**
Source: Gruber, 2005, p. 95.

Page Layout

Every page has two kinds of space: white space and space for text and graphics. The best way to design a page is to make a grid—a drawing of what the page will look like. In making a grid, you decide how to use white space and determine how many columns to have on the page.

Page Grids   As the phrase suggests, a page grid is like a map on which you plan where text, graphics, and white space will go. To devise an effective grid, consider your audience, their purpose in reading, and their reading behavior.

 **On TechComm Web**

For more about page layout, see the Document Design Tutorial on <bedfordstmartins.com/techcomm>.

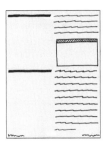
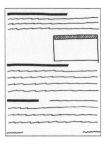
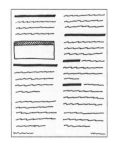
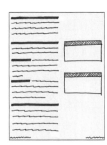

■ **Figure 12.8 Thumbnail Sketches**

Many writers like to begin with a *thumbnail sketch*, a rough drawing that shows how the text and graphics will look on the page. Figure 12.8 shows several thumbnail sketches for a page from the body of a manual.

Keep experimenting by sketching the different kinds of pages your document contains: body pages, front matter, and so on. When you are satisfied, make page grids. You can use either a computer or a pencil and paper, or you can combine the two techniques.

Figure 12.9 shows two simple grids: one using picas (the unit that printing professionals use, which equals one-sixth of an inch) and one using inches.

Experiment with different grids until the design is attractive, able to meet the needs of your readers, and appropriate for the information you are conveying. Figure 12.10 shows some possibilities.

White Space Sometimes called *negative space*, white space is the area of the paper with no writing or graphics: the space between two lines of text, the space between text and graphics, and, most obviously, the margins. White space directs readers' eyes to a particular element, emphasizing it. White space also helps readers see relationships among elements on the page.

■ **Figure 12.9 Sample Grids Using Picas and Inches**
Source: Kerman and Tomlinson, 2004, p. 388.

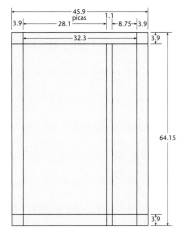

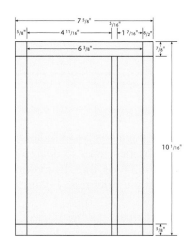

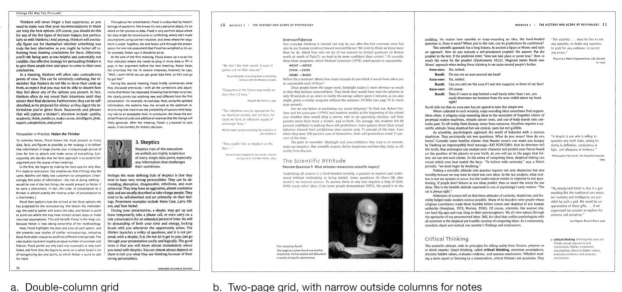

a. Double-column grid
Source: Williams and Miller, 2002, p. 70.

b. Two-page grid, with narrow outside columns for notes
Source: Myers, 2003, pp. 10–11.

c. Three-panel brochure
Source: Norman Rockwell Museum, 2005.

■ **Figure 12.10   Popular Grids**

Margins make up close to half the area on a typical page. Why so much? Margins serve four main purposes:

- They limit the amount of information on the page, making it easier to read and use.

- They provide space for binding and allow readers to hold the page without covering up the text.

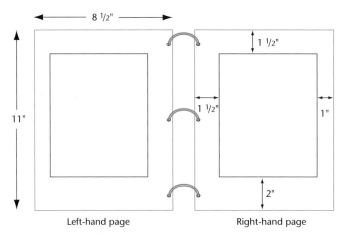

■ Figure 12.11   Typical Margins for a Document That Is Bound Like a Book

Increase the size of the margins when the subject becomes more difficult or when your readers become less knowledgeable about it.

- They provide a neat frame around the type.
- They provide space for marginal glosses. (Marginal glosses are discussed later in this chapter.)

Figure 12.11 shows common margin widths for left-hand and right-hand pages.
White space can also set off and emphasize an element on the page. For instance, white space around a graphic separates it from the text and draws readers' eyes to it. White space between columns helps readers to read the text easily. And white space between sections of text helps readers to see that one section is ending and another is beginning.

Columns

Many workplace documents have multiple columns. A multicolumn design offers three major advantages:

- Text is easier to read because the lines are shorter.
- Columns allow you to fit more information on the page. Many graphics can fit in one column or extend across two or more columns. In addition, a multicolumn design can contain more words on a page than a single-column design.
- Columns let you use the principle of repetition to create a visual pattern, such as text in one column and accompanying graphics in an adjacent column.

Typography

Typography, the study of type and the way people read it, encompasses type-faces, type families, case, and type size, as well as the white space of typography: line length, line spacing, and justification.

TECH TIP
How to Format Columns

To create multiple columns, use the **Columns** dialog box.

From the **Format** menu, select **Columns**.

You can use **preset** layouts.

You can also select the **number of columns** and specify the **width** and **spacing** yourself.

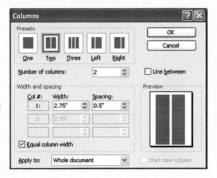

When you divide your document into columns, text flows from the bottom of one column to the top of the next column.

If you want to end a column of text in a specific location or create columns of equal length, use a **column break** to move the text below to the next column.

KEYWORDS: columns, break, column break

Typefaces   A typeface is a set of letters, numbers, punctuation marks, and other symbols, all bearing a characteristic design. There are thousands of typefaces, and more are designed every year. Figure 12.12 shows three contrasting typefaces.

As Figure 12.13 illustrates, typefaces are generally classified into two categories: *serif* and *sans serif*.

> *This paragraph is typed in French Script typeface. You are unlikely to see this style of font in a technical document because it is too ornate and too hard to read. It is better suited to wedding invitations and other formal announcements.*
>
> This paragraph is Times Roman. It looks like the kind of type used by the *New York Times* and other newspapers in the nineteenth century. It is an effective typeface for text in the body of technical documents.
>
> This paragraph is Univers, which has a modern, high-tech look. It is best suited for headings and titles in technical documents.

■ **Figure 12.12   Typefaces**

Serif typefaces are often considered easier to read because the serifs—the short extensions on the letters—encourage the movement of the reader's eyes along the line.

The effect of serifs on readability might differ from culture to culture, because if you see one kind of type often, you become used to it and read it quickly and easily.

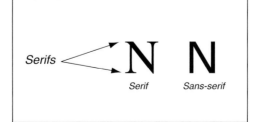

Sans-serif typefaces are harder on our eyes because the letters are less distinct from one another than they are in a serif typeface. However, sans-serif typefaces are easier to read on the screen and when printed on dot-matrix printers, because the letters are simpler.

Sans-serif typefaces are used mostly for short documents and for headings.

■ **Figure 12.13   Serif and Sans-Serif Typefaces**

Helvetica Light	*Helvetica Bold Italic*
Helvetica Light Italic	**Helvetica Heavy**
Helvetica Regular	***Helvetica Heavy Italic***
Helvetica Regular Italic	Helvetica Regular Condensed
Helvetica Bold	*Helvetica Regular Condensed Italic*

■ **Figure 12.14   Helvetica Family of Type**

On TechComm Web

See John Magnik's Typography 1st for information on typography and design. Click on Links Library for Ch. 12 on <bedfordstmartins.com/techcomm>.

Most of the time, you will use standard typefaces such as Times Roman and Arial, which are included in your software and which your printer can reproduce. Remember, however, that different typefaces convey different impressions and that some can cause more eye fatigue than others.

Type Families   Each typeface belongs to a family of typefaces, which consist of variations on the basic style, such as italic and boldface. Figure 12.14, for example, shows Helvetica.

Be careful not to overload your text with too many different members of the same family. Used sparingly and consistently, however, they can help you with filtering: calling attention to various kinds of text, such as warnings and notes, or even characters that readers are to type on the computer keyboard. Use italic for book titles and other elements, and use boldface for emphasis and headings. However, you can go years without needing condensed and expanded versions of typefaces. And you can live a full, rewarding life without ever using outlined or shadowed versions.

On TechComm Web

For more about typography, see the Document Design Tutorial on <bedfordstmartins.com/techcomm>.

Case   To ensure that your document is easy to read, use uppercase and lowercase letters as you would in any other kind of writing (see Figure 12.15).

The average person requires 10 to 25 percent more time to read text using all uppercase letters than to read text using both uppercase and lowercase. In addition, uppercase letters take up as much as 35 percent more space than lowercase letters (Haley, 1991). And if the text includes both uppercase and lowercase, readers will find it easier to see where new sentences begin (Poulton, 1968).

Type Size   Type size is measured with a basic unit called a *point*. There are 12 points in a *pica* and 72 points in an inch.

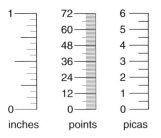

Lowercase letters are easier to read than uppercase because the individual variations from one letter to another are greater.

Individual variations are greater in lowercase words

THAN THEY ARE IN UPPERCASE WORDS.

■ **Figure 12.15   Individual Variations in Lowercase and Uppercase Type**

In most technical documents, 10-, 11-, or 12-point type is used for the body of the text:

This paragraph is printed in 10-point type. This size is easy to read, provided it is reproduced on a high-quality ink-jet printer or laser printer.

This paragraph is printed in 12-point type. If the document will be read by people over age 40, 12-point type is a good size because it is more legible than a smaller size.

This paragraph is printed in 14-point type. This size is appropriate for titles or headings.

Type sizes used in other parts of the document include the following:

footnotes	8- or 9-point type
indexes	2 points smaller than body text
slides or transparencies	24- to 36-point type

In general, aim for at least a 2- to 4-point difference between the headings and the body. Too many size variations, however, suggest a sweepstakes advertisement rather than serious text.

Line Length   The line length most often used on an 8.5 × 11-inch page—about 80 characters—is somewhat difficult to read. A shorter line of 50 to 60 characters is less demanding, especially in a long document (Biggs, 1980).

Line Spacing   Sometimes called *leading* (pronounced *ledding*), *line spacing* refers to the white space between lines or between a line of text and a graphic. If lines are too far apart, the page looks diffuse, the text loses coherence, and readers tire quickly. If lines are too close together, the page looks crowded and becomes difficult to read. Some research suggests that smaller type, longer lines, and sans serif typefaces all benefit from extra line spacing. Figure 12.16 on page 274 shows three variations in line spacing.

Line spacing is usually determined by the kind of document you are writing. Memos and letters are single-spaced, whereas reports, proposals, and similar documents are often double-spaced or one-and-a-half-spaced.

Figure 12.17 on page 275 shows how line spacing can be used to distinguish one section of text from another and to separate text from graphics.

Justification   Justification refers to the alignment of words along the left and right margins of the text. In technical communication,

TECH TIP
How to Format Fonts

To improve the readability of your document, use the **Font** dialog box to specify typographical elements such as typeface, style, size, color, character spacing, and text effects.

From the **Format** menu, select **Font.**

You can change the appearance of a typeface by checking various **Effects** boxes.

You can also specify basic font formatting, such as typeface, type size, bold, italic, and underlining, by using drop-down menus and buttons in the **Formatting** toolbar.

KEYWORDS: font, font style

Using Type Sizes Responsibly

According to the design principle of contrast, text set in large type contrasts with text set in small type. It makes sense to use large type to emphasize headings and other important information that you want to stand out. But be careful with small type. It is unethical to use excessively small type (6 points or smaller) to disguise information that you *don't* want to stand out. When you read the fine print in an ad for cell-phone service, you get annoyed when you figure out that the low rates are guaranteed for only three months or that you are committing to a long-term contract. You *should* get annoyed; it's annoying. Don't do it.

text is often *left-justified* (also called *ragged right*). Except for paragraph indentations, the lines begin along a uniform left margin but end on an irregular right border. Ragged right is most common in word-processed text (even though word processors can justify the right margin).

In *justified* text (also called *full-justified*), both the left and right margins are justified. Justified text is seen most often in typeset, formal documents, such as books.

---

a.   **Excessive line spacing**

Aronomink Systems has been contracted by Cecil Electric Cooperative, Inc.

(CECI) to design a solid waste management system for the Cecil County

plant, Units 1 and 2, to be built in Cranston, Maryland. The system will consist

of two 600 MW pulverized coal-burning units fitted with high-efficiency elec-

trostatic precipitators and limestone reagent FGD systems.

b.   **Appropriate line spacing**

Aronomink Systems has been contracted by Cecil Electric Cooperative, Inc. (CECI) to design a solid waste management system for the Cecil County plant, Units 1 and 2, to be built in Cranston, Maryland. The system will consist of two 600 MW pulverized coal-burning units fitted with high-efficiency electrostatic precipitators and limestone reagent FGD systems.

c.   **Inadequate line spacing**

Aronomink Systems has been contracted by Cecil Electric Cooperative, Inc. (CECI) to design a solid waste management system for the Cecil County plant, Units 1 and 2, to be built in Cranston, Maryland. The system will consist of two 600 MW pulverized coal-burning units fitted with high-efficiency electrostatic precipitators and limestone reagent FGD systems.

■ **Figure 12.16   Line Spacing**

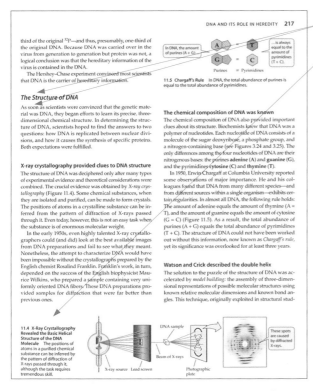

The line spacing between two sections should be greater than the line spacing within a section.

Line spacing separates text from the graphic.

This page uses no extra line spacing between single-spaced paragraphs. Instead, it uses paragraph indents. This format can make the page look dense and uninviting.

■ **Figure 12.17   Line Spacing Used to Distinguish One Section from Another**
Source: Purves et al., 2004, p. 217.

The following passage (U.S. Department of Agriculture, 2002) is presented first in left-justified form and then in justified form:

Notice that the space between words is uniform in left-justified text.

We recruited participants to reflect the racial diversity of the area in which the focus groups were conducted. Participants had to meet the following eligibility criteria: have primary responsibility or share responsibility for cooking in their household; prepare food and cook in the home at least three times a week; eat meat and/or poultry; prepare meat and/or poultry in the home at least twice a week; and not regularly use a digital food thermometer when cooking at home.

In justified text, the spacing between words is irregular, slowing down the reader. Because a big space suggests a break between sentences, not a break between words, the reader can become confused, frustrated, and fatigued.

We recruited participants to reflect the racial diversity of the area in which the focus groups were conducted. Participants had to meet the following eligibility criteria: have primary responsibility or share responsibility for cooking in their household; prepare food and cook in the home at least three times a week; eat meat and/or poultry; prepare meat and/or poultry in the home at least twice a week; and not regularly use a digital food thermometer when cooking at home.

Notice that the irregular spacing not only slows down reading but also can create "rivers" of white space. Readers are tempted to concentrate on the rivers running south rather than on the information itself.

TECH TIP
How to Modify Line Spacing

When designing the page, you can adjust the white space between lines of text and before or after each paragraph by using the **Paragraph** dialog box.

From the **Format** menu, select **Paragraph.**

In the **Paragraph** dialog box, you can change the **spacing before** and **after** paragraphs.

You can also specify the **space between lines** of text.

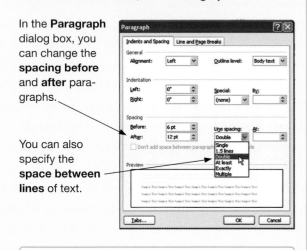

KEYWORDS: line spacing, leading, paragraph spacing

 In This Book

For more about titles, see Ch. 10, p. 205. For more about using headings, see Ch. 10, p. 206.

 **On TechComm Web**

For more about designing headings, see the Document Design Tutorial on <bedfordstmartins.com/techcomm>.

Justification can make the text harder to read in one more way. Some word processors and typesetting systems automatically hyphenate words—sometimes incorrectly—that do not fit on the line. Hyphenation slows down and distracts readers. Left-justified text does not require as much hyphenation as justified text does.

Titles and Headings

Titles and headings should stand out visually on the page because they present a new idea.

Titles   Because a title is the most important heading in a document, it should be displayed clearly and prominently. If it is on a cover page or a title page, use boldface in a large size, such as 18 or 24 points. If it also appears at the top of the first page, make it slightly larger than the rest of the text—perhaps 16 or 18 points for a document printed in 12-point type—but smaller than it is on the cover or title page. Many designers center titles on the page between the right and left margins.

Headings   Readers should be able to tell when you are beginning a new topic. The most effective way to distinguish one level of headings from another is to use size variations (Williams & Spyridakis, 1992). Most readers will notice a 20 percent size difference between a first-level heading and a second-level heading. Boldface also sets off headings effectively. The least effective way to set off headings is underlining, because in many word processors the underline obscures the *descenders*, the portions of letters that extend below the body, such as in *p* and *y*.

In general, the more important the heading level, the closer it is to the left margin: first-level headings usually begin at the left margin, second-level headings are often indented one-half inch, and third-level headings are often indented an inch. Indented third-level headings also can be run into the text.

In designing headings, use line spacing carefully. A perceivable distance between a heading and the text that follows increases the impact of the heading. Consider these three examples:

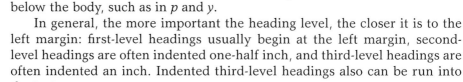

TECH TIP
How to Modify Justification

To increase the readability of your document, you can specify the alignment of words along the left and right margins by using the **Paragraph** dialog box or the appropriate buttons on the **Formatting** toolbar.

To modify justification using the **Paragraph** dialog box, select **Paragraph** from the **Format** menu. You can specify that lines begin along the left margin or right margin, are centered on the page, or are justified.

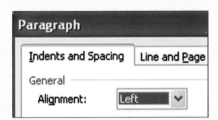

You can also modify justification by using buttons on the **Formatting** toolbar.

 To left align text.

 To right align text.

 To center text.

 To justify text.

KEYWORDS: alignment, justify text

Summary

In this example, the writer has skipped a line between the heading and the text that follows it. The heading stands out clearly.

Summary
In this example, the writer has not skipped a line between the heading and the text that follows it. The heading stands out, but not as emphatically.

Summary. In this example, the writer has begun the text on the same line as the heading. This run-in style makes the heading stand out the least.

Other Design Features

Table 12.3 on pages 278–79 shows five other design features that are used frequently in technical communication: rules, boxes, screens, marginal glosses, and pull quotes.

■ **Table 12.3 Rules, Boxes, Screens, Marginal Glosses, and Pull Quotes**

Two types of rules are used here: the vertical rules to separate the columns, and the blue horizontal rules to separate each item. Rules enable you to fit a lot of information on a page, but when overused they make the page look cluttered.

Source: Institute, 2005, p. 43.

Rules. A *rule* is a design term for a straight line. Using the drawing tools on a word processor, you can add rules. Horizontal rules can separate headers and footers from the body of the page or divide two sections of text. Vertical rules can separate columns on a multicolumn page or identify revised text in a manual. Rules exploit the principles of alignment and proximity.

Source: Valley, 2005, p. 61.

Boxes. Adding rules on all four sides of an item creates a box. Boxes can enclose graphics or special sections of text, or form a border for the whole page. Boxed text is often positioned to extend into the margin, giving it further emphasis. Boxes exploit the principles of contrast and repetition.

The use of three different colors of screens clearly distinguishes the three sets of equations.

Source: Purvis et al., 2004, p. 466.

Screens. The background shading behind text or graphics for emphasis is called a *screen*. The density can range from 1 percent to 100 percent; 5–10 percent is usually enough to provide emphasis without making the text illegible. You can use screens with or without boxes. Screens exploit the principles of contrast and repetition.

■ **Table 12.3** *(continued)*

This author uses the marginal gloss for presenting definitions of keywords.

interest underlies all
and minimize costs.
utilitarianism. Social
ng whether to donate
and anxiety) against
u anticipate rewards

and give directions to
ribe how we ought to
learn the *reciprocity*
to those who have
rocity norm compels
as we receive. With
eive, we also learn a
our help, even if the
ho each week attend
ty norm: They report
r and infirm than do
& Weitzman, 1992).

■ **bystander effect** the tendency for any given bystander to be less likely to give aid if other bystanders are present.

■ **social exchange theory** the theory that our social behavior is an exchange process, the aim of which is to maximize benefits and minimize costs.

■ **superordinate goals** shared goals that override differences among people and require their cooperation.

Source: Myers, 2003, p. 603.

Marginal glosses. A marginal gloss is a brief comment on the main discussion. Marginal glosses are usually set in a different typeface—and sometimes in a different color—from the main discussion. Although marginal glosses can be helpful in providing a quick overview of the main discussion, they can also compete with the text for the reader's attention. Marginal glosses exploit the principles of contrast and repetition.

This pull quote is placed in the margin, but it can go anywhere on the page, even spanning several columns or the whole page.

Puritan leaders, however, interpreted
an error caused either by a misguided
r by the malevolent power of Satan.
the cause, errors could
lerated. As one Puritan
proclaimed, "God doth
in his word tolerate
States, to give
s to . . . adversaries of
if they have power in
s to suppress them. The
saith . . . there is no
one."
y after banishing Roger
Winthrop confronted another dis-
s time—as one New Englander ob-
"Woman that Preaches better Gospell
of your black-coates that have been at
eversity." The woman was Anne
n, a devout Puritan steeped in Scripture
orbed by religious questions.
n had received an excellent education
ather in England. The mother of four-

Almost from the beginning, John Winthrop and other leaders had difficulty enforcing their views of Puritan orthodoxy.

Source: Roark et al., 2005, p. 115.

Pull quotes. A pull quote is a brief quotation (usually just a sentence or two) that is pulled from the text and displayed in a larger type size, and usually in a different typeface and enclosed in a box. Newspapers and magazines use pull quotes to attract readers' attention. Pull quotes are inappropriate for reports and similar documents because they look too informal. They are increasingly popular, however, in newsletters. Pull quotes exploit the principles of contrast and repetition.

ANALYZING SOME PAGE DESIGNS

Figures 12.18–12.22 on pages 281–85, showing typical page designs used in technical documents, illustrate the concepts discussed in this chapter.

 On TechComm Web

To view Figs. 12.18 and 12.19 in context on the Web, click on Links Library for Ch. 12 on <bedfordstmartins.com/ techcomm>.

TECH TIP
How to Create Boxes and Screens

To emphasize page elements by enclosing them in a box or adding background shading, use the **Borders and Shading** dialog box.

To create a **border** around a page element or an entire page, select the area that you want to enclose and then select **Borders and Shading** from the **Format** menu.

Select the **Borders** or **Page Border** tab.

You can specify the type of border, line style, color, and/or line width.

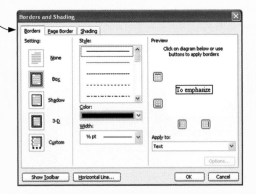

To create a **screen**, also called **shading**, select the area you want to screen and then select **Borders and Shading** from the **Format** menu.

Select the **Shading** tab.

You can specify the color within the box, as well as the style of the pattern.

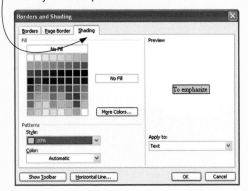

> **KEYWORDS:** borders, page border, shading

TECH TIP
How to Create Text Boxes

To emphasize graphics or special sections of text, or to position such elements independently of your margins, use the **Text Box** feature in the **Drawing** toolbar.

To **create** a text box, select the **Text Box** button from the **Drawing** toolbar.

Click and drag your cursor to create a text box.

Click inside the text box and begin typing text.

You can select the text box and move it around the page.

To **format** your text box, select the box and then click on the **Text Box** button in the **Format** menu.

The **Format Text Box** dialog box allows you to specify design elements such as fill colors, border style, box size, and internal margins, as well as the wrapping style of the surrounding text.

You can also use buttons in the **Drawing** toolbar to specify design elements such as fill color, line color, font color, line style, shadow style, and 3-D style.

> **KEYWORDS:** text box, drawing toolbar, fill color, line color

This page from a report is designed to use space efficiently.

The two-column format is economical because a lot of words fit on a page and because it lets the designer use narrow or wide graphics without wasting space.

178 Federal Reserve Bulletin □ March 2002

proportions incorporated in the IP index from 1994 forward.

Beginning with this revision, the methods and data used to obtain estimates of value added in the electric utility industry have been improved. A change was necessary for several reasons. First, many of the data that had been used to compute value added were contained in an EIA publication that has been discontinued. Second, the EIA data on "utilities" include regulated entities only, and data covering all producers of electric power (that is, including the unregulated power generators) are required to avoid a severe understatement of the value added by the entire industry in 2000. Finally, a review of the earlier methods suggested value added was understated for the period preceding the deregulation of the industry.

The Federal Reserve's new estimates of value added for the electric utility industry were constructed according to the Census definition of value added, that is, industry revenue minus the cost of purchased material inputs. Data on industry revenue (including all establishments that distribute power to final users) were obtained from Statistical Yearbooks issued by the Edison Electric Institute; these data were combined with EIA measures of fuel costs to obtain an estimate of Census value added. The new figures were applied on a best-change basis for the period from 1992 forward; the 2002 revision will introduce refined results as well as revised figures for earlier years.

Changes to Individual Series

With this revision, the capacity series for natural gas extraction (part of SIC 13) incorporates new estimates developed by the EIA; the new estimates are substantially lower than the agency's previous figures that were used to derive the capacity for natural gas extraction. The new figures are designed to better reflect the ability of producing wells to deliver gas into the gathering and pipeline system, whereas previous EIA figures measured capacity at the wellhead only.

The source data for one other capacity series has changed. The index for silver capacity is now based on data from the USGS; previously it was derived using a trend-through-peak method.

The monthly production indicators for construction machinery and original equipment motor vehicle parts were refined. The weights used to combine the available product data for construction machinery were updated. The indicator for motor vehicle parts is

2. U.S. LAN equipment, 1992–2001

Period	Production index	Price index	Value of production (millions of dollars)
Annual estimates (1992 = 100)			
1992	100.000	100.000	1,648.8
1993	190.691	83.556	2,684.4
1994	298.728	74.243	3,736.6
1995	604.349	62.153	6,328.3
1996	953.621	57.123	9,177.7
1997	1,610.035	47.548	12,897.7
1998	2,480.329	34.327	14,344.5
1999	3,191.443	28.130	15,124.9
2000	4,163.164	24.406	17,118.2
Quarterly estimates (1996:Q1 = 100)			
1996:Q1	100.000	100.000	7,923.2
Q2	113.744	98.967	8,919.0
Q3	128.626	93.735	9,552.8
Q4	150.302	86.623	10,315.7
1997:Q1	161.797	84.029	10,772.1
Q2	183.502	79.683	11,585.3
Q3	224.022	77.535	13,762.2
Q4	262.123	74.493	15,471.1
1998:Q1	290.487	62.795	14,452.9
Q2	326.083	59.075	15,262.7
Q3	328.499	53.487	13,921.3
Q4	329.790	52.587	13,741.0
1999:Q1	417.721	48.619	16,091.2
Q2	419.060	47.117	15,644.2
Q3	394.817	46.808	14,642.6
Q4	402.795	44.249	14,121.6
2000:Q1	449.375	43.459	15,473.4
Q2	493.979	41.718	16,327.9
Q3	599.868	39.456	18,752.6
Q4	604.171	37.433	17,919.0
2001:Q1	538.767	34.889	14,893.0
Q2	465.929	34.232	12,651.6
Q3	471.295	31.602	11,814.1

The designer uses white space effectively to separate text from graphics and to set off headings.

now developed from monthly product data (engines, brakes, axles, and transmissions), production-worker hours, and motor vehicle assemblies; previously, the series was derived from the product only.

The annual estimates of motor vehicle repair parts were also improved; their derivation now includes information on the average age of the motor vehicle fleet.

LAN Equipment

The 2000 revision introduced a new IP series for the production of local area network (LAN) equipment (routers, switches, and hubs). The new series is not published in the monthly statistical release, but it is included in the broader IP aggregate for communications equipment and updated on an ongoing basis (see the March 2001 Bulletin article). Table 2 shows updates of the results for LAN equipment originally issued a year ago.   □

The use of the second color — green — is effective in the graphic, but it doesn't provide much emphasis for the heading. The designer might use a darker green or increase the size of the heading.

■ **Figure 12.18   A Two-Column Design**
Source: U. S. Federal Reserve Board, 2002 <www.federalreserve.gov/pubs/bulletin/2002/0302_2nd.pdf>.

This page from a white paper uses a simple double-spaced, one-column design.

The header is separated from the main portion of the page by a horizontal rule.

FREE ANTI-VIRUS TIPS & TECHNIQUES

Create a Personal.xls File

This technique is equivalent to creating a Payload macro to address Word macro viruses. Laroux.A checks for the existence of a file by the name of *personal.xls* in Excel's *XLSTART* directory. If one exists, it does not infact. Thus, if we put a file by that name in that directory, we will be immunized from Laroux.A. As with ConceptA, Laroux.A is the most widespread of all Excel macro viruses.

To create such a file, simply take an empty Excel file and place it in the *XLSTART* subdirectory under where Excel is located.

As in the case of Word, many other viruses have since appeared, and other variants of Laroux now exist that would not be affected by this approach.

PROS: Works against Laroux.A

CONS: Ineffective against any other virus

Excel Macro Virus Protection

Some designers do not use a paragraph indent in the first line after a heading.

Like Word97, Excel97 also has the Macro virus protection option as a check box available under Tools/Options.../General (see also the section entitled "Word7.0a and Word97"). This check box enables the user to be alerted if any macros exist in the spreadsheet about to be opened. If such a spredsheet is encountered, the user is given the choice of stopping, disregarding the warning, or continuing with the macros disabled.

However, Excel users often use more macros than Word users. Therefore, Excel users are more likely to get the alert involving useful macros than their counterparts who use Word. Thus, though users should be encouraged to use this option, system administrators would likely find rebellious users if they tried to enforce this technique.

PRO: Generally effective. If there's a macro in the spreadsheet, it tells you so.

CON: Many Excel spreadsheets have useful macros, so many false alarms

This page includes two levels of headings. The designer uses size to distinguish the two levels.

PowerPoint Macro Viruses

The column devoted to marginal annotations is separated from the main portion of the text by a vertical rule.

It took about two years after the introduction of PowerPoint97 for the first PowerPoint virus to appear. Because PowerPoint is much less widely used than Word or Excel, and because PowerPoint97 shares the same macro programming language as its Office97 brethren, the first PowerPoint97 viruses happen to be cross-infectors which can also infect Word or Excel.

PowerPoint only started to support macros in the version distributed as PowerPoint97.

PowerPoint only started to support macros in the version distributed as PowerPoint97.

The footer consists only of a page number.

❿

■ **Figure 12.19   A One-Column Design**
Source: Kuo, 2004 <www.nai.com/common/media/vil/pdf/free_AV_tips_techniques.pdf>.

This page from a Dell sales catalog is well designed.

The heading and the text just below it present the main idea: you can upgrade the sound as you configure your computer.

The sound-cards section uses two columns of text to accommodate more textual information.

The speaker-systems section includes photos of the four options because computer users might want to see what they are getting. The sound-cards section does not lend itself to visual representation.

■ **Figure 12.20   A Complex Design**
Source: Dell, 2005, p. 32.

This page from Scientific American *uses space effectively with a three-column design.*

The technical description of black holes is clearly distinguished from the rest of the text by the box rule and a different typeface.

Color is used sparingly.

A TALE OF TWO BLACK HOLES

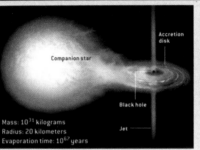

Companion star

Accretion disk

Black hole

Jet

Mass: 10^{31} kilograms
Radius: 20 kilometers
Evaporation time: 10^{67} years

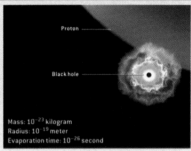

Proton

Black hole

Mass: 10^{-23} kilogram
Radius: 10^{-19} meter
Evaporation time: 10^{-26} second

ASTROPHYSICAL BLACK HOLES are thought to be the corpses of massive stars that collapsed under their own weight. As matter falls into them, they act like cosmic hydroelectric plants, releasing gravitational potential energy—the only power source that can account for the intense x-rays and gaseous jets that astronomers see spurting out of celestial systems such as the x-ray binary shown here.

MICROSCOPIC BLACK HOLES have masses ranging up to that of a large asteroid. They might have been churned out by the collapse of matter early in the big bang. If space has unseen extra dimensions, they might also be created by energetic particle collisions in today's universe. Rather than swallowing matter, they would give off radiation and decay away rapidly.

would evaporate shortly after they formed, lighting up the particle detectors like Christmas trees. In so doing, they could give clues about how spacetime is woven together and whether it has unseen higher dimensions.

A Tight Squeeze

IN ITS MODERN FORM, the concept of black holes emerges from Einstein's general theory of relativity, which predicts that if matter is sufficiently compressed, its gravity becomes so strong that it carves out a region of space from which nothing can escape. The bound-ary of the region is the black hole's event horizon: objects can fall in, but none can come out. In the simplest case, where space has no hidden dimensions or those dimensions are smaller than the hole, its size is directly proportional to its mass. If you compressed the sun to a radius of three kilometers, about four-millionths of its present size, it would become a black hole. For Earth to meet the same fate, you would need to squeeze it into a radius of nine millimeters, about a billionth its present size.

Thus, the smaller the hole, the higher the degree of compression that is re-quired to create it. The density to which matter must be squeezed scales as the inverse square of the mass. For a hole with the mass of the sun, the density is about 10^{19} kilograms per cubic meter, higher than that of an atomic nucleus. Such a density is about the highest that can be created through gravitational collapse in the present universe. A body lighter than the sun resists collapse because it gets stabilized by repulsive quantum forces between subatomic particles. Observationally, the lightest black hole candidates are about six solar masses.

Stellar collapse is not the only way that holes might form, however. In the early 1970s Stephen W. Hawking of the University of Cambridge and one of us (Carr) investigated a mechanism for generating holes in the early universe. These are termed "primordial" black holes. As space expands, the average density of matter decreases; therefore, the density was much higher in the past, in particular exceeding nuclear levels within the first microsecond of the big bang. The known laws of physics allow for a matter density up to the so-called Planck value of 10^{97} kilograms per cubic meter—the density at which the strength of gravity becomes so strong that quantum-mechanical fluctuations should break

Overview/*Black Hole Factories*

- Black holes need not be gargantuan, ravenous monsters. Theory implies that they can come in a huge variety of sizes, some even smaller than subatomic particles. Tiny holes should be wracked by quantum effects, and the very smallest would explode almost as soon as they formed.
- Small black holes might be left over from the early stages of the big bang, and astronomers might be able to detect some of them exploding today.
- Theorists have recently proposed that small black holes might be created in collisions in the present universe, even on Earth. They had thought that the requisite energies were too high, but if space has extra dimensions with the right properties, then the energy threshold for black hole production is much lower. If so, holes might be produced by the Large Hadron Collider (LHC) at CERN and in cosmic-ray collisions high in the atmosphere. Physicists could use the holes to probe the extra dimensions of space.

■ **Figure 12.21 A Multicolumn Design**
Source: Carr and Giddings, 2005, p. 50.

The involvement of undergraduate students is an important feature of RUI, which provides them with research-rich learning environments. However, the primary purpose of RUI is to support faculty research, thereby maintaining the intellectual vibrancy of faculty members in the classroom and research community.

RUI provides the following types of support:

•   **Single-Investigator and Collaborative Faculty Research Projects**—Provides support through NSF research programs in response to proposals submitted by individual faculty members or by groups of collaborating investigators. RUI proposals differ from standard NSF proposals in that they include an RUI Impact Statement describing the expected effects of the proposed research on the research and education environment of the institution.

•   **Shared Research Instrumentation and Tools**—Provides support for (1) the purchase or upgrade of instrumentation or equipment necessary to support research that will be conducted by several faculty members and (2) the development of new instrumentation.

•   **Research Opportunity Awards (ROA's)**—Enable faculty members at predominantly undergraduate institutions to pursue research as visiting scientists with NSF-supported investigators at other institutions. ROA's are usually funded as supplements to ongoing NSF research grants. ROA's are intended to increase the visitors' research capability and effectiveness; improve research and teaching at their home institution; and enhance the NSF-funded research of the host principal investigator.

For More Information

For further information about the RUI activity, including guidelines for the preparation and submission of proposals, see program announcement NSF 00-144.

Prospective applicants for RUI grants and principal investigators interested in hosting an ROA visiting researcher are urged to contact a program officer in the appropriate discipline.

4.   **Minority Research Planning Grants and Career Advancement Awards**—These awards are part of NSF's overall effort to give members of minority groups that are underrepresented in science and engineering greater access to scientific research support.

•   **Minority Research Planning Grants (MRPG's)**—Enable eligible minorities who have not had prior independent Federal research support to develop competitive research projects by supporting preliminary studies and similar activities. These are one-time awards of up to $18K for a maximum of 18 months.

•   **Minority Career Advancement Awards (MCAA's)**—Support activities that can expand the research career potential of promising applicants. These awards are

This page has no header or footer with page numbers or section headings.

Chunking is poor. The reader cannot easily see where one section begins and ends. There should be greater leading between sections than within sections.

The same typeface and size are used in the two different headings and at the start of the bullet items, violating the principle of repetition.

The effect of the bullets is diminished because the turnovers are not indented.

■ **Figure 12.22   A Poorly Designed Page**
Source: National Science Foundation, 2001 <www.nsf.gov/pubs/2001/nsf013/nsf013.pdf>.

INTERACTIVE SAMPLE DOCUMENT
Analyzing a Page Design

The following page (Doyle, 2005) is from *Scientific American.* The questions in the margin ask you to think about page design (as discussed on pages 265–279). E-mail your responses to yourself and/or your instructor, and see suggested responses on TechComm Web.

1. Describe the use of columns. In what ways do they work well?

2. Describe the text justification. In what ways, if any, would you revise the justification?

3. Describe the design and placement of the graphic. In what ways, if any, would you change its size and placement?

4. Why are the two sets of information in the left margin presented there rather than in the body of the text?

On TechComm Web

To e-mail your responses to yourself and/or your instructor and to see suggested responses, click on Interactive Sample Documents for Ch. 12 on <bedfordstmartins.com/techcomm>.

news SCAN

BY THE NUMBERS

Measuring Beauty

LIFE WITH SUN, WATER AND OTHER NATURAL AMENITIES   BY RODGER DOYLE

FAST FACTS:
PLACES TO LIVE

The high and low ratings of U.S. counties are listed according to their natural amenities. The scores are scaled from 0 to 100; the national average is 37.

Top Five
Ventura (California): 100
Humboldt (California): 100
Santa Barbara (California): 99
Mendocino (California): 99
Del Norte (California): 98

Bottom Five
Mower (Minnesota): 7
Norman (Minnesota): 6
Tipton (Indiana): 6
Wilkin (Minnesota): 2
Red Lake (Minnesota): 0

SOURCE: Economic Research Service, U.S. Department of Agriculture.

Books such as *Places Rated Almanac* and *America's Most Charming Towns and Villages* have long been publishing staples, but in recent years the U.S. government has joined the trend by rating each county in the contiguous 48 states in terms of its natural amenities. The ratings, made by the Economic Research Service of the U.S. Department of Agriculture, are based on six measures: January temperature, January sunshine, temperature gain between January and July (less is better), July humidity, water area, and topographic variation.

The map, which summarizes the ratings, reveals a distinct pattern, with the western states and southern Florida at the top of the scale and scoring well on most measures. In contrast, the upper Midwest, from Ohio through the Dakotas, shows a relative lack of amenities. This region, of course, tends to have cold winters. But even when January temperatures are removed from the equa-

verse recreational opportunities such as fishing, skiing and big game hunting. The eastern third of the country, aside from Florida, has no top-rated counties except for several in southern Appalachia, which has a hospitable climate, many lakes and rivers, and considerable topographic diversity.

With the study, the USDA hopes to understand the factors underlying the economic viability of rural counties. It demonstrated that natural amenities correlate strongly with population change: Counties having very high amenities scores typically doubled in population during the period from 1970 to 1996, apparently because of their ability to attract retirees and recreational facilities. Those at the low end of the amenities scale lost population or barely held even. Furthermore, the degree of natural amenities helps to explain rural population shifts at least as much as economic factors, such as changing employment opportunities in farming, mining and lumbering.

Natural amenities do not play much of a role in metropolitan areas, where economic considerations such as transportation and skilled labor are vital. Of the big cities, Los Angeles and San Francisco score the highest. Manhattan (New York County) ranks only 1,689 out of 3,111 counties (but who goes there for the scenery?); Cook County, Illinois (Chicago), and Washington, D.C., rank even lower. Of the remaining major metropolitan counties, Franklin County, Ohio (Columbus), and Hennepin County, Minnesota (Minneapolis), have the lowest ratings. Most major suburban counties in the Northeast and Midwest get low ratings. Among the few exceptions are two New York City areas, Fairfield County, Connecticut, and Suffolk County, New York.

Rodger Doyle can be reached at rdoyle2@adelphia.net

Rating of Counties on the Natural Amenities Scale
Bottom decile   Next decile   Middle six deciles   Next decile   Top decile
SOURCE: Economic Research Service, U.S. Department of Agriculture. Counties listed are those that rated highest in each of the nine U.S. Census regions (separated by dark lines). In cases where two counties have the same rating, both are shown.

FURTHER READING
Natural Amenities Drive Rural Population Change. David A. McGranahan. Economic Research Service, U.S. Department of Agriculture, 1999. www.ers.usda.gov/publications/aer781/

tion, the ratings in the region do not improve significantly (the region generally lacks topographic variation). Among the few northern areas to rank high is Glacier County, Montana, which includes the eastern face of the Rocky Mountains, extensive plains area, buttes, lakes and rivers, together with di-

Writer's Checklist

Did you

☐ analyze your audience: their knowledge of the subject, attitudes, and reasons for reading, as well as the kinds of tasks they will be carrying out? (p. 260)

☐ think about what your readers will expect to see when they pick up the document? (p. 260)

☐ determine your resources in time, money, and equipment? (p. 260)

☐ consider the best size for the document? (p. 261)

☐ consider the best paper for the document? (p. 262)

☐ consider the best binding for the document? (p. 262)

☐ think about which accessing tools would be most appropriate, such as icons, color, dividers, tabs, and cross-reference tables? (p. 263)

☐ devise a style for headers and footers? (p. 265)

☐ devise a style for page numbers? (p. 265)

☐ draw thumbnail sketches and page grids that define columns and white space? (p. 267)

☐ choose typefaces that are appropriate to your subject? (p. 271)

☐ use appropriate styles from the type families? (p. 272)

☐ use type sizes that are appropriate for your subject and audience? (p. 272)

☐ decide on whether to use left-justified text or full-justified text? (p. 273)

☐ choose a line length that is suitable for your subject and audience? (p. 273)

☐ choose line spacing that is suitable for your line length, subject, and audience? (p. 273)

☐ design your title for clarity and emphasis? (p. 276)

☐ work out a logical, consistent style for each heading level? (p. 276)

☐ use rules, boxes, screens, marginal glosses, and pull quotes where appropriate? (p. 278)

☐ use color, if you have access to it, to highlight certain items, such as warnings? (p. 264)

Exercises

 In This Book For more about memos, see Ch. 14, p. 352.

1. Your word processor contains a number of templates for documents such as reports, letters, and memos. Study two templates for the same kind of document—for example, memos. What are the main differences between them? For what writing situations—audience, purpose, and subject—is each one most suited?

2. Study the first and second pages of an article in a journal in your field. Describe 10 different design features you identify on these two pages. Which design features are most effective for the audience and purpose? Which are least effective?

3. **GROUP EXERCISE** Form small groups for this collaborative exercise in analyzing design. Photocopy or scan a page from a book or a magazine. Choose a page that does not contain advertisements. Each person works independently for the first part of this project:

   • One person describes the design elements.

   • One person evaluates the design. Which aspects of the design are effective, and which could be improved?

   • One person creates a new design using thumbnail sketches.

   Then the group members meet and compare notes. Do all members of the group agree with the first member's description of the design? With the second member's analysis of the design? Do all members like the third member's redesign? What have your discussions taught you about design? Write a memo to your instructor presenting your findings. Include the photocopied or scanned page with your memo.

4. Study the following page from a Micron data sheet (Micron, 2005, p. 26). Describe its major design characteristics: its typography and its use of margins and white space. What are the strengths of this design? What are the weaknesses? What design features do you recommend changing or adding to make it more attractive and easier to read? If appropriate, devise headings that can be added to the page. Present your analysis and recommendations in a memo to your instructor.

256Mb, 128Mb, 64Mb, 32Mb
Q-FLASH MEMORY

CLEAR STATUS REGISTER Command

The ISM sets the status register bits SR5, SR4, SR3, and SR1 to "1s." These bits, which indicate various failure conditions, can only be reset by the CLEAR STATUS REGISTER command. Allowing system software to reset these bits can perform several operations (such as cumulatively erasing or locking multiple blocks or writing several bytes in sequence). To determine if an error occurred during the sequence, the status register may be polled. To clear the status register, the CLEAR STATUS REGISTER command (50h) is written. The CLEAR STATUS REGISTER command functions independently of the applied VPEN voltage and is only valid when the ISM is off or the device is suspended.

BLOCK ERASE Command

The BLOCK ERASE command is a two-cycle command that erases one block. First, a block erase setup is written, followed by a block erase confirm. This command sequence requires an appropriate address within the block to be erased. The ISM handles all block preconditioning, erase, and verify. Time tWB after the two-cycle block erase sequence is written, the device automatically outputs status register data when read. The CPU can detect block erase completion by analyzing the output of the STS pin or status register bit SR7. Toggle OE# or CEx to update the status register. Upon block erase completion, status register bit SR5 should be checked to detect any block erase error. When an error is detected, the status register should be cleared before system software attempts corrective actions. The CEL remains in read status register mode until a new command is issued. This two-step setup command sequence ensures that block contents are not accidentally erased. An invalid block erase command sequence results in status register bits SR4 and SR5 being set to "1." Also, reliable block erasure can only occur when VCC is valid and VPEN = VPENH. Note that SR3 and SR5 are set to "1" if block erase is attempted while VPEN ≤ VPENLK. Successful block erase requires that the corresponding block lock bit be cleared. Similarly, SR1 and SR5 are set to "1" if block erase is attempted when the corresponding block lock bit is set.

BLOCK ERASE SUSPEND Command

The BLOCK ERASE SUSPEND command allows block erase interruption in order to read or program data in another block of memory. Writing the BLOCK ERASE SUSPEND command immediately after starting the block erase process requests that the ISM suspend the block erase sequence at an appropriate point in the algorithm. When reading after the BLOCK ERASE SUSPEND command is written, the device outputs status register data. Polling status register bit SR7, followed by SR6, shows when the BLOCK ERASE operation has been suspended. In the default mode, STS also transitions to VOH. tLES defines the block erase suspend latency. At this point, a READ ARRAY command can be written to read data from blocks other than that which is suspended. During erase suspend to program data in other blocks, a program sequence can also be issued. During a PROGRAM operation with block erase suspended, status register bit SR7 returns to "0" and STS output (in default mode) transitions to VOL. However, SR6 remains "1" to indicate block erase suspend status. Using the PROGRAM SUSPEND command, a program operation can also be suspended. Resuming a SUSPENDED programming operation by issuing the Program Resume command enables the suspended programming operation to continue. To resume the suspended erase, the user must wait for the programming operation to complete before issuing the Block ERASE RESUME command. While block erase is suspended, the only other valid commands are READ QUERY, READ STATUS REGISTER, CLEAR STATUS REGISTER, CONFIGURE, and BLOCK ERASE RESUME. After a BLOCK ERASE RESUME command to the Flash memory is completed, the ISM continues the block erase process. Status register bits SR6 and SR7 automatically clear and STS (in default mode) returns to VOL. After the ERASE RESUME command is completed, the device automatically outputs status register data when read. VPEN must remain at VPENH (the same VPEN level used for block erase) during block erase suspension. Block erase cannot resume during block erase suspend until PROGRAM operations are complete.

Case 12: Designing a Report Template

 In This Book   For more about memos, see Ch. 14, p. 352.

Background

You are part of the information staff for the Animal and Plant Health Inspection Service's Plant Protection and Quarantine (PPQ), which is part of the U.S. Department of Agriculture. The organization's goal is to protect the health and value of American agriculture and natural resources. Working with other federal agencies, Congress, the states, agricultural interests, and the general public, PPQ responds to potential acts of agricultural bioterrorism, invasive species, and diseases of wildlife and livestock. The organization's information staff helps PPQ scientists communicate research findings to both a general audience and expert audiences from agriculture, industry, government, science, and education.

Amid growing concerns of new pest introductions to domestic plant resources, PPQ is undertaking a safeguarding review. This review's goal is to propose specific recommendations on how to improve PPQ's ability to protect the nation's plant resources from harmful plant pests. Drawing on the expertise of representatives from government, industry, and academia, PPQ plans to publish a final report documenting the review's findings and recommendations, as well as several follow-up reports.

"Creating this report will be a little tricky," your supervisor, Charlotte McQuarrie, explains. "This report will include findings and recommendations from four separate committees: Pest Exclusion, Pest Detection and Response, International Pest Information, and Permit. Unless we give the committees some guidance, we are likely to get four different page designs—"

"—and that means we'll spend hours reformatting all the material so that the report has a consistent design," you say, interrupting.

"You got it. I think we need to start thinking about the design of the whole report right now. If we can decide on its overall design and page layout, we can give each committee a Word template to follow. Our job will be a lot easier when it comes time to compile all the information in a single report. I'm also planning to use this design for other follow-up reports that PPQ will publish over the next year and a half."

"Do you have any ideas for the design of the report?"

"Not yet. I want you to come up with a design and develop a template based on that design. I have some unformatted text and some graphics from the Pest Exclusion Committee for you to experiment with. I've added some brief comments using Word's reviewing toolbar to get you started." (See Document 12.1.)

"What do you have in mind?"

"I'd like to be able to e-mail each committee a Word template for the report. This template would reflect the design of the report. For example, if we go with a two-column design, the template would already have a two-column layout. All the writers would need to do is add content. They could use styles that we've defined for headings, body text, lists, captions, and so on. Your first step is to create the report's page design."

|Pest Exclusion Committee Report|

|<<snip snip>>|

|2.26 Detector Dogs|

|The use of dogs to detect meat and plant products is employed at a number of POEs. Dogs are used to monitor international mail, air passengers, and certain cargo entries. The APHIS-PPQ plans to integrate The Beagle Brigade Program into a number of AQI operations including airport baggage clearance, international mail facilities, cargo inspection, land border surveillance, and smuggling interdiction. It also has plans to explore other areas outside AQI where use of dogs may be helpful and to explore cross-utilization possibilities.|

At this time PPQ's program is constrained by a commitment to use beagles and a specific passive training technique. Customs and California's dog programs use both passive and aggressive search and alert techniques specific to the assigned task and select breeds based on the traits desired for a specific task. As a result, APHIS is self-limited in its ability to expand its use of dog scenting.

■ **Document 12.1**
Unformatted Content for the PPQ's Safeguarding Review Report
Source: Based on NPB, 1999
<www.aphis.usda.gov/ppq/safeguarding/MainReport.PDF>.

Comment: This is the first-level heading for the chapter. You will need to create a design for first-through third-level headings.

Comment: I deleted text here (sections 2.1-2.25) so that I could show you two shorter sections containing the elements we need to include in the page design.

Comment: This is a second-level heading.

Comment: You need to decide how to design the body text. Consider such elements as page grids, white space, columns, typography, and other design features. Don't forget to include accessing aids in your design.

On TechComm Web

For digital versions of case documents, click on Downloadable Case Documents on <bedfordstmartins.com/techcomm>.

|The San Ysidro, CA, border crossing from Mexico with the normal daily volume of vehicular traffic. Note the Customs officer with a detector dog conducting a primary inspection for controlled substances.|

> **Comment:** This is a caption for the graphic.

|Recommendations|

> **Comment:** This is a third-level heading.

Place detector dog teams at all high-risk ports of entry to facilitate passenger and baggage clearance.

Review APHIS's training and breed selection program to maximize use of different screening techniques and breed capabilities.

Negotiate with Customs to cross-train its dogs to screen for agricultural products at smaller ports of entry.

2.27 X-Ray Application

X-ray equipment is currently used to screen passenger baggage for pre-departure and at some ports of entry, at international mail facilities, and for cargo containers at various high volume locations and devanning sites along the U.S./Mexico border.

|Truck x-ray, Otay Mesa, CA, used principally by U.S. Customs for drug interdiction. A detailed X-ray of an entire semitruck with cargo requires 10 minutes.|

> **Comment:** Another caption

Customs plans to install additional truck x-ray equipment at additional southern border locations and at northern border crossing locations as funding allows.

The development of tomographic x-ray equipment to facilitate inspection at POEs is currently stalled. Originally under development by the Federal Aviation Agency to facilitate explosion detection, funding by that agency was rescinded when this technology failed to detect sheet explosives at the required levels.

Vivid Technology has developed a dual energy x-ray system that will enable a high speed analysis of baggage for quarantine commodities which uses the atomic number, mass, and density of objects to discriminate targeted materials from non-targeted objects. Implementation of this x-ray technology is planned to begin at JFK's Terminal One as a pilot program and then expand to other international airports.

Other x-ray technology under development in addition to heavy pallet x-ray and improved truck x-ray capability include imaging and relocatable inspection systems (IRIS or VACIS) and a railcar inspection system that uses gamma rays to detect objects as a train moves slowly through the equipment.

Recommendations

Develop or abandon development of tomographic x-ray technology.

Acquire and begin using Vivid Technology's dual energy x-ray system, and any other identified smart x-ray equipment to expedite screening and clearance of cargo, baggage, and mail.

Negotiate with Customs to use its truck x-ray capability to screen cargo containers.

|2.28 Future Possibilities and Research Needed|

|<<snip snip>>|

> **Comment:** This is another second-level heading.

> **Comment:** I deleted the rest of the text in this chapter.

Your Assignment

1. Using the techniques discussed in this chapter, create a page design for the body of the report. Write Charlotte a memo in which you justify your design decisions. Attach a copy of your sample page design to your memo.

2. Using Microsoft's Word's Styles and Formatting and document template features, create a report template based on your design for committee writers to use when they draft their reports.

13

Creating Graphics

Graphics are the "pictures" in technical communication: drawings, maps, photographs, diagrams, charts, graphs, and tables. Graphics range from realistic, such as photographs, to highly abstract, such as organization charts. In terms of function, graphics range from the decorative, such as clip art that shows people seated at a conference table, to highly informative, such as a table or a schematic diagram of an electronic device.

 On TechComm Web

See the Preparing Effective Charts and Graphs Tutorial on <bedfordstmartins.com/ techcomm>.

Graphics are important in technical communication because they do the following:

- catch the reader's attention and interest
- help you communicate information that is difficult to communicate with words
- help you clarify and emphasize information
- help nonnative speakers of English understand the information
- help you communicate information to multiple audiences with different interests, aptitudes, and reading habits

THE FUNCTIONS OF GRAPHICS

We have known for decades that graphics motivate people to study documents more closely. Some 83 percent of what we learn derives from what we see, whereas only 11 percent derives from what we hear (Gatlin, 1988). Because we are good at acquiring information through sight, a document that includes a visual element beyond words on the page is more effective than one that does not. People studying a text with graphics learn about one-third more than people studying a text without graphics (Levie & Lentz, 1982). And people remember 43 percent more when a document includes graphics (Morrison & Jimmerson, 1989). Readers like graphics. According to one survey, readers of computer documentation consistently want more graphics and fewer words (Brockmann, 1990, p. 203).

Graphics offer benefits that words alone cannot:

- *Graphics are indispensable in demonstrating logical and numerical relationships.* For example, an organization chart effectively represents the lines of authority in the organization. If you want to communicate the number of power plants built in each of the past 10 years, a bar graph works better than a paragraph.
- *Graphics can communicate spatial information more effectively than words alone.* If you want to show the details of a bicycle derailleur, a diagram of the bicycle with a close-up of the derailleur is more effective than a verbal description.
- *Graphics can communicate steps in a process more effectively than words alone.* A troubleshooting guide, a common kind of table, explains what might be causing a problem in a process and how you might fix it. Or a diagram can show clearly how acid rain forms.
- *Graphics can save space.* Consider the following paragraph:

  > In the Wilmington area, some 90 percent of the population aged 18 to 34 watches movies on a VCR or DVD player. They watch an average of 2.86 movies a week. Among 35- to 49-year-olds, the percentage is 82, and the average number of movies is 2.19. Among the 50- to 64-year-old age group, the percentage is 67, and the number of movies watched averages 2.5. Finally, among people 65 years old or older, the percentage is 48, and the average number of movies watched weekly is 2.71.

  Presented as a paragraph, this information is uneconomical and hard to remember. Presented as a table, however, the information is more concise and more memorable.

Age	Percentage watching movies	Number of movies watched per week
18–34	90	2.86
35–49	82	2.19
50–64	67	2.50
65+	48	2.71

- *Graphics can reduce the cost of documents intended for international readers.* Translation costs can reach 30 to 40 cents per word. Used effectively, graphics can reduce the number of words you have to translate (Corante, 2005).

As you plan and draft your document, look for opportunities to use graphics to clarify, emphasize, summarize, and organize information.

CHARACTERISTICS OF AN EFFECTIVE GRAPHIC

Effective graphics must be clear, understandable, and meaningfully related to the larger discussion. Follow these five principles:

- *A graphic should serve a purpose.* Don't include a graphic unless it will help your reader understand or remember information. Avoid content-free clip art, such as drawings of businesspersons shaking hands.

- *A graphic should be simple and uncluttered.* Three-dimensional bar graphs are easy to make, but they are harder to understand than two-dimensional ones, as shown in Figure 13.1.

- *A graphic should present a manageable amount of information.* Presenting too much information can confuse readers. Consider audience and purpose: what kinds of graphics are readers familiar with, how much do they already know about the subject, and what do you want the document to do? Because readers learn best if you present information in small chunks, create several simple graphics rather than a single complicated one.

- *A graphic should meet the reader's format expectations.* Through experience, readers learn how to read different kinds of graphics. Follow the conventions—for instance, use diamonds to represent decision points in a flowchart—unless you have a good reason not to.

- *A graphic should be clearly labeled.* Give every graphic (except a brief, informal one) a unique, clear, informative title. Fully label the columns of a table and the axes and lines of a graph. Don't make readers guess whether you are using meters or yards, or whether you are also including statistics from the previous year.

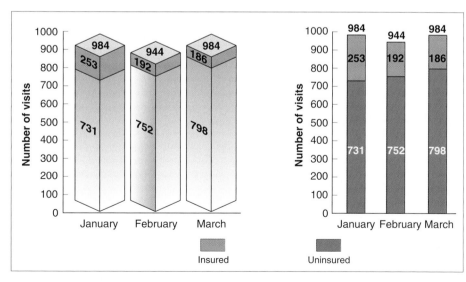

Unnecessary 3-D is one example of chartjunk, a term used by Tufte (1983) to describe the ornamentation that clutters up a graphic, distracting readers from the message.

The two-dimensional bar graph is clean and uncluttered, whereas the three-dimensional graph is more difficult to understand because the additional dimension obscures the main data points. The number of uninsured emergency-room visits in February, for example, is very difficult to see in the three-dimensional graph.

■ **Figure 13.1   Chartjunk and Clear Art**

Ethics Note

Creating Honest Graphics

- If you did not create the graphic or generate the data, cite your source and, if you want to publish it, obtain permission. For more on citing graphics, see page 300.

- Include all relevant data. For example, if you have a data point that you cannot explain, do not change the scale to eliminate it.

- Begin the axes in your graphs at zero, or mark them clearly, so that you represent quantities honestly.

- Do not use a table to hide a data point that would be obvious in a graph.

- Show items as they really are. Do not manipulate a photograph of a computer monitor to make the screen look bigger than it is.

- Do not use color or shading to misrepresent an item's importance. A light-shaded bar in a bar graph, for example, appears larger and nearer than a dark-shaded bar of the same size.

Common problem areas are pointed out in the discussions of various kinds of graphics throughout this chapter.

Guidelines

Integrating Graphics and Text

▶ **Place the graphic in an appropriate location.** If readers need the graphic to understand the discussion, put it directly after the relevant point in the discussion, or as soon after it as possible. If the graphic merely supports or elaborates a point, include it as an appendix.

▶ **Introduce the graphic in the text.** Whenever possible, refer to a graphic before it appears (ideally, on the same page). Refer to the graphic by number (such as *Figure 7*). Do not refer to "the figure above" or "the figure below," because the graphic might be moved during the production process. If the graphic is in an appendix, cross-reference it: "For complete details of the operating characteristics, see Appendix, Part B, page 19."

▶ **Explain the graphic in the text.** State what you want readers to learn from it. Sometimes a simple paraphrase of the title is enough: "Figure 2 compares the costs of the three major types of coal gasification plants." At other times, however, you might need to explain why the graphic is important or how to interpret it. If the graphic is intended to make a point, be explicit:

> As Figure 2 shows, a high-sulfur bituminous coal gasification plant is more expensive than either a low-sulfur bituminous or anthracite plant, but more than half of its cost is cleanup equipment. If these expenses could be eliminated, high-sulfur bituminous would be the least expensive of the three types of plants.

Graphics often are accompanied by captions, explanations ranging from a sentence to several paragraphs.

▶ **Make the graphic clearly visible.** Distinguish the graphic from the surrounding text by adding white space or rules (lines) or by enclosing it in a box.

▶ **Make the graphic accessible.** If the document is more than a few pages long and contains more than four or five graphics, consider including a list of illustrations so that readers can find them easily.

In This Book

For more about white space and rules, see Ch. 12, pp. 268 and 278.

For more about lists of illustrations, see Ch. 18, p. 470.

UNDERSTANDING THE PROCESS OF CREATING GRAPHICS

Creating graphics involves planning, creating, revising, and citing.

Planning Graphics

Whether you think first about the text or the graphics, consider the following four aspects of the document as you plan.

- *Audience.* Will readers understand the kinds of graphics you want to use? Will they know the standard icons in your field? Are they motivated to read your document, or do you need to enliven the text—for example, by adding color for emphasis—to hold their attention?

- *Purpose.* What point are you trying to make with the graphic? As Figure 13.2 on page 298 shows, even a few simple facts can yield a number of different points. Your responsibility is to determine what you want to show and how best to show it. Don't rely on your software to do your thinking; it can't.

- *The kind of information you want to communicate.* Your subject will help you decide what type of graphic to include. For example, in writing about languages spoken by your state's citizens, you might use tables for the statistical data, maps for the patterns of language use, and graphs for statistical trends over time.

- *Physical conditions.* The physical conditions in which readers will use the document—amount of lighting, amount of surface space available, and so forth—will influence the type of graphic as well as its size and shape, the thickness of lines and size of type, and the color.

As you plan how you are going to create the graphics, consider four important factors:

- *Time.* Because making a complicated graphic can take a lot of time, you need to establish a schedule.

- *Money.* A high-quality graphic can be expensive. How big is the project budget? How can you use that money effectively?

Rail Line	November		December		January	
	Disabled by electrical problems	Total disabled	Disabled by electrical problems	Total disabled	Disabled by electrical problems	Total disabled
Bryn Mawr	19	27	17	28	20	26
Swarthmore	12	16	9	17	13	16
Manayunk	22	34	26	31	24	33

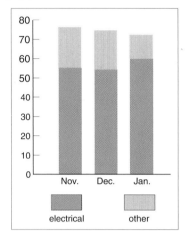

a. Number of railcars disabled, November–January

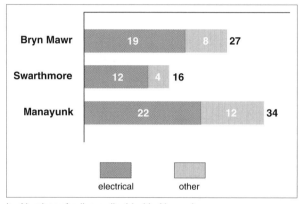

b. Number of railcars disabled in November

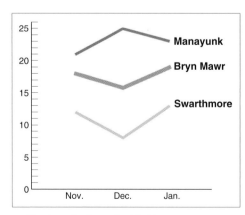

c. Number of railcars disabled by electrical problems, November–January

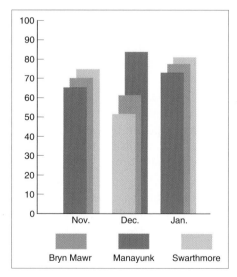

d. Range in percentage of railcars, by line, disabled by electrical problems, November–January

■ **Figure 13.2   Different Graphics Emphasizing Different Points**

Each of these four graphs emphasizes a different point derived from the data in the table. Graph (a) focuses on the total number of cars disabled each month, classified by cause; graph (b) focuses on the three rail lines during one month; and so forth. For information on bar graphs, see pages 309 and 311–14; for information on line graphs, see pages 314, 316, and 318.

- *Equipment.* Determine what tools and software you will require, such as spreadsheets for tables and graphs, and graphics software for diagrams.
- *Expertise.* How much do you know about creating graphics? Do you have access to the expertise of others?

Creating Graphics

Usually, you won't have all the resources you would like. You will have to choose one of the following four approaches:

- *Using existing graphics.* For a student paper that *will not be published*, some instructors allow the use of photocopies or scans of existing graphics; other instructors do not. For a document that *will be published*, whether written by a student or a professional, using an existing graphic is permissible if the graphic is in the public domain, if it is the property of the writer's organization, or if that organization has obtained permission to use it. Be particularly careful about graphics you find on the Web. Many people mistakenly think that anything on the Web can be used without permission. The same copyright laws that apply to printed material apply to Web-based material, whether words or graphics. For more on citing graphics, see page 300.

  Aside from the issue of copyright, think carefully before you use existing graphics. The style of the graphic might not match that of the others you want to use, and the graphic might lack some features you want or include some you don't. If you use an existing graphic, assign it your own number and title.

- *Modifying existing graphics.* You can redraw an existing graphic or use a scanner to digitize the graphic and then modify it electronically with graphics software.

- *Creating graphics on a computer.* You can create many kinds of graphics using your spreadsheet software and the drawing tools on your word processor. Consult the Selected Bibliography on page 678 for a list of books about computers and technical communication.

- *Having someone else create the graphics.* Professional-level graphics software can cost hundreds of dollars and require hundreds of hours of practice. Some companies have technical-publications departments with graphics experts, but others subcontract this work. Many print shops and service bureaus have graphics experts on staff or can direct you to them.

In This Book

For more about work made for hire, see Ch. 2, p. 19.

Revising Graphics

As with any other aspect of technical communication, build in enough time and budget enough money to revise the graphics. Create a checklist and evaluate each graphic for effectiveness. The Writer's Checklist at the end of this

TECH TIP

How to Insert and Modify Graphics

To insert and modify graphics, use the **Insert Picture** command and the **Format Picture** dialog box or **Picture** toolbar.

To **insert a graphic** such as a photograph, drawing, chart, or graph, place your cursor where you want to insert the graphic, then select **Picture** from the the the **Insert** menu.

To insert a graphic from a file on your computer, network, or removable memory card, select **From File**.

You can also insert clip art, images from a scanner or camera, drawings, AutoShapes, WordArt, and charts.

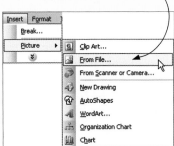

To **modify an image** that is already in your document, double-click on it and then use the **Format Picture** dialog box.

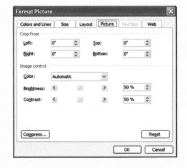

The **Format Picture** dialog box allows you to modify the appearance of a picture, crop and rotate it, and wrap text around it.

The **Picture** toolbar also allows you to modify the appearance, size, and layout of a picture.

KEYWORDS: insert picture, format picture, modifying pictures, Picture toolbar

chapter (page 330) is a good starting point. Show the graphics to people whose backgrounds are similar to your intended readers' and ask them for suggestions. Revise the graphics and solicit more reactions.

Citing Graphics

In This Book

For more about copyright, see Ch. 2.

If you wish to publish a graphic that is protected by copyright (even if you have revised it), you need to obtain written permission (see page 20). Related to the issue of permission is the issue of citing. Of course, you *do not* cite a graphic if you created it yourself from scratch or if your own organization owns the copyright.

In all other cases, you should include a citation, even if the document is a course assignment and will not be published. Citing graphics, even those you have revised substantially, shows your instructor that you understand professional conventions and your ethical responsibilities.

In This Book

For more about style manuals, see Appendix, Part B, p. 579.

If you are following a style manual, such as the APA style manual, check to see whether it presents a format for citing graphics. Most style manuals call for a source statement in the caption:

Source: Anderson Machine Tools, 2005: "Reconfiguration Project: Progress Report"

If your graphic is based on an existing graphic, the source statement should state that your graphic is "based on" or "adapted from" your source.

USING COLOR EFFECTIVELY

 On TechComm Web

See Color Connection by Xerox <www.colorconnection.xerox.com>, the Design 101 section, for articles about color and graphics software. Click on Links Library for Ch. 13 on <bedfordstmartins.com/ techcomm>.

Color draws attention to information you want to emphasize, establishes visual patterns to promote understanding, and adds interest. But it is also easy to misuse. The following discussion is based on Jan V. White's excellent text *Color for the Electronic Age* (1990).

In using color in graphics and page design, keep these seven principles in mind:

- *Don't overdo it.* Readers can interpret only two or three colors at a time. Use colors for small items, such as portions of graphics and important words. And don't use colors where black and white will work better.

- *Use color to emphasize particular items.* People interpret color before they interpret shape, size, or placement on the page. Color effectively draws a reader's attention to a particular item or group of items on a page. In Figure 13.3, for example, color adds emphasis to several different kinds of items.

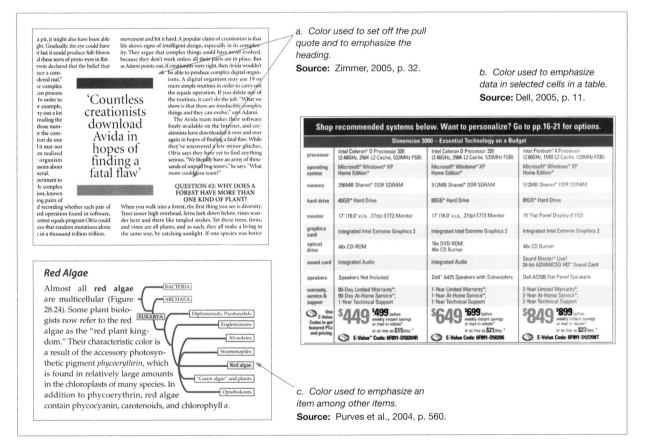

a. *Color used to set off the pull quote and to emphasize the heading.*
Source: Zimmer, 2005, p. 32.

b. *Color used to emphasize data in selected cells in a table.*
Source: Dell, 2005, p. 11.

c. *Color used to emphasize an item among other items.*
Source: Purves et al., 2004, p. 560.

■ **Figure 13.3   Color Used for Emphasis**

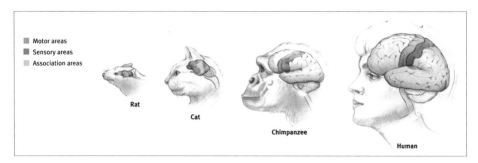

■ **Figure 13.4   Color Used to Establish Patterns**
Source: Myers, 2003, p. 57.

- *Use color to create patterns.* The principle of repetition—readers learn to recognize patterns—applies in graphics and document design. In creating patterns, also consider shape. For instance, use red for safety comments, but place them in octagons resembling a stop sign. This way, you give your readers two visual cues to help them recognize the pattern. Figure 13.4 shows a page in a biology textbook that uses color to establish patterns.

  Color is also an effective way to emphasize design features such as text boxes, rules, screens, and headers and footers.

- *Use contrast effectively.* The visibility of a color is a function of the background against which it appears (see Figure 13.5). The strongest contrasts are between black and white and between black and yellow.

  The need for effective contrast also applies to graphics used in presentations, as shown here:

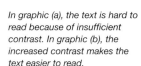
In This Book

For more about designing your document, see Ch. 12.

In graphic (a), the text is hard to read because of insufficient contrast. In graphic (b), the increased contrast makes the text easier to read.

In This Book

For more about presentation graphics, see Ch. 21, p. 543.

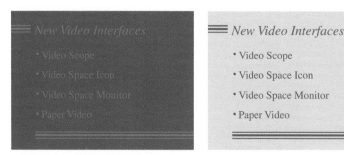

a. Insufficient contrast   b. Effective contrast

In This Book

For more about cultural patterns, see Ch. 5, p. 83.

- *Take advantage of any symbolic meanings colors may already have.* In American culture, for example, red signals danger, heat, or electricity; yellow signals caution; and orange signals warning. Using these warm colors in ways that depart from their familiar meanings could be confusing. The

Notice that a color washes out if the background color is too similar.

■ **Figure 13.5   The Effect of Background in Creating Contrast**

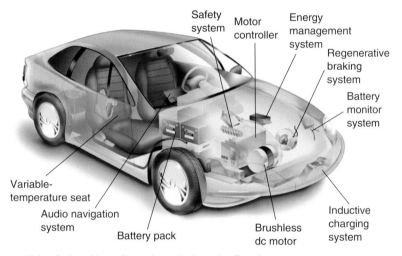

The batteries are red. The warm red contrasts effectively with the cool green of the car body.

■ **Figure 13.6   Colors Have Clear Associations for Readers**

cooler colors—blues and greens—are more conservative and subtle. Figure 13.6 illustrates these principles. Keep in mind, however, that different cultures interpret colors differently.

• *Be aware that color can obscure or swallow up text.*

If you are using print against a colored background, you might need to make the type a little bigger, because color makes text look smaller.

Text printed against a white background looks bigger than the same size text printed against a colored background. White letters counteract this effect.

- *Use bright colors to make objects look bigger.*

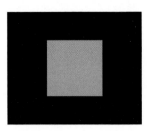 

The orange box looks bigger than the blue box even though they are the same size.

Categories of technical information:

- Numerical information
- Logical relationships
- Process descriptions and instructions
- Visual and spatial characteristics
- Motion in graphics

CHOOSING THE APPROPRIATE KIND OF GRAPHIC

Graphics used in technical documents fall into two categories: tables and figures. Tables are lists of data, usually numbers, arranged in columns. Figures are everything else: graphs, charts, diagrams, photographs, and the like. Typically, tables and figures are numbered separately: the first table in a document is Table 1; the first figure is Figure 1. In documents of more than one chapter (like this book), the graphics are usually numbered within each chapter. That is, Figure 3.2 is the second figure in Chapter 3.

There is no simple system for choosing a graphic, because in many situations several types would work. In general, however, graphics can be categorized according to the kind of information they contain. (Some kinds of graphics can convey several kinds of information. For instance, a table can include both numerical values and procedures.)

The discussion that follows is based on the classification system in William Horton's "Pictures Please—Presenting Information Visually" in *Techniques for Technical Communicators* (Barnum & Carliner, 1993). Figure 13.7 presents an overview of this discussion.

Illustrating Numerical Information

The kinds of graphics used most often to display numerical values are tables, bar graphs, pictographs, line graphs, and pie charts.

Tables　Tables convey large amounts of numerical data easily, and they are often the only way to present several variables for a number of items. For example, if you want to show how many people are employed in six industries in 10 states, a table would probably be most effective. Although tables lack the visual appeal of other kinds of graphics, they can handle much more information.

■ **Figure 13.7**   **Choosing the Appropriate Kind of Graphic (Based on Horton [1993])**

Purpose	Type of graphic		What the graphic does best
Illustrating numerical information	Table	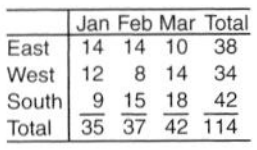	Shows large amounts of numerical data, especially when there are several variables for a number of items
	Bar graph	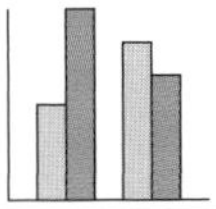	Shows the relative values of two or more items.
	Pictograph		Enlivens statistical information for the general reader.
	Line graph	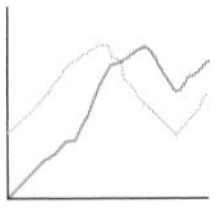	Shows how the quantity of an item changes over time. A line graph can accommodate much more data than a bar graph can.
	Pie chart	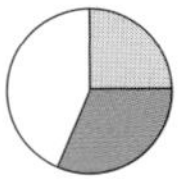	Shows the relative size of the parts of a whole. Pie charts are instantly familiar to most readers.
Illustrating logical relationships	Diagram	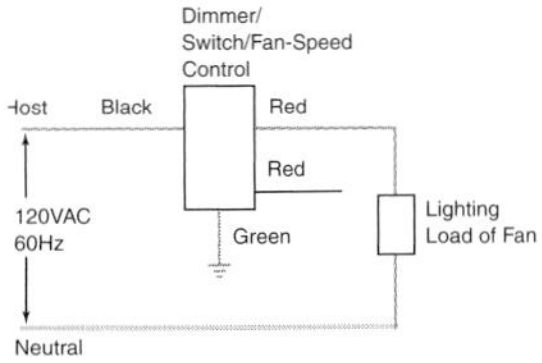	Represents items or properties of items.
	Organization chart	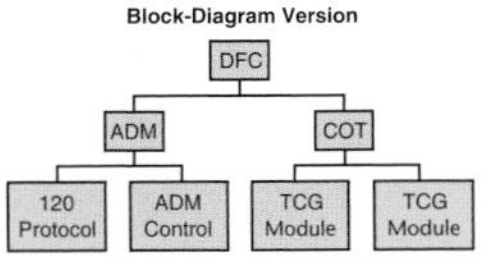	Shows the lines of authority and responsibility in an organization.
Illustrating instructions and process descriptions	Checklist	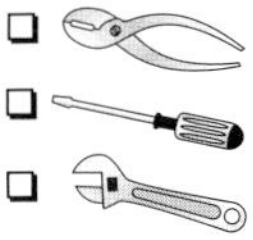	Lists or shows what equipment or materials to gather, or describes an action.
	Table	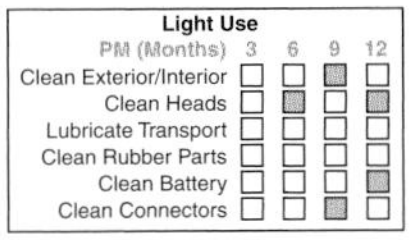	Shows numbers of items or indicates the state (on/off) of an item.

■ **Figure 13.7** *(continued)*

Purpose	Type of graphic		What the graphic does best
Illustrating instructions and process descriptions (continued)	Flowchart 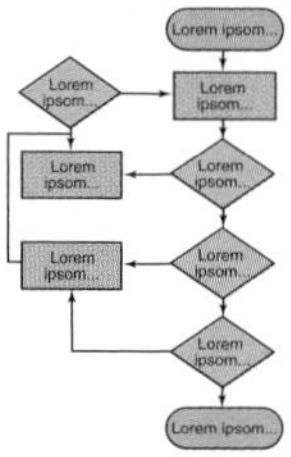		Shows the stages of a procedure or a process.
	Logic tree 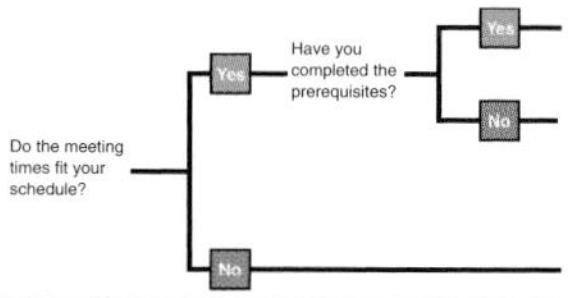		Shows which of two or more paths to follow.
Illustrating visual and spatial characteristics	Drawing 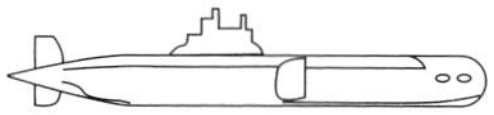		Shows simplified representations of objects.
	Map 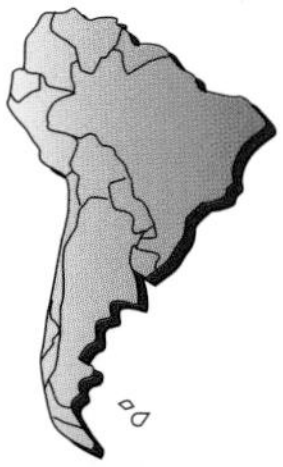		Shows geographic areas.
	Photograph 		Shows precisely the external surface of objects.
	Screen shot 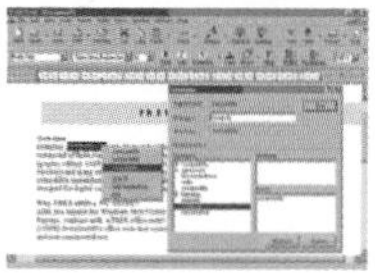		Shows what appears on a computer screen.

Table number

Table title

Column heads

Column subheads

Row

Data cell

Stub

Source statement

Caption

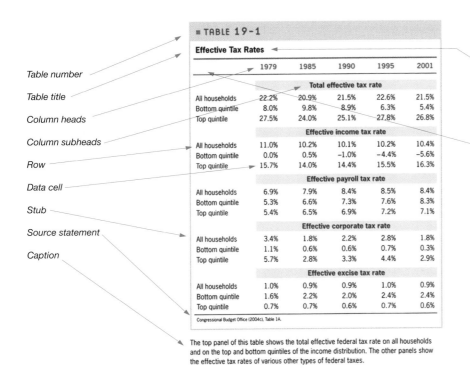

■ TABLE 19-1

Effective Tax Rates

	1979	1985	1990	1995	2001
Total effective tax rate					
All households	22.2%	20.9%	21.5%	22.6%	21.5%
Bottom quintile	8.0%	9.8%	8.9%	6.3%	5.4%
Top quintile	27.5%	24.0%	25.1%	27.8%	26.8%
Effective income tax rate					
All households	11.0%	10.2%	10.1%	10.2%	10.4%
Bottom quintile	0.0%	0.5%	−1.0%	−4.4%	−5.6%
Top quintile	15.7%	14.0%	14.4%	15.5%	16.3%
Effective payroll tax rate					
All households	6.9%	7.9%	8.4%	8.5%	8.4%
Bottom quintile	5.3%	6.6%	7.3%	7.6%	8.3%
Top quintile	5.4%	6.5%	6.9%	7.2%	7.1%
Effective corporate tax rate					
All households	3.4%	1.8%	2.2%	2.8%	1.8%
Bottom quintile	1.1%	0.6%	0.6%	0.7%	0.3%
Top quintile	5.7%	2.8%	3.3%	4.4%	2.9%
Effective excise tax rate					
All households	1.0%	0.9%	0.9%	1.0%	0.9%
Bottom quintile	1.6%	2.2%	2.0%	2.4%	2.4%
Top quintile	0.7%	0.7%	0.6%	0.7%	0.6%

Congressional Budget Office (2004c), Table 1A.

The top panel of this table shows the total effective federal tax rate on all households and on the top and bottom quintiles of the income distribution. The other panels show the effective tax rates of various other types of federal taxes.

The data in this table consist of numbers, but tables can also present textual information or a combination of numbers and text.

Tables are usually titled at the top because readers scan them from top to bottom. This table should contain a more complete title: Effective Tax Rates, 1979–2001.

Some writers would include a stub head. The stub—the left-hand column—lists the items for which data are displayed. The stub head in this table would be "Households." It would be displayed above the first "All households" in the stub.

Notice that a screen is used behind the column subheads for emphasis.

In most cases, the caption is placed directly after the table title. The writer here places it beneath the table.

■ **Figure 13.8   Parts of a Table**
Source: Gruber, 2005, p. 541.

Figure 13.8 illustrates the standard parts of a table. Tables are identified by number (Table 1) and an informative title that includes the items being compared and the basis (or bases) of comparison:

Mallard Population in Rangeley, 2002–2004

The Growth of the Robotics Industry in Japan and the United States, 2005

Guidelines

Creating Effective Tables

▶ **Indicate the units of measure.** If all the data are expressed in the same unit, indicate that unit in the title:

Farm Size in the Midwestern States (in Hectares)

If the data in different columns are expressed in different units, indicate the units in the column heads:

Population (in millions)	Per Capita Income (in thousands of U.S. dollars)

If all the *data cells* in a column use the same unit, indicate that unit in the column head, not in each data cell:

Speed (knots)

15
18
14

You can express data in both real numbers and percentages. A column head and the first data cell under it might read as follows:

Number of Students (Percentage)

53 (83)

▶ **In the stub — the left-hand column — list the items being compared.** Arrange the items in a logical order: big to small, important to unimportant, alphabetical, chronological, geographical, and so forth. If the items fall into several categories, include the names of the categories in the stub:

Snowbelt States . . . .
    Connecticut . . . .
    New York . . . .
    Vermont . . . .

Sunbelt States . . . .
    Arizona . . . .
    California . . . .
    New Mexico . . . .

In This Book

For more about screens, see Ch. 12, p. 278.

If the items in the stub are not grouped in logical categories, skip a line after every five rows to help the reader follow the rows across the table. Or use a screen or a colored background for every other set of five rows. Also useful are dot leaders: a row of dots that links the stub and the next column.

▶ **In the columns, arrange the data clearly and logically.** Use the decimal-tab feature to line up the decimal points:

  3,147.4
    365.7
46,803.5

In general, don't change units unless the quantities are so dissimilar that your readers would have a difficult time understanding them if expressed in the same units.

  3.4 hr
12.7 min
  4.3 sec

This list would probably be easier for most readers to understand than one in which all quantities were expressed in the same unit.

▶ **Do the math.** If your readers will need to know the totals for the columns or the rows, provide them. If your readers will need to know percentage changes from one column to the next, present them:

Number of Students (Percentage Change from Previous Year)

2000	2001	2002
619	644 (+4.0)	614 (−4.7)

▶ **Use dot leaders if a column contains a "blank" spot—a place where there are no appropriate data:**

3,147
. . .
46,803

But don't substitute dot leaders for a quantity of zero.

▶ **Don't make the table wider than it needs to be.** The reader should be able to scan across a row easily. As White (1984) points out, there is no reason to make the table as wide as the text column in the document. If a column head is long— more than five or six words — stack the words:

Computers Sold
Without a CD-RW Drive

▶ **Minimize the use of rules.** Grimstead (1987) recommends using rules only when necessary: to separate the title and the heads, the heads and the body, and the body and the notes. When you use rules, make them thin rather than thick.

▶ **Provide footnotes where necessary.** All the information your readers need to understand the table should accompany it.

▶ **If you did not generate the information yourself, indicate your source.** See the discussion of citing graphics on page 300.

Bar Graphs Like tables, bar graphs can communicate numerical values, but they are better at showing the relative values of two or more items. Figure 13.9 on page 311 shows typical horizontal and vertical bar graphs that you can make easily using your spreadsheet. Figure 13.10 on page 311 shows an effective bar graph that uses grid lines.

The five variations on the basic bar graph shown in Table 13.1 on page 312 can help you accommodate different communication needs. You can make all these types using your spreadsheet.

TECH TIP
How to Use Tab Stops

To control the placement of text on a page or in a table, you can align the text by using the **tab stops** in the horizontal ruler.

1. Click the **tab indicator** on the horizontal ruler to change the type of tab stop displayed.

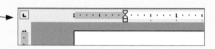

The following table describes common tab stops.

Tab stop	Description
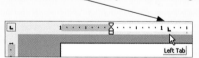	

Tab stop	Description
L	Lines up text to the left
⅃	Lines up text to the right
⊥	Centers text at tab stop
⊥.	Aligns numbers on their decimal points

2. When the appropriate tab stop appears, click the horizontal ruler where you want to align text.

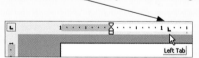

To remove a tab stop, drag it away from the ruler.

3. After you have set a tab stop, place the cursor to the left of the text you want to align and press the **tab** key.

KEYWORDS: set tab stops, horizontal ruler, indent text or numbers in a table

TECH TIP
How to Create Tables

To create tables, use the **Table** feature.

To **create a table**, place your cursor where you want to position the table, then use the **Insert** command on the **Table** menu.

Use the **Insert Table** dialog box to specify the number of columns and rows.

You can also create a table by left-clicking the **Table** button on the toolbar, then dragging your cursor to specify the number of columns and rows.

To **modify a table**, double-click on it, then use the **Tables and Borders** toolbar. This toolbar allows you to modify the appearance of a table, split and merge cells, and organize data.

KEYWORDS: tables, tables and borders, merge cells, split cells

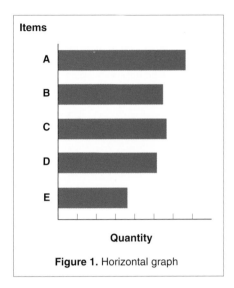

Items

A

B

C

D

E

Quantity

Figure 1. Horizontal graph

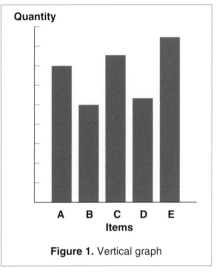

Quantity

A   B   C   D   E

Items

Figure 1. Vertical graph

Horizontal bars are best for showing quantities such as speed and distance. Vertical bars are best for showing quantities such as height, size, and amount. However, these distinctions are not ironclad; as long as the axes are clearly labeled, readers should have no trouble understanding the graph.

■ **Figure 13.9   Structures of Horizontal and Vertical Bar Graphs**

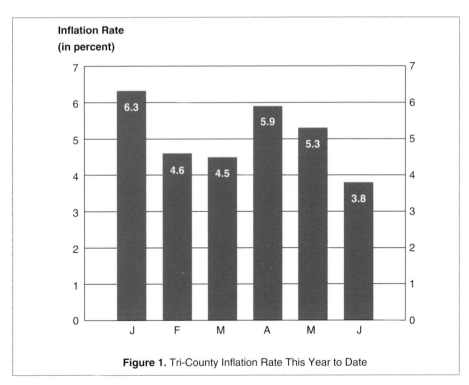

**Inflation Rate
(in percent)**

Figure 1. Tri-County Inflation Rate This Year to Date

■ **Figure 13.10   Effective Bar Graph**

■ **Table 13.1 Variations on the Basic Bar Graph**

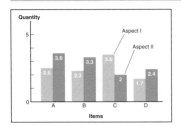

Grouped bar graph. The *grouped* bar graph lets you compare two or three quantities for each item. Grouped bar graphs would be useful, for example, for showing the numbers of full-time and part-time students at several universities. One bar could represent full-time students; the other, part-time students. To distinguish between the bars, use hatching (striping), shading, or color, and either label one set of bars or provide a key.

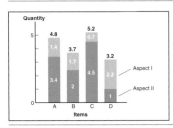

Subdivided bar graph. In the *subdivided* bar graph, Aspect I and Aspect II are stacked like wooden blocks placed on top of one another. Although totals are easy to compare in a subdivided bar graph, individual quantities are not.

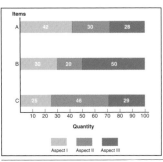

100-percent bar graph. The *100-percent* bar graph, which shows the relative proportions of the elements that make up several items, is useful in portraying, for example, the proportion of full-scholarship, partial-scholarship, and no-scholarship students at a number of colleges.

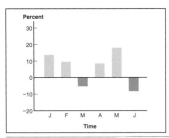

Deviation bar graph. The *deviation* bar graph shows how various quantities deviate from a norm. Deviation bar graphs are often used when the information contains both positive and negative values, such as profits and losses. Bars on the positive side of the norm line represent profits, bars on the negative side, losses.

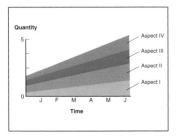

Stratum graph. The *stratum graph,* also called an *area graph,* shows the change in quantities of several items over time. Although stratum graphs are used frequently in business and scientific fields, general readers sometimes have trouble understanding how to read them.

Guidelines

Creating Effective Bar Graphs

▶ **Make the proportions fair.** Make your vertical axis about 25 percent shorter than your horizontal axis. An excessively long vertical axis exaggerates the differences in quantities; an excessively long horizontal axis minimizes the differences. Make all the bars the same width, and make the space between them about half as wide as a bar. Here are two poorly proportioned graphs.

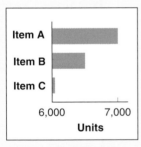

a. Excessively long vertical axis

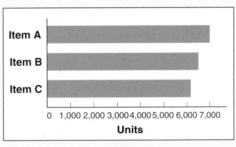

b. Excessively long horizontal axis

▶ **If possible, begin the quantity scale at zero.** Doing so ensures that the bars accurately represent the quantities. Notice how misleading a graph can be if the scale doesn't begin at zero.

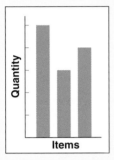

a. Misleading

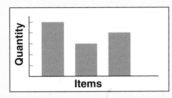

b. Accurately representative

If it is not practical to start the quantity scale at zero, break the quantity axis clearly at a common point on all bars.

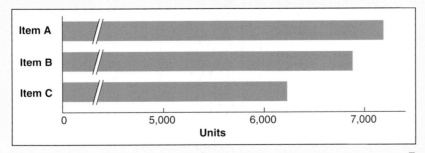

> ▶ **Use tick marks — marks along the axis — to signal the amounts.**

> Use grid lines — tick marks that extend through the bars — if the table has several bars, some of which are too far away from the tick marks to allow readers to gauge the quantities easily. (See Figure 13.10 on page 311.)
>
> ▶ **Arrange the bars in a logical sequence.** For a vertical bar graph, use chronology if possible. For a horizontal bar graph, arrange the bars in order of descending size, beginning at the top of the graph, unless some other logical sequence seems more appropriate.
>
> ▶ **Place the title below the figure.** Unlike tables, which are usually read from top to bottom, figures are usually read from the bottom up.
>
> ▶ **Indicate the source of your information if you did not generate it yourself.**

Pictographs   Pictographs—bar graphs in which the bars are replaced by a series of symbols—are used primarily to present statistical information to the general reader. The quantity scale is usually replaced by a statement indicating the numerical value of each symbol. Thousands of clip-art symbols and pictures are available for use in pictographs. Figure 13.11 shows an example of a pictograph.

Represent quantities in a pictograph honestly. Figure 13.12 shows an inherent problem: a picture drawn to scale can appear many times larger than it should.

Line Graphs   Line graphs are used almost exclusively to show changes in quantity over time—for example, the month-by-month production figures for a product. A line graph focuses the reader's attention on a change in quantity, whereas a bar graph emphasizes the quantities themselves.

Clip-art pictures and symbols are available online for use in pictographs. Arrange pictographs horizontally rather than vertically. Pictures of computer monitors balanced on top of each other can look foolish.

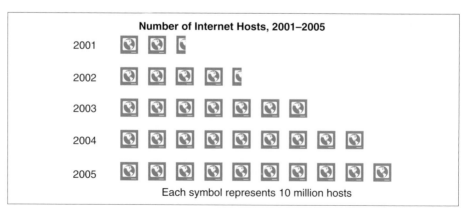

■ **Figure 13.11   Pictograph**

TECH TIP

How to Create Graphics in Excel

You can create many of the types of graphics discussed in this chapter using a spreadsheet program such as Microsoft Excel. First you enter the data that the graphic will display, then you select the type of graphic to create.

1. After you have entered your data in a spreadsheet, select the **Chart Wizard** button from the toolbar.

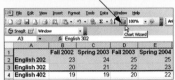

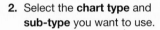

2. Select the **chart type** and **sub-type** you want to use.

3. Select the **data range** and **series** you wish to include in your graphic.

4. Select **chart options** for your graphic.

5. Select where you want to **place** your graphic in your spreadsheet.

After creating a graphic, you can use the **Copy** and **Paste Special** commands to insert your graphic in your document.

On TechComm Web

For more help with displaying data graphically, click on Preparing Effective Charts and Graphs in Tutorials on <bedfordstmartins.com/techcomm>.

KEYWORDS: Chart Wizard, chart type, data series, data range, data labels, legends

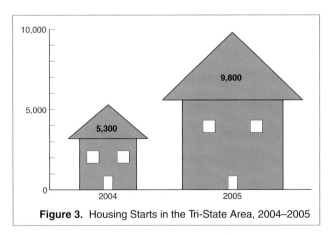

The reader sees the total area of the symbol rather than its height.

Figure 3. Housing Starts in the Tri-State Area, 2004–2005

■ **Figure 13.12   Misleading Pictograph**

TECH TIP

How to Use Drawing Tools

Although you can make many types of graphics using a spreadsheet, some types, such as pictographs, call for drawing tools. Your word processor includes basic drawing tools.

To **create shapes**, use the **Drawing** toolbar.

Select a **drawing tool**—such as a line, arrow, rectangle, or oval—then drag your cursor to create the shape.

You can also select complex shapes from the **AutoShapes** menu.

Once you have created a shape, you can position the shape in your document by selecting and dragging it.

To **modify a shape**, double-click on it, then use the **Format AutoShape** dialog box.

The **Format AutoShape** dialog box allows you to modify the appearance, size, and layout of a shape.

Buttons on the **Drawing** toolbar also allow you to modify the appearance of a shape.

KEYWORDS: Drawing toolbar, drawing tool, AutoShapes, drawing canvas

---

You can plot three or four lines on a line graph. If the lines intersect, use different colors or patterns to distinguish them. If the lines intersect too often, however, the graph will be unclear; in this case, draw separate graphs. Figure 13.13 shows a line graph.

Using different colors for the lines helps readers distinguish them.

If you can put the labels near the lines themselves, as this writer has done with "Men" and "Women," readers do not have to look elsewhere to see what the lines represent. If you cannot put the labels near the lines, let your software create a legend off to the side that explains what the lines represent.

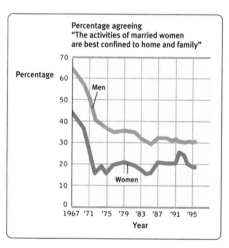

FIGURE 5.7

Changing attitudes about gender roles
U.S. college students' endorsement of the traditional view of women's role has declined dramatically. Men's and women's attitudes have also converged. (From Dey & others, 1991; Sax & others, 1999.)

■ **Figure 13.13   Line Graph**
Source: Myers, 2003, p. 91.

INTERACTIVE SAMPLE DOCUMENT
Balancing Clarity and Drama in Graphics

The following graphic, a bar graph accompanied by a drawing, is included on a Web site addressed to general readers. The questions in the margin ask you to think about the principles of graphics (page 295), color (page 301), and bar graphs (page 313). E-mail your responses to yourself and/or your instructor, and see suggested responses on TechComm Web.

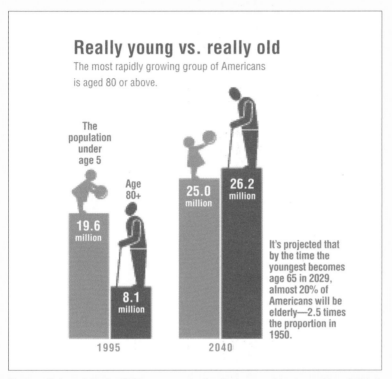

1. How effectively has the designer used the two colors?

2. How do the drawings of the child and the elderly man help communicate the point?

3. Create a rough sketch of a graph that communicates the text on the right. Should this information be communicated in words or in a graphic? Why?

 **On TechComm Web**

To e-mail your responses to yourself and/or your instructor and to see suggested responses, click on Interactive Sample Documents for Ch. 13 on <bedfordstmartins.com/techcomm>.

Source: Holmes & Bagby, 2002 <www.understandingusa.com/chaptercc=2&cs=18.html>.

Guidelines

Creating Effective Line Graphs

- **If possible, begin the quantity scale at zero.** Doing so is the best way to portray the information honestly. If you cannot begin at zero, clearly indicate a break in the axis.
- **Use reasonable proportions for the vertical and horizontal axes.** As with bar graphs, make the vertical axis about 25 percent shorter than the horizontal axis.
- **Use grid lines—horizontal, vertical, or both—rather than tick marks when your readers need to read the quantities precisely.**

Pie Charts The pie chart is a simple but limited design used for showing the relative size of the parts of a whole. You can make pie charts with your spreadsheet. Figure 13.14 shows two typical examples.

Pie charts are often used to show how proportions of quantities that make up a whole change over time.

Note that the labels are presented within the slices when they will fit and outside the slices when they will not.

Your spreadsheet will automatically maintain consistent colors for the slices from one pie chart to the next in a set of charts like this.

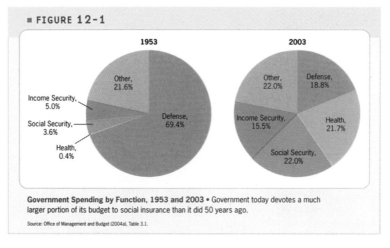

FIGURE 12-1
1953
Other, 21.6%
Income Security, 5.0%
Social Security, 3.6%
Health, 0.4%
Defense, 69.4%
2003
Other, 22.0%
Defense, 18.8%
Income Security, 15.5%
Health, 21.7%
Social Security, 22.0%
Government Spending by Function, 1953 and 2003 • Government today devotes a much larger portion of its budget to social insurance than it did 50 years ago.
Source: Office of Management and Budget (2004a), Table 3.1.

■ **Figure 13.14 Pie Charts**
Source: Gruber, 2005, p. 302.

Guidelines

Creating Effective Pie Charts

- **Restrict the number of slices to six or seven.** As the slices get smaller, judging their relative sizes becomes more difficult.
- **Begin with the largest slice at the top and work clockwise in decreasing order, unless you have a good reason to arrange them otherwise.**
- **Include a miscellaneous slice for very small quantities that would make the chart unclear.** Explain its contents in a footnote. This slice, sometimes called "other," follows the other sections.

▶ **Label the slices (horizontally, not radially) inside the slice, if space permits.** Include the percentage that each slice represents and, if appropriate, the raw numbers.

▶ **To emphasize one slice, use a bright, contrasting color or separate the slice from the pie.** Do this, for example, when you introduce a discussion of the item represented by that slice.

▶ **Check to see that your software follows the appropriate guidelines for pie charts.** Some spreadsheets add fancy visual effects that can reduce comprehension. For instance, many spreadsheets portray the pie in three dimensions, as shown here.

In this three-dimensional pie chart about the percentages of a college's student body, by year, the sophomore slice looks bigger than the freshman slice, even though it isn't, because it appears closer to the reader. To communicate clearly, make the pies two-dimensional.

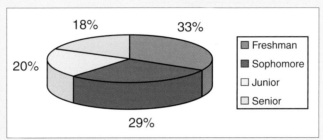

▶ **Don't overdo fill patterns.** Fill patterns are designs, shades, or colors that distinguish one slice from another. In general, use simple, understated patterns, or none at all.

▶ **Check that your percentages add up to 100.** If you are doing the calculations yourself, check your math.

Illustrating Logical Relationships

Graphics can help you present logical relationships among items. For instance, in describing a piece of hardware, you might want to show its major components. The two kinds of graphics that best show logical relationships are diagrams and organization charts.

Diagrams   A diagram is a visual metaphor that uses symbols to represent items or their properties. In technical communication, common kinds of diagrams are blueprints, wiring diagrams, and schematics. Figure 13.15 on page 320 is a diagram.

Organization Charts   A popular form of diagram is the organization chart, in which simple geometric shapes, usually rectangles, suggest logical relationships, as shown in Figure 13.16 on page 320. The drawing program in your word processor can create organization charts.

The artist has used drawings of laboratory equipment to create simple flowcharts to represent laboratory procedures.

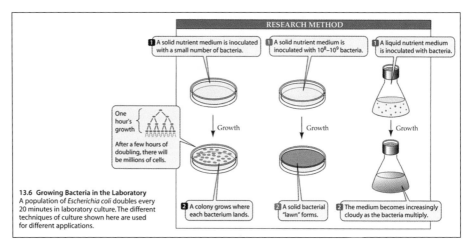

13.6 **Growing Bacteria in the Laboratory**
A population of *Escherichia coli* doubles every 20 minutes in laboratory culture. The different techniques of culture shown here are used for different applications.

■ **Figure 13.15   Diagram**
Source: Purves, 2004, p. 264.

Illustrating Process Descriptions and Instructions

Graphics often accompany process descriptions (see Chapter 9) and instructions (see Chapter 19). The following discussion looks at some of the graphics used in writing about actions: checklists, tables, flowcharts, and logic trees.

Checklists   In explaining how to carry out a task, you often need to show the reader what equipment or materials to gather, or describe an action or series of actions to take. A checklist is a list of items, each preceded by a check box. If readers might be unfamiliar with the items you are listing, include

An organization chart is often used to show the hierarchy in an organization, with the president of a company, for example, in the box at the top.

Alternatively, as shown here, an organization chart can show the functional divisions of a system, such as the human nervous system.

Note that the two boxes at the bottom should be drawn so that they align clearly under "Autonomic." As drawn here, they appear to align under "Autonomic" and "Somatic."

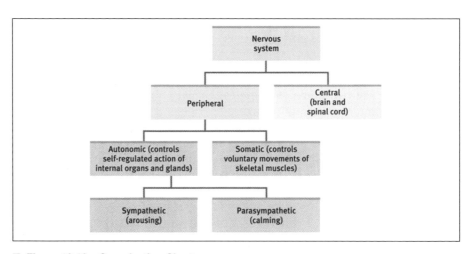

■ **Figure 13.16   Organization Chart**
Source: Myers, 2003, p. 41.

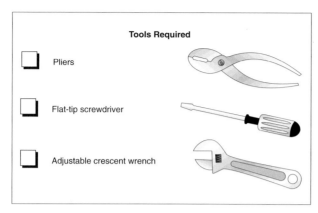

■ **Figure 13.17   Checklist**

drawings of the items, as shown in Figure 13.17. The list function in your word processor can create check boxes.

Often you need to indicate that your reader is to carry out certain tasks at certain intervals. A table is a useful graphic for this kind of information, as illustrated in Figure 13.18.

Flowcharts   A flowchart, as the name suggests, shows the various stages of a process or a procedure. Flowcharts are useful, too, for summarizing instructions. In a basic flowchart, stages are represented by labeled geometric shapes. Flowcharts can portray open systems (those that have a "start" and a "finish") or closed systems (those that end where they began). Figure 13.19 on page 322 is an open-system flowchart that shows the stages of a procedure.

Regular Maintenance, First 40,000 Miles

	Mileage							
	5,000	10,000	15,000	20,000	25,000	30,000	35,000	40,000
change oil, replace filter	✓	✓	✓	✓	✓	✓	✓	✓
rotate tires	✓	✓	✓	✓	✓	✓	✓	✓
replace air filter				✓				✓
replace spark plugs				✓				✓
replace coolant fluid								✓
replace ignition cables								✓
replace timing belt								✓

■ **Figure 13.18   A Table Used to Illustrate a Maintenance Schedule**

■ **Figure 13.19**
A Flowchart Used to
Illustrate a Procedure
Source: Illinois State Board of
Education, 2005 <www.isbe.net/
ayp/making_ayp.htm>.

On TechComm Web

To view Figure 13.19 in context on
the Web, click on Links Library for
Ch. 13 on <**bedfordstmartins.com/
techcomm**>.

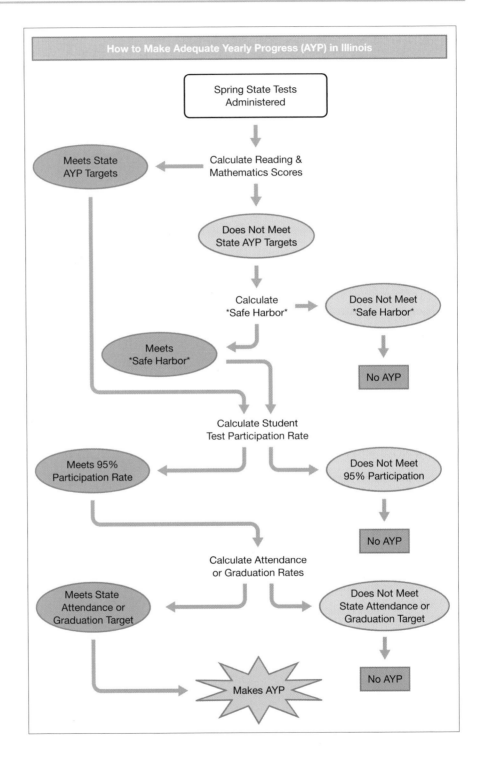

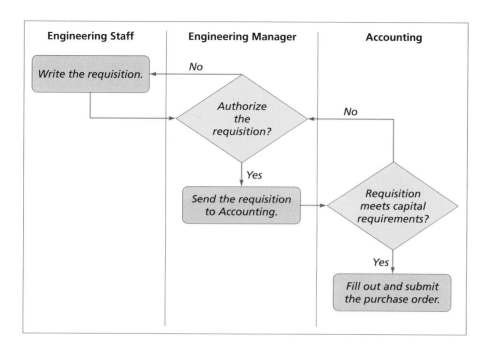

■ **Figure 13.20**
Deployment Flowchart

A deployment flowchart shows who is responsible for carrying out which tasks. Here the engineering staff writes the requisition, then sends it to the Engineering Manager.

Figure 13.20 shows a deployment flowchart, which you can make using the drawing tools in your word processor.

Logic Trees   Logic trees use a branching metaphor. The logic tree shown in Figure 13.21 helps students think through the process of registering for a course.

Illustrating Visual and Spatial Characteristics

To illustrate visual and spatial characteristics, use photographs, screen shots, line drawings, and maps.

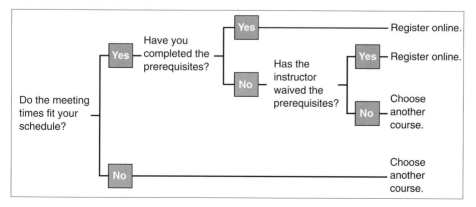

■ **Figure 13.21   Logic Tree**

Photographs   *Photographs* are unmatched for reproducing visual detail. Sometimes, however, a photograph can provide too much information. In a sales brochure for an automobile, a glossy photograph of the dashboard might be very effective. But in an owner's manual, if you want to show how to use the trip odometer, a diagram that focuses on that item would be more useful.

Sometimes a photograph can provide too little information. The item you want to highlight might be located inside the mechanism or obscured by another component.

Guidelines

Presenting Photographs Effectively

▶ **Eliminate extraneous background clutter that can distract readers.** Crop the photograph, or digitize it and delete unnecessary detail. Figure 13.22 shows examples of cropped and uncropped photographs.

▶ **Do not electronically manipulate the photograph.** There is nothing unethical about digitizing a photograph, removing blemishes, and cropping it. However, manipulating a photograph—for example, enlarging the size of the monitor that comes with a computer system—is unethical.

▶ **Help readers understand the perspective.** Most objects in magazines and journals are photographed at an angle to show the object's depth as well as its height and width.

▶ **If appropriate, include some common object, such as a coin or a ruler, in the photograph to give readers a sense of scale.**

▶ **If appropriate, label components or important features.**

Cropping a photograph lets you direct the reader's attention to the information you wish to emphasize. The image on the right is a cropped and enlarged version of the photo on the left.

The original version emphasizes the vastness of space; the cropped version emphasizes the shape of the space station.

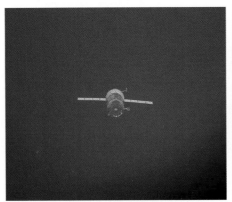 

■ **Figure 13.22   Cropping a Photograph**
Source: NASA, 2004 <http://spaceflight.nasa.gov/gallery/images/station/crew9/html/iss009e05034.html>.

TECH TIP

How to Create Screen Shots

To show your reader what appears on a computer monitor, you can create a screen shot of an entire screen or an active window using the **Print Screen** feature of your computer.

To **create a screen shot of the** ——→ **entire screen**, press the **Print Screen** button on your keyboard.

To **create a screen shot of an active window**, click in the window you wish to copy and then simultaneously press the **Alt** and **Print Screen** buttons on your keyboard.

An active window has a dark-blue border.

After you have copied a screen or window, open your document, click your cursor where you want to insert the shot, and then select **Paste** from the **Edit** menu.

You can modify screen shots already placed in your document by using the **Format Picture** dialog box or the **Picture** toolbar.

KEYWORD: screen captures

Screen Shots   Screen shots—images of what appears on a computer monitor— are often used in software manuals to show readers what the screen looks like at various points during the use of a program. Figure 13.23 on page 326 is an example of a screen shot.

Line Drawings   Line drawings are simplified visual representations of objects. They can have three advantages over photographs:

- Line drawings can focus readers' attention on desired information better than photographs can.
- Line drawings can highlight information that might be obscured by bad lighting or a bad angle in photographs.
- Line drawings can be easier for readers to understand than photographs are.

Figure 13.24 on page 326 shows the effectiveness of a line drawing.

You have probably seen the three variations on the basic line drawing shown in Figure 13.25 on page 327.

Maps   Maps are readily available as clip art that can be modified with a graphics program. Figure 13.26 on page 327 shows a map derived from clip art.

■ **Figure 13.23**
Screen Shot
Source: Software602, Inc., 2005
<http://download.software602
.com/pdf/pcs/4/pcs4_manual
.pdf>.

*In this portion of a page from a
user's manual for a Software602
product, the writer uses a
screen shot to help orient
readers. The screen shot gives
readers confidence that they are
performing the task correctly.*

**Saving a
Document**

You may save a document using the commands **Save** or **Save As** from
the **File** menu, or using the **Save** button on the tool bar. Using the
Save command will activate the save dialog:

New to this version of 602Text is the ability to save in the Rich Text
Format (*.RTF). Many other formats are also available.

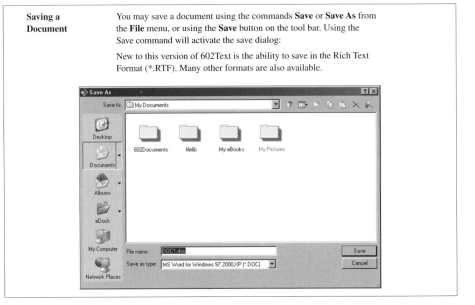

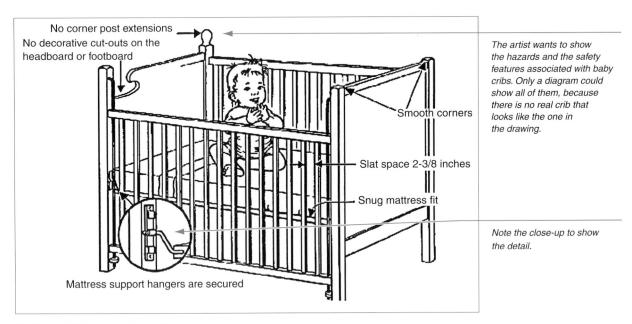

■ **Figure 13.24   Line Drawing**
Source: U.S. Consumer Product Safety Commission, 1999 <www.cpsc.gov/cpscpub/pubs/usedcrib.pdf>.

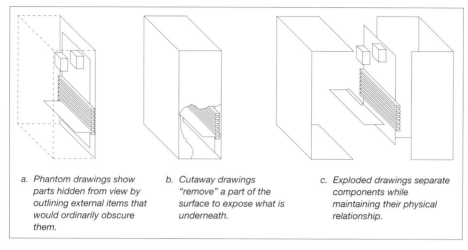

a. *Phantom drawings show parts hidden from view by outlining external items that would ordinarily obscure them.*

b. *Cutaway drawings "remove" a part of the surface to expose what is underneath.*

c. *Exploded drawings separate components while maintaining their physical relationship.*

■ **Figure 13.25   Phantom, Cutaway, and Exploded Views**

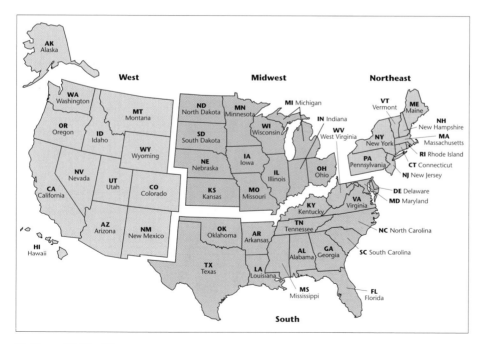

Include a scale and a legend if the map is one that is not thoroughly familiar to your readers. Also, use conventional colors, such as blue for water.

■ **Figure 13.26   Map**

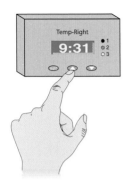

■ **Figure 13.27 Showing the Action from the Reader's Perspective**

In many cases, you need to show only the person's hands, not the whole body.

Showing Motion in Your Graphics

In technical documents, you will often want to show motion. For instance, in an instruction manual for helicopter technicians, you might want to illustrate the process of removing an oil dipstick or tightening a bolt, or you might want to show a warning light flashing. Although document designers frequently use animation or video, printed graphics are still needed to communicate this kind of information.

If the reader is to perform the action, show the action from the reader's point of view, as in Figure 13.27.

Figure 13.28 illustrates four additional techniques for showing action. These techniques are conventional but not universal. If you are addressing readers from another culture, consult a qualified person from that culture to make sure your graphics are clear and inoffensive.

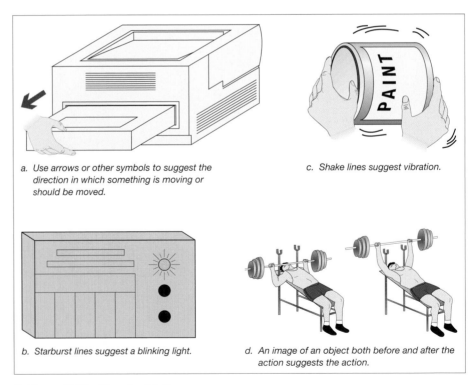

a. *Use arrows or other symbols to suggest the direction in which something is moving or should be moved.*

c. *Shake lines suggest vibration.*

b. *Starburst lines suggest a blinking light.*

d. *An image of an object both before and after the action suggests the action.*

■ **Figure 13.28 Showing Motion**

Strategies for Intercultural Communication

Creating Effective Graphics for Multicultural Readers

Whether you are writing for people within your organization or outside it, consider the needs of readers whose first language is different from your own. Like words, graphics have cultural meanings. If you are unaware of these meanings, you could communicate something very different from what you intend. The following guidelines are based on William Horton's (1993) article "The Almost Universal Language: Graphics for International Documents."

- **Be aware that reading patterns differ.** In some countries, people read from right to left or from top to bottom. In some cultures, direction signifies value: the right-hand side is superior to the left, or the reverse. You need to think about how to sequence graphics that show action, or where you put "before" and "after" graphics. If you want to show a direction, as in an informal flowchart, consider using arrows to indicate how to read the chart.

- **Be aware of varying cultural attitudes toward giving instruction.** Instructions for products made in Japan are highly polite and deferential: "Please attach the cable at this time." Some cultures favor spelling out general principles but leaving the reader to supply the details. For people in these cultures, instructions containing a detailed close-up of how to carry out a task might appear insulting.

- **Deemphasize trivial details.** Because common objects, such as plugs on the ends of power cords, come in different shapes around the world, draw them to look generic rather than specific to one country.

- **Avoid culture-specific language, symbols, and references.** Don't use a picture of a mouse to symbolize a computer mouse because the device is not known by that name everywhere. Avoid the casual use of national symbols (such as the maple leaf or national flags), because you might make an error in a detail that would insult your readers. Use colors carefully: red means danger to most people from Western cultures, but it is a celebratory color to the Chinese.

- **Portray people very carefully.** Every aspect of a person's appearance, from clothing to hairstyle to features, is culture or race specific. A photograph of a woman in casual Western attire seated at a workstation would be ineffective in an Islamic culture, where only the hands and eyes of a woman may be shown. Horton (1993) recommends using stick figures or silhouettes that do not suggest any one culture, race, or sex.

- **Be particularly careful in portraying hand gestures.** Many Western hand gestures, such as the "okay" sign, are considered obscene in other cultures, and long red fingernails are inappropriate. Use hands in graphics only when necessary—for example, carrying out a task—and obscure the person's sex and race.

Cultural differences are many and subtle. Learn as much as possible about your readers and about their culture and outlook, and have the graphics reviewed by someone from the culture.

Writer's Checklist

This checklist focuses on the characteristics of an effective graphic.

☐ Does the graphic have a purpose? (p. 295)
☐ Is the graphic honest? (p. 296)
☐ Is the graphic simple and uncluttered? (p. 295)
☐ Does the graphic present a manageable amount of information? (p. 295)
☐ Does the graphic meet the reader's format expectations? (p. 295)
☐ Is the graphic clearly labeled? (p. 295)

☐ For an existing graphic, do you have the legal right to use it? (p. 299) If so, have you cited the source appropriately? (p. 300)
☐ Does the graphic appear in a logical location in the document? (p. 296)
☐ Is the graphic introduced clearly in the text? (p. 296)
☐ Is the graphic explained in the text? (p. 296)
☐ Is the graphic clearly visible in the text? (p. 297)
☐ Is the graphic easily accessible to your readers? (p. 297)

Exercises

 In This Book   For more about memos, see Ch. 14, p. 352.

1. Find out from the admissions department at your college or university the number of students enrolled from the different states or from the different counties in your state. Present this information in four different kinds of graphics:

   a. map

   b. table

   c. bar graph

   d. pie chart

   In three or four paragraphs, explain why each graphic is appropriate for a particular audience and purpose and how each emphasizes different aspects of the information.

2. Design a flowchart for a process you are familiar with, such as applying for a summer job, studying for a test, preparing a paper, or performing some task at work. Your audience is someone who will be carrying out the process.

3. The following table (U.S. Bureau of the Census, 2004, p. 140) provides statistics on injuries. Study the table, then perform the following tasks:

   a. Create two different graphics, each of which communicates information about the cost of lost wages and productivity.

   b. Create two different graphics, each of which compares wage and productivity losses to the total of other losses due to unintentional injuries.

No. 176. Costs of Unintentional Injuries: 2002
[586.3 represents $586,300,000,000. Covers costs of deaths or disabling injuries together with vehicle accidents and fires]

Cost	Amount (bil. dol.)					Percent distribution				
	Total[1]	Motor vehicle	Work	Home	Other	Total[1]	Motor vehicle	Work	Home	Other
Total	**586.3**	**242.7**	**146.6**	**126.7**	**88.3**	**100**	**100**	**100**	**100**	**100**
Wage and productivity losses[2] . .	286.4	79.6	74.0	80.3	56.3	48.8	32.8	50.5	63.4	63.8
Medical expense	106.6	28.0	27.7	30.2	22.3	18.2	11.5	18.9	23.8	25.3
Administrative expenses[3]	88.7	62.0	26.3	5.5	4.3	15.1	25.5	17.9	4.3	4.9
Motor vehicle damage	71.1	71.1	2.8	(NA)	(NA)	12.1	29.3	1.9	(NA)	(NA)
Employer cost[4]	22.6	2.0	12.5	4.7	3.8	3.9	0.8	8.5	3.7	4.3
Fire loss	10.9	(NA)	3.3	6.0	1.6	1.9	(NA)	2.3	4.7	1.8

NA Not available.[1]Excludes duplication between work and motor vehicle ($18.0 billion in 2002). [2]Actual loss of wages and household production, and the present value of future earnings lost. [3]Home and other costs may include costs of administering medical treatment claims for some motor-vehicle injuries filed through health insurance plans. [4]Estimate of the uninsured costs incurred by employers, representing the money value of time lost by noninjured workers.

   Source of Tables 175 and 176: National Safety Council, Itasca, IL, *Injury Facts, 2003 Edition* (copyright).

4. For each of the following four graphics, write a paragraph evaluating its effectiveness and describing how you would revise it.

a.

	2003	2004	2005
Civil Engineering	236	231	253
Chemical Engineering	126	134	142
Comparative Literature	97	86	74
Electrical Engineering	317	326	401
English	714	623	592
Fine Arts	112	96	72
Foreign Languages	608	584	566
Materials Engineering	213	227	241
Mechanical Engineering	196	203	201
Other	46	42	51
Philosophy	211	142	151
Religion	86	91	72

b.

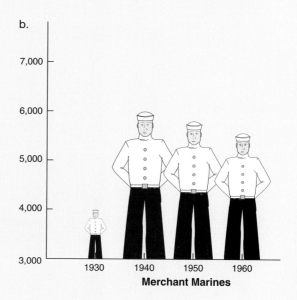

Merchant Marines

c.

Expenses at Hillway Corporation

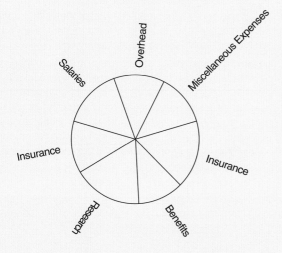

d.

Costs of the Components of a PC

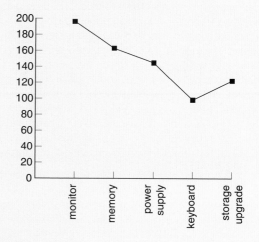

5. The three graphs on page 332 illustrate the sales of two products—Series 1 and Series 2—for each quarter of 2006. Which is the most effective in conveying the information? Which is the least effective? What additional information would make the most effective graph better?

a.
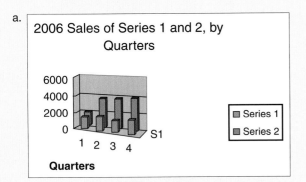

b.
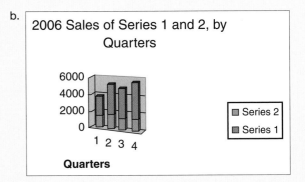

c.
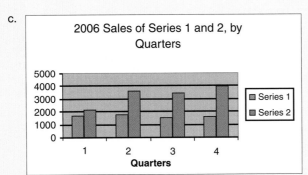

6. **GROUP EXERCISE** Form small groups. Go to one of the campus's computer centers and study a popular piece of software, such as a spreadsheet or graphics package. Have each group member, working separately, print out three of the basic kinds of graphics, such as graphs, tables, and pie charts, and take notes on the process. Come together as a group and share your experiences in learning how to use the software. What techniques did you try: using a tutorial, reading a manual, trial and error, asking someone for help? If appropriate, have the group go back to the lab together and work through some of the questions that arose in the group meeting. Write a memo to your instructor describing how easy or how difficult it was to learn how to produce these graphics and evaluate their quality. How well do the graphics conform to the basic guidelines presented in this chapter? Would you recommend the software to other members of your class? Why or why not?

7. **INTERNET EXERCISE** Locate a graphic on the Web that you consider inappropriate for an international audience because it might be offensive or unclear in some cultures. Imagine an intended audience for the graphic, such as people from the Middle East, and write a brief statement explaining the potential problem. Finally, revise the graphic so that it would be appropriate for its intended audience.

Case 13: Evaluating Graphics Made with a Spreadsheet Program

 In This Book For more about memos, see Ch. 14, p. 352.

Background

The National Highway Traffic Safety Administration (NHTSA), under the U.S. Department of Transportation, carries out safety programs focusing on improving the safety performance of motor vehicles and motor-vehicle equipment. NHTSA also conducts research on driver behavior, vehicle use, and highway safety. You work in the documentation group for the Research and Development (R&D) program at NHTSA. The R&D program provides scientific evidence to support NHTSA's safety initiatives. You help R&D scientists prepare documents reporting the results of research and crash investigations. Often the scientists' first opportunity to present their findings is at various professional conferences. They use spreadsheet programs to create the graphics they need for their presentations and conference papers.

Recently, some scientists have retired and been replaced by new hires. Your boss, Elsa Beardsley, has asked you to help some of the new scientists. "I want you to work with Dana Shapiro, Megan Hamilton, and Allison Yamamoto. All three of them are preparing papers for the 20th International Technical Conference on the Enhanced Safety of Vehicles in Nagoya, Japan. Specifically, I'd like you to review their graphics."

You ask Elsa why she thinks they need help with their graphics. "They're all good researchers. However, when they report their findings, they don't always choose the most appropriate kind of graphics. They also unnecessarily complicate their graphics by adding a bunch of chartjunk. The spreadsheet application gives them too many choices when it comes to selecting a type of graphic or modifying a graphic, but the program doesn't offer them any help in choosing what kind of chart works best for different kinds of information and readers."

Dana Shapiro and you are good friends, so you decide to stop by her office first. Dana shows you three graphics (Documents 13.1–13.3) she is planning to use in her conference paper. She also shows you the spreadsheet data she used to create each graphic.

Dana tells you that the Conference on the Enhanced Safety of Vehicles brings together about 1,000 representatives from government agencies, industry, and safety-advocacy groups worldwide to discuss research findings and advanced technologies related to vehicle safety. Her paper reports on the development phase of NHTSA's research program on improved frontal protection. Specifically, her research assesses the crash conditions that result in the highest number of injuries/fatalities to drivers with air bags.

"What are you trying to convey in each figure?" you ask.

"In the first figure," Dana explains, "I want to show the distribution of frontal crashes in three different crash modes. In the second figure, I'm showing how the presence of air bags affects drivers' risk of sustaining serious or fatal injuries in four body regions. I want to show that arm injuries are slightly more likely with air bags than without them, but that lower-extremity injuries—the type that lead to lifelong disabilities—are lower with air bags. In the last figure, I just want to show the average number of moderate lower-extremity injuries occurring annually to front-seat occupants in air-bag-equipped vehicles in our data set. I want to communicate the scope of the problem. I want people to know that an average of 17,669 lower-extremity injuries occur annually in frontal crashes involving air-bag-equipped vehicles."

"What type of injuries are 'tib.plat' and 'tib.shaft'?" you ask.

"They're both types of injuries to the tibia, the lower leg."

"Thanks. I'll take a look at these graphics more closely and get back to you later this week."

You also briefly visit with Megan Hamilton and Allison Yamamoto. You note that their graphics have some of the same flaws as Dana's graphics. You decide that brief guidelines for choosing graphics in a spreadsheet program would be useful to the new R&D scientists. Besides, the guidelines might save you from repeating the same information to several scientists.

Your Assignment
1. Using the techniques explained in this chapter, create guidelines to help the R&D scientists decide which type of chart or graph to create.
2. Revise Dana Shapiro's graphics. Write Dana a brief memo explaining your revisions.

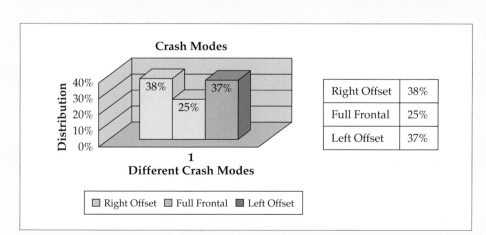

Right Offset	38%
Full Frontal	25%
Left Offset	37%

■ **Document 13.1**
Vertical Bar Graph

 On TechComm Web

For digital versions of case documents, click on Downloadable Case Documents on <bedfordstmartins.com/techcomm>.

Serious-to-Fatal Injury Risk

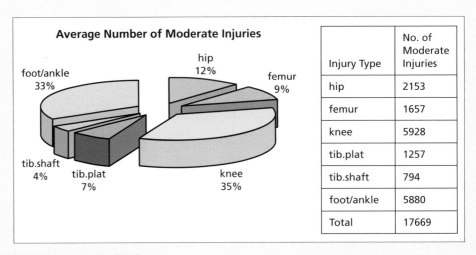

	Arms	Thorax	Head	Legs
Air Bag	0.65%	0.80%	0.49%	0.87%
No Air Bag	0.43%	1.25%	0.90%	1.20%

■ **Document 13.2   Combination Bar and Line Graph**

Average Number of Moderate Injuries

Injury Type	No. of Moderate Injuries
hip	2153
femur	1657
knee	5928
tib.plat	1257
tib.shaft	794
foot/ankle	5880
Total	17669

■ **Document 13.3   Pie Chart**

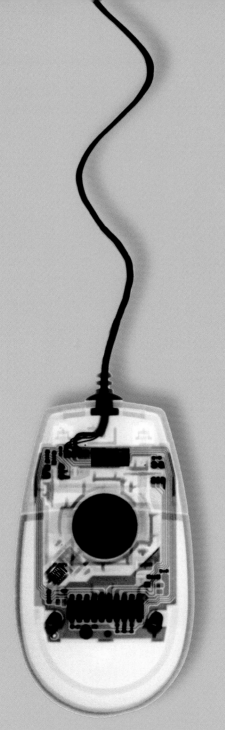

PART FIVE

Applications

14 Writing Letters, Memos, and E-mails

TECH COMM AT WORK

You can expect to write correspondence every day on the job. A wholesaler who wants to communicate with someone outside his organization—for example, to thank a customer for placing an order—will likely use a letter. An IT specialist who needs to correspond with people within her own organization—for example, to request resources to carry out a project or to convey the status of that project—will likely write a memo. And a manager of a political action committee who wants to confirm details of a meeting with her colleagues will likely use e-mail. It makes sense, then, to understand the conventions of letters, memos, and e-mails and to learn some strategies for writing effective workplace correspondence.

To communicate with others in the workplace, you will use a number of different media. Along with written correspondence, face-to-face meetings, and phone conversations, you will likely use text messaging and instant messaging, two computer-based synchronous (real-time) media that are somewhere between talking on the phone and writing an e-mail message. This chapter discusses the three major formats for written correspondence: letters, memos, and e-mails. These three formats are essentially similar, but they differ in some important ways.

UNDERSTANDING THE PROCESS OF WRITING LETTERS, MEMOS, AND E-MAILS

The process of writing letters, memos, and e-mails is much like that of writing any other kind of workplace document. Figure 14.1 on page 338 presents an overview of this process.

SELECTING THE TYPE OF CORRESPONDENCE

When you need to correspond with others in the workplace, your first task is to decide on the appropriate format. Figure 14.2 on page 339 offers guidelines for helping you make that decision.

PRESENTING YOURSELF EFFECTIVELY IN CORRESPONDENCE

Chapter 1 discusses the measures of excellence for effective technical communication—including honesty, clarity, accuracy, accessibility, and correctness. These measures also apply to business correspondence. This section focuses on five characteristics that are particularly important when you write letters, memos, and e-mails in the workplace.

In writing business correspondence:

Use the appropriate level of formality.

Communicate correctly.

Project the "you attitude."

Avoid correspondence clichés.

Communicate honestly.

■ Figure 14.1   An
Overview of the Process
for Writing Letters,
Memos, and E-mails

Analyze Your Audience

Consider the readers' characteristics and attitudes and how they will use the document. Remember that the tone, content, and format of letters, memos, and e-mails differ from culture to culture.

Analyze Your Purpose

What do you want to accomplish in the document? After others read it, what do you want them to know, believe, or do?

Gather Information About Your Subject

Use appropriate techniques of primary and secondary research. For more information, see Chapter 6.

Choose a Type of Document

Letters are best for formal situations. Memos are less formal than letters. E-mails are the least formal of the three, but they still require a moderately formal tone and correctness.

Draft the Document

Clearly state your purpose, use headings to help your readers, summarize your message, provide adequate background, organize the discussion, and highlight action items.

Format the Document

Use a conventional format but adapt it to meet the special needs of your audience, purpose, and subject.

Revise, Edit, and Proofread the Document

Let it sit for as long as you can. Many careful writers draft e-mails in a text editor such as Notepad, then revise them later. For more-formal occasions, ask subject-matter experts to review your documents.

Send the Document

Go on to the next task.

Format	Main use of the format	Advantages of the format	Disadvantages of the format
Letter	Formal communication with people either within or outside your own organization.	• Because letters are the only format that uses centuries-old conventions such as the salutation and complimentary close, they are the most appropriate format for communicating with people outside your organization or, in some formal situations, with people in your own organization. • Because letters are paper documents, they can be filed easily in an archive.	Although letters can be faxed or attached to e-mails, many organizations still consider them paper documents that require a signature in ink. Paper versions of letters require time and other resources: • They need to be signed individually (although there are mechanical ways to simulate a signature). • They require paper. • They require handling. • They take time to be delivered. • They require postage if they are sent outside your organization.
Memo	Moderately formal written communication, usually with people within your organization.	• Because a memo is word processed, the writer can control its design and appearance. • Because memos are paper documents, they can be filed easily in an archive.	Although memos can be faxed or attached to e-mails, those that are printed on paper require time and other resources: • They need to be signed. • They require paper. • They require handling. • They take time to be delivered.
E-mail	Quick, relatively informal communication with one or many recipients.	• E-mail systems are available almost everywhere in the working world. • Sending an e-mail doesn't cost anything, once the system is in place. • Recipients can store and forward e-mail easily. They can capture the text and reuse it in other documents. • E-mails can carry other digital files as attachments.	Because e-mails are informal, they are not appropriate for many kinds of correspondence that require a written record.

■ **Figure 14.2   Choosing the Most Appropriate Format for Business Communication**

Use the Appropriate Level of Formality

As shown in Figure 14.2, one factor that distinguishes e-mails, memos, and letters is the formality of the language. E-mails are the least formal, and letters are the most formal. When you use any of these formats, however, you are representing your organization and, for this reason, should always avoid informal writing.

People are most tempted to use informal writing in e-mails. Remember that e-mails, like memos and letters, are legally the property of the organization for which you work, and they are almost always archived digitally, even after recipients have deleted them from their computers. Remember that your e-mails might be read by the company president, or they might appear in a newspaper or be used in a court of law. Therefore, use a moderately formal tone to avoid potential embarrassment.

TOO INFORMAL	Our meeting with United went south right away when they threw a hissy fit, saying that we blew off the deadline for the progress report.
MODERATELY FORMAL	In our meeting, the United representatives expressed concern that we had missed the deadline for the progress report.
TOO INFORMAL	I doubt if Bob gives a flying squirrel how you handle it. Do whatever you want.
MODERATELY FORMAL	I don't think Bob prefers any particular method. Please use your judgment.

In memos and letters, strive for the same moderately formal tone. Don't try to sound like a dictionary.

TOO FORMAL	It was indubitably the case that our team was successful in presenting a proposal that was characterized by quality of the highest order. My appreciation for your industriousness is herewith extended.
MODERATELY FORMAL	I think we put together an excellent proposal. Thank you very much for your hard work.

Communicate Correctly

One issue closely related to formality is correctness. As discussed in Chapter 1, correct writing is writing that is free of errors in grammar, punctuation, style, usage, and spelling. The most problems with correctness arise when people use e-mail.

Some writers think that because e-mail is a quick, informal medium, they need not worry about correctness. They are wrong. You have to plan your e-mails just as you plan any other written communication. And you have to revise, edit, and proofread them as well. Sending an e-mail that contains errors of correctness is unprofessional because doing so shows a lack of respect for your reader and for yourself. It also causes your reader to think that you are careless about your job.

 In This Book
For more about editing and proofreading, see Ch. 3, p. 33.

Project the "You Attitude"

Correspondence must convey a courteous, positive tone. The key to accomplishing this task is using the *you attitude*—that is, looking at the situation from the reader's point of view and adjusting the content, structure, and tone to meet his or her needs. For example, if you are writing to a supplier who has failed to deliver some merchandise on the agreed-upon date, the "you attitude" dictates that you not discuss problems you are having with other suppliers—those problems don't concern your reader. Instead, concentrate on explaining clearly and politely that the reader has violated your agreement and that not having the merchandise is costing you money. Then propose ways to expedite the shipment.

Following are examples of thoughtless sentences, each followed by an improved version that shows the "you attitude."

ACCUSING	You must have dropped the engine. The housing is badly cracked.
BETTER	The badly cracked housing suggests that your engine must have fallen onto a hard surface from some height.
SARCASTIC	You'll need two months to deliver these parts? Who do you think you are, the post office?
BETTER	Surely you would find a two-month delay for the delivery of parts unacceptable in your business. That's how I feel, too.
BELLIGERENT	I'm sure you have a boss, and I doubt if he'd like to hear about how you've mishandled our account.
BETTER	I'm sure you would prefer to settle the account between us rather than have it brought to your supervisor's attention.

A calm, respectful tone makes the best impression and increases the chances that you will achieve your goal.

Avoid Correspondence Clichés

Over the centuries, a number of words and phrases have come to be associated with business correspondence; one common example is *as per your request*. These phrases sound stilted and insincere. If you would feel awkward or uncomfortable saying these clichés to a friend, avoid them in your correspondence.

Figure 14.3 is a list of common clichés and their more natural equivalents. Figure 14.4 on page 342 shows two versions of the same letter—one written in clichés, the other in plain language.

 In This Book

For more about choosing the right words and phrases, see Ch. 11, p. 235.

■ **Figure 14.3 Letter Clichés and Natural Equivalents**

Letter clichés	Natural equivalents
attached please find	attached is
enclosed please find	enclosed is
pursuant to our agreement	as we agreed
referring to your ("referring to your letter of March 19, the shipment of pianos . . .")	"As you wrote in your letter of March 19, the . . ." (or subordinate the reference at the end of your sentence)
wish to advise ("We wish to advise that . . .")	(The phrase doesn't say anything. Just say what you want to say.)
the writer ("The writer believes that . . .")	"I believe . . ."

■ Figure 14.4 Sample Letters with and Without Clichés

The letter on the right side avoids clichés and shows an understanding of the "you attitude." Instead of focusing on the violation of the warranty, it presents the conclusion as good news: the snowmobile is not ruined, and it can be repaired and returned in less than a week for a small charge.

Letter containing clichés

Dear Mr. Smith:

Referring to your letter regarding the problem encountered with your new Trailrider Snowmobile, our Customer Service Department has just submitted its report.

It is their conclusion that the malfunction is caused by water being present in the fuel line. It is our conclusion that you must have purchased some bad gasoline. We trust you are cognizant of the fact that while we guarantee our snowmobiles for a period of not less than one year against defects in workmanship and materials, responsibility cannot be assumed for inadequate care. We wish to advise, for the reason mentioned hereinabove, that we cannot grant your request to repair the snowmobile free of charge.

Permit me to say, however, that the writer would be pleased to see that the fuel line is flushed at cost, $30. Your Trailrider would then give you many years of trouble-free service.

Enclosed please find an authorization card. Should we receive it, we shall perform the above-mentioned repair and deliver your snowmobile forthwith.

Sincerely yours,

Letter in natural language

Dear Mr. Smith:

Thank you for writing to us about the problem with your new Trailrider Snowmobile.

Our Customer Service Department has found water in the fuel line. Apparently some of the gasoline was bad. While we guarantee our snowmobiles for one year against defects in workmanship and materials, we cannot assume responsibility for problems caused by bad gasoline. We cannot, therefore, grant your request to repair the snowmobile free of charge.

However, no serious harm was done to the snowmobile. We would be happy to flush the fuel line at cost, $30. Your Trailrider would then give you many years of trouble-free service. If you will authorize us to do this work, we will have your snowmobile back to you within four working days. Just fill out the enclosed authorization card and drop it in the mail.

Sincerely yours,

Communicate Honestly

You should communicate honestly when you write any kind of document, and business correspondence is no exception. Communicating honestly shows respect for your reader and for yourself.

On TechComm Web

For more about letter writing, search for "business letters" at Purdue University's OWL. Click on Links Library for Ch. 14 on <bedfordstmartins.com/techcomm>.

WRITING LETTERS

Letters are still a basic means of communication between organizations, with millions written each day. Writing a letter is much like writing any other technical document. First you have to analyze your audience and

Ethics Note

Writing Honest Business Correspondence

Why is dishonesty a big problem in business correspondence? Maybe it has something to do with the fact that the subjects discussed in e-mails, memos, and letters often relate to the writer's professionalism and the quality of his or her work. For instance, when a salesperson working for a supplier writes to a customer explaining why the product did not arrive on time, he is tempted to make it seem as if his company—and he personally—is blameless. Similarly, when a manager has to announce a new policy that employees will dislike, she might be tempted to distance herself from the policy.

The most professional thing a writer can do is tell the truth. If you mislead a reader in explaining why the shipment didn't arrive on time, the reader will likely double-check the facts, conclude that you are trying to avoid responsibility, and end your business relationship. If you try to convince readers that you had nothing to do with a new, unpopular policy, some of them will know if you are being misleading, and you will lose your most important credential: your credibility.

determine your purpose. Next you have to gather your information, make an outline, write a draft, and then revise, edit, and proofread the draft.

Understanding the Elements of the Letter

Most letters include a heading, an inside address, a salutation, a body, a complimentary close, a signature, and reference initials. Some letters also include one or more of the following: attention line, subject line, enclosure line, and copy line. Figure 14.5 on page 344 shows the elements of a letter.

Learning the Format of the Letter

Two common formats are used for letters: modified block and full block. Figure 14.6 on page 346 illustrates these formats.

Understanding Common Types of Letters

Organizations send out many different kinds of letters. This section focuses on four types of letters written frequently in the workplace.

Common types of letters:

Inquiry letter

Response to an inquiry

Claim letter

Adjustment letter

Heading. *Most organizations use letterhead stationery with their heading printed at the top. This preprinted information and the date the letter is sent make up the heading. If you are using blank paper rather than letterhead, your address (without your name) and the date form the heading. Use letterhead for the first page and do not number it. Use blank paper for the second and all subsequent pages.*

Inside Address. *If you are writing to an individual who has a professional title—such as Professor, Dr., or, for public officials, Honorable—use it. If not, use Mr. or Ms. (unless you know the recipient prefers Mrs. or Miss). If the reader's position fits on the same line as the name, add it after a comma; otherwise, drop it to the line below. Spell the name of the organization the way the organization itself does: for example, International Business Machines calls itself IBM. Include the complete mailing address: street number and name, city, state, and zip code.*

Attention Line. *Sometimes you will be unable to address a letter to a particular person because you don't know (and cannot easily find out) the name of the individual who holds that position in the company.*

DAVIS TREE CARE
1300 Lancaster Avenue
Berwyn, PA 19092
www.davisfortrees.com

May 12, 2006

Fairlawn Industrial Park
1910 Ridgeway Drive
Rollins, MO 84639

Attention: Director of Maintenance

Subject: Fall pruning

Dear Director of Maintenance:

Do you know how much your trees are worth? That's right—your trees. As a maintenance director, you know how much of an investment your organization has in its physical plant. And the landscaping is a big part of your total investment.

Most people don't know that even the hardiest trees need periodic care. Like shrubs, trees should be fertilized and pruned. And they should be protected against the many kinds of diseases and pests that are common in this area.

At Davis Tree Care, we have the skills and experience to keep your trees healthy and beautiful. Our diagnostic staff is made up of graduates of major agricultural and forestry universities, and all of our crews attend special workshops to keep current with the latest information on tree maintenance. Add to this our proven record of 43 years of continuous service in the Berwyn area, and you have a company you can trust.

Subject Line. *Use either a project number (for example, "Subject: Project 31402") or a brief phrase defining the subject (for example, "Subject: Price Quotation for the R13 Submersible Pump").*

Salutation. *If you decide not to use an attention line or a subject line, put the salutation, or greeting, two lines below the inside address. The traditional salutation is Dear, followed by the reader's courtesy title and last name, followed by a colon (not a comma):*
Dear Ms. Hawkins:

■ **Figure 14.5   Elements of a Letter**

Letter to Fairlawn Industrial Park
Page 2
May 13, 2006

May we stop by to give you an analysis of your trees—absolutely without cost or obligation? A few minutes with one of our diagnosticians could prove to be one of the wisest moves you've ever made. Just give us a call at 555-9187, and we'll be happy to arrange an appointment at your convenience.

Sincerely yours,

Jasmine Brown

Jasmine Brown
President

Enclosure: Davis Tree Care brochure

c: Darrell Davis, Vice President

Header *for second page.*

Body. *In most cases, the body contains at least three paragraphs: an introductory paragraph, a concluding paragraph, and one or more body paragraphs.*

Complimentary Close. *The conventional phrases* Sincerely, Sincerely yours, Yours sincerely, Yours very truly, *and* Very truly yours *are interchangeable.*

Signature. *Type your full name on the fourth line below the complimentary close. Sign the letter, in ink, above the typewritten name. Most organizations prefer that you include your position under your typed name.*

Copy Line. *If you want the primary recipient to know that other people are receiving a copy of the letter, include a copy line. Use the symbol c (for "copy") followed by the names of the other recipients (listed either alphabetically or according to organizational rank).*

Enclosure Line. *If the envelope contains documents other than the letter, include an enclosure line that indicates the number of enclosures. For more than one enclosure, add the number: "Enclosures (2)." In determining the number of enclosures, count only separate items, not pages. A 3-page memo and a 10-page report constitute only two enclosures. Some writers like to identify the enclosures:*

> *Enclosure: 2005 Placement Bulletin*
> *Enclosures (2): "This Year at Ammex"*
> *2005 Annual Report*

■ **Figure 14.5**   *(continued)*

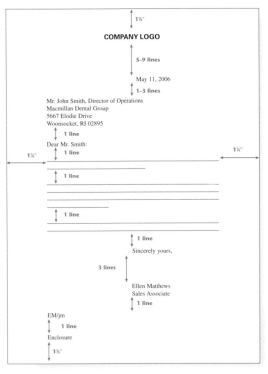

a. Modified block format

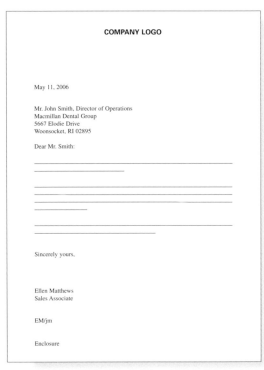

b. Full block format—everything aligned along the left margin

■ **Figure 14.6   Common Letter Formats**

The dimensions and spacing shown for the modified block format also apply to the full block format.

Inquiry Letter   Figure 14.7 shows an inquiry letter, in which you ask questions. The key to an inquiry letter is persuasion.

 In This Book

Two other types of letters are discussed in this book: the transmittal letter (see Ch. 18, p. 467) and the job-application letter (see Ch. 15, p. 387).

Response to an Inquiry   Figure 14.8 on page 348 shows a response to the inquiry letter in Figure 14.7.

Claim Letter   Figure 14.9 on page 349 is an example of a claim letter that the writer faxed to the reader.

14 Hawthorne Ave.
Belleview, TX 75234
November 2, 2006

Dr. Andrea Shakir
Director of Technical Services
Orion Corporation
721 West Douglas Avenue
Maryville, TN 31409

Dear Dr. Shakir:

I am writing to you because of Orion's reputation as a leader in the manufacture of adjustable x-ray tables. I am a graduate student in biomedical engineering at the University of Texas, and I am working on an analysis of diagnostic equipment for a seminar paper. Would you be able to answer a few questions about your Microspot 311?

1. Can the Microspot 311 be used with lead oxide cassettes, or does it accept only lead-free cassettes?
2. Are standard generators compatible with the Microspot 311?
3. What would you say is the greatest advantage, for the operator, of using the Microspot 311? For the patient?

My project is due on January 15. I would greatly appreciate your assistance in answering these questions. Of course, I would be happy to send you a copy of my report when it is completed.

Yours very truly,

Albert K. Stern

Albert K. Stern

You write an inquiry letter to acquire information. Explain who you are and why you are writing. Make your questions precise and clear, and therefore easy to answer. Explain what you plan to do with the information and how you can compensate the reader for answering your questions.

This writer's task is to motivate the reader to provide some information. That information is not likely to lead to a sale because the writer is a graduate student doing research, not a potential customer.

Notice the flattery in the first sentence.

The writer presents specific questions in a list format, making the questions easy to read and understand.

In the final paragraph, the writer politely indicates his schedule and requests the reader's response. Note that he offers to send the reader a copy of his report.

If the reader provides information, the writer should send a thank-you letter.

■ **Figure 14.7   Inquiry Letter**

In responding to an inquiry letter, answer the questions if you can. If you cannot, either because you don't know the answers or because you cannot divulge proprietary information, explain the reasons and offer to assist with other requests.

ORION

**721 WEST DOUGLAS AVE.
MARYVILLE, TN 31409**

**(615) 619-8132
www.orioninstruments.com**

November 7, 2006

Mr. Albert K. Stern
14 Hawthorne Ave.
Belleview, TX 75234

Dear Mr. Stern:

The writer responds graciously.

I would be pleased to answer your questions about the Microspot 311. We think it is the best unit of its type on the market today.

The writer answers the three questions posed in the inquiry letter.

1. The 311 can handle lead oxide or lead-free cassettes.
2. At the moment, the 311 is fully compatible only with our Duramatic generator. However, special wiring kits are available to make the 311 compatible with our earlier generator models—the Olympus and the Saturn. We are currently working on other wiring kits.
3. For the operator, the 311 increases the effectiveness of the radiological procedure while at the same time cutting down the amount of film used. For the patient, it reduces the number of repeat exposures and therefore reduces the total dose.

The writer encloses other information to give the reader a fuller understanding of the product.

I am enclosing a copy of our brochure on the Microspot 311. If you would like additional copies, please let me know. I would be happy to receive a copy of your analysis when it is complete. Good luck!

Sincerely yours,

Andrea Shakir, M.D.

Andrea Shakir, M.D.
Director of Technical Services

The writer uses the enclosure notation to signal that she is attaching an item to the letter.

Enclosure

The writer indicates that she is forwarding a copy to her supervisor.

c: Robert Anderson, Executive Vice President

■ **Figure 14.8   Response to an Inquiry**

ROBBINS CONSTRUCTION, INC.

255 Robbins Place, Centerville, MO 65101 | (417) 555-1850 | www.robbinsconstruction.com

August 18, 2006

Mr. David Larsyn
Larsyn Supply Company
311 Elmerine Avenue
Anderson, MO 63501

Dear Mr. Larsyn:

As steady customers of yours for over 15 years, we came to you first when we needed a quiet pile driver for a job near a residential area. On your recommendation, we bought your Vista 500 Quiet Driver, at $14,900. We have since found, much to our embarrassment, that it is not substantially quieter than a regular pile driver.

We received the contract to do the bridge repair here in Centerville after promising to keep the noise to under 90 dB during the day. The Vista 500 (see enclosed copy of bill of sale for particulars) is rated at 85 dB, maximum. We began our work and, although one of our workers said the driver didn't seem sufficiently quiet to him, assured the people living near the job site that we were well within the agreed sound limit. One of them, an acoustical engineer, marched out the next day and demonstrated that we were putting out 104 dB. Obviously, something is wrong with the pile driver.

I think you will agree that we have a problem. We were able to secure other equipment, at considerable inconvenience, to finish the job on schedule. When I telephoned your company that humiliating day, however, a Mr. Meredith informed me that I should have done an acoustical reading on the driver before I accepted delivery.

I would like you to send out a technician—as soon as possible—either to repair the driver so that it performs according to specifications or to take it back for a full refund.

Yours truly,

Jack Robbins

Jack Robbins, President

Enclosure

■ **Figure 14.9   Claim Letter**

A claim letter is a polite, reasonable complaint. If you purchase a defective or falsely advertised product or receive inadequate service, you write a claim letter. If the letter is convincing, your chances of receiving an equitable settlement are good because most organizations realize that unhappy customers are bad for business. In addition, claim letters help companies identify weak points in their product or service.

The writer indicates clearly in the first paragraph that he is writing about an unsatisfactory product. Note that he identifies the product by model name.

The writer presents the background, filling in specific details about the problem. Notice how he supports his earlier claim that the problem embarrassed him professionally.

The writer states that he thinks the reader will agree that there was a problem with the equipment.

Then the writer suggests that the reader's colleague did not respond satisfactorily.

The writer proposes a solution: that the reader take appropriate action. The writer's clear, specific account of the problem and his professional tone increase his chances of receiving the solution he proposes.

 On TechComm Web

For excellent advice on adjustment letters, see Business Communication: Managing Information and Relationships. Click on Links Library for Ch. 14 on <bedfordstmartins.com/techcomm>.

An adjustment letter, a response to a claim letter, tells the customer how you plan to handle the situation. Your purpose is to show that your organization is fair and reasonable and that you value the customer's business.

If you can grant the request, the letter is easy to write. Express your regret, state the adjustment you are going to make, and end on a positive note by encouraging the customer to continue doing business with you.

The writer wisely expresses regret about the two problems cited in the claim letter.

The writer describes the actions he has already taken and formally states that he will do whatever the reader wishes.

The writer expresses empathy in making the offer of adjustment. Doing so helps to create a bond: you and I are both professionals who rely on our good reputations.

This polite conclusion appeals to the reader's sense of fairness and good business practice.

Larsyn Supply Company

311 Elmerine Avenue
Anderson, MO 63501
(417) 555-2484
www.larsynsupply.com

August 22, 2006

Mr. Jack Robbins, President
Robbins Construction, Inc.
255 Robbins Place
Centerville, MO 65101

Dear Mr. Robbins:

I was very unhappy to read your letter of August 18 telling me about the failure of the Vista 500. I regretted most the treatment you received from one of my employees when you called us.

Harry Rivers, our best technician, has already been in touch with you to arrange a convenient time to come out to Centerville to talk with you about the driver. We will of course repair it, replace it, or refund the price. Just let us know your wish.

I realize that I cannot undo the damage that was done on the day that a piece of our equipment failed. To make up for some of the extra trouble and expense you incurred, let me offer you a 10 percent discount on your next purchase or service order with us, up to a $1,000 total discount.

You have indeed been a good customer for many years, and I would hate to have this unfortunate incident spoil that relationship. Won't you give us another chance? Just bring in this letter when you visit us next, and we'll give you that 10 percent discount.

Sincerely,

Dave Larsyn

Dave Larsyn, President

■ **Figure 14.10   "Good News" Adjustment Letter**

Adjustment Letter   Figures 14.10 and 14.11 show examples of "good news" and "bad news" adjustment letters. The first is a reply to the claim letter shown in Figure 14.9 on page 349.

Quality Storage Media

2077 Highland, Burley, ID 84765
208·555·1613
www.qualstorage.com

February 3, 2006

Ms. Dale Devlin
1903 Highland Avenue
Glenn Mills, NE 69032

Dear Ms. Devlin:

Thank you for writing us about the portable disc you purchased on January 11, 2006. I know from personal experience how frustrating it is when a disc fails.

According to your letter, you used the disc to store the business plan for your new consulting business. When you attempted to copy that file to your hard drive, the portable disc failed, and the business plan was lost. You have no other copy of that file. You are asking us to reimburse you $1,500 for the cost of re-creating that business plan from notes and rough drafts.

As you know, our discs carry a lifetime guarantee covering parts and workmanship. We will gladly replace the defective portable disc. However, the guarantee states that the manufacturer and the retailer will not assume any incidental liability. Thus we are responsible only for the retail value of the blank disc, not for the cost of duplicating the work that went into making the files stored on the disc.

However, your file might still be recoverable. A reputable data-recovery firm might be able to restore the data from the file at a very reasonable cost. To prevent such problems in the future, we always recommend that you back up all valuable files periodically.

We have already sent out your new portable disc by overnight delivery. It should arrive within the next two days.

Please contact us if we can be of any further assistance.

Sincerely yours,

Paul R. Blackwood

Paul R. Blackwood, Manager
Customer Relations

If you are writing a "bad news" adjustment letter, salvage as much goodwill as you can by showing that you have acted reasonably. In denying a request, explain your side of the matter, thus educating the customer about how the problem occurred and how to prevent it in the future.

The writer does not begin by stating that he is denying the reader's request. Instead, he begins politely by trying to form a bond with the reader. In trying to meet the customer on neutral ground, be careful about admitting that the customer is right. If you say "We are sorry that the engine you purchased from us is defective," it would bolster the customer's claim if the dispute ended up in court.

The writer summarizes the facts of the incident, as he sees them.

The writer explains that he is unable to fulfill the reader's request. Notice that the writer never explicitly denies the request. It is more effective to explain why granting the request is not appropriate. Also notice that the writer does not explicitly say that the reader failed to make a backup copy of the plan and therefore the problem is her fault.

The writer shifts from the bad news to the good news. The writer explains that he has already responded appropriately to the reader's request.

The writer ends with a polite conclusion. A common technique is to offer the reader a special discount on another, similar product.

■ **Figure 14.11   "Bad News" Adjustment Letter**

WRITING MEMOS

Even in the age of e-mail, memos are likely to survive, because sometimes writers want a slightly more formal document. The following discussion explains how to write effective memos.

Like letters, memos have a characteristic format, which consists of the elements shown in Figure 14.12.

Print the second and all subsequent pages of a memo on plain paper rather than on letterhead. Include three items in the upper right-hand or left-hand corner of each page: the name of the recipient, the page number, and the date of the memo. See Figure 14.5 on page 345.

Figure 14.13 shows a sample memo.

Write out the month instead of using the all-numeral format (6/12/06); multicultural readers might use a different notation for dates and could be confused.

AMRO   MEMO

To: B. Pabst
From: J. Alonso **J. A.**
Subject: MIXER RECOMMENDATION FOR PHILLIPS
Date: 12 June 2006

INTEROFFICE

List the names of persons receiving photocopies of the memo, either alphabetically or in descending order of organizational rank.

To:	C. Cleveland	c:	B. Aaron
From:	H. Rainbow **H. R.**		K. Lau
Subject:	Shipment Date of Blueprints		J. Manuputra
	to Collier		W. Williams
Date:	2 October 2006		

NORTHERN PETROLEUM COMPANY
INTERNAL CORRESPONDENCE

Most writers put their initials or signature next to the typed name (or at the end of the memo) to show that they have reviewed the memo and accept responsibility for it.

Date: January 3, 2006
To: William Weeks, Director of Operations
From: Helen Cho, Chemical Engineering Dept. **H. C.**
Subject: Trip Report — Conference on Improved Procedures
for Chemical Analysis Laboratory

■ **Figure 14.12   Identifying Information in a Memo**

Some organizations prefer the full names of the writer and reader; others want only the first initials and last names. Some prefer job titles; others do not. If your organization does not object, include your job title and your reader's. The memo will then be informative for someone who refers to it after either of you has moved on to a new position, as well as for others in the organization who might not know you.

Dynacol Corporation

INTEROFFICE COMMUNICATION

To: G. Granby, R&D
From: P. Rabin, Technical Services   *P.R.*
Subject: Trip Report—Computer Dynamics, Inc.
Date: September 22, 2006

The purpose of this memo is to present my impressions of the Computer Dynamics technical seminar of September 19. The goal of the seminar was to introduce their new PQ-500 line of high-capacity storage drives.

Summary

In general, I was impressed with the technical capabilities and interface of the drives. Of the two models in the 500 series, I think we ought to consider the external drives, not the internal ones. I'd like to talk to you about this issue when you have a chance.

Discussion

Computer Dynamics offers two models in its 500 series: an internal drive and an external drive. Both models have the same capacity (10 G of storage), and they both work the same way: they extend the storage capacity of a server by integrating an optical disk library into the file system. The concept is that they move files between the server's faster, but limited-capacity, storage devices (hard disks) and its slower, high-capacity storage devices (magneto-optical disks). This process, which they call data migration and demigration, is transparent to the user.

For the system administrator, integrating either of the models would require no more than one hour. The external model would be truly portable; the user would not need to install any drivers, as long as his or her device is docked on our network. The system administrator would push the necessary drivers onto all the networked devices without the user having to do anything.

Although the internal drive is convenient—it is already configured for the computer—I think we should consider only the external drive. Because so many of our employees do teleconferencing, the advantage of portability outweighs the disadvantage of inconvenience. The tech rep from Computer Dynamics walked me through the process of configuring both models. A second advantage of the external drive is that it can be salvaged easily when we take a computer out of service.

Recommendation

I'd like to talk to you, when you get a chance, about negotiating with Computer Dynamics for a quantity discount. I think we should ask McKinley and Rossiter to participate in the discussion. Give me a call (x3442) and we'll talk.

This memo is a trip report, a record of a business trip written after the employee returns to the office. Readers are less interested in an hour-by-hour narrative of what happened than in a carefully structured discussion of what was important.

The subject line is specific: the reader can tell at a glance that the memo reports on a trip to Computer Dynamics, Inc.

The memo begins with a clear statement of purpose, as discussed in Ch. 5, p. 88.

The writer provides a summary, which helps him to convey his main request: he would like to meet with the reader.

Headings make the memo easier to read. The reader can skip sections she doesn't need and quickly understand what each section is about. Headings also make the memo easier to write, because the writer can focus on the kind of information the reader needs.

The writer describes the background: a comparison of the two models.

The writer states his conclusion: the company should consider only the external drive.

The recommendations section states what the writer would like the reader to do next: discuss with her how to proceed.

Memos often conclude with action steps: bulleted or numbered lists of what the writer will do or what the writer would like others to do. Here is an example:

Action Items
I would appreciate it if you would work on the following tasks and have your results ready for the meeting on Monday, June 9.

- *Henderson: recalculate the flow rate.*
- *Smith: set up meeting with the regional EPA representative for sometime during the week of February 13.*
- *Falvey: ask Armitra in Houston for his advice.*

■ **Figure 14.13   Sample Memo**

 In This Book   For more examples of memos, see Ch. 18.

WRITING E-MAILS

Before you write an e-mail in the workplace, find out your organization's e-mail policies. Most companies have written policies that discuss circumstances under which you may and may not use e-mail, principles you should use in writing e-mail messages, and monitoring of employee e-mail.

Regardless of your company's policies, you should adhere to netiquette guidelines. *Netiquette* refers to etiquette on a network.

On TechComm Web

For statistics on e-mail usage in business, see the ePolicy Institute. Click on Links Library for Ch. 14 on <bedfordstmartins.com/techcomm>.

On TechComm Web

See Albion.com's discussion of netiquette. Click on Links Library for Ch. 14 on <bedfordstmartins.com/techcomm>.

Guidelines

Following Netiquette

▶ **Stick to business.** Don't send jokes or other nonbusiness messages.

▶ **Don't waste bandwidth.** Keep the message brief. When you reply to another e-mail, don't quote long passages from it. Instead, establish the context of the original e-mail by paraphrasing it briefly or by including a short quotation from it. (When you excerpt a small portion of an e-mail, add a phrase such as <*snip*> at the start and end of the quotation.) When you quote, delete the routing information from the top and the signature block from the bottom. And make sure to send the e-mail only to people who need to read it.

▶ **Use appropriate formality.** As discussed on pages 339–40, avoid informal writing.

▶ **Write correctly.** As discussed on page 340, revise, edit, and proofread your e-mails before sending them.

▶ **Don't flame.** To *flame* is to scorch a reader with scathing criticism, usually in response to something that person wrote in a previous message. Flaming is rude. When you are angry, keep your hands away from the keyboard.

▶ **Use the subject line.** Readers like to be able to decide whether they want to read the message. Therefore, write specific, accurate, and informative subject lines, just as you would in a memo.

▶ **Make your message easy on the eyes.** Use uppercase and lowercase letters, and skip lines between paragraphs. Don't use italics, underlining, or boldface for emphasis, even if your e-mail software can accommodate them, because you can't be sure your reader's e-mail system can. Instead, use uppercase letters for emphasis. Keep the line length under 65 characters so that lines do not get broken up if the recipient's monitor has a smaller screen.

▶ **Don't forward a message to another person or to an online discussion forum without the writer's permission.** Doing so is unethical, and it might be illegal (the courts haven't decided yet).

▶ **Don't send a message unless you have something to say.** Resist the temptation to write that you agree with another message. If you can add something new, fine, but don't send a message just to be part of the conversation.

Figure 14.14a shows an e-mail that violates netiquette guidelines. The writer is a technical professional working for a microchip manufacturer. Figure 14.14b shows a revised version of this e-mail message.

To: Supers and Leads		The writer does not clearly state his purpose in the subject line and the first paragraph.
Subject:	
LATELY, WE HAVE BEEN MISSING LASER REPAIR FILES FOR OUR 16MEG WAFERS. AFTER BRIEF INVESTIGATION, I HAVE FOUND THE MAIN REASON FOR THE MISSING DATA.	
OCCASIONALLY, SOME OF YOU HAVE WRONGLY PROBED THE WAFERS UNDER THE CORRELATE STEP AND THE DATA IS THEN COPIED INTO THE NONPROD STEP USING THE QTR PROGRAM. THIS IS REALLY STUPID. WHEN DATE IS COPIED THIS WAY THE REPAIR DATA IS NOT COPIED. IT REMAINS UNDER THE CORRELATE STEP.	Using all uppercase letters gives the impression that the writer is yelling at the readers.
TO AVOID THIS PROBLEM, FIRST PROBE THE WAFERS THE RIGHT WAY. IF A WAFER MUST BE PROBED UNDER A DIFFERENT STEP, THE WAFER IN THE CHANGE FILE MUST BE RENAMED TO THE ** FORMAT.	The writer has not proofread.
EDITING THE WAFER DATA FILE SHOULD BE USED ONLY AS A LAST RESORT, IF THIS BECOMES A COMMON PROBLEM, WE COULD HAVE MORE PROBLEMS WITH INVALID DATA THAT THERE ARE NOW.	
SUPERS AND LEADS: PLEASE PASS THIS INFORMATION ALONG TO THOSE WHO NEED TO KNOW.	With long lines and no spaces between paragraphs, this e-mail is difficult to read.
ROGER VANDENHEUVAL	

a. E-mail that violates Netiquette guidelines

	The writer has edited and proofread the e-mail.
To: Supers and Leads	
Subject: Missing Laser Repair Files for 16MB Wafers	The subject line and first paragraph clearly state the writer's purpose.
Supers and Leads:	
Lately, we have been missing laser repair files for our 16MB wafers. In this e-mail I want to briefly describe the problem and recommend a method for solving it.	
Here is what I think is happening. Some of the wafers have been probed under the correlate step; this method copies the data into the Nonprod step and leaves the repair data uncopied. It remains under the correlate step.	Double-spacing between paragraphs and using short lines make the e-mail easier to read.
To prevent this problem, please use the probing method outlined in Spec 344-012. If a wafer must be probed using a different method, rename the wafer in the CHANGE file to the *.* format. Edit the wafer data file only as a last resort.	
I'm sending along copies of Spec 344-012. Would you please pass along this e-mail and the spec to all of your operators.	
Thanks. Please get in touch with me if you have any questions.	The writer concludes politely.
Roger Vandenheuval	

b. E-mail that adheres to Netiquette guidelines

■ **Figure 14.14   Netiquette**

INTERACTIVE SAMPLE DOCUMENT
Following Netiquette in an E-mail Message

This message was written in response to a question e-mailed to several colleagues by a technical communicator seeking advice on how to write meeting minutes effectively. A response to an e-mail message should adhere to the principles of effective e-mails and proper netiquette. The questions in the margin ask you to think about these principles (explained on pages 354–55). E-mail your responses to yourself and/or your instructor, and see suggested responses on TechComm Web.

1. How effectively has the writer conserved bandwidth?

2. How effectively has the writer stated her purpose?

3. How effectively has the writer projected a "you attitude" (explained on page 340)?

4. How effectively has the writer made her message easy to read?

 **On TechComm Web**

To e-mail your responses to yourself and/or your instructor and to see suggested responses, click on Interactive Sample Documents for Ch. 14 on <**bedfordstmartins .com/techcomm**>.

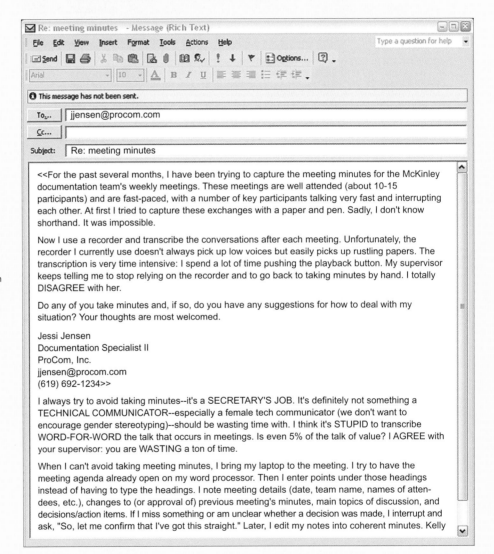

Re: meeting minutes   - Message (Rich Text)

File   Edit   View   Insert   Format   Tools   Actions   Help

Type a question for help

Send   Arial   10   Options...

This message has not been sent.

To... | jjensen@procom.com

Cc... |

Subject: | Re: meeting minutes

<<For the past several months, I have been trying to capture the meeting minutes for the McKinley documentation team's weekly meetings. These meetings are well attended (about 10-15 participants) and are fast-paced, with a number of key participants talking very fast and interrupting each other. At first I tried to capture these exchanges with a paper and pen. Sadly, I don't know shorthand. It was impossible.

Now I use a recorder and transcribe the conversations after each meeting. Unfortunately, the recorder I currently use doesn't always pick up low voices but easily picks up rustling papers. The transcription is very time intensive: I spend a lot of time pushing the playback button. My supervisor keeps telling me to stop relying on the recorder and to go back to taking minutes by hand. I totally DISAGREE with her.

Do any of you take minutes and, if so, do you have any suggestions for how to deal with my situation? Your thoughts are most welcomed.

Jessi Jensen
Documentation Specialist II
ProCom, Inc.
jjensen@procom.com
(619) 692-1234>>

I always try to avoid taking minutes--it's a SECRETARY'S JOB. It's definitely not something a TECHNICAL COMMUNICATOR--especially a female tech communicator (we don't want to encourage gender stereotyping)--should be wasting time with. I think it's STUPID to transcribe WORD-FOR-WORD the talk that occurs in meetings. Is even 5% of the talk of value? I AGREE with your supervisor: you are WASTING a ton of time.

When I can't avoid taking meeting minutes, I bring my laptop to the meeting. I try to have the meeting agenda already open on my word processor. Then I enter points under those headings instead of having to type the headings. I note meeting details (date, team name, names of attendees, etc.), changes to (or approval of) previous meeting's minutes, main topics of discussion, and decisions/action items. If I miss something or am unclear whether a decision was made, I interrupt and ask, "So, let me confirm that I've got this straight." Later, I edit my notes into coherent minutes. Kelly

Strategies for Intercultural Communication

Writing Culture-Specific Letters, Memos, and E-mails

Letters, memos, and e-mails differ from one culture to another. Here are a few examples of how:

- **Letters.** The role, format, and tone of letters in the target culture might be different. In many high-context cultures, such as that of Japan, letters are expected to begin with a paragraph about the seasons and not to make explicit sales pitches.

- **Memos.** In the United States, most memos are less formal in style and tone than letters. In cultures in which documents tend to be formal, letters might be preferred to memos, or memos might be more formal than in the United States. For instance, they might not use contractions.

- **E-mails.** In some cultures, e-mails are not as popular as they are in the United States. In Asia, for instance, face-to-face meetings are more common for short, informal communications because they show more respect for the other person.

  Try to study letters, memos, and e-mails written by people from the culture you will be addressing. Also try to have important letters, memos, and e-mails reviewed by a person from that culture before you send them.

 In This Book

For more about cultural variables in letter writing and about high-context and low-context cultures, see Ch. 5, p. 78.

Writer's Checklist

Letter Format

☐ Is the first page typed on letterhead stationery? (p. 344)
☐ Is the date included? (p. 344)
☐ Is the inside address complete and correct? (p. 344)
☐ Is the appropriate courtesy title used? (p. 344)
☐ If appropriate, is an attention line included? (p. 344)
☐ If appropriate, is a subject line included? (p. 344)
☐ Is the salutation appropriate? (p. 344)
☐ Is the complimentary close typed with only the first word capitalized? (p. 345)
☐ Is the complimentary close followed by a comma? (p. 345)
☐ Is the signature legible, and is the writer's name typed beneath the signature? (p. 345)
☐ If appropriate, is an enclosure line included? (p. 345)
☐ If appropriate, is a copy line included? (p. 345)
☐ Is the letter typed in one of the standard formats? (p. 346)

Types of Letters

Does the inquiry letter

☐ explain why you chose the reader to receive the inquiry? (p. 347)
☐ explain why you are requesting the information and to what use you will put it? (p. 347)
☐ specify by what date you need the information? (p. 347)
☐ list the questions clearly and, if appropriate, provide room for the reader's responses? (p. 347)
☐ offer, if appropriate, the product of your research? (p. 347)

☐ Does the response to an inquiry letter answer the reader's questions or explain why they cannot be answered? (p. 348)

Does the claim letter

☐ identify specifically the unsatisfactory product or service? (p. 349)

☐ explain the problem(s) clearly? (p. 349)
☐ propose an adjustment? (p. 349)
☐ conclude courteously? (p. 349)

Does the "good news" adjustment letter
☐ express your regret? (p. 350)
☐ explain the adjustment you will make? (p. 350)
☐ conclude on a positive note? (p. 350)

Does the "bad news" adjustment letter
☐ meet the reader on neutral ground, expressing regret but not apologizing? (p. 351)
☐ explain why the company is not at fault? (p. 351)
☐ clearly deny the reader's request? (p. 351)
☐ attempt to create goodwill? (p. 351)

Memos

☐ Does the identifying information adhere to your organization's standards? (p. 352)
☐ Did you clearly state your purpose at the start of the memo? (p. 353)

☐ Did you use headings to help your reader? (p. 353)
☐ If appropriate, did you summarize your message? (p. 353)
☐ Did you provide appropriate background for the discussion? (p. 353)
☐ Did you organize the discussion clearly? (p. 353)
☐ Did you highlight items requiring action? (p. 353)

E-mail

☐ Did you refrain from discussing nonbusiness subjects? (p. 354)
☐ Did you keep the e-mail as brief as possible and send it only to appropriate people? (p. 354)
☐ Did you use appropriate formality? (p. 354)
☐ Did you write correctly? (p. 354)
☐ Did you avoid flaming? (p. 354)
☐ Did you write a specific, accurate subject line? (p. 354)
☐ Did you use uppercase and lowercase letters? (p. 354)
☐ Did you skip lines between paragraphs? (p. 354)
☐ Did you set the line length under 65 characters? (p. 354)
☐ Did you check with the writer before forwarding his or her message? (p. 354)

Exercises

1. A beverage container you recently purchased for $8.95 has a serious leak. The grape drink you put in it ruined a $35 white tablecloth. Inventing any reasonable details, write a claim letter to the manufacturer of the container.

2. As the recipient of the claim letter described in Exercise 1, write an adjustment letter granting the customer's request.

3. You are the manager of a private swimming club. A member has written saying that she lost a contact lens (value $75) in your pool and she wants you to pay for a replacement. The contract that all members sign explicitly states that the management is not responsible for loss of personal possessions. Write an adjustment letter denying the request. Invent any reasonable details.

4. As manager of a stereo equipment retail store, you guarantee that you will not be undersold. If a customer who buys something from you can prove within one month that another retailer sells the same equipment at a lower price, you will refund the difference. A customer

has written to you and enclosed an ad from another store showing that it is selling the CD-RW drive he purchased for $26.50 less than he paid at your store. The advertised price at the other store was a one-week sale that began five weeks after the date of his purchase. He wants a $26.50 refund. Inventing any reasonable details, write an adjustment letter denying his request. You are willing, however, to offer him a 25-pack of blank CD-R disks worth $7.95 for his equipment if he would like to come pick it up.

5. **GROUP EXERCISE** Form small groups for this exercise on claim and adjustment letters. Have each member of your group study the following two letters. Meet and discuss your reactions to the letters. How effectively does the writer of the claim letter present his case? How effective is the adjustment letter? Does its writer succeed in showing that the company's procedures for ensuring hygiene are effective? Does its writer succeed in projecting a professional tone? Write a memo to your instructor discussing the two letters. Attach a revision of the adjustment letter to the memo.

Seth Reeves
19 Lowry's Lane
Morgan, TN 30610

April 13, 2006

Sea-Tasty Tuna
Route 113
Lynchburg, TN 30563

Gentlemen:

I've been buying your tuna fish for years, and up to now it's been OK.

But this morning I opened a can to make myself a sandwich. What do you think was staring me in the face? A fly. That's right, a housefly. That's him you see taped to the bottom of this letter.

What are you going to do about this?

Yours very truly,

SEA-TASTY TUNA
Route 113
Lynchburg, TN 30563
www.seatastytuna.com

April 21, 2006

Mr. Seth Reeves
19 Lowry's Lane
Morgan, TN 30610

Dear Mr. Reeves:

We were very sorry to learn that you found a fly in your tuna fish.

Here at Sea-Tasty we are very careful about the hygiene of our plant. The tuna are scrubbed thoroughly as soon as we receive them. After they are processed, they are inspected visually at three different points. Before we pack them, we rinse and sterilize the cans to ensure that no foreign material is sealed in them.

Because of these stringent controls, we really don't see how you could have found a fly in the can. Nevertheless, we are enclosing coupons good for two cans of Sea-Tasty tuna.

We hope this letter restores your confidence in us.

Truly yours,

6. Bill, the writer of the following e-mail, is the primary technical supervisor on the production line in a microchip manufacturing facility. He is responding to Larry, a supervisor who reports to him. Larry has sent him the following note: "Bill, I can't seem to find a spec that describes coat tracks. Some of the new hires don't know what they are. What should I tell them?" Bill's reply:

Larry—

Coat tracks are the machines used in the first step of the photo process. The wafers coem to coat to have a layer of a photosensitive resist applyed. This requires several operations to be done by the same machine. First the wafer is coated with a layer of primer or hmds. This ensures that the resist will adhere to the wager. The wafer is then caoted with resist. There are 5 different types of resist in use, each has its won characteristics, and all are used on different levels and part types. I dont really have time to go into all the details now. The photo resist must be applyed ina uniform layer as the unfioromity of the resist can effect several other steps to include exsposure on the stepper to the etch rate on a lam. To insure the proper unfiromity and resist volumes the tracks are inspected at 24 hour intervals, all the functions are checked and partical monitors are ran to ensure proper operation and cleanlyness. After the wafer is coated it is soft baked, this rids the wafer of solvents in the primer and resist and also hardens the resist. The wafers are then ready to go to the next step at the p&e or the stepper.

If, in fact, there is no specification that Bill can give to Larry, what would be the best way to communicate the information to him? What impression will his e-mail make on Larry? Why?

7. Louise and Paul work for the same manufacturing company. Louise, a senior engineer, is chairing a committee to investigate ways to improve the hiring process at the company. Paul, a technical editor, also serves on the committee. The excerpts quoted in Louise's e-mail are from an e-mail written by Paul to all members of the committee in response to Louise's request that members describe their approach to evaluating job-application materials. How would you revise Louise's e-mail to make it more effective?

To: Paul

From: Louise

Sometimes I just have to wonder what you're thinking, Paul.

>Of course, it's not possible to expect perfect
>resumes. But I have to screen them, and last
>year I had to read over 200. I'm not looking for
>perfection, but as soon as I spot an error I make
>a mental note of it and, when I hit a second and
>then a third error I can't really concentrate on
>the writer's credentials.

Listen, Paul, you might be a sharp editor, but the rest of us have a different responsibility: to make the products and move them out as soon as possible. We don't have the luxury of studying documents to see if we can find errors. I suggest

you concentrate on what you were hired to do, without imposing your "standards" on the rest of us.

>From my point of view, an error can include a
>misused tradmark.

Misusing a "tradmark," Paul? Is that Error Number 1?

8. **INTERNET EXERCISE** Because students use e-mail to communicate with other group members when they write collaboratively, your college or university would like to create a one-page handout on how to use e-mail responsibly. Using a search engine, find three or four netiquette guides on the Internet that focus on using e-mail. Study these guides and write a one-page student guide to using e-mail to communicate with other students. Somewhere in the guide, be sure to list the sites you studied, so that students can visit them for further information about netiquette.

Case 14: Projecting the "You Attitude" When Corresponding with Customers and Colleagues

Background

You work for the Customer Service Department at United Tools, a successful manufacturer and marketer of tools and equipment for professional tool users in the United States. Product lines include hand and power tools for vehicle-service, industrial, agricultural, electrical, and construction applications. Recently, United Tools received a letter from a hardware store that carries its products (Document 14.1). You try to speak to your supervisor, Russ Ong, about the situation. Unfortunately, Russ has just learned about a shipping error that loaded all tool orders from West Coast retailers on a truck heading to New York. While rushing off to a meeting, Russ tells you, "Anytime a weekend warrior gets hurt using one of our tools, the tool is always assumed to be the problem. People need to learn to use tools for the jobs they're designed for. Pipe wrenches are for gripping and turning a pipe. They are not designed to be used as crowbars, hammers, or pliers. I don't have time for this."

You decide to investigate the situation. A colleague in Marketing sends you an e-mail message (Document 14.2) providing some background on the pipe wrench in question, the UT904 pipe wrench.

You decide to investigate the situation further. One of the company engineers replies to your request for information on the UT904 (Document 14.3).

At lunch you explain the situation to Maureen Perez, a colleague in the Customer Service Department: "I think I may have uncovered a problem with our UT9 pipe wrenches. But I don't think Russ, Marketing, or R&D believes a problem exists."

"Be careful how you handle this," Maureen Perez cautions. "Remember what happened to Bev when she accused Richard—in a widely circulated e-mail message—of designing an unsafe brake-line flaring tool. Switched to the night shift, one negative performance evaluation, and three weeks later Bev was gone."

Handee Hardware, Inc.
Millersville, AL 61304
www.handeehardware.com

December 4, 2006
United Tools
20 Central Avenue
Dover, TX 76104

Gentlemen:

I have a problem I'd like to discuss with you. I've been carrying your line of hand tools for many years.

Your 9" pipe wrench has always been a big seller. But there seems to be something wrong with its design. I have had two complaints in the last few months about the handle snapping off when pressure is exerted on it. In one case, the user cut his hand seriously enough to require stitches.

Frankly, I'm hesitant to sell any more of the 9" pipe wrenches but still have more than two dozen in inventory.

Have you had any other complaints about this product?

Sincerely yours,

Chel Thomas

Chel Thomas

■ **Document 14.1**
Claim Letter from Handee Hardware

On TechComm Web
For digital versions of case documents, click on Downloadable Case Documents on <bedfordstmartins.com/techcomm>.

Your Assignment

1. Write a memo or letter to an appropriate officer in the company alerting him or her to the situation you have uncovered and presenting appropriate recommendations. (For a discussion on ethical and legal considerations, see Chapter 2.)

2. Assume that your supervisor has authorized you to draft a letter to be sent to retailers and retail customers who have written claim letters to your company, offering an appropriate adjustment. Draft the letter.

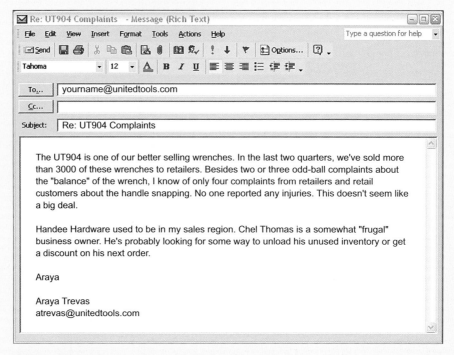

■ Document 14.2   E-mail from Marketing Department

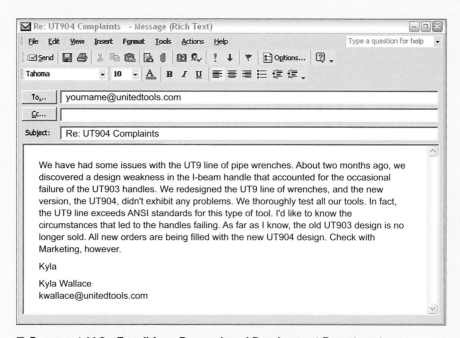

■ Document 14.3   E-mail from Research and Development Department

Preparing Job-Application Materials

15

TECH COMM AT WORK

Almost certainly, you will not work for one employer, or even a few employers, for your whole career. According to the U.S. Department of Labor (2004), the typical American worker holds more than ten different jobs while he or she is between the ages of 18 and 38. These jobs obviously don't last long. Even when American workers begin a job at mid-career (ages 33 to 38), nearly 40 percent of them will not be with that company at the end of one year, and 70 percent of them will not be with that company in five years. Every time you change jobs—whether it's one time or twenty times—you will need to change your résumé and other job-application materials.

For most of you, the first nonacademic test of your technical-communication skills comes when you prepare job-application materials. And it's an important test. A survey of 120 major U.S. corporations concluded that writing ability is related to workplace success: "People who cannot write and communicate clearly will not be hired, and if already working, are unlikely to last long enough to be considered for promotion" (College Entrance, 2004).

UNDERSTANDING THE PROCESS OF PREPARING JOB-APPLICATION MATERIALS

Preparing job-application materials requires weeks and months, not days, and there is no way to cut corners. Figure 15.1 presents an overview of the process.

PLANNING THE JOB SEARCH

In planning a job search, you have three main tasks:

- *Do a self-inventory.* Before you can start thinking of where you want to work, you need to answer some questions about yourself:
  - *What are your strengths and weaknesses?* Are your skills primarily technical? Do you work best with others or on your own?
  - *What subjects do you like?* Think about what you have liked or disliked about your jobs and college courses.
  - *What kind of organization would you like to work for?* Profit or nonprofit? Government or private industry? Small or large?
  - *What are your geographical preferences?* If you are free to relocate, where would you like to live? How do you feel about commuting?

■ **Figure 15.1   An Overview of the Process for Preparing Job-Application Materials**

Plan the Job Search

Do a self-inventory, learn as much as you can about potential employers, and begin to plan your materials.

↓

Decide How to Look for a Position

Use as many resources as you can, including the college-placement office on campus, published ads, and company Web sites.

↓

Learn as Much as You Can About the Organizations to Which You Will Apply

Use appropriate techniques of primary and secondary research. See Chapter 6.

↓

Draft the Résumé and Application Letter

Decide whether to write a chronological or a skills résumé. Include the traditional sections—identifying information, objectives, education, employment history, personal information, and references—and other appropriate sections, such as military service, language skills, or computer skills. For a skills résumé, include a skills section. Decide whether to write a scannable résumé.

Write the letter to elaborate on several key points from the résumé. Include the traditional introductory and concluding paragraphs, as well as at least one paragraph about your job experience and one about your education.

↓

Revise, Edit, and Proofread the Résumé and Letter

You want these documents to be perfect. Try to have several people help you review them. See the Writer's Checklist on pages 398–99.

↓

Prepare for Job Interviews

Study job interviews, research the organizations you applied to, think about what you can offer these organizations, study lists of common interview questions, compile a list of questions to ask, and rehearse the interview.

↓

Write Appropriate Follow-up Letters

With any luck, you'll get to write a letter of appreciation after an interview and then a letter accepting a job offer.

- *Learn about the employers.* Don't base your job search exclusively on information in employment ads. Learn about the organizations through other means as well:

On TechComm Web

To find the *Occupational Handbook*, click on Links Library for Ch. 15 on <bedfordstmartins.com/techcomm>.

—*Attend job fairs.* Your college and your community probably hold job fairs, where employers provide information about their organizations. Sometimes a single organization will hold a job fair to find qualified candidates for a wide variety of jobs.

—*Find out about trends in your field.* Read the *Occupational Handbook*, published by the U.S. Department of Labor, for information about your field and related fields. Talk with professors and with the people at your college's job-placement office.

—*Research the companies that interest you.* Visit their Web sites. Search the index of the *Wall Street Journal* for articles about them. Study their annual reports on their Web sites.

• *Prepare your materials.* You know you will write application letters and résumés and go on interviews. Start planning early by obtaining materials from the career-placement office. Talk with friends who have gone through the process successfully; study their application materials. Read books and visit Web sites about different aspects of the job search.

  One more very important part of preparing your materials is to make a *portfolio*, a collection of your best work. You'll want to give prospective employers a copy of the portfolio to showcase your skills. For technical communicators, the portfolio will include a variety of documents created in courses and in previous positions. For technical professionals, it might include proposals and reports as well as computer simulations, Web sites, and presentation graphics. A portfolio can be presented in a loose-leaf notebook, with each item preceded by a descriptive and evaluative statement. Often it is digital, presented on a CD or a Web site.

In This Book

For more about electronic portfolios, see p. 397.

Strategies for Intercultural Communication

Applying for International Positions

When you apply for a position in another country, keep in mind that the conventions of the process vary—sometimes quite a bit. You will need to adapt your résumé and letter to the expectations of the country in which you would like to work. Consult one of the following sources for advice on drafting résumés when applying for international positions:

• Krannich, R. L., & Enelow, W. S. (2002). *Best resumes and CVs for international jobs.* Manassas Park, VA: Impact Publications.

• Krannich, R. L., & Krannich, C. (2002). *Directory of websites for international jobs: The click and easy guide.* Manassas Park, VA: Impact Publications.

• Goinglobal.com <www.goinglobal.com/topic/resumes.asp>.

• Monster.com Work Abroad <http://international.monster.com>.

• Thompson, M. A. (2002). *The global résumé and CV guide.* Hoboken, NJ: John Wiley & Sons.

UNDERSTANDING SEVEN WAYS TO LOOK FOR A POSITION

Once you have done your planning, you can start to look for a position. There are seven major ways to find a job.

- *Through a college or university placement office.* Placement offices bring companies and students together. Student résumés are made available to representatives of business, government, and industry who arrange on-campus interviews. Students who do best in the campus interviews are then invited to visit the organization for a tour and another interview. The advantages of this system are that it is free and it is easy.

- *Through a professional placement bureau.* A professional placement bureau offers essentially the same service as a college placement office but charges a fee to either the employer or the employee. Placement bureaus cater primarily to more-advanced professionals who are changing jobs.

- *Through a published job ad.* Organizations publish ads in public-relations catalogs (such as *College Placement Annual*), technical journals, and newspapers. Check the major journals in your field and the large metropolitan newspapers. In responding to an ad, you most likely will send a résumé and a job-application letter.

- *Through an organization's Web site.* Many organizations list their job offerings on their Web sites and explain how to apply.

- *Through a job board on the Internet.* Job boards are sites sponsored by federal agencies, Internet service providers, and private organizations. Some sites merely list positions, to which you respond by regular mail or by e-mail; others let you submit your résumé electronically, so that employers can get in touch with you. Use a search engine to search for "employment," "careers," and "jobs." Or combine one of these terms with the name of your field, as in "careers and forestry." Among the biggest job boards are the following:

  —Indeed (a metasearch engine for job seekers)
  —America's Job Bank (sponsored by the U.S. Department of Labor)
  —Monster
  —CareerBuilder
  —AfterCollege
  —CareerMag

  Many of these sites contain articles about searching for jobs electronically, including how to research companies, how to write electronic résumés, and how to prepare for interviews.

  One caution about using job boards: once you post something to an Internet site, you have probably lost control of it. Here are four questions to ask before you post your résumé:

<div class="sidebar">

Search for a position through:

A college or university placement office

A professional placement bureau

A published job ad

An organization's Web site

A job board on the Internet

An unsolicited letter to an organization

Connections

 In This Book

For more about job-application letters, see p. 387. For more about electronic résumés, see p. 383.

 On TechComm Web

To find these sites and additional job-related resources on the Web, click on Links Library for Ch. 15 on <bedfordstmartins.com/techcomm>.

</div>

—Who has access to your résumé? You might want to remove your home address and phone number from it if anyone can view it.

—How will you know if an employer requests your résumé? Will you be notified by the job board?

—Can your current employer see your résumé? If your employer knows you are looking for a new job, your current position could be jeopardized.

—Can you update your résumé at no cost? Some job boards charge you each time you update it.

- *Through an unsolicited letter to an organization.* Instead of waiting for an ad or a notice on a Web site, consider sending an unsolicited application. The disadvantage is obvious: there might not be an opening. Yet many professionals favor this technique because there are fewer competitors for jobs that do exist and because organizations do not advertise all available positions. Sometimes an impressive unsolicited application can even prompt an organization to create a position.

    Before you write an unsolicited application, learn as much as you can about the organization: current and anticipated major projects, hiring plans, and so forth. The business librarian at your college or university will be able to point out additional sources of information, such as the Dun and Bradstreet guides, the *F&S Index of Corporations*, and indexed newspapers such as the *New York Times*, *Washington Post*, and *Wall Street Journal*. You should also study the organization's Web site.

- *Through connections.* A relative or an acquaintance can exert influence, or at least point out a new position. Other good contacts include past employers and professors. Also consider becoming active in the student chapter of your field's professional organization, through which you can meet professionals in your area.

WRITING PAPER RÉSUMÉS

This section discusses the fundamentals for preparing paper résumés. The next section discusses electronic résumés.

Many students wonder whether to write their résumés themselves or use a résumé-preparation agency. It is best to write your own résumé, for three reasons:

- *You know yourself better than anyone else does.* No matter how professional the work of a résumé-preparation agency, you can do a better job communicating important information about yourself.

- *Employment officers know the style of the local agencies.* Readers who realize that you did not write your own résumé might wonder whether you are hiding any deficiencies.

- *If you write your own résumé, you will be more likely to adapt it to different situations.* You are unlikely to return to a résumé-preparation agency and pay an additional fee to make a minor revision.

The résumé communicates in two ways: through its appearance and through its content.

Appearance of the Résumé

Because potential employers normally see your résumé before they see you, it has to make a good first impression. Employers believe that the résumé's appearance reflects the writer's professionalism. When employers look at a résumé, they see the documents they will be reading if they hire you. Résumés should appear neat and professional and have the following characteristics:

- *Generous margins.* Leave a one-inch margin on all four sides.
- *Clear type.* Use a good-quality laser printer.
- *Balance.* Arrange the information so that the page has a balanced appearance.
- *Clear organization.* Use adequate white space. The line spacing between items should be greater than the line spacing within an item. That is, there should be more space between your education section and your employment section than between items within either of those sections. You should be able to see the different sections clearly if you stand and look down at the résumé on the floor by your feet.

Indent appropriately. When you arrange items in a vertical list, indent *turnovers*, the second and subsequent lines of any item, a few spaces. The following list, from the computer-skills section of a résumé, could be confusing:

Computer Experience

Systems: PC, Macintosh, UNIX, Andover AC-256, Prime 360
Software: Lotus 1-2-3, DBase V, PlanPerfect, Micrografx Designer, Adobe Page-
Maker, Microsoft Word
Languages: Pascal, C++, HTML, XHTML

When the second line of the long entry is indented, the arrangement is much easier to understand:

Computer Experience

Systems: PC, Macintosh, UNIX, Andover AC–256, Prime 360
Software: Lotus 1–2–3, DBase V, PlanPerfect, Micrografx Designer, Adobe Page
    Maker, Microsoft Word
Languages: Pascal, C++, HTML, XHTML

 In This Book

For more about page design, see Ch. 12, p. 265.

Figure 15.2 on page 370 shows how an unattractive résumé creates a negative impression, whereas an attractive one creates a positive impression.

■ **Figure 15.2**
Unattractive and
Attractive Résumés

The unattractive résumé,
with its inadequate margins,
poor balance, and poor line
spacing, is a chore to read.
The attractive résumé is
much easier to read.

James K. Wislo	1628 Rossi Street
	Boise, ID 83706
	(208) 284-2697
	jameswislo@mail.boisestate.edu
Objective	Entry-level position as a general assistant
Education	Boise State University, Boise, ID
	BS in Biomechanical Engineering
	Current GPA: 3.1
	Expected date of graduation: 8/2008

Related course work   Machine Design: ProVAX and DGI
AutoCAD   Introduction to machining operation
Solidworks design   Plastic manufacturing processes
Technical communication

Employment   1/2004-Present (20 hours per week): Custodial and maintenance
Boise State University, recreation center, Boise ID
Install and maintain soap dispenser machines.
Treat all floors (wooden and linoleum) with appropriate chemicals.
Pressure-wash showers and sauna using TENNANT 750 machine.
Report damaged equipment in the building.
Report any shortage or lack of cleaning detergent and equipment.
Organize daily and weekly cleaning schedule.
10/2003-1/2004: Food server
Aramark Food Service, Boise, ID
Serve food across counter. Prepare all condiments to be served.
Clean kitchen and eating area after regular open hours.
Act as a liaison between students and chef: report on likes and
dislikes of students.

Honors   National Dean's List 2003-2004.
Awarded $4,500 GEM scholarship from Boise State University.

Activities   Member, Boise State University international student organization.
Certified member, American Red Cross.

References			
	Mr. Jeff Emacio	Mr. Bill Wingate	Prof. Karen Seagate
	Building Foreman	Catering Manager	Department of
	1910 University	1700 University	History
	Drive	Drive, Suite 215	Boise State University
	Boise, ID 83725	Boise, ID 83725	Boise, ID 83725
	(208) 555-3833	(208) 555-1225	(208) 555-1435

a. Unattractively designed résumé

■ **Figure 15.2**
(continued)

James K. Wislo

1628 Rossi Street   (208) 284-2697
Boise, ID 83706   jameswislo@mail.boisestate.edu

Objective   Entry-level position as a general assistant

Education   Boise State University, Boise, ID
BS in Biomechanical Engineering
Current GPA: 3.1
Expected date of graduation: 8/2008

Related course work
AutoCAD   Machine Design: ProVAX and DGI
Solidworks design   Introduction to machining operation
Technical   Plastic manufacturing processes
  communication

Employment   1/2004–Present (20 hours per week): Custodial and maintenance
Boise State University, recreation center, Boise ID
  • Install and maintain soap dispenser machines.
  • Treat all floors (wooden and linoleum) with appropriate chemicals.
  • Pressure-wash showers and sauna using TENNANT 750 machine.
  • Report damaged equipment in the building.
  • Report any shortage or lack of cleaning detergent and equipment.
  • Organize daily and weekly cleaning schedule.

10/2003–1/2004: Food server
Aramark Food Service, Boise, ID
  • Serve food across counter.
  • Prepare all condiments to be served.
  • Clean kitchen and eating area after regular open hours.
  • Act as a liaison between students and chef: report on likes and dislikes of students.

Honors   • National Dean's List 2003–2004.
  • Awarded $4,500 GEM scholarship from Boise State University.

Activities   • Member, Boise State University international student organization.
  • Certified member, American Red Cross.

References   Mr. Jeff Emacio   Mr. Bill Wingate   Prof. Karen Seagate
Building Foreman   Catering Manager   Department of History
1910 University Drive 1700 University Drive, Boise State University
Boise, ID 83725   Suite 215   Boise, ID 83725
(208) 555-3833   Boise, ID 83725   (208) 555-1435
                       (208) 555-1225

b. Attractively designed résumé

Ethics Note

Writing Honest Job-Application Materials

Many résumés contain lies or exaggerations. Job applicants say they attended colleges they didn't and were awarded degrees they weren't, give themselves inflated job titles, say they were laid off when they were really fired for poor performance, and inflate their accomplishments (Sahadi, 2004). Companies take this problem seriously. One survey found that of the top ten qualities employers look for in job applicants, number one is communication skills (both written and oral), and number two is honesty and integrity (JobWeb.com, 2004). Many employers today routinely check applicants' credentials. For instance, Northrop Grumman, a global defense company headquartered in Los Angeles, does a complete background check on all job applicants before making an offer. The company verifies each candidate's education and employment history, checks for a criminal record, and checks with the appropriate department of motor vehicles. If the company finds any problems, it does not offer the candidate a position. If the person is already working for the company, he or she is fired (Wait and Dizard, 2003).

Content of the Résumé

Although experts advocate different approaches to résumé writing, they all agree that résumés must be informative and attractive.

- *The résumé must provide clear, specific information, without generalizations or self-congratulation.* Your résumé is a sales document, but you are both the salesperson and the product. You cannot gracefully say "I am a terrific job candidate." Instead, you have to provide the details that will lead the reader to conclude that you are a terrific job candidate.

- *The résumé must be completely free of errors.* Writing errors cast doubt on the accuracy of the information in the résumé. Ask for assistance after you have written your draft, and proofread the finished product at least twice. Then have someone else proofread it, too.

A résumé should be long enough to include all pertinent information but not so long that it bores or irritates the reader. If you have less than 10 years' experience or are applying for an entry-level position, most readers will expect a one-page résumé. If you have more than 10 years' experience or the job is more advanced than an entry-level position, readers will expect a two-page résumé (Isaacs, 2004). If the information comes to just over a page, either eliminate or condense some of the material to make it fit on one page or modify the layout so that it fills a substantial part of the second page.

Two common résumé styles are chronological and skills. In a *chronological résumé*, you use time as the organizing pattern for each section, including education and experience, and discuss your responsibilities for each job you have held. In a *skills résumé*, you merely list your previous jobs, then include a skills section in which you describe your talents and achievements.

 In This Book

Fig. 15.4 on p. 380 and Fig. 15.5 on p. 381 show chronological résumés. Fig. 15.6 on p. 382 shows a skills résumé.

Recent graduates usually use the chronological résumé because in most cases they lack the record of skills and accomplishments needed for a skills résumé. If you have a lot of professional work experience, you might consider the skills style.

Elements of the Chronological Résumé

Most chronological résumés have six basic elements, plus other elements that are appropriate for some job seekers.

A chronological résumé contains:

Identifying information

Objectives or summary of qualifications

Education

Employment history

Interests and activities

References

Other elements

Identifying Information   Include your full name, address, phone number, and e-mail address. Use your complete address, with the zip code. If your address during the academic year differs from your home address, list both and identify them clearly. An employer might call during an academic holiday to arrange an interview.

Objectives or Summary of Qualifications   After the identifying information, add a statement of objectives or a summary of qualifications.

A *statement of objectives*, which is used most often by candidates new to the field, is a brief phrase or sentence—for example, "Entry-level position as a hospital dietitian" or "Summer internship in manufacturing processes." In drafting your statement, follow these three suggestions:

- *State only the goals or duties explicitly mentioned, or clearly implied, in the job advertisement.* If you unintentionally suggest that your goals are substantially different from the job responsibilities, the reader might infer that you would not be happy working there and not consider you further.

- *Focus on the reader's needs, not on your goals.* Instead of stating that you are looking for a position with "opportunities for advancement" or that "offers a high salary," find out what the company needs: for example, "Position in Software Engineering specializing in database-applications development that enables me to use my four years of experience developing large enterprise-database solutions based on a normalized relational design."

- *Be specific.* You accomplish little by writing "Position offering opportunities in the field of health science, where I can use my communication and analytical skills." Specify what kind of position you want—nurse, physician, hospital administrator, pharmaceutical researcher?

Job candidates with more experience tend to write a summary of their qualifications. This statement is usually a brief paragraph that highlights three or four important skills or accomplishments.

Summary of Qualifications

Six years' experience creating testing documentation to qualify production programs that run on Automated Test and Handling Equipment. Four years' experience running QA tests on software, hardware, and semiconductor products. Bilingual English and Italian. Secret security clearance.

Education   If you are a student or a recent graduate, place the education section next. If you have substantial professional experience, place the employment experience section before the education section.

Include at least the following information in the education section:

- *The degree.* After the degree abbreviation (for example, BS, BA, AA, or MS), list your academic major (and, if you have one, your minor): "BS in Materials Engineering, minor in General Business."
- *The institution.* Identify the institution by its full name: "Louisiana State University," not "LSU."
- *The location of the institution.* Include the city and state.
- *The date of graduation.* If your degree has not yet been granted, add "Anticipated date of graduation" or a similar phrase.
- *Information about other schools you attended.* List any other institutions you attended beyond high school, even those from which you did not earn a degree. The description for other institutions should include the same information as in the main listing. Arrange entries in reverse chronological order: that is, list first the school you attended most recently.

Guidelines

Elaborating on Your Education

The following guidelines can help you develop the education section of your résumé.

▶ **List your grade-point average.** If your average is significantly above the median for the graduating class, list it. Or list your average in the courses in your major, or in all your courses for the past two years. Calculate it however you wish, but be honest and clear.

▶ **Compile a list of courses.** Include courses that will interest an employer, such as advanced courses in your major, or communication courses, such as technical communication, public speaking, and organizational communication. For example, a list of business courses on an engineer's résumé shows special knowledge and skills. But don't bother listing required courses. Include the substantive titles of listed courses; employers won't know what "Chemistry 450" is. Call it by its official title: "Chemistry 450. Organic Chemistry."

▶ **Describe a special accomplishment.** For a special senior design or research project, present the title and objective of the project, any special or advanced techniques or equipment you used, and, if you know them, the major results: "A Study of Shape Memory Alloys in Fabricating Actuators for Underwater Biomimetic Applications—a senior design project to simulate the swimming styles and anatomy of fish." A project discussion makes you seem more like a professional: someone who designs and carries out projects.

> ▶ **List honors and awards you received.** Scholarships, internships, and academic awards suggest exceptional ability. If you have received a number of honors, or some that were not exclusively academic, you might list them separately (in a section called "Honors" or "Awards") rather than in the education section. Decide where this information will make the best impression.

The education section is the easiest part of the résumé to adapt in applying for different positions. For example, a student majoring in electrical engineering who is applying for a position requiring strong communication skills can list communication courses in one version of the résumé and advanced electrical engineering courses in another version. As you compose the education section, emphasize those aspects of your background that meet the requirements for a particular job.

Employment History   Present at least the basic information about each job you have held: the dates of employment, the organization's name and location, and your position or title. Then add carefully selected details. Readers want to know what you did and accomplished. Provide at least a two- to three-line description for each position. For particularly important or relevant jobs, give a more extensive description, focusing on one or more of the following factors:

- *Skills.* What technical skills did you use on the job?
- *Equipment.* What equipment did you operate or oversee? In particular, mention any computer equipment or software with which you are familiar.
- *Money.* How much money were you responsible for? Even if you considered your data-entry position fairly easy, the fact that the organization grossed, say, $2 million a year shows that the position involved real responsibility.
- *Documents.* What kinds of documents did you write or assist in writing? Especially list any long reports, manuals, proposals, or Web sites.
- *Personnel.* How many people did you supervise?
- *Clients.* What kinds of, and how many, clients did you do business with in representing your organization?

Whenever possible, emphasize *results.* If you reorganized the shifts of the weekend employees you supervised, state the results:

> Reorganized the weekend shift, resulting in a cost savings of more than $3,000 per year.

> Wrote and produced (with Adobe FrameMaker software) a 56-page parts catalog that is still used by the company and that increased our phone inquiries by more than 25 percent.

When you describe positions, functions, or responsibilities, use the active voice ("supervised three workers") rather than the passive voice ("three workers were supervised by me"). The active voice highlights action. Also

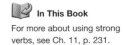

In This Book

For more about using strong verbs, see Ch. 11, p. 231.

administered	coordinated	evaluated	maintained	provided
advised	corresponded	examined	managed	purchased
analyzed	created	expanded	monitored	recorded
assembled	delivered	hired	obtained	reported
built	developed	identified	operated	researched
collected	devised	implemented	organized	solved
completed	directed	improved	performed	supervised
conducted	discovered	increased	prepared	trained
constructed	edited	instituted	produced	wrote

■ **Figure 15.3   Strong Action Verbs Used in Résumés**

note that résumés often omit the *I* at the start of sentences: "Prepared bids" rather than "I prepared bids." Whichever style you use, be consistent. Figure 15.3 lists some strong verbs to use in describing your experience.

Here is a sample listing of employment history:

> June–September 2005: Student Dietitian
> Millersville General Hospital, Millersville, TX
> Gathered dietary histories and assisted in preparing menus for a 300-bed hospital.
> Received "excellent" on all items in evaluation by head dietitian.

In just a few lines, you can show that you sought and accepted responsibility and that you acted professionally. Do not write "I accepted responsibility"; instead, present facts that lead the reader to that conclusion.

Naturally, not all jobs entail professional skills and responsibilities. Many students find summer work as laborers, salesclerks, and so forth. If you have not held a professional position, list the jobs you have held, even if they are unrelated to your career plans. If the job title is self-explanatory, such as waitperson or service-station attendant, don't elaborate. If you can write that you contributed to your tuition or expenses, such as by earning 50 percent of your annual expenses through a job, employers will be impressed by your self-reliance.

One further suggestion: if you have held a number of nonprofessional as well as several professional positions, group the nonprofessional ones:

> Other Employment: cashier (summer 2001), salesperson (part-time, 2002), clerk (summer 2003)

This strategy prevents the nonprofessional positions from drawing the reader's attention away from the more important positions.

List jobs in reverse chronological order on the résumé to highlight the most recent employment.

Two circumstances frequently call for some subtlety:

- *You have some gaps in your employment history.* If you were not employed for several months or years because you were raising children, attending school, recovering from an accident, or for other reasons, consider using a skills résumé, which focuses more on your skills and less on your job history. Also, you can explain the gaps in the cover letter. For instance, you could write, "I spent 2001 and part of 2002 caring for my elderly parent, but during that time I was able to do some substitute teaching and study at home to prepare for my A+ and Network+ certification, which I earned in late 2002." Do not lie or mislead about your dates of employment.

- *You have had several positions with the same employer.* If you want to show that you have had several positions with the same employer, you can present one description that encompasses all the positions or present a separate description for each position.

Presenting One Description

BLUE CROSS OF IOWA, Ames, Iowa (January 1997–present)

- *Internal Auditor II (2001–present)*
- *Member Service Representative/Claims Examiner II (1999–2001)*
- *Claims Examiner II (1997–1999)*

As Claims Examiner II, processed national account inquiries and claims in accordance with. . . . After promotion to Member Service Representative/Claims Examiner II position, planned policies and procedures. . . . As Internal Auditor II, audit claims, enrollment, and inquiries; run data-set population and sample reports. . . .

This format enables you to mention your promotions and to create a clear narrative that emphasizes your progress within the company.

Presenting Separate Descriptions

BLUE CROSS OF IOWA, Ames, Iowa (January 1997–present)

- *Internal Auditor II (2001–present)*

  Audit claims, enrollment, and inquiries . . .

- *Member Service Representative/Claims Examiner II (1999–2001)*

  Planned policies and procedures . . .

- *Claims Examiner II (1997–1999)*

  Processed national account inquiries and claims . . .

This format, which enables you to create a more detailed description of each position, is effective if you are trying to show that the positions were distinct and you wish to describe your more recent positions more fully.

Interests and Activities   Résumés do not include personal information such as the writer's height, weight, date of birth, and marital status. Federal legislation prohibits organizations from requiring this information. In addition, most people feel that such information is irrelevant to a person's ability.

However, the "interests and activities" section of your résumé is the appropriate place for several kinds of information:

- participation in community-service organizations (such as Big Brothers/Big Sisters) or volunteer work in a hospital
- hobbies related to your career (for example, electronics for an engineer)
- sports, especially those that might be socially useful in your professional career, such as tennis, racquetball, and golf
- university-sanctioned activities, such as membership on a team, work on the college newspaper, or election to a responsible position in an academic organization or residence hall

Do not include activities that might create a negative impression, such as hunting, gambling, or performing in a rock band. And always omit such mundane activities as meeting people and reading; everybody does these things.

References   Potential employers will want to learn more about you from your professors and previous employers. In providing references, follow three steps:

- *Decide how you want to present your references.* On your résumé, you can list the names of three or four references—people who have written letters of recommendation or who have agreed to speak on your behalf. Or you may say that you will furnish references upon request.

  Furnishing your references' names and contact information makes you appear open and forthright. It shows that you have already secured your references, and the reader can easily phone them or write them a letter. Listing your references makes it easy for the prospective employer to proceed with the hiring process. The only disadvantage is that it takes up space. (If you don't have space, you can list your references on a separate sheet of paper.)

  Writing "References furnished upon request" requires only one line and puts you in a more flexible position. You can still secure references after you have submitted the résumé. You also can send selected letters of reference to prospective employers according to your analysis of what they want. However, some readers will interpret the lack of names as evasive or perhaps assume that you have not yet secured your references. A bigger disadvantage is that if readers are impressed by your résumé and want to learn more about you, they cannot do so quickly and directly.

  What do personnel officers prefer? According to Bowman (2004), 70 percent of hiring officials want to see full references, including name, title, organization, mailing address, and phone number.

- *Choose your references carefully.* Solicit references only from those who know your work best and for whom you have done your best work—for instance, a previous employer with whom you worked closely or a professor from whom you received A's. Don't solicit references from prominent professors who do not know your work well; they will be unable to write informative letters.

- *Give the person an opportunity to decline gracefully.* Sometimes a person has not been as impressed with your work as you think. If you simply ask the person to serve as a reference, he or she might accept and then write a lukewarm letter. It is better to say "Would you be able to write an enthusiastic letter for me?" or "Do you feel you know me well enough to write a strong recommendation?" If the person shows any hesitation or reluctance, withdraw the request. It may be a little embarrassing, but it is better than receiving a weak recommendation.

Other Elements   The sections discussed so far appear on almost everyone's résumé. Other sections are discretionary or appropriate for only some job seekers.

- *Computer skills.* Classify your skills in categories such as hardware, software, languages, and operating systems. List any professional certifications you have been awarded.

- *Military experience.* If you are a veteran, describe your military service as if it were any other job, citing dates, locations, positions, ranks, and tasks. List positive job-performance evaluations.

- *Language ability.* A working knowledge of another language can be very valuable, particularly if the potential employer has international interests and you could be useful in translation or foreign service.

- *Willingness to relocate.* If you are willing to relocate, say so. Many organizations will find you a more attractive candidate.

Elements of the Skills Résumé

The skills résumé differs from the chronological résumé in that it includes a separate section, usually titled "Skills" or "Skills and Abilities," that emphasizes job skills and knowledge. In a skills résumé, the employment section becomes a brief list of information about your employment history: company, dates of employment, and position. Here is an example of a skills section:

A skills résumé contains:
Identifying information
Objective or summary of qualifications
Skills
Education
Employment history
Interests and activities
References
Other elements

Skills and Abilities

Management
> Served as weekend manager of six employees in the retail clothing business. Also trained three summer interns at a health maintenance organization.

Writing and Editing
> Wrote status reports, edited performance appraisals, participated in assembling and producing an environmental-impact statement using desktop publishing.

Teaching and Tutoring
> Tutored in the University Writing Center. Taught a two-week course in electronics for teenagers. Coach youth basketball.

The writer uses design to emphasize his name.

The writer could modify the objective statement to name the company to which he is applying.

The writer emphasizes his advanced engineering courses. For another position, he might emphasize other courses.

The writer creates a category that calls attention to his academic awards and his membership in his field's major professional organization.

The writer's choice of references emphasizes his professional skills. Other students might choose a mix of supervisors and professors.

In This Book

Many of the job boards listed on p. 367 include samples of résumés.

CARLOS RODRIGUEZ

3109 Vista Street   Philadelphia, PA 19136   (215) 555-3880   crodrig@dragon.du.edu

Objective
Entry-level position in signal processing

Education
BS in Electrical Engineering
Drexel University, Philadelphia, PA
Anticipated 6/2006
Grade-Point Average: 3.67 (on a scale of 4.0)
Senior Design Project: "Enhanced Path-Planning Software for Robotics"

Advanced Engineering Courses
Digital Signal Processing   Computer Hardware
Introduction to Operating Systems I, II   Systems Design
Digital Filters   Computer Logic Circuits I, II

Employment
6/2003–1/2004   Electrical Engineering Intern II
RCA Advanced Technology Laboratory, Moorestown, NJ
Designed ultra-large-scale integrated circuits using VERILOG and VHDL hardware description languages. Assisted senior engineer in CMOS IC layout, modeling, parasitic capacitance extraction, and PSPICE simulation operations.

6/2002–1/2003   Electrical Engineering Intern I
RCA Advanced Technology Laboratory, Moorestown, NJ
Verified and documented several integrated circuit designs. Used CAD software and hardware to simulate, check, and evaluate these designs. Gained experience on the VAX and Applicon.

Honors and Organizations
Eta Kappa Nu (Electrical Engineering Honor Society)
Tau Beta Pi (General Engineering Honor Society)
Institute of Electrical and Electronics Engineers, Inc.

References
Ms. Anita Feller   Mr. Fred Borelli   Mr. Sam Shamir
Engineering Consultant   Unit Manager   Comptroller
700 Church Road   RCA Corporation   RCA Corporation
Cherry Hill, NJ 08002   Route 38   Route 38
(609) 555-7836   Moorestown, NJ 08057   Moorestown, NJ 08057
                           (609) 555-2435   (609) 555-7849

■ **Figure 15.4   Chronological Résumé of a Traditional Student**

In a skills section, you choose the headings, the arrangement, and the level of detail. Your goal, of course, is to highlight whatever skills the employer is seeking.

Figures 15.4, 15.5 (see page 381), and 15.6 (see page 382) show three examples of effective résumés.

**Alice P.
Linder**

1781 Weber Road
Warminster, PA 18974
(215) 555-3999
linderap423@aol.com

Objective

An internship in molecular research that uses my computer skills

The writer uses a table format for her résumé. Notice that all her headings are contained within the left-hand column.

The writer indicates that she is interested in an internship, not a continuing position.

Education

Harmon College, West Yardley, PA
BS in Bioscience and Biotechnology
Expected Graduation Date: 6/2006

Related Course Work
General Chemistry I, II, III   Biology I, II, III
Organic Chemistry I, II   Statistical Methods for Research
Physics I, II   Technical Communication
Calculus I, II

The writer's list of courses includes several outside her technical subject area to emphasize the skills she has demonstrated in her career.

**Employment
Experience**

6/2003–present (20 hours per week): Laboratory Assistant Grade 3
GlaxoSmithKline, Upper Merion, PA
Analyze molecular data on E & S PS300, Macintosh, and IBM PCs.
Write programs in C++ and wrote a user's guide for an instructional
computing package. Train and consult with scientists and deliver
in-house briefings.

All of the writer's positions show an interest in working with people.

8/2000–present: Volunteer, Physical Therapy Unit
Children's Hospital of Philadelphia, Philadelphia, PA
Assist therapists and guide patients with their therapy. Use play therapy to
enhance strengthening progress.

The volunteer position says something about the writer's character.

6/1992–1/1996: Office Manager
Anchor Products, Inc., Ambler, PA
Managed 12-person office in $1.2 million company. Also performed general
bookkeeping and payroll.

Before attending college, the writer worked as an office manager. Notice how the description of her position suggests that she is a skilled and responsible worker.

Honors

Awarded three $5,000 tuition scholarships (2002–2004) from the Gould
Foundation.

The writer believes that the skills required in raising children are relevant in the workplace. Others might think that because a résumé describes job credentials, this information should be omitted.

**Additional
Information**

Member, Harmon Biology Club, Yearbook Staff
Raising three school-age children
Tuition 100% self-financed

References

Available upon request

To keep the résumé on one page, the writer doesn't list her references. They might be included on a second page, however. Particularly for a nontraditional student, references might be among the person's best selling points.

■ **Figure 15.5   Chronological Résumé of a Nontraditional Student**

This is another version of the résumé in Figure 15.5

Alice P. Linder

1781 Weber Road
Warminster, PA 18974

(215) 555-3999
linderap423@aol.com

Objective

A position in molecular research that uses my computer skills

---

In a skills résumé, you present the skills section at the start. This organization lets you emphasize your professional attributes. Notice that the writer uses specific details—names of software, number of credits, types of documents, kinds of activities—to make her case.

Skills and Abilities

Laboratory Skills
- Analyze molecular data on E & S PS300, Macintosh, and IBM PCs. Write programs in C++.
- Have taken 12 credits in biology and chemistry labs.

Communication Skills
- Wrote a user's guide for an instructional computing package.
- Train and consult with scientists and deliver in-house briefings.

Management Skills
- Managed 12-person office in $1.2 million company.

Education

Harmon College, West Yardley, PA
BS in Bioscience and Biotechnology
Expected Graduation Date: 6/2006

Related Course Work

General Chemistry I, II, III	Biology I, II, III
Organic Chemistry I, II	Statistical Methods for Research
Physics I, II	Technical Communication
Calculus I, II	

Notice that the employment section is now a list of positions rather than a description of what the writer did in each position.

Employment Experience

6/2003–present (20 hours per week)
GlaxoSmithKline, Upper Merion, PA
Laboratory Assistant Grade 3

8/2000–present
Children's Hospital of Philadelphia, Philadelphia, PA
Volunteer, Physical Therapy Unit

6/1992–1/1996
Anchor Products, Inc., Ambler, PA
Office Manager

Honors

Awarded three $5,000 tuition scholarships (2002–2004) from the Gould Foundation.

Additional Information

Member, Harmon Biology Club, Yearbook Staff
Raising three school-age children
Tuition 100% self-financed

References

Available upon request

■ **Figure 15.6   Skills Résumé of a Nontraditional Student**

WRITING ELECTRONIC RÉSUMÉS

Some 70 percent of U.S. employers now use computerized *applicant-tracking systems* to evaluate the dozens, hundreds, or even thousands of job applications they receive every day (Lorenz, 2005). Companies store the information from these applications in databases, which they search electronically to generate a pool of applicants for specific positions. An electronic résumé can take several forms:

- *A formatted résumé attached to an e-mail message.* You attach the word-processing file to an e-mail message. Keep in mind, however, that some e-mail software is unable to read attached files. If the job notice requests "a plain-text document sent in the body of the message," do not attach a file.

- *An ASCII résumé.* You can attach or send an ASCII résumé, one that uses the limited ASCII character set and is saved as a .txt file, which can be entered directly into the organization's database.

- *A scannable résumé—one that will be scanned into an organization's database.* There are several popular database programs for this purpose, such as Res-Trac and Resumix. Even when you submit a printed résumé to a company, you should consider how well the document will scan electronically.

- *A Web-based résumé.* You can put your résumé on your own Web site and hope that employers will come to you, or you can post it on a job board on the Web.

Ways of creating and sending résumés will undoubtedly change as the technology changes. For now, you need to know that the traditional printed résumé is only one of several ways to present your credentials, and you should keep abreast of new techniques for applying for positions. Which form should your résumé take? Whichever form the organization prefers. If you learn of a position from a notice on an organization's Web site, the notice will tell you how to apply.

Content of the Electronic Résumé

Most of the earlier discussion of the content of a printed résumé also applies to an electronic résumé. The résumé must be honest and free of errors, and it must provide clear, specific information.

If the résumé is to be entered into a database instead of read by a person, include industry-specific jargon: all the keywords an employment officer might use in searching for qualified candidates. If an employment officer is looking for someone with experience writing Web pages, be sure you include the terms "Web page," "Internet," "HTML," "Java," and any other relevant keywords. If your current position requires an understanding of programming languages, name the languages you know. Also use keywords that refer to your communication skills, such as "public speaking," "oral communication," and "communication skills." In short, whereas a traditional printed résumé focuses on *verbs*—tasks you have done—an electronic résumé focuses on *nouns*.

The approach used by defense contractor Telos shows the importance of keywords in an electronic résumé (Vaas, 2002). Two days after the company posts a job opening on a job board, it receives about 100 résumés. The company performs a keyword search, reducing the stack to about 60 résumés, and then reads them. What happens to the other 40? Nothing.

On TechComm Web

For more about formatting electronic résumés, see The Riley Guide: Resumes, Cover Letters. Click on Links Library for Ch. 15 on <bedfordstmartins.com/techcomm>.

Format of the Electronic Résumé

Because electronic résumés must be easy to read and scan, they require a very simple design. Consequently, they are not as attractive as paper-based résumés, and they are longer, because they use only a single narrow column of text.

Guidelines

Preparing an ASCII Résumé

▶ **Use ASCII text only.** ASCII text includes letters, numbers, and basic punctuation marks. Avoid boldface, italic, underlining, and special characters such as "smart" quotation marks and math symbols. Also avoid horizontal or vertical lines or graphics. To be sure you are using only ASCII characters, save your file as "plain text." Then open it using your software's text editor, such as Notepad, and check to be sure it contains only ASCII characters.

▶ **Left-align the information.** Do not try to duplicate the formatting of a traditional paper résumé. You can't. Instead, left-align each new item. For example, here is a sample listing from the employment-experience section:

6/03–present
(20 hours per week)
GlaxoSmithKline
Upper Merion, PA
Analyst I

Analyze molecular data on E & S PS300, Macintosh, and IBM PCs. Write programs in C++ and wrote a user's guide for an instructional computing package. Train and consult with scientists and deliver in-house briefings.

▶ **Send yourself a test version of the résumé.** When you finish writing and formatting the résumé, send yourself a copy, then open it in your text editor and see if it looks professional.

If you are mailing a paper résumé that will be scanned, follow seven additional guidelines. (See page 387.)

Figure 15.7 is an example of a scannable résumé.

■ Figure 15.7   Scannable Résumé

This is an electronic version of the résumé in Figure 15.6. Notice that the writer uses ASCII text and left justification.

Alice P. Linder
1781 Weber Road
Warminster, PA 18974
(215) 555-3999
linderap423@aol.com

Objective: A position in molecular research that uses my computer skills

Skills and Abilities:
Laboratory Skills. Analyze molecular data on E & S PS300, Macintosh, and IBM PCs.
Write programs in C++. Have taken 12 credits in biology and chemistry labs.

Communication Skills. Wrote a user's guide for an instructional computing package.
Train and consult with scientists and deliver in-house briefings.

Management Skills. Managed 12-person office in $1.2 million company.

Education:
Harmon College, West Yardley, PA
BS in Bioscience and Biotechnology
Expected Graduation Date: June 2006

Related Course Work:
General Chemistry I, II, III
Organic Chemistry I, II
Physics I, II
Calculus I, II
Biology I, II, III
Statistical Methods for Research
Technical Communication

Employment Experience:
June 2003-present (20 hours per week)
GlaxoSmithKline, Upper Merion, PA
Laboratory Assistant Grade 3

August 2000-present
Children's Hospital of Philadelphia, Philadelphia, PA
Volunteer, Physical Therapy Unit

June 1992-January 1996
Anchor Products, Inc., Ambler, PA
Office Manager

Honors:
Awarded three $5,000 tuition scholarships (2002-2004) from the Gould Foundation.

Additional Information:
Member, Harmon Biology Club, Yearbook Staff
Raising three school-age children
Tuition 100% self-financed

Keywords: ◄
C++, IBM, PC, Macintosh, molecular research, programming, presentations,
management, laboratory assistant, volunteer, physical therapy

The writer includes a keywords list.

References:
Available upon request

INTERACTIVE SAMPLE DOCUMENT
Preparing an ASCII Résumé

The following résumé was written by a graduating college senior who wanted to work for a wildland firefighting agency such as the U.S. Bureau of Land Management or the U.S. Forest Service. The writer plans to save the résumé as a .txt file and enter it directly into these agencies' employment databases. The questions in the margin ask you to think about electronic résumés (as outlined on pages 383–84). E-mail your responses to yourself and/or your instructor, and see suggested responses on Tech-Comm Web.

1. How effectively has the writer formatted this résumé?

2. What elements are likely to be problematic when the writer saves the résumé as a .txt file?

3. What is the function of the industry-specific jargon in this résumé?

4. Why does the writer place the education section after the sections on career history and fire and aviation qualifications?

 **On TechComm Web**

To e-mail your responses to yourself and/or your instructor and to see suggested responses, click on Interactive Sample Documents for Ch. 15 on <bedfordstmartins .com/techcomm>.

BURTON L. KREBS

34456 West Jewell St.   208-555-9627
Boise, ID 83704   burtonkrebs@mail.com

Objective
Lead crew position on rappel crew

Career History
- Senior Firefighter, Moyer Rappel Crew, 05/05–Present
- Senior Firefighter, Boise Helitack, 05/03–10/03
- Hotshot Crew Member, Boise Interagency Hotshot Crew, 07/02–09/02
- Helirappel Crew Member, Moyer Rappel Crew, 06/98–09/01

Fire and Aviation Qualifications
Crew Boss (T)
Helicopter Manager
Helicopter Rappeller
Helirappel Spotter
Helispot Manager
Type 2 Helibase Manager (T)
Incident Commander Type 4 (T)

Education
Bachelor of Arts in Communication Training and Development, Boise State University, Boise, Idaho, GPA 3.57, May 2006

Skills
- Excellent oral and written communication skills
- Proficient in Word, Excel, and PowerPoint
- Knowledgeable of helicopter contract administration
- Perform daily and cumulative flight invoice cost summaries

Awards
"Outstanding Performance" Recognition, U.S. Bureau of Land Management, 2003
"Outstanding Performance" Recognition, U.S. Forest Service, 2000, 2001, 2002

Guidelines

Preparing a Scannable Résumé

▶ **Use a good-quality laser printer.** The better the resolution, the better the scanner will work.

▶ **Use white paper.** Even a slight tint to the paper can increase the chances that the scanner will misinterpret a character.

▶ **Do not fold the résumé.** The fold line can confuse the scanner.

▶ **Use a simple sans-serif typeface.** Scanners can easily interpret large, open typefaces such as Arial.

▶ **Use a single-column format.** A double-column text will scan inaccurately. Left-align everything.

▶ **Use wide margins.** Instead of an 80-character width, set your software for 60 or 65 characters. This way, regardless of the equipment the reader is using, the lines will break as you intend them.

▶ **Use the space bar instead of the tab key.** Tabs will be displayed according to the settings on the reader's equipment, not the settings on your equipment. Therefore, use the space bar to move text horizontally.

WRITING JOB-APPLICATION LETTERS

Most job applications call for a résumé and a letter. The letter is crucial because it is the first thing your reader sees. If the letter is ineffective, the reader will not bother to read the résumé. Make your letter appeal as directly and specifically as possible to a particular person.

The Concepts of Selectivity and Development

The keys to a good letter are selectivity and development. *Select* two or three points of special interest to the potential employer and *develop* them into paragraphs. Emphasize results, such as improved productivity or quality or decreased costs. If one of your previous part-time positions called for skills the potential employer is looking for, write a substantial paragraph about that position, even though the résumé devotes only a few lines to it.

For most candidates, a job-application letter should fill the better part of a page. For more-experienced candidates, it might fill two pages. Regardless, if you write at length on a minor

TECH TIP

How to Save a Document as ASCII Text

When you wish to save a document using a simple plain-text format that does not use formatting specific to any particular application, you can save your document as **ASCII text**.

Before saving a document as ASCII text, remember to use only letters, numbers, and basic punctuation marks.

1. To **save your document as ASCII text**, select **Save As** from the **File** menu.

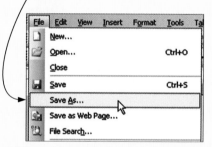

2. Select **Plain Text** from the drop-down menu and click on **Save**.

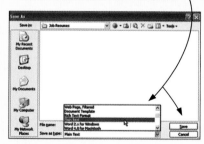

You can check the appearance of your plain-text document by opening the file using a text editor such as Notepad.

> **KEYWORDS:** plain text, ASCII, about saving documents

In This Book

For more about formatting letters, see Ch. 14, p. 343.

point, you become boring and appear to have poor judgment. Employers seek candidates who can say a lot in a small space.

Elements of the Job-Application Letter

The inside address—name, title, organization, and address of the recipient—is important because you want to be sure your materials get to the right person. And you don't want to offend that person with a misspelling or an incorrect title. If you are uncertain about any of the information—the reader's name, for example, might have an unusual spelling—verify it by phoning the organization.

When you do not know who should receive the letter, phone the company to find out who manages the department. If you are unsure of the appropriate department or division to write to, address the letter to a high-level executive, such as the president. The letter will get to the right person. Also, because the application includes both a letter and a résumé, use an enclosure notation.

In This Book

For more about developing paragraphs, see Ch. 10, p. 210.

The four-paragraph example that will be discussed here is only a basic model, consisting of an introductory paragraph, two body paragraphs (education and employment), and a concluding paragraph. At a minimum, your letter should include these four paragraphs, but there is no reason it cannot have five or six.

Plan the letter carefully. Draft it and then revise it. Let it sit for a while, revise it again, and then edit and proofread it. Spend as much time on it as you can.

The Introductory Paragraph   The introductory paragraph has four specific functions.

- *It identifies your source of information.* In an unsolicited application, all you can do is ask if a position is available. For a solicited application, however, name your source of information.

- *It identifies the position you are interested in.* Often the organization you are applying to is advertising several positions. If you omit the title of the position you are interested in, your reader might not know which one you are seeking.

- *It states that you wish to be considered for the position.* Although the context makes your wish obvious, you should mention it because the letter would be awkward without it.

- *It forecasts the rest of the letter.* Choose a few phrases that forecast the body of the letter, so that the letter flows smoothly. For example, if you use the phrase *retail experience* in the opening paragraph, you are preparing your reader for the discussion of your retail experience later in the letter.

These four points need not appear in any particular order, nor does each need to be covered in a single sentence. The following sample paragraphs demonstrate different ways of providing the necessary information:

Response to a Job Ad

I am writing in response to your notice in the May 13 *New York Times*. I would like to be considered for the position in system programming. I hope you find that my studies in computer science at Eastern University, along with my programming experience at Airborne Instruments, qualify me for the position.

Note that the writer identifies the date of the ad, the name of the publication, and the name of the position. Then she forecasts the main points she will make in the body of the letter.

Unsolicited

My academic training in hotel management and my experience with Sheraton International have given me a solid background in the hotel industry. Would you please consider me for any management trainee position that might be available?

The writer politely requests that the reader consider his application.

Unsolicited Personal Contact

Mr. Howard Alcott of your Research and Development Department suggested that I write to you. He thinks that my degree in Organic Chemistry and my practical experience with Brown Laboratories might be of value to XYZ Corporation. Do you have an entry-level position in organic chemistry for which I might be considered?

Notice the tone in all three of these samples: quiet self-confidence. Don't oversell yourself ("I am the candidate you have been hoping for") or undersell yourself ("I don't know that much about computers, but I am willing to learn").

The Education Paragraph   For most students, the education paragraph should come before the employment paragraph because the education paragraph will be stronger. However, if your employment experience is stronger, present it first.

In writing your education paragraph, take your cue from the job ad (if you are responding to one). What aspect of your education most directly fits the job requirements? If the ad stresses versatility, you might structure your paragraph around the range and diversity of your courses. Also, you might discuss course work in a subject related to your major, such as business or communication skills. Extracurricular activities are often very valuable; if you were an officer in a student organization, you could discuss the activities and programs you coordinated. Perhaps the most popular strategy for developing the education paragraph is to discuss skills and knowledge gained from advanced course work in your major field.

Example 1

At Eastern University, I have taken a wide range of science courses, but my most advanced work has been in chemistry. In one laboratory course, I developed a new aseptic brewing technique that lowered the risk of infection by more than 40 percent. This new technique was the subject of an article in the *Eastern Science Digest*. Representatives from three national breweries have visited our laboratory to discuss the technique with me.

Note that the writer develops one idea, presenting enough information about it to interest the reader. Paragraphs that merely list a number of courses that the writer has taken are ineffective: everyone takes courses.

Example 2

To broaden my education at Southern University, I took eight business courses in addition to my requirements for a degree in Civil Engineering. Because your ad mentions that the position will require substantial client contact, I believe that my work in marketing, in particular, would be of special value. In an advanced marketing seminar, I used FrameMaker to produce a 20-page sales brochure describing the various kinds of building structures for sale by Oppenheimer Properties to industrial customers in our section of the city. That brochure is now being used at Oppenheimer, where I am an intern.

Example 3

The most rewarding part of my education at Western University occurred outside the classroom. My entry in a fashion-design competition sponsored by the university won second place. More important, through the competition I met the chief psychologist at Western Regional Hospital, who invited me to design clothing for people with disabilities. I have since completed six different outfits, which are now being tested at the hospital. I hope to be able to pursue this interest once I start work.

An additional point: if you haven't already specified your major and your college or university in the introductory paragraph, be sure to do so here.

The Employment Paragraph   Like the education paragraph, the employment paragraph should begin with a topic sentence and develop a single idea. That idea might be that you have a broad background or that one job in particular has given you special skills that make you especially well suited for the available job.

Example 1

For the past three summers and part-time during the academic year, I have worked for Redego, Inc., a firm that specializes in designing and planning industrial complexes. I began as an assistant in the drafting room. By the second summer, I was accompanying a civil engineer on field inspections. Most recently, I have used AutoCAD to assist an engineer in designing and drafting the main structural supports for a 15-acre, $30 million chemical facility.

Example 2

Although I have worked every summer since I was 15, my most recent position, as a technical editor, has been the most rewarding. I was chosen by Digital Systems, Inc., from among 30 candidates because of my dual background in computer science and writing. My job was to coordinate the editing of computer manuals. Our copy editors, most of whom are not trained in computer science, need someone to help verify the technical accuracy of their revisions. When I was unable to answer their questions, I was responsible for interviewing our systems analysts to find the correct answers and to make sure the computer novice could follow them. This position gave me a good understanding of the process by which operating manuals are created.

Example 3

I have worked in merchandising for three years as a part-time and summer sales-person in men's fashions and accessories. I have had experience running inventory-control software and helped one company switch from a manual to an online system. Most recently, I assisted in clearing $200,000 in out-of-date men's fashions: I coordinated a campaign to sell half of the merchandise at cost and was able to convince the manufacturer's representative to accept the other half for full credit. For this project, I received a certificate of appreciation from the company president.

Although you will discuss your education and experience in separate paragraphs, try to link these two halves of your background. If an academic course led to an interest that you were able to pursue in a job, make that point in the transition from one paragraph to the next. Similarly, if a job experience helped shape your academic career, tell the reader about it.

The Concluding Paragraph   The purpose of the concluding paragraph is to motivate the reader to invite you for an interview. In the preceding paragraphs, you provided the information that should have convinced the reader to give you another look. In the last paragraph, you want to make it easy for him or her to do so. The concluding paragraph contains three main elements:

- *A reference to your résumé.* If you have not yet referred to it, do so now.
- *A polite but confident request for an interview.* Use the phrase *at your convenience.* Don't make the request sound as if you're asking for a personal favor.
- *Your phone number and e-mail address.* State the time of day you can be reached. Adding an e-mail address gives the employer one more way to get in touch with you.

Example 1

The enclosed résumé provides more information about my education and experience. Could we meet at your convenience to discuss the skills and experience I could bring to Pentamax? You can leave a message for me anytime at (303) 555-5957 or cfilli@claus.cmu.edu.

Example 2

More information about my education and experience is included on the enclosed résumé, but I would appreciate the opportunity to meet with you at your convenience to discuss my application. You can reach me after noon on Tuesdays and Thursdays at (212) 555-4527 or leave a message anytime.

The examples of effective job-application letters in Figures 15.8 and 15.9 on pages 392–393 correspond to the résumés in Figures 15.4 and 15.5 on pages 380–381.

In this paragraph, the writer suggests that she has technical and interpersonal skills and that her company thought she did an excellent job on a project she coordinated.

The theme of all these samples is that an effective paragraph has a sharp focus and specific evidence and that it clearly suggests the writer's qualifications.

All job letters end with a paragraph that urges the reader to contact the writer and provides the information that makes it easy for the reader to do so.

■ **Figure 15.8**
Job-Application Letter

Notice that the writer's own name does not appear at the top of his letter.

In the inside address, he uses the reader's courtesy title, "Mr."

The writer points out that he has taken two graduate courses. Notice that he discusses his senior design project, which makes him look more like an engineer solving a problem than a student taking a course.

Notice the use of "In addition" to begin the third sentence. This phrase breaks up the "I" openings of several sentences.

An enclosure notation refers to his résumé.

 In This Book

Many of the job boards listed on p. 367 include samples of application letters.

3109 Vista Street
Philadelphia, PA 19136

January 20, 2005

Mr. Stephen Spencer, Director of Personnel
Department 411
Boeing Naval Systems
103 Industrial Drive
Wilmington, DE 20093

Dear Mr. Spencer:

I am writing in response to your advertisement in the January 16 *Philadelphia Inquirer.* Would you please consider me for the position in Signal Processing? I believe that my academic training in electrical engineering at Drexel University, along with my experience with the RCA Advanced Technology Laboratory, would qualify me for the position.

My education at Drexel has given me a strong background in computer hardware and system design. I have concentrated on digital and computer applications, developing and designing computer and signal-processing hardware in two graduate-level engineering courses. For my senior design project, I am working with four other undergraduates in using OO programming techniques to enhance the path-planning software for an infrared night-vision robotics application.

While working at the RCA Advanced Technology Laboratory, I was able to apply my computer experience to the field of VLSI design. I designed ultra-large-scale integrated circuits using VERILOG and VHDL hardware description languages. In addition, I assisted a senior engineer in CMOS IC layout, modeling, parasitic capacitance extraction, and PSPICE simulation operations.

The enclosed résumé provides an overview of my education and experience. Could I meet with you at your convenience to discuss my qualifications for this position? Please write to me at the above address or leave a message anytime at (215) 555-3880. My e-mail address is crodrig@dragon.du.edu.

Yours truly,

Carlos Rodriguez

Carlos Rodriguez

Enclosure (1)

■ **Figure 15.9**
Job-Application Letter

1781 Weber Road
Warminster, PA 18974

January 17, 2006

Ms. Hannah Gail
Fox Run Medical Center
399 N. Abbey Road
Warminster, PA 18974

Dear Ms. Gail:

Last April I contacted your office regarding the possibility of an internship as a laboratory assistant at your center. Your assistant, Mary McGuire, told me then that you might consider such a position this year. With the experience I have gained since last year, I believe I would be a valuable addition to your center in many ways.

At Harmon College, I have earned a 3.7 GPA in 36 credits in chemistry and biology; all but two of these courses had laboratory components. One skill stressed at Harmon is the ability to communicate effectively, both in writing and orally. Our science courses have extensive writing and speaking requirements; my portfolio includes seven research papers and lab reports of more than 20 pages each, and I have delivered four oral presentations, one of 45 minutes, to classes.

At GlaxoSmithKline, where I currently work part-time, I analyze molecular data on an E & S PS300, a Macintosh, and an IBM PC. I have tried to remain current with the latest advances; my manager at GlaxoSmithKline has allowed me to attend two different two-day in-house seminars on computerized data analysis using SAS. My experience as the manager of a 12-person office for four years helped me acquire interpersonal skills that would benefit Fox Run.

More information about my education and experience is included on the enclosed résumé, but I would appreciate the opportunity to meet with you at your convenience to discuss my application. If you would like any additional information about me or Harmon's internship program, please write to me at the above address, call me at (215) 555-3999, or e-mail me at linderap423@aol.com.

Very truly yours,

Alice P. Linder

Alice P. Linder

Enclosure

The writer gracefully suggests that she would be an even better candidate this year than last year.

The writer is making two points: she is experienced in the lab, and she is an experienced communicator.

By mentioning her portfolio, she is suggesting that she would be happy to show the reader her documents. This statement is an example of understated self-confidence.

PREPARING FOR A JOB INTERVIEW

If your job-application letter is successful, you will be invited to a job interview, where both you and the organization can start to see whether your working there would be a good fit.

On TechComm Web

For links to Web sites about job interviews, click on Links Library for Ch. 15 on <bedfordstmartins .com/techcomm.

In This Book

For more about research techniques, see Ch. 6.

In This Book

For more about communicating persuasively, see Ch. 8.

Guidelines

Preparing for a Job Interview

For every hour you spend in a job interview, you need to do many hours of preparation.

▶ **Study job interviews.** The dozens of books and Web sites devoted to job interviews cover everything from how to do your initial research to common interview questions and how to dress. Although you can't prepare for everything that will happen, you can prepare for a lot of things.

▶ **Study the organization to which you applied.** If you inadvertently show that you haven't done your homework, the interviewer will assume that you're always unprepared. Learn what products or services the organization provides, how well it has done in recent years, what its plans are, and so forth. Start with the organization's own Web site, and then proceed to online and print resources. Search for the organization's name on the Internet.

▶ **Think about what you can offer the organization.** Your goal during the interview is to show how you can help the organization accomplish its goals. Think about how your academic career, your work experience, and your personal characteristics and experiences have prepared you to solve problems and carry out projects to help the organization succeed. Make notes about projects you carried out in courses, experiences on the job, and experiences in your personal life that can serve as persuasive evidence to support claims about your qualifications.

▶ **Study lists of common interview questions.** Interviewers study these lists; you should, too. You're probably familiar with some of the favorites:
   —Can you tell me about yourself?
   —Where do you see yourself in five years?
   —Why did you apply to our company?
   —What do you see as your greatest strengths and weaknesses?
   —Tell me about an incident that taught you something important about yourself.
   —What was your best course in college? Why?

▶ **Compile a list of questions you wish to ask.** Near the end of the interview, the interviewer will probably ask if you have any questions. The interviewer expects you to have compiled a brief list of questions about working for the organization. Do not focus on salary, vacation days, or sick leave. Instead, ask about ways you can continue to develop as a professional, improving your ability to contribute to the organization.

▶ **Rehearse the interview.** It's one thing to think about how you might answer an interview question. It's another to have to answer it. Rehearse the interview by asking friends or colleagues to play the role of the interviewer, making up questions you haven't thought about. Then ask these people for constructive criticism.

The job boards on the Internet are excellent resources when preparing for a job interview. They discuss questions such as the following:

In This Book

For a list of Internet job boards, see p. 367.

- When should you arrive for the interview?
- What should you wear?
- How do interviewers interpret your body language?
- What questions are you likely to be asked?
- How long should your answers be?
- How do you know when the interviewer wishes to end the interview?
- How can you get the interviewer's contact information to write a follow-up letter?

WRITING FOLLOW-UP LETTERS AFTER AN INTERVIEW

After an interview, you should write a letter of appreciation. If offered the job, you also may have to write a letter accepting or rejecting the position.

- *Letter of appreciation after an interview.* Thank the representative for taking the time to see you, and emphasize your particular qualifications. You can also restate your interest in the position. A follow-up letter can do more good with less effort than any other step in the job-application process because so few candidates take the time to write one.

In This Book

Many of the job boards listed on p. 367 include samples of follow-up letters for various situations that occur during the job search.

   Dear Mr. Weaver:

   Thank you for taking the time yesterday to show me your facilities and to introduce me to your colleagues.

   Your advances in piping design were particularly impressive. As a person with hands-on experience in piping design, I can appreciate the advantages your design will have.

   The vitality of your projects and the good fellowship among your employees further confirm my initial belief that Cynergo would be a fine place to work.

   Sincerely yours,

   Harriet Bommarito

   Harriet Bommarito

- *Letter accepting a job offer.* This one is easy: express appreciation, show enthusiasm, and repeat the major terms of your employment.

   Dear Mr. Weaver:

   Thank you very much for the offer to join your design team. I accept.

I look forward to starting work on Monday, July 19. The salary, as you indicate in your letter, is $48,250.

As you have recommended, I will get in touch with Mr. Matthews in Personnel to get a start on the paperwork.

I appreciate the trust you have placed in me, and I assure you that I will do whatever I can to be a productive team member at Cynergo.

Sincerely yours,

Mark Greenberg

- *Letter rejecting a job offer.* If you decide not to accept a job offer, express your appreciation and, if appropriate, explain why you are declining the offer. Remember, you might want to work for this company sometime in the future.

  Dear Mr. Weaver:

  I appreciate very much the offer to join your staff.

  Although I am certain that I would benefit greatly from working at Cynergo, I have decided to take a job with a firm in Pittsburgh, where I have been accepted at Carnegie-Mellon to pursue my master's degree at night.

  Again, thank you for your generous offer.

  Sincerely yours,

  Cynthia O'Malley

  Cynthia O'Malley

- *Letter acknowledging a rejection.* Why write back after you have been rejected for a job? To maintain good relations. You might get a phone call the next week explaining that the person who accepted the job has had to change her plans and offering you the position.

  Dear Mr. Weaver:

  I was disappointed to learn that I will not have a chance to join your staff, because I feel that I could make a substantial contribution. However, I realize that job decisions are complex, involving many candidates and many factors.

  Thank you very much for the courtesy you have shown me.

  Sincerely yours,

  Paul Goicochea

  Paul Goicochea

CREATING ELECTRONIC PORTFOLIOS

An increasingly popular way to search for a job is to create an *electronic portfolio*, a collection of materials including the applicant's résumé and other samples of his or her work. Students and professionals alike display their electronic portfolios on the Web or copy them to disk and make them available to prospective employers.

Items typically presented in an electronic portfolio include the following:

- résumé
- letters of recommendation
- transcripts and professional certifications
- reports, papers, Web sites, slides of oral presentations, and other documents the applicant has written or created as a student or an employee

Because the portfolio is electronic, it can include all kinds of media, from simple word-processed documents to HTML files, video, audio, and animation. Updating an electronic portfolio is relatively easy: just add new items as you create them. One important point comes across clearly in a carefully prepared electronic portfolio: you know how to create a Web site.

Figure 15.10 is the template for student portfolios provided by Florida State University.

 On TechComm Web

For more about online portfolios, see "Developing Your Online Portfolio" by Kevin M. Barry and Jill C. Wesolowski. Click on Links Library for Ch. 15 on <bedfordstmartins.com/techcomm>.

In This Book

For information about creating Web sites, see Ch. 20.

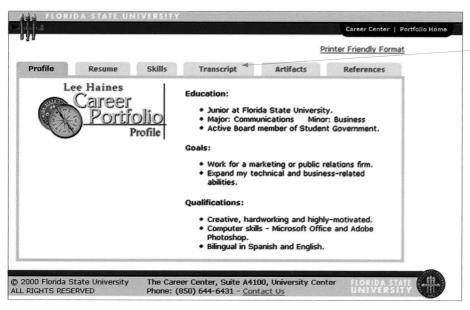

This template provides tabs for the most common kinds of information presented in an online portfolio.

Figure 15.10   Template for a Student Electronic Portfolio
Source: Florida State University, 2004 <www.career-recruit.fsu.edu/careerportfolio/enter/output/main.html>.

Guidelines

Creating an Electronic Portfolio

To create an electronic portfolio, follow these seven steps:

▶ **Analyze your audience and purpose.** Are you writing to potential employers? To a supervisor at work? Are you trying to showcase your technical skills? Your ability to write different kinds of documents?

▶ **Gather your materials.** Always include your current résumé. Consider, too, evidence of your accomplishments, such as transcripts, licenses or certifications, and reference letters. Finally, gather your work samples from courses or the workplace. Think of reports and other kinds of documents you have written, Web sites you have created, and graphics from oral presentations.

▶ **Organize your materials.** With all your materials before you, organize them to display your credentials effectively. Most readers will expect a topical organization, with categories such as background, certifications and honors, course projects, and workplace samples. Some categories, such as workplace samples, might be subdivided into subcategories such as computer skills, oral presentations, and project reports.

▶ **Write introductory statements for each major item and for the whole portfolio.** The statement about each item helps readers understand what the item is, when and why you created it, what tools you used, what skills you learned, and what you would do differently if you had other resources. The statement about the whole portfolio is your opportunity to explain how the various items fit together and how they demonstrate your professionalism.

▶ **Prepare the materials for electronic display.** For print documents, use software such as Adobe Acrobat to create portable documents that can be stored and displayed online but that retain their print formatting. For online documents, such as Web pages, use a Web editor or work in a text editor such as Notepad to create hypertext. Use graphics software to code graphics to add to the site.

▶ **Review and revise the portfolio draft.** Test the draft to make sure all the links work and the materials are well organized, attractive, and professional. Ask others to help you determine areas to improve.

▶ **Assemble the portfolio.** After revising the portfolio, either upload it to a Web site or burn it to a CD.

Writer's Checklist

Printed Résumé
- [ ] Does the résumé meet the needs of its readers? (p. 372)
- [ ] Does the résumé have a professional appearance, with generous margins, a symmetrical layout, adequate white space, and effective indentation? (p. 369)
- [ ] Is the résumé honest? (p. 372)
- [ ] Is the résumé free of errors? (p. 372)
- [ ] Does the identifying information contain your name, address(es), phone number(s), and e-mail address(es)? (p. 373)
- [ ] Does the résumé include a clear statement of your job objectives or a summary of your credentials? (p. 373)

☐ Does the education section include your degree, your institution and its location, and your (anticipated) date of graduation, as well as any other information that will help a reader appreciate your qualifications? (p. 374)

☐ Does the employment section include, for each job, the dates of employment, the organization's name and location, and (if you are writing a chronological résumé) your position or title, as well as a description of your duties and accomplishments? (p. 375)

☐ Does the interests and activities section include relevant hobbies or activities? (p. 377) Have you omitted any personal information that might reflect poorly on you? (p. 378)

☐ Does the references section include the names, job titles, organizations, mailing addresses, and phone numbers of three or four references? (p. 378) If you are not listing this information, does the strength of the rest of the résumé offset the omission? (p. 378)

☐ Does the résumé include any other appropriate sections, such as skills and abilities, military service, language skills, or honors? (p. 379)

Electronic Résumé

In addition to the items mentioned in the checklist for a printed résumé, did you

☐ use ASCII format? (p. 384)
☐ use a simple sans-serif typeface? (p. 387)
☐ use a single-column format? (p. 387)
☐ use wide margins? (p. 387)
☐ use the space bar instead of the tab key? (p. 387)

Job-Application Letter

☐ Does the letter meet your reader's needs? (p. 387)
☐ Is the letter honest? (p. 372)
☐ Does the letter look professional? (p. 388)

☐ Does the introductory paragraph identify your source of information and the position you are applying for, state that you wish to be considered, and forecast the rest of the letter? (p. 388)

☐ Does the education paragraph meet your reader's needs with a unified idea introduced by a topic sentence? (p. 389)

☐ Does the employment paragraph meet your reader's needs with a unified idea introduced by a topic sentence? (p. 390)

☐ Does the concluding paragraph include a reference to your résumé, a request for an interview, your phone number, and your e-mail address? (p. 391)

☐ Does the letter include an enclosure notation? (p. 392)

Preparing for a Job Interview

Did you

☐ study job interviews? (p. 394)
☐ study the organization to which you applied? (p. 394)
☐ think about what you can offer the organization? (p. 394)
☐ study lists of common interview questions? (p. 394)
☐ compile a list of questions you wish to ask? (p. 394)
☐ rehearse the interview? (p. 394)

Follow-up Letters

☐ Does your letter of appreciation for a job interview thank the interviewer and briefly restate your qualifications? (p. 395)

☐ Does your letter accepting a job offer show enthusiasm and repeat the major terms of your employment? (p. 395)

☐ Does your letter rejecting a job offer express your appreciation and, if appropriate, explain why you are declining the offer? (p. 396)

☐ Does your letter acknowledging a rejection have a positive tone that will help you maintain good relations? (p. 396)

Exercises

 In This Book For more about memos, see Ch. 14, p. 352.

1. **INTERNET EXERCISE** Using a job board on the Web, list and briefly describe five positions available in your field in your state. What skills, experience, and background does each position require? What is the salary range for each position?

2. **INTERNET EXERCISE** Locate and provide the URLs of three job boards that provide interactive forms for creating a résumé automatically. In a brief memo to your instructor, describe the strengths and weaknesses of each. Which job board appears to be the easiest to use? Why?

3. The following résumé was submitted in response to an ad describing these duties: "CAM Technician to work with other technicians and manage some GIS and mapping projects. Also perform updating of the GIS database. Experience required." In a brief memo to your instructor, describe how effective the résumé is. What are some of its problems?

Kenneth Bradley

530 Maplegrove   Bozeman, Mont. 59715 (406)-484-2916
kbradley@montanastate.edu

Objective	Entry level position as a CAM Technician. I am also interested in possibly staying with the company until after graduation, possibly moving into a position as a Mechanical Engineer.
Education	Enrolled at Montana State University in Bozeman August 2004- Present
Employment	Fred Meyer 65520 Chinden Garden City, MT (406)-323-7030 *Janitor-7/03-6/04* Responsible for cleaning entire store, as well as equipment maintenance and floor maintenance and repair. *Assistant Janitorial Manager- 6/04-9/04* Responsible for cleaning entire store, equipment maintenance, floor maintenance and repair, scheduling, and managing personnel *Head of Freight- 9/04-Present* In charge of braking down all new freight, stocking shelves, cleaning the stock room, and managing personnel **Montana** State University Bozeman, MT *Teachers Aide ME 120- 1/03-5/03* *Teachers Aide ME 120* In charge of keeping students in line and answering any questions related to drafting.
References	Timothy Rayburn Janitorial Manager (406)-555-8571 John Guarnio Coworker (406)-555-8970 Eduardo Perez Coworker (406)-555-2032

4. The following application letter responds to an ad describing these duties: "CAM Technician to work with other technicians and manage some GIS and mapping projects. Also perform updating of the GIS database. Experience required." In a brief memo to your instructor, describe how effective the letter is, and how it could be improved.

530 Maplegrove
Bozeman, Mont. 59715
November 11, 2006

Mr. Bruce Hedley
Adecco Technical
5578 S. Vista Ave
Bozeman, Mont. 59715

Dear Mr. Hedley,

I am writing you in response to your advertisement on Monsterjobs.com. Would you please consider me for the position of CAM technician? I believe that my academic schooling at Montana State University, along with my work experience would make me an excellent candidate for the position.

While at Montana State University, I took one class in particular that applies well to this job. It was a CAD drafting class, which I received a 97% in. The next semester I was a Teachers Aid for that same class, where I was responsible for answering questions about drafting from my peers. This gave me a much stronger grasp on all aspects of CAD work than I could have ever gotten from simply taking the class.

My employment at Fred Meyer is also a notable experience. While there is no technical aspects of either positions I have held, I believe that my experience there will shed light on my work ethic and interpersonal skills. I started out as a graveyard shift janitor, with no previous experience. All of my coworkers were at least thirty years older than me, and had a minimum of five years of janitorial experience. However after working there for only one year I was promoted to assistant manager. Three months after I received this position, I was informed that Fred Meyer was going to contract out the janitorial work and that all of us would be losing our jobs. I decided that I wanted to stay within the company, and I was able to receive a position as head of freight.

The enclosed résumé provides an overview of my education and work experience. I would appreciate an opportunity to meet with you at your convience to disscuss my qualifications for this position. Please write me at the above address or leave a message anytime. If you would like to contact me by e-mail, my e-mail address is kbadley@montanastate.edu.

Yours truly,

Ken Bradley

5. How effective is the following letter of appreciation? How could it be improved? Present your findings in a brief memo to your instructor.

914 Imperial Boulevard
Durham, NC 27708

November 13, 2006

Mr. Ronald O'Shea
Division Engineering
Safeway Electronics, Inc.
Holland, MI 49423

Dear Mr. O'Shea:

Thanks very much for showing me around your plant. I hope I was able to convince you that I'm the best person for the job.

Sincerely yours,

Robert Harad

6. **INTERNET EXERCISE** In a newspaper or journal or on the Internet, find a job ad for a position in your field for which you might be qualified. Write a résumé and a job-application letter in response to the ad; include the job ad or a photocopy. You will be evaluated not only on the content and appearance of the materials but also on how well you have targeted them to the ad.

Case 15: Identifying Transferable Skills for a Career Changer

Background

"I'm thinking about changing careers," your friend Mercedes tells you. After ten years of teaching mathematics, she wants a job in industry. "I'm looking for something that's a little more challenging. I can't stand the thought of teaching beginning algebra for another year, not to mention another twenty years. Besides, I don't see much opportunity for career advancement as a teacher. Because I'm not interested in switching to administration, the best I can hope for is to become the chair of the mathematics department someday. A job in industry would offer me new challenges, and I might have more opportunities for advancement."

"What career are you thinking of?" you ask.

"I've done a little research, and I'm thinking of using my math skills as an actuary."

"What's an actuary?"

"Actuaries work in the insurance field. They calculate insurance premiums, set reserve funds, and estimate the costs of implementing new benefits. In last Sunday's newspaper, I found a job advertisement for an actuarial analyst." (See Document 15.1.)

"Do you qualify for this job?"

"I think I do. But I'm not sure how to describe ten years of teaching mathematics so that the skills I've acquired seem relevant to the position."

"I remember when my friend Terry left the army and made the transition from military to civilian life. Because there are not many job openings for artillery officers in the business world, Terry had to focus on transferable skills. Terry used the experience she acquired in the army, along with college course work, volunteer activities, and hobbies, to apply for a management position she was interested in. You can do something similar. You need to identify which of your qualifications and experiences are relevant to the actuarial analyst position."

"You seem to know what you're talking about. Would you be willing to help me apply for this position?"

"Sure. Send me your current résumé (Document 15.2), and I'll see what I can do. In the meantime, I'll e-mail you a few resources on the Internet that describe the concept of transferable skills."

■ **Document 15.1   Job Advertisement for an Actuarial Analyst**

 **On TechComm Web**

For digital versions of case documents, click on Downloadable Case Documents on <bedfordstmartins.com/techcomm>.

Actuarial Analyst

Collects and analyzes data and other necessary information for pricing, reserving, underwriting, and forecasting at Gold Star Insurance. Requires undergraduate degree in Mathematics, Statistics, Industrial Engineering, Computer Science, Economics, or equivalent area. College-level mathematics, including calculus, statistics, and/or numerical analysis. Proficient in the use of spreadsheet and statistical software; general keyboarding skills. Ability to analyze and resolve complex issues pertaining to pricing, experience monitoring, reserving, and forecasting. Projects will include management reporting, various health data trend studies, financial analysis and planning, supervising special projects, and some travel. Detail-oriented and able to clearly and concisely communicate highly technical issues orally and in writing.

Send a letter of application and a résumé to Ms. Roberta Klein, Director of Actuarial Services, Gold Star Insurance, PO Box 2233, St. Louis, MO 63136.

■ Document 15.2
Mercedes's Chronological
Teaching Résumé

Mercedes Viana

927 Emerald Street   208-555-1510
Boise, ID 83704   mviana@hotmail.com

Education

MA **Mathematics Education,** *State University of New York at Albany, December 1996.* GPA 3.96.
>   Courses include: Chaos and Complexity, Vector Analysis.

BA **Mathematics,** Minor in Economics, *State University of New York at Albany, Academic Excellence in Mathematics Award, May 1995.*
>   Overall GPA 3.66, Major GPA 3.78.
>   Courses include: Production and Operations Management for Engineers, Engineering Project Management, Introduction to Engineering Analysis, Human Resource Management, Writing and Critical Thinking.

Teaching Experience

Boise State University, Adjunct Faculty, Mathematics, Boise, ID, 2001–Present.
>   Researched, designed, and taught courses including College Algebra, Pre-Calculus, Finite Mathematics, and Introduction to Mathematical Thought. Selected texts and created online and print materials. Developed innovative methods to present technical material to nonexperts. Student evaluations consistently listed my strengths as the following: organization, preparedness, and clarity of presentation.

Boise City Schools, Mathematics Teacher, Boise, ID, 2002–Present.
>   Developed project plan for academic year, adjusting approach based on student progress data. Provided instruction and written and oral feedback, maintained progress records, and supervised activities of over 120 students daily. Generated written reports on student progress with curriculum recommendations and presented this material to administration and parents. Participated in school, district, and regional team meetings to address educational mandates. Communicated with parents, teachers, and administration daily via e-mail, phone, and written correspondence. Supervised three cheerleader squads of 20 students. Directed two coaches, practice and event scheduling, and fund-raising opportunities.

Rockingham County Schools, Mathematics Teacher, Bridgewater, VA, 1999–2001.
>   Guided over 90 students to above-state-average results on Virginia Standards of Learning (SOL) examinations in Algebra and Geometry. Worked with multidisciplinary team to create material addressing SOL objectives. Supervisor evaluations highlighted strengths including "works very hard to make sure each student understands the problem being worked."

Pulaski Technical College, Instructor, N. Little Rock, AR, 1998–1999.
>   Designed material to address the needs of approximately 80 diverse adult learners. Provided group instruction, arranged and led small-group tutoring sessions, and created assessment tools. Also taught Advanced Placement Calculus at local high school to accelerated sophomores.

■ Document 15.2
(continued)

Pulaski County School District, Mathematics Teacher, Little Rock, AR, 1997–1998. Taught mathematics with an emphasis on integrating technology. Wrote reports to district administration on innovative plans to include multicultural material in the traditional math classroom. Supervisor evaluations highlighted strengths including "constantly on the growing edge of learning, . . . personable, possesses a pleasing and positive attitude, . . . relates well with people."

SUNY Albany, School of Education, Computer Consultant, Albany, NY, 1995–1996. Assisted math and science faculty with advanced computer skills such as programming, computer networking, and use of statistical programs.

Technical Skills

- MS Office Software: Word, Excel, PowerPoint.
- Desktop Publishing Software: FrameMaker, Photoshop, Adobe Acrobat.
- Web-Authoring Software: FrontPage, Blackboard (Web-Based Training).
- Mathematics and Database Software: SAS, Maple V, Access.
- Computer-Aided Drafting: Pro/Engineer.
- Programming Languages: C++, Java, Fortran.

Honors

- *Kappa Delta Pi,* National Educational Honor Society, 1996.
- *Phi Theta Kappa,* National Honor Society, 1993.
- Science Award, Mathematics Award, and Academic Award, Cazenovia College, 1993.
- Dean's List, Cazenovia College, Rensselaer Polytechnic Institute, and SUNY at Albany, 1992–1995.

Professional Development

- International Society for Technology in Education Certified, 2002.
- Graduate Course Work in Computer Science, James Madison University, 2000–2001.
- Society for Technical Communicators National Annual Conference, Chicago, IL, 2001.
- National Teacher Training Institute in Mathematics, Science, and Technology, Harrisonburg, VA, 2001.
- Teachers Teaching with Technology Statistics Institute, Hot Springs, AR, 1998.

References

Available upon request.

Your Assignment

1. Using an Internet search engine such as Google, locate three or four Internet resources describing the concept of transferable skills for career changers. Write Mercedes a brief e-mail message in which you list the resources you located and provide a one-paragraph summary of each resource.

2. Revise Mercedes's current résumé (Document 15.2) so that it emphasizes transferable skills relevant to the actuarial analyst position (Document 15.1).

3. Draft a job-application letter that Mercedes could use to respond to the actuarial analyst ad.

16 Writing Proposals

TECH COMM AT WORK

When professionals want resources to improve how they do their jobs, they often write proposals. For instance, a physical therapist might write a proposal to his supervisor for funding to attend a convention to learn about current rehabilitation practices. A physics teacher might write a proposal to the National Science Foundation for funding to research ways to improve the teaching of superstring science. A director of a homeless shelter might write a proposal for funding to increase the services offered by the shelter. And a team of co-workers might write a proposal for a large construction project funded by a federal agency. Whether the project is small or big, within your own company or outside it, you are likely to write proposals throughout your career.

Most projects undertaken by organizations, and most major changes made within organizations, begin with a proposal. A proposal is an offer to carry out research or to provide a product or service.

UNDERSTANDING THE PROCESS OF WRITING PROPOSALS

Writing a proposal calls for the same process of planning, drafting, revising, editing, and proofreading that you use for other kinds of documents. Figure 16.1 presents an overview of this process.

Analyze Your Audience

In particular, consider the reader's knowledge about, and attitudes toward, what you are proposing.

↓

Analyze Your Purpose

Make clear exactly what you are asking the readers of your proposal to do. In most cases, you are asking for resources and authorization to carry out a research project or to perform a task.

↓

Gather Information About Your Subject

A successful proposal is based on solid research about the reader's needs and about the subject. Use the primary and secondary research techniques discussed in Ch. 6.

↓

Choose The Appropriate Type of Proposal

Internal proposals are submitted to the writer's own organization; external proposals are directed to another organization.

↓

■ **Figure 16.1   An Overview of the Process for Writing Proposals**

> **Draft the Proposal**
>
> Follow the instructions in any RFP or IFB. If there is none, include an **introduction,** which shows specifically that you understand your reader's problem or opportunity; a **proposed program,** which describes what you will do if the proposal is accepted; a **qualifications and experience** section, including evidence of other successful projects; a **budget**; and **appendices,** such as a task schedule and a description of evaluation techniques.

> **Format the Proposal**
>
> For external proposals, study the RFP. For internal proposals, study other proposals submitted in your organization.

> **Revise, Edit, Proofread, and Submit the Proposal**
>
> External proposals usually have a firm deadline. You need to build in time to revise the proposal thoroughly and still get it to readers on time. See the Writer's Checklist on p. 426.

THE LOGISTICS OF PROPOSALS

Proposals can be classified as either external or internal; external proposals are either solicited or unsolicited. (See Figure 16.2.)

External and Internal Proposals

Proposals are either external (if submitted to another organization) or internal (if submitted to the writer's own organization).

External Proposals   No organization produces all the products or provides all the services it needs. Office furniture and equipment have to be purchased, and offices need to be cleaned and maintained. Sometimes projects require unusual expertise, such as sophisticated market analyses. Because many companies supply these products and services, most organizations require that each prospective supplier compete for the business by submitting a proposal, a document arguing that the supplier deserves the business.

Internal Proposals   One day, while working on a project in the laboratory, you realize that if you had a fiber-curl measurement system, you could do your job better and faster. The increased productivity would save your company the cost of the system in a few months. Your supervisor asks you to write a memo describing what you want, why you want it,

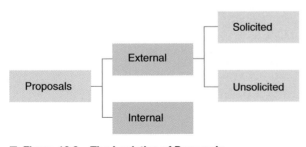

■ **Figure 16.2   The Logistics of Proposals**

what you're going to do with it, and what it costs. If your request seems reasonable and the money is available, you'll likely get the new system.

Your memo is an *internal proposal*—a formal argument, submitted within an organization, for carrying out an activity that will benefit the organization. An internal proposal might recommend that the organization conduct research, purchase a product, or change some aspect of its policies or procedures.

Often the scope of the proposal determines its format. A request for a small amount of money might be conveyed orally, either in person or on the phone, or in writing, either by e-mail or in a brief memo. A request for a large amount, however, is usually presented in a formal proposal.

Solicited and Unsolicited Proposals

External proposals are either solicited or unsolicited. A *solicited proposal* is submitted in response to a request from the customer. An *unsolicited proposal* is submitted by a prospective supplier that believes the customer has a need for goods or services.

Solicited Proposals   When an organization wants to purchase a product or service, it publishes one of two basic kinds of statements:

- An *information for bid (IFB)* is used for standard products. When an agency of the federal government needs desktop computers, for instance, it informs computer manufacturers of the configuration it needs. All other things being equal, the supplier that offers the lowest bid wins the contract.

- A *request for proposals (RFP)* is used for more-customized products or services. For example, if the air force needs a friend-or-foe radar device, the RFP it publishes might be a long, detailed set of technical specifications. The supplier that can design, produce, and deliver the device most closely resembling the specifications—at a reasonable price—will probably win the contract.

Most organizations issue RFPs and IFBs in print and online. Government RFPs and IFBs are published in the journals *Commerce Business Daily* (for contracts under $25,000) and *FedBizOpps* (for contracts over $25,000), both of which are available online. Figure 16.3 on page 408 shows a sample entry.

 On TechComm Web

For links to these government journals, click on Links Library for Ch. 16 on <bedfordstmartins .com/techcomm>.

Unsolicited Proposals   An unsolicited proposal is like a solicited proposal except that it does not refer to an RFP. Even though the potential customer never formally requested the proposal, in most cases the supplier was invited to submit the proposal after people from the two organizations met and discussed the project. Because proposals are expensive to write, suppliers are reluctant to submit them without assurances that they will be considered carefully. Thus, the word *unsolicited* is only partially accurate.

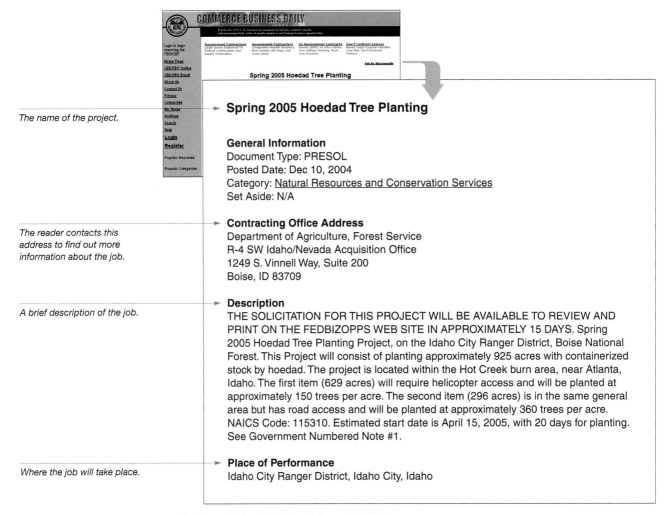

The name of the project.

The reader contacts this address to find out more information about the job.

A brief description of the job.

Where the job will take place.

■ **Figure 16.3   IFB Extract from CBDNET**
Source: CBD/FBO Online, 2004 <www.cbdweb.com/index.php/search/show/730240>.

External proposals, both solicited and unsolicited, can culminate in contracts of several types: a flat fee for a product or a one-time service; a leasing agreement; or a "cost-plus" contract, under which the supplier is reimbursed for the actual cost plus a profit set at a fixed percentage of the costs.

THE "DELIVERABLES" OF PROPOSALS

A *deliverable* is what the supplier will deliver at the end of the project. Deliverables can be classified into two major categories, as shown in Figure 16.4.

Research Proposals

In a research proposal, you are promising to perform research, then provide a report about it. For example, a biologist for a state bureau of land management writes a proposal to the National Science Foundation requesting resources to build a window-lined tunnel in the forest to study tree and plant roots and the growth of fungi. The biologist also

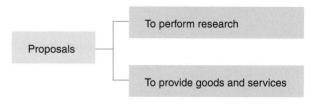

■ **Figure 16.4   "Deliverables" of a Proposal**

wishes to investigate the relationship between plant growth and the activity of insects and worms. The deliverable will be a report submitted to the National Science Foundation and perhaps an article published in a professional journal.

A research proposal often leads to two other kinds of documents: progress reports and completion reports.

After the proposal has been approved and the researchers have begun work, they often submit one or more *progress reports*, which tell the sponsor of the project how the work is proceeding. Is it following the plan of work outlined in the proposal? Is it going according to schedule? Is it staying within budget?

At the end of the project, researchers prepare a *completion report*, often called a *final report*, a *project report*, or simply a *report*. A completion report tells the whole story of the research project, beginning with the problem or opportunity that motivated it, the methods used in carrying it out, and the results, conclusions, and recommendations.

People carry out research projects to satisfy their curiosity and to advance professionally. Organizations often require that their professional employees carry out research and publish it in appropriate reports, journals, or books. Government researchers and university professors, for instance, are expected to remain active in their fields. Writing proposals is one way to get the resources—time and money for travel, equipment, and assistants—to carry out research.

 On TechComm Web

For sample proposals and writing checklists, see Writing Guidelines for Engineering and Science Students. Click on Links Library for Ch. 16 on <bedfordstmartins .com/techcomm>.

 In This Book

For more about progress reports and completion reports, see Ch. 17, p. 438, and Ch. 18, p. 455.

Goods and Services Proposals

A goods and services proposal leads to a tangible product (a fleet of automobiles), a service (building maintenance), or some combination of the two (the construction of a building).

A vast network of goods and services contracts spans the working world. The U.S. government, the world's biggest customer, spent $77 billion in 2004 buying military equipment from organizations that submitted proposals (U.S. Census Bureau, 2004, p. 310). But goods and services contracts are by no means limited to government contractors. One auto manufacturer buys engines from another; a company that makes spark plugs buys its steel from another company.

Another kind of goods and services proposal requests funding to support a local organization. The director of a museum might apply to the state humanities organization for a *grant*, or cash payment, to help finance a special exhibit at the museum.

PERSUASION AND PROPOSALS

In This Book

For more about persuasion, see Ch. 8.

A successful proposal is a persuasive argument. You must convince readers that the future benefits will outweigh the immediate and projected costs. Basically, you must clearly show the following:

- that you understand the readers' needs
- that you have decided what to do and you are able to do it
- that you are a professional and you are committed to fulfilling your promises

Understanding Readers' Needs

In This Book

For more about analyzing your audience, see Ch. 5, p. 68.

The most important element of a proposal is the definition of the problem or opportunity to which the proposed project responds. Although this point seems obvious, people who evaluate proposals agree that the most common weakness they see is an inadequate or inaccurate understanding of the problem or opportunity.

Readers' Needs in an External Proposal   Most readers will reject a proposal as soon as they realize that it doesn't address their needs. When you receive an RFP, study it thoroughly. If you don't understand something in it, contact the organization. They will be happy to clarify the RFP, because a poor proposal wastes everyone's time.

When you write an unsolicited proposal, analyze your audience carefully. How can you define the problem or opportunity so that the client will understand it? Keep in mind the readers' needs and, if possible, their backgrounds. Concentrate on how the problem has decreased productivity or quality or how your ideas would create new opportunities. When you submit an unsolicited proposal, your task in many cases is to convince readers that a need exists. Even when you have reached an understanding with some of your customer's representatives, your proposal will still have to persuade other officials in the company.

Readers' Needs in an Internal Proposal   Writing an internal proposal is both simpler and more complicated than writing an external one. It is simpler because you have more access to your readers than you do to external readers, and you can get more information more easily. However, it is more complicated because you might find it hard to understand the situation in

---

Strategies for Intercultural Communication

Writing International Proposals

When you address a proposal to a reader from another culture, keep in mind the following two suggestions:

- **Be sure you have read and understood the proposal requirements.** The following proposal guidelines published by the National Research Foundation (2002) in South Africa describes the management plan that is required for one of its grants:

  This section requires detail on the time that will be spent by various resources on the following list of activities:
  - Project Co-ordination/Management
  - Research and Development
  - Financial Reporting
  - Project Reporting
  - Marketing/Commercialisation
  - Product Management
  - Other (please specify)

  An organogram illustrating which tasks will be completed by particular resources and the hierarchy of the project team would be useful.

  An *organogram* is a combination of *organizational* and *diagram*. In the United States, it's called an *organization chart*.

- **Understand that persuasive messages may require more than just attention to the bottom line.** Paying attention to the welfare of the company or the community may be more persuasive. An American company was surprised to learn that the Venezuelan readers of its proposal had selected a French company that "had been making personal visits for years, bringing their families, and engaging in social activities long before there was any question of a contract" (Thrush, 2000).

---

your organization. Some colleagues might not be willing to tell you that your proposal is a long shot or that your ideas might threaten someone in the organization. Before you write an internal proposal, discuss your ideas with as many potential readers as you can to learn what the organization really thinks of them.

Describing What You Plan to Do

Once you have shown that you understand what needs to be done and why, describe what you plan to do. Convince your readers that you can respond effectively to the situation you have just described. Discuss procedures and equipment you would use. If appropriate, justify your choices. For example, if you say you want to do ultrasonic testing on a structure, explain why, unless the reason is obvious.

Present a complete picture of what you would do from the first day of the project to the last. You need more than enthusiasm and good faith; you need a detailed plan showing that you have already started to do the work. Although no proposal can anticipate every question about what you plan to do, the more planning you have done before you submit the proposal, the greater the chances that you will be able to do the work successfully if it is approved.

Demonstrating Your Professionalism

Once you have shown that you understand readers' needs and can offer a well-conceived plan, demonstrate that you are the kind of person (or that yours is the kind of organization) who is committed to delivering what you promise. Convince readers that you have the pride, ingenuity, and perseverance to solve the problems that are likely to occur. In short, show that you are a professional.

Guidelines

Demonstrating Your Professionalism in a Proposal

Demonstrate your ability to carry out a project by providing four kinds of information in a proposal:

▶ **Credentials and work history.** Show that you know how to do this project because you have done similar ones. Which people in your organization have the qualifications to carry out the project? What equipment and facilities will enable you to do the work? What management structure will you use to coordinate the activities and keep the project running smoothly?

▶ **Work schedule.** Sometimes called a *task schedule*, a work schedule is a graph or chart that shows when the various phases of the project will be carried out. The work schedule reveals more about your attitudes toward your work than about what you will be doing on any given day. A detailed work schedule shows that you have tried to foresee problems that might threaten the project.

▶ **Quality-control measures.** Describe how you will evaluate the effectiveness and efficiency of your work. Quality-control procedures might consist of technical evaluations carried out periodically by the project staff, on-site evaluations by recognized authorities or by the potential client, or progress reports.

▶ **Budget.** Most proposals conclude with a detailed budget, a statement of how much the project will cost. This is another way to show that you have done your homework on a project.

Ethics Note

Writing Honest Proposals

When an organization approves a proposal, it needs to trust that the people who will carry out the project will do it professionally. Over the centuries, however, dishonest proposal writers have perfected a number of ways to trick organizations into thinking a project is going to go smoothly:

- saying that certain qualified people will participate in the project, even though they will not
- saying that the project will be finished by a certain date, even though it will not
- saying that the deliverable will have certain characteristics, even though it will not
- saying that the project will be completed under budget, even though it will not

There are three reasons to be honest in writing a proposal:

- to avoid serious legal trouble stemming from breach-of-contract suits
- to avoid acquiring a bad reputation, thus ruining your business
- to do the right thing

WRITING A PROPOSAL

Although writing a proposal requires the same writing process that you use for most other kinds of technical documents, a proposal can be so large that two aspects of the writing process—resource planning and collaboration— are even more important than they are with smaller documents.

As discussed in Chapter 5, planning a project requires a lot of work. You need to see whether your organization can devote resources to writing the proposal and then to carrying out the project if the proposal is approved. Sometimes an organization writes a proposal, wins the contract, and then loses money because it lacks the resources to do the project and must subcontract major portions of it. The resources you need fall into three basic categories:

- *Personnel.* Do you have the technical personnel, managers, and support people?
- *Facilities.* Do you have the facilities, or can you lease them? Can you profitably subcontract tasks to companies that have the right facilities?
- *Equipment.* Do you have the right equipment? If not, can you buy or lease it, or subcontract the work? Some contracts provide for the purchase of equipment, but others don't.

 On TechComm Web

For a proposal-writing checklist, see Alice Reid's "A Practical Guide for Writing Proposals." Click on Links Library for Ch. 16 on <bedfordstmartins.com/ techcomm>.

In This Book

For more about collaboration, see Ch. 4.

In This Book

For more about boilerplate, see Ch. 2, p. 19.

On TechComm Web

To view the proposal guidelines of the Society for Human Resource Management, click on Links Library for Ch. 16 on <bedfordstmartins .com/techcomm>.

Structure of a proposal:
Summary
Introduction
Proposed program
Qualifications and experience
Budget
Appendices

In This Book

For more about summaries, see Appendix, Part A, p. 576, and Ch. 18, p. 470.

Don't write a proposal unless you are confident that you can carry out the project if you get the go-ahead.

Collaboration is critical in large proposals because no one person has the time and expertise to do all the work. Writing major proposals requires the expertise of technical personnel, writers, editors, graphic artists, managers, lawyers, and document-production specialists. Usually, a project manager coordinates the process.

Proposal writers almost always reuse existing information, including *boilerplate*, such as descriptions of other projects the company has done, histories and descriptions of the company, and résumés of the important personnel who will work on the project. This reuse of information is legal and ethical—as long as it is the intellectual property of the company.

THE STRUCTURE OF THE PROPOSAL

Proposal structures vary greatly from one organization to another. A long, complex proposal might have 10 or more sections, including introduction, problem, objectives, solution, methods and resources, and management. If the authorizing agency provides an IFB, an RFP, or a set of guidelines, follow it closely. If you have no guidelines, or if you are writing an unsolicited proposal, use the structure shown here as a starting point. Then modify it according to your subject, your purpose, and the needs of your audience. An example of a proposal is presented on pages 419–23.

Summary

For a proposal of more than a few pages, provide a summary. Many organizations impose a length limit, such as 250 words, and ask the writer to present the summary, single-spaced, on the title page. The summary is crucial, because it might be the only item that readers study in their initial review of the proposal.

The summary covers the major elements of the proposal but devotes only a few sentences to each. Define the problem in a sentence or two. Then describe the proposed program and provide a brief statement of your qualifications and experience. Some organizations wish to see the completion date and the final budget figure in the summary; others prefer that this information be presented separately on the title page along with other identifying information about the supplier and the proposed project.

Introduction

The purpose of the introduction is to help readers understand the context, scope, and organization of the proposal.

Guidelines

Introducing a Proposal

The introduction to the proposal should answer the following seven questions:

▶ **What is the problem or opportunity?** Describe the problem or opportunity in specific monetary terms, because the proposal itself will include a budget, and you want to convince your readers that spending money on what you propose is smart. Don't say that a design problem is slowing down production; say that it is costing $4,500 a day in lost productivity.

▶ **What is the purpose of the proposal?** The purpose of the proposal is to describe a problem or opportunity and to propose activities that will culminate in a deliverable. Be specific in explaining what you want to do.

▶ **What is the background of the problem or opportunity?** Although you probably will not be telling your readers anything they don't already know, show them that you understand the problem or opportunity: the circumstances that led to its discovery, the relationships or events that will affect the problem and its solution, and so on.

▶ **What are your sources of information?** Review the relevant literature, ranging from internal reports and memos to published articles or even books, so that readers will understand the context of your work.

▶ **What is the scope of the proposal?** If appropriate, indicate what you are—and are not—proposing to do.

▶ **What is the organization of the proposal?** Explain the organizational pattern you will use.

▶ **What are the key terms that you will use in the proposal?** If you will use any specialized or unusual terms, define them in the introduction.

Proposed Program

In the proposed program, sometimes called the *plan of work*, explain what you want to do. Be specific. You won't persuade anyone by saying that you plan to "gather the data and analyze it." How will you gather and analyze the data? Justify your claims. Every word you say—or don't say—will give your readers evidence on which to base their decision. If you know your subject, the proposed program will show it. If you don't, you will probably slip into meaningless generalities or include erroneous information that undermines the whole proposal.

If your project concerns a subject written about in the professional literature, show your familiarity with the scholarship by referring to the pertinent studies. However, don't just string together a bunch of citations. For example, don't write, "Carruthers (2002), Harding (2003), and Vega (2003) have all researched the relationship between acid-rain levels and groundwater contamination." Rather, use the recent literature to sketch the necessary background and provide the justification for your proposed program. For instance:

> Carruthers (2002), Harding (2003), and Vega (2003) have demonstrated the relationship between acid-rain levels and groundwater contamination. None of these studies,

 On TechComm Web

For a sample literature review, see Writing Guidelines for Engineering and Science Students. Click on Links Library for Ch. 16 on <bedfordstmartins.com/ techcomm>.

however, included an analysis of the long-term contamination of the aquifer. The current study will consist of...

You might include only a few references to recent research. However, if you have researched your topic thoroughly, you might devote several paragraphs or even several pages to recent scholarship.

In This Book

For more about researching a subject, see Ch. 6.

Whether your project calls for primary research, secondary research, or both, the proposal will be unpersuasive if you haven't already done a substantial amount of the research. For instance, say you are writing a proposal to do research on industrial-grade lawn mowers. You are not being persuasive if you write that you are going to visit Wal-Mart, Lowe's, and Home Depot to see what kinds of lawn mowers they carry. This statement is unpersuasive for two reasons:

- You need to justify why you are going to visit those three retailers rather than others. Anticipate your readers' questions: Why did you choose those three retailers? Why didn't you choose more-specialized dealers?

- You should already have visited the appropriate stores and completed any other preliminary research. If you haven't done the homework, readers have no assurance that you will do it or that it will pay off. If your supervisor authorizes the project and then learns that none of the lawn mowers on the market meets your organization's needs, you will have to go back and submit a different proposal—an embarrassing move.

Unless you can show in your proposed program that you have done the research—and that the research indicates that the project is likely to succeed—your readers have no reason to authorize the project.

Qualifications and Experience

After you have described how you would carry out the project, show that you can do it. The more elaborate the proposal, the more substantial the discussion of your qualifications and experience has to be. For a small project, include a few paragraphs describing your technical credentials and those of your co-workers. For larger projects, include the résumés of the project leader, often called the *principal investigator*, and the other important participants.

External proposals also should discuss the qualifications of the supplier's organization, describing similar projects the supplier has successfully completed. For example, a company bidding on a contract to build a large suspension bridge should describe other suspension bridges it has built. It also should focus on the equipment and facilities the company already has and on the management structure that will ensure the project will go smoothly.

Budget

Good ideas aren't good unless they're affordable. The budget section of a proposal specifies how much the proposed program will cost.

Budgets vary greatly in scope and format. For simple internal proposals, add the budget request to the statement of the proposed program: "This study will take me two days, at a cost of about $400" or "The variable-speed recorder currently costs $225, with a 10 percent discount on orders of five or more." For more-complicated internal proposals and for all external proposals, include a more explicit and complete budget.

Most budgets are divided into two parts: direct costs and indirect costs.

- *Direct costs* include expenses such as salaries and fringe benefits for program personnel, travel costs, and necessary equipment, materials, and supplies.

- *Indirect costs* cover the intangible expenses that are sometimes called *overhead*: general secretarial and clerical expenses not devoted exclusively to any one project, as well as operating expenses such as utilities and maintenance. Indirect costs are usually expressed as a percentage—ranging from less than 20 percent to more than 100 percent—of direct costs.

Appendices

Many types of appendices might accompany a proposal. Most companies have boilerplate descriptions of their organizations and of other projects they have completed. Another popular appendix is the supporting letter: a testimonial to the supplier's skill and integrity written by a reputable and well-known person in the field. Two other appendices deserve special mention: the task schedule and the description of evaluation techniques.

Task Schedule   The task schedule is almost always drawn in one of three graphical formats: table, bar chart, or network diagram.

Tables   The simplest but least informative way to present a schedule is in a table, as shown in Figure 16.5. As with all graphics, provide a textual reference that introduces and, if necessary, explains the table.

Although displaying information in a table is better than writing it out in sentences, readers still cannot "see" the information. They have to read it to figure out how long each activity will take, and they cannot tell whether any of the activities are interdependent. They have no way of determining what would happen to the overall project schedule if one of the activities faced delays.

Bar Charts   Bar charts, also called *Gantt charts* after the early twentieth-century civil engineer who first used them, are more informative than tables. The basic bar chart shown in Figure 16.6 on page 418 allows readers to see how long each task will take and when different tasks occur simultaneously. Like tables, however, bar charts do not indicate the interdependency of tasks.

 On TechComm Web

To see a tutorial on using Microsoft Excel to create a Gantt chart, click on Links Library for Ch. 16 on <bedfordstmartins .com/techcomm>.

■ **Figure 16.5   Table**

TASK SCHEDULE

Activity	Start date	Finish date
Design the security system	4 Oct. 06	19 Oct. 06
Research available systems	4 Oct. 06	3 Jan. 07
Etc.		

TECH TIP

How to Create a Gantt Chart

You can create a simple **Gantt chart** using the **Table** feature in Word.

1. Create a table with enough cells to include your tasks and dates.

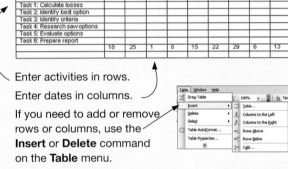

Enter activities in rows.

Enter dates in columns.

If you need to add or remove rows or columns, use the **Insert** or **Delete** command on the **Table** menu.

2. To create cells that span several columns, select the cells you wish to merge and then select **Merge Cells** on the **Table** menu.

To create column headings and horizontal bars, merge cells.

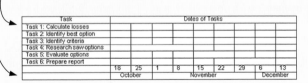

3. To differentiate completed tasks (black bars) from tasks yet to be completed (gray bars) or to hide borders, select the cells you wish to modify and then choose **Borders and Shading** on the **Format** menu.

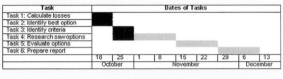

The **Borders** tab allows you to hide borders of selected cells.

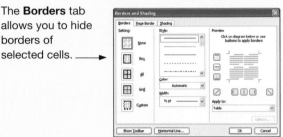

The **Shading** tab allows you to shade selected cells.

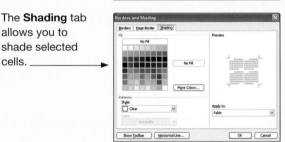

KEYWORDS: Table, cells, merge cells, borders, shading

On TechComm Web

To create Gantt charts, you can use a spreadsheet program such as Excel. See the Preparing Effective Charts and Graphs Tutorial on <bedfordstmartins .com/techcomm>.

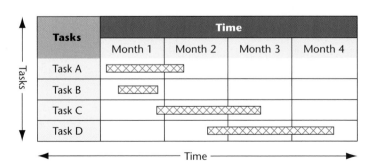

■ **Figure 16.6** **Bar Chart**
Source: SmartDraw.com, 2004 <www.smartdraw.com/tutorials/gantt/tutorial1.htm#what>.

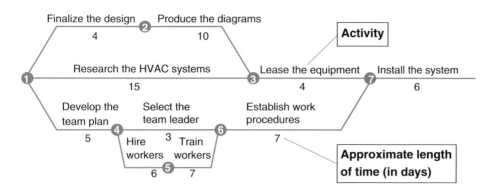

Network Diagrams   Network diagrams show interdependence among various activities, clearly indicating which activities must be completed before others can begin. Even the relatively simple network diagram shown in Figure 16.7 can be difficult to read. You would probably not use this type of diagram in a document intended for general readers.

Description of Evaluation Techniques   *Evaluation* can mean different things to different people, but an *evaluation technique* typically refers to any procedure used to determine whether the proposed program is both effective and efficient. Evaluation techniques can range from simple progress reports to sophisticated statistical analyses. Some proposals call for evaluation by an outside agent, such as a consultant, a testing laboratory, or a university. Other proposals describe evaluation techniques that the supplier itself will perform, such as cost-benefit analyses.

The issue of evaluation is complicated by the fact that some people think in terms of *quantitative evaluations*—tests of measurable quantities, such as production increases—whereas others think in terms of *qualitative evaluations*—tests of whether a proposed program is improving, say, the workmanship of a product. And some people include both qualitative and quantitative testing when they refer to evaluation. An additional complication is that projects can be tested while they are being carried out (*formative evaluations*) as well as after they have been completed (*summative evaluations*).

When an RFP calls for "evaluation," experienced proposal writers contact the sponsoring agency's representatives to determine precisely what the word means.

SAMPLE INTERNAL PROPOSAL

The following example of an internal proposal (Bethke, Cowles, Frachiseur, and Stoffel, 2004) has been formatted as a memo rather than as a formal proposal. (See Chapter 17, page 441, for the progress report written after this project was under way and Chapter 18, page 475, for the completion report.)

FOUR SQUARE WOODWORKING

P.O. Box 1966   (208) 440-1056
Eagle, ID 83616   foursquare@cableone.net

Memo

An effective subject line indicates the purpose ("proposal") and the subject of the memo ("feasibility study on table-saw capability").

Date: October 17, 2004
To: Chris Bethke, Shop Foreman
From: David Bethke, Steve Cowles, Amy Frachiseur, and Justin Stoffel
Subject: Proposal for Feasibility Study on Table-Saw Capability

Purpose

Memos of more than one page should begin with a clear statement of purpose and a summary.

The purpose of our proposal is to request authorization and funding to study whether repairing or replacing our existing table saw would reduce unnecessary labor and wasted materials and improve safety conditions in the shop.

Summary

The background of the problem.

Four Square Woodworking has a reputation for high-quality products and efficient customer service. We pride ourselves on our ability to make custom furniture and decorative trim. However, such flexibility is time-consuming. As you know, our shop has become quite successful in this past fiscal year. The number of estimate inquiries we received was 15% above 2003's total. We filled *three times* the orders in fiscal year 2004 as we did in 2003 (see Figure 1 on page 2).

The problem at the heart of the project.

As you know, in a shop with 20 employees, efficiency is even more important under this increased workload. Unfortunately, our table saw is now almost ten years old, and its age is beginning to show. Our woodworkers spend extra time adjusting and readjusting the saw to achieve precise cuts and repairing wood marred by the saw. Some wood is ruined and must be discarded. And we almost had a serious accident last month, a close call that would not have happened with a safer saw.

The proposal. Note that the writers have already planned what they will do if the proposal is accepted.

Because of growing employee concern over the shop's table saw, we propose to research options for repairing or replacing it. We would begin by calculating the cost of extra labor and ruined wood related to our table saw and identifying our options for addressing the table-saw problem. Next, we would establish necessary and desirable criteria for evaluating table saws, research available table-saw options, and evaluate these options according to our criteria.

A summary of the schedule, the budget, and the credentials of the writers.

To perform this research and present a report on our findings, we estimate that we would require 40 hours over the next eight weeks, for a total cost of $600. Our research team would consist of shop assistants David Bethke, Steve Cowles, and Justin Stoffel, as well as technical-communication intern Amy Frachiseur.

Memo to Mr. Chris Bethke
October 17, 2004
Page 2

If you accept this proposal, we would begin immediately, submitting to you a progress report on November 1, 2004, and a completion report on December 13, 2004. The completion report would include the details of our research and a recommendation for addressing our table-saw problem.

Introduction

We are seeking approval for a project to study whether repairing or replacing our existing table saw would reduce unnecessary labor and wasted materials as well as improve the shop's safety conditions. This proposal is based on growing concerns over the safety and effectiveness of our current table saw.

The introduction begins with a clear statement of the two aspects of the problem: financial and safety.

As Figure 1 shows, our workload has increased nearly threefold in the last year. We are very proud of all of our work, especially our scrollwork antique-replica dining chairs and exterior gingerbread trim. Unfortunately, this detailed work takes quite a lot of time. We have found that the time needed to produce this work is growing longer and longer as our ten-year-old table saw is growing older. At times, lines form as our co-workers wait to use it.

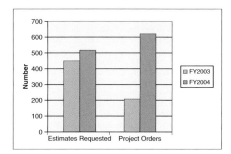

Figure 1.   Estimates Requested and Project Orders
for FY 2003 Compared to FY 2004

The bar graph helps the writers show that as the saw becomes less effective, the company needs to use it more.

Although our sales have been on the rise, so has the level of danger in the shop. Nearly half of all woodworking injuries happen at a table saw (*Tablesaw Safety*, n.d.). Last month, after a power outage, the table saw powered up unexpectedly. Jo Bucket came within a few inches of losing a hand. Newer saws have magnetic safety switches that automatically cut the power to the saw after an outage. Jo's near miss was very disturbing to all of us, reinforcing our concern about the outmoded safety features on our table saw.

In describing their safety concerns, the writers show that they have already begun to research the problem.

In addition to safety concerns, our current table saw's bearings are wearing out, causing excessive deflection of the blade and occasional binding of the lumber. These problems

Memo to Mr. Chris Bethke
October 17, 2004
Page 3

increase the time spent adjusting the saw, waiting to use the saw, and fixing mistakes caused by improper cuts and saw marks. The shop also loses money each month due to wood severely damaged or ruined by the saw.

The introduction concludes with an advance organizer for the rest of the proposal.

We propose to study options for improving our table-saw capabilities. Our research will help our shop foreman determine whether we should take no action, repair our current table saw, or replace it. The following sections of this memo include the proposed procedure, the schedule, our qualifications, the proposed budget for the research, and the references.

By presenting the project as a set of tasks, the writers show that they are well organized. This organization by tasks will be used in the progress report (see p. 442) and the completion report (see p. 475).

Proposed Tasks

With your approval, we will perform the following tasks to determine the best solution to addressing our shop's table-saw problem.

1. *Investigate the extent of the problem by calculating unnecessary labor and wasted materials.*

The writers will start with primary research to determine the cost of the problem.

We will use the table-saw log to determine the number and type of cuts performed in 2003 and 2004. We will also collect data from the woodworker logs to calculate the number of hours spent finishing marred wood. Using this data, we will compare the time spent in 2004 with 2003 in the initial cutting and finishing of our pieces. We will use the shop's material inventory to calculate wasted materials.

2. *Identify our options for addressing this problem.*

The writers will define and describe their options.

We will consider the current condition of the table saw, the likelihood of its continued deterioration, the cost to repair it, as well as the costs and benefits of replacing it. We have already searched major woodworking journals such as *Woodworker's Journal* and *Fine Woodworking*, as well as tool catalogs. These resources suggest that there are several table-saw brands safer and more effective than our current saw, for less than $2,000. Consequently, we request authorization to consider saws retailing for up to $2,000. We will need to determine whether our shop's woodworkers will be best served by continuing to use our current table saw or whether we should invest in a newer and safer table saw.

The proposal sounds credible because the writers have already begun their secondary research.

3. *Identify the main criteria against which we will evaluate different saws.*

In a feasibility study, it is smart to determine your criteria first, before you study the options. The writers describe more of their research.

To help us determine the necessary and desirable criteria, we have already identified a few articles that discuss safety (*How to Buy*, 2003; *Tablesaw Safety*, n.d.) and important features to consider when selecting a table saw (Loganbill, n.d.; Strickland, n.d.; Strong, 2003; Wright, 2003). We will also distribute a questionnaire to shop employees and interview Nathan Abram, an expert woodworker. David Bethke has already spoken by phone with Nathan, who says he is happy to discuss our table-saw problem with us when we are ready.

4. *Research available table-saw options.*

After describing the criteria, the writers describe techniques they will use to identify their specific options.

Steve Cowles already has plans to attend the Portland Metropolitan Expo Center's Woodworking Show, October 22–24, on other shop-related business. He will use this

Memo to Mr. Chris Bethke
October 17, 2004
Page 4

opportunity to talk to experts at the show about table-saw options. The program from the conference lists the manufacturers, and the major ones will attend. We will also seek Nathan Abram's advice and visit at least three experts at local retail outlets to create a list of table-saw options.

5. *Evaluate saw options using our evaluation criteria.*
Using a point system and a scoring key that we will create for each criterion, we will compare saw options and calculate a numeric score for each table saw under consideration.

6. *Prepare a completion report.*
We will prepare a completion report that explains the table-saw problem, our research methods, and our findings. We will include information about our current table-saw situation, about how we established criteria, and about how we selected table saws to study. We will include our evaluations of table-saw options that shaped our conclusions and final recommendation. This report will be submitted to you by December 14, 2004.

Schedule

The following is a schedule of the tasks for the project.

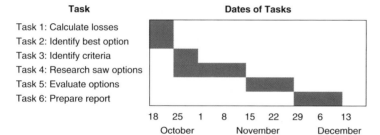

Task	Dates of Tasks
Task 1: Calculate losses	
Task 2: Identify best option	
Task 3: Identify criteria	
Task 4: Research saw options	
Task 5: Evaluate options	
Task 6: Prepare report	

18   25   1   8   15   22   29   6   13
October   November   December

Figure 2   Schedule of Project Tasks

Experience

We bring over twenty years of combined woodworking experience to the project:

- David Bethke has eight years of experience in furniture creation, specializing in intricate trim work; he helped to found Four Square Woodworking.
- Steve Cowles has five years of experience preparing and finishing wood; he spent three years in a lumber mill.

The writers state that they will evaluate each option against each criterion. This method will help them keep the analysis as objective as possible.

Preparing the completion report is part of the project.

Organizing the project by tasks makes it easy for the writers to present a Gantt chart.

Note that each task is presented with parallel grammar.

The creation of the Gantt chart is explained in the Tech Tip on p. 418.

The writers summarize their credentials.

Memo to Mr. Chris Bethke
October 17, 2004
Page 5

- Amy Frachiseur has four years of experience in woodshops; she is currently completing a degree in technical communication.
- Justin Stoffel has six years of experience in woodworking, four years of which were spent as a general contractor. He also has two years of experience as a sales representative for Craftsman power saws.

Budget

Following is an itemized budget for our proposed research.

Name	Hours	Hourly Rate	Cost
David Bethke	10	$15	$150
Steve Cowles	12	$15	$180
Amy Frachiseur	8	$15	$120
Justin Stoffel	10	$15	$150
		Total:	$600

References

How to Buy a Table Saw. (2003). Retrieved October 13, 2004, from http://www.rd.com/americanwoodworker/toolguide/HTB_Tablesaw.pdf

Loganbill, J. (n.d.). *Setting up a table saw & squaring crosscut devices*. Retrieved October 16, 2004, from http://thewoodshop.20m.com/calibrate_sled1.htm

Strickland, S. (n.d.). *Table saw tuneup*. Retrieved October 12, 2004, from http://www.puzzlecraft.com/Projects/HTMAP/07saw.htm

Strong, J. (2003). *Eyeing table saw specifications*. Retrieved October 9, 2004, from http://www.dummies.com/WileyCDA/DummiesArticle/id-2324.html

Tablesaw safety. (n.d.). Retrieved October 12, 2004, from http://www.woodmagazine.com/wood/story.jhtml?storyid=/templatedata/wood/story/data/333.xml&catref=wd25

Wright, D. (2003). *Choosing a tablesaw: Contractor or cabinet?* Retrieved October 15, 2004, from http://www.woodcentral.com/bparticles/con_vs_table.shtml

---

A simple budget makes it easy for readers to understand the cost of carrying out the research.

References provide the bibliographic data for sources cited in the proposal.

INTERACTIVE SAMPLE DOCUMENT
Analyzing an External Proposal

The author of the following sample proposal (Miner, 2002) works for a nonprofit organization that studies police-community relations. The proposal is addressed to a foundation that funds law-enforcement research and projects. The author is requesting $66,240 to carry out a research project. The questions in the margin ask you to think about some of the ways an external proposal differs from an internal proposal. E-mail your responses to yourself and/or your instructor, and see suggested responses on TechComm Web.

February 3, 2002

Mr. Hubert Williams, President
Law Enforcement Foundation
1001 23rd Street, NW, Suite 200
Washington, DC 20037

Dear Mr. Williams:

The Center for Urban Problems (CUP), as Washington's largest organization dealing with police-community relations, invites your investment in a $66,240 special project to improve community relations with minorities. We are encouraged that the Law Enforcement Foundation supports innovative projects that improve the delivery of police services. Over 85 percent of your grant dollars during the past three years have been invested at the local community level. Clearly, your support fills a valuable niche in light of the more conservative funding offered by the federal government. This strong commitment to unique projects is shared by the researchers and evaluation specialists at CUP.

The Problem: Spiraling Tensions. Despite proactive community relations programs, an unchecked tension exists between municipal police and minority community members. Relationships between law enforcement officers and minorities—Chicano, African American, Puerto Rican—are at a critical stage. One out of every three arrests in Washington, DC, currently involves a member of a minority community; the incidence is even higher in such cities as San Antonio, Kansas City, and Los Angeles.

Many factors contribute to the growing minority community–police tensions: increasing complexity of urban life, unemployment discrimination, and housing problems. Although these nationwide social problems were not created by the police, the police must cope with the consequences of these problems. This vast social dislocation spawns minority attitudes of prejudice and contempt. To counterbalance these problems, many police communities have adopted public relations programs to "sell" their departments to the minority communities without the concomitant need to be ready to work with those communities. As a result, there is an ever-widening gap between present and potential minority community acceptance of police behavior.

1. Beginning in the second sentence of this paragraph, the writer describes the reader's own organization. What is the function of this description?

2. The writer's description of the problem does not provide specific statistical evidence. Is this a weakness of the proposal, or is there a good reason for the lack of specifics?

3. At the end of the solution section, the writer refers to Attachment A, a task schedule. What are the advantages and disadvantages of attaching an appendix, compared with incorporating this information into the body of the proposal?

4. Assuming that the reader is not familiar with CUP (the writer's organization), how effective is this description of CUP in establishing its credentials?

 **On TechComm Web**

To e-mail your responses to yourself and/or your instructor and to see suggested responses, click on Interactive Sample Documents for Ch. 16 on <bedfordstmartins .com/techcomm>.

The Solution: Evaluating Police-Community Relations Bureaus. Successful claims regarding the effectiveness of police-community relations bureaus remain undocumented. Police departments are latching on to a new fad without understanding the key components of a police-community relations program. Some features of the bureau approach work; others don't. The goal of this project is to identify the successful features of existing bureaus, so that success can be delivered more quickly to police departments serving substantial numbers of minority citizens. The CUP research staff will follow standard social science research techniques as detailed in our time-and-task chart, Attachment A.

CUP Credentials: National Experience and Networks. CUP is uniquely suited to conduct this evaluation project on police-community relations bureaus. As a nonpolice-linked organization, it can objectively and independently assess current practices. This project represents a systematic continuation of prior CUP efforts in this area with state and municipal organizations as well as private police-related associations. Its staff has a cumulative 100 years of experience in evaluating police-related projects. Finally, local and national networking with 28 regional offices make it well postured to effectively conduct this assessment.

Budget Request: $66,240 Payable over Six Months. With the demonstrated concern that you've shown in the delivery of police services to minorities, I am requesting a grant of $66,240. Quite frankly, the project extends beyond the financial boundaries of CUP. Accordingly, we must now reach out to the community for assistance in what surely is a vital service to the police community. The outcome of this project will touch the operations of over 6,000 law enforcement groups nationwide, resulting in a $13 investment in each existing municipal and state police organization, or a cost of seven cents (7¢) per police official.

In making this investment, the Law Enforcement Foundation will be supporting a cost-effective approach to the delivery of police services for the minority communities where major problems exist. Mr. Lloyd Solomon, National Program Director for CUP, can be reached at (202) 123-4567 to answer questions or give further information.

Sincerely,

Carolyn Smith, President

P.S. Please come visit us and see this important project for yourself.

Enclosures:
Attachment A: Time-and-Task Chart
Attachment B: IRS Nonprofit Certification

Writer's Checklist

The following checklist covers the basic elements of a proposal. Guidelines established by the recipient of the proposal should take precedence over these general suggestions.

Does the summary provide an overview of

☐ the problem or the opportunity? (p. 414)
☐ the proposed program? (p. 414)
☐ your qualifications and experience? (p. 414)

Does the introduction indicate

☐ the problem or opportunity? (p. 415)
☐ the purpose of the proposal? (p. 415)
☐ the background of the problem or opportunity? (p. 415)
☐ your knowledge of the professional literature? (p. 415)
☐ the scope of the proposal? (p. 415)
☐ the organization of the proposal? (p. 415)
☐ the key terms that will be used in the proposal? (p. 415)

☐ Does the description of the proposed program provide a clear, specific plan of action and justify the tasks you propose performing? (p. 415)

Does the description of qualifications and experience clearly outline

☐ your relevant skills and past work? (p. 416)
☐ the skills and background of the other participants? (p. 416)
☐ your department's (or organization's) relevant equipment, facilities, and experience? (p. 416)

Is the budget

☐ complete? (p. 417)
☐ correct? (p. 417)
☐ accompanied by an in-text reference? (p. 416)

☐ Do the appendices include the relevant supporting materials, such as a task schedule, a description of evaluation techniques, and evidence of other successful projects? (p. 417)

Exercises

 In This Book   For more about memos, see Ch. 14, p. 352.

1. **INTERNET EXERCISE** Study the National Science Foundation's Grant Proposal Guide (click on Links Library for Chapter 16 on <bedfordstmartins.com/techcomm>). What are the important ways in which this guide differs from the advice provided in this chapter? What accounts for these differences? Present your findings in a 500-word memo to your instructor.

2. **INTERNET/GROUP EXERCISE** Form groups according to major. Using *Commerce Business Daily* or *FedBizOpps,* find an RFP for a project related to your academic field (click on Links Library for Chapter 16 on <bedfordstmartins .com/techcomm>). Study the RFP. What can you learn about the needs of the organization that issued it? How effectively does the RFP describe what the issuing organization expects to see in the proposal? Is the RFP relatively general or specific? What sorts of evaluation techniques does the RFP call for? In your response, include a list of questions that you would ask the issuing organization if you were considering responding to the RFP. Present your results in a memo to your instructor.

3. Write a proposal for a research project that will constitute a major assignment in this course. Your instructor will tell you whether the proposal is to be written individually or collaboratively. Start by defining a technical subject that interests you. (This subject could be one that you are involved in at work or in another course.) Using abstract services and other bibliographic tools, compile a bibliography of articles and books on the subject. (See Chapter 6 for a discussion of finding information.) Create a reasonable real-world context. Here are three common scenarios from the business world:

   • Our company uses Technology X to perform Task A. Should we instead be using Technology Y to perform Task A? For instance, our company uses traditional surveying tools in its contracting business. Should we be using GPS surveying tools instead?

   • Our company has decided to purchase a tool to perform Task A. Which make and model of the tool should we purchase, and from which supplier should we buy or lease it? For instance, our company has decided to purchase 10 multimedia computers.

Which brand and model should we buy, and from whom should we buy them?

- Our company does not currently perform Function X. Is it feasible to perform Function X? For instance, we do not currently offer day care for our employees. Should we? What are the advantages and disadvantages of doing so? What forms can day care take? How is it paid for?

Following are some additional ideas for topics:

- the need to provide legal file-sharing access to students
- the value of using the Internet to form ties with another technical-communication class on another campus
- the need for expanded opportunities for internships in your major
- the need to create an advisory board of people from industry to provide expertise about your major
- the need to raise money to keep the college's computer labs up-to-date
- the need to evaluate your major to ensure that it is responsive to students' needs

- the advisability of starting a campus branch of a professional organization in your field
- the need to improve parking facilities on campus
- the need to create or improve organizations for minorities or women on campus

These topics can be approached from different perspectives. For instance, the first one—providing file-sharing access to students—could be approached in several ways:

- Our college currently purchases journals but does not provide legal file-sharing access for students. Should we consider reducing the library's journal budget to subsidize legal file-sharing access?
- Our college has decided to provide legal file-sharing access for students. How should it do so? What vendors provide such services? What are the strengths and weaknesses of each vendor?
- Our college does not offer legal file-sharing access for students. Should we make it a goal to do so? What are the advantages and disadvantages of doing so?

Case 16: Selecting a Funding Source

 In This Book   For more about memos, see Ch. 14, p. 352.

Background

A seaside community, the city of Port Hueneme, California, is located in a fertile coastal plain. Year-round temperatures moderated by the ocean help the region produce as many as six fresh fruit and vegetable crops a year. You have just started work as a technical-communication intern at the Port Hueneme Discovery Center, an interactive science center. Focusing on the region's natural resources, the center's mission is to provide educational opportunities that inspire lifelong learning and interest in science, math, and technology. Your role is to help the center write proposals to fund upcoming exhibits and educational programs.

"Near the end of her internship, Heather Blanchard, our last intern, started to research funding sources for our upcoming exhibit on saltwater intrusion," explains John Orr, the center's Exhibits and Education Director. "Saltwater intrusion is probably the most common and widespread contamination in aquifers, our source of groundwater wells and springs. When fresh water is withdrawn from the ground at a faster rate than it can be replenished, salt water from the ocean intrudes into the freshwater aquifer, resulting in our water supplies' becoming contaminated with salt water."

"I assume that saltwater intrusion could wreak havoc on our agricultural crops?" you ask.

"It already has. Although our water district has built water-diversion structures, spreading grounds, and distribution facilities to augment the natural recharge of our aquifers, the region still needs to combat seawater intrusion. We want to educate our visitors about saltwater intrusion. Unfortunately, Heather's internship ended before she could recommend a funding source. I'd like you to pick up where she left off."

"What work has already been accomplished?"

"Heather wrote a brief outline of our project to help focus her search for funding. After not having much success locating sources of state or federal dollars, she decided to take advantage of our 501-c-3 status and concentrate on private funding sources, especially those interested in environmental education" (Document 16.1).

"What does 501-c-3 indicate?" you ask.

"A 501-c-3 designation by the Internal Revenue Service indicates that an organization is both tax-exempt and non-profit. Such a designation helps the Discovery Center apply for funding from many private funding sources. Heather consulted *Environmental Grantmaking Foundations* and created profiles of four possible funding sources. I'd like you to take a look at the profiles and recommend which, if any, of the potential funders is a good match" (Document 16.2).

■ **Document 16.1**
Proposed Saltwater Intrusion Exhibit

Proposed Saltwater Intrusion Exhibit

Background
The overpumping of water in Ventura County, especially the Oxnard Plain, has caused the water levels in underground aquifers to drop well below sea level. As a result, seawater has intruded into underground basins and contaminated the groundwater used for everything from farming to drinking water.

Goals
1. To help Discovery Center visitors realize the nature and importance of groundwater to Ventura County, the state of California, and the nation
2. To help Discovery Center visitors understand the saltwater intrusion problem in Ventura County as well as possible solutions

Approaches
1. Provide Discovery Center visitors the opportunity to use a hand pump to draw drinkable water to the surface. Such an activity shows where drinkable water comes from and introduces the concept of an aquifer.
2. Use large samples of local bedrock with water seeping through to demonstrate how water percolates down through seemingly solid layers of rock and gravel.
3. Use transparent tubes filled with rock, sand, soil, gravel, and water in such a way that visitors can appreciate how aquifers can store and supply groundwater.
4. Construct a small-scale representation of a coastal plain with an adjacent body of salt water. Visitors can pump water from the coastal plain's aquifer and watch as salt water invades the groundwater supply.
5. Install four graphic panels describing the effect of saltwater intrusion and strategies for combating it.
6. Include bedrock drill samples taken around the Oxnard Plain so visitors can both see and touch the bedrock directly below their feet.

Cost
We estimate that the exhibit described above, exclusive of the drilling of the well, will cost approximately $40,000. We estimate drilling the well will cost $16,000.

■ **Document 16.2**
Profiles of Four Potential Funding Sources

Name: Phantom Creek Trust

Contact information: c/o Kathleen Gainter & Associates, P.O. Box 93312, Seattle, WA 98101-3312.

History and philosophy: Established in 1962 by George Moomey, founder of Crown Fisheries in Seattle, Washington. The foundation has one primary goal: to protect and restore the natural environment of the Pacific Coast, especially in the Pacific Northwest.

Interests: Funding priorities include projects that educate the public, support quality environmental education, foster sustainable agricultural policies and practices, protect aquatic resources, and protect environmentally sensitive areas.

Issues funded: Climate and atmosphere, biodiversity, endangered lands, agriculture, water, oceans and coasts, energy.

Activities funded: Direct action, education, media projects.

Funding analysis:

	FY 2004	FY 2005
Environmental grants authorized	$5,297,101	$5,843,390
Number	108	129
Award range	$3,000–$205,000	$2,500–$1,000,000
Median award	$55,000	$55,000

Sample grants: *Kooskooskie Commons* ($20,000), bring together local farming, environmental, and business organizations to focus on restoration of salmon habitat and stream flows in the Walla Walla River; *Ecological Awareness Resources* ($62,000), planning and implementation of an ecosystem-wide K–12 environmental educational plan for the Seattle, Washington, area.

Emphases: Educational institutions, nonprofit organizations, advocacy, Pacific Northwest, environmental education, special projects.

Restrictions: No individuals.

Name: Faria Family Foundation

Contact information: Joe Faria, Program Director, 7634 PCH, Ventura, CA 93001.

History and philosophy: Established in 1967 by Joe Faria, a prosperous citrus farmer, this organization is committed to conserving California's freshwater supplies through voluntary actions, fostering sustainable use of our natural resource base, and conservation education targeting young people, educators, community leaders, and private landowners.

Interests: Support for water resources, environmental education excellence, and education on all levels.

Issues funded: Biodiversity, endangered lands, agriculture, water, oceans and coasts, energy, toxic substances.

Activities funded: Education.

Funding analysis:

	FY 2004	FY 2005
Environmental grants authorized	$2,730,000	$3,532,000
Number	43	52
Award range	$20,000–$80,000	$20,205–$80,000
Median award	$60,000	$60,000

■ Document 16.2
(continued)

Sample grants: The Tides Foundation ($61,000), develop and test a water-quality and pollution prevention–training package for students engaged in community-based service learning; *River Watch Network* ($55,000), assist communities in educating themselves about the connections between environmental contamination and public health and to develop water-quality monitoring tools.

Emphases: Educational institutions, nonprofit organizations, demonstration programs, education, innovative programs, training, special projects.

Restrictions: No individuals, no land acquisition, lobbying, litigation, basic research, annual campaigns, mortgage reduction, operating costs.

Name: Lorenzo Foundation

Contact information: Martha Gimigan, Director, 504 Pacific Avenue, San Francisco, CA 94133.

History and philosophy: Established in 1972, the Lorenzo Foundation is a private philanthropy interested primarily in the advancement and preservation of the governance of society by partici-pation in the democratic process, with protection of basic rights as provided by the Constitution and Bill of Rights.

Interests: Supports government accountability projects with respect to the environment, espe-cially public education and mobilization seeking to ensure that environmental laws and regulations are enforced.

Issues funded: Climate and atmosphere, biodiversity, endangered lands, water, toxic substances.

Activities funded: Advocacy, education, litigation, media projects.

Funding analysis:

	FY 2004	FY 2005
Environmental grants authorized	$393,180	$751,000
Number	11	27
Award range	$5,000–$65,000	$5,000–$120,000
Median award	$25,000	$20,000

Sample grants: Los Padres Biodiversity Project ($25,000), public education to help ensure U.S. Forest Service compliance with existing environmental laws and regulations; *Military Toxics Project* ($70,000), monitoring, education, and citizen organizing to investigate health effects of U.S. Department of Defense activities along Pacific Coast.

Emphases: Nonprofit organizations, special projects, action-oriented projects.

Restrictions: Not reported.

Name: National Organization for Environmental Education & Training

Contact information: Eugene Robertson, President, 50 Olive Street, Suite 128, Phoenix, AZ 85064.

History and philosophy: Established in 1998 by a dot-com venture capitalist and an active philanthropist who left most of his estate to the organization.

Interests: Watershed protection, conservation of natural resources, environmental education.

Issues funded: Endangered lands, water, agriculture, oceans and coasts.

Activities funded: Direct action, education, media projects, research.

■ **Document 16.2**
(continued)

Funding analysis:

	FY 2004	FY 2005
Environmental grants authorized	$6,225,000	$8,449,397
Number	7	11
Award range	$100,000–$5,000,000	$100,000–$5,000,000
Median award	$150,000	$300,000

Sample grants: *Upper Sespe Riverkeeper* ($200,000), expansion of watershed education programs; *National Fish and Wildlife Foundation* ($450,000), Coastal Plain Stewards Project to help private farmers manage land for wildlife as well as agriculture.

Emphases: Educational institutions, museums, nonprofit organizations, public agencies.

Restrictions: No individuals, no support for loans or operating costs.

Your Assignment

1. John Orr wishes to submit a proposal to one of the four funding sources profiled by Heather (Document 16.2). Write a memo to John Orr explaining which funding source would be most appropriate and why. If you feel that none of the profiled organizations is a good funding source for the saltwater intrusion exhibit, write a memo in which you explain your decision and recommend an alternative funding source.

2. Major funding sources often ask potential funding recipients to submit a brief *letter of inquiry* before submitting a full proposal. Outlining a program and its funding needs, this letter helps a funding source to determine whether it would be interested in the project and would like to receive a full proposal. Using strategies discussed in this chapter, as well as information you have learned about your recommended funding source, write a letter of inquiry.

Writing Informal Reports

TECH COMM AT WORK

People start writing informal reports almost as soon as they start work. An intern at the local newspaper might be asked to take minutes at a department meeting or contribute to the monthly status report for his department. A manager who wishes to communicate a new policy on reporting travel expenses will issue a directive in the form of an e-mail or a memo. A chemist will give her supervisor a report summarizing the findings of her research on whether the department should invest in a new spectrophotometer. Throughout your career, you will write hundreds of informal reports.

A report is a statement—oral or written—that helps listeners or readers understand, analyze, or take action on some situation or idea. This book classifies reports into two categories: formal and informal. This chapter discusses informal reports; Chapter 18 discusses formal reports.

Informal reports cover many subjects, have many purposes, and take many forms. Although an informal report is a routine communication about an everyday matter, it can be very important. An incident report written by police officers at the scene of an automobile accident might have enormous implications for many people.

In This Book

For more about e-mails, memos, and letters, see Ch. 14.

Informal reports can be communicated orally or as one of five kinds of documents:

- *E-mails.* E-mails are increasingly popular because they are easy to distribute and can be revised and pasted into another document.
- *Memos.* Memos are relatively informal documents used for communicating with other people in the same organization. They can range from less than a page to as long as 10 pages or more.
- *Forms.* Routine informal reports are often written or typed on preprinted forms or on templates on a computer.
- *Letters.* Letters are preferred when writer and readers work at different organizations.
- *Reports.* Some companies prefer that all reports, formal and informal, include the document elements associated with formal reports, including transmittal letters, title pages, and tables of contents.

UNDERSTANDING THE PROCESS OF WRITING INFORMAL REPORTS

Writing informal reports involves the same process used in most other kinds of technical communication. Figure 17.1 outlines the process of writing informal reports.

Analyze Your Audience

In some cases, it is easy to identify your audience and purpose. For instance, meeting minutes are addressed to all the members of the committee or department. In other cases, determining your audience is not as easy. For example, you might be reporting on an accident on the job. To whom should you address the report: Your direct supervisor? Your direct supervisor and others? Once you have identified your audience, analyze their knowledge of the subject, their attitudes toward it, and how they will use the information. See Chapter 5 for more information on audience.

Analyze Your Purpose

What is your purpose: To describe what happened? To recommend some course of action? In this situation, you need to analyze your purpose just as carefully as you would for any other kind of document. See Chapter 5 for more information on purpose.

Research the Subject and Compile Your Information

Sometimes assembling information is as simple as printing a file. Other times it requires sophisticated information-gathering techniques using primary and secondary research. See Chapter 6 for more about research methods.

Choose an Appropriate Format

The most common formats for informal reports are e-mails and memos. In some organizations, covers, title pages, and other elements usually associated with more-formal reports are used for all reports. Therefore, the choice of format is often determined by your organization, as well as by your audience and purpose.

Draft the Report

For routine reports, you can sometimes use sections of previous reports. In a status report, for instance, you can copy the description of your current project from the previous report and then update it as necessary. This reuse of information is ethical. Some informal reports are drafted on-site. For instance, an engineer might use a hand-held computer to "draft" an informal report as she walks around a site.

Revise, Edit, and Proofread the Report

Informal does not mean careless.

■ **Figure 17.1   An Overview of the Process for Writing Informal Reports**

Types of informal reports:

Directives

Field and lab reports

Progress and status reports

Incident reports

Meeting minutes

WRITING DIRECTIVES

In a *directive,* you explain a policy or a procedure you want your readers to follow. Even though you have the authority to require your readers to follow the new policy, you want to explain why the policy is desirable or at least necessary. As discussed in Chapter 8, you are most persuasive when you present clear, compelling evidence (in the form of commonsense arguments, numerical data, and examples); when you consider opposing arguments effectively; and when you present yourself as cooperative, moderate, fair-minded, and modest. If appropriate, include arguments that appeal to your readers' broader goals of security, recognition, and personal and professional growth.

Figure 17.2 is an example of a directive.

Quimby Interoffice

Date: March 19, 2006
To: All supervisors and sales personnel
From: D. Bartown, Engineering
Subject: Avoiding Customer Exposure to Sensitive Information Outside Conference Room B

Recently I have learned that customers meeting in Conference Room B have been allowed to use the secretary's phone directly outside the room. This practice presents a problem: the proposals that the secretary is working on are in full view of the customers. Proprietary information such as pricing can be jeopardized unintentionally.

In the future, would you please escort any customers or non-Quimby personnel needing to use a phone to the one outside the Estimating Department? Thanks very much.

The writer begins with a clear explanation of the problem the directive addresses. Presenting the reasons for the new policy shows respect for the readers and therefore makes the directive more persuasive.

The writer's polite but informal tone throughout the memo is likely to motivate readers to cooperate. Notice the use of "please" and "thanks" in the second paragraph.

■ Figure 17.2   A Directive

WRITING FIELD AND LAB REPORTS

A common kind of informal report describes inspections, maintenance, and site studies. This type of report, often known as a *field report* or *lab report*, explains the problem, methods, results, and conclusions, but it deemphasizes the methods and may include recommendations. The report in Figure 17.3 illustrates possible variations on this standard report structure.

LOBATE CONSTRUCTION
3311 Industrial Parkway
Speonk, NY 13508

Quality Construction Since 1957

April 11, 2006

Ms. Christine Amalli, Head
Civil Engineering
New York Power
Smithtown, NY 13507

Dear Ms. Amalli:

We are pleased to report the results of our visual inspection of the Chemopump after Run #9, a 30-day trial on Kentucky #10 coal.

The inspection was designed to determine if the new Chemopump is compatible with Kentucky #10, the lowest-grade coal that you anticipate using. In preparation for the 30-day test run, the following three modifications were made by your technicians:

• New front-bearing housing buffer plates of tungsten carbide were installed.
• The pump-casting volute liner was coated with tungsten carbide.
• New bearings were installed.

Our summary is as follows. A number of small problems with the pump were observed, but nothing serious and nothing surprising. Normal break-in accounts for the wear. The pump accepted the Kentucky #10 well.

The following four minor problems were observed:

• The outer lip of the front-end bell was chipped along two-thirds of its circumference.
• Opposite the pump discharge, the volute liner received a slight wear groove along one-third of its circumference.
• The impeller was not free-rotating.
• The holes in the front-end bell were filled with insulating mud.

The following three components showed no wear:

• 5½" impeller
• suction neck liner
• discharge neck liner

■ **Figure 17.3**
A Field Report

Because the writer and the reader work for different companies, the letter is the appropriate format for this brief informal report.

The word visual *describes the methods.*

The writer states the purpose of the inspection.

This writer has chosen to incorporate the words summary *and* conclusion *in the body of the letter rather than use headings as a method of organization.*

■ **Figure 17.3** *(continued)*

page 2

Our conclusion is that the problems can be attributed to normal break-in for a new Chemo-pump. The Kentucky #10 coal does not appear to have caused any extraordinary problems. In general, the new Chemopump seems to be operating well.

We would recommend, however, that the pump be modified as follows:

1. Replace the front-end bell with a tungsten carbide-coated front-end bell.
2. Replace the bearings on the impeller.
3. Install insulation plugs in the holes in the front-end bell.

Further, we recommend that the pump be reinspected after another 30-day run on Kentucky #10.

The writer concludes politely.
If you have any questions, or would like to authorize these modifications, please call me at 555-1241. As always, we appreciate the trust you have placed in us.

Sincerely,

Marvin Littridge
Director of Testing and Evaluation

Guidelines

Responding to Readers' Questions in a Field or Lab Report

Be sure to answer the following questions:

- What is the purpose of the report?

- What are the main points covered in the report?

- What were the problems leading to the decision to perform the procedure?

- What methods were used?

- What were the results?

- What do the results mean?

- What should be done next?

WRITING PROGRESS AND STATUS REPORTS

 In This Book

For more about proposals, see Ch. 16. For more about completion reports, see Ch. 18.

A *progress report* describes an ongoing project. A *status report,* sometimes called an *activity report,* describes the entire range of operations of a department or division. For example, the director of marketing for a manufacturing company might submit a monthly status report.

A progress report is an intermediate communication between the proposal (the argument that a project be undertaken) and the completion report

Ethics Note

Reporting Your Progress Honestly

Withholding bad news is unethical because it can mislead readers. As sponsors or supervisors of a project, readers have a right to know how it is going. If you find yourself faced with any of the following three common problems, consider responding in these ways:

- *The deliverable—the document or product you will submit at the end of the project—won't be what you thought it would be.* Without being defensive, describe the events that led to the situation and explain how the deliverable will differ from what you described in the proposal.

- *You won't meet your schedule.* Explain why you are going to be late and state when the project will be complete.

- *You won't meet the budget.* Explain why you need more money and state how much more you will need.

(the comprehensive record of a completed project). A progress report lets you check in with your audience.

Regardless of how well the project is proceeding, explain clearly and fully what has happened and how it will affect the overall project. Your tone should be objective, neither defensive nor casual. Unless ineptitude or negligence caused the problem, you're not to blame. Regardless of the news you are delivering—good, bad, or mixed—your job is the same: to provide a clear and complete account of your activities and to forecast the next stage of the project.

When things go wrong, you might be tempted to cover up problems and hope that you can solve them before the next progress report. This course of action is unwise and unethical. Chances are that problems will multiply, and you will have a harder time explaining why you didn't alert your readers earlier.

Organizing Progress and Status Reports

The time pattern and the task pattern, two organizational patterns frequently used in progress and status reports, are illustrated in Figure 17.4 on page 440. A status report is usually organized according to task; by its nature, a status report covers a specified time period.

Concluding Progress and Status Reports

In the conclusion of a progress or status report, evaluate how the project is proceeding. In the broadest sense, there are two possible messages: things are going well, or things are not going as well as anticipated.

In the time pattern, you describe all the work that you have completed in the present reporting period and then sketch in the work that remains. Some writers include a section on present work, which enables them to focus on a long or complex task still in progress.

The time pattern	The task pattern
Discussion	Discussion
A. Past Work	A. Task 1
B. Future Work	1. Past work
	2. Future work
	B. Task 2
	1. Past work
	2. Future work

The task pattern allows you to describe, in order, what has been accomplished on each task. Often a task-oriented structure incorporates the chronological structure.

■ **Figure 17.4   Organizational Patterns in Progress and Status Reports**

Guidelines

Projecting an Appropriate Tone in a Progress or Status Report

▶ **If the news is good, convey your optimism but avoid overstatement.**

OVERSTATED   We are sure the device will do all that we ask of it and more.

REALISTIC   We expect that the device will perform well and that, in addition, it might offer some unanticipated advantages.

Beware of promising early completion. Such optimistic forecasts rarely prove accurate, and it is always embarrassing to have to report a failure to meet the optimistic deadline.

▶ **Don't panic if the preliminary results are not as promising as you had planned or if the project is behind schedule.** Even the best-prepared proposal writers cannot anticipate all problems. As long as the original proposal was well planned and contained no wildly inaccurate computations, don't feel responsible. Just do your best to explain unanticipated problems and the status of the project. If your news is bad, give the reader as much time as possible to deal with it effectively.

On TechComm Web

To see another sample progress report, for a study on American Sign Language, click on Links Library for Ch. 17 on <bedfordstmartins .com/techcomm>.

Find other samples of progress reports at Writing Guidelines for Engineering and Science Students. Click on Links Library for Ch. 17 on <bedfordstmartins .com/techcomm>.

If appropriate, use appendices for supporting materials such as computations, printouts, schematics, diagrams, tables, or a revised task schedule. Be sure to cross-reference these appendices in the body of the report, so that readers can find them easily.

Sample Progress Report

The following progress report (Bethke, Cowles, Frachiseur, and Stoffel, 2004) was written for the project proposed on pages 420–24 in Chapter 16. (The completion report for this study begins on page 475 in Chapter 18.)

FOUR SQUARE WOODWORKING

P.O. Box 1966   (208) 440-1056
Eagle, ID 83616   foursquare@cableone.net

Memo

Date: November 1, 2004
To: Chris Bethke, Shop Foreman
From: David Bethke, Steve Cowles, Amy Frachiseur, and Justin Stoffel
Subject: Progress Report for Feasibility Study on Table-Saw Capability

The subject line and the purpose statement identify the purpose of the document: to report on progress.

Purpose
This is a progress report on our feasibility study on table-saw capability for Four Square Woodworking.

Summary
We have been researching whether repairing or replacing our existing table saw would improve the shop's safety conditions and reduce unnecessary labor and wasted materials. We have investigated our table-saw problem and identified our options for addressing this problem. We are researching table-saw options.

Our study is currently on budget and on schedule, and we expect to submit a completion report by the December 14 deadline noted in the proposal.

The summary briefly explains the purpose of the project and answers the question, "How is the project going, and will it be completed on schedule and under budget?"

Introduction
On October 18, we received approval of our proposal to study options for improving our table-saw capabilities. This proposal was based on growing employee concern over the shop's table saw. The results of this research will be presented in a completion report delivered to Chris Bethke, Shop Foreman, on December 14.

Because of Four Square Woodworking's reputation for high-quality work, the shop has experienced a threefold increase in projects in the last year. Unfortunately, our 10-year-old table saw has been unable to handle this increased workload. The saw's bearings are worn, resulting in increased time to adjust the blade for precision cuts and increased incidences of marred and wasted wood. The saw also lacks newer safety features. Jo Bucket's near miss while using the table saw reinforced our concern about the outmoded safety features on our table saw. The shop foreman asked us to study the problem and see whether we could propose a solution that costs no more than $2,000 in initial capital outlay.

Most of the information in the introduction is taken directly from the proposal. This reuse of text is ethical.

Results of Research
First we discuss the completed work: Tasks 1–3. Then we discuss our future work: Tasks 4–6.

The writers begin by describing the organization of the results section.

Completed Work

Task 1. Investigate the extent of the problem by calculating unnecessary labor and wasted materials.

The time spent ripping lumber, sanding out blade marks, and finishing dusty material, adjusted for the increase in workload from 2003 to 2004, grew by four hours per month per employee. For 20 employees, working for $15 per hour, it adds up to $1,200 per month. The cost of wasted materials, again adjusted for workload and type of product, is $200 per month. Collectively these losses amount to $1,400 per month.

Task 2. Identify our options for addressing this problem.

We considered three options:

- *Continuing to use the current saw without repairing it.* We immediately ruled out this option because it does not address the safety concerns and is costing the company more than $16,000 per year.
- *Repairing the current saw.* We ruled out this option because it does not address the safety concerns and because of what we learned from talking to representatives from table-saw repair services. We consulted with representatives of the two major repair services in the city—Appleby's Engine Repair and Modern Industrial Supply—as well as Craftsman, the manufacturer of our current saw. Both Ron Appleby of Appleby's and Harry Callanan of Modern told us that fixing a saw of that age is unwise. Also, the Craftsman representative said that the company would warranty only the bearings themselves and the labor for six months.
- *Replacing the current saw.* A quick look at major woodworking journals such as *Woodworker's Journal* and *Fine Woodworking* confirmed what we already knew: there are numerous brands and models superior to our current saw and available for less than our $2,000 budget. Consequently, we decided to focus our research on finding the best available table saw for our needs.

Task 3. Identify the main criteria against which we will evaluate different saws.

We distributed a questionnaire (see page 5) to shop employees asking them about how they use the table saw and what features would be important to them in a new saw. David Bethke then interviewed Nathan Abram, a well-known, award-winning woodworker and frequent contributor to several woodworking publications. We determined our necessary criteria. To be considered an option and for us to further evaluate it, a table saw will have to meet our necessary safety and cost criteria:

- *Safety.* Our primary technical question will be the following: does the saw incorporate the best safety features that currently exist? Three important safety features are identified in "How to Buy a Table Saw" (2003) in the *American Woodworker's Tool Buyer's Guide 2003*: a tool-free blade guard, an easy-to-access switch, and a magnetic switch that automatically cuts the power to the saw after an outage. Our insurance representative, James Mullen, added that effective antikick-back pawls that stay sharp, as well as an effective dust-collection system, are important safety features (personal communication, October 26, 2004). We want a saw with as many of these safety features as possible.
- *Cost.* We know that any solution we recommend will need to cost less than $2,000.

Next we determined four desirable criteria against which we will evaluate the different options.

The writers organize their discussion by task, as they did in the proposal.

These data will be presented again in the completion report.

This cross-reference to the questionnaire helps readers find the information quickly.

The writers have devised a logical approach: classifying the criteria into two categories, necessary and desirable. If a saw does not meet the necessary criteria, it will not be considered further.

Memo to Mr. Chris Bethke   November 1, 2004   Page 3

- *Power.* We want at least a 3 hp motor and prefer a 5 hp motor. Writing in *woodcentral.com*, David Wright (2003) suggests that cheaper saws with less powerful motors "make rough cuts, wear out quickly, don't hold their adjustments, and are more prone to dangerous kickbacks" (para. 2). In addition, a high-powered saw cuts more quickly, putting less strain on the motor. Although a 2 hp motor is adequate for a home woodshop, 3 or 5 hp motors can run all day (*How to Buy*, 2003).
- *Accuracy.* An accurate cut saves money because it reduces the need for hand-finishing and decreases the incidence of wasted materials. The size and material of a saw's table-top, for instance, are among the most important factors in determining a saw's accuracy (Strong, 2003). For an accurate cut, we considered the following characteristics:
  a. Fence length. A longer fence is better able to guide longer pieces of material. As our work is custom, we use many different sizes of boards. Because 100 percent of our woodworkers (see page 5) want the fence to be at least 50", we made that our preferred length.
  b. Blade height adjustment. Seventy-five percent of our woodworkers adjust the blade for precise height cuts at least 10 to 15 times a day (see page 5). Consequently, we place a high value on the saw's blade-height adjustment. The greater the number of turns of the handwheel required to adjust the blade height, the greater the precision. We want at least seven turns to full height.
  c. Vibration tendency. Excessive vibration in a saw can cause an improper cut. The vibration is directly related to the saw's weight: a heavier saw vibrates less. We want a saw weighing at least 500 pounds and with less than .001" vibration in any direction. We plan to use Strickland's (n.d.) easy measure of vibration when evaluating saws.
  d. Arbor run-out. The amount the blade moves from side to side as material is being fed through the table should be kept as small as possible to ensure accuracy. Loganbill (n.d.) recommends that the arbor run-out be less than .003".
- *Quality.* When evaluating the quality of a saw, we will consider the overall design and materials of the following components:
  a. Fence and extension table. Laminate material warps less and results in a more precise cut than other materials such as plastic. Seventy-five percent of questionnaire respondents preferred laminate material (see page 5).
  b. Splitter and guard. The operator needs to be able to see the cut and still be protected. Sixty percent of survey respondents preferred see-through plastic guards (see page 5).
  c. Trunnion. If the trunnion bolts are easy to reach, they are easier to adjust, which allows for less downtime.
  d. Dust-collection system. Dusty wood takes extra time to clean for finishing.
- *Ease of use.* We want to buy a saw that our woodworkers find easy to use. It is difficult to evaluate a saw's ease of use just by looking at pictures. For this criterion, we will visit local retail shops and ask one of our senior woodworkers, Andreas Luther, to perform a series of standard cuts using each saw being considered. We will then ask him to rate each saw's ease of use on a 10-point scale (1 very hard to use, 10 very easy to use).

Future Work
We are now at work on Task 4, researching available table-saw options.

Task 4. Research available table-saw options.
         Steve Cowles talked to experts at the Portland Metropolitan Expo Center's
         Woodworking Show (see page 6). Later this week, we will interview Nathan

Notice that the writers skillfully integrate their secondary research into their discussion of the criteria. By doing so, they enhance their credibility.

The primary research —based on the questionnaire distributed to the woodworkers —also enhances the writers' credibility by showing that they went to the trouble of finding out what their fellow employees want in a table saw.

Here the writers explain what they need to do to complete the project.

Again, the writers add a cross-reference.

Abram and visit experts at our three local retail outlets to complete our list of possible table-saw options.

Task 5. Evaluate saw options using our evaluation criteria.
We will compare available styles, brands, and models against our criteria. For each criterion, we will use a scoring key to aid us in assigning point values.

Task 6. Prepare a completion report.
We will prepare a completion report that explains the problem, the methods, and our findings. We will include detailed information about our current table-saw problem, about how we established criteria, and about how we selected table-saw options. We will include the comparisons of selected saws that helped define our recommendation. We will submit the completion report by December 14, 2004.

Updated Schedule
Black bars represent completed tasks; gray bars represent tasks yet to be completed.

Task	Dates of Tasks
Task 1: Calculate losses	
Task 2: Identify best option	
Task 3: Identify criteria	
Task 4: Research saw options	
Task 5: Evaluate options	
Task 6: Prepare report	

18   25   1   8   15   22   29   6   13
October   November   December

The Gantt chart shows the progress toward completing each of the project tasks. See the Tech Tip in Ch. 16, p. 418, for advice on how to create Gantt charts.

Conclusion
Our team has successfully completed Tasks 1–3 and begun Task 4. We are on schedule to complete Tasks 4–6 by the December 14 deadline. We have investigated our shop's table-saw problem, identified our options for addressing this problem, and determined necessary and desirable criteria for selecting a table saw. We are currently assembling a list of table-saw options. Next we will evaluate these options using our criteria. We will include our recommendation for addressing the shop's table-saw problem in the December 14 completion report.

The conclusion summarizes the status of the project.

Please contact David Bethke, extension 1220, if you have questions or comments.

The writers end with a polite offer to provide additional information.

References
How to buy a table saw. (2003). Retrieved October 13, 2004, from
 http://www.rd.com/americanwoodworker/toolguide/HTB_Tablesaw.pdf

Loganbill, J. (n.d.). *Setting up a table saw & squaring crosscut devices.* Retrieved October 16, 2004, from http://thewoodshop.20m.com/calibrate_sled1.htm

Strickland, S. (n.d.). *Table saw tuneup.* Retrieved October 12, 2004, from http://www.puzzlecraft.com/Projects/HTMAP/07saw.htm

Strong, J. (2003). *Eyeing table saw specifications.* Retrieved October 9, 2004, from
 http://www.dummies.com/WileyCDA/DummiesArticle/id-2324.html

Wright, D. (2003). *Choosing a tablesaw: Contractor or cabinet?* Retrieved October 15, 2004, from http://www.woodcentral.com/bparticles/con_vs_table.shtml

Memo to Mr. Chris Bethke   November 1, 2004   Page 5

Employee Questionnaire

This is a copy of the questionnaire we asked our shop's 20 woodworkers to complete. Their responses (in percentages) are included with each question.

Four Square Woodworking Table-saw Questionnaire

Directions: We are considering replacing our shop's current table saw. We would like your help in deciding which features we should consider when evaluating our replacement options. For each question, please circle only one option.

1. On which type of saw do you prefer to perform crosscutting, ripping, and grooving?
   A. Contractor **0%**   B. Hybrid **0%**   C. Cabinet **100%**

2. How many times *per week* do you make rip cuts?
   A. 0–5 **0%**   B. 6–10 **30%**   C. 11–15 **60%**   D. 16+ **10%**

3. Do you prefer a right tilt or a left tilt?
   A. Right **10%**   B. Left **90%**

4. What type of blade guard do you prefer on table saws?
   A. Steel **40%**   B. Plastic **60%**

5. What type of fence material do you prefer on table saws?
   A. Wood & laminate   **70%**
   B. Steel   **10%**
   C. Aluminum   **10%**
   D. Plastic/Teflon   **10%**

6. What type of material do you prefer for a table saw's extension table?
   A. Plywood & laminate   **30%**
   B. Particleboard & laminate   **30%**
   C. Melamine & MDF   **40%**

7. How large a fence system is necessary for your typical table saw?
   A. 24" **0%**   B. 30" **0%**   C. 40" **0%**   D. 50" **100%**

8. How many times *per day* do you estimate that you need to adjust the table saw's blade for precise height cuts?
   A. 1–5 **10%**   B. 6–10 **20%**   C. 11–15 **60%**   D. 16+ **10%**

Presenting the questionnaire — complete with the data it generated — enhances the writers' credibility.

Each question is designed so that it yields quantitative data. Notice that the writers present the data, a design that makes it simple for readers to understand the woodworkers' preferences.

This trip report also enhances the writers' credibility. For more information on memos, see Ch. 14, p. 352.

Memo

To: Chris Bethke, Shop Foreman
From: Steve Cowles, Shop Assistant
Subject: Portland Metropolitan Expo Center's Woodworking Show Trip Report
Date: October 26, 2004

This memo reports on my recent activities and findings while attending the Portland Metropolitan Expo Center's Woodworking Show on October 22–24, 2004. Attending the woodworking show in Portland, Oregon, allowed me to examine new table saws and ask experts for their recommendations on solving our table-saw problem.

Summary

Based on my talks with distributors for Craftsman, Delta, and Grizzly, as well as recommendations by expert woodworkers attending the show, I feel we should further investigate the Powermatic Model 66, Grizzly 1023SLX, Jet JTAS-10XL50-1, and Delta Unisaw 36-L31X-BC50 and ask for recommendations from our local retailers.

Findings

I was able to talk to the distributors for the Craftsman, Delta, and Grizzly brands. Each had its own selling points, but Delta seemed to have more of the characteristics that we are looking for. It had one of the stiffest fences that deflected only 1/64" at the arbor, built for heavy-duty use and designed to reduce assembly time.

Most of the other saws at the show were about the same. They all had deflecting guards from 1/64" to 3/64" at 20 pounds of pressure. All had problems with blade scoring, some less than others, but many manufacturers are in the process of fixing this problem.

Gerald, the Delta representative, had some very useful information from a recent comparison test; compared to the other brands at the show, the Delta 36-L31X-BC50 scored the highest ratings. The only drawback was the table extension length. The other representatives were all very impressive, but Gerald offered the most information. I concluded that his company backs the performance of its machines as well as it builds them.

I also asked David Hogg, Editor of *Popular Woodworking Magazine,* and Linda Oats, Host of *Tools & Techniques* on the DIY Network, for their recommendations. David recommended the Powermatic Model 66, Grizzly G1023SLX, Jet JTAS-10XL50-1, and Delta Unisaw 36-L31X-BC50. Linda recommended the Powermatic Model 66, Jet JTAS-10XL50-1, and Bosch 4000.

Recommendation

We have a good list of table-saw options started. However, I'd like to ask some of the experts at our local retail shops for their recommendations as well. I trust their opinions, and they are familiar with the work we do at Four Square. With your permission, I'll schedule meetings with several of our local retailers.

WRITING INCIDENT REPORTS

An incident report describes events such as workplace accidents, health or safety emergencies, and equipment problems. (Specialized kinds of incident reports go by other names, such as *accident reports* or *trouble reports*.) The purpose of an incident report is to explain what happened, why it happened, and what the organization did—or is going to do—to follow up on the incident.

Figure 17.5 on page 448 is the executive summary from an accident report written after a dust explosion.

WRITING MEETING MINUTES

Minutes, an organization's official record of a meeting, are distributed to all those who belong to the committee or any other unit represented at the meeting. Sometimes minutes are written by administrative assistants; other times they are written by technical professionals.

In writing minutes, be clear, comprehensive, objective, and diplomatic. Do not interpret what happened; just report it. Because meetings rarely follow their agendas perfectly, you might find it challenging to provide an accurate record of the meeting. If necessary, interrupt the discussion to request clarification.

Do not record emotional exchanges between participants. Because minutes are the official record of the meeting, you want them to reflect positively on the participants and the organization. Figure 17.6 on page 449 is an example of an effective set of minutes.

 **In This Book**

For more about conducting meetings, see Ch. 4, p. 48.

U.S. Chemical Safety and Hazard Investigation Board

INVESTIGATION REPORT

The writer begins with a brief summary of the accident incident.

A January 29, 2003, dust explosion at the West Pharmaceutical Services, Inc., plant in Kinston, North Carolina, killed six workers and injured 38 others, including two firefighters.

The writer presents background information about the company's operations.

The Kinston facility manufactured rubber drug-delivery components such as syringe plungers, septums, and vial seals. Production operations included rubber compounding, molding, and extrusion. The rubber compounding process consisted of two separate production lines, each with a mixer, a mill, and batchoff equipment. Raw materials were prepared in another area of the plant.

The writer presents the main conclusion about what caused the accident.

The U.S. Chemical Safety and Hazard Investigation Board (CSB) determined that accumulated polyethylene dust above a suspended ceiling fueled the explosion. Because of the extent of damage to the Kinston facility, it was not possible to definitively determine the event that dispersed the dust or what ignited it.

The writer explains the root causes of the accident.

CSB determined the following root causes of the January 29 incident:

- West did not perform adequate engineering assessment of the use of powdered zinc stearate and polyethylene as antitack agents in the rubber batchoff process.
- West engineering management systems did not ensure that relevant industrial fire safety standards were consulted.
- West management systems for reviewing material safety data sheets did not identify combustible dust hazards.
- The Kinston plant's hazard communication program did not identify combustible dust hazards or make the workforce aware of such.

The writer summarizes the main recommendations presented in the report.

CSB makes substantive recommendations to West Pharmaceutical Services, Inc., to:

- Develop/revise policies and procedures for new material safety reviews, and safety reviews of engineering projects.
- Ensure that its manufacturing facilities that generate combustible dusts meet the requirements of National Fire Protection Association (NFPA) Standard 654.
- Improve hazard communication programs.

CSB recommends to the North Carolina Building Code Council that the State fire code be amended to require compliance with NFPA 654. Additionally, recommendations are made to the North Carolina Department of Labor, Occupational Safety and Health Division; North Carolina Code Officials Qualification Board; and Crystal, Inc.–PMC.

■ **Figure 17.5   Executive Summary from an Accident Report**
Source: U.S. Chemical Safety and Hazard Investigation Board, 2004 <www.csb.gov/completed_investigations/docs/CSB_WestReport.pdf>.

Robbins Junior High School
Weekly Planning Committee Minutes
Minutes of the February 14, 2006 Meeting

The meeting was called to order by Ms. De Grazia at 3:40 P.M. in the conference room. In attendance were Mr. Sipe, Ms. Leahy, Mr. Zaerr, Mr. Simon, and Principal Barson. Ms. Evett was absent.

In the title and the first paragraph, the writer records the logistical details of the meeting: name of the body that met, date, names of those attending, and so forth.

The minutes of the February 7, 2006, meeting were read. The following correction was made: In paragraph 2, "800 hours" was replaced with "80 hours." The minutes were then unanimously approved.

The writer records the reading, revision, and approval of the previous meeting's minutes.

There was one topic: authorization for the antidrug presentations by motivational speaker Alan Winston. Principal Barson reported on his discussion with Peggy Giles of the School District. She offered positive comments about Winston's presentations at other schools in the district last year. Principal Barson has also been in contact with the three other principals who invited Mr. Winston last year; they all spoke highly of his presentations.

The writer records the main topic of the meeting: the authorization of funding for a guest speaker.

Principal Barson moved that the committee authorize Winston's visit, to be scheduled in late May. The motion was seconded by Louis Simon.

Mr. Sipe asked whether the individual school or the district was to pay for the expenses (approximately $2,800) for the visit. Principal Barson replied that the school and the district would split the costs evenly, as had been done last year. The school has more than $4,000 surplus in operating expenses.

The writer records the action taken at the meeting.

Mr. Zaerr expressed serious concerns about the effect of the visit on the teaching schedule. The visit would disrupt one whole day for all three grades in the school. Principal Barson acknowledged this but replied that in his weekly meeting with department chairs earlier in the week, they gave their approval to the idea. Since student participation would be voluntary, teachers were to offer review sessions to those students who elected not to attend Winston's presentation.

The writer downplays an emotional exchange. She briefly explains the arguments made in a discussion but doesn't comment on angry exchanges or quote people.

There being no more discussion, Ms. De Grazia called for a vote on the motion. The motion carried 4–0, with one abstention.

Principal Barson asked the committee if they would assist him in planning and publicizing Winston's visit. The committee agreed. Ms. De Grazia asked if there was any new business. There was none.

The writer records the logistical details about how the meeting concluded.

Ms. De Grazia adjourned the meeting at 4:20 P.M.

Zenda Hill
Recording Secretary

■ **Figure 17.6   Set of Meeting Minutes**

INTERACTIVE SAMPLE DOCUMENT
Writing Meeting Minutes

The following set of minutes serves as the official record of a King County Fish and Wildlife Commission meeting on August 5, 2005. The questions in the margin ask you to think about the discussion of writing meeting minutes (on page 447). E-mail your responses to yourself and/or your instructor, and see suggested responses on TechComm Web.

1. How much care has the writer taken with the quality and accuracy of his writing?

2. Has the writer written minutes that reflect positively on the participants and the organization?

3. What are the functions of the boldfaced text and the action item in the body of the minutes?

 On TechComm Web

To e-mail your responses to yourself and/or your instructor and to see suggested responses, click on Interactive Sample Documents for Ch. 17 on <bedfordstmartins.com/techcomm>.

Attendance
Commission: Shirley Ozment, Chair, Fred Burkhart, Vice Chair, Miranda Tayer, Ken Solomon, John Kraege, and Mary Lou Frymire. **Commission staff:** Chris Beach. **Department:** Jeff Stone, Director, and Ryan Walker. **Public:** Brock Wagenaar.

Chair Ozment called the meeting to order at 10:05 A.M.

Approval of Minutes
Commissioner Burkhart moved, seconded by Commissioner Tayer, to approve minutes of July 7, 2005. The motion carried unanimously.

Director's Report
Director Stone reviewed significant Department issues and activities. Director Stone also presented Dr. Jim Loveless with the KCFWC 2005 Contributor of the Year award for his work on the sage grouse.

Budget Update
Director Stone discussed the status of the Department's budget.

Proposed Land Transactions
Ryan Walker presented two proposed land transactions for the Commission's consideration and approval.

Commissioner Frymire moved, seconded by Commissioner Ozment, to approve the following land transaction: Acquisition of the 2,362-acre W. K. Lilly property for a price not to exceed $850,000. The motion carried unanimously.

Amendment to Mandatory Report of Hunting Activity
Director Stone presented proposed permanent amendments to KAC 232-28-992, Mandatory Report of Hunting Activity, to encourage timely reporting that would allow the Department to develop accurate harvest estimates used to recommend the following year's permit levels and season adjustments. Commissioner Ozment asked, "Do you think this will help you get the permit numbers right this time?" Director Stone replied, "It's an inexact science." Commissioner Ozment didn't seem pleased by the response.

Commissioner Solomon moved, seconded by Commissioner Burkhart, to adopt the permanent amendments to KAC 232-28-992 as proposed. The motion carried unanimously, with only Commissioner Ozment dissenting.

Hunter Education Student Manual Development
Brock Wagenaar (Hunter Education instructor) briefed the commission on the development of a new hunter education student manual. Brock requested that Director Stone tell him the quantity to print no later than December 2006.

Action item: Jeff Stone

Amendments to Nontoxic Shot Requirements

Ryan Walker presented a proposed permanent amendment to KAC 232-16-505, Nontoxic Shot Requirements. No oral testimony of the proposed amendments was received during the meeting.

Commissioner Frymire moved, seconded by Commissioner Solomon, to adopt the permanent amendments to KAC 232-16-505 as proposed.

Chair Ozment adjourned the meeting at 11:20 A.M.
Respectfully submitted by Chris Beach, Commission Staff

Writer's Checklist

☐ Did you choose an appropriate format for the informal report? (p. 435)

Does the directive

☐ clearly and politely explain your message? (p. 436)
☐ explain your reasoning, if appropriate? (p. 436)

Does the field or lab report

☐ clearly explain the important information? (p. 437)
☐ use, if appropriate, a problem-methods-results-conclusion-recommendations organization? (p. 437)

Does the progress or status report

☐ clearly announce that it is a progress or status report? (p. 439)
☐ use an appropriate organization? (p. 439)

☐ clearly and honestly report on the subject and forecast the problems and possibilities of the future work? (p. 439)
☐ append supporting materials that substantiate the discussion? (p. 440)

Does the incident report

☐ explain what happened? (p. 447)
☐ explain why it happened? (p. 447)
☐ explain what the organization did about it or will do about it? (p. 447)

Do the minutes

☐ provide the necessary housekeeping details about the meeting? (p. 447)
☐ explain the events of the meeting accurately? (p. 447)
☐ reflect positively on the participants and the organization? (p. 447)

Exercises

 In This Book For more about memos, see Ch. 14, p. 352.

1. As the manager of Lewis Auto Parts Store, you have noticed that some of your salespeople smoke in the showroom. You have received several complaints from customers. Write a directive in the form of a memo defining a new policy: salespeople may smoke in the employees' lounge but not in the showroom.

2. Write a progress report about the research project you proposed in response to Exercise 3 on page 427 in Chapter 16. If the proposal was a collaborative effort, collaborate with the same group members on the progress report.

3. **INTERNET/GROUP EXERCISE** You are one of three members of the Administrative Council of your college's student association. Recently, the three of you have concluded that your weekly meetings have become chaotic, largely because you do not follow parliamentary procedure and because controversial issues have arisen that have attracted numerous students (the meetings are open to all students). You have decided that it is time to consider adopting some parliamentary procedures to make the meetings more orderly and more effective. Look on the Web for models of parliamentary procedure. Is there one that you can adopt? Could you combine elements of several to create an effective model? Find or put together a brief set of procedures, being sure to cite your sources. In a memo to your instructor, discuss the advantages and disadvantages of the model you propose and submit it along with the procedures.

Case 17: Revising an Injury Report Form

 In This Book   For more about memos, see Ch. 14, p. 352.

Background

"Did you know that more than 50 percent of the serious injuries to female athletes happen to cheerleaders?" asks Joan Jacqua, the Clubs and Activities Coordinator for Acorn Valley Academy, a private, coeducational high school.

"I had no idea that cheerleading was so risky," Principal John Robinson responds.

"Cheerleading is no longer just pom-poms, megaphones, and high kicks. Cheerleading is gymnastics with stunts and tricks. Last year, more than twenty-five thousand cheerleaders were treated in emergency rooms for injuries to the ankle, shoulder, head, and neck. I just came from a meeting with Robin Dungan, our new cheerleading coach. She told me some of these statistics, and frankly, they scared me. She asked if we have a written emergency plan for what to do if a cheerleader is injured at practice or while cheering at an event."

"Do we?"

"Yes, we have detailed emergency plans for each of our clubs and athletic teams. These plans describe specific roles for each staff member or volunteer in case of emergency. However, according to Robin, we don't have a very good injury report form (Document 17.1). Robin looked at our current form and said that it doesn't encourage a standardized approach to providing all the necessary information about an injury. She thinks our injury form, even if completely filled out, won't meet the needs of everyone who reads or uses these reports."

"What do you think?" Principal Robinson asks.

"After looking at the form, I agree with Robin. These injury reports need to satisfy a diverse audience. The adage 'If you didn't write it down, you didn't do it' seems to apply here," Joan says.

"Asking advisers to 'give a full account' seems too broad. It would be helpful if the form prompted advisers to document specific information and details. In addition, the form needs to work not only for cheerleading but also for our other athletic teams and for clubs such as theater, chess, and science."

"I agree. I think this form should be revised."

"I'd like to have a revised injury report form ready for when parents and students attend our clubs and activities orientation at the start of next year. We might want to discuss the form at the orientation, or we might just want to go over the form at the first coaches and advisers meeting. I'm not sure. Would you ask one of our school volunteers with a background in technical communication to look into this situation and make some recommendations?"

Later that afternoon, Joan picks up the phone and dials your number.

Your Assignment

1. Write Joan a memo in which you describe the purpose of the injury report form, identify the audiences for the report, and describe each audience's needs.

2. Based on your analysis of the report's purpose and audience, redesign the academy's report form (Document 17.1). Attach a memo to Joan justifying your design choices and recommending who, if anyone, should review this form before it is finalized.

3. Write Joan a brief memo in which you recommend whether the injury report should be discussed at the student-parent orientation on Clubs and Activities Night. If you feel that it should be discussed with students and parents, justify your recommendation and explain which elements of the form should be addressed. If you feel that the form should not be discussed at the orientation, justify your recommendation and discuss how the form should be introduced to advisers and coaches.

■ **Document 17.1   Acorn Valley Academy's Injury Report Form**

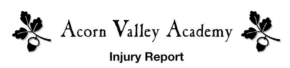

Acorn Valley Academy
Injury Report

Directions: Please type or write in block capitals using black ink.
Routing: Originator to Clubs and Activities Coordinator to Principal

Section I: Injured Student

Student's Name: _____

Address: _____

Phone:_____

Parent Day Phone #1: _____

Parent Day Phone #2: _____

Section II: Injury Details (to be completed by club or activity adviser)
In the space below, give a full account of the injury.

_____

_____

_____

_____

_____

_____

_____

_____

_____

Section III: Adviser's Contact Information

Adviser's Name: _____

Department: _____

Extension:_____

E-mail:_____

Section IV: Signature

Signature: _____

Date: _____

 On TechComm Web

For digital versions of case documents, click on Downloadable Case Documents on <bedfordstmartins.com/ techcomm>.

18 Writing Formal Reports

TECH COMM AT WORK

Professionals write formal reports almost as soon as they start work. An IT professional who has completed research into expanding the company's wireless services communicates her results in a report to her supervisors. An engineering team that has finished studying two alternative sites for locating a new bridge presents its recommendation in a report to the city planning and zoning commission that authorized the study. A manager of a health club presents quarterly sales information in a report to his supervisor. Reports are challenging to write because they often consist of different parts that are read by different audiences. For instance, one reader might be interested only in the executive summary, another only in the conclusions and recommendations. Writing a formal report is, therefore, an exercise in presenting technical information to a wide variety of audiences, each of which has its own purposes in reading the report.

A formal report can be the final link in a chain of documents that begins with a proposal and continues with one or more progress reports. This last, formal report is often called a *final report, project report,* or *completion report.* The sample document beginning on page 475 is the final report in the series about selecting a table saw. (The proposal appears in Chapter 16, and a progress report appears in Chapter 17.)

A formal report can also be a freestanding document, one that was not preceded by a proposal or by progress reports. For instance, you might be asked to research employee attitudes toward comp time: compensating employees who work overtime with time off rather than with overtime pay. This task would call for you to research the subject and write a single complete report.

In This Book

For more about proposals, see Ch. 16. For more about progress reports, see Ch. 17, p. 438.

UNDERSTANDING THE TYPES OF FORMAL REPORTS

One challenge in talking about reports is that there is no standard terminology. Some terms refer to the topic of the report (*environmental-impact statement, lab report*), some to the phase of the investigation (*progress report, annual report*), and some to the function or purpose of the report (*informational report, analytical report*). Some terms have special meanings in particular fields and in particular organizations. When you are asked to write a report, talk to more-experienced people before you begin.

This section describes three kinds of reports, classified according to their main purpose.

On TechComm Web

See Business Communication: Managing Information and Relationships. Click on Links Library for Ch. 18 on <bedfordstmartins.com/ techcomm>.

Informational Report: | Presents results

Analytical Report: | Presents results + draws conclusions

Recommendation Report: | Presents results + draws conclusions + makes recommendations

Informational Reports

An informational report presents facts, often referred to as *results*, to help readers understand a situation. For instance, the circulation department at a library might present an informational report to its planning board, communicating the number of patrons who visit the library, the kinds of items they borrow, the number and kinds of items the library purchases, the number and kinds of items stolen, and so forth.

In This Book

For more about status reports, see Ch. 17, p. 438.

Here are examples of the kinds of questions an informational report addresses:

- *What is the status of Project X?* What is the status of the project to reinforce the levees on the river?
- *How do we do Function X?* What quality-control procedures do we use for the laptops we manufacture?
- *What are the most popular ways of doing Function X?* What is the ratio of surgical to laser operations for treating gallstones in the United States?
- *What do our people think of Situation X?* How satisfied are our employees with our medical benefits?

An informational report usually involves the primary- and secondary-research techniques discussed in Chapter 6, including using the library and the Internet, conducting interviews, and distributing questionnaires.

Analytical Reports

Like informational reports, analytical reports provide information, but then they analyze it and present conclusions. A *conclusion* is an interpretation of the results. For instance, in writing the report to the planning board of the library, the staff in the circulation department might present all the statistics but emphasize that thefts of CDs have increased substantially. With further analysis, the writers might conclude why some types of media are stolen more than others. An analytical report, therefore, tries to describe *why* something happens, *how* it happens, or *what it means*.

Here are some examples of the kinds of questions an analytical report addresses:

- *What is the best way to do Function X?* What is the most effective way to track manuscripts being edited by different people?
- *What causes Situation X?* Why is there a high turnover in the Information Systems Department?
- *What are the results of Situation X?* If we create a Web site for our company, how much can we expect business to increase?
- *Could we do Function X?* Do we have the infrastructure to compete with Company A in bidding on these government contracts?

Analytical reports usually include an informational element. For instance, if you work for a software manufacturer, you might write an analytical report to explain why your customer-support costs are high. In the informational section—the results—you describe your customer-support costs, focusing on which products (and which aspects of them) are causing your customers the most problems. In the analytical section—the conclusion—you use these data to explain why customers encounter these problems.

 In This Book

For more about causal reasoning, see Ch. 7, p. 145.

Recommendation Reports

A recommendation report goes a step further than presenting information and analyzing it: it advocates a certain course of action. What is the difference between drawing conclusions and presenting recommendations? If your conclusion is that Product A meets our needs better than Product B or C, you might recommend that we buy Product A. But you also might recommend that we buy product B if it does 90 percent of what A does but costs only 50 percent as much.

Here are examples of the kinds of questions a recommendation report addresses:

- *What should we do about Problem X?* What should we do about the large number of calls to Technical Support?
- *Should we do Function X?* Although we cannot afford to reimburse tuition for all college courses our employees wish to take, can we reimburse them for classes directly related to their work?
- *Should we use Technology A or Technology B to do Function X?* Should we buy several high-output copiers or a larger number of low-output copiers?
- *We currently use Method A to do Function X. Should we be using Method B?* We sort our bar-coded mail by hand; should we buy an automatic sorter?

Organizational culture affects how reports are written. In some organizations, only certain people are authorized to draw conclusions and make recommendations. In other organizations, managers like to segment the report-writing process so that different groups work on results, conclusions, and recommendations. One group writes the informational report, and then hands the project over to a different group, which writes the analytical report. A third group writes the recommendation report. Each group, in effect, checks the work of the group or groups that preceded it. This method can reduce the chances that inaccurate or incomplete results are used to derive conclusions and that invalid conclusions are used to formulate unwise recommendations.

USING A PROBLEM-SOLVING MODEL FOR PREPARING FORMAL REPORTS

On TechComm Web

See NASA's guide to report writing. Click on Links Library for Ch. 18 on <bedfordstmartins.com/techcomm>.

Many writers find that a problem-solving approach helps them to put together an effective report. A problem-solving approach has six basic steps. Figure 18.1 on page 458 shows a basic problem-solving model.

■ **Figure 18.1**
An Overview of a
Problem-Solving
Model for Formal
Reports

Analyze Your Audience

Consider how well your readers know the subject and why they are reading the report. People who need only a general understanding of the subject need less information than people who need a detailed understanding (see Chapter 5). Consider the readers' attitudes toward the project, which might affect the organizational pattern, the amount of detail, and the vocabulary you choose (see Chapter 7).

Analyze Your Purpose

Think about why your readers requested it and what they are likely to do with it. Are you trying merely to answer questions for your readers, or are you trying to alter their beliefs or motivate them to take action? Before you proceed too far, make sure your principal reader agrees with your understanding of your purpose. (For information on doing so, see Chapter 5.)

Identify Questions That Need to Be Answered

If you are writing an informational report on library antitheft systems, here are a few of the questions you will likely consider:

- What are antitheft systems, what technologies do they use, what kinds of materials do they protect, and how effective are they?
- What have been the experiences of libraries like ours that have used them?
- How easy is it to install and maintain the systems? How often do they break down?
- Do they pose any health risks?

State these questions precisely. "How do library antitheft systems work?" is too vague. "What different technologies are used in the library antitheft systems currently available?" is better because it is more specific. See Chapter 6.

Carry Out Appropriate Research

The questions you need to answer will determine the kinds of research you should perform. Often you will consult company records, interview people, distribute questionnaires, perform experiments, make observations, and consult books, journals, and Internet sources. Then you will analyze the information to be sure it is valid and current. See Chapter 6.

Draw Conclusions from the Research

Some kinds of evidence are more valuable than others. For example, benchmark tests by independent groups are more persuasive than claims from manufacturers about their own products. Look for a number of different kinds of evidence that all point to a causal relationship. See Chapter 8.

Formulate Recommendations Based on Conclusions

Often, your recommendation will flow directly from your conclusions. But sometimes other factors come into play. Your company might not have the funds to implement your recommendation, your company might have changed its priorities, or the problem might have changed. See the Ethics Note on page 463.

UNDERSTANDING FEASIBILITY REPORTS

One kind of recommendation report is written so often that it deserves special discussion. A *feasibility report* documents a study that evaluates at least two alternative courses of action. For example, should we expand our product line to include a new item? Should we make changes in an existing product?

A feasibility report is an argument that answers three kinds of questions:

- *Questions of possibility.* We would like to build a new rail line to link our warehouse and our retail outlet, but if we cannot raise the money, the project is not possible. Even if we have the money, do we have government authorization? If we do, are the soil conditions appropriate for the rail link?

- *Questions of economic wisdom.* Even if we can afford to build the rail link, should we do so? If we use all our resources on this project, what other projects will have to be postponed or canceled? Is there a less expensive or a less financially risky way to achieve the same goals?

- *Questions of perception.* If your company's workers have recently accepted a temporary wage freeze, they might view the rail link as unnecessary. The truckers' union might see it as a threat to truckers' job security. Some members of the public also might be interested parties because any large-scale construction might affect the environment.

The following discussion explains the six steps that are particular to preparing feasibility reports. Begin by analyzing your audience and purpose, as you would for any technical document. Then perform the following tasks.

Identify the Problem or Opportunity

What is not working, or not working as well as it might? What situation presents an opportunity for us to decrease costs or improve the quality of our product or service? Without a clear statement of your problem or opportunity, you cannot plan your research.

For example, your company's employees who smoke are absent and ill more often than those who don't. Your supervisor has asked you to investigate whether the company should offer a free smoking-cessation program. The company can offer the program only if the company's insurance carrier will pay for it. The first thing you need to do is talk with the insurance agent. If the insurance carrier will pay for the program, you can proceed with your investigation. If the agent says no, you have to determine whether another insurance carrier offers better coverage or whether there is some other way to encourage employees to stop smoking.

Establish Criteria for Responding to the Problem or Opportunity

Criteria are standards against which you measure your options. Criteria can take two forms: *necessary* and *desirable.* For example, if you want to buy a

On TechComm Web

For sample reports, see Writing Guidelines for Engineering and Science Students. Click on Links Library for Ch. 18 on <bedfordstmartins.com/techcomm>.

In This Book

For more about considering opposing viewpoints, see Ch. 8, p. 160.

To prepare a feasibility report:

Identify the problem or opportunity.

Establish criteria for responding to the problem or opportunity.

Determine the options.

Study each option according to the criteria.

Draw conclusions about each option.

Formulate recommendations based on the conclusions.

In This Book

For more about establishing criteria, see Ch. 7, p. 136.

photocopier for your business, necessary criteria might be that each copy cost less than two cents to produce and that the photocopier be able to handle oversize documents. If the photocopier doesn't fulfill those two criteria, you will not consider it further. Desirable criteria might include that the photocopier do double-sided copying and stapling. Desirable criteria let you make distinctions among a variety of similar objects, objectives, actions, or effects. If a photocopier does not fulfill a desirable criterion, you will still consider it, although it will be less attractive.

Until you can establish your criteria, you don't know what your options are. Sometimes you inherit your criteria; your supervisor tells you how much money you can spend, for instance, and that figure becomes part of your necessary criteria. Sometimes you derive your criteria from your research.

Determine the Options

After you establish your criteria, you determine your options. *Options* are potential courses of action you can take in responding to a problem or an opportunity. Determining your options might be simple or complicated.

Sometimes your options are presented to you. For instance, your supervisor asks you to study two vendors for accounting services and recommend one of them. The options are Vendor A or Vendor B. Simple.

In other cases, you have to consider a series of options. For example, your department's photocopier is old and breaking down. Your first decision: whether to repair it or replace it. Once you have decided that question, you have to make more decisions. If you are going to replace it, what features are you going to look for in a new one? Each time you make a decision, you have to answer more questions, until eventually you arrive at your final decision. For a complicated scenario like this, you might find it helpful to use logic boxes to sketch the logic of your options, as shown in Figure 18.2.

As you perform research, your understanding of your options will likely change. At this point, however, it is useful to at least understand the basic logic of your options or series of options.

Study Each Option According to the Criteria

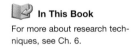
In This Book
For more about research techniques, see Ch. 6.

Once you have identified your options (or series of options), study each one according to the criteria. For the photocopier project, secondary research would include studying articles about photocopiers in technical journals and specification sheets from the different manufacturers. Primary research might include observing product demonstrations, as well as interviewing representatives from different manufacturers and managers who have purchased different brands.

To make the analysis of the options as objective as possible, investigators sometimes create a *matrix*, a method for systematically evaluating

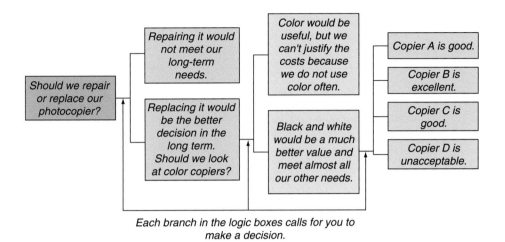

Each branch in the logic boxes calls for you to
make a decision.

■ **Figure 18.2   Using Logic Boxes to Plot a Series of Options**

each option according to each criterion. A matrix is a table (or a spread-sheet), as shown in Figure 18.3 on page 462. Here the writer is nearly at the end of his series of options: he is evaluating four similar photocopiers according to four criteria.

Does using a matrix ensure an objective analysis? No. Bias can creep in at three stages:

- *Determining which criteria to examine.* In Figure 18.3, the Xerox Model 4500 (option 2) did very poorly on criterion 4. If criterion 4 were removed from the analysis, or if many other criteria were added, the Xerox might score much higher.

- *Deciding the range of values for each criterion.* As explained in Figure 18.3, there is no one "correct" way to determine the range of values for each criterion. If one of your criteria is whether the copier can staple, how do you decide to score a machine that does stapling and a machine that does not? If you give 10 points to a machine that does stapling and 0 points to a machine that does not, you have probably eliminated the nonstapling machine. However, if stapling is unimportant, it might be more reasonable to assign a value of 8 points to nonstapling machines. To help readers understand your thinking, include a brief statement explaining your reasoning for each criterion. For example, for the duplexing criterion, explain that you give a copier 9 points if it can print duplex and 8 points if it cannot, because printing duplex is an unimportant criterion. However, for the color criterion, you give a copier 9 points if it can print in color and 2 points if it cannot, because color printing is very important.

■ **Figure 18.3   A Matrix**

To use a matrix, you assign a value (0–10 is a common range) for each criterion for each option. Then you add up the values for each option and compare the totals. In this case, option 3 scores the highest, with 35 points; option 2 scores the lowest, with 26 points.

To help your readers understand how you derived your values, you need to explain the scoring system in the report.

Option	Criterion 1: Pages per Minute	Criterion 2: Ability to Duplex	Criterion 3: Extra Paper Bins	Criterion 4: Color Printing	Total Points
Option 1: Ricoh Model 311	9	8	7	9	33
Option 2: Xerox Model 4500	8	9	7	2	26
Option 3: Savin Model 12X	10	8	8	9	35
Option 4: Sharp Model S350	7	8	8	9	32

In This Book

The sample report in this chapter includes a decision matrix on p. 487.

- *Assigning values to criteria.* If, for example, one of your criteria is ease of operation, you might give one machine a 9, whereas someone else might give it a 3. Other criteria are equally difficult to assess objectively. For example, what value do you give to the cost criterion if one machine costs $12,500 per year to operate and another costs $14,300?

Evaluating options according to criteria is always subjective. The main advantage of a matrix is that it helps you do a methodical analysis. For your readers, a matrix makes your analysis easier to follow because it clearly presents your methods and results.

Draw Conclusions About Each Option

Whether you use a matrix or some other, less formal means of recording your evaluations, the next step is to draw conclusions about the options you studied—by interpreting your results and writing evaluative statements about the options.

For the study of photocopiers, your conclusion might be that the Ricoh model is the best copier: it meets all your necessary criteria and the greatest number of desirable criteria, or it scores highest on your matrix. Depending on your readers' preferences, present your conclusions in one of three ways.

- *Rank all the options.* The Ricoh copier is the best option, the Savin copier is second best, and so forth.
- *Classify all the options in two categories.* Those categories might be *acceptable* and *unacceptable*.
- *Present a compound conclusion.* The Ricoh offers the most technical capabilities; the Savin is the best value.

Ethics Note

Presenting Honest Recommendations

As you formulate your recommendations, you might know what your readers want you to say. For example, they might want you to recommend the cheapest solution, one that uses a certain kind of technology, or one that is supplied by a certain vendor. Naturally, you want to be able to recommend what they want. But sometimes the facts won't let you. Your responsibility is to tell the truth—to do the research honestly and competently, then present the findings honestly. Your name goes on the report. You want to be able to defend your recommendations based on the evidence and your reasoning.

One worrisome situation that arises frequently is that none of the options would be a complete success, or none would work at all. What do you do? You tell the truth about the options, warts and all. Give the best advice you can, even if that advice is to do nothing.

Formulate Recommendations Based on the Conclusions

The discussion about recommendations in Figure 18.1 on page 458 applies to feasibility reports. If you conclude that Plan A is better than Plan B and you see no obvious problems with Plan A, recommend Plan A. But if the problem has changed or your company's priorities or resources have changed, you might decide to recommend a course of action that is inconsistent with the conclusions you derived. Your responsibility is to use your judgment and recommend the best course of action.

WRITING FORMAL REPORTS

The following discussion presents a basic structure for a formal report. Remember that every document you write should reflect its audience, purpose, and subject. Therefore, you are likely to need to modify, add, or delete some of the elements discussed here.

The easiest way to draft a report is to think of it as consisting of three sections: the front matter, the body, and the back matter. Table 18.1 on page 464 shows the purposes and typical elements of the three sections. The sample completion report beginning on page 475 shows many of the components of a formal report.

You will probably draft the body before the front matter and the back matter. This sequence is easiest because you think through what you want to say in the body, then draft the front matter and back matter based on it.

> **Writing formal reports:**
> Writing the body
> Writing the front matter
> Writing the back matter

Writing the Body

The elements that make up the body of a report are discussed here in the order in which they usually appear in a report. However, you should draft the elements in whatever order you find most comfortable.

■ **Table 18.1   Elements of a Typical Report**

Section of the report	Purposes of the section	Typical elements in the section
Front matter	• to orient the reader to the subject • to provide summaries for technical and managerial readers • to help readers navigate the report • to help readers decide whether to read the document	• letter of transmittal (p. 467) • cover (p. 467) • title page (p. 467) • abstract (p. 467) • table of contents (p. 468) • list of illustrations (p. 470) • executive summary (p. 470)
Body	• to provide the most comprehensive account of the project, from the problem or opportunity that motivated it, to the methods and the most important findings	• introduction (p. 464) • methods (p. 465) • results (p. 465) • conclusions (p. 466) • recommendations (p. 466)
Back matter	• to present supplementary information, such as more-detailed explanations than are provided in the body • to enable readers to consult the secondary sources the writers used	• glossary (p. 473) • list of symbols (p. 473) • references (p. 474) • appendices (p. 474)

Introduction   The introduction helps readers understand the technical discussion that follows. Start by analyzing who the readers are, then consider these standard questions:

- *What is the subject of the report?* If the report follows a proposal and progress report, you can probably copy this information from one of these documents and modify it as necessary. Reusing this information is efficient and ethical.

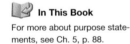
In This Book
For more about purpose statements, see Ch. 5, p. 88.

- *What is the purpose of the report?* The purpose of the report is not the purpose of the project. The purpose of the report is to present information to enable readers to understand a subject, to affect their attitudes toward a subject, or to enable them to carry out a task.

- *What is the background of the report?* Include this information, even if you have presented it before. Some of your readers might not have read your previous documents or might have forgotten them.

- *What are your sources of information?* Briefly describe your primary and secondary research, to prepare your readers for a more detailed discussion of your sources in subsequent sections of the report.

- *What is the scope of the report?* Indicate the topics you are including, as well as those you are not.

- *What are the most significant findings?* Summarize the most significant findings of the project.

- *What are your recommendations?* In a short report containing a few simple recommendations, include those recommendations in the introduction. In a lengthy report containing many complex recommendations, briefly summarize them in the introduction, then refer readers to the more detailed discussion in "Recommendations."

- *What is the organization of the report?* Indicate your organizational pattern so that readers can understand where you are going and why.

- *What key terms are you using in the report?* The introduction is an appropriate place to define new terms. If you need to define many terms, place the definitions in a glossary and refer readers to it in the introduction.

 On TechComm Web

For examples of research reports, see Online Computer Library Center. Click on Links Library for Ch. 18 on <bedfordstmartins .com/techcomm>.

Methods   The methods section answers the question "What did you do?" In drafting the methods section, consider your readers' knowledge of the field, their perception of you, and the uniqueness of the project, as well as their reasons for reading the report and their attitudes toward the project. Provide enough information to help readers understand what you did and why you did it that way. If others will be using the report to duplicate your methods, include sufficient detail.

Results   Results are the data you have discovered or compiled. Present the results objectively, without comment. Save the interpretation of the results—your conclusions—for later. If you combine results and conclusions, your readers might be unable to follow your reasoning and might not be able to tell whether the evidence justifies your conclusions.

Whereas the methods section answers the question "What did you do?" the results section answers the question "What did you see?"

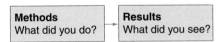

Your audience's needs will help you decide how to structure the results. How much they know about the subject, what they plan to do with the report, what they expect your recommendation(s) to be—these and many other factors will affect how you present the results. For instance, suppose that your company is considering installing a VoIP phone system that will allow you to transmit telephone calls over the Internet. In the introduction, you explain the disadvantages and limitations of the company's current phone system. In the methods section, you describe how you established the criteria you applied to the available phone systems, as well as your research procedures. In the results section, you provide the details of each phone system you are considering, as well as the results of your evaluation of each system.

In This Book

For more about evaluating evidence and drawing conclusions, see Ch. 8, p. 159.

Conclusions   Conclusions are the implications of the results. To draw conclusions, you need to think carefully about your results, weighing whether they point clearly to a single meaning. The conclusions answer the question "What does it mean?"

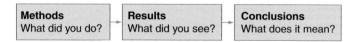

| Methods
What did you do? | Results
What did you see? | Conclusions
What does it mean? |

Recommendations   Recommendations are suggestions to take particular actions. The recommendations section answers the question "What should we do?" As discussed earlier in this chapter, recommendations do not always flow directly from conclusions. Always consider recommending that the organization take no action, or no action at this time.

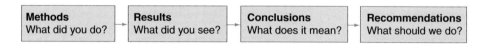

| Methods
What did you do? | Results
What did you see? | Conclusions
What does it mean? | Recommendations
What should we do? |

Guidelines

Writing Recommendations

As you draft your recommendations, consider the following four factors:

▶ **Content.** Be clear and specific. If the project has been unsuccessful, don't simply recommend that your readers "try some other alternatives." What alternatives do you recommend and why?

▶ **Tone.** When you recommend a new course of action, be careful not to offend whoever formulated the earlier course. Do not write that acting on your recommendations will "correct the mistakes" that have been made. Instead, your recommendations "offer great promise for success." A restrained, understated tone is more persuasive. It shows that you are interested only in the good of your company, not personal rivalries.

▶ **Form.** If the report leads to only one recommendation, use traditional paragraphs. If the conclusion of the report leads to more than one recommendation, consider a numbered list.

▶ **Location.** Consider including a summary of the recommendations—or, if they are brief, the full list—after the executive summary or in the introduction as well as at the end of the body of the report.

Writing the Front Matter

Front matter is common in reports, proposals, and manuals. As discussed in Table 18.1 on page 464, front matter helps readers understand the whole document and find the information they seek.

Most organizations have established formats for front matter. Study the style guide used in your company or, if there isn't one, examples from the files to see how other writers have assembled their documents.

Letter of Transmittal   The letter of transmittal, which can take the form of a letter or memo, introduces the primary reader to the purpose and content of the document. It is attached to the document, bound in with it, or simply placed on top of it. Even though the letter likely contains no information that is not included elsewhere in the document, it is important because it is the first thing the reader sees. It establishes a courteous and professional tone. Letters of transmittal are customary even when the writer and reader both work for the same organization. See page 475 for an example of a transmittal letter in the sample completion report.

 In This Book
For more about formatting a letter, see Ch. 14, p. 343.

Cover   The cover protects the document from normal wear and tear and from harsher environmental conditions such as water or grease. The cover usually contains the title of the document, the name and position of the writer, the date of submission, and the name or logo of the writer's company. Sometimes the cover also includes a security notice or a statement of proprietary information.

 In This Book
For information about types of bindings, see Ch. 12, p. 262.

Title Page   A title page states at least the title of the report, the name of the author, and the date of submission. A more complex title page also might include a project number, a list of additional personnel who contributed to the document, and a distribution list. See page 476 for an example of a title page in the sample completion report.

Abstract   An abstract is a brief technical summary of the document, usually no more than 200 words. It addresses readers who are familiar with the technical subject and who need to decide whether they want to read the full document. In an abstract, you can use technical terminology and refer to advanced concepts in the field. Abstracts are sometimes published by abstract services, which are useful resources for researchers.

 In This Book
For more about abstract services, see Ch. 6, p. 107.

There are two types of abstracts: descriptive and informative. A *descriptive abstract*—sometimes called a *topical*, *indicative*, or *table-of-contents abstract*—describes the kinds of information contained in the document. It does not provide the major findings (important results, conclusions, or recommendations). It simply lists the topics covered, giving equal emphasis to each. Figure 18.4 on page 468 is a descriptive abstract from a

This abstract is descriptive rather than informative because it does not explain the criteria or describe the system.

ABSTRACT

"Design of a Radio-Based System for Distribution Automation"

by Brian D. Crowe

At this time, power utilities' major techniques of monitoring their distribution systems are after-the-fact indicators such as interruption reports, meter readings, and trouble alarms. These techniques are inadequate because they are expensive and they fail to provide the utility with an accurate picture of the dynamics of the distribution system. This report describes a project to design a radio-based system for a pilot project. This report describes the criteria we used to design the system, then describes the hardware and software of the system.

Keywords: distribution automation, distribution systems, load, meters, radio-based systems, utilities

■ **Figure 18.4   Descriptive Abstract**
Source: Crowe, 1985.

report by a utility company about its pilot program for measuring how much electricity its customers are using. A descriptive abstract is used most often when space is at a premium. Some government proposals, for example, call for a descriptive abstract to be placed at the bottom of the title page.

An *informative abstract* presents the major findings. If you don't know which kind of abstract the reader wants, write an informative one.

Abstracts often contain a list of a half-dozen or so keywords, which are entered into electronic databases. As the writer, one of your tasks is to think of the various keywords that will lead people to the information in your document.

The distinction between descriptive and informative abstracts is not absolute. Sometimes you might have to combine elements of both in a single abstract. For instance, if there are 15 recommendations—far too many to list—you might simply note that the report includes numerous recommendations.

The sample completion report contains an informative abstract on page 477.

Table of Contents   The table of contents, the most important guide to navigating the document, has two main functions: to help readers find the information they want and to help them understand the scope and organization of the document.

A table of contents uses the same headings as the document itself. Therefore, to create an effective table of contents, you must first make sure that the headings are clear and that you have provided enough of them. If the table of contents shows no entry for five or six pages, you probably need to partition the document into additional subsections. In fact, some tables of contents have one entry, or even several, for every document page.

The following table of contents, which relies exclusively on generic headings (those that describe an entire class of items), is too general to be useful.

Table of Contents

Introduction 1
Materials 3
Methods 4   ◄— *This methods section, which goes from page 4 to page 18, should have sub-entries to break up the text and to help readers find the information they seek.*
Results 19
Recommendations 23
References 26
Appendices 28

For more-informative headings, combine the generic and the specific:

Recommendations: Five Ways to Improve Information-Retrieval Materials Used in the Calcification Study

Results of the Commuting-Time Analysis

Then build more subheadings into the report itself. For instance, in the "Recommendations" example above, you could create a subheading for each of the five recommendations. Once you establish a clear system of headings within the document, use the same text attributes—capitalization, boldface, italic, and outline style (traditional or decimal)—in the table of contents.

When adding page numbers to your document, remember two points:

- The table of contents does not contain an entry for itself.
- Front matter is numbered using lowercase roman numerals (*i*, *ii*, and so forth), often centered at the bottom of the page. The title page of a document is not numbered, although it represents page *i*. The abstract is usually numbered page *ii*. The table of contents is usually not numbered, although it represents page *iii*. The body of the document is numbered with Arabic numerals (1, 2, and so on), typically in the upper outside corner of the page.

A table of contents appears on page 478 in the completion report.

TECH TIP

How to Format Headers, Footers, and Page Numbers

In writing a report, you might want to use different headers, footers, and page-numbering schemes and styles in the different sections of the report. To do this, you will create different **sections** in your Word file. Within each section, you can modify the headers, footers, and page numbers by using the **Header and Footer** toolbar.

To **modify the format** of headers, footers, and page numbers, select **Header and Footer** from the **View** menu.

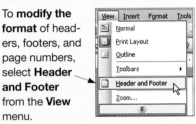

The **Header and Footer** toolbar allows you to add and modify text, insert page numbers and dates, and choose the format of page numbers.

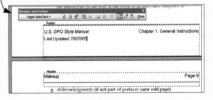

 The **Page Setup** button allows you to adjust the location of headers and footers and specify different headers and footers for odd and even pages, as well as the first page.

 The **Format Number** button allows you to change the format of page numbers.

KEYWORDS: header and footer toolbar, header, footer, page setup, page number, format page numbers, sections

TECH TIP

How to Create a Table of Contents

To make a table of contents automatically in Word, you must use the **Styles** feature to format the headings in your document.

1. Place your cursor where you want to create your table of contents.

2. Select **Reference** from the **Insert** menu, then select **Index and Tables.**

3. Click on the **Table of Contents** tab. You can choose the format for your table of contents, select the level of detail to include, and preview the appearance of the table.

    You can also **modify** the text attributes of the table-of-contents levels to match the text attributes in your document.

If you later change your document and its pagination, you can update the page numbers or the entire table of contents by right-clicking in the table of contents, then selecting **Update Field**.

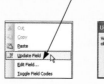

> **KEYWORDS:** table of contents, index and tables, update fields

List of Illustrations   The list of illustrations is a table of contents for the figures and tables. List the figures first, then the tables. (If the document contains only figures, call it a *list of figures*. If it contains only tables, call it a *list of tables*.) You may begin the list of illustrations on the same page as the table of contents, or you may begin the list on a separate page and list it in the table of contents. Figure 18.5 shows a list of illustrations.

Executive Summary   The executive summary (sometimes called the *epitome, executive overview, management summary*, or *management overview*) is a brief condensation of the document addressed to managers. Most managers need only a broad understanding of the projects the organization undertakes and how they fit together into a coherent whole.

An executive summary for a document under 20 pages is typically one page (double-spaced). For longer documents, the maximum length is often calculated as a percentage of the document, such as 5 percent.

The executive summary presents information to managers in two parts:

- *Background.* This section explains the problem or opportunity—what was not working, or not working effectively or efficiently; or what potential modification of a procedure or product had to be analyzed.

- *Major findings and implications.* This section might include a brief description (only one or two sentences) of the methods, followed by a full paragraph about the conclusions and recommendations.

■ **Figure 18.5   List of Illustrations**

An executive summary differs from an informative abstract. An abstract focuses on the technical subject (such as whether the new radio-based system monitors energy usage effectively); an executive summary concentrates on whether the system can improve operations *at a particular company.*

Guidelines

Writing an Executive Summary

Follow these five suggestions in writing executive summaries:

- **Use specific evidence in describing the background.** For most managers, the best evidence includes costs and savings. Instead of writing that the equipment you are now using to cut metal foil is ineffective, write that the equipment jams once every 72 hours on average, costing $400 in materials and $2,000 in productivity. Then add up these figures for a monthly or an annual total.

- **Be specific in describing the research.** For instance, research suggests that if your company had a computerized energy-management system, you could cut your energy costs by 20 to 25 percent. If your energy costs last year were $300,000, you could save $60,000 to $75,000.

- **Describe the methods briefly.** If you think your readers are interested, include a brief description—no more than a sentence or two.

- **Describe the findings according to your readers' needs.** If your readers want to know your results, provide them. If your readers are unable to understand the technical data or are uninterested, go directly to the conclusions and recommendations.

- **Ask an outside reader to review your draft.** Give it to someone who has had no connection to the project. That person should be able to read your summary and understand what the project means to the organization.

INTERACTIVE SAMPLE DOCUMENT
Analyzing an Executive Summary

The following executive summary comes from a corporate report on purchasing BlackBerry devices for employees. The questions in the margin ask you to think about the discussion of executive summaries (beginning on page 470). E-mail your responses to yourself and/or your instructor, and see suggested responses on TechComm Web.

1. How clearly does the writer explain the back-ground? Identify the problem or opportunity described in this executive summary.

2. Does the writer discuss the methods? If so, identify the discussion.

3. Identify the findings: the results, conclusions, and recommendations. How clearly has the writer explained the benefits to the company?

 On TechComm Web

To e-mail your responses to yourself and/or your instructor and to see suggested responses, click on Interactive Sample Documents for Ch. 18 on <bedfordstmartins .com/techcomm>.

Executive Summary

On May 11, we received approval to study whether BlackBerry devices could help our 20 engineers receive e-mail, monitor their schedules, take notes, and store files they need in the field. In our study, we addressed these problems experienced by many of our engineers:

- They have missed deadlines and meetings and lost client information.
- They have been unable to access important files from the field.
- They have complained about the weight of the binders and other materials— sometimes weighing more than 40 pounds—that they have to carry.
- They have to spend time keyboarding notes that they took in the field.

In 2005, missed meetings and other schedule problems cost the company over $400,000 in lost business. And our insurance carrier settled a claim for $50,000 from an engineer who experienced back and shoulder problems due to the weight of his pack.

We researched the capabilities of BlackBerry devices, then established these criteria for our analysis:

- The device must weigh less than 6 ounces.
- It must be compatible with Windows back to 98.
- It must have a 240 × 240-pixel color screen.
- It must have TCP/IP capability.
- It must have a full QWERTY keyboard.
- It must be GPS-enabled.
- It must have a built-in speakerphone.
- It must have at least 32 MB of memory.
- It must have Bluetooth® capability.
- It must cost $200 or less.

On the basis of our analysis, we recommend that the company purchase five BlackBerry 7100g devices, for a total cost of $1,000. These devices best meet all our technical and cost criteria. We further recommend that after a six-month trial period, the company decide whether to purchase an additional 15 devices for the other engineers.

An executive summary is included on page 479 in the sample completion report.

Writing the Back Matter

The back matter can include any or all of the following items: glossary, list of symbols, references, and appendices.

Glossary and List of Symbols   A *glossary*, an alphabetical list of definitions, is particularly useful if some of your readers are unfamiliar with the technical vocabulary in your document. Instead of slowing down your discussion by defining technical terms as they appear, you can use boldface, or some similar method of highlighting words, to indicate that the term is defined in the glossary. The first time a boldfaced term appears, explain this system in a footnote. For example, the body of the document might say, "Thus the **positron*** acts as the...," while a note at the bottom of the page explains:

> *This and all subsequent terms in boldface are defined in the Glossary, page 26.

Although the glossary is usually placed near the end of the document, before the appendices, it can also be placed immediately after the table of contents if the glossary is brief (less than a page) and if it defines essential terms. Figure 18.6 shows an excerpt from a glossary.

A *list of symbols* is formatted like a glossary, but it defines symbols and abbreviations rather than terms. It, too, may be placed before the appendices or after the table of contents. See Figure 18.7.

Glossary

Applicant: A state agency, local government, or eligible private nonprofit organization that submits a request to the Grantee for disaster assistance under the state's grant.

Case Management: A systems approach to providing equitable and fast service to applicants for disaster assistance. Organized around the needs of the applicant, the system consists of a single point of coordination, a team of on-site specialists, and a centralized, automated filing system.

Cost Estimating Format (CEF): A method for estimating the total cost of repair for large, permanent projects by use of construction industry standards. The format uses a base cost estimate and design and construction contingency factors, applied as a percentage of the base cost.

Declaration: The President's decision that a major disaster qualifies for federal assistance under the Stafford Act.

Hazard Mitigation: Any cost-effective measure that will reduce the potential for damage to a facility from a disaster event.

■ **Figure 18.6   Glossary**
Source: Based on Federal Emergency Management Agency, 2002 <www.fema.gov/r-n-r/pa/glossary.htm>.

List of Symbols

β	beta
CRT	cathode-ray tube
γ	gamma
Hz	hertz
rcvr	receiver
SNR	signal-to-noise ratio
uhf	ultra high frequency
vhf	very high frequency

■ **Figure 18.7   List of Symbols**

References   Many documents contain a list of references (sometimes called a *bibliography* or *list of works cited*) as part of the back matter. References and the accompanying textual citations throughout the document are called *documentation.* Documentation acknowledges your debt to your sources, establishes your credibility as a writer, and helps readers locate and review your sources. See Appendix, Part B, page 579, for a discussion of documentation.

Appendices   An appendix is any section that follows the body of the document (and the list of references or bibliography, glossary, or list of symbols). Appendices (or *appendixes*) convey information that is too bulky for the body or that will interest only a few readers. Appendices might include maps, large technical diagrams or charts, computations, computer printouts, test data, and texts of supporting documents.

Appendices, usually labeled with letters rather than numbers (Appendix A, Appendix B, and so on), are listed in the table of contents and are referred to at the appropriate points in the body of the document. Therefore, they are accessible to any reader who wants to consult them.

SAMPLE FORMAL REPORT

The following example (Bethke, Cowles, Frachiseur, and Stoffel, 2004) is the completion report on the project proposed in Chapter 16 on pages 420–24. The progress report for the same project appears in Chapter 17 on pages 441–46.

FOUR SQUARE WOODWORKING

P.O. Box 1966   (208) 440-1056
Eagle, ID 83616   foursquare@cableone.net

Memo ◄

Date: December 13, 2004

To: Mr. Chris Bethke, Shop Foreman

From: David Bethke, Shop Assistant ◄
           Steven Cowles, Shop Assistant
           Amy Frachiseur, Technical Writer
           Justin Stoffel, Shop Assistant

Subject: Completion Report for the Feasibility Study Regarding Table-Saw Replacement ◄

We have attached our completion report for our feasibility study about replacing our current table saw. We completed the tasks described in our proposal of October 17, 2004: investigating safety and production problems related to our outdated table saw and researching options for improving our lumber-sawing capability.

First, we investigated the extent of the problem by calculating unnecessary labor and wasted materials related to our table-saw problem. At an hourly rate of $15 for each woodworker, we calculated a monthly expense of $1,200 due to inefficiency. In addition, we calculated the cost of ruined wood due to poor cuts to be $200 per month. Then we identified our options for addressing this problem. We found that the problem was too important to ignore and that repair would not address the safety problem and would not be cost-effective. Therefore, we decided to focus on the purchase of a new table saw. Next, we established saw-selection criteria and researched available table saws according to our criteria.

Based on the information we gathered and reviewed, we recommend the Delta Unisaw 36-L31X-BC50, at a cost of $1,550. Its extensive safety features, power, accuracy, quality of construction, and ease of use put it well ahead of the competition. It also includes an industry-leading five-year warranty. Measured by the length of its warranty, the Delta would cost less than $26 per month. This new saw would pay for itself in approximately five weeks.

We appreciate the opportunity to research options for improving operations at Four Square Woodworking. We look forward to working on other projects in the future. If you have any questions or comments, please contact David Bethke at extension 1220. ◄

Transmittal "letters" can be presented as memos.

The writers include their titles and that of their primary reader. This way, future readers will be able to tell the positions of the reader and writers.

The subject heading indicates the subject of the report—the feasibility study about table-saw replacement—and the purpose of the report—completion report.

The purpose of the study. Notice that the writers link the completion report to the proposal, giving them an opportunity to state the problems that led to the study.

The methods the writers used to carry out the research. Note that the writers clarify the logic they used: how they decided to study the topic.

The major recommendation.

A polite offer to provide more information.

A good title indicates the subject and purpose of the document. One way to indicate the purpose is to use a generic term—such as analysis, recommendation, summary, *or* instructions—*in a phrase following a colon. For more about titles, see Ch. 10, p. 205.*

**Feasibility Study for Table-Saw Replacement:
A Completion Report**

Prepared for: **Mr. Chris Bethke, Shop Foreman**

Prepared by: David Bethke, Shop Assistant
Steven Cowles, Shop Assistant
Amy Frachiseur, Technical Writer
Justin Stoffel, Shop Assistant

December 13, 2004

The names and positions of the principal reader and the writers of the document.

The date the document was submitted.

FOUR SQUARE WOODWORKING
P.O. Box 1966   (208) 440-1056
Eagle, ID 83616   foursquare@cableone.net

The name or logo of the writers' organization.

Abstract

"Feasibility Study for Table-Saw Replacement: A Completion Report"

Prepared by: David Bethke, Shop Assistant
Steven Cowles, Shop Assistant
Amy Frachiseur, Technical Writer
Justin Stoffel, Shop Assistant

In October of 2004, Chris Bethke, shop foreman of Four Square Woodworking, commissioned a study of whether to repair or replace our aging table saw. The saw is unsafe and is costing us money because it slows down our woodworkers and ruins materials. He authorized $2,600 for the study, including $2,000 for the saw and $600 for research labor. The company's present Craftsman contractor saw's bearings are wearing out, causing excessive deflection of the blade and occasional binding of the lumber. Over $1,200 per month in labor is being spent among the company's 20 employees in increased time using the saw, waiting to use the saw, and fixing mistakes caused by improper cuts and saw marks. An additional $200 is lost because of wasted materials. First we researched options for repairing the saw but concluded that replacing it would be more fiscally responsible given costs of repair and lost production time while the saw would be unavailable. We then researched other table saws for replacement. Based on a questionnaire given to shop employees, an interview with woodworking expert Nathan Abram, a research trip to a woodworking exposition, research at retail outlets, and an evaluation of four table saws, we recommend the Delta Unisaw 36-L31X-BC50 as the best choice for the company. It has a built-in dust chute to direct more than 80 percent of dust out of the base to the back of the machine for easy cleaning from the floor instead of spreading into the air. It also has the industry-standard Biesemeyer fence, which has only 1/64" deflection of the blade at the arbor with 20 pounds of pressure applied. Such a fence will greatly improve the accuracy of our cuts. Its total cost is $1,550, or $26 per warranted month, which will be saved in less than two months due to decreased labor costs and wasted materials. With this increased efficiency and speed of output, our company can more easily continue to grow and provide its customers with the quality they have come to expect from Four Square Woodworking.

Keywords: crosscut, Delta, fence, woodworking, rip, table saw, safety

ii

The title of the report is often placed within quotation marks because the abstract might be placed outside the report, in which case the report is a separate document.

Abstracts are often formatted as a single paragraph.

The purpose of the study.

The methods.

The major recommendation.

Note that the writers provide technical information about the table saw they recommend.

A keywords list ensures that if the report is searched electronically, it will register "hits" for each term listed.

Note that the typeface and design of the headings here match the typeface and design of the headings in the report itself.

In this table of contents, the two levels of headings are distinguished by type size, type style (roman versus italic), and indentation.

A list of tables allows the reader to refer quickly to them.

Contents

List of Tables

iii

1

Executive Summary

The number of projects commissioned at Four Square Woodworking rose 25 percent in 2004 compared with 2003. Much of this growth has come from positive word of mouth. Our flexibility, speed, and consistently high-quality work continue to draw more and more customers.

Unfortunately, our table saw is not as safe as today's models. In addition, our output has been steadily decreasing, largely because our table saw is 10 years old and is wearing out. Time spent cutting lumber has increased 35 percent, as precise cuts grow more and more difficult to achieve on the machine. Most of this increased labor is devoted to sanding out blade marks and finishing gouged wood. This extra labor is costing us more than $1,200 per month. In addition, we are losing $200 per month in wasted wood.

We researched options for repair and concluded that replacing the saw would address the safety problem and be most cost-effective. Through secondary research in woodworking journals, a questionnaire distributed to our 20 woodworkers, an interview with woodworking expert Nathan Abram, and visits to a woodworking exposition and retail outlets, we identified several qualified models that would solve our problem.

After analyzing the data we collected, we recommend the Delta Unisaw 36-L31X-BC50 for its excellent safety features, power, accuracy, quality of construction, and ease of use. It has an industry-leading five-year warranty to ensure its quality. All of our woodworkers report that they would welcome the new saw; there would be no learning curve for any of them. The Delta costs $1,550, $450 below our $2,000 capital budget. Buying this saw would cut production time by over four hours per employee per month and significantly reduce wasted materials. At the woodworkers' average pay rate of $15 per hour and factoring in a cost reduction of wasted materials of $200, the new saw would save $1,400 per month, meaning that it would pay for itself in a little more than one month.

The executive summary describes the project with a focus on the managerial aspects, particularly the recommendation. Note the writers' emphasis on the problem and their use of dollar figures.

Mentioning the safety problem gets the reader's attention. The writers then describe the symptoms of the problem in financial terms. Notice the use of specific dollar figures.

The writers summarize their methods briefly.

The discussion of the technology is brief. Most managers are not interested in the technical details.

Managers want the bottom line: how much will it cost to implement your recommendation, and how long will the payback period be?

2

In some organizations, all first-level headings begin a new page.

The background and purpose of the report.

An overview of the methods.

A more detailed statement of the background and problem.

A more detailed statement of the methods.

The introduction can present the major findings of the report.

Notice the writers' use of the phrases We concluded *at the beginning of the paragraph and* We therefore recommend *at the end. Repeating key terms in this way helps readers understand the logic of a report and therefore concentrate on the technical information it contains.*

An advance organizer for the rest of the report.

Introduction

On October 28, 2004, we received approval of our proposal to research options for repairing or replacing the table saw at Four Square Woodworking. This report presents the findings of our study. We weighed the cost of lost productivity against the cost of repairing or replacing our present saw. We researched our options and concluded that it would be best to buy a new saw. We then researched available features and associated costs of available table saws.

One current table saw poses a safety risk. Last month, after a power outage, the table saw powered up unexpectedly. Jo Bucket came within a few inches of losing a hand. Newer saws have magnetic safety switches that automatically cut the power to the saw after an outage. Jo's near miss was very disturbing to all of us, reinforcing our concern about the outmoded safety features on our table saw.

In addition, the saw, now almost 10 years old, is wearing out. The table saw is the most basic tool in the shop, used for virtually every piece we build. We rely on it for accurate, clean ripping, crosscutting, mitering, grooving, and dadoing. But our records indicate that each of our 20 woodworkers is spending an average of four extra hours per month adjusting and readjusting the saw to achieve a precise cut, and sanding out and finishing wood marred from the saw. At an hourly rate of $15 for each woodworker, we calculated a monthly expense of $1,200 due to inefficiency. In addition, we calculated the cost of ruined wood due to poor cuts to be $200 per month.

Considering this problem, we researched options for repair and concluded that replacing the saw would be the most cost-effective option. Through secondary research in woodworking journals, a questionnaire distributed to our 20 woodworkers, an interview with woodworking expert Nathan Abram, and visits to a woodworking exposition and retail outlets, we identified several qualified models that would solve our problem.

We concluded that a Delta Unisaw 36-L31X-BC50, at a cost of $1,550, is the best fit for our company. Its extensive safety features, power, accuracy, quality of construction, and ease of use put it well ahead of the competition. It also includes an industry-leading five-year warranty. Measured by the length of its warranty, the Delta would cost less than $26 per month. Given the shop's current loss of $1,200 per month in wages and $200 in wasted material, the saw would pay for itself in less than one and a half months. This would allow faster creation of our work at our high standards of quality and help us maintain our reputation and growth. We therefore recommend that we purchase the Delta Unisaw 36-L31X-BC50.

In the following sections, we provide additional details about our research methods, the results we obtained, the conclusions we drew from those results, and our recommendation.

3

Research Methods

To better understand our table-saw problems and consider our options, we performed the following research:

1. We investigated the extent of the problem by calculating unnecessary labor and wasted materials. To calculate the unnecessary labor, we compared the time spent in 2004 and 2003 in the initial cutting and finishing of our pieces. We normed the data to account for the number and types of cuts we performed each year. We used the machine log to determine the number and types of cuts as well as the woodworker logs to calculate the number of hours spent on finishing the marred wood. To determine the amount of wasted materials, we studied the materials inventory, norming the figures to account for the change in the number and types of pieces we made in 2003 and 2004.

2. We identified our options for addressing this problem:
    *   *Continuing to use the current saw without repairing it.* We considered the current condition of the saw, as well as the likelihood of continued deterioration as it ages.
    *   *Repairing the current saw.* For some tools, repair is less expensive and just as effective as replacement. We consulted representatives of the two major repair services in the city—Appleby's Engine Repair and Modern Industrial Supply—as well as Craftsman, the manufacturer of our current saw. We asked each of them the same question: what would it cost to bring the saw up to its original specs?
    *   *Replacing the current saw.* Because the table saw remains the essential tool for woodworking, there are many on the market, and they continue to improve in quality. We conducted secondary research in woodworking journals to learn whether replacing our current saw is a feasible option.

3. We identified the main criteria against which we would evaluate the different saws. We started by identifying two necessary criteria:
    *   *Safety.* Table saws are inherently dangerous. According to WoodMagazine.com, "Of the 720,000 injuries per year associated with woodworking, 42 percent happen at the table saw" (*Tablesaw Safety,* n.d.). However, we have not sustained a major injury, and we will do everything we can to maintain the safety of workers at our shop. Because we value safety highly, we decided to consider only those saws that have the best safety features. Therefore, our primary technical question was this: does the saw incorporate the best safety features that currently exist?
    *   *Cost.* We needed to work within a capital budget of $2,000.

    Next we identified four desirable criteria to help us make distinctions among available table saws. To learn what criteria are important to consider when evaluating a table saw, we consulted online resources, distributed a questionnaire to each of our 20 woodworkers (see Appendix A, page 13), and conducted a phone interview with master cabinetmaker Nathan Abram (see Appendix B, page 14). We present the desirable criteria from most important to least important.

The writers use the same task organization as in the proposal and progress report.

Because the project is now completed, they have dropped the word task *from their numbered system.*

Notice how the writers describe their primary-research methods. In many organizational reports, writers rely on company records for information.

The writers begin their analysis by determining what their major options were.

The writers' research is woven throughout the discussion.

Unless a saw met these two necessary criteria, the writers would not consider it further.

In most projects, writers need to work within a budget. For this reason, cost is often a necessary criterion.

The logic of the research strategy makes sense: use the necessary criteria to narrow down the list of options, then use the desirable criteria to rank all the remaining options.

4

- *Power.* Because we often work with substantial pieces of hardwood, we need a saw with considerable power. Writing in *Woodcentral.com,* David Wright (2003) suggests that cheaper saws with less powerful motors "make rough cuts, wear out quickly, don't hold their adjustments, and are more prone to dangerous kickbacks" (para. 2).
- *Accuracy.* An accurate cut saves money because it reduces the need for hand-finishing and decreases the incidence of wasted materials. The size and material of a saw's tabletop, for instance, are among the most important factors in determining a saw's accuracy (Strong, 2003).
- *Quality.* We need a saw that can withstand the day-to-day rigors of a busy wood-working shop. A saw made of high-quality material saves the shop money by reducing downtime.
- *Ease of use.* Although our woodworkers have an average of eight years' experience — and none have fewer than two years' — we do not want to buy a saw that they find hard to use.

The writers assembled a list of options: table saws that met the necessary criteria. Note how they discuss their research methods.

4. We researched available options. To create a list of table saws to evaluate, we attended the Portland Metropolitan Expo Center's Woodworking Show on October 22–24 (for a trip report, see Appendix C, page 16) and visited local dealers. Attending the woodworking show in Portland gave us an opportunity to look at the latest tools and equipment from over 40 vendors, talk to expert woodworkers, and attend how-to sessions. Similarly, our visits to local table-saw dealers allowed us to try out table saws and talk to people who have been selling and using table saws for years.

The writers then compared each option against each criterion to see which option best fulfilled the company's needs.

5. We compared available styles, brands, and models against our criteria. For each criterion, we agreed upon a scoring key to aid us in assigning point values. To help us evaluate the saws, we asked a woodworker to try out each of the saws at a local dealer.

Finally, the writers drew conclusions and formulated a recommendation.

6. Finally, we analyzed our data, drew conclusions, and formulated a recommendation.

5

Results

In this section, we present the results of our research. We cover the costs of lost productivity and wasted materials, options for repair and replacement, criteria for selecting a table saw, and a comparison of qualified saws. The following results correspond to the tasks described in the research methods section.

The writers present an advance organizer for the results section.

1.   *Calculating Costs of Lost Productivity and Wasted Materials*
For high-end products such as those we craft, lost productivity is very expensive. We need to be able to deliver our products on schedule. We found that time spent ripping lumber, sanding out blade marks, and finishing dusty material, adjusted for the increase in workload, grew by an average of four hours per month per employee. For 20 employees, working for $15 per hour, it adds up to $1,200 per month. We calculated the cost of wasted materials, again adjusted for workload and type of product, to be $200 per month.

The writers present their data on lost productivity and wasted materials.

These calculations, based on a comparison of 2003 and 2004, understate the costs associated with the table saw because they use a baseline of 2003 (when the table saw was already out of spec) and do not account for further deterioration. Using 2003 as a baseline, we can see only the deterioration of the saw over the last year. In fact, we have noticed problems with the saw over the last three or four years. In short, we believe that a properly functioning saw would save us considerably more money than our calculations suggest.

The writers explain that their calculations are conservative: the costs are likely to be greater than they calculated.

2.   *Identifying Our Best Option*
We studied our three options.
- *Continuing to use the current saw without repairing it.* We immediately ruled out this option because it would not address the safety problem and because it is costing the company more than $16,000 per year in lost productivity and ruined materials. For a company of our size, this figure is unacceptable.
- *Repairing the current saw.* We ruled out this option because it would not address our safety concerns. In addition, this option would not effectively address the cost problems. We consulted with representatives of the two major repair services in the city—Appleby's Engine Repair and Modern Industrial Supply—as well as Craftsman, the manufacturer of our current saw. Ron Appleby of Appleby's and Harry Callanan of Modern (each of whom has more than 25 years of experience with saws) told us the same thing: fixing a saw of that age is unwise. Appleby (personal communication, October 20, 2004) estimated $800 for the repairs; Callanan (personal communication, October 21, 2004) estimated $700. Both of them pointed out that we could expect other components to fail in the next few years. We also spoke to the Craftsman representative, Audrey Weller (personal communication, October 21, 2004), who gave us a price of $750 to replace the bearings. Craftsman would warranty the bearings themselves and the labor for six months, but they would not warranty any other parts or problems. Also, it would take up to one week for the work to be completed.

The writers ruled out the first two options because neither would address the safety and productivity problems.

References to the writers' primary research enhance their credibility.

6

- *Replacing the current saw.* A quick look at major woodworking journals such as *Woodworker's Journal* and *Fine Woodworking* confirmed what we already knew: there are numerous brands and models superior to our current saw and available for less than $2,000, our budget. We therefore decided to concentrate our research on finding the best available saw on the market for our needs.

3.   Determining Our Necessary and Desirable Criteria

We distributed a questionnaire (Appendix A, page 13) to our fellow employees asking them how they use the table saw and what features would be important to them in a new saw. David Bethke then conducted a phone interview with Nathan Abram, a well-known, award-winning woodworker and frequent contributor to several woodworking publications. David had formerly been an assistant to Mr. Abram. He asked for his advice and opinions about different styles, brands, and features. A transcript of this interview is presented as Appendix B (page 14).

Based on our research, we determined our necessary criteria. To be considered an option and for us to evaluate it further, a table saw had to meet our necessary safety and cost criteria:

- *Safety.* We valued safety highly. Our primary technical question was this: does the saw incorporate the best safety features that currently exist? Three important safety features are identified in "How to Buy a Table Saw" (2003) in the *American Woodworker's Tool Buyer's Guide 2003:* a tool-free blade guard, a magnetic switch, and an easy-to-access switch. Our insurance representative, James Mullen, added that effective antikickback pawls that stay sharp, as well as an effective dust-collection system, are important safety features (personal communication, October 26, 2004). We found that these five safety features are not standard on all saws. We wanted, however, a saw with at least four of these five safety features.
- *Cost.* We needed to work within a capital budget of $2,000.

Next we determined four desirable criteria against which we evaluated the different options.

- *Power.* We wanted at least a 3 hp motor and preferred a 5 hp motor. A more powerful motor can move lumber faster, increasing feed rate. In addition, a high-powered saw cuts more quickly, putting less strain on the motor. Although a 2 hp motor is adequate for a home woodshop, 3 or 5 hp motors can withstand hour after hour of daily production use (*How to Buy,* 2003).
- *Accuracy.* An accurate cut saves money because it reduces the need for hand-finishing and decreases the incidence of wasted materials. For an accurate cut, we considered the following characteristics:
  a. Fence length. A fence is a straight guide used to keep a board a specified distance from the table-saw blade. A longer fence is better able to guide longer pieces of material. As our work is custom, we use many different sizes of boards. Because 100 percent of our woodworkers (see Appendix A, page 13) wanted the fence to be at least 50", we made that our preferred length.
  b. Blade height adjustment. Seventy-five percent of our woodworkers adjust the blade for precise height cuts at least 10 to 15 times a day (see Appendix A,

The writers explain how their secondary research helped them understand what safety features to look for.

The writers present their findings based on their desirable criteria.

Cross-referencing the appendix improves the accessibility of the report.

7

page 13). Consequently, we placed a high value on the saw's blade height adjustment. The greater the number of turns of the hand-wheel required to adjust the blade height, the greater the precision. We wanted at least seven turns to full height.

c. Vibration tendency. Excessive vibration in a saw can cause an improper cut. The vibration is directly related to the saw's weight: a heavier saw vibrates less. We wanted a saw weighing at least 500 pounds and with less than .001" vibration in any direction. Strickland (n.d.) offers one easy measure of vibration: balance a nickel on edge on the tabletop and turn the saw on. If the nickel falls, the saw is vibrating too much.

d. Arbor run-out. The amount the blade moves from side to side as material is being fed through the table should be kept as small as possible to ensure accuracy. Loganbill (n.d.) recommends that the arbor run-out be less than .003".

- *Quality.* When evaluating the quality of a saw, we considered the overall design and materials of the following components:

a. Fence and extension table. Laminate material warps less and results in a more precise cut than other materials such as plastic. Seventy-five percent of survey respondents preferred laminate material (see Appendix A, page 13).

b. Splitter and guard. It is important for the operator to be able to see the cut and still be protected. Sixty percent of survey respondents preferred see-through plastic guards (see Appendix A, page 13).

c. Trunnion. The trunnion is the assembly that holds the saw's arbor (the rotating shaft that serves as the blade's axis) to the underside of the table. If the trunnion bolts are easy to reach, they are easier to adjust, which allows for less downtime.

d. Dust-collection system. Dusty wood takes extra time to clean for finishing.

- *Ease of use.* We want to buy a saw that our woodworkers find easy to use. It is difficult to evaluate a saw's ease of use just by looking at pictures. For this criterion, we visited local retail shops and asked one of our senior woodworkers, Andreas Luther, to perform a series of standard cuts using each saw being considered. We then asked him to rate each saw's ease of use on a 10-point scale (1 very hard to use, 10 very easy to use).

4. Selecting Table-Saw Options

We talked to experts at the Portland Metropolitan Expo Center's Woodworking Show (see Appendix C, page 16), sought the advice of Nathan Abram, and visited experts at our three local retail outlets to create a list of possible table-saw options. In each instance, we explained our shop's needs and asked for the person to recommend three or four table saws that might meet our needs. Table 1 on page 8 lists the recommendations of the people from whom we sought advice.

The writers skillfully document their process of compiling a list of saws to investigate further.

8

Table 1. Table-Saw Recommendations

Recommender	Rationale for Selecting as Recommender	Date	Recommendations
David Hogg	Editor, *Popular Woodworking Magazine,* more than 20 years of experience in cabinet shops	10/22/04	• Powermatic Model 66 • Grizzly G1023SLX • Jet JTAS-10XL50-1 • Delta Unisaw 36-L31X-BC50
Linda Oats	Host, *Tools & Techniques,* the DIY Network, author of 60 woodworking books	10/24/04	• Powermatic Model 66 • Jet JTAS-10XL50-1 • Bosch 4000
Nathan Abram	Award-winning woodworker with over 30 years of experience	11/02/04	• Powermatic Model 66 • DeWalt DW746 • Grizzly G1023SLX • Delta Unisaw 36-L31X-BC50
Clive Luceno	Owner, Intermountain Tool & Hardware Co., sells all major brands of table saws, former sales representative for Craftsman	11/07/04	• Grizzly G1023SLX • Delta Unisaw 36-L31X-BC50 • Bridgewood TSC-10CL
Terry McDowell	Sales Specialist, Home Depot, retired woodshop owner with 35 years of experience	11/07/04	• Powermatic Model 66 • Jet JTAS-10XL50-1 • Grizzly G1023SLX • Delta Unisaw 36-L31X-BC50
Ty Schweighofer	Owner, Union Machinery Company, been in business for over 20 years	11/08/04	• Jet JTAS-10XL50-1 • Delta Unisaw 36-L31X-BC50 • Bosch 4000

Based on the information gathered, we chose the four most commonly recommended models to investigate further:
• Powermatic Model 66
• Grizzly G1023SLX
• Jet JTAS-10XL50-1
• Delta Unisaw 36-L31X-BC50

5. Evaluating Each Table Saw Against Our Criteria

We started by investigating whether our four recommended models met our necessary criteria for safety and cost (Table 2). Next we evaluated each model using our four desirable criteria. To make our evaluation of remaining options as objective as possible, we

9

created a decision matrix (Table 3). Included in our matrix is an explanation of how we scored each saw against each criterion.

Table 2. Table-Saw Necessary-Criteria Evaluation

Model	Safety Features[1]	Meets Safety Criterion?[2]	Cost	Meets Cost Criterion?[3]	Consider Further?
Powermatic Model 66	a, b, c, e	Yes	$2,100	No	No
Grizzly G1023SLX	a, b, c, e	Yes	$1,125	Yes	Yes
Jet JTAS-10XL50-1	a, b, c, e	Yes	$1,500	Yes	Yes
Delta Unisaw 36-L31X-BC50	a, b, c, d, e	Yes	$1,550	Yes	Yes

[1] (a) tool-free blade guard, (b) magnetic switch, (c) easy-to-access switch, (d) antikickback pawls, and (e) dust-collection system.
[2] To meet our necessary *safety* criterion, the saw must feature at least four of the following five safety features: a tool-free blade guard, a magnetic switch, an easy-to-access switch, antikickback pawls, and a dust-collection system.
[3] To meet our necessary *cost* criterion, the saw must retail for less than $2,000.

The writers explain the logic behind their scoring system. Without an explanation, this decision matrix would be of little value.

Table 3. Table-Saw Decision Matrix

Model	Power Score[1]	Accuracy Score[2]	Quality Score[3]	Ease of Use Score[4]	Total Score
Grizzly G1023SLX	4	6	8	8	26
Jet JTAS-10XL50-1	8	6	4	7	25
Delta Unisaw 36-L31X-BC50	8	8	8	9	33

[1] Saw scored four points for a 3 hp motor and eight points for a 5 hp motor.
[2] Saw scored two points for a 50"+ fence, two points for 7+ turns blade adjustment precision, two points for passing "balanced-nickel" vibration test, and two points for an arbor run-out of less than .003".
[3] Saw scored two points for a laminate table, two points for a see-through splitter and guard, two points for easy trunnion adjustment, and two points for an effective dust-collection system.
[4] Saw scored points equal to expert woodworker's rating on a 10-point scale.

The writers explain their scoring system. This explanation is necessary because the total score for each option will determine the writers' conclusions and recommendations.

10

Conclusions

The function of a conclusion is to explain what the data mean. Here the writers explain why they think the Delta Unisaw is the best choice for their shop. Notice that a conclusion is not the same as a recommendation.

All four models—Powermatic Model 66, Grizzly 1023SLX, Jet JTAS-10XL50-1, and Delta Unisaw 36-L31X-BC50—are high-quality saws, but the Delta Unisaw fared best in our assessment of each saw's safety, cost, power, accuracy, quality, and ease of use.

The Delta Unisaw was the only saw we tested that has a built-in dust chute to direct more than 80 percent of dust out of the base to the back of the machine for easy cleaning from the floor instead of spreading into the air. The Unisaw also has the industry-standard Biesemeyer fence, which has only 1/64" deflection of the blade at the arbor with 20 pounds of pressure applied. Such a fence will greatly improve the accuracy of our cuts.

Although the Unisaw is the second-most-expensive saw that we tested, it has a five-year warranty covering all parts, whereas the other three models carried only one-year warranties. The $1,550 spent on the Unisaw can be calculated as $26 per warranted month, compared to $94 per warranted month for the next-highest-rated saw, the Grizzly.

11

Recommendation

This recommendation states explicitly what the writers think the reader should do next.

The recommendation largely repeats information presented in other places in the report. In technical communication, repetition can reinforce important information and increase your chances of reaching readers who read only selected portions of long documents.

We recommend buying a Delta Unisaw 36-L31X-BC50 for $1,550 for our shop. We conclude that it would reduce safety risks. In addition, it would reduce work time on ripping and finishing by four hours per employee per month, as well as reduce wasted materials, a combined savings of $1,400 per month. Although we could repair our current saw for only $750, the time lost in repair and its continued deterioration without warranty coverage would be far more costly than buying a new Delta Unisaw. The Delta Unisaw would pay for itself in a little more than one month.

12

References

How to buy a table saw. (2003). Retrieved October 13, 2004, from http://www.rd.com/
americanwoodworker/toolguide/HTB_Tablesaw.pdf

Loganbill, J. (n.d.). *Setting up a table saw & squaring crosscut devices.* Retrieved October
16, 2004, from http://thewoodshop.20m.com/calibrate_sled1.htm

Strickland, S. (n.d.). *Table saw tuneup.* Retrieved October 12, 2004, from http://www
.puzzlecraft.com/Projects/HTMAP/07saw.htm

Strong, J. (2003). *Eyeing table saw specifications.* Retrieved October 9, 2004, from http://
www.dummies.com/WileyCDA/DummiesArticle/id-2324.html

Tablesaw safety. (n.d.). Retrieved October 12, 2004, from http://www.woodmagazine.com/
wood/story.jhtml?storyid=/templatedata/wood/story/data/333.xml&catref=wd25

Wright, D. (2003). *Choosing a tablesaw: Contractor or cabinet?* Retrieved October 15,
2004, from http://www.woodcentral.com/bparticles/con_vs_table.shtml

This list of references is written according to the APA documentation style, which is discussed in Appendix, Part B, p. 582.

13

Appendix A: Employee Questionnaire

[Here the writers present the questionnaire that they presented in the progress report that appears in Chapter 17, page 445. Reusing information from previous documents related to the project is efficient and ethical.]

14

One of the writers tape-recorded this interview (with the respondent's permission). Because the respondent is well known in the woodworking community, the writers are wise to include this transcript.

Appendix B: Interview with Nathan Abram

The following interview took place on November 2, 2004. A transcript of the interview follows.

D - Dave Bethke, interviewer
N - Nathan Abram, expert woodworker

D - Nathan, it has been a while since we have talked, and I appreciate your taking time out of your busy schedule to talk with me.

N - It's my pleasure, Dave. I can always make time for old friends.

D - Well, as I told you over the phone, our shop is in need of a new table saw. Can you give me a few tips to consider when looking for a new saw, as well as your own preferences?

N - The main points to look for depend on your application of the saw. You work as a professional carpenter, so the saw will get a lot of use. There are three types of table saws: contractor, hybrid, and cabinet.

The contractor saw has an open base, which leads to poor dust collection. It is also made for light-duty applications, so they are usually less than 1.5 hp.

The hybrid saws are a little beefier, such that the motors are 2 hp, and they try to incorporate a dust chute to direct the dust away from the blade. They are slightly heavier to help reduce the vibrations.

The cabinet saws are the Cadillacs of the table saws. They have motors ranging from 3 to 5 hp. They are typically 600-plus pounds, virtually eliminating vibrations. They also have a dust-management system that helps remove almost all the dust away from the saw.

Once you pick the type of saw, I would say motor, fence material, quality of construction, table size, ease of use, and blade are the major factors in choosing a new saw.

D - Let's start with the motor.

N - Well, you know as well as I do that ripping woods like hard maple, walnut, and cherry requires a lot of power. If you don't have enough power, the blade will bind up and cause severe damage to the wood, saw, and, most dangerously, the operator. I would look for at least 3 hp and, if it is in the budget, 5 hp.

D - How about the fence? What should we be looking for?

N - There are three things to keep in mind when looking for a table-saw fence: length, height, and face material. You need to find a fence that you are comfortable working with. If the fence is not easily adjustable, it most likely will not be adjusted when it gets out of alignment. Try to get the largest fence system possible; I use a 50-inch Unifence.

15

The Unifence is nice because the fence face is aluminum, and you can rotate it for different applications. I have used Biesemeyer fences and think that they are great. A lot of other brands, OEM and aftermarket, copy the Biesemeyer T-square fence because it is an industry standard. I like the laminate face of the Biesemeyer; the knockoffs use materials like plastic and Teflon. But both of these materials seem to move with temperature fluctuations, causing the fence to have waves across the face of the material. As I stated earlier, I currently use the Unifence, but I switch back and forth because of my sponsors. Dave, ultimately I would use the Biesemeyer-brand fence.

D - You mentioned table size. What did you mean here; out-feed or extension?

N - Both. You need a good out-feed table when cutting sheet goods or long sticks of lumber. There are two different options here, laminate and roller. I use a laminate table.

Extension wings are necessary to widen your tabletop. I would look for solid cast iron, not webbed. I have had problems with webbed extension wings warping on me in the past.

D - What are your thoughts on blades?

N - Well, I would look for a saw with a 10-inch blade. The reason I say that is because 12-inch and 14-inch blades are hard to come by and they are *very* expensive, where a very nice 10-inch blade will cost about $120. Make sure your arbor will hold a dado set of at least 3/4″. I would also get a zero-clearance insert to help reduce chip-out on the bottom of the cut.

D - I would like to say thank you for your time; I really appreciate it.

N - No problem, Dave. Remember to make sure that you get a good miter gauge, dust collector, splitter, and push sticks for your saw. Safety is always number one. Remember: the most important safety rule is to wear your safety glasses.

16

Appendix C: Portland Coliseum Exposition Trip Report

[Here the writers present the trip report that they presented in the progress report that appears in Chapter 17, page 446.]

Writer's Checklist

Does the transmittal letter

- [ ] clearly state the title and, if necessary, the subject and purpose of the document? (p. 475)
- [ ] clearly state who authorized or commissioned the document? (p. 475)
- [ ] briefly state the methods you used? (p. 475)
- [ ] summarize your major results, conclusions, and recommendations? (p. 475)
- [ ] acknowledge any assistance you received? (p. 475)
- [ ] courteously offer further assistance? (p. 475)

Does the cover include

- [ ] the title of the document? (p. 467)
- [ ] your name and position? (p. 467)
- [ ] the date of submission? (p. 467)
- [ ] the company name or logo? (p. 467)

Does the title page

- [ ] include a title that clearly states the subject and purpose of the document? (p. 476)
- [ ] list the names and positions of both you and your principal reader? (p. 476)
- [ ] include the date of submission of the document and any other identifying information? (p. 476)

Does the abstract

- [ ] list the document title, your name, and any other identifying information? (p. 477)
- [ ] clearly define the problem or opportunity that led to the project? (p. 477)
- [ ] briefly describe (if appropriate) the research methods? (p. 477)
- [ ] summarize the major results, conclusions, and recommendations? (p. 477)

Does the table of contents

- [ ] clearly identify the executive summary? (p. 478)
- [ ] contain a sufficiently detailed breakdown of the major sections of the body of the document? (p. 469)
- [ ] reproduce the headings as they appear in your document? (p. 478)
- [ ] include page numbers? (p. 469)

- [ ] Does the list of illustrations (or list of tables or list of figures) include all the graphics found in the body of the document? (p. 470)

Does the executive summary

- [ ] clearly state the problem or opportunity that led to the project? (p. 470)
- [ ] explain the major results, conclusions, recommendations, and managerial implications of your document? (p. 470)
- [ ] avoid technical vocabulary and concepts that a managerial audience is not likely to know? (p. 471)

In planning your informational, analytical, or recommendation report, did you

- [ ] analyze your audience? (p. 458)
- [ ] analyze your purpose? (p. 458)
- [ ] identify the questions that need to be answered? (p. 458)
- [ ] carry out appropriate research? (p. 458)
- [ ] draw valid conclusions about the results (if appropriate)? (p. 458)
- [ ] formulate recommendations based on the conclusions (if appropriate)? (p. 458)

Does the introduction

- [ ] explain the subject of the report? (p. 464)
- [ ] explain the purpose of the report? (p. 464)
- [ ] explain the background of the report? (p. 464)
- [ ] describe your sources of information? (p. 464)
- [ ] indicate the scope of the report? (p. 465)
- [ ] briefly summarize the most significant findings of the project? (p. 465)
- [ ] briefly summarize your recommendations? (p. 465)
- [ ] explain the organization of the report? (p. 465)
- [ ] define key terms used in the report? (p. 465)

- [ ] Does the methods section describe your methods in sufficient detail? (p. 465)
- [ ] Have you justified your methods where necessary, explaining, for instance, why you chose one method over another? (p. 465)

Are the results presented

- [ ] clearly? (p. 465)
- [ ] objectively? (p. 465)
- [ ] without interpretation? (p. 465)

Are the conclusions

- [ ] presented clearly? (p. 466)
- [ ] drawn logically from the results? (p. 466)

Are the recommendations

- ☐ clear? (p. 466)
- ☐ objective? (p. 466)
- ☐ polite? (p. 466)
- ☐ in an appropriate form (list or paragraph)? (p. 466)
- ☐ in an appropriate location? (p. 466)

- ☐ Does the glossary include definitions of all the technical terms your readers might not know? (p. 473)
- ☐ Does the list of symbols include all the symbols and abbreviations your readers might not know? (p. 473)
- ☐ Do the appendices include the supporting materials that are too bulky to present in the document body or are of interest to only a small number of your readers? (p. 474)

Exercises

 In This Book   For more about memos, see Ch. 14, p. 352.

1. An important element in carrying out a feasibility study is determining the criteria by which to judge each option. For each of the following topics, list five necessary criteria and five desirable criteria you might apply in assessing the options.

    a. buying a computer printer

    b. selecting a major

    c. choosing a company to work for

    d. buying a car

    e. choosing a place to live while you attend college

2. **INTERNET EXERCISE** In Links Library for Chapter 6 on <bedfordstmartins.com/techcomm>, find a site that links to government agencies and departments. Find a government report on a subject that interests you. Determine whether it is an informative, an analytical, or a recommendation report. In what ways does the structure of the report differ from the structure described in this chapter? In other words, does it lack some of the elements described in this chapter, or does it have additional elements? Are the elements arranged in the same order in which they are described in this chapter? In what ways do the differences reflect the audience, purpose, and subject of the report?

3. **GROUP EXERCISE** Write the completion report for the research project you proposed in response to Exercise 3 on page 427 in Chapter 16. Your instructor will tell you whether the report is to be written individually or collaboratively, but work with a partner in reviewing and revising your report. You and your partner will work together closely at the end of the project as you revise your reports, but keep in mind that a partner can be very helpful during the planning phase, too, as you choose a topic, refine it, and plan your research.

4. **INTERNET EXERCISE** Secure a completion report for a project subsidized by a city or federal agency, a private organization, or a university committee or task force. (Be sure to check your university's Web site; universities routinely publish strategic planning documents and other sorts of self-study reports. Also check <www.nas.edu>, which is the site for the National Academy of Sciences, the National Academy of Engineering, the Institute of Medicine, and the National Research Council, all of which publish reports on the Web.) In a memo to your instructor, analyze the report. Overall, how effective is it? How could the writers have improved the report? If possible, submit a copy of the report along with your memo.

Case 18: Analyzing Options and Drawing Conclusions

 In This Book   For more about memos, see Ch. 14, p. 352.

Background

Pioneer Construction, based in Syracuse, New York, offers a range of construction services, including feasibility studies, negotiated design construction, traditional-plan and spec-bid construction, and construction management. With more than 100 full-time employees and sales reaching $38 million annually, Pioneer builds everything from shopping centers and warehouses to restaurants and churches. In addition to heavy-duty construction equipment and vehicles, Pioneer maintains a fleet of 10 pickup trucks. Pioneer's construction supervisors use these trucks to travel to construction sites, haul tools and equipment, and transport clients.

Currently, Pioneer is using an aging fleet of trucks. Bought before many of the safety and comfort features standard in new pickups were available, these trucks do not reflect the focus on safety and quality that the company wishes to convey to clients, nor do they allow the construction supervisors to carry out their duties efficiently. At a recent meeting, a construction supervisor lamented, "My truck spends more time out of service than in service." This remark prompted dozens of other comments critical of the company's trucks. These comments only reinforced what the company president, Mattias van Noordennen, already knew: it was time to replace the company's trucks.

"What type of truck should we buy?" Mattias asked.

"Ram 2500 Quad Cab," one supervisor suggested.

"I like the GMC Sierra 2500's tight turning radius," another said.

Someone else added, "The ground clearance of the Chevrolet Silverado 2500HD is impressive."

A fourth supervisor began, "I agree. The Silverado's 3,125-pound payload capacity—"

"Wait a second," Mattias interrupted. "Do we know if we need that heavy a capacity for our pickups? I think we should first determine what we *need* our new trucks to be able to do. Then we can decide what we'd *like* them to be able to do. I know that your job duties vary, but I am confident that each of you can describe typical ways in which you use your pickup at work." Mattias then outlined how he would like to proceed: each construction supervisor will send him an e-mail message in which the supervisor briefly summarizes how he or she typically uses his or her truck.

After the meeting, Mattias stopped by your office. He asked you and your colleagues in the Documentation Department to help him develop evaluation criteria. "Because of your team's experience in responding to evaluation criteria in our clients' RFPs, as well as in developing criteria for our company's IFBs, I thought you could help us come up with evaluation criteria to use when we select a replacement truck for our pickup fleet. Take a look at the construction supervisors' comments (Document 18.1) and figure out what they are looking for in a pickup truck. Our budget will limit the cost of each truck to no more than $35,000."

Your Assignment

1. Based on the information provided by the construction supervisors and your own research on heavy-duty pickups, write Mattias a memo in which you recommend the *necessary* and *desirable* criteria the company should use to select a replacement vehicle for the pickup fleet.

2. Create a decision matrix for company officials to evaluate each vehicle option systematically according to each *desirable* criterion you have established. Include a scoring key that lists the range of values for each criterion and explains how to use the guide to score the vehicle options objectively.

3. Based on data from your decision matrix, write the conclusions and recommendations sections of a feasibility report on replacing the pickup fleet at Pioneer.

On TechComm Web

For digital versions of case
documents, click on
Downloadable Case Documents
on <bedfordstmartins.com/
techcomm>.

Chris Wetzler

I practically live in my truck, so comfort and safety are important to me. I need a truck that is comfortable enough for daily use and rugged enough for off-road use. I probably spend 60% of my time on paved roads and the rest on dirt or snow. Although many of us don't often fill the truck's bed to full capacity, when I do, I need at least 6 feet 6 inches to comfortably haul materials—a short bed won't do. This stuff isn't very heavy (half a ton at most).

Geordie Olsson

I carry a lot of tools with me, both in the cab and in the bed. I also tow up to 10,000 lbs. a couple of times a month. I use the front seat of my truck as a desk. I'm frequently on dirt roads requiring high clearance. In the winter, 4WD has helped me get to sites that I couldn't reach with 2WD. When visiting sites, I use the cab to carry blueprints and other large items that are too fragile or sensitive to leave exposed to the elements.

Libby Sabanosh

Towing equipment every day, I lug a healthy 7,000 to 9,000 pounds to work sites. A truck with lots of muscle would be great. It seems that it's never just me in the truck. I usually take a few folks from the office to a site. I also taxi people back to the office. At times, I need to carry one-ton loads in the bed. The items are not bulky but can be almost seven feet in length.

Hank de Vre

I frequently take two or three clients to a site. I'm a little embarrassed to ask all of them to squeeze into the front seat with me. The backseat is just not big enough for adults to ride comfortably. I also notice the look on their faces when they discover that my truck is missing its seat belts in back. I tow up to 9,500 lbs. and loads up to 2,000 lbs. in the bed.

Sara Fedarko

I haul building supplies or other cargo of significant length and weight: up to seven feet and 2,500 pounds. Although I usually travel by myself, a couple of times a month I drive with passengers. I frequently use 4WD at muddy sites, especially in the winter. Electronic traction control would be nice. Thankfully, I've never needed air bags, but I'd appreciate front and side air bags.

19 Writing Instructions and Manuals

TECH COMM AT WORK

As a professional, you will read and write instructions and manuals on the job. A librarian might write sets of instructions for patrons on how to access the library's resources and collections. A manager in Human Relations might write instructions to help employees understand how to request permission to travel on company business and how to request reimbursement after they return. A technical communicator might write instructions to help other technical professionals use document templates effectively. This person also might write or edit employee manuals, as well as user's manuals to accompany products made by the company.

A computer-industry analyst (Greiner, 2004, p. 12) laments the poor state of the instruction sheets he works with:

> Insert a circuit card the wrong way, and it could be damaged beyond salvation. Put batteries in backwards, and you could get a nice explosion. Plug in wires wrong, and your equipment could flunk the smoke test.

Because instructions and manuals have acquired a bad reputation over the years, many people don't even bother trying to read them. This situation is regrettable, because instructions and manuals are fundamentally important in carrying out procedures and using products safely and effectively.

Chapter 9 discusses process descriptions, which explain how a process occurs—for example, how a water heater burns natural gas to heat the water inside. This chapter discusses instructions, which are process descriptions written to help the reader perform a specific task—for instance, installing a water heater in a house. This chapter also discusses manuals, which are larger documents that often include instructions. Figure 19.1 on page 498, a page from a user's manual, illustrates some of the basic concepts that will be presented in this chapter.

 On TechComm Web

For examples of instructions, see Writing for Engineering and Science Students. Click on Links Library for Ch. 19 on <bedfordstmartins.com/techcomm>.

UNDERSTANDING THE PROCESS OF WRITING INSTRUCTIONS AND MANUALS

When you write instructions and manuals, you use the same planning, drafting, revising, editing, and proofreading process that you use with other kinds of technical documents. However, some aspects of the process are applied somewhat differently, as shown in Figure 19.2 on page 499.

DESIGNING A SET OF INSTRUCTIONS

As you plan to write a set of instructions, think about how readers will be using the document. Analyzing your audience and purpose, and gathering and organizing your information, will help you decide whether you should

This is a page from the user's manual for a Casio digital piano.

The headings for the two tasks described on this page include gerunds ("-ing" verbs).

Safety information is presented to help the reader avoid injury.

Instructional writing consists of words and graphics. This document uses a two-column design, with one task presented in each column. A vertical rule helps the reader see how to read the page.

Notice that the design is open and attractive. Each numbered step begins at the top of a column. As a result, there is a lot of white space under the graphic and words that make up step 3.

In instructional writing, steps are numbered clearly. Sometimes, as in this case, a numbered step can have sub-steps. Here the sub-steps are presented in bulleted lists.

Diagrams allow the designer or illustrator to include detailed drawings of important components.

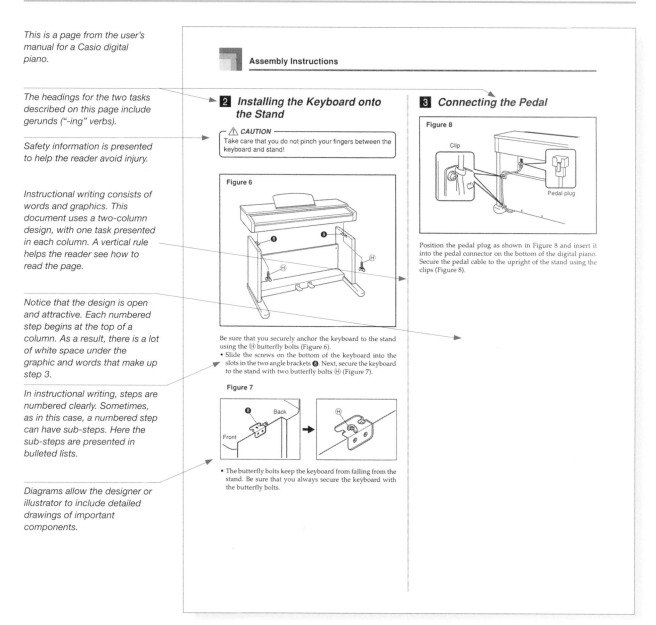

Assembly Instructions

2 **Installing the Keyboard onto the Stand**

⚠ CAUTION
Take care that you do not pinch your fingers between the keyboard and stand!

Figure 6

Be sure that you securely anchor the keyboard to the stand using the ⊞ butterfly bolts (Figure 6).
• Slide the screws on the bottom of the keyboard into the slots in the two angle brackets ❺. Next, secure the keyboard to the stand with two butterfly bolts ⊞ (Figure 7).

Figure 7

Front   Back

• The butterfly bolts keep the keyboard from falling from the stand. Be sure that you always secure the keyboard with the butterfly bolts.

3 **Connecting the Pedal**

Figure 8

Clip

Pedal plug

Position the pedal plug as shown in Figure 8 and insert it into the pedal connector on the bottom of the digital piano. Secure the pedal cable to the upright of the stand using the clips (Figure 8).

■ **Figure 19.1   Characteristics of Instructional Writing**
Source: Casio, 2005 <ftp.casio.co.jp/pub/world_manual/emi/en/ap_24/01_e.pdf>.

write a one-page set of instructions or a longer document that needs to be bound. You might realize that the information would work better as a Web-based document that allows readers to link to the information they need. Or you might decide to write several versions of the information: a brief,

Analyze Your Audience and Purpose

Who are your readers? What do they already understand about the subject? What is their attitude toward the subject? What are their language skills? Where and how will they be using the instructions or manual? Try to state your purpose, such as "to explain the procedure to follow in case of chemical contamination in the lab." You will need to state the purpose in the instructions or manual. For more information, see Chapter 5.

Gather and Organize Your Information

Use the primary- and secondary-research techniques discussed in Chapter 6. Read existing documents about similar subjects, perform observations, and interview or distribute questionnaires to the people in your organization who designed and fabricated the items and processes you are discussing. Perform the tasks that you plan on explaining. For more information, see Chapters 6 and 7.

Design the Document

Your design will depend on the medium you choose (paper or online), the amount of information you want to communicate, the reading ability of your readers, the conditions under which the document will be read, and other factors. For more information, see Chapter 12 and the discussion in this chapter beginning on page 500.

Draft the Document

As you draft, carry out the process you are describing. You are likely to be more effective in drafting the document than someone who knows the process better because you will confront the same challenges that the eventual reader will confront. For more information, see Chapter 3.

Revise, Edit, and Proofread the Document

In revising, check the document to see whether you can carry out the process it describes. In addition, show it to subject-matter experts to see whether it contains any errors or omissions. For more information, see Chapter 3.

Test the Document

Usability testing, which involves observing people as they carry out the tasks explained in the document, will help you determine whether users can read the document easily and use it effectively. Usability testing is discussed in this chapter beginning on page 521.

■ **Figure 19.2 An Overview of the Process for Writing Instructions and Manuals**

paper-based set of instructions and a longer, Web-based document with links that users can access from the company intranet.

As always in technical communication, imagining how readers will use what you write will help you plan how to create a document. For example,

In This Book

For more about planning, see Ch. 3.

having decided that your audience, purpose, and subject call for a paper-based set of instructions of perhaps 1,000 words and a dozen drawings and photographs, you can start to design the document. You will need to consider your resources, especially your budget: long documents cost more than short ones; color costs more than black and white; heavy paper costs more than light paper; secure bindings cost more than staples.

Designing a set of instructions is much like designing any other kind of technical document. As discussed in Chapter 12, you want to create a document that is attractive and easy to use. When you design a set of instructions, you need to consider a number of issues related to document and page design.

Designing the Document

In designing a set of instructions, you need to consider many factors, including the following:

- *What are your reader's expectations?* For instructions that accompany a simple, inexpensive product such as a light switch, readers will expect instructions written on the back of the package or, at most, printed in black and white on a small sheet of paper folded inside the package. For instructions that accompany an expensive consumer product such as a high-definition TV, readers will expect a more sophisticated full-color document printed on high-quality paper.

- *Do you need to create more than one set of instructions for different audiences?* If you are writing about complex devices such as electronic thermostats, you might decide to create one set of instructions for electricians (who will install and maintain the device) and one set for homeowners (who will operate the device). You might decide to create a paper-based document that can also be read easily on the Internet.

- *What languages should you use?* In most countries, including the United States, several or many languages are spoken. You might decide to include instructions in two or more languages. Doing so will help you communicate better with more people, and it can help you avoid legal problems. In liability cases, U.S. courts sometimes find that if a company knew that many of its customers speak only Spanish, for example, the instructions should appear in Spanish as well as in English. If you are making multilingual instructions, you will have to decide whether to combine the different versions on the same page or print all the instructions in English first, then in the second language. Obviously, the more languages in which you present the information, the longer the document will be. Length will affect your budget because it affects the kind of binding and the size and weight of paper to use.

- *Will the environment in which the instructions are read affect the document design?* If people will be using the instructions outdoors, you will need to use a coated paper that can tolerate a little water. If people will be reading the instructions while sitting in a small, enclosed area, you might select a small paper size and a binding that allows the reader to fold the pages over to save space. If people have a lot of room, you might decide to create poster-size instructions that can be taped to the wall and that are easy to read from across the room.

Designing the Pages

The previous discussion of document design hints at some of the important issues regarding page design that you need to consider:

- *Should you make your pages multilingual?* You have two choices: simultaneous or sequential. In a *simultaneous design,* you might create a multicolumn page. One column presents the graphics; another presents the text in English; another presents the text in Spanish. Obviously, this won't work if you have more than two or three languages. But it is efficient because you can present each graphic only once. In a *sequential design,* you present all the information in English (say, on pages 1–8), then all the information in Spanish (on pages 9–16). The sequential design is easier for readers to use because they are not distracted by text in other languages, but you will have to present all the graphics several times, which will make the instructions longer.

- *Will readers be anxious about the information?* If readers will find the information intimidating, make the design unintimidating. For instance, if you are writing to general readers about how to set up a wireless network for home computers, create open pages with a lot of white space and graphics. Use large type and narrow text columns so that each page contains a relatively small amount of information.

- *Will the environment in which the instructions are read affect the page design or typography?* If your readers will be reading the instructions in good light, you can use normal type sizes. If they will be reading in poor light, you will want to use larger type.

Regardless of how you answer these questions, design your pages so that they are clear and attractive.

 **In This Book**
For more about design, see Ch. 12.

For more about design, see Ch. 12.

Guidelines

Designing Clear, Attractive Pages

To design pages that are clear and attractive, follow these two guidelines:

▶ **Create an open, airy design.** Do not squeeze too much information onto the page. Build in space for wide margins and effective line spacing, use large type, and chunk the information effectively.

> ▶ **Clearly relate the graphics to the text.** In the step-by-step portions of a set of instructions, present graphics to accompany every step or almost every step. Create a design that makes it clear which graphics go with each text passage. One easy way to do this is to use a table, with the graphics in one column and the text in the other. A horizontal rule or extra line spacing separates the text and graphics for one step from the text and graphics for the next step.
>
> Figure 19.3 shows these points.

a. Cluttered design

This page is cluttered, containing far too much information. The page is not chunked effectively. As a result, the reader's eyes don't know where to focus. Would you look forward to using these instructions to assemble this cabinet?

Source: Slide-Lok, 2005

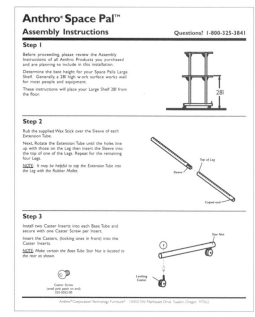

b. Attractive design

This page is well designed, containing an appropriate amount of information presented in a simple two-column format. Notice the effective use of white space and the horizontal rules separating the steps.

Source: Anthro, 2005
<www.anthro.com/assemblyinstructions/ 300-5237-00.pdf>.

■ **Figure 19.3   Cluttered and Attractive Page Designs in a Set of Instructions**

PLANNING FOR SAFETY

Even though some kinds of tasks do not involve safety risks, many do. If they do, your most important responsibility in writing documentation is to make sure you do everything you can to ensure your readers' safety.

Plan for safety by:

Writing effective safety information

Designing effective safety information

Placing safety information in the appropriate location

Ethics Note

Protecting Your Readers' Safety

Whether you are writing to other people in your own organization, to customers, to vendors, or to the general public, you should do whatever you can to ensure that readers stay safe. To a large extent, the way to do this is to be honest and write clearly. If readers will encounter safety risks, explain what those risks are and how to minimize them. Doing so is a question of rights. Readers have a right to the best information they can get.

Protecting your readers' safety is also a question of law. People who get hurt can sue the company that made the product or provided the service. As discussed in Chapter 2, this field of law is called *liability law*. Your company is likely to have legal professionals on staff or on retainer who are charged with ensuring that the company is not responsible for putting people at unnecessary risk.

Writing Effective Safety Information

Be clear and concise. Avoid complicated sentences.

COMPLICATED	It is required that safety glasses be worn when inside this laboratory.
SIMPLE	You must wear safety glasses in this laboratory.
SIMPLE	Wear safety glasses in this laboratory.

Sometimes a phrase works better than a sentence: "Safety glasses required."

Because a typical set of instructions or a manual can contain dozens of comments—both safety and nonsafety—experts have devised *signal words* to indicate the seriousness of the advice. Unfortunately, signal words are not used consistently. For instance, the American National Standards Institute (ANSI) and the U.S. military's MILSPEC publish definitions that differ significantly, and many private companies have their own definitions. Figure 19.4 on page 504 presents the four most popular signal words; the first three words are accompanied by symbols showing the color combinations endorsed by ANSI in its Standard Z535.4.

Designing Effective Safety Information

Whether printed in a document or on machinery or equipment, safety information should be prominent and easy to read. Many organizations use visual symbols to represent levels of danger, but these symbols are not standardized.

Organizations that create products sold only in the United States use safety information that conforms with standards published by ANSI and with the federal Occupational Safety and Health Administration (OSHA). Organizations that create products that are also sold outside the United States use safety information that conforms with standards published by the International

 On TechComm Web

For advice about communicating safety information on Web pages, see Lisa A. Tallman's "Designing for the Web: Special Considerations for Safety Information." Click on Links Library for Ch. 19 on <bedfordstmartins.com/techcomm>.

 In This Book

For more about color, see Ch. 12, p. 264.

Signal Word	Explanation	Example
Danger **⚠ DANGER**	*Danger* is used to alert readers about an immediate and serious hazard that will likely be fatal. Notice that writers often use all-uppercase letters for danger statements.	DANGER: EXTREMELY HIGH VOLTAGE. STAND BACK.
Warning **⚠WARNING**	*Warning* is used to alert readers about the potential for serious injury or death or serious damage to equipment. Notice that writers often use all-uppercase letters for warning statements.	WARNING: TO PREVENT SERIOUS INJURY TO YOUR ARMS AND HANDS, YOU MUST MAKE SURE THE ARM RESTRAINTS ARE IN PLACE BEFORE OPERATING THIS MACHINE.
Caution **⚠CAUTION**	*Caution* is used to alert readers about the potential for anything from moderate injury to serious equipment damage or destruction.	Caution: Do not use nonrechargeable batteries in this charging unit; they could damage the charging unit.
Note	*Note* is used for a tip or suggestion to help the readers carry out the procedure successfully.	Note: Two kinds of washers are provided—regular washers and locking washers. Be sure to use the locking washers here.

■ **Figure 19.4 Signal Words**

The yellow triangle is consistent with the ISO approach. Because ISO creates standards for international use, its safety labels use icons, not words, to represent safety dangers.

The Danger signal word and the text are consistent with the ANSI approach. The information is presented in English.

■ **Figure 19.5 A Typical Safety Label**
Source: HCS, LLC, 2004
<www. safetylabel.com/search/index.
php?pn=H6010-CDDHPL>.

 **On TechComm Web**

To view Fig. 19.5 in context on the Web, click on Links Library for Ch. 19 on <bedfordstmartins.com/techcomm>.

For information on designing safety labels, see HCS at safetylabel .com. Click on Links Library for Ch. 19 on <bedfordstmartins.com/techcomm>.

Organization for Standardization (ISO). Figure 19.5 shows a safety label that incorporates ANSI and ISO standards.

Placing Safety Information in the Appropriate Location

What is the appropriate location for safety information? This question has no easy answer because you cannot control how your audience reads your document. Be conservative: put safety information wherever you think the reader is likely to see it, and don't be afraid to repeat yourself. A reasonable amount of repetition—such as including the same safety comment at the top of each page—is effective. But don't repeat the same piece of advice in each of 20 steps, because readers will stop paying attention to it. If your company's format for instructions calls for a safety section near the beginning of the document, place the information there and repeat it just before the appropriate step in the step-by-step section.

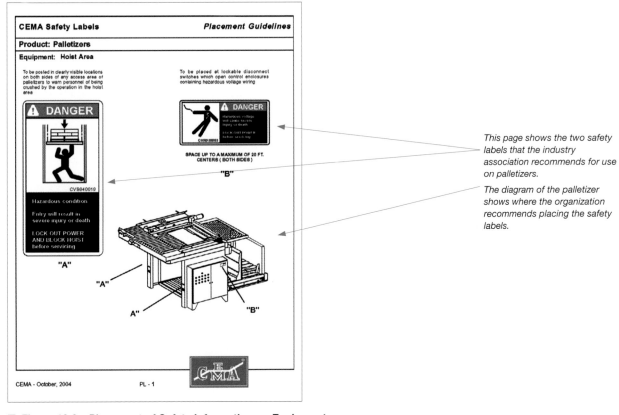

The page shows the two safety labels that the industry association recommends for use on palletizers.

The diagram of the palletizer shows where the organization recommends placing the safety labels.

■ **Figure 19.6   Placement of Safety Information on Equipment**
Source: CEMA, 2004 <www.cemanet.org/safety/p11.pdf>.

Figure 19.6 shows one industry association's guidelines for placing safety information on palletizers.

DRAFTING EFFECTIVE INSTRUCTIONS

Instructions can be brief—a small sheet of paper—or extensive, up to 20 pages or more. Brief instructions might be produced by a writer, a graphic artist, and a subject-matter expert. Longer instructions might call for additional people, such as marketing and legal personnel.

Regardless of the size of the project, most instructions are organized like process descriptions. The main difference is that the conclusion of a set of instructions is not a summary but an explanation of how to make sure the reader has followed the instructions correctly. Most sets of instructions contain four elements: title, general introduction, step-by-step instructions, and conclusion.

Elements of a set of instructions:

Title

General introduction

Step-by-step instructions

Conclusion

 **In This Book**

For more about process descriptions, see Ch. 9, p. 187.

Drafting the Title

A good title for instructions is simple and clear. Two forms are common:

- *How-to*. This is the simplest form: "How to Install the J112 Shock Absorber."
- *Gerund*. The gerund form uses the "-ing" form of a verb: "Installing the J112 Shock Absorber."

One form to avoid is the noun string, which is awkward and hard for readers to understand: "J112 Shock Absorber Installation Instructions."

 **In This Book**

For more about noun strings, see Ch. 11, p. 239.

Drafting the General Introduction

The general introduction provides the preliminary information that readers will need to follow the instructions safely and easily.

Guidelines

Drafting Introductions for Instructions

Every set of instructions is different and calls for a different introduction. Where appropriate, consider answering the following six questions:

▶ **Who should carry out the task?** Sometimes you need to identify or describe the person or persons who are to carry out a task. Aircraft maintenance, for example, may be performed only by those certified to do it.

▶ **Why should the reader carry out this task?** Sometimes the reason is obvious: you don't need to explain why a backyard barbecue grill should be assembled. But you do need to explain the rationale for many tasks, such as changing radiator antifreeze in a car.

▶ **When should the reader carry out this task?** Some tasks, such as rotating tires or planting crops, need to be performed at particular times or particular intervals.

▶ **What safety measures or other concerns should the reader understand?** In addition to the safety measures that apply to the whole task, mention any tips that will make the job easier:

    NOTE: For ease of assembly, leave all nuts loose. Give only 3 or 4 complete turns on bolt threads.

▶ **What items will the reader need?** List necessary tools, materials, and equipment so that the reader will not have to interrupt his or her work to hunt for something. If you think the reader might not be able to identify these items easily, include drawings next to the names.

▶ **How long will the task take?** Consider stating how long the task will take readers with no experience, some experience, and a lot of experience.

 In This Book

For more about graphics, see Ch. 13.

Drafting Step-by-Step Instructions

The heart of a set of instructions is the step-by-step information.

Guidelines

Drafting Steps in Instructions

▶ **Number the instructions.** For long, complex instructions, use two-level numbering, such as a decimal system.

1
    1.1
    1.2
2
    2.1
    2.2
etc.

If you need to present a long set of steps, such as 50, group them logically into, say, six sets of eight or nine steps, and begin each set with a clear heading.

▶ **Present the right amount of information in each step.** Each step should define a single task the reader can carry out easily, without having to refer to the instructions.

TOO MUCH INFORMATION	1. Mix one part cement with one part water, using the trowel. When the mixture is a thick consistency without any lumps bigger than a marble, place a strip of the mixture about 1" high and 1" wide along the face of the brick.
TOO LITTLE INFORMATION	1. Pick up the trowel.
RIGHT AMOUNT OF INFORMATION	1. Mix one part cement with one part water, using the trowel, until the mixture is a thick consistency without any lumps bigger than a marble.
	2. Place a strip of the mixture about 1" high and 1" wide along the face of the brick.

▶ **Use the imperative mood.** For example, "Attach the red wire...." The imperative is more direct and economical than the indicative mood ("You should attach the red wire..." or "The operator should attach the red wire..."). Avoid the passive voice ("The red wire is attached..."), because it can be ambiguous: is the red wire already attached?

▶ **Do not confuse steps and feedback statements.** A *step* is an action that the reader is to perform. A *feedback statement* describes an event that occurs in response to a step. For instance, a step might read "Insert the disk in the drive." That step's feedback statement might read "The system will now update your user information." Do not make a feedback statement a numbered step. Present it as part of the step to which it refers. Some writers give feedback statements their own design.

 On TechComm Web

For examples of instructions, see HowStuffWorks and Knowledge Hound. Click on Links Library for Ch. 19 on <bedfordstmartins.com/techcomm>.

 In This Book

For more about the imperative mood and the passive voice, see Ch. 11, pp. 235 and 236.

📖 **In This Book**

For more about graphics, see
Ch. 13.

▶ **Include graphics.** When appropriate, add a photograph or a drawing to show the reader what to do. Some activities, such as adding two drops of a reagent to a mixture, do not need an illustration, but they might be clarified by charts or tables.

▶ **Do not omit articles (*a, an, the*) to save space.** Omitting articles can make the instructions unclear and hard to read. In the sentence "Locate midpoint and draw line," for example, the reader cannot tell whether "draw line" is a noun (as in "locate the draw line") or a verb and its object (as in "draw the line").

Drafting the Conclusion

Instructions often conclude by stating that the reader has completed the task or by describing what the reader should do next. For example:

> Now that you have replaced the glass and applied the glazing compound, let it sit for at least five days so that the glazing can cure. Then prime and paint the window.

Some conclusions end with *maintenance tips* or a *troubleshooting guide*. This guide, usually in the form of a table, identifies common problems and explains how to solve them.

REVISING, EDITING, AND PROOFREADING INSTRUCTIONS

You want to revise, edit, and proofread all the documents you write to make sure they are honest, clear, accurate, comprehensive, accessible, concise, professional in appearance, and correct. When you write instructions, you should be extra careful, for two reasons.

First, your readers rely on your instructions to carry out the task. If they can't complete it—or they do complete it, but the device doesn't work correctly—they'll be unhappy. Nobody likes to spend a few hours assembling a garage-door opener, then find half a dozen parts left over. Second, readers rely on you to help them complete the task safely. To prevent injuries—and liability actions—build into the budget time to revise, edit, and proofread your instructions carefully.

One form of revision that is often used for instructional writing is usability testing, which is discussed later in this chapter, beginning on page 521.

SAMPLE INSTRUCTIONS

Figure 19.7 is a full set of instructions. Figure 19.8 on page 510 is a list of parts from a set of instructions. Figure 19.9 on page 511 is a list of tools and materials from a set of instructions. Figure 19.10 on page 512 is an excerpt from the safety information in a set of instructions. Figure 19.11 on page 513 is the conclusion from a set of installation instructions. Figure 19.12 on page 513 is a portion of the troubleshooting guide in the instructions for a lawn mower.

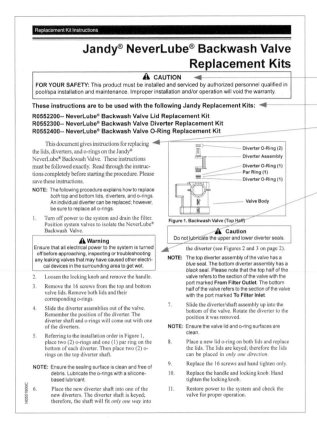

This is the first page of a two-page set of instructions for installing a replacement valve assembly used in swimming pools.

The title is indicated in the header and in the large type at the top.

The caution box indicates that the instructions are intended only for authorized personnel. Notice the use of the mandatory word must.

This statement indicates which models of the product are covered by these instructions.

The writer explicitly states the purpose of the document.

Note that there is no list of tools and materials. Because the instructions are intended for experienced technicians, the writer assumes they will have the appropriate tools and materials.

A warning, with its own design, informs the reader of the electrical hazard. The warning should state that the risks include electrocution, which might lead to serious injury or death. A qualified installer knows these risks, of course, but the writer should state them anyway.

The writer uses a two-column design, which allows all the text to fit on one side of the sheet of paper. This design is inconvenient for the reader, however, who has to turn the paper over to study Figures 2 and 3. It also creates a cluttered page.

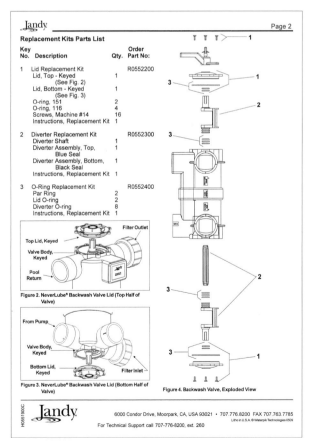

The second page contains the parts list and most of the graphics.

This page also is cluttered. In addition, because of the proximity of the parts list to all the figures, it is unclear which one(s) it relates to. (See Ch. 12, p. 258, for a discussion of proximity.)

These instructions would be easier to use if they were printed on a bigger sheet of paper. That way, the text and Figures 1–3 could all fit on one side.

Notice that the graphics are drawings, not photographs. Drawings emphasize the important information, and they are easy to label with part names.

These instructions end with contact information for the company. Instructions addressed to technicians rather than the general public often do not include troubleshooting guides. The assumption is that technicians can figure out how to solve any problems.

■ **Figure 19.7 Set of Installation Instructions**

Source: Jandy, 2005 <www.jandy-downloads.com/pdfs/NL_BWV_Replacement_Kit.pdf>.

■ **Figure 19.8   List of Parts**
Source: General Electric, 2003a.

PARTS INCLUDED

HARDWARE PACKET

PART		QUANTITY
	Wood Screws (¼" x 2")	2
	Toggle Bolts (and wing nuts) (¼" x 3")	4
	Self-aligning Machine Screws (¼"-28 x 3¼")	3
	Nylon Grommet (for metal cabinets)	2
	Metal Screws (⅛" x ½")	1 black 2 bronze
	Power Cord Strap (plastic)	1

You will find the installation hardware contained in a packet with the unit. Check to make sure you have all these parts.
NOTE: Some extra parts are included.

ADDITIONAL PARTS

PART		QUANTITY
TOP CABINET TEMPLATE	Top Cabinet Template	1
INSTALLATION INSTRUCTIONS	Installation Instructions	1
	Separately Packed Grease Filters	2
	Charcoal Filter (on some models)	1

This list of parts makes life simple for readers because they can see what the parts look like and what they are called.

Instruction writers sometimes mistakenly assume that general readers know the names of parts and other hardware; many people do not.

On TechComm Web

For ways of measuring the value of effective documentation, see Jay Mead's "Measuring the Value Added by Technical Documentation: A Review of Research and Practice." Click on Links Library for Ch. 19 on <bedfordstmartins.com/techcomm>.

In This Book

For more about collaboration, see Ch. 4.

In This Book

For more about front matter, see Ch. 18.

DRAFTING EFFECTIVE MANUALS

A good manual reduces the possibility of injuries and liability, but it also should attract customers and reduce costs (because the organization needs fewer customer-support people). A poorly written manual is expensive because it must be revised more often and because it alienates customers.

Most of the principles of effective instructions also apply to manuals. For example, when writing a manual, you have to analyze your audience, explain procedures clearly, and include graphics. However, manuals require more planning because they are larger and more complex.

Writing a manual is almost always a collaborative project. A full-size manual can require too many skills for one person to write: technical skills in the subject area, writing skills, graphics skills, production skills, even a knowledge of contracts and law to prevent lawsuits.

Drafting the Front Matter

Front matter helps readers understand the content and organization of a manual and the best ways to use it. Most manuals have a cover or title page, a table of contents, a preface, and a section about how to use the manual.

Installation Instructions

PREPARE TO INSTALL THE RANGE

FOR YOUR SAFETY:

All rough-in and spacing dimensions must be met for safe use of your range. Electricity to the range can be disconnected at the outlet without moving the range if the outlet is in the preferred location (remove lower drawer).

To reduce the risk of burns or fire when reaching over hot surface elements, cabinet storage space above the cooktop should be avoided. If cabinet storage space is to be provided above the cooktop, the risk can be reduced by installing a range hood that sticks out at least 5" beyond the front of the cabinets. Cabinets installed above a cooktop must be no deeper than 13".

Be sure your appliance is properly installed and grounded by a qualified technician.

Make sure the cabinets and wall coverings around the range can withstand the temperatures (up to 200°F.) generated by the range.

TOOLS YOU WILL NEED

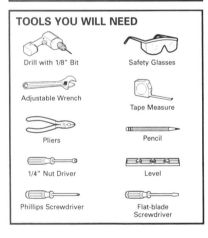

Drill with 1/8" Bit — Safety Glasses
Adjustable Wrench — Tape Measure
Pliers — Pencil
1/4" Nut Driver — Level
Phillips Screwdriver — Flat-blade Screwdriver

MATERIALS YOU MAY NEED

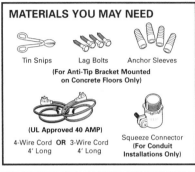

Tin Snips — Lag Bolts — Anchor Sleeves
(For Anti-Tip Bracket Mounted on Concrete Floors Only)

(UL Approved 40 AMP)
4-Wire Cord **OR** 3-Wire Cord
4' Long — 4' Long

Squeeze Connector **(For Conduit Installations Only)**

PARTS INCLUDED

Anti-Tip Bracket Kit

1 REMOVE SHIPPING MATERIALS

Remove packaging materials. Failure to remove packaging materials could result in damage to the appliance.

■ **Figure 19.9   List of Tools and Materials**
Source: General Electric, 2003b.

Drawings of the tools and materials are more effective than lists.

To decide whether to use a cover or just a title page, consider the manual's size and intended use. Manuals that will receive some wear and tear, such as those used outside, need a hard cover, usually of a water-resistant material. Manuals used around an office usually don't need hard covers, unless they are large and require extra strength.

The title page contains the title of the manual, plus the company's name, address, and logo. An extensive table of contents is also important

 In This Book

For more about creating headings, see Ch. 10, p. 206, and Ch. 12, p. 276.

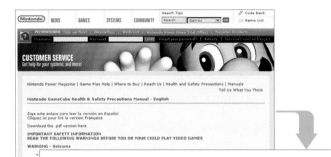

This excerpt from a longer set of safety information describes dangers inherent in playing video games. The more serious the safety risk, the longer and more detailed the safety information.

This sentence should use mandatory language: "You must read the following warnings..."

Although this excerpt uses appropriate signal words, it should also use icons to emphasize the importance of the information.

IMPORTANT SAFETY INFORMATION
READ THE FOLLOWING WARNINGS BEFORE YOU OR YOUR CHILD PLAY VIDEO GAMES

WARNING - Seizures

- Some people (about 1 in 4000) may have seizures or blackouts triggered by light flashes or patterns, such as while watching TV or playing video games, even if they have never had a seizure in the past.
- Anyone who has had a seizure, loss of awareness, or other symptom linked to an epileptic condition should consult a doctor before playing a video game.
- Parents should watch when their children play video games. Stop playing and consult a doctor if you or your child has any of the following symptoms:

Convulsions	Eye or muscle twitching
Loss of awareness	Altered vision
Involuntary movements	Disorientation

- To reduce the likelihood of a seizure when playing video games:
  1. Sit or stand as far from the screen as possible.
  2. Play video games on the smallest available television screen.
  3. Do not play if you are tired or need sleep.
  4. Play in a well-lit room.
  5. Take a 10 to 15 minute break every hour.

WARNING - Repetitive Motion Injuries and Eyestrain
Playing video games can make your muscles, joints, skin or eyes hurt after a few hours. Follow these instructions to avoid problems such as tendinitis, carpal tunnel syndrome, skin irritation or eyestrain:

- Avoid excessive play. It is recommended that parents monitor their children for appropriate play.
- Take a 10 to 15 minute break every hour, even if you don't think you need it.
- If your hands, wrists, arms or eyes become tired or sore while playing, stop and rest them for several hours before playing again.
- If you continue to have sore hands, wrists, arms or eyes during or after play, stop playing and see a doctor.

■ **Figure 19.10   Excerpt from Safety Information**
Source: Nintendo, 2005 <www.nintendo.com/consumer/manuals/precautions_gcn_english.jsp>.

There is more information about using iPod nano in onscreen help and on the web.

The following table describes where to get more iPod-related software and service information.

To Learn About	Do This
Service and support, forums, and Apple software downloads	Go to www.apple.com/support/ipod.
Using iPod nano through an interactive online tutorial	Go to www.apple.com/support/ipod.
Using iTunes	Open iTunes and choose Help > "iTunes and Music Store Help." For an online iTunes tutorial (not available in all areas), go to www.apple.com/support/itunes.
Using iPhoto (on Mac OS X)	Open iPhoto and choose Help > iPhoto Help.
Using iSync (on Mac OS X)	Open iSync and choose Help > iSync Help.
Using iCal (on Mac OS X)	Open iCal and choose Help > iCal Help.
The latest information on iPod nano	Go to www.apple.com/ipod.
Registering iPod nano	If you didn't register when you installed software from the iPod CD, go to www.apple.com/register.
Finding your iPod nano serial number	Look at the back of your iPod nano or select Settings > About.
Obtaining warranty service	First follow the advice in this booklet, the onscreen help, and online resources, and then go to www.apple.com/support.

■ **Figure 19.11 Conclusion from a Set of Instructions**
Source: Apple Computer, Inc., 2005 <http://manuals.info.apple.com/en/iPod_nano_Features_Guide.pdf>.

This page from the conclusion of a set of instructions uses a table to organize the information.

because people don't read a manual straight through but refer to it for specific information. To be effective, contents headings should focus on the tasks the readers want to accomplish.

Front matter might also include an introduction or a preface, or information presented in "about" phrases, as in "About Product X" or "About the

Problem	Cause	Correction
The mower does not start.	1. The mower is out of gas. 2. The gas is stale. 3. The spark plug wire is disconnected from the spark plug.	1. Fill the gas tank. 2. Drain the tank and refill it with fresh gas. 3. Connect the wire to the plug.
The mower loses power.	1. The grass is too high. 2. The air cleaner is dirty. 3. There is a buildup of grass, leaves, or trash in the underside of the mower housing.	1. Set the mower to a "higher cut" position. See page 10. 2. Replace the air cleaner. See page 11. 3. Disconnect the spark plug wire, attach it to the retainer post, and clean the underside of the mower housing. See page 8.

■ **Figure 19.12   Excerpt from a Troubleshooting Guide**

INTERACTIVE SAMPLE DOCUMENT
Presenting Clear Instructions

The following page is from a set of instructions contained in a user's manual. The questions in the margin ask you to think about the discussion of instructions (on page 505). E-mail your responses to yourself and/or your instructor, and see suggested responses on TechComm Web.

1. How has the designer tried to ensure that readers will follow the steps in the correct order?

2. Is the amount of information presented in each step appropriate?

3. What kind of information is presented in the imperative mood? What kind of information is not?

4. How effectively are graphics used to support the textual information on this page?

On TechComm Web

To e-mail your responses to yourself and/or your instructor and to see suggested responses, click on Interactive Sample Documents for Ch. 19 on <bedfordstmartins .com/techcomm>.

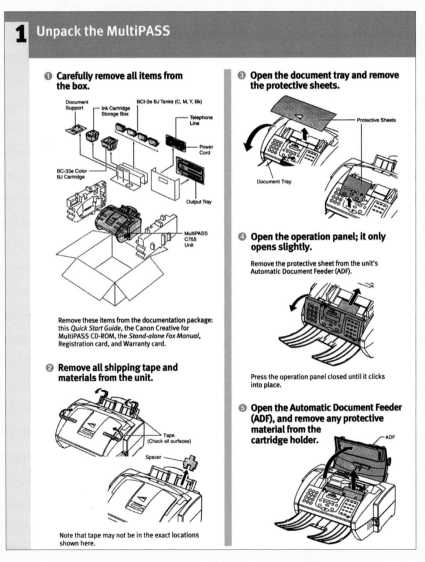

Source: Canon U.S.A., Inc., 2002 <www.usa.canon.com/cpr/pdf/Manuals/C755_Setup.pdf>.

Product X Documentation Set." This introductory information should answer five basic questions:

- Who should use this manual?
- What product, procedure, or system does the manual describe?
- What is the manual's purpose?
- What are the manual's major components?
- How should the manual be used?

Some manuals need to answer an additional question: what does the typography signify? If the typography signifies different kinds of information (10-point Courier type might represent the text the reader is supposed to type) and you want your readers to understand your conventions, define them in the front matter.

Figure 19.13 on page 516 is a preface from a manual.

Drafting the Body

The structure, style, and graphics of the body of a manual will depend on its purpose and audience. For instance, the body of a manual might include summaries and diagnostic tests to help readers determine whether they have understood the discussion. A long manual might have more than one "body"— that is, each chapter might be a self-contained unit with its own introduction, body, and conclusion.

Guidelines

Drafting the Body of a Manual

▶ **Structure the body according to how the reader will use it.** If the reader will carry out a process, organize it chronologically, beginning with the first step in the process. If the reader needs to understand a concept, use a more-important-to-less-important organization. Consider the patterns discussed in Chapter 7, but be ready to combine or alter them to meet the needs of your audience.

▶ **Write clearly.** Simple, short sentences work best. Use the imperative mood to give instructions.

▶ **Be informal, if appropriate.** For some kinds of manuals, especially those intended for readers unfamiliar with the subject, an informal style that uses contractions and everyday vocabulary is effective. One caution: safety warnings and information about serious subjects, such as disease, usually require a formal style.

▶ **Use graphics.** Graphics break up the text and help readers understand the information. Whenever readers are to perform an action with their hands, include a drawing or photograph showing the action. Where appropriate, use tables and figures.

 **In This Book**

For more about graphics, see Ch. 13.

This is the preface from a manual for a software product.

This manual explains how to use one of the features of the software.

A preface often answers the question "Who is the audience for this manual?"

"How to Use This Manual" is a popular feature because it presents an overview of the contents. Because this manual is a PDF document presented online, it contains hyperlinks to its main contents.

A preface often directs readers to related documentation.

The footer contains the title of the manual and the page number.

Preface

This publication provides instructions on using the Layout Control feature.

NOTE: This feature is optional. Please contact your sales representative to order this feature.

Who Should Use This Manual

This document is intended for SAN administrators who plan, discover, configure, or monitor SANs.

How to Use This Manual

This publication is organized as follows:

Chapter 1, Customizing the Topology Layout, describes how to customize the topology.

Chapter 2, Viewing Port Information, describes how to view port properties and status and how to determine the connected ports between two devices.

An *Index* is also provided.

For a glossary of terms, refer to SANavigator the SANUser Manual.

Related Documentation

Other publications that provide additional information about this product are:

• *Topology Layout Customization Online Help*

Topology Layout Customization User Manual   IX

■ **Figure 19.13   Preface from a Manual**
Source: McDATA Corporation, 2004 <www.mcdata.com/downloads/tpub/umanual/layout_sanav42.pdf>.

Manual Conventions   The following notational conventions are used in this document.

Convention	Meaning
Italic	Outside book references, names of user interface windows, panels, buttons, and dialog boxes.
`monospace`	On-screen or user-entered text or code.
Bold	Keyboard keys.
Click. As in "click the icon on the navigation control panel."	Click with the left mouse button on the object to activate a function.
Right click. As in "right click the product icon."	Click with the right mouse button on the object to activate a function.
Select. As in "select the log entry."	Click once on the object to select it.

A conventions section helps readers understand the typographic styles that are used in the manual.

Where to Get Help   For technical support, McDATA® end-user customers should call the phone number located on the service label attached to the front or rear of the hardware product.

McDATA's "Best in Class" Solution Center provides a single point of contact for customers seeking help. The Solution Center will research, explore, and resolve inquiries or service requests regarding McDATA products and services. The Solution Center is staffed 24 hours a day, 7 days a week, including holidays.

NOTE: To expedite warranty entitlement, please have your product serial number available.

McDATA Corporation
380 Interlocken Crescent
Broomfield, CO 80021

Phone: **(800) 752-4572 or (720) 566-3910**
Fax: (720) 566-3851
E-mail: supportmcdata.com

A preface often helps readers understand how to get help with the product. This section usually contains Web addresses, mailing addresses, phone and fax numbers, and e-mail addresses.

Note that this preface does not contain safety information because the product is a software program that does not pose any safety risks. If the product did pose risks, safety information would be presented in the preface or in a separate safety section.

■ **Figure 19.13**   *(continued)*

This preface explains how to order a paper copy of the manual.

Ordering Documentation

To order a paper copy of this manual, contact your McDATA representative, or use the contact information listed below.

Phone: (800) 545-5773 and select the option for information on our complete family of enterprise-to-edge SAN solutions.

Fax: (720) 566-3860

This preface requests that readers comment on the quality of the manual. These comments help the company improve the manual.

Forwarding Publication Comments

We sincerely appreciate any comments about this publication. Did you find this manual easy or difficult to use? Did it lack necessary information? Were there any errors? Could its organization be improved?

Please send your comments via e-mail, our home page, or FAX. Identify the manual, and provide page numbers and details. Thank you.

E-mail:	pubsmgrmcdata.com
Home Page:	http://www.mcdata.com
FAX:	Technical Communications Manager (303) 465-4996

A preface often includes legal information identifying trademarks and registered trademarks used in the manual. For more information on trademarks, see Ch. 2, p. 20.

Trademarks

The following terms, indicated by a registered trademark symbol (®) or trademark symbol (™) on first use in this publication, are trademarks of McDATA Corporation, SANavigator, Inc., or both, in the United States, other countries, or both:

Registered Trademarks	Trademarks
McDATA®	E/OS™
SANavigator®	

All other trademarked terms, indicated by a registered trademark symbol (®) or trademark symbol (™) on first use in this publication, are trademarks of their respective owners in the United States, other countries, or both.

Topology Layout Customization User Manual   XI

■ **Figure 19.13**   *(continued)*

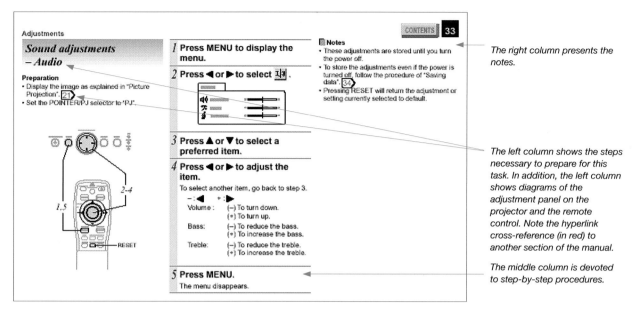

The right column presents the notes.

The left column shows the steps necessary to prepare for this task. In addition, the left column shows diagrams of the adjustment panel on the projector and the remote control. Note the hyperlink cross-reference (in red) to another section of the manual.

The middle column is devoted to step-by-step procedures.

■ **Figure 19.14   A Page from the Body of a Manual**

Note the generous use of white space and the use of colors to signal types of information: green for the task being explained, red for hyperlinks, and blue for step-by-step instructions.

Source: Toshiba America Consumer Products, Inc., 2005 <http://tacpservice.toshiba.com/ConsumerProductSupport/Manuals/projectors/650ee.pdf>.

Figure 19.14 shows a page from the body of a user's manual for a data-projection unit. The task described here is adjusting the sound.

Drafting the Back Matter

Four items typically appear in the back matter: glossary, index, warranty information, and appendices. A *glossary* is an alphabetized list of definitions of important terms in the document. An *index* is common for most manuals of 20 to 30 pages or more.

The word *appendices* refers to a range of elements. Appendices in procedures manuals often have flowcharts or other graphics that illustrate the processes described in the body. Appendices in user's guides often have diagnostic tests and reference materials, such as explanations of error messages or troubleshooting guides.

Drafting Revisions of Manuals

In high-tech industries, a new generation of a product might come along as often as every 18 months. As products evolve, technical communicators need

 In This Book

For more about glossaries, see Ch. 18, p. 473.

to revise the manuals that go with them. When a new version of the product is released, you can take one of two approaches to revising.

- *Publish a "new" manual.* Although a new manual will most likely contain elements from the old manual, it might never mention the old manual. Although a new manual can reflect the look of the new product, people who are switching from the old product to the new one might have to spend time finding the information that applies specifically to the new product.

- *Publish a "revised" manual.* Revised manuals contain information from the old version, but new information is marked, usually with an icon in the margin or with a change bar (a vertical rule in the margin). Sometimes a section in the front matter describes the changes to this version of the product. Although a revised manual is easier for previous users to use, it can look like a patch job.

If you want to reuse any information from an existing document, you need to determine who owns the copyright to that information. As discussed in Chapter 2, most documents in the workplace are written as "work made for hire" and are therefore the property of the organization. Sometimes, however, documents are written by contractors who retain the copyright. In these cases, you need to get permission from the copyright holder to reuse any text or graphics.

Strategies for Intercultural Communication

Writing Instructions and Manuals for Multicultural Readers

Organizations work hard to make their instructions and manuals appropriate for multicultural readers. Because important instructions and manuals can be read by readers from several or even dozens of cultures, you need to answer three important questions as you plan the documents:

In This Book

For more about Simplified English, see Ch. 11, p. 246.

- **In what language should the information be written?** You can either translate the document into the readers' native language or try to make the English easy to understand. Although translation is sometimes the best or only alternative, companies often use Simplified English or some other form of English with a limited grammar and vocabulary.

- **Do the graphics or text need to be modified?** As discussed in Chapter 5, communicators need to be aware of cultural differences. For example, a printer manual translated for an Italian audience presented nude models with strategically placed rectangles showing the various colors the machine could reproduce. But the manual carefully avoided explicit advice about how to use the printer, because Italian readers prefer suggestions (Delio, 2002).

On TechComm Web

Read Michelle Delio's article about cultural factors and manuals in *Wired News.* Click on Links Library for Ch. 19 on <bedfordstmartins.com/techcomm>.

- **What is the readers' technological infrastructure?** If your readers don't have Internet access, there is no point in making a Web version of the information. If your readers pay by the minute for Internet access, you want to create Web-based information that downloads quickly.

USABILITY TESTING

Usability testing is the process of performing experiments with people who represent real users to see how well they understand a document and how easily they can use it. It is used frequently as part of the revision process for instructions and manuals. This section covers five topics:

- the goals of usability testing
- the basic concepts of usability testing
- preparing for a usability test
- conducting a usability test
- interpreting and reporting the data from a usability test

The information in this section is based on Rubin (1994) and Dumas and Redish (1993).

The Goals of Usability Testing

The two main goals of usability testing are to improve product safety and to save money. An effective document reduces the risk that a customer will be injured in assembling or using the product. As discussed in Chapter 2, courts are now finding companies guilty of publishing "defective" instructions and manuals. Usability testing also can save money by helping the company understand and exploit the product's competitive advantages and by reducing the number of service calls and customer-support staff. In addition, usability testing can improve related products, increase customer satisfaction, and reduce the need to update the product.

The Basic Concepts of Usability Testing

There are three basic principles of usability testing:

- *Usability testing permeates product development.* Usability testing involves testing the document rigorously and often to make sure it works and is easy to use.
- *Usability testing involves studying real users as they use the product.* A company learns important information from real users that it would not have learned from people in the organization.
- *Usability testing involves setting measurable goals and determining whether the product meets them.* Usability testing involves determining in advance what the user is supposed to be able to do. For instance, in testing a help system for a word-processing program, the testers might decide that the user should be able to find the section on saving a file and perform that task successfully in less than two minutes.

 On TechComm Web

For an article describing the Online Computer Library Center's usability testing program, click on Links Library for Ch. 19 on <bedfordstmartins.com/techcomm>.

Preparing for a Usability Test

Usability testing requires careful planning. According to Kantner (1994), planning accounts for one-half to three-quarters of the time devoted to testing. Eight main tasks must be accomplished in planning a usability test:

- *Understand your users' needs.* Testers conduct *focus groups,* bringing people together for a few hours to discuss a product or an issue. In addition, they test existing products, have experts review the product, and conduct on-site interviews and observations of real users in the workplace.

- *Determine the purpose of the test.* Testers can test an idea even before the product is designed, to see if people understand it and like it. Or they can test a prototype to see if it is easy to use, or a finished product to see if it needs any last-minute improvements.

- *Staff the test team.* Extensive programs in usability testing involve many specialists, each doing one job. Smaller programs involve only a handful of people, each doing many jobs.

- *Set up the test environment.* A basic environment includes a room for the test participant and another room for the test observers. Figure 19.15 shows a basic usability lab.

- *Develop a test plan.* A *test plan* is a proposal requesting resources; it describes and justifies what the testers plan to do.

- *Select participants.* Testers recruit participants who match the profile of the intended users. Generally, it is best not to use company employees, who might know more about the product than a real user could.

In This Book

For more about proposals, see Ch. 16, p. 405.

A usability lab consists of two rooms: one where the participant works and one where the testers observe.

Testers observe the participant through a one-way mirror and make video recordings of the participant's actions.

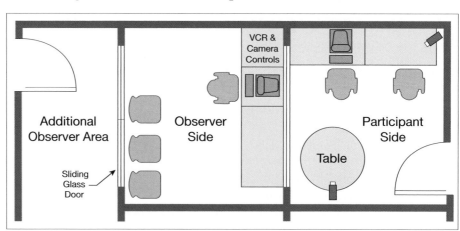

■ **Figure 19.15   A Basic Usability Lab**
Source: Microsoft, 2005 <www.microsoft.com/usability/lab.mspx>.

- *Prepare the test materials.* Most tests require legal forms, an orientation script to help the participant understand the purpose of the test, background questionnaires, instructions for the participant to follow, and a log for the testers to record data during the test.
- *Conduct a pilot test.* A pilot test is a usability test for the usability test. A pilot test can uncover problems with the equipment, the document being tested, the test materials, and the test design.

Conducting a Usability Test

There are three important aspects of conducting a usability test:

- *Staying organized.* Testers make a checklist and a schedule for the test day, including every task that every person, including the test participant, is to carry out.
- *Interacting with the participant.* Among the most popular techniques for eliciting information from the test participant is the *think-aloud protocol,* in which the participant says aloud what he or she is thinking: "I guess I'm supposed to press Enter here, but I'm not sure, because the manual didn't say to do it."
- *Debriefing the participant.* After the test, testers usually have questions about the participant's actions. For this reason, they debrief—that is, interview—the participant.

Interpreting and Reporting the Data from a Usability Test

After a usability test, testers have a great deal of data, including notes, questionnaires, and videos. Turning that data into useful information requires three steps:

- *Tabulating the information.* Testers gather all the information from the test, including *performance* measures, such as how long it took a participant to complete a task, and *attitude* measures, such as how easy the participant found it to perform the task.
- *Analyzing the information.* Testers analyze the information, concentrating on the most important problems revealed in the test and trying to determine the severity and frequency of each one.
- *Reporting the information.* Writing a clear, comprehensive report often leads the testers to insights they might not have achieved otherwise.

Although usability testing might seem extremely expensive and difficult, testers who are methodical, open-minded, and curious about how people use the document find that it is the least expensive and most effective way to improve its quality.

Writer's Checklist

Instructions

☐ Are the instructions designed effectively, with adequate white space and a clear relationship between the graphics and the accompanying text? (p. 501)
☐ Do the instructions have a clear title? (p. 506)

Does the introduction to the set of instructions

☐ state the purpose of the task? (p. 506)
☐ describe safety measures or other concerns that readers should understand? (p. 506)
☐ list necessary tools and materials? (p. 506)

Are the step-by-step instructions

☐ numbered? (p. 507)
☐ expressed in the imperative mood? (p. 507)
☐ simple and direct? (p. 507)

☐ Are appropriate graphics included? (p. 508)

Does the conclusion

☐ include any necessary follow-up advice? (p. 508)
☐ include, if appropriate, a troubleshooting guide? (p. 508)

Manuals

☐ Does the manual include, if appropriate, a cover? (p. 510)
☐ Does the title page provide all the necessary information to help readers determine whether they are reading the appropriate manual? (p. 511)
☐ Is the table of contents clear and explicit? (p. 511)
☐ Are the items phrased clearly to indicate the tasks readers are to carry out? (p. 515)

Does the other front matter clearly indicate

☐ the product, procedure, or system the manual describes? (p. 515)

☐ the purpose of the manual? (p. 515)
☐ the major components of the manual? (p. 515)
☐ the best way to use the manual? (p. 515)

☐ Is the body of the manual organized clearly? (p. 515)
☐ Are appropriate graphics included? (p. 515)
☐ Is a glossary included, if appropriate? (p. 519)
☐ Is an index included, if appropriate? (p. 519)
☐ Are all other appropriate appendix items included? (p. 519)
☐ Is the writing style clear and simple throughout? (p. 515)

Usability Testing

Did you prepare for the usability test by

☐ understanding your users' needs? (p. 522)
☐ determining the purpose of the test? (p. 522)
☐ staffing the test team? (p. 522)
☐ setting up the test environment? (p. 522)
☐ developing a test plan? (p. 522)
☐ selecting participants? (p. 522)
☐ preparing the test materials? (p. 523)
☐ conducting a pilot test? (p. 523)

Did you conduct the usability test effectively by

☐ staying organized? (p. 523)
☐ interacting appropriately with the participant? (p. 523)
☐ debriefing the participant? (p. 523)

Did you interpret and report the test data by

☐ tabulating the information? (p. 523)
☐ analyzing the information? (p. 523)
☐ reporting the information? (p. 523)

Exercises

 In This Book   For more about memos, see Ch. 14, p. 352.

1. **INTERNET EXERCISE** Study a set of instructions from HowStuffWorks <www.howstuffworks.com> or Knowledge Hound <www.knowledgehound.com>. Write a memo to your instructor evaluating the quality of the instructions. Attach a printout of representative pages from the instructions.

2. You work in the customer-relations department of a company that makes plumbing supplies. The head of product development has just handed you the draft of installation instructions for a sliding tub door (p. 525). She has asked you to comment on their effectiveness. Write a memo to her, evaluating the instructions and suggesting improvements.

INSTALLATION INSTRUCTIONS

CAUTION: SEE BOX NO. 1 BEFORE CUTTING ALUMINUM HEADER OR SILL

1 Measure the wall to wall opening at the tub rim.

CAUTION: Do not forget to add 2" to inside tape measurement when required.

USE YOUR TAPE CORRECTLY.

2 Cut the bottom sill track 1/4" less than opening.

3 If desired, use a good all purpose caulk on the under side of sill. Press sill down on tub rim. Be sure drain holes face into tub.

4 Set wall jambs against the wall. Align vertically, mark wall with pencil or crayon.

5 Peel backing from installation tape on jambs, install by setting each jamb firmly over and down upon the sill. Press firmly to the wall for a good bond.

6 Measure the width inside the installed jambs, cut header bar 1/8" less.

7 Wall Jamb / Header Bar / Bottom Sill / Door Panel

Mount nylon rollers on top of each door panel (see sketch) using the center hole. Other holes will raise or lower the doors for wall alignment. Thread door panels onto header bar with smooth side of panels facing inside the tub.

8 Push doors to the center of header bar. Lift and lower into place, easing bottom nylon door guides into the proper channel of sill.

TRIDOR MODEL ONLY:

To reverse direction of panels, raise panels out of bottom track and slide catches past each other thereby reversing direction so that shower head does not throw water between the panels.

HARDWARE KIT CONTENTS
TUDOR MODEL
4 nylon bearings
4 ball bearing screws # 8–32 × 3/8"
TRIDOR MODEL
6 nylon bearings
6 ball bearing screws # 8–32 × 3/8"

3. Write a brief manual for a process familiar to you. Consider writing a procedures manual for a school activity or a part-time job, such as your work as the business manager of the school newspaper or as a tutor in the Writing Center.

4. GROUP EXERCISE Write instructions for one of the following activities or for a process used in your field. Include appropriate graphics. In a brief note preceding the instructions, indicate your audience and purpose. Exchange these materials with a partner. Observe your partner and take notes as he or she attempts to carry out the instructions. Then revise your instructions and share them with your partner; discuss whether the revised instructions are easier to understand and apply and, if so, how? Submit your instructions to your instructor.

a. how to change a bicycle tire

b. how to delete the contents of the cache in your browser

c. how to light a fire in a fireplace

d. how to copy a compact disc to a blank disc

e. how to find an online discussion group and subscribe to it

f. how to locate, download, and install a file from CNET's Shareware.com <www.shareware.com>, CNET's Download.com <www.download.com>, or a similar site.

Case 19: Writing Instructions for Installing a Programmable Thermostat

 In This Book For more about memos, see Ch. 14, p. 352.

Background

You are the new technical-communication intern at Owyhee Engineers, a diversified manufacturer of control technologies for buildings, homes, and industry. The company is developing a programmable thermostat, the Energy Control 37 (EC37), for use in homes. Your documentation group is responsible for writing the installation and operation instructions for the EC37. Your supervisor, Warren Fu, has asked you to interview Alexis Jaeger, a product engineer, about the thermostat. After the interview, you report back to Warren.

"In short, a programmable thermostat automatically sets back the temperature in your home based upon a predetermined schedule," you summarize. "The chief advantage of a programmable thermostat is that you no longer need to adjust the setting before leaving the house or before bedtime. In fact, by automatically adjusting the temperature to a lower setting while you are sleeping or out of the house, you can reduce energy use by 17 to 25 percent. That translates into more money in your pocket.

"I took notes while Alexis explained the installation procedure and she gave me some possible graphics for the instructions" (Documents 19.1 and 19.2).

"I'd like you to start by writing the installation instructions and choosing the graphics to accompany the instructions," Warren says. "Before you start writing, spend some time thinking about our customers. Most are do-it-yourself homeowners and not professional contractors."

"What else can you tell me about our customers?"

"A lot of homeowners are afraid of doing the installation themselves." They imagine all the things that can go wrong, especially when they picture a tangled mass of electrical wiring lurking behind their walls. They decide it's too much

to handle. They return our thermostats and ask for a refund. They need to understand that the seemingly complicated installation is really just a series of small steps. If they take their time and follow the directions, they can do it."

"Thanks," you respond. "This information will help me plan the instructions."

Your Assignment

1. Using principles discussed in this chapter, revise the information in Document 19.1. Design the installation instructions so that they are professional in appearance and easy to read. Add any necessary information that is missing, especially safety information.

2. Review the possible graphics for the instructions (Document 19.2) and decide which, if any, of the graphics are appropriate, given the instructions' audience and purpose. In a memo to Warren, recommend which graphic(s) to use and where the graphic(s) should be placed. If none of the graphics seems appropriate to you, or if you think additional graphics are needed, describe the kind of information that should be provided and where it should be placed. For example, if you think the instructions would benefit from a line graph comparing the monthly heating and cooling costs for a home with a programmable thermostat versus a home without a programmable thermostat, write the following: "Insert at the top of the page a line graph showing monthly heating and cooling costs for a house with a programmable thermostat versus a comparable house without a programmable thermostat. Show a 12-month period and use different colors to distinguish the two lines." The more specific your statement, the easier it will be for Warren to understand how to revise the instructions.

■ **Document 19.1   Notes for Installing a Programmable Thermostat**

 On TechComm Web

For digital versions of case documents, click on Downloadable Case Documents on <bedfordstmartins.com/techcomm>.

Installation Notes

Need #1 Phillips (small) screwdriver, drill, 3/16" bit

Homeowner has two options: (1) Install new thermostat in place of the old one, unless the current thermostat is located in a place with unusual heating conditions (e.g., near stove, direct sunlight, fireplace, hot-water pipes) or unusual cooling conditions (e.g., draft from stairwell, door, or window); in a damp area such as a bathroom (this leads to corrosion); or in a place with poor air circulation (e.g., corner, alcove, behind door). (2) Pick a new location. If picking a new location, locate unit on an inside wall about 5 feet above the floor in an often-used room. However, wait to install until all work such as painting has been completed.

To avoid shock and damage to furnace, AC, and thermostat, power should be turned off at circuit breaker, fuse box, or appliance before installation begins. Remove the old thermostat's cover: some covers snap on and pull off; others have locking screws on the side that must be loosened.

Wires must be labeled before they are removed. Use the labels that come packaged with the EC37. Letters (G, Y, W, RH, B, O, RC) will be printed near the terminals on the old unit. Label each wire as it is removed from the old unit's terminal, making sure wires don't fall back into hole in the wall. Then remove the old unit by loosening all the screws that attach it to the wall. Discard.

Prepare to install the EC37 by stripping insulation (about 3/8") from the wires coming out of the wall. This will clean off any corrosion. In addition, fill wall opening with non-flammable insulation. This will prevent drafts from affecting the unit. Separate the EC37's body from the baseplate by pressing latch at bottom on the unit. New holes for the screws used to attach the baseplate to the wall might need to be drilled if mounting unit to soft material such as plasterboard. If so, drill 3/16" holes for each screw, and use the plastic anchors included in the package. Hold the base against the wall with the wires coming through the opening in the baseplate and attach to wall with the two screws included.

Attach the wires to the matching terminals (e.g., wire labeled G to terminal labeled G). Wires should not touch each other or other parts of the terminal. Make sure wires are trapped between black spacer and brass terminal. Tighten wires securely. Snap the unit's body onto the baseplate.

Warning of Electrical Shock Hazard #1

Warning of Electrical Shock Hazard #2

Warning of Electrical Shock Hazard #3

Thermostat Placement

Wire-Terminal Attachment Showing Black Spacer

Base of EC37 Showing Wires Attached to Terminals

Stripping Insulation from Wire #1

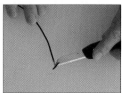
Stripping Insulation from Wire #2

■ **Document 19.2   Possible Graphics for the Installation Instructions**

20 Designing Web Sites

The Web is a gigantic publishing medium, made up of billions of Web pages. Nobody has precise figures about Web usage, because it changes too quickly and there is no "Internet headquarters." In 2005, the search engine Google's database included links to some 8 billion pages. If the average Web site consists of 100 pages, that would mean there were some 80 million Web sites that year (Google, 2005a). Because the Web is such an important publishing medium for organizations, professionals should understand the basics of creating a Web site.

UNDERSTANDING THE PROCESS OF CREATING WEB SITES

Figure 20.1 on page 530 presents an overview of the process of creating a Web site. This chapter focuses on the principles of effective design.

DESIGNING EFFECTIVE WEB SITES AND WEB PAGES

Most of the principles of good Web page design are similar to the principles of good page design for printed documents. For instance, start with a page grid, use white space liberally, and use typography effectively. However, you need to apply these principles a little differently in designing your Web site.

Aim for Simplicity

When you create a site, it doesn't cost anything to use all the colors in the rainbow, to add sound effects and animation, or to make text blink on and off. Although these effects can sometimes help you communicate information, most often all they do is slow the download and annoy the visitor. If a special effect serves no useful function, avoid it.

To design effective Web sites and Web pages:

Aim for simplicity.

Make the text easy to read and understand.

Create informative headers and footers.

Help visitors navigate the site.

Create clear, informative links.

Avoid Web clichés.

Include extra features your visitors might need.

■ **Figure 20.1**
An Overview of the Process for Creating a Web Site

 On TechComm Web

For links to online tutorials that explain how to code text and graphics, click on Links Library for Ch. 20 on <bedfordstmartins.com/ techcomm>.

Analyze Your Audience and Purpose

Who are your visitors, and why are they visiting? Do they have any disabilities that you need to consider? Do they speak English, or should you include other languages? Think about your purpose. What are your goals in launching the site: To project a positive image for your organization? To sell or publicize your products or services? To elicit donations? For more about audience and purpose, see Chapter 5.

Design the Site and Its Pages

Visitors should find it easy to locate the information they need. Figure out what kinds of information visitors will require and how they will look for it. Try to give all your pages a consistent appearance. The site's navigation elements should appear in the same place on each page to create a pattern that will help guide visitors. For more information, see Mike Markel's Web Design Tutorial on <bedfordstmartins.com/techcomm>.

Create and Code the Content

People don't "read" Web sites; they scan them, looking for the information they want. Aim for simplicity. Rewrite information so that it consists of brief, easy-to-understand chunks. Create clear, informative links. For links to tutorials on designing Web pages, click on Links Library for Ch. 20 on <bedfordstmartins.com/techcomm>.

Revise and Test the Site

Test the site as you would a print document to make sure it accomplishes your purposes. Can visitors understand the main point? Can they understand how the pages of the site work together? Do the technical aspects of the site work correctly? Do all the links work? Does the e-mail form for contacting you work? Test the site with different kinds of computers, monitors, and browsers. For information on usability testing, see Chapter 19, page 521.

Launch the Site

You will use file transfer protocol (FTP) to transport your file to an Internet service provider (ISP), or, if the Internet server is within your own organization, carry a disk down the hall. Once the site is launched on the Web, test it again.

Register the Site with Search Engines

Publicize your site by adding the URL to all your product information and advertising. But also make it easy for people to find the site by notifying search engines that you have launched it.

Maintain the Site

To encourage frequent visits, actively maintain the site. Add new information and announce the additions in a "what's new" box on the home page that directs visitors to them. Delete old information. Test for link rot: links to sites that no longer exist or that have moved. And solicit comments from users. Ask visitors to e-mail you about any features that are not working and to make suggestions for adding content to your site. Be sure to reply with a thank-you note.

Guidelines

Designing a Simple Site

▶ **Use simple backgrounds.** A plain white background or a pale pastel is best. Avoid loud patterns that distract the visitor from the words and graphics of the text. You don't want visitors to "see" the background.

▶ **Use conservative color combinations to increase text legibility.** The greater the contrast between the text color and the background color, the more legible the text. The most legible color combination is black text on a white background. Bad idea: black on purple.

▶ **Avoid decorative graphics.** Don't waste space using graphics that convey no useful information. Hesitate before you use clip art.

▶ **Use thumbnail graphics.** Instead of a large graphic, which takes a long time to download, use a thumbnail so that visitors can click on it to open a larger version of the image.

 On TechComm Web

For an introduction to color theory as it applies to the Web, see Jane Rock Kennedy's "Introduction to Color." Click on Links Library for Ch. 20 on <bedfordstmartins .com/techcomm>.

Make the Text Easy to Read and Understand

Web pages are harder to read than paper documents because screen resolution is much less sharp—usually 72 dots per inch (dpi) versus 1200 dpi on a basic laser printer and 2400 dpi in some books.

Guidelines

Designing Easy-to-Read Text

▶ **Keep the text short.** Poor screen resolution makes reading long stretches of text difficult. In general, pages should contain no more than two or three screens of information.

▶ **Chunk information.** When you write for the screen, chunk information to make it easier to understand. Use frequent headings, brief paragraphs, and lists. Figure 20.2 on page 532 shows poor chunking and effective chunking.

▶ **Make the text as simple as possible.** Use common words and short sentences to make the information as simple as the subject allows.

 On TechComm Web

For more on writing for the Web, see John Morkes and Jakob Nielsen's "Concise, SCANNABLE, and Objective: How to Write for the Web." Click on Links Library for Ch. 20 on <bedfordstmartins .com/techcomm>.

Create Informative Headers and Footers

Headers and footers help visitors understand and navigate your site, and they help establish your credibility. You want your visitors to know that they are visiting the official site of your organization and that it was created by professionals. Figure 20.3 on page 533 shows a typical Web site header, and Figure 20.4 on page 533 shows a typical Web site footer.

 On TechComm Web

To view Figures 20.3 and 20.4 in context on the Web, click on Links Library for Ch. 20 on <bedfordstmartins.com/ techcomm>.

On the Web, a string of long, complex paragraphs, as seen in (a), won't win you any friends. Chunk the information by adding headings, writing short paragraphs, and using lists, as seen in (b). Note, too, that the writer uses a narrow column width in (b) to reduce the line length.

Consideration should be given to the comparative risk represented by the exposure and information regarding the exposure source, including history of and response to antiretroviral therapy based on clinical response, CD4+ T-cell counts, viral load measurements, and current disease stage. When the source person's virus is known or suspected to be resistant to one or more of the drugs considered for the PEP regimen, the selection of drugs to which the source person's virus is unlikely to be resistant is recommended; expert consultation is advised. If this information is not immediately available, initiation of PEP, if indicated, should not be delayed; changes in the regimen can be made after PEP has started, as appropriate. For HCP who initiate PEP, re-evaluation of the exposed person should occur within 72 hours postexposure, especially if additional information about the exposure or source person becomes available.

PHS continues to recommend stratification of HIV PEP regimens based on the severity of exposure and other considerations (e.g., concern for antiretroviral drug resistance in the exposure source). The majority of HIV exposures will warrant a two-drug regimen, using two NRTIs or one NRTI and one NtRTI (Tables 1 and 2; Appendix). Combinations that can be considered for PEP include ZDV and 3TC or emtricitabine (FTC); d4T and 3TC or FTC; and tenofovir (TDF) and 3TC or FTC. In the previous PHS guidelines, a combination of d4T and ddI was considered one of the first-choice PEP regimens; however, this regimen is no longer recommended because of concerns about toxicity (especially neuropathy and pancreatitis) and the availability of more tolerable alternative regimens (3).

The addition of a third (or even a fourth) drug should be considered for exposures that pose an increased risk for transmission or that involve a source in whom antiretroviral drug resistance is likely. The addition of a third drug for PEP after a high-risk exposure is based on demonstrated effectiveness in reducing viral burden in HIV-infected persons. However, no definitive data exist that demonstrate increased efficacy of three- compared with two-drug HIV PEP regimens. Previously, IDV, nelfinavir (NFV), EFV, or abacavir (ABC) were recommended as first-choice agents for inclusion in an expanded PEP regimen (3).

PHS now recommends that expanded PEP regimens be PI-based. The PI preferred for use in expanded PEP regimens is lopinavir/ritonavir (LPV/RTV). Other PIs acceptable for use in expanded PEP regimens include atazanavir, fosamprenavir, RTV-boosted IDV, RTV-boosted SQV, or NFV (Appendix). Although side effects are common with NNRTIs, EFV may be considered for expanded PEP regimens, especially when resistance to PIs in the source person's virus is known or suspected. Caution is advised when EFV is used in women of childbearing age because of the risk of teratogenicity.

Drugs that may be considered as alternatives to the expanded regimens, with warnings about side effects and other adverse events, are EFV or PIs as noted in the Appendix in combination with ddI and either 3TC or FTC. The fusion inhibitor enfuvirtide (T20) has theoretic benefits for use in PEP because its activity occurs before viral-host cell integration; however, it is not recommended for routine HIV PEP because of the mode of administration (subcutaneous injection twice daily). Furthermore, use of T20 has the potential for production of anti-T20 antibodies that cross react with HIV gp41. This could result in a false-positive, enzyme immunoassay (EIA) HIV antibody test among HIV-uninfected patients. A confirmatory Western blot test would be expected to be negative in such cases. T20 should only be used with expert consultation.

Antiviral drugs not recommended for use as PEP, primarily because of the higher risk for potentially serious or life-threatening adverse events, include ABC, delavirdine, ddC, and, as noted previously, the combination of ddI and d4T. NVP should not be included in PEP regimens except with expert consultation because of serious reported side effects, including hepatotoxicty (with one instance of fulminant liver failure requiring liver transplantation), rhabdomyolysis, and

a. Poor chunking

Who is eligible?

Qualified candidates meet two or more of the following criteria:

- Degree in technical communication, graphic arts or design, or a related field
- Three or more years working in technical communication
- Teaching experience in communication, graphic arts or design, or a related field
- Previous winner in another STC competition
- Previous experience as a judge in another STC competition
- Certification by a communication-related professional organization
- STC member

What type of commitment is required?

- Judges attend an orientation meeting during the first week of November where they receive training and guidelines for judging. During this meeting, judges in the physical-media art and technical publications competitions receive the entries they will judge.
- Judges in the online communication competition meet again on Saturday, December 3 to judge all entries as a team and form a consensus. Allow most of the day for this activity.
- Judges in the technical art competition meet in early December for consensus judging. The length of time required depends on the number of entries.
- Judges in the technical publications competition have approximately one month to evaluate the entries, working individually. These judges meet again in early December for consensus judging. Consensus judging requires about three hours, or one evening, to complete.
- Best of Show judges meet following the consensus judging to determine if any entries qualify for the Best of Show award.

b. Effective chunking

■ Figure 20.2   Chunking on a Web Page

■ **Figure 20.3   Web Site Header**
Source: Corel, 2005 <http://apps.corel.com/partners/default.asp>.

All pages should include a link to the home page.

This row of links helps visitors to see their accounts and use the site easily.

This row of links helps visitors to see the major content areas of the site.

PRODUCTS :: FREE TRIALS :: STORE :: COMMUNITY :: ABOUT :: PARTNERS :: MEDIA :: CONTACT US :: CAREERS :: PRIVACY

COREL Copyright © 2005 Corel Corporation. All rights reserved. Terms of use

■ **Figure 20.4   Web Site Footer**
Source: Corel, 2005 <www.corel.com/servlet/Satellite?pagename=Corel2/Home>.

Footers often contain copyright notices and links to enable visitors to contact the Webmaster. This footer also contains links to the company's privacy policy and several other areas of the site.

Help Visitors Navigate the Site

Visitors to a Web site cannot hold the Web page in their hands; all they can do is view the page on the screen. Therefore, each page should help visitors see where they are in the site and get where they want to go. One important way to help visitors navigate the site is to create and sustain a consistent visual design on every page. Make the header, footer, background color or pattern, typography (typeface, size, and color), and placement of the navigational links the same on every page.

Guidelines

Making Your Site Easy to Navigate

▶ **Include a site map or index.** A *site map,* which lists the pages on the site, can be a graphic or a textual list of the pages, grouped according to logical categories. An *index* is an alphabetized list of the pages. Figure 20.5 on page 534 is a section of the Google site map.

▶ **Use a table of contents at the top of a long page.** If your page extends more than a couple of screens, include a table of contents—a set of links to the items on that page—so that a visitor does not have to scroll down to find the topic he or she wants. A table of contents can link one page to information farther down on the same page or on other pages. Figure 20.6 on page 534 shows an excerpt from a table of contents at the top of a frequently asked questions (FAQ) page.

▶ **Help visitors get back to the top of a long page.** If a page is long enough to justify a table of contents, include a "Back to top" link (a textual link, a button, or an icon) before each new chunk of information.

▶ **Include a link to the home page on every page.** This link can be a simple "Back to home page" textual link, a button, or an icon.

▶ **Include textual navigational links at the bottom of the page.** If you are using buttons or icons for links, include textual versions of those links at the bottom of the page. Visitors who have turned off the images to speed up the download

On TechComm Web

For advice on how to design an effective site map, see Jakob Nielsen's "Site Map Usability." Click on Links Library for Ch. 20 on <bedfordstmartins.com/ techcomm>.

won't be able to understand the graphical link (unless you have added an alt [*alternate*] tag—a tag that instructs the browser to display a word or phrase defining the graphic). In addition, visitors with impaired vision might be using special software that reads the information on the screen. This software interprets text only, not graphics.

■ **Figure 20.5   Site Map**
Source: Google, 2005b <www.google.com/sitemap.html>.

 On TechComm Web

To view Figure 20.5 in context on the Web, click on Links Library for Ch. 20 on <bedfordstmartins.com/techcomm>.

Google Site Map

Search Guides	Services	Tools	Help Centers
Basics of Search	Alerts	Maps	Blogger
Advanced Search	Answers	Mobile	Code
Search Results Page	Catalogs	News Search	Desktop Search
Setting Preferences	Directory	Scholar	Hello
Search Features	Froogle	Special Searches	Keyhole
Services & Tools	Groups	University Search	Picasa Photo Organizer
Help Center	Images	Web Search	Google Toolbar
	Google Labs		Translate Tool
	Local		Web APIs

Corporate Overview	Investor Relations	Press Center	Hiring
Company	Financial Info	Media Resources	U.S. Jobs
Features	Financial Data	News from Google	International Jobs
Technology	News & Events	Images and B-roll	Benefits
Business	Investor FAQ	Awards	Students
Culture	Code of Conduct	Permissions	Culture
Quick profile	Guidelines	Product Descriptions	Engineer's Life
Address	Board of Directors	Reviewer's Guides	Video
Management	Board Committees	Software Principles	
Milestones	Report Concerns	Milestones	
Our Philosophy	Email Notification	Executive Bios	
No pop-ups	Documents	Testimonials	
Software principles	Contact Us	Permissions	
		Google Permissions	
		Guidelines	
		Request Form	
		Brand Terms	
		Promotion	

■ **Figure 20.6   Table of Contents**
Source: U.S. Copyright Office, 2005 <www.copyright.gov/help/faq/>.

In this excerpt from the U.S. Copyright Office FAQ, visitors can click on the red bullets to reveal or hide the red links. This design lets visitors choose the level of detail they wish to see.

Each link on this page sends the visitor to a separate page that answers the question.

 On TechComm Web

To view Figure 20.6 in context on the Web, click on Links Library for Ch. 20 on <bedfordstmartins.com/techcomm>.

Frequently Asked Questions about Copyright

The Copyright Office offers introductory answers to frequently asked questions about copyright, registration, and services of the Office. Click on a subject heading below to view questions and answers relating to your selection. Links throughout the answers will guide you to further information on our website or from other sources. Should you have any further questions, please consult our Contact Us page.

- Copyright in General
- What Does Copyright Protect?
  - What does copyright protect?
  - Can I copyright my website?
  - Can I copyright my domain name?
  - How do I protect my recipe?
  - Can I copyright the name of my band?
  - How do I copyright a name, title, slogan or logo?
  - How do I protect my idea?
  - Does my work have to be published to be protected?
  - Can I register a diary I found in my grandmother's attic?
  - How do I protect my sighting of Elvis?
  - Does copyright protect architecture?
  - Can I get a star named after me and claim copyright to it?

Create Clear, Informative Links

Well-phrased links are easy to read and understand. By clearly telling the visitor what kind of information the linked site provides, they help him or her decide whether to follow the link. The following guidelines are based on Sun Microsystems' "Guide to Web Style" (Sun, 1999).

Guidelines

Writing Clear, Informative Links

▶ **Structure your sentences as if there were no links in your text.**

AWKWARD	Click here to go to the Rehabilitation Center page, which includes numerous links to research centers across the nation.
SMOOTH	The Rehabilitation Center page includes numerous links to research centers across the nation.

▶ **Indicate what information the linked page contains.** Visitors get frustrated if they wait for a file to download and then discover that it doesn't contain the information they expected.

UNINFORMATIVE	See the Rehabilitation Center.
INFORMATIVE	See the Rehabilitation Center's hours of operation.

▶ **Don't change the colors of the text links.** Visitors are used to two common colors: blue for links that have not yet been clicked and purple for links that have already been clicked.

Avoid Web Clichés

The Web has already developed its own clichés. Tired, empty words or phrases can obscure the site's purpose and make visitors suspect that they are wasting their time. The following Web clichés are particularly annoying because they insult visitors' intelligence by stating the obvious.

- *"Check out our site."* If the information looks interesting and useful, they will.
- *"Under construction."* If the site is a mess, don't launch it. If you want to tell visitors that you update the contents periodically, state when the site was last revised.
- *"Cool."* Uncool.
- *"Come back often."* If their visit was worthwhile, they will. If it wasn't, they won't.

Include Extra Features Your Visitors Might Need

Because visitors with a range of interests and needs will visit your site, consider adding several or all of the following five features:

- *An FAQ.* A list of frequently asked questions helps new visitors by providing basic information, explaining how to use the site, and directing them to more-detailed discussions. Figure 20.6 on page 534 is an excerpt from an FAQ page.

- *A search page or engine.* A search page or search engine lets visitors enter a keyword or phrase and find all the pages on the site that contain it.

- *Resource links.* If the main purpose of your site is to educate visitors, provide links to other sites.

- *A printable version of your site.* A Web site is designed for a screen, not a page. Consider making a printable version of your site, with black text on a white background and all the text and graphics consolidated into one big file.

- *A text-only version of your site.* Many visitors with slow Internet connections set their browsers to view text only. In addition, as is discussed more fully in the next section, many visitors with impaired vision rely on text because their specialized software cannot interpret graphics. Therefore, consider creating a text-only version of your site and include a link to it on your home page.

DESIGNING WEB SITES FOR VISITORS WITH DISABILITIES

On TechComm Web

For a detailed look at accessibility, see the Web Content Accessibility Guidelines from the World Wide Web Consortium. A site called Bobby will check your Web site for free to evaluate its adherence to accessibility options. Click on Links Library for Ch. 20 on <bedfordstmartins.com/techcomm>.

The Internet has proved to be a terrific technology for people with disabilities because it brings a world of information to their desktops, allowing them to work from home and participate in virtual communities. However, as sites have become more sophisticated over the past few years, many people with disabilities have found the Internet harder to use. In 1996, a court ruled that the Americans with Disabilities Act covers commercial Web sites, which must now be accessible to people with disabilities. Over the next few years, more effort will go into making hardware and software to help people with disabilities use the Internet.

The following discussion highlights several ways to make your site easier to use for people with disabilities. Consider three main types of disabilities as you design your site:

- *Vision impairment.* People who cannot see, or cannot see well, rely on text-to-speech conversion programs. Provide either a text-only version of the site or textual equivalents of all your graphics. Use the alt (alternate) tag to create a textual label that appears when the visitor holds the mouse over the graphic.

Do not rely on color or graphics alone to communicate information. For example, if you use a red icon to signal a warning, also use the word *warning.* If you use tables to create columns on the screen, label each column clearly using a text label rather than just an image.

Use 12-point type or larger throughout your site, and provide audio feedback—for example, have a button beep when the visitor presses it.

- *Hearing impairment.* If you use video, provide captions and, if the video includes sound, a volume control. Also use visual feedback techniques; for example, make a button flash when the visitor presses it.

- *Mobility impairment.* Some people with mobility impairments find it easier to use the keyboard than a mouse. Therefore, build in keyboard shortcuts wherever possible. If visitors have to click on an area of the screen using a pointing device, make the area large so that it is easy to see and click.

DESIGNING WEB SITES FOR MULTICULTURAL AUDIENCES

Almost two-thirds of the people using the Internet are nonnative speakers of English, and that number continues to grow as more people from developing nations go online (Global, 2004). Therefore, it makes sense to plan your site as if many of your visitors will not be proficient in English.

Strategies for Intercultural Communication

Communicating Online Across Cultures

Planning for a multicultural Web site is similar to planning for a multicultural paper document.

- **Use short sentences and paragraphs, as well as common words.**

- **Avoid idioms, both verbal and visual, that might be confusing.** For instance, don't use sports metaphors, such as *full-court press,* or a graphic of an American-style mailbox to suggest an e-mail link.

- **If a large percentage of your visitors speak a language other than English, consider creating a version of your site in that language.** The expense can be considerable, but so can the benefits.

 On TechComm Web

See the World Wide Web Consortium's internationalization page for more about the challenges of creating markup languages that meet the needs of international users.

Also see "Guidelines for Accessible Web Sites: Technology & Users" by Michele Ward, Philip Rubens, and Sherry Southard.

Click on Links Library for Ch. 20 on <bedfordstmartins.com/techcomm>.

On TechComm Web

See Stan Morris's essay "The
Importance of International Laws
for Web Publishers." Click on
Links Library for Ch. 20 on
<bedfordstmartins.com/
techcomm>.

In This Book

For more about copyright law, see
Ch. 2, p. 18.

COPYRIGHT LAW AND THE WEB

The words and images that you see on the Internet are covered by copyright, even if you see no copyright symbol. The only exceptions are information that is in the public domain because it is not covered by copyright (such as information created by federal government sources), because the copyright has expired (the author has been dead for more than 70 years), or because the creator of the information explicitly states that the information is in the public domain and you are free to copy it.

Even if you cite the information appropriately when using it, you still must abide by copyright law. If you cite it correctly but violate copyright, you are not a plagiarist, but you are a copyright violator and can be sued by the copyright holder.

This much we know. However, a number of complex issues related to the Internet and copyright law are still unclear. Benedict O'Mahoney (2005) has written several thoughtful essays on some of the complicated issues involved in interpreting copyright law. Here are just three of the questions he addresses:

- *Is the design of a Web page protected by copyright law?* Some would say no, because what visitors see is determined by their hardware and software, and visitors can customize the image. However, the design of a Web page is an original work and thus should be protected, regardless of how visitors might change it after it is transmitted.

- *Are lists of links protected?* Is each link protected by copyright? No. Is the whole list of links protected? Probably, if the writer showed some originality in creating the list. For example, a set of links to resources for agriculture students would be protected if the writer did some original thinking in creating categories for the individual links.

- *May you link to anyone else's Web site? May anyone link to yours?* Although the Web was originally envisioned as an open environment, in which anyone can link to anyone else, a site owner might not want the extra traffic on its server or might not want to be associated with the linking site. Are you responsible for finding out who has linked to you, or should the linking site have to get permission to link to you?

As this discussion suggests, copyright questions related to digital documents are likely to remain unresolved for years. Over the next decade, the courts will be hearing many cases in which copyright law has to be reinterpreted in light of the unique technical, economic, and social implications of electronic media. Your responsibility is to be sure to consult your company's legal counsel if you have even the slightest doubts about whether your use of digital information is legal.

ETHICS AND THE WEB

Copyright is an area of law, but the word *copyright* literally refers to the *right* to *copy,* and the word *right* brings up the issue of ethics.

Guidelines

Creating an Ethical Site

▶ **Don't plagiarize.** If you want to publish material you found on the Internet, ask the copyright owner for written permission.

▶ **Ask permission to link.** Notify an organization if you wish to link to its site, then abide by its wishes. And ask before *deep linking*—linking to a page other than the home page.

▶ **Don't steal someone else's designs.** Create your own designs for attractive, functional pages and sites.

▶ **Don't misuse meta tags.** If you look at the source code of a typical Web page, you will see a meta tag near the top. This is the place where you put keywords that describe the contents of your site. If you are a Ford dealer, you list "Ford," "dealer," and the names of Ford models. It is unethical and, according to some intellectual-property attorneys, illegal for a Ford dealer to list "Chevrolet" to get potential Chevrolet customers to come to the Ford site.

SAMPLE WEB PAGES

The best way to learn about designing Web sites and their pages is to study them. Figures 20.7, 20.8, and 20.9 on pages 540 and 542 offer examples of good Web page design.

This page is simple and attractive, with a clear purpose, effective organization, and large, clear type.

The name of the organization.

The name of the page.

Frames are used effectively here. Users can scroll down to read additional information, but the header, the photograph, and the footer remain visible.

Large, easy-to-read textual links.

 On TechComm Web

To view Figures 20.7–20.9 in context on the Web, click on Links Library for Ch. 20 on <bedfordstmartins.com/ techcomm>.

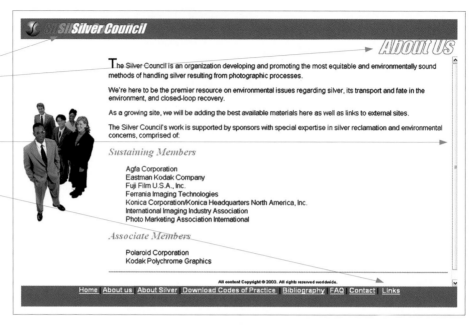

■ **Figure 20.7   The Silver Council Home Page**

Source: Silver Council, 2005 <www.silvercouncil.org/html/default.htm>.

The navigation links are clear. You always know where you are.

The page has four clearly designated sections:
- the header and main set of links
- a link to a new Palm product
- links to other main content areas
- the footer

■ **Figure 20.8   The PalmSource Page**

Source: Palm, Inc., 2005 <www.palmsource.com/>.

INTERACTIVE SAMPLE DOCUMENT
Designing Effective Web Sites

Following is the home page for the National Oceanic and Atmospheric Administration (NOAA) Fisheries Service, a division of the Department of Commerce. The NOAA Fisheries Service is responsible for managing, conserving, and protecting living marine resources within the United States' Exclusive Economic Zone. The questions in the margin ask you to think about creating and designing effective Web sites and Web pages. E-mail your responses to yourself and/or your instructor, and see suggested responses on TechComm Web.

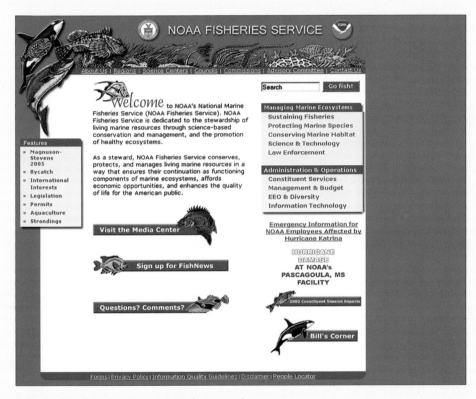

Source: NOAA Fisheries, 2005 <www.nmfs.noaa.gov/>.

1. Evaluate the navigation links of this site. How easy do you think it would be to find what you need?

2. How effectively has the author designed the information in the text window? What additional information, if any, would you include?

3. How effective are the graphics?

 On TechComm Web

To e-mail your responses to yourself and/or your instructor and to see suggested responses, click on Interactive Sample Documents for Ch. 20 on <bedfordstmartins .com/techcomm>.

This page is designed to contain a large number of links to tutorials and other reference information. Tutorials are presented in the left-hand column, an explanation of how to use the site is presented in the middle column, and other reference material is presented in the right-hand column.

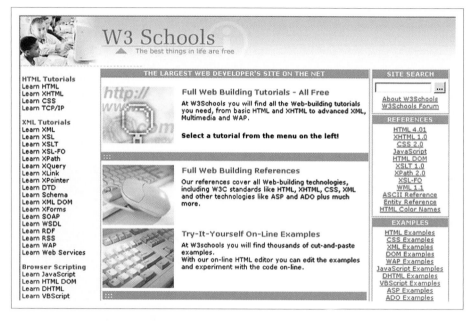

■ **Figure 20.9   The W3 Schools Home Page**
Source: W3 Schools, 2005 <www.w3schools.com/>.

Web Designer's Checklist

In designing the site, did you

☐ analyze your audience and purpose before planning your site? (p. 530)

☐ use a plain, simple background? (p. 531)

☐ allow for effective contrast between the background color and the text color? (p. 531)

☐ avoid decorative graphics? (p. 531)

☐ use thumbnail graphics rather than large ones? (p. 531)

☐ make the text easy to read by using brief chunks of text? (p. 531)

☐ use simple language and short sentences? (p. 531)

☐ create informative headers and footers? (p. 531)

☐ include a site map or index? (p. 533)

☐ use a table of contents at the top of every long page? (p. 533)

☐ link to the top of every long page? (p. 533)

☐ link to the home page on every page? (p. 533)

☐ include textual navigational links at the bottom of the page? (p. 533)

☐ create clear and informative links? (p. 535)

☐ avoid Web clichés? (p. 535)

☐ include extra features your visitors might need, such as an FAQ page, a list of links, a printable version of the site, and a text-only version of the site? (p. 536)

☐ design the site so that it is easy for people with impaired vision, hearing, or movement to use? (p. 536)

☐ design the site to accommodate the needs of multicultural visitors? (p. 537)

☐ get permission to publish any information that you did not generate? (p. 539)

☐ ask permission to link? (p. 539)

☐ link to another site's home page rather than a secondary page? (p. 539)

☐ avoid including misleading information in the meta tags? (p. 539)

☐ revise and test the information? (p. 530)

☐ get the files to an Internet server? (p. 530)

☐ register the site with search engines? (p. 530)

Exercises

 In This Book   For more about memos, see Ch. 14, p. 352.

1. **INTERNET EXERCISE** Find the sites of three manufacturers within a single industry, such as personal watercraft, cars, computers, or medical equipment. Study the three sites, focusing on one of these aspects of site design:

   - use of color
   - effectiveness of the graphics in communicating information
   - quality of the writing
   - quality of the site map or index
   - navigation, including the clarity and placement of links to other pages in the site
   - use of Web clichés
   - accommodation of multicultural visitors
   - accommodation of people with disabilities
   - the phrasing of the links

   Which of the three sites is most effective? Which is least effective? Why? Compare and contrast the three sites in terms of their effectiveness.

2. **INTERNET EXERCISE** Using a search engine, find a site that serves the needs of people with a particular physical ailment or disability—for example, the Glaucoma Foundation <www.glaucomafoundation.org/index.php>. What attempts have the designers made to accommodate the needs of visitors to the site? How effective do you think those attempts have been?

3. **INTERNET EXERCISE** Using a search engine, find five tutorials on creating Web pages. For each site, determine the level of expertise of the intended audience and analyze the strengths and weaknesses of the tutorial. Present your results in a memo to your instructor.

4. **GROUP/INTERNET EXERCISE** Form small groups and describe and evaluate your college's or university's Web site. Different members of the group might carry out the following tasks:

   - E-mail the site's Webmaster to ask about the process of creating the site. For example, how involved with the content and design of the site was the Webmaster? What is the Webmaster's role in maintaining the site?
   - Analyze the kinds of information the site contains and determine whether the site is intended primarily for faculty, students, alumni, or prospective students.
   - Determine the overlap between the information on the site and the information in printed documents published by the school. In those cases in which they overlap, is the information on the site merely a duplication of the printed information, or has it been revised to take advantage of the unique capabilities of the Web?

   Present your conclusions and recommendations for improving the site in a memo to your instructor.

Case 20: Designing a Site

 In This Book   For more about memos, see Ch. 14, p. 352.

Background

The Foundation for Research, Education, Sustainability, and Health (FRESH), founded in 1986 in a small barn, has always used a two-page newsletter to communicate with growers. As the business expanded, FRESH leased a few acres from a neighbor. Several loyal friends helped FRESH build a greenhouse, and the business began to grow and sell nursery plants to local customers. As FRESH continued to gain popularity in the mid-1990s, it emerged as a leader in the field of organic supplies and organic-farming advocacy. Recently, FRESH transformed itself into a nonprofit organization whose mission is to sponsor organic-farming research, distribute research results to people interested in adopting organic-farming practices, and educate the public about organic farming.

You have been volunteering a few hours each week at the foundation's office. Most of the time, you help the office staff produce *FRESH Ideas,* a monthly newsletter distributed to organic farmers and other supporters of organic agriculture. Occasionally, you help write the guidelines for applying to the foundation's competitive grant program. The cofounder and Executive Director, Erik McBride, has asked you to help the foundation with an important project.

"The foundation's board of directors has authorized funding to create a FRESH Web site," Erik explains. "I just came from a meeting at which board members brainstormed some ideas for the site. We focused on coming up with ideas for all the pages or topics we want on the site. I want you to take a look at the notes from our meeting and create a site design incorporating our ideas." (See Document 20.1.)

After briefly looking over the notes, you ask, "You generated a bunch of different topics. Do you want the site design to include all of them?"

"It doesn't have to. After you start working on the design, you might find that some of the topics just don't fit. Or you might decide to break up topics or combine two or more topics. Use the foundation's mission to guide your decisions. Also, we need your advice on how to label the navigation links clearly so our visitors can accurately predict what information a page contains."

Your Assignment

1. For each of the numbered ideas in Erik's notes (Document 20.1), write a clear, informative link label that could be used on the site's navigational elements. If appropriate, you may combine or break up ideas.

2. Design the basic structure for the FRESH Web site. Using a graphics program to make a diagram in which each box represents a page on the Web site, create a visual display that will communicate your design to the board of directors. Include a brief memo in which you justify your design.

■ **Document 20.1   Notes from the Brainstorming Session**

 On TechComm Web

For digital versions of case documents, click on Downloadable Case Documents at <bedfordstmartins.com/techcomm>.

General Thoughts

- Reflect our core mission: sponsor organic-farming research, distribute the results to interested parties, and educate the public.
- Reflect our foundation's strong commitment to organic-farming advocacy.
- Serve the interests of our local, longtime supporters, as well as broaden our focus to consumers, who are quickly becoming more aware of the uncertainties surrounding our food-supply system.

Ideas for Content

1. A place for visitors to access current and back issues of *FRESH Ideas*. Author guidelines for submitting to the newsletter. Info about different subscriptions: print, online, and e-mail.
2. Contact info, biographies of board of directors, FRESH staff.
3. Information on our competitive grant program: application guidelines, areas of interest, restrictions, past grants, etc.
4. A mechanism for people to donate.
5. Definition of organic farming.
6. Place to include public-education materials, such as guides to organic farming, recipes, cookbooks, lists of places to buy organic foods.
7. Pictures of FRESH employees, FRESH events, etc.
8. Information for people interested in jobs and internships with FRESH.
9. A way for people to contact us.
10. Description of how to volunteer.
11. Place to address general questions on organic farming.
12. Place to tell the story of FRESH.
13. Updates on FRESH activities such as briefing USDA officials on important issues, sponsoring tours of local organic farms, and lobbying activities in the Senate.
14. A place to post organic-farming research.
15. Notices of upcoming relevant conferences, meetings, etc.
16. Way for readers to subscribe to FRESH mailing list.
17. Examples of letters to state and federal representatives and tips on how to write such letters.
18. Links to other sites of interest.
19. List of FRESH accomplishments.
20. FRESH press releases.
21. Space to promote *FRESH Feast*, our signature fund-raising event.

Making Oral Presentations

21

TECH COMM AT WORK

Professionals in all types of businesses make oral presentations. A member of a farm collective might brief other members on whether the collective has the experience, equipment, and facilities to provide produce to a local restaurant chain. An exercise physiologist might make a presentation to coaches about new findings on how to increase the effectiveness of training techniques. An English teacher might make a presentation to colleagues about which textbooks students and teachers should use next year. With some preparation and practice, you can give presentations that will help you significantly in the workplace. As a confident, competent presenter, you can sell your ideas — from proposals to progress and completion reports — to clients, suppliers, and supervisors.

To some extent, the technique for preparing written documents and oral presentations is quite similar: you analyze your audience and purpose, gather information, organize it, and create graphics. The big difference, of course, is the form of delivery. There are four basic types of presentations:

- *Impromptu presentations.* You deliver the presentation without advance notice. For instance, your supervisor calls on you during a meeting to speak about a project you are working on.
- *Extemporaneous presentations.* You plan and rehearse the presentation. Although you might refer to notes or an outline during the presentation, you create the sentences as you speak. At its best, an extemporaneous presentation is clear and sounds spontaneous.
- *Scripted presentations.* You read a text that was written in advance (by you or someone else). Scripted presentations sacrifice naturalness for increased clarity and precision.
- *Memorized presentations.* You speak without notes or a script. Memorized presentations are not appropriate for most technical subjects because most people cannot memorize presentations of more than a few minutes.

This chapter discusses extemporaneous and scripted presentations.

UNDERSTANDING THE ROLE OF ORAL PRESENTATIONS

An oral presentation has one big advantage over a written one: it permits a dialogue between the speaker and the audience, both before and after the presentation. Oral presentations are common in technical communication. You can expect to give oral presentations to four types of audiences:

- *Clients and customers.* You present your products' features and its advantages over the competition. After the sale, you might provide oral operating instructions and maintenance tips to users.

- *Colleagues in your organization.* You instruct fellow workers on a subject you know well. After you return from an important conference or an out-of-town project, your supervisors want a briefing—an oral report. If you have an idea for improving operations at your organization, you write an informal proposal and then present it orally to a small group of managers. Your presentation helps them determine whether to study the idea.

- *Fellow professionals at technical conferences.* You speak about your own research project or about a team project. You might address other professionals in your field or professionals in other fields.

- *The public.* You deliver oral presentations to civic organizations and government bodies.

You might not have had much experience in public speaking, and perhaps your few attempts have been difficult. You might even have read that people fear giving presentations more than they fear anything else, including death. This claim is nonsense, of course, and it is counterproductive. True, many people don't look forward to giving presentations. But you're going to give a lot of them, so the smartest thing is to figure out how to get comfortable doing so. Here is a secret: you can get pretty good at it if you prepare and rehearse. Once you learn that people in the room are there to hear what you have to say—not to stare at you, evaluate your clothing, or catch you making a grammar mistake—you can calm down and deliver your information effectively. After giving a few presentations, you will be able to take advantage of the many opportunities that come your way to project your professionalism while communicating effectively.

UNDERSTANDING THE PROCESS OF PREPARING AND DELIVERING ORAL PRESENTATIONS

Figure 21.1 on page 548 presents an overview of the process of preparing and delivering oral presentations. The rest of this chapter discusses this process, beginning with how to prepare a presentation.

PREPARING A PRESENTATION

When you see an excellent 20-minute presentation, you are seeing only the last 20 minutes of a process that took many hours. Experts recommend 20 to 60 minutes of preparation for each minute of the presentation (Smith, 1991). At an average of 40 minutes of preparation time, you would need more than 13 hours to prepare a 20-minute presentation. Obviously, there are many variables, including your knowledge of the subject and your experience creating graphics and giving presentations on that subject. But the point is that good presentations don't just happen.

Preparing an oral presentation requires five steps.

 On TechComm Web

The Virtual Presentation Assistant offers advice on presentations and provides links to text and videos of speeches. Click on Links Library for Ch. 21 on <bedfordstmartins.com/techcomm>.

**■ Figure 21.1
An Overview of the
Process for Preparing
and Delivering Oral
Presentations**

Analyze the Speaking Situation

How much does your audience know about the subject? What are your listeners' goals? What is your purpose—to inform or persuade, or both? Budget your time for the presentation.

↓

Organize and Develop the Presentation

Use or adapt one or several of the organizational patterns described in Chapter 7. Gather the information you will need.

↓

Prepare the Presentation Graphics

Effective graphics are visible, legible, simple, clear, and correct. Choose the appropriate technology based on the speaking situation and the available resources.

↓

Choose Effective Language

Use language to signal advance organizers, summaries, and transitions. Choose memorable language by involving the audience, referring to people, and using interesting facts, figures, and quotations.

↓

Rehearse the Presentation

Rehearse at least three times to make sure you are comfortable with the information. Use the Speaker's Checklist on page 567.

↓

Deliver the Presentation

First, calm your nerves. In the presentation, use your voice effectively. Maintain eye contact and use natural gestures. Don't block the audience's view of the screen. At the end, politely solicit questions and answer them effectively.

Analyzing the Speaking Situation

To prepare an oral presentation:

Analyze the speaking situation.

Organize and develop the presentation.

Prepare presentation graphics.

Choose effective language.

Rehearse the presentation.

First analyze your audience and purpose, then determine how much information you can deliver in the allotted time.

Analyzing Your Audience and Purpose   In planning an oral presentation, consider audience and purpose, just as you would in writing a document.

- *Audience.* What does the audience know about your subject? Your answer helps you determine the level of technical vocabulary and concepts you will use, as well as the types of graphics. Why are audience members listening to your presentation? Are they likely to be hostile, enthusiastic, or neutral? A presentation on the virtues of free trade, for instance, will be received one way by conservative economists and another way by U.S. steelworkers.

Are they nonnative speakers of English? If so, prepare to slow down your delivery and use a simple vocabulary.

- *Purpose.* Are you attempting to inform, persuade, or do both? If you are explaining how windmill farms work, you might describe the process. If you are explaining why your windmills are an economical way to generate power, you might compare their results with those of other power sources.

Your analysis of your audience and purpose will affect the content and form of your presentation. For example, you might have to emphasize some aspects of your subject and ignore others. Or you might have to arrange topics to accommodate an audience's needs.

Budgeting Your Time   At most professional meetings, each speaker is given a maximum time, such as 20 minutes. If the question-and-answer period is part of your allotted time, plan accordingly. Even at an informal presentation, you will probably have to work within an unstated time limit that you must determine from the speaking situation. If you take more than your time, eventually your listeners will resent you or simply stop paying attention.

For a 20-minute presentation, the time allotment shown in Table 21.1 is typical. For a scripted presentation, most speakers need a little over a minute to deliver a double-spaced page of text effectively.

■ Table 21.1   Time Allotment for a 20-Minute Presentation

Task	Time (minutes)
• Introduction	2
• Body	
– First Major Point	4
– Second Major Point	4
– Third Major Point	4
• Conclusion	2
• Questions	4

On TechComm Web

See Dave Zielinski's essay on addressing multicultural audiences. Click on Links Library for Ch. 21 on <bedfordstmartins.com/techcomm>.

Organizing and Developing the Presentation

The speaking situation will help you decide how to organize and develop the information you will present.

Start by reviewing the organizational patterns discussed in Chapter 7. One of them might fit the speaking situation. For instance, if you are a quality-assurance engineer for a computer-chip manufacturer and are addressing your technical colleagues on why one of the company's products is experiencing a higher than normal failure rate, think in terms of cause and effect: the high failure rate is the effect, but what is the cause? Or think in terms of problem-method-solution: the high failure rate is the problem; the research you conducted to determine its cause is the method; your recommended action is the solution. Of course, you can combine and adapt several organizational patterns.

While you devise an effective organizational pattern for your presentation, note the kinds of information you will need for each section. Some of this information will be data; some of it will be graphics that you can use in your slides; some might be objects that you want to pass around the audience.

Some presenters like to outline their presentations on paper or in a word-processing program. More and more, however, people use their presentation-graphics software for outlining. Figure 21.2 on page 550 shows the Outline view in Microsoft PowerPoint.

This is also a good time to plan the introduction and conclusion of your presentation.

■ **Figure 21.2**
The Outline View in
Microsoft PowerPoint

You can draft in the outline view.

What you type appears in the image of the slide.

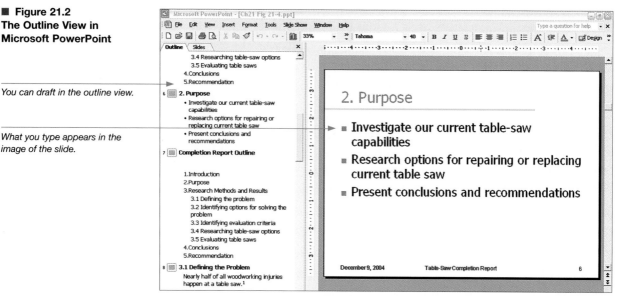

Guidelines

Introducing a Presentation

In introducing a presentation, consider these five suggestions.

▶ **Introduce yourself.** Unless you are speaking to the colleagues you work with every day, begin with an introduction, such as "Good morning, my name is Omar Castillo, and I'm the Director of Facilities here at United." If you are using slides, put your name and position on the title slide.

▶ **State the title of your presentation.** Presentation titles should explain the audience and purpose, such as "Replacing the HVAC System in Building 3: Findings from the Feasibility Study." Include this title on your title slide.

▶ **Explain the purpose of the presentation.** This explanation can be brief: "My purpose is to present the results of the feasibility study carried out by the Facilities Group. As you may recall, last quarter we were charged with determining whether it would be wise to replace the HVAC system in Building 3."

▶ **State your main point.** An explicit statement can help your audience understand the rest of the presentation: "Our main finding is that the HVAC system should be replaced as soon as possible. Replacing it would cost approximately $120,000. The payback period would be 2.5 years. We recommend that we start soliciting bids now, for an installation date in the third week of November."

▶ **Provide an advance organizer.** Listeners need specific statements of where you are going: "First I'd like to describe our present system, highlighting the recent problems we have experienced. Next I'd like to.... Then I'd like to.... Finally, I'd like to conclude and invite your questions."

Planning the Introduction   Like an introduction to a written document, an introduction to an oral presentation helps your audience understand what you are going to say, why you are going to say it, and how you are going to say it.

Planning the Conclusion   Like all conclusions, a conclusion to an oral presentation reinforces what you have said and looks to the future.

Guidelines

Concluding a Presentation

In concluding a presentation, consider these four suggestions.

▶ **Announce that you are concluding.** You might say, "At this point, I'd like to conclude my talk." This statement helps the audience focus on your conclusions.

▶ **Summarize the main points.** Because listeners cannot rewind what you have said, it's important to briefly summarize your main points. If you are using slides, list each main point in one short phrase per slide.

▶ **Look to the future.** If appropriate, speak briefly about what you think (or hope) will happen next: "If the president accepts our recommendation, you can expect the renovation to begin in late November. After a few hectic weeks, we'll have the ability to control our environment much more precisely than we can now."

▶ **Invite questions.** Questions from the audience can help you clarify what you said or communicate information that you did not include in the formal presentation.

Preparing Presentation Graphics

Graphics clarify or highlight important ideas or facts. Graphics are particularly helpful in presenting statistical data, abstract relationships, and descriptions of equipment or processes. Research reported by Smith (1991) indicates that presentations that include graphics are judged to be more professional, persuasive, and credible than those that do not. In addition, Smith notes, audiences remember the information better:

	Retention after	
	3 hours	3 days
Without graphics	70%	10%
With graphics	85%	65%

One other advantage of using presentation graphics is that the audience is not always looking at you. Giving the audience another visual focus can reduce your nervousness.

In This Book
For more about creating graphics, see Ch. 13.

Characteristics of an Effective Graphic Effective graphics have five characteristics:

- *Visibility.* The most common problem with presentation graphics is that they are too small. Don't transfer information from an 8.5 × 11-inch page to a slide or transparency. In general, text has to be in 24-point type or larger to be visible on the screen. Figure 21.3 shows that transferring text from a page to a slide makes for a poor slide.

    To save space, compress sentences into brief phrases:

TEXT IN A DOCUMENT	The current system has three problems: • It is expensive to maintain. • It requires nonstandard components. • It is not compliant with the new MILSPEC.
SAME TEXT ON A SCREEN	Three Problems: • Expensive Maintenance • Nonstandard Components • Noncompliance with MILSPEC

- *Legibility.* Use clear, legible lines for drawings and diagrams: black on white works best. Use legible typefaces for text; a boldfaced sans-serif typeface such as Arial or Helvetica is effective because it reproduces clearly on a screen. Avoid shadowed and outlined letters.

This slide contains far too much text. A common guideline is to put no more than seven words on a line, and no more than seven lines on a slide. Otherwise, the text becomes too small to read easily.

There's another problem with this slide. What is the presenter supposed to do or say while this slide is visible? The presenter cannot read the text, because many people in the audience will find it offensive to have someone read to them.

If you have lengthy text—such as long quotations or a list of sources—distribute a handout at the end of your presentation. During the presentation itself, reduce the text to brief phrases.

The "Workbook" Approach

In explaining the U.S. approach to privacy the "Workbook" describes privacy protection not as ethical practice but as good business:

"In the United States, the importance of protecting the privacy of individuals' personal information is a priority for the federal government and consumers. Consumers repeatedly cite fears that their personal information will be misused as a reason for not doing business online. In this way, moves to bolster on-line privacy protect consumer interests and fuel the broader growth of on-line communications, innovation, and business. Self-regulatory initiatives are an effective approach to putting meaningful privacy protections in place. In certain highly sensitive areas, however, legislative solutions are appropriate. These sensitive areas include financial and medical records, genetic information, Social Security numbers, and information involving children." [8]

■ **Figure 21.3   Text Copied from a Page to a Slide**

- *Simplicity.* Text and drawings must be simple. Each graphic should present only one idea. Your listeners have not seen the graphic before and will not be able to linger over it.

- *Clarity.* In cutting words and simplifying concepts and visual representations, make sure the point of the graphic remains clear.

- *Correctness.* Everyone makes mistakes, but mistakes are particularly embarrassing when they are 10 inches tall on a screen.

In This Book

For more about typefaces, see Ch. 12, p. 271. For more about using color in graphics, see Ch. 13, p. 301.

Two points from Chapter 13 are important here. First, when you use graphics templates in your software, remember that some of them violate basic principles of design. Second, don't use clip art just to fill blank space on a transparency or slide.

One more point: you cannot use copyrighted material—images, text, music, video, or other material—in your presentation without written permission to do so.

On TechComm Web

See Dave Zielinski's essay on how copyright law applies to presentations. Click on Links Library for Ch. 21 on <bedfordstmartins .com/techcomm>.

Graphics and the Speaking Situation   To plan your graphics, analyze four aspects of the speaking situation:

- *Length of the presentation.* How many graphics should you have? Smith (1991) suggests showing a different graphic approximately every 30 seconds. This figure is only a guideline; you should base your decision on your subject and audience. Still, the general point is valid: it is far better to have a series of simple graphics than to have one complicated graphic that stays on the screen for five minutes.

- *Audience aptitude and experience.* What kinds of graphics can your audience understand easily? You don't want to present scatter graphs, for example, if your listeners do not know how to interpret them.

- *Size and layout of the room.* Graphics to be used in a small meeting room differ from those to be used in a 500-seat auditorium. Think first about the size of the images, then about the layout of the room. For instance, will a window create glare that you will have to consider as you plan the type or placement of the graphics?

- *Equipment.* Find out what kind of equipment will be available in the presentation room. Ask about backups in case of equipment failure. If possible, bring your own equipment. That way, you know it works and you know how to use it. Some speakers bring graphics in two media just in case; that is, they have slides and transparencies of the same graphics.

Using Graphics to Signal the Organization of the Presentation   Used effectively, graphics can help you communicate how your presentation is organized. For example, you can use the transition from one graphic to the next to indicate the transition from one point to the next. Figure 21.4 on pages 554–55 shows the

**Feasibility Study
on Table-Saw Capability:
A Completion Report**

Prepared by:
**David Bethke, Shop assistant
Steven Cowles, Shop assistant
Amy Frachiseur, Technical writer
Justin Stoffel, Shop assistant**

The first slide—the title slide—shows the title of the presentation and the name and affiliation of each speaker.

At the bottom of each slide is a footer with the date, the title of the presentation, and the number of the slide.

Completion Report Outline

➡ 1. Introduction
2. Purpose
3. Research Methods and Results
  3.1 Defining the problem
  3.2 Identifying options for solving the problem
  3.3 Identifying evaluation criteria
  3.4 Researching table-saw options
  3.5 Evaluating table saws
4. Conclusions
5. Recommendation

The next slide presents an overview, which outlines the presentation. The blue arrow identifies the point the speaker is addressing.

---

1. Introduction

Shop workload:

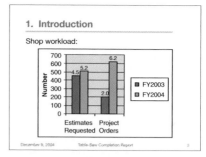

Notice that the title of the third slide is numbered according to the outline introduced in the previous slide. Such cues help the audience understand the structure of your presentation.

This slide uses a simple multiple-bar graph. Although the speakers could have used words in a bulleted list, graphics are more visually interesting and easier to understand.

---

1. Introduction (cont'd)

Table-Saw Problem:
  Unsafe conditions, lost productivity, wasted materials
  • Inadequate safety features
  • Worn bearings, excessive fence deflection, excessive arbor run-out, low feed rate

If a topic extends onto a second slide, as you see here, use a "cont'd" notation. Don't try to squeeze all the information onto one slide.

Slide 5, not included here, is identical to Slide 2, except for the placement of the blue arrow. The speakers use Slide 5—and Slides 7, 24, and 26—to help orient the listener.

---

2. Purpose

• Investigate our current table-saw capabilities
• Research options for repairing or replacing current table saw
• Present conclusions and recommendations

Notice that the bulleted list on this slide uses parallel structure: all the phrases begin with the present tense of the verb.

3.1 Defining the Problem

Nearly half of all woodworking injuries happen at a table saw.

Unfortunately, our saw lacks standard safety features:
• a magnetic switch (Jo nearly lost her hand because our saw lacks this feature)
• a tool-free blade guard
• an easy-to-access power switch
• anti-kickback pawls
• an effective dust-collection system

When you wish to cite sources, you have two choices: add source statements at the bottom of the appropriate slides or make a sources slide that you show at the end of the presentation. If the list of sources is long, or if you think your listeners might want a copy of it, make a paper copy to distribute.

3.1 Defining the Problem (cont'd)

Lost Productivity:
  20 workers each spend 4 hours/month =
    80 hours/month at $15/hour =
        $1,200/month
Wasted Materials:
        $200/month

In this presentation, the speakers use color—sparingly—for emphasis.

Slide 10, not shown here, concludes Section 3.1 of the presentation.

3.2 Identifying Options for Solving the Problem

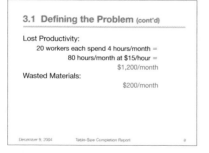

Option	Decision	Rationale
1. Use saw as is	Ruled Out	• Lacks safety features. • Current losses of $16,800/year in lost productivity and wasted material.
2. Repair saw	Ruled Out	• Lacks safety features. • Fixing a 10-year-old saw out of warranty is unwise.
3. Replace saw	Best Option	Safer and more efficient saws available for less than $2,000.

When you use tables, keep them simple. If you have a lot of rows and columns, present the data on several slides.

3.3 Identifying Evaluation Criteria

Necessary Criteria
• Safety. We wanted at least four of the following features:
  - tool-free blade guard
  - magnetic switch
  - easy-to-access switch
  - anti-kickback pawls
  - effective dust-collection system
• Cost. We worked within a capital budget of $2,000.

If you are projecting your presentation graphics from a computer, you can set the software so that each bulleted item appears only after you click the mouse. This way, the audience will not read ahead.

■ **Figure 21.4   Selected Slides for a Brief Presentation**

3.3 Identifying Evaluation Criteria
(cont'd)

Desirable Criteria

- Power. We wanted at least a 3-hp motor and preferred a 5-hp motor.
- Accuracy. We considered fence length, blade adjustment, vibration tendency, and arbor run-out.

3.4 Researching Table-Saw Options

Three Woodworking Experts	Recommendations
David Hegg Editor, *Popular Woodworking Magazine*, more than 20 years of experience in cabinet shops	• Powermatic Model 66 • Grizzly G1023SLX • Jet JTAS-10XL50-1 • Delta Unisaw 36-L31X-BC50
Linda Oats Host, *Tools & Techniques*, The DIY Network, author of 60 woodworking books	• Powermatic Model 66 • Jet JTAS-10XL50-1 • Bosch 4000
Nathan Abram Award-winning woodworker with over 30 years of experience	• Powermatic Model 66 • DeWalt DW746 • Grizzly G1023SLX • Delta Unisaw 36-L31X-BC50

3.4 Researching Table-Saw Options
(cont'd)

We chose the four most commonly recommended models to further investigate:

- Powermatic Model 66
- Grizzly G1023SLX
- Jet JTAS-10XL50-1
- Delta Unisaw 36-L31X-BC50

Notice how the speakers split up the information between Slides 12 and 13 so that each slide contains only a small amount. If all the information were on one slide, the slide would look too busy, and the type would be too small.

Slide 14, not shown here, completes Section 3.3.

The slide number enables audience members to ask questions by referring to the number.

The formatting that appears throughout the slide set—the background color, the horizontal rules, and the footer—is created in the Slide-Master view. This formatting appears in every slide unless you modify or delete it for that slide.

3.4 Researching Table-Saw Options
(cont'd)

Powermatic Model 66

Source: www.wmhtoolgroup.com/index

3.4 Researching Table-Saw Options
(cont'd)

Grizzly G1023SLX

Source: www.grizzly.com/products/item

3.5 Evaluating Table Saws

Necessary Criteria

Model	Safety Features	Meets Safety Criterion?	Cost	Meets Cost Criterion?	Consider Further?
Powermatic Model 66	a,b,c,e	yes	$2,100	No	No
Gizzly G1023SLX	a,b,c,e	yes	$1,125	Yes	Yes
Jet JTAS-10XL50-1	a,b,c,e	yes	$1,500	Yes	Yes
Delta Unisaw 36-LS31X-BC50	a,b,c,d,e	yes	$1,550	Yes	Yes

If you think the audience will be interested in viewing an item, include a photograph. Do not use a photo unless it shows something interesting or informative.

All graphics are protected by copyright law. Therefore, you must get permission to use them and cite the sources in your presentation.

Slides 20 and 21, not shown here, present photographs of the two other table saws being considered.

Most of these slides are based on information presented in the completion report. As in most cases, excerpts from a written document had to be reformatted and revised to work effectively on a screen.

3.5 Evaluating Table Saws
(cont'd)

Desirable Criteria

Model	Power Score	Accuracy Score	Quality Score	Ease-of-Use Score	Total Score
Grizzly G1023SLX	4	6	8	8	26
Jet JTAS-10XL50-1	8	6	4	7	25
Delta Unisaw 36-LS31X-BC50	8	8	8	9	33

4. Conclusions

- All three options are high-quality saws.
- Although the Delta Unisaw is the second most expensive saw, it fared best in our evaluation.
- The Delta Unisaw comes with the best warranty: 5 years. The cost per warranted month is $26, compared to $94 for the next highest-rated saw.

5. Recommendation

Purchase a Delta Unisaw 36-L31X-BC50, at a cost of $1,550.

Savings: $1,400/month
Payback period: 5 weeks

As discussed in Ch. 18, conclusions are inferences that you draw from results.

Also as discussed in Ch. 18, recommendations are statements about what you think should be done next.

■ **Figure 21.4** *(continued)*

To create speaking notes for each slide, type the notes in the box under the picture of the slide, then print the notes page.

You can print the slides on your notes pages in color or black and white.

The problem with using speaking notes is that you cannot read your notes and maintain eye contact at the same time.

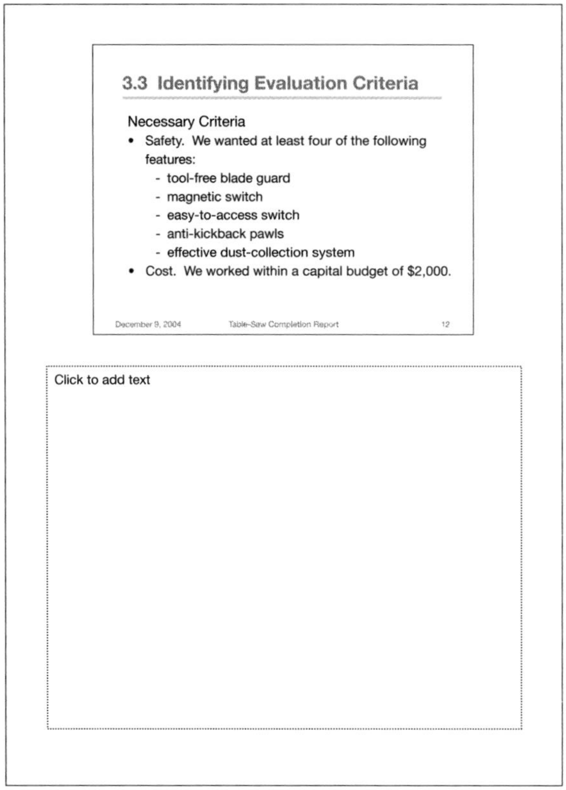

3.3 Identifying Evaluation Criteria

Necessary Criteria
- Safety. We wanted at least four of the following features:
    - tool-free blade guard
    - magnetic switch
    - easy-to-access switch
    - anti-kickback pawls
    - effective dust-collection system
- Cost. We worked within a capital budget of $2,000.

December 9, 2004   Table-Saw Completion Report   12

Click to add text

■ **Figure 21.5   Speaking Notes**

slides for a presentation that accompanied the report on selecting a table saw presented in Chapter 18 (see pages 475–91). The outline in Slide 2 is used in Slides 5, 7, and 16 to signal the transition to the next major section of the presentation.

For your last graphic, consider a summary of your main points or a brief set of questions that restate your main points and prompt the audience to synthesize the information you have presented.

Presentation software allows you to create two other kinds of documents—*speaking notes* and *handouts*—that can enhance a presentation. Figure 21.5 shows a page of speaking notes. Figure 21.6 shows a handout.

Basic Media Used for Presentations   Table 21.2 on page 558 describes the basic media used to create oral presentations.

If you are using presentation-graphics software, keep in mind that many of the templates provided with the software are unnecessarily ornate—full of fancy shading, designs, and colors. Choose a simple template, then modify it for your situation. You want the audience to focus on the information, not the design of the graphic.

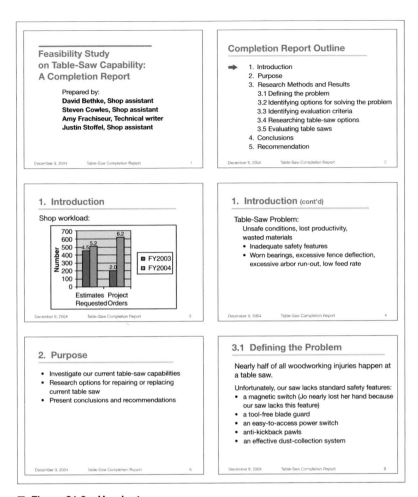

■ Figure 21.6   Handout

You can print multiple slides on each page, in color or black and white. Here the software is set to print six slides on a page.

The advantage of using handouts is that if you announce at the start of the presentation that you will make them available at the end, your audience will concentrate on what you are saying and not be distracted by trying to take notes.

In addition, set the software so that you use the mouse to advance from one graphic to the next. If you set it so that it advances automatically at a specified interval, such as 60 seconds, you will have to speed up or slow down your presentation to keep up with the graphics.

Choosing Effective Language

Delivering an oral presentation is more challenging than writing a document, for two reasons:

- Listeners can't go back to listen again to something they didn't understand.
- Because you are speaking live, you must maintain your listeners' attention, even if they are hungry or tired or the room is too hot.

■ **Table 21.2 Basic Media for Oral Presentations**

Medium	Advantages	Disadvantages
Computer presentations: images are projected from a computer to a screen.	• Very professional appearance. • You can produce any combination of static or dynamic images, from simple graphs to sophisticated, three-dimensional animations, as well as sound and video. • You can launch an Internet browser and show images from the Web.	• The equipment is expensive and not available everywhere. • Preparing the graphics can be time-consuming. • Presentations prepared using one piece of software might not run on all systems.
Slide projector: projects previously prepared slides onto a screen.	• Very professional appearance. • Versatile—can handle photographs or artwork, color or black and white. • With a second projector, you can eliminate the pause between slides. • During the presentation, you can easily advance and reverse the slides. • Graphics software lets you create small paper copies of your slides to distribute to the audience after the presentation.	• Slides can be expensive to produce. • The room has to be kept relatively dark during the slide presentation.
Overhead projector: projects transparencies onto a screen.	• Transparencies are inexpensive and easy to create. • You can draw transparencies "live." • You can create overlays by placing one transparency over another. • Lights can remain on during the presentation.	• Not as professional-looking as slides. • Each transparency must be loaded separately by hand.
Chalkboard or other hard writing surface.	• Almost universally available. • You have complete control—can add, delete, or modify the graphic easily.	• Complicated or extensive graphics are difficult to create. • Ineffective in large rooms. • Very informal appearance.
Objects: models or samples of material that can be held up or passed around the audience.	• Interesting for the audience. • Provides a close look at the object.	• Audience members might not be listening while they are looking at the object. • It can take a long while to pass an object around a large room. • The object might not survive intact.
Handouts: photocopies of written material given to each audience member.	• Much material can fit on the page. • Audience members can write on their copies and keep them.	• Audience members might read the handout rather than listen to the speaker.

Using language effectively helps you meet these two challenges.

Using Language to Signal Advance Organizers, Summaries, and Transitions
Even if you use graphics effectively, listeners cannot "see" the organization of a presentation as well as readers can. For this reason, use language to alert your listeners to advance organizers, summaries, and transitions.

INTERACTIVE SAMPLE DOCUMENT
Integrating Graphics and Text on a Presentation Slide

The following slide is part of a presentation about the Human Genome Project. The questions in the margin ask you to think about the discussion of preparing presentation graphics on pages 551–57. E-mail your responses to yourself and/or your instructor, and see suggested responses on TechComm Web.

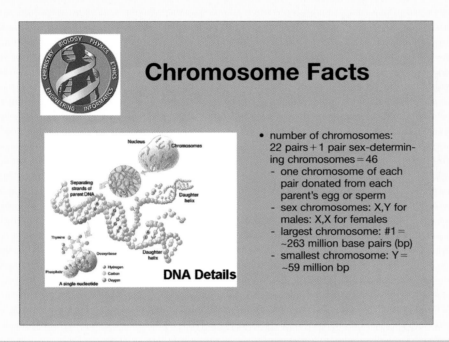

1. How effective is the Human Genome Project logo in the upper left-hand corner of the slide?

2. How well does the graphic of DNA support the accompanying text on chromosome facts?

3. Overall, how effective is the presentation graphic?

 **On TechComm Web**

To e-mail your responses to yourself and/or your instructor and to see suggested responses, click on Interactive Sample Documents for Ch. 21 on <bedfordstmartins .com/techcomm>.

- *Advance organizers.* Use an advance organizer (a statement that tells the listener what you are about to say) in the introduction. In addition, use advance organizers when you introduce main ideas in the body of the presentation.

- *Summaries.* The major summary is in the conclusion, but you might also summarize at strategic points in the body of the presentation. For instance, after a 3- to 4-minute discussion of a major point, you might summarize it in one sentence before going on to the next major point. Here is a sample summary from a conclusion:

  > Let me conclude by summarizing my three main points about the implications of the new RCRA regulations on the long-range waste-management strategy for Radnor Township. The first point is: . . . The second point is: . . . The third point is: . . . I hope this presentation will give you some ideas as you think about the challenges of implementing the RCRA.

- *Transitions.* As you move from one point to the next, signal the transition clearly. Summarize the previous point, then announce that you are moving to the next point:

  > It is clear, then, that the federal government has issued regulations without indicating how it expects county governments to comply with them. I'd like to turn now to my second main point: . . .

Using Memorable Language   Effective presentations require memorable language.

Guidelines

Using Memorable Language in Oral Presentations

Draw on these three techniques to help make a lasting impression on your audience.

▶ **Involve the audience.** People are more interested in their own concerns than in yours. Talk to the audience about their problems and their solutions. In the introduction, establish a link between your topic and the audience's interests. For instance, a presentation to a city council about waste management might begin like this:

> Picture yourself on the Radnor Township Council two years from now. After exhaustive hearings, proposals, and feasibility studies, you still don't have a waste-management plan that meets federal regulations. What you do have is a mounting debt: the township is being fined $1,000 per day until you implement an acceptable plan.

▶ **Refer to people, not to abstractions.** People remember specifics; they forget abstractions. To make a point memorable, describe it in human terms:

> What could you do with that $365,000 every year? In each computer lab in each school in the township, you could replace each PC every three years instead of every four years. Or you could expand your school-lunch program to feed every needy child in the township. Or you could extend your after-school programs to cover an additional 3,000 students.

▶ **Use interesting facts, figures, and quotations.** Search the Internet for interesting information about your subject. For instance, you might find a brief quotation from an authoritative figure in the field or a famous person not generally associated with the field (for example, Theodore Roosevelt on waste management and the environment).

A note about humor: only a few hundred people in the United States make a good living being funny. Don't plan to tell a joke. If something happens during the presentation that provides an opening for a witty remark and you are good at making witty remarks, fine. But don't *prepare* to be funny.

Rehearsing the Presentation

Even the most gifted speakers need to rehearse. It is a good idea to set aside enough time to rehearse your speech thoroughly.

Rehearsing an Extemporaneous Presentation   Rehearse your extemporaneous presentation at least three times.

- *First rehearsal.* Don't worry about posture or voice projection. Just compose your presentation aloud with your presentation slides. Your goal is to see if the speech makes sense—if you can explain all the points and create effective transitions. If you have trouble, stop and try to figure out the problem. If you need more information, get it. If you need a better transition, create one. You are likely to learn that you need to revise the order of your slides. Pick up where you left off and continue the rehearsal, stopping again where necessary to revise.

- *Second rehearsal.* This time, the presentation should flow more easily. Make any necessary changes to the slides. When you have complete control over the organization and flow, check to see if you are within the time limits.

- *Third rehearsal.* After a satisfactory second rehearsal, try the presentation under more realistic circumstances—if possible, in front of people. The listeners might offer questions or constructive advice about your speaking style. If people aren't available, tape-record or videotape the presentation and then evaluate your own delivery. If you can visit the site of the presentation to rehearse there, you will find giving the actual speech a little easier.

Rehearse again until you are satisfied with your presentation; don't try to memorize it.

Rehearsing a Scripted Presentation   Rehearsing a scripted presentation is a combination of revising and editing the text and rehearsing it. As you revise, read the script aloud to hear how it sounds. Once you think the presentation says what you want it to say, try reading it into an audio or video recorder. Revise it until you are satisfied, then rehearse in front of real people. Do not memorize the presentation. There is no need to; you will have your script in front of you on the podium.

DELIVERING A PRESENTATION

When giving the presentation, you need to concentrate on what you have to say. However, you also need to address three other issues.

To deliver a presentation:
Calm your nerves.
Use your voice effectively.
Use your body effectively.

Calming Your Nerves

Most professional actors admit to being nervous before a performance, so it is no wonder that most technical speakers are nervous. You might well fear that you will forget everything or that no one will be able to hear you. These fears are common. But keep in mind three facts about nervousness:

- *You are much more aware of your nervousness than the audience is.* They are farther away from your trembling hands.

- *Nervousness gives you energy and enthusiasm.* Without energy and enthusiasm, your presentation will be flat. If you seem bored and listless, your audience will become bored and listless.

- *After a few minutes, your nervousness will pass.* You will be able to relax and concentrate on the subject.

This advice is unlikely to make you feel much better if you are distracted by nerves as you wait to give your presentation. Experienced speakers offer three tips for coping with nervousness:

- *Realize that you are prepared.* If you have done your homework, prepared the presentation carefully, and rehearsed it several times, you'll be fine.

- *Realize that the audience is there to hear you, not to judge you.* Your listeners want to hear what you have to say. They are much less interested in your nervousness than you are.

- *Realize that your audience is made up of individual people who happen to be sitting in the same room.* You'll feel better if you realize that audience members also get nervous before making presentations.

Guidelines

Releasing Nervous Energy

Experienced speakers suggest the following strategies for dealing with nervousness before a presentation.

▶ **Walk around.** A brisk walk of a minute or two can calm you by dissipating some of your nervous energy.

▶ **Go off by yourself for a few minutes.** Getting away can help you compose your thoughts and realize that you can handle the nervousness.

▶ **Talk with someone for a few minutes.** For some speakers, distraction works best. Find someone to talk to.

▶ **Take several deep breaths, exhaling slowly.** Doing so will help you control your nerves.

When it is time to begin, don't jump up to the lectern and start speaking quickly. Walk up slowly and arrange your text, outline, or note cards before you. If water is available, take a sip. Look out at the audience for a few seconds before you start. Begin with "Good morning" (or "Good afternoon" or "Good evening"), and refer to the officers and dignitaries present. If you have not been introduced, introduce yourself. In less formal contexts, just begin your presentation.

So that the audience will listen to you and have confidence in what you say, use your voice and your body to project an attitude of restrained self-confidence. Show interest in your topic and knowledge about your subject.

Using Your Voice Effectively

Inexperienced speakers often have problems with five aspects of vocalizing.

- *Volume.* Because acoustics vary greatly from room to room, you won't know how well your voice will carry until you have heard someone speaking there. In some rooms, speakers can use a conversational volume. Other rooms require greater voice projection. These circumstances aside, more people speak too softly than too loudly. After your first few sentences, ask if the people in the back of the room can hear you. When people speak into microphones, they tend to speak too loudly. Glance at your audience to see if you are having volume problems. The body language of audience members will be clear.

- *Speed.* Nervousness makes people speak quickly. Even if you think you are speaking at the right rate, you might be going a little too fast for some listeners. Although you know your subject well, your listeners are trying to understand new information. For particularly difficult points, slow down for emphasis. After finishing one major point, pause before introducing the next one.

- *Pitch.* In an effort to control their voices, many speakers end up flattening their pitch. The resulting monotone is boring and, for some listeners, distracting. Try to let the pitch of your voice go up or down as it would in a normal conversation.

- *Articulation.* Nervousness can accentuate sloppy pronunciation. If you want to say *environment,* don't say *envirament.* A related problem involves technical words and phrases, especially the important ones. When a speaker uses a phrase over and over, it tends to get clipped and becomes difficult to understand. Unless you articulate carefully, *Scanlon Plan* will end up as *Scanluhplah.*

- *Nonfluencies.* Avoid such meaningless fillers as *you know, like, okay, right, uh,* and *um.* These phrases do not hide the fact that you aren't saying anything. A thoughtful pause is better than an annoying verbal tic.

Using Your Body Effectively

Besides listening to you, the audience will be looking at you. Effective speakers use their body language to help listeners follow the presentation.

Guidelines

Facing an Audience

As you give a presentation, keep in mind four guidelines about physical movement.

▶ **Maintain eye contact.** Eye contact helps you see how the audience is receiving the presentation. You will see, for instance, if listeners in the back are having trouble hearing you. For small groups, look at each listener randomly; for larger groups, look at each segment of the audience frequently during your speech. Do not stare at the screen, at the floor, or out the window.

▶ **Use natural gestures.** When people talk, they often gesture with their hands. Most of the time, gestures make the presentation look natural and improve listeners' comprehension. You can supplement your natural gestures by using your arms and hands to signal pauses and to emphasize important points. When referring to graphics, walk toward the screen and point to direct the audience's attention. Avoid mannerisms — physical gestures that serve no useful purpose, such as jiggling the coins in your pocket or pacing back and forth. Like verbal mannerisms, physical mannerisms are often unconscious. Constructive criticism from friends can help you pinpoint them.

▶ **Don't block the audience's view of the screen.** Stand off to the side of the screen. Use a pointer to indicate key words or images on the screen.

▶ **Control the audience's attention.** People will listen to and look at anything that is interesting. If you hand out photocopies at the start of the presentation, some people will start to read them and stop listening to you. If you leave an image on the screen after you finish talking about it, some people will keep looking at it instead of listening to you. When you want the audience to look at you and listen to you, remove the graphics or make the screen blank.

ANSWERING QUESTIONS AFTER A PRESENTATION

When you finish a presentation, thank the audience simply and directly: "Thank you for your attention." Then invite questions. Don't abruptly say "Any questions?" This phrasing suggests that you don't really want to answer

Strategies for Intercultural Communication

Making Oral Presentations to Multicultural Audiences

If your audience includes people of different cultures and native languages, keep the following three suggestions in mind:

- **Hire translators and interpreters if necessary.** If many people in the audience do not understand your language, hire interpreters (people who can translate your words as you speak them) and translators (people who can translate your written material if they can work on it in advance).

- **Use graphics effectively to reinforce your points for nonnative speakers.** Try to devise ways to present information using graphics — flowcharts, diagrams, and so forth — to help your listeners understand you.

- **Be aware that gestures can have cultural meanings.** As discussed in Chapter 13, hand gestures (such as the thumbs-up or the "okay" gesture) have different — and sometimes insulting — meanings in some cultures. Therefore, it's a good idea to limit the use of these gestures. You can't go wrong with an arms-out, palms-up gesture that projects openness and inclusiveness.

> ## Ethics Note
>
> ### Answering Questions Honestly
>
> If an audience member asks a question to which you do not know the answer, admit it. Simply say "I don't know" or "I'm not sure, but I think the answer is . . . ." Smart people know that they don't know everything. If you have some ideas about how to find out the answer—by checking a certain reference source, for example—share them. If the question is obviously important to the person who asked it, you might offer to meet with him or her to discuss ways for you to give a more complete response, perhaps by e-mail.

questions. Instead, say something like this: "If you have any questions, I'd be happy to try to answer them now." If invited politely, people will be much more likely to ask. In that way, you will be more likely to communicate your information effectively.

When you respond to questions, you might encounter any of these four situations:

- *You're unsure everyone heard the question.* Ask if people have heard it. If they haven't, repeat or paraphrase it, perhaps as an introduction to your response: "Your question is about the efficiency of these three techniques. . . ." Some speakers always repeat the question, which also gives them an extra moment to prepare an answer.

- *You don't understand the question.* Ask for a clarification. After responding, ask if you have answered the question adequately.

- *You get a question that you have already answered in the presentation.* Restate the answer politely. Begin your answer with a phrase such as the following: "I'm sorry I didn't make that point clear. I wanted to explain how. . . ." Never insult the person by pointing out that you already answered it.

- *A belligerent member of the audience rejects your response and insists on restating his or her original point.* Politely offer to discuss the matter further after the session. This way, the person won't bore or annoy the rest of the audience.

If it is appropriate to stay after the session to talk individually with members of the audience, offer to do so. Remember to thank them for their courtesy in listening to you.

SAMPLE EVALUATION FORM

Figure 21.7 on page 566 is a list of questions that can help you focus your thoughts as you watch and listen to a presentation.

■ **Figure 21.7   Sample Evaluation Form**

On TechComm Web

To download this form in an electronic format, see Forms for Technical Communication on <bedfordstmartins.com/techcomm>.

Oral Presentation Evaluation Form

Speaker:
Topic:
Grade:

To the left of each of the following statements, write a number from 1 to 5, with 5 signifying strong agreement and 1 signifying strong disagreement.

Organization and Development
( )   1. In the introduction, the speaker tried to relate the topic to the audience's concerns.
( )   2. In the introduction, the speaker explained the main points he or she wanted to make in the presentation.
( )   3. In the introduction, the speaker explained the organization of the presentation.
( )   4. Throughout the presentation, I found it easy to understand the organization of the presentation.
( )   5. Throughout the presentation, the speaker used appropriate and sufficient evidence to clarify the subject.
( )   6. In the conclusion, the speaker summarized the main points effectively.
( )   7. In the conclusion, the speaker thanked the audience for their courtesy in listening.
( )   8. In the conclusion, the speaker invited questions politely.
( )   9. In the conclusion, the speaker answered questions effectively.
( ) 10. The speaker stayed within the stipulated time requirements.

Verbal and Physical Presence
( ) 11. The speaker used interesting, clear language to get the points across.
( ) 12. The speaker used clear and distinct enunciation.
( ) 13. The speaker seemed relaxed and poised.
( ) 14. The speaker exhibited no distracting vocal mannerisms.
( ) 15. The speaker exhibited no distracting physical mannerisms.
( ) 16. The speaker made eye contact throughout the presentation.
( ) 17. The speaker seemed to be enthusiastic throughout the presentation.

Use of Presentation Graphics
( ) 18. The speaker used presentation graphics effectively to reinforce and explain the main points.
( ) 19. The speaker used presentation graphics effectively to highlight the organization of the presentation.
( ) 20. The presentation graphics were easy to see.
( ) 21. The presentation graphics were easy to understand.
( ) 22. The presentation graphics looked correct and professional.
( ) 23. The speaker used appropriate kinds of content graphics such as tables and illustrations.

For Group Presentations
( ) 24. The group seemed well rehearsed.
( ) 25. The graphics were edited so that they looked consistent from one group member to the next.
( ) 26. The transitions from one group member to the next were smooth.
( ) 27. Each group member seemed to have done an equal amount of work in preparing and delivering the presentation.

On the other side of this sheet, answer the following two questions.
28. What did you particularly like about this presentation?
29. What would you have done differently if you had been the speaker?

Speaker's Checklist

☐ Did you analyze the speaking situation—the audience and purpose of the presentation? (p. 548)

☐ Did you determine how much information you can communicate in your allotted time? (p. 549)

☐ Did you organize and develop the presentation? (p. 548)

Did you prepare graphics that are

☐ visible? (p. 552)
☐ legible? (p. 552)
☐ simple? (p. 553)
☐ clear? (p. 553)
☐ correct? (p. 553)

☐ In planning your graphics, did you consider your audience's aptitude and experience, the size and layout of the room, and the equipment? (p. 553)

☐ Did you plan your graphics to help the audience understand the organization of your presentation? (p. 553)

☐ Did you choose appropriate media for your graphics? (p. 558)

☐ Did you make sure that the presentation room will have the necessary equipment for the graphics? (p. 553)

☐ Did you choose language to signal advance organizers, summaries, and transitions? (p. 558)

☐ Did you choose language that is vivid and memorable? (p. 560)

☐ Did you rehearse your presentation several times with a tape recorder, video camera, or live audience? (p. 561)

Exercises

1. Learn some of the basic functions of a presentation-graphics software program. For instance, modify a template, create your own original design, add footer information to a master slide, insert a graphic onto a slide, and set the animation feature to make each bulleted item appear only after a mouse click.

2. Using presentation-graphics software, create a design to be used for the master slide of a computer presentation. Then, for the same information, create a design to be used in a transparency made on a black-and-white photocopier.

3. Prepare a five-minute presentation, including graphics, on one of the topics listed here. For each presentation, your audience consists of the other students in your class, and your purpose is to introduce them to an aspect of your academic field.

   a. Define a key term or concept in your field.

   b. Describe how a particular piece of equipment is used in your field.

   c. Describe how to carry out a procedure common in your field.

   The instructor and the other students will evaluate the presentation by filling out the form in Figure 21.7.

4. **GROUP EXERCISE** Prepare a five-minute presentation based either on your proposal for a research-report topic in response to Exercise 3 on page 427 in Chapter 16 or on your completion report in response to Exercise 3 on page 493 in Chapter 18. Your audience consists of the other students in your class, and your purpose is to introduce them to your topic. The instructor and the other students will evaluate the presentation by filling out the form in Figure 21.7. If your instructor wishes, this assignment can be done collaboratively.

Case 21: Choosing Effective Slide Layouts

Background

Once or twice a month, you and your longtime friend Sang Jun Lee meet for lunch to catch up on what is new in your professional and personal lives. As a crime-scene examiner for a county crime lab, Sang collects, examines, and investigates physical evidence at a crime scene that may help locate and convict criminals. During one lunch date, Sang tells you about an article he recently read about the "evils" of PowerPoint. "The author argued that PowerPoint emphasizes format over content," Sang says. "The software encourages speakers to reduce everything to a bulleted list or an incoherent graphic."

"I've heard that before," you reply. "In one of my courses, we read a few articles on PowerPoint. Most of the articles had titles like 'PowerPoint-Induced Sleep,' 'Power-Point Pitfalls,' 'The Pentagon Declares War on Electronic Slide Shows,' and 'Friends Don't Let Friends Use Power-Point.' The articles made the same points as the article you just read. The authors said that the templates are ugly and that they dumb down presentations and convey information poorly."

"That article made me a little nervous," Sang says. "I'm scheduled to talk to students enrolled in an introductory course on crime-scene investigation next week. The professor asked me to give a brief overview of fingerprinting. I've started to put together a PowerPoint presentation, but now I'm worried that I might be going about it the wrong way. Would you be able to help me?"

"Sure. I'll do some Internet research and see if I can find some advice on creating useful slides."

"What I really need help with is how to present my information. I use the default title-and-text slide for almost all my slides. I know the software includes many other slide layouts—two-column text, content over text, text over content—but I'm just not sure when to use these layouts."

"E-mail me a few of your slides, and I'll take a look."

Your Assignment

1. Use the Internet to research guidelines for preparing effective graphics using presentation software. Focus your research on guidelines related to slide *layout* (the way information is arranged and presented on a slide), not slide *design* (the use of color schemes). Write Sang an e-mail message reporting your findings.

2. Using strategies discussed in this chapter, revise Sang's sample slides (Document 21.1). Include a brief memo to Sang explaining your revisions.

Some Fingerprint Background

- 2,000 BC—Ancient Babylonians used fingerprints on clay tablets during business transactions.
- 1858—Sir William Herschel required laborers in India to sign contracts with fingerprints.
- 1892—Sir Francis Galton created the foundation of modern fingerprinting science by arguing that fingerprints are unique.
- 1902—Fingerprinting used in the United States.
- 1924—Congress establishes the Identification Division of the F.B.I.
- 2005—Integrated Automated Fingerprint Identification System (IAFIS) maintained by F.B.I. compares a single fingerprint with a database of 47 million fingerprints.

Go over brief history of fingerprints.

■ **Document 21.1   Slides and Speaking Notes for Part of a Presentation**

 On TechComm Web

For digital versions of case documents, click on Downloadable Case Documents on <**bedfordstmartins.com/techcomm**>.

Cyanoacrylate-Fuming Method

- Known as the Super-Glue Method.
- Used by most state and local police in United States.
- A chemical technique used to make latent fingerprints visible.

First used by the Japanese National Police Agency's Criminal Identification Division in 1978. Introduced to the US by the United States Army Criminal Investigation and Bureau of Alcohol, Tobacco, and Firearms Laboratories.

There are three different types of fingerprints: *visible, impression,* and *latent.* Crime scene examiners need permanent, portable copies of fingerprints. *Visible* and *impression* fingerprints can be photographed without too much effort. *Latent* prints must first be made visible before photographing them.

There are three general techniques for making latent fingerprints visible: physical techniques, chemical techniques, and instrumental techniques. Cyanoacrylate fuming is a chemical technique.

Cyanoacrylate fuming works by chemically reacting with the chemicals found in a latent print. Organic compounds exuded through the pores in the fingertips are left when a person's hand touches something. In the case of Cyanoacrylate fuming, the super glue reacts with the traces of fatty acids, proteins, and amino acids in the latent fingerprints. Combined with the moisture in the air, the result is a visible, sticky white material that forms along the ridges of the fingerprint, forming an image that can be photographed.

2

■ **Document 21.1** *(continued)*

Different Patterns of Fingerprints

- In a loop, the ridges enter from either side, curve, and exit the same side they entered.
- In a whorl, the ridges are usually circular.
- In an arch, the ridges enter from one side, make a rise in the center, and exit on the opposite side.

Every person's hand (as well as feet) feature minute ridges and valleys. In the fingers and thumbs, these ridges form patterns of loops, whorls, and arches. Explain to class each of these patterns.

Identifications

- Scotland Yard requires 16 points
- Australia requires 16 points
- Germany requires 12 points
- Netherlands requires 10 points
- Bulgaria requires 8 points
- South Africa requires 7 points
- United States has no set standard

U.S. courts assume as fact the argument that no two fingers can have identical characteristics. Fingerprint identification is not determined by shape or pattern but by the study of a print's ridge characteristics. Courts require forensic technicians to find a minimum number of "Galton points"—matching characteristics on a fingerprint. Thus, a fingerprint specialist must make a point-by-point comparison to match a fingerprint found at the scene of a crime to a suspect.

However, just how many points are necessary to establish a "match" varies from state to state and country to country. Go over examples of different number of points required. In the United States, for example, the FBI moved away from match requirements based on a minimum number of Galton points half a century ago. Worldwide, labs are doing away with point systems and are, instead, relying upon the opinion of the forensic examiner.

4

■ **Document 21.1**   *(continued)*

The Future of Fingerprinting

Most commonly used biometric identification
   methods:
- Fingerprint scan: 58%
- Facial scan: 13.4%
- Hand scan: 12%
- Iris scan: 8.3%
- Voice scan: 5.1%
- Signature scan: 2.4%
- Keystroke scan: .3%

Does not total 100% due to rounding

In addition to criminal investigations, fingerprints play a key role in biometric-
security technology. Biometric technology examines a measurable, physical
characteristic or personal behavioral trait used to recognize the identity or
verify the claimed identity of a person. For example, hand geometry, retinal
scan, iris scan, fingerprint patterns, facial characteristics, DNA sequence
characteristics, voice prints, and hand-written signature.

Among all the biometric techniques, fingerprint-based identification (e.g.,
fingerprint scanning) is expected to continue as the biometric technology of
choice in the near future. Other biometric technologies will continue to see
limited use.

5

Appendix:
Reference Handbook

Part A: Skimming Your Sources and Taking Notes

To record the information that will eventually go into your document, you need to skim your potential sources and take notes. Don't try to read every potential source. A careful reading of a work that looks promising might prove disappointing. You might also get halfway through a book and realize that you must start writing immediately to submit your document on time.

Guidelines

Skimming Books and Articles

To skim effectively, read the following parts of books and articles.

In a book, skim:

- *the preface and introduction:* to understand the writer's approach and methods
- *the acknowledgments section:* to learn about help the author received from other experts in the field, or about the author's use of primary research or other resources
- *the table of contents:* to understand the book's scope and organization
- *the notes at the ends of chapters or at the end of the book:* to understand the nature and extent of the author's research
- *the index:* to determine the extent of the coverage of the information you need
- *a few paragraphs from different portions of the text:* to gauge the quality and relevance of the information

In an article, skim:

- *the abstract:* to get an overview of the article's content
- *the introduction:* to understand the article's purpose, main ideas, and organization
- *the notes and references:* to understand the nature and extent of the author's research
- *the headings and several of the paragraphs:* to understand the article's organization and the quality and relevance of the information

Skimming will not always tell you whether a book or article is going to be useful, but it can tell you if a work is *not* going to be useful—because it doesn't cover your subject, for example, or because it is too superficial or too advanced. Eliminating the sources you don't need will give you more time to spend on the ones you do.

Note taking is often the first step in writing the document. The best way to take notes is electronically. If you can download files from the Internet, download bibliographic references from a CD-ROM database, and take notes on a laptop computer, you will save a lot of time and prevent many errors. If you do not have access to these electronic tools, get a pack of note cards.

Most note taking involves three kinds of activities: paraphrasing, quoting, and summarizing. Knowing how to paraphrase, quote, and summarize is important for two reasons:

- To a large extent, the work you do at this point will determine the quality of your finished product. You want to record the information accurately and clearly. Mistakes made at this point can be hard to catch later, and they can ruin your document.

- You want to use your sources responsibly. You don't want to plagiarize unintentionally.

 In This Book

For a discussion of plagiarism, see Appendix, Part B, p. 581.

Guidelines

Recording Bibliographic Information

Record the bibliographic information for each source from which you take notes.

Information to record for a book	*Information to record for an article*
• author	• author
• title	• title of the article
• publisher	• title of the periodical
• place of publication	• volume
• year of publication	• number
• call number	• date of publication
	• pages on which the article appears
	• call number of the periodical

PARAPHRASING

A paraphrase is a restatement, in your own words, of someone else's words. If you simply copy someone else's words—even a mere two or three in a row—you must use quotation marks.

In taking notes, what kind of material should you paraphrase? Any information that you think might be useful: background data, descriptions of mechanisms or processes, test results, and so forth.

Figure A.1 on page 576 shows a paraphrased passage based on the following discussion. The author is explaining the concept of performance-centered design.

Original Passage

In performance-centered design, the emphasis is on providing support for the structure of the work as well as the information needed to accomplish it. One of the best examples is TurboTax®, which meets all the three main criteria of effective performance-centered design:

- **People can do their work with no training on how to use the system.** People trying to do their income tax have no interest in taking any kind of training.

They want to get their taxes filled out correctly and quickly, getting all the deductions they are entitled to. These packages, over the years, have moved the interface from a forms-based one, where the user had to know what forms were needed, to an interview-based one that fills out the forms automatically as you answer questions. The design of the interface assumes no particular computer expertise.

- **The system provides the right information at the right time to accomplish the work.** At each step in the process, the system asks only those questions that are relevant based on previous answers. The taxpayer is free to ask for more detail or may proceed through a dialog that asks more-detailed questions if the taxpayer doesn't know the answer to the higher-level question. If a taxpayer is married filing jointly, the system presents only those questions for that filing status.

- **Both tasks and systems change as the user understands the system.** When I first used TurboTax 6 years ago I found myself going to the forms themselves. Doing my taxes generally took about 2 days. Each year I found my need to go to the forms to be less and less. Last year, it took me about 2 hours to do my taxes, and I looked at the forms only when I printed out the final copy.

This paraphrase is inappropriate because the three bulleted points are taken word for word from the original. The fact that the student omitted the explanations from the original is irrelevant. These are direct quotes, not paraphrases.

> Lovgren, "Achieving Performance-Centered Design"
> <www.reisman-consulting.com/pages/a-Perform.html>
>
> example of performance-centered design:
> TurboTax® meets three main criteria:
>
> - People can do their work with no training on how to use the system.
> - The system provides the right information at the right time to accomplish the work.
> - Both tasks and systems change as the user understands the system.

a. Inappropriate paraphrase

This paraphrase is appropriate because the words are different from those used in the original.

When you turn your notes into a document, you are likely to reword your paraphrases. Be sure you don't accidentally use wording from the original source. As you revise your document, check a copy of the original source document to be sure you haven't unintentionally reverted to the wording from the source.

> Lovgren, "Achieving Performance-Centered Design"
> <www.reisman-consulting.com/pages/a-Perform.html>
>
> example of performance-centered design:
> TurboTax® meets three main criteria:
>
> - You don't have to learn how to use the system.
> - The system knows how to respond at the appropriate time to what the user is doing.
> - As the user gets smarter about using the system, the system gets smarter, making it faster to complete the task.

b. Appropriate paraphrase

■ **Figure A.1   Inappropriate and Appropriate Paraphrased Notes**
Source: Adapted from Lovgren, 2000 <www.reisman-consulting.com/pages/a-Perform.html>.

Guidelines

Paraphrasing Accurately

▶ **Study the original until you understand it thoroughly.**

▶ **Rewrite the relevant portions of the original.** Use complete sentences, fragments, or lists, but don't compress the material so much that you'll have trouble understanding it later.

▶ **Title the information so that you'll be able to identify its subject at a glance.** The title should include the general subject and the author's attitude or approach to it, such as "Criticism of open-sea pollution-control devices."

▶ **Include the author's last name, a short title of the article or book, and the page number of the original.** You will need this information later in citing your source.

QUOTING

Sometimes you will want to quote a source, either to preserve the author's particularly well-expressed or emphatic phrasing or to lend authority to your discussion. Avoid quoting passages of more than two or three sentences, or your document will look like a mere compilation. Your job is to integrate an author's words and ideas into your own thinking, not merely to introduce a series of quotations.

Although you probably won't be quoting long passages in your document, recording a complete quotation in your notes will help you recall its meaning and context more accurately when you are ready to integrate it into your own work.

The simplest form of quotation is an author's exact statement:

> As Jones states, "Solar energy won't make much of a difference for at least a decade."

To add an explanatory word or phrase to a quotation, use brackets:

> As Nelson states, "It [the oil glut] will disappear before we understand it."

Use ellipses (three spaced dots) to show that you are omitting part of an author's statement:

ORIGINAL STATEMENT	"The generator, which we purchased in May, has turned out to be one of our wisest investments."
ELLIPTICAL QUOTATION	"The generator . . . has turned out to be one of our wisest investments."

According to the documentation style recommended by the Modern Language Association (MLA), if the author's original statement has ellipses, you should add brackets around the ellipses that you introduce:

 In This Book

For more about formatting quotations, see "Quotation Marks," "Ellipses," and "Brackets" in Appendix, Part C. For a discussion of how to document quotations, see Appendix, Part B, p. 581.

ORIGINAL STATEMENT	"I think reuse adoption offers . . . the promise to improve business in a number of ways."
ELLIPTICAL QUOTATION	"I think reuse adoption offers . . . the promise to improve business [. . .]."

SUMMARIZING

Summarizing is the process of rewriting a passage in your own words to make it shorter while still retaining its essential message. Writers summarize to help them learn a body of information or create a draft of one or more of the summaries that will go into the document.

Most long technical documents contain several kinds of summaries:

- a letter of transmittal (see page 467) that provides an overview of the document
- an abstract (see page 467), a brief technical summary
- an executive summary (see page 470), a brief nontechnical summary directed to the manager
- a conclusion (see page 466) that draws together a complicated discussion

The guidelines and examples in this section explain how to summarize the printed information you uncover in your research.

Guidelines

Summarizing

The following advice focuses on extracting the essence of a passage by summarizing it.

▶ **Read the passage carefully several times.**

▶ **Underline key ideas.** Look for them in the titles, headings, topic sentences, transitional paragraphs, and concluding paragraphs.

▶ **Combine key ideas.** Study what you have underlined. Paraphrase the underlined ideas. Don't worry about your grammar, punctuation, or style at this point.

▶ **Check your draft against the original for accuracy and emphasis.** Check that you record statistics and names correctly and that your version of a complicated concept faithfully represents the original. Check that you get the proportions right; if the original devotes 20 percent of its space to a particular point, your draft should not devote 5 percent or 50 percent to that point.

▶ **Record the bibliographic information carefully.** Even though a summary might contain all your own words, you still must cite it, because the main ideas are someone else's. If you don't have the bibliographic information in an electronic form, put it on note cards.

A BRIEF HISTORY OF TELEVISION

Although it seems as if television has been around for a long time, it's a relatively new science, younger than rocketry, internal medicine, and nuclear physics. In fact, some of the people that helped develop the first commercial TV sets and erect the first TV broadcast antennas are still living today.

The Early Years

The first electronic transmission of a picture was believed to have been made by a Scotsman, John Logie Baird, in the cold month of February 1924. His subject was a Maltese Cross, transmitted through the air by the magic of television (also called "Televisor" or "Radiovision" in those days) the entire distance of ten feet.

To say that Baird's contraption was crude is an understatement. His Televisor was made from a cardboard scanning disk, some darning needles, a few discarded electric motors, piano wire, glue, and other assorted odds and ends. The picture reproduced by the original Baird Televisor was extremely difficult to see—a shadow, at best.

Until about 1928, other amateur radiovision enthusiasts toyed around with Baird's basic design, whiling away long hours in the basement transmitting Maltese Crosses, model airplanes, flags, and anything else that would stay still long enough under the intense light required to produce an image. (As an interesting aside, the lighting for Baird's 1924 Maltese Cross transmission required 2,000 volts of power, produced by a roomful of batteries. So much heat was generated by the lighting equipment that Baird eventually burned his laboratory down.)

Baird's electromechanical approach to television led the way to future developments in transmitting and receiving pictures. The nature of the Baird Televisor, however, limited the clarity and stability of images. Most of the sets made and sold in those days required the viewer to peer through a glass lens to watch the screen, which was seldom over seven by ten inches in size. What's more, the majority of screens had an annoying orange glow that often marred reception and irritated the eyes.

Modern Television Technology

In the early 1930s, Vladimir Zworykin developed a device known as the iconoscope camera. About the same time, Philo T. Farnsworth was putting the finishing touches on the image dissector tube, a gizmo that proved to be the forerunner of the modern cathode ray tube or CRT—the everyday picture tube. These two devices paved the way for the TV sets we know and cherish today.

The first commercially available modern-day cathode ray tube televisions were available in about 1936. Tens of thousands of these sets were sold throughout the United States and Great Britain, even though there were no regular television broadcasts until 1939, when RCA started what was to become the first American television network, NBC. Incidentally, the first true network transmission was in early 1940, between NBC's sister stations WNBT in New York City (now WNBC-TV) and WRGB in Schenectady.

■ **Figure A.2**
Original Passage
Source: Based on McComb, 1991.

Figure A.2 is a narrative history of television technology addressed to the general reader. Figure A.3 on page 580 is a summary that includes the key terms. This summary is 10 percent of the length of the original.

Postwar Growth
World War II greatly hampered the development of television, and during 1941–1945, no television sets were commercially produced (engineers were too busy perfecting radar, which, interestingly enough, contributed significantly to the development of conventional TV). But after the war, the television industry boomed. Television sets were selling like hotcakes, even though they cost an average of $650 (based on average wage earnings, that's equivalent to about $4,000 today).

Progress took a giant step in 1948 and 1949 when the four American networks, NBC, CBS, ABC, and Dumont, introduced quality, "class-act" programming, which at the time included *Kraft Television Theatre*, *Howdy Doody*, and *The Texaco Star Theatre* with Milton Berle. These famous stars of the stage and radio made people want to own a television set.

Color and Beyond
Since the late 1940s, television technology has continued to improve and mature. Color came on December 17, 1953, when the FCC approved RCA's all-electronic system, thus ending a bitter, four-year bout between CBS and RCA over color transmission standards. Television images beamed via space satellite caught the public's fancy in July of 1962, when Telstar 1 relayed images of AT&T chairman Frederick R. Kappell from the U.S. to Great Britain. Pay-TV came and went several times in the 1950s, 1960s, and 1970s; modern-day professional commercial videotape machines were demonstrated in 1956 by Ampex; and home video recorders had appeared on retail shelves by early 1976.

■ **Figure A.2**   *(continued)*

Summary: A Brief History of Television

In 1924, Baird made the first electronic transmission of a picture. The primitive equipment produced only a shadow. Although Baird's design was modified by others in the 1920s, the viewer had to look through a glass lens at a small screen that gave off an orange glow.

Zworykin's iconoscopic camera and Farnsworth's image dissector tube—similar to the modern CRT—led in 1936 to the development of modern TV. Regular broadcasts began in 1939 on the first network, NBC. Research stopped during WWII, but after that, sales grew, even though sets cost approximately $650, the equivalent of $4,000 today.

Color broadcasts began in 1953; satellite broadcasting began in 1962; and home VCRs were introduced in 1976.

Key terms: television, history of television, NBC, color television, satellite broadcasting, videocassette recorders, Baird, Zworykin, Farnsworth.

■ **Figure A.3   Summary of the Original Passage**

Part B: Documenting Your Sources

Documentation identifies the sources of the ideas and the quotations in your document. Integrated throughout your document, documentation consists of citations in the text and a reference list (or list of works cited) at the back of your document. Documentation serves three basic functions:

For more help with documenting sources, click on Re:Writing on <bedfordstmartins.com/techcomm>.

- *To help you acknowledge your debt to your sources.* Complete and accurate documentation is a professional obligation, a matter of ethics. Failure to document a source, whether intentional or unintentional, is plagiarism. At most colleges and universities, plagiarism means automatic failure of the course and, in some instances, suspension or expulsion. In many companies, it is grounds for immediate dismissal.

- *To help you establish credibility.* Effective documentation helps you place your document within the general context of continuing research and define it as a responsible contribution to knowledge in the field. Knowing how to use existing research is one mark of a professional.

- *To help your readers find your source in case they want to read more about a particular subject.*

Three kinds of material should always be documented:

- *Any quotation from a written source or an interview, even if it is only a few words.*

In This Book

For more about quoting and paraphrasing sources, see Appendix, Part A, p. 575.

- *A paraphrased idea, concept, or opinion gathered from your reading.* There is one exception. An idea or concept so well known that it has become general knowledge, such as Einstein's theory of relativity, needs no citation. If you are unsure about whether an item is general knowledge, document it, just to be safe.

- *Any graphic from a written or an electronic source.* Cite the source for a graphic next to the graphic or in the reference list. For an online source, be sure to include a retrieval statement in the bibliographic entry. If you are publishing your work, you must also request permission to use any graphic protected by copyright.

In This Book

For more about using graphics from other sources, see Ch. 13, p. 299.

Just as organizations have their own preferences for formatting and punctuation, many organizations also have their own documentation styles. The documentation systems included in this section of the appendix are based on the following style manuals:

- *Publication manual of the American Psychological Association* (5th ed.). (2001). Washington, DC: APA. This system, referred to as APA style, is used widely in the social sciences.

- *Scientific style and format: The CBE manual for authors, editors, and publishers* (6th ed.). (1994). New York: Cambridge University Press; *National Library of Medicine recommended formats for bibliographic citation supplement:*

Internet formats. (2001). Bethesda, MD: U.S. Department of Health and Human Services. This system, from the Council of Science Editors (formerly the Council of Biology Editors), is referred to as CSE style and is widely used in the natural sciences.

- Gibaldi, J. (2003). *MLA handbook for writers of research papers* (6th ed.). New York: MLA. This system, referred to as MLA style, is used widely in the humanities.

Other organizations may use one of the following published style guides.

GENERAL

Chicago manual of style (15th ed.). (2003). Chicago: University of Chicago Press. See also http://www.press.uchicago.edu/Misc/Chicago/cmosfaq/cmosfaq.html

BUSINESS

American Management Association. (1996). *The AMA style guide for business writing.* New York: AMACOM. See also http://www.amanet.org

CHEMISTRY

American Chemical Society. (1997). *ACS style guide: A manual for authors and editors* (2nd ed.). Washington, DC: Author. See also http://www.acs.org

ENGINEERING

Institute of Electrical and Electronics Engineers. (2005). *IEEE standards style manual.* Piscataway, NJ: Author. See also http://standards.ieee.org

GEOLOGY

Adkins-Heljeson, M., Bates, R. L., & Buchanan, R. (Eds.). (1995). *Geowriting: A guide to writing, editing, and printing in earth science* (5th rev. ed.). Alexandria, VA: American Geological Institute. See also http://www.agiweb.org

GOVERNMENT DOCUMENTS

U.S. Government Printing Office. (2000). *Style manual* (29th ed.). Washington, DC: Author. See also http://www.gpo.gov

JOURNALISM

Goldstein, N. (Ed.). (2002). *Associated press stylebook and briefing on media law* (35th rev. ed.). New York: Associated Press. See also http://www.ap.org

LAW

Columbia Law Review, Harvard Law Review, University of Pennsylvania Law Review, and Yale Law Journal. (2005). *The bluebook: A uniform system of citation* (18th ed.). Cambridge: Harvard Law Review Association. See also http://www.legalbluebook.com

MATHEMATICS

Higham, N. J. (1998). *Handbook of writing for the mathematical sciences* (2nd ed.). Philadelphia: Society for Industrial and Applied Mathematics. See also http://www.siam.org

MEDICINE

American Medical Association. (1998). *American Medical Association manual of style* (9th ed.). Baltimore: Williams. See also http://www.ama-assn.org

PHYSICS

American Institute of Physics, Publication Board. (1990). *Style manual for guidance in the preparation of papers* (4th ed.). New York: Author. See also http://www.aip.org

POLITICAL SCIENCE

American Political Science Association. (2001). *Style manual for political science* (rev. ed.). Washington, DC: Author. See also http://www.apsanet.org

SCIENCE AND TECHNICAL WRITING

National Information Standards Organization. (1995). *Scientific and technical reports—Elements, organization, and design*. Bethesda, MD: Author. See also http://www.niso.org

Rubens, P. (Ed.). (2000). *Science and technical writing: A manual of style* (2nd ed.). New York: Routledge.

SOCIAL WORK

National Association of Social Workers. (1995). *Writing for the NASW Press: Information for authors* (rev. ed.). Washington, DC: National Association of Social Workers Press. See also http://www.naswpress.org

SOCIOLOGY

American Sociological Association. (1997). *American Sociological Association style guide* (2nd ed.). Washington, DC: Author. See also http://www.asanet.org

Check with your instructor to see which documentation system to use in the documents you write for class. For documents prepared in the workplace, find out your organization's style and abide by it.

APA STYLE

 On TechComm Web

For more information, see the APA site. Click on Links Library for the Appendix on <bedfordstmartins .com/techcomm>.

APA style consists of two elements: the citation in the text and the list of references at the end of the document.

APA Textual Citations

In APA style, a textual citation typically includes the name of the source's author and the date of its publication. Textual citations vary depending on the type of information cited, the number of authors, and the context of the citation. The following models illustrate a variety of common textual citations; for additional examples, consult the *Publication Manual of the American Psychological Association.*

1. Summarized or Paraphrased Material   For material or ideas that you have summarized or paraphrased, include the author's name and publication date in parentheses immediately following the borrowed information.

> This phenomenon was identified more than 50 years ago (Wilkinson, 1948).

If your sentence already includes the source's name, do not repeat it in the parenthetical notation.

> Wilkinson (1948) identified this phenomenon more than 50 years ago.

2. Quoted Material or Specific Fact   If the reference is to a specific fact, idea, or quotation, add the page number(s) of the source to your citation.

> This phenomenon was identified more than 50 years ago (Wilkinson, 1948, p. 36).
> Wilkinson (1948) identified this phenomenon more than 50 years ago (p. 36).

3. Source with Multiple Authors   For a source written by two authors, cite both names. Use an ampersand (&) in the parenthetical citation itself, but use the word *and* in regular text.

> (Halloway & Ratey, 2005)
> Halloway and Ratey (2005) argued . . .

For a source written by three, four, or five authors, include all the names the first time you cite the reference; after that, include only the last name of the first author followed by *et al.*

First Reference

> Bradley, Edmunds, and Soto (2001) argued . . .

Subsequent References

> Bradley et al. (2001) found . . .

For a source written by six or more authors, use only the first author's name followed by *et al.*

> (Smith et al., 2003)

4. Source Issued by an Organization   If the author is an organization rather than a person, use the name of the organization.

The causes of narcolepsy are discussed in a recent booklet (Association of Sleep Disorders, 2001).

In a recent booklet, the Association of Sleep Disorders (2001) discusses the causes of narcolepsy.

If the organization name has a common abbreviation, you may include it in the first citation and use it in any subsequent citations.

First Reference

(International Business Machines [IBM], 2006)

Subsequent References

(IBM, 2006)

5. Source with an Unknown Author   If the source does not identify an author, use a shortened version of the title in your parenthetical citation.

This trend has been evident in American society since the beginning of the 20th century ("Modernism," 2002).

If the author is identified as anonymous—a rare occurrence—treat *Anonymous* as a real name.

(Anonymous, 2006)

6. Multiple Authors with Same Last Name   Use first initials if two or more sources have authors with the same last name.

S. Jones (2006) performed a functional genomic analysis. M. R. Jones (2006) studied cell morphology using RNA interference.

7. Multiple Sources in One Citation   When you refer to two or more sources in one citation, present the sources in alphabetical order, separated by semicolons.

This phenomenon has been well documented (Halloway & Ratey, 2005; Meyer, 2005; Sax, 2005).

8. Personal Communication   Include the words *personal communication* and the date of the communication when citing personal interviews, phone calls, letters, memos, and e-mails.

A. M. Suleiman (personal communication, May 12, 2005) pointed out that . . .

9. Electronic Document   Cite the author and date of the source as you would for other kinds of documents. If the author is unknown, give a shortened version of the title in your parenthetical citation. If the date is unknown, use *n.d.* (for "no date").

Children with autism have a wide range of needs (Eckstein, n.d.).

If the document is posted as a PDF file, include a page number in the citation. If a page number is not available but the source contains paragraph numbers, give the paragraph number: (Tong, 2001, ¶ 4) or (Tong, 2001, para. 4). If no paragraph or page number is available and the source has headings, cite the appropriate heading and paragraph.

Vidoli (2000) warned against using jargon "because it may be misinterpreted" (Writing Naturally section, para. 2).

The APA Reference List

A reference list provides the information your readers will need in order to find each source you have cited in the text. It should not include sources you read but did not use. Following are some guidelines for an APA-style reference list.

In This Book

For a sample APA-style reference list, see p. 598.

- *Arranging Entries.* The entries are arranged alphabetically by author's last name. Two or more works by the same author are arranged by date, earliest to latest. Two or more works by the same author in the same year should be listed alphabetically by title and should also include a lowercase letter after the date: Smith 2004a, Smith 2004b, and so on. Works by an organization are alphabetized by the first significant word in the name of the organization.

- *Book Titles.* Titles of books should be italicized. The first word of the book's title and subtitle are capitalized, but all other words (except proper nouns) should be lowercase.

- *Publication Information.* Give the publisher's full name or consult your style guide for the preferred abbreviation. Include both the publisher's city and state or country unless the city is well known (such as New York, Boston, or London).

- *Periodical Titles.* Titles of periodicals should be italicized, and all major words should be capitalized.

- *Article Titles.* Titles of articles should not be italicized or placed in quotation marks. The first word of the article's title and subtitle are capitalized, but all other words (except proper nouns) should be lowercase.

- *Electronic Sources.* Include as much information as you can about electronic sources, such as author, date of publication, identifying numbers, and retrieval information. Also be sure to record the date you retrieved the information, because electronic information changes frequently.

- *Indenting.* Use a hanging indent, with the second and subsequent lines of each entry indented 5 to 7 spaces:

Simons, L. M. (2005, May). Fossil wars: Dispatch from the front lines. *National Geographic, 207,* 48–69.

Paragraph indents, in which the first line of each entry is indented 5 to 7 spaces, may be preferred by your instructor:

Simons, L. M. (2005, May). Fossil wars: Dispatch from the front lines. *National Geographic, 207,* 48–69.

- *Spacing.* Double-space the entire reference list. Do not add extra spacing between entries.
- *Page Numbers.* When citing a range of page numbers for articles, always give the complete numbers (for example, 121–124, *not* 121–24). If an article continues on subsequent pages interrupted by other articles or advertisements, use a comma to separate the page numbers. Use the abbreviation *p.* or *pp.* only with articles in newspapers, chapters in edited books, and articles from proceedings published as a book.
- *Dates.* Follow this format: year, month, day, with a comma after only the year (2005, October 31).

Following are models of reference list entries for a variety of sources. For further examples of APA-style citations, consult the *Publication Manual of the American Psychological Association.*

BOOKS

10. Book by One Author   Begin with the author's last name, followed by the first initial or initials. If the author has a first and a middle initial, include a space between the initials. Place the year of publication in parentheses, then give the title of the book, followed by the location and name of the publisher.

Matlen, T. (2005). *Survival tips for women with AD/HD: Beyond piles, palms, and Post-its.* New York: Specialty Press.

11. Book by Multiple Authors   To cite two or more authors, use the ampersand (&) instead of *and* between their names. Use a comma to separate the authors' names.

Grandin, T., & Johnson, C. (2005). *Animals in translation: Using the mysteries of autism to decode animal behavior.* New York: Scribner.

To cite more than six authors, list only the first six, followed by *et al.*

12. Multiple Books by Same Author   List the entries by the author's name and then by date, with the earliest date first.

Beder, J. (2004). *Voices of bereavement: A casebook for grief counselors.* Oxford: Routledge.

Beder, J. (2006). *Hospital social work: The interface of medicine and caring.* Oxford: Routledge.

APA: CITING A BOOK BY ONE AUTHOR

When citing a book, use the information from the title page and the copyright page (on the reverse side of the title page), not from the book's cover or a library catalog.

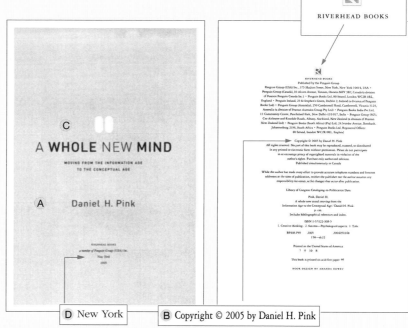

Record the following information:

A **The author.** Give the last name first, followed by a comma and initials for first and middle names. Separate initials with a space (Tufte, E. R.).

B **The date of publication.** Put the most recent copyright year in parentheses and end with a period (outside the parentheses).

C **The title.** Give the full title; include the subtitle (if any), preceded by a colon. Italicize the title and subtitle, capitalizing only the first word of the title, the first word of the subtitle, and any proper nouns. End with a period.

D **The city of publication.** If more than one city is given, use the first one listed. For a city that may be unfamiliar to your readers or confused with another city, add an abbreviation of the state, province (if Canada), or country: Portland, England. Insert a colon.

E **The publisher.** Give the publisher's name. Omit words such as *Inc.* and *Co.* Include and do not abbreviate terms such as *University* and *Press.* End with a period.

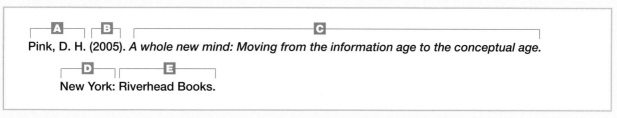

Pink, D. H. (2005). *A whole new mind: Moving from the information age to the conceptual age.*
New York: Riverhead Books.

In This Book For more APA-style models for citing other types of books, see pp. 588, 590, and 592.

If you use multiple works by the same author written in the same year, list the books alphabetically by title and include *a*, *b*, and so forth after the year—both in your reference list and in your parenthetical citations.

> McGraw, P. (2005a). *Family first: Your step-by-step plan for creating a phenomenal family.* New York: Free Press.
>
> McGraw, P. (2005b). *Love smart: Find the one you want—Fix the one you got.* New York: Free Press.

13. Book Issued by an Organization   Use the full name of the organization in place of an author's name. If the organization is also the publisher, use the word *Author* in place of the publisher's name.

> American Psychological Association. (2005). *Concise rules of APA style.* Washington, DC: Author.

14. Book by an Unknown Author   If the author of the book is unknown, begin with the title in italics.

> *PDR psychotropic prescribing guide.* (2005). Montvale, NJ: Thompson.

15. Edited Book   Place the abbreviation *Ed.* or *Eds.* in parentheses after the name(s), followed by a period.

> De Mijolla, A. (Ed.). (2005). *International dictionary of psychoanalysis.* New York: Macmillan.

16. Chapter or Section in an Edited Book

> Goldwater, R. (2004). The development of ethnological museums. In B. M. Carbonell (Ed.), *Museum studies: An anthology of contexts* (pp. 133–138). Malden, MA: Blackwell Publishing.

17. Book in Edition Other Than First   Include the edition number in parentheses following the title.

> Ormrod, J. (2005). *Educational psychology: Developing learners* (5th ed.). New York: Prentice Hall.

18. Multivolume Work   Include the number of volumes after the title.

> Hurley, S., & Chater, N. (2005). *Perspectives on imitation: From neuroscience to social science* (Vols. 1–2). Cambridge, MA: MIT Press.

19. Translated Book   Name the translator after the title.

> Freud, S. (2006). *The interpretation of dreams* (J. Forrester, Trans.). New York: Penguin.

APA: CITING AN ARTICLE FROM A PERIODICAL

Periodicals include journals, magazines, and newspapers. This page gives an example of a citation for a print journal article.

Record the following information:

A **The author.** Give the last name first, followed by a comma and initials for first and middle names. Separate initials with a space (Tufte, E. R.). Separate the names of multiple authors with commas; use an ampersand (&) before the final author's name.

B **The date of publication.** Put the year in parentheses and end with a period (outside the parentheses). For magazines and newspapers, include the month and, if relevant, the day (2006, May 23).

C **The article title.** Give the full title; include the subtitle (if any), preceded by a colon. Do not underline or italicize the title or put it in quotation marks. Capitalize only the first word of the title, the first word of the subtitle, and any proper nouns. End with a period.

D **The periodical title.** Italicize the periodical title and capitalize all major words. Insert a comma.

E **The volume number and issue number.** For journals, include the volume number, italicized. If each issue starts with page 1, include the issue number in parentheses, not italicized. Insert a comma.

F **Inclusive page numbers.** Give all the numbers in full (316–337, *not* 316–37). For newspapers, include the abbreviation *p.* for page (or *pp.* for pages) and the section letter, if relevant (p. D4). End with a period.

Jones, S. L. (2005). From writers to information coordinators: Technology and the changing

face of collaboration. *Journal of Business and Technical Communication, 19*, 449–467.

In This Book For more APA-style models for citing other types of periodical articles, see p. 592.

20. Non-English Book   Give the original title, then the English translation in brackets.

> Silva, J., & Miele, P. (2005). *El método Silva de control mental* [The Silva mind control method]. Mexico City: Diana.

21. Entry in a Reference Work   Begin with the title of the entry if it has no author.

> Machine model organization. (2004). In *Dictionary of international business terms* (3rd ed.). Hauppauge, NY: Barron's.

PERIODICALS

22. Journal Article   Follow the author's name and date with the article title; then give the journal title. If the journal issue is identified by a word such as *Spring*, include that word in the date. Include the volume number, set off by commas, after the journal name. Volume numbers should be italicized, but issue and page numbers should not.

> Yaworski, J. (2002, Spring). How to build a Web site in six easy steps. *Journal of College Reading and Learning, 32*, 148–153.

In citing an article from a journal paginated by issue, follow the volume number immediately with the issue number (not italicized) in parentheses.

> Reed, I. C. (2005). Creativity: Self-perceptions over time. *International Journal of Aging and Human Development, 60*(1), 1–18.

23. Magazine Article   Include the month in the date. If it's a weekly magazine, include the day. Include the volume number, if there is one, after the magazine title.

> Bowden, M. (2004, December). Among the hostage-takers. *The Atlantic Monthly, 294*, 76–96.

24. Newspaper Article   Include the specific publication date following the year.

> Deutsch, C. (2005, December 22). It's getting crowded on the environmental bandwagon. *The New York Times*, p. C5.

25. Newsletter Article   Cite a newsletter article as you would a magazine article.

> Webbe, F. (2005, Spring). I run marathons because I can. *Exercise and Sport Psychology Newsletter, 19*, 1.

ELECTRONIC SOURCES

26. Nonperiodical Web Document   To cite a nonperiodical Web document, provide as much of the following information as possible: author's name,

APA: CITING A NONPERIODICAL WEB DOCUMENT

You will likely need to search the Web site to find some of the citation information you need. For some sites, all of the details may not be available; find as many as you can. Remember that the citation you provide should allow readers to retrace your steps electronically to locate the source.

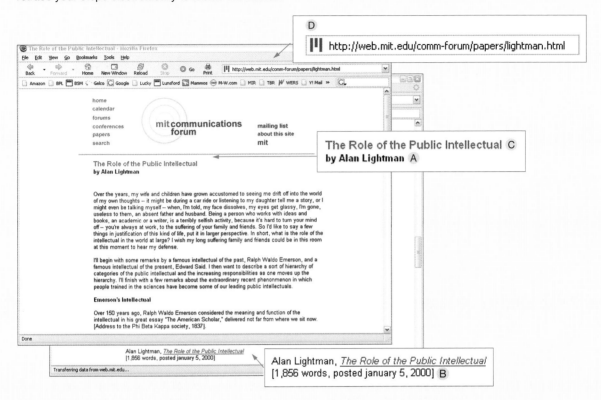

Record the following information:

A **The author.** Give the last name first, followed by a comma and initials for first and middle names. Separate initials with a space (Tufte, E. R.). Separate the names of multiple authors with commas; use an ampersand (&) before the final author's name.

B **The date of publication or most recent update.** Put the date in parentheses and end with a period (outside the parentheses). If there is no date, use *n.d.*

C **The document title.** Give the full title; include the subtitle (if any), preceded by a colon. Italicize the title and subtitle, capitalizing only the first word of the title, the first word of the subtitle, and any proper nouns. End with a period.

D **The retrieval date and URL.** Include the word *Retrieved* before the date, insert a comma after the year, and include the word *from* before the complete URL.

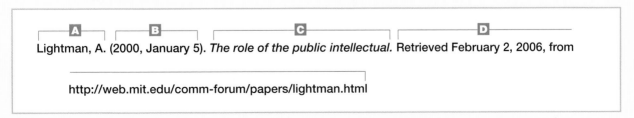

Lightman, A. (2000, January 5). *The role of the public intellectual.* Retrieved February 2, 2006, from

http://web.mit.edu/comm-forum/papers/lightman.html

In This Book   For more APA-style models for citing other types of Web sources, see pp. 592, 594, and 596.

date of publication or most recent update (use *n.d.* if there is no date), document title (in italics), retrieval date, and URL for the document.

> Bly, R. W. (n.d.). *The fundamentals of persuasive writing.* Retrieved December 22, 2005, from http://bly.com/Pages/documents/TFOPW.html

If the author of a document is not identified, begin the reference with the title of the document.

> *What is resilience?* (2004). Retrieved July 9, 2005, from http://apahelpcenter.org/featuredtopics/feature.php?id=6&ch=2

If the document is from a university program's Web site, identify the host institution and program or department, followed by a colon and the URL for the document.

> Whitburn, M. (2005). *Definitional techniques.* Retrieved May 23, 2006, from Rensselaer Polytechnic Institute, Virtual Writing Center Web site: http://www.rpi.edu/dept/llc/writecenter/web/definition.html

27. Article in an Online Periodical   To cite online articles, provide the same information as you would for print articles. (See items 22–25 on page 592.) If an identical version of the article also appears in print, do not include a URL; instead, follow the title of the article with the words *Electronic version* in brackets.

> Cooke, L. (2005, November). Eye tracking: How it works and how it relates to usability [Electronic version]. *Technical Communication, 52*(4), 456–463.

If there is no print version, or if you are citing an online article that is different from the print version (for example, the format is different or the online version contains additional materials, such as animations), include the date you retrieved the article and its URL.

> Ace, M. (2004, June). Where the jobs are. *The Willamette Galley, 7*(3). Retrieved April 10, 2006, from http://www.stcwvc.org/galley/0406/C05_State_TechPubs.html

If you are citing an article you retrieved from a searchable Web site, such as a newspaper's site, give the URL for the site rather than for the specific source.

> Klein, A. (2005, December 11). Hospitals save money, but safety is questioned. *The Washington Post.* Retrieved December 21, 2005, from http://www.washingtonpost.com

28. Article from a Database   To cite an article from an electronic database, provide the publication information followed by the access date, the name of the database, and the item number, if any.

> Pinckney, B. (2005, January 14). *Daily Gazette* redesign: Easier for readers to navigate. *The Business Review, 31*(41), 3–4. Retrieved March 22, 2005, from General BusinessFile ASAP database (A128229144).

APA: CITING AN ARTICLE FROM A DATABASE

Libraries subscribe to services such as LexisNexis, ProQuest, InfoTrac, and EBSCOhost that provide access to databases of electronic texts. The databases provide publication information, abstracts, and the complete texts of documents in a specific subject area, discipline, or profession.

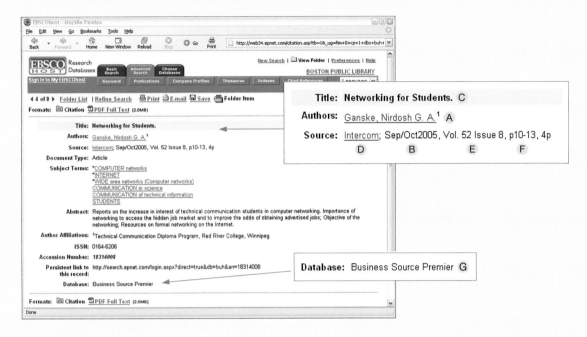

Record the following information:

A **The author.** Give the last name first, followed by a comma and initials for first and middle names. Separate initials with a space (Tufte, E. R.). Separate the names of multiple authors with commas; use an ampersand (&) before the final author's name.

B **The date of publication.** Put the year in parentheses and end with a period (outside the parentheses). For magazines and newspapers, include the month and, if relevant, the day (2006, May 23).

C **The article title.** Give the full title; include the subtitle (if any), preceded by a colon. Do not underline or italicize the title or put it in quotation marks. Capitalize only the first word of the title, the first word of the subtitle, and any proper nouns. End with a period.

D **The periodical title.** Italicize the periodical title and capitalize all major words. Insert a comma.

E **The volume number and issue number.** For journals, include the volume number, italicized. If each issue starts with page 1, include the issue number in parentheses, not italicized. Insert a comma.

F **Inclusive page numbers.** Give all the numbers in full (316–337, *not* 316–37). For newspapers, include the abbreviation *p.* for page (or *pp.* for pages) and the section letter, if relevant (p. D4). End with a period.

G **The retrieval date and name of the database.** Include the word *Retrieved* before the date, a comma, and then the word *from* before the database name.

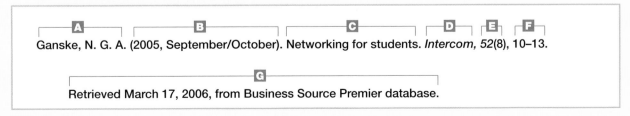

In This Book   For more APA-style models for citing other types of electronic sources, see pp. 592, 594, and 596.

29. Software   List only specialized, not off-the-shelf, software in your reference list. Include the words *Computer software* in brackets after the title.

> PsychMate [Computer software]. (2003). Pittsburgh: Psychology Software Tools.

30. Software Manual   Include the words *Software manual* in brackets after the title.

> Jones, J. B. (2005). Engineering thermodynamics [Software manual]. Upper Saddle River, NJ: Prentice Hall.

31. E-mail Message or Real-Time Communication   E-mail messages are not cited in the reference list. Instead, they should be cited in the text as personal communications. (See item 8 on page 586.)

32. Online Posting   If an online posting is not archived, and therefore is not retrievable, cite it as a personal communication and do not include it in the reference list. If the posting can be retrieved from an archive, provide the author's name or screen name, the exact date of the posting, the title or subject line, and any identifier in brackets. Finish with *Message posted to*, followed by the address.

> Kasprzak, A. (2005, June 4). Comparing companies for a project [Msg 1734]. Message posted to http://groups.yahoo.com/group/online-learning/

OTHER SOURCES

33. Technical or Research Report   Include identifying numbers in parentheses after the report title. If appropriate, include the name of the service used to locate the item in parentheses after the publisher.

> Sullins, C., & Miron, G. (2005, March). *Challenges of starting and operating charter schools: A multicase study* (Report No. 49008-5237). Kalamazoo, MI: The Evaluation Center. (ERIC Document Reproduction Service No. ED486071)

34. Government Document   For most government agencies, use the abbreviation *U.S.* instead of spelling out *United States*. Include identifying document numbers after the publication title.

> U.S. Department of Energy. (2002, May 1). *Wind power today: Wind energy program highlights 2001* (Technical Publication 102002-1556). Washington, DC: U.S. Government Printing Office.

35. Brochure or Pamphlet   After the title of the document, include the word *Brochure* or *Pamphlet* in brackets.

> American Psychological Association. (2005). *What is clinical hypnosis and what is it used for?* [Brochure]. Washington, DC: Author.

36. Article from Conference Proceedings   After the proceedings title, give the page numbers on which the article appears.

> Zabulis, X., Patterson, A., & Daniildis, K. (2005). Digitizing archaeological excavations from multiple views. In *Proceedings of the Fifth International Conference on 3-D Digital Imaging and Modeling* (pp. 81–88). Thessaloniki, Greece: Informatics and Telematics Institute.

37. Lecture or Speech

> Euben, R. (2004, December 15). Travel, theory, and the search for knowledge: Western and Islamic journeys to "the other shore." Lecture presented at Harvard University, Cambridge, MA.

38. Dissertation Abstract   If you use *Dissertation Abstracts International* (*DAI*), include the *DAI* volume, issue, and page number. If you use UMI's digital dissertation services, include the UMI number in parentheses at the end.

> Knievel, M. S. (2002). Rethinking the "humanistic": Technical communication and computers and writing as sites of change in English studies (Doctoral dissertation, Texas Tech University, 2002). *Dissertation Abstracts International, 63* (06), 2229. (UMI No. 3056071)

39. Audio Recording   Give the function of the originator or primary contributor in parentheses after the name. Give the medium in brackets after the title.

> Hallowell, E. M. (Speaker). (2005). *Delivered from distraction: Getting the most out of life with attention deficit* [CD]. New York: Random House Audio.

40. Motion Picture   Give the names of the primary contributors, such as the producer and director, and follow the film's title with the words *Motion picture* in brackets. List the country in which the film was produced and the studio's name. If the film was not widely distributed, give instead the distributor's name and address in parentheses.

> Cataldo, M. (Producer), & Massingham, G. (Director). (2000). *Technical rescue: Awareness* [Motion picture]. (Available from Emergency Film Group, 140 Cooke Street, Edgartown, MA 02539)

41. Television Program   Start with the director, producer, or other principal contributor, and the date the program aired. Include the words *Television broadcast* or *Television series* in brackets after the program title.

> Lennon, T. (Director), & Angier, J. (Producer). (2004). *Becoming American: The Chinese experience* [Television series]. Alexandria, VA: Public Broadcasting Service.

For a single episode in a television series, start with the writer and director of the episode. Include the words *Television series episode* in brackets after the episode title. Also include information about the series.

> Cort, J. (Writer), & Pannone, G., & Visalberghi, M. (Directors). (2002). Sinking city of Venice [Television series episode]. In P. S. Aspell (Executive Producer), *Nova*. Boston: WGBH.

42. Published Interview   If it is not clear from the title, or if there is no title, include the words *Interview with* and the subject's name in brackets.

> Jardin, X. (2005, December). Thinking outside the box office [Interview with Steven Soderbergh]. *Wired*, 256–257.

43. Personal Interview   Interviews you conduct, whether in person or over the telephone, are considered personal communications and are not included in the reference list. Instead, they should be cited in the text. (See item 8 on page 586.)

44. Personal Correspondence   Personal letters and memos are not included in the reference list. Instead, they should be cited in the text. (See item 8 on page 586.)

45. Unpublished Data   Include a description of the data in brackets.

> Dailey, J. A. (2006). [Operational statistics for Hornell Municipal Airport]. Unpublished raw data.

Sample APA Reference List

Following is a sample reference list using the APA citation system.

References

Chapter in an edited book

Brinkmann, J. (2006). Business ethics and intercultural communication: Exploring the overlap between two academic fields. In L. A. Samovar, R. E. Porter, & E. R. McDaniel (Eds.), *Intercultural communication: A reader* (pp. 430–439). Boston: Wadsworth.

Book in edition other than first

Guirdham, M. (2005). *Communicating across cultures at work* (2nd ed.). West Lafayette, IN: Purdue University Press.

Journal article, paginated by issue

Jacobs, G., Opdenacker, L., & Van Waes, L. (2005). A multilanguage online writing center for professional communication: Development and testing. *Business Communication Quarterly, 68*(1), 5–22.

Nonperiodical Web document

Payne, N. (2004, October 10). *Cross culture communication across languages.* Retrieved January 14, 2006, from http://www.buzzle.com/editorials/10-8-2004-60268.asp

Starke-Meyerring, D. (2005). Meeting the challenges of globalization: A framework for global literacies in professional communication programs. *Journal of Business and Technical Communication, 19*, 468–499. ◄───── *Journal article, paginated by volume*

Winters, E. (2005, April). Communicating across cultures. *Mexico Connect, 8*(12). Retrieved January 14, 2006, from http://www.mexconnect.com/mex_/travel/ewinters/ewcrossculture.htm ◄───── *Article in an online periodical*

CSE STYLE

CSE style consists of two elements: the citation in the text and the list of references at the end of the document.

On TechComm Web

For more information, see the CSE site. Click on Links Library for the Appendix on <bedfordstmartins.com/techcomm>.

CSE Style for Reference List Entries

BOOKS

1. Book by One Author   601
2. Book by Multiple Authors   603
3. Book Issued by an Organization   603
4. Edited Book   603
5. Chapter or Section in an Edited Book   603
6. Book in Edition Other Than First   603

PERIODICALS

7. Journal Article   603
8. Magazine Article   603
9. Newspaper Article   605

ELECTRONIC SOURCES

10. Online Book (Monograph)   605
11. Article in an Online Journal or Magazine   605
12. Article in an Online Newspaper   605
13. Article from a Database   605
14. Web Site   605
15. Government Site   605
16. E-mail Message   607
17. Online Posting   607

OTHER SOURCES

18. Scientific or Technical Report   607
19. Paper Published in Conference Proceedings   607
20. Government Document   607
21. Unpublished Document   607
22. Map or Chart   607
23. Other Media   607

CSE Textual Citations

For CSE-style textual citations, you may use either the citation-sequence system or the name-year system. Find out which method your instructor or organization prefers.

- *Citation-Sequence System.* In this method, superscript or parenthetical numbers are inserted into the text to indicate borrowed material.

  . . . travels at the speed of light[1], but still others contend that gravity is responsible for the phenomenon[2-4].

  or

. . . travels at the speed of light (1), but still others contend that gravity is responsible for the phenomenon (2–4).

Later textual references to the same sources repeat the numbers already used.

. . . as experiments have shown[23]. If the velocity theory[1,6] is to be taken . . .

In the list of references at the end of the document, the cited sources are numbered in the order in which they first appear in the text.

- *Name-Year System.* In this method, the author's last name and year of publication are mentioned either in the text or in a parenthetical citation immediately following the borrowed material.

  . . . travels at the speed of light (Posdevna 2005), but still others contend that gravity is responsible for the phenomenon (Walters 1990; Chang 2005; Rivera 2006).

  . . . as experiments have shown (Rao and Leschley 2004). If Posdevna's velocity theory (2005) is to be taken . . .

  . . . the most recent study on this topic was inconclusive (Matthews and others 2006).

  In the list of references at the end of the document, the cited sources are listed alphabetically by author's last name.

The CSE Reference List

 In This Book

For a sample CSE-style reference list, see p. 608.

Whether you use the citation-sequence system or the name-year system in the body of your paper, you will also need to prepare a list of references at the end. The following guidelines will help you prepare a CSE-style reference list.

- *Arranging Entries: Citation-Sequence System.* The entries are arranged in numerical order, with each entry having a number that corresponds to its first appearance in the text. Sources are not repeated in the list of references, even if one is referred to many times in the text.

- *Arranging Entries: Name-Year System.* The entries are arranged alphabetically by author's last name. Two or more works by the same author are arranged by date, earliest to latest. Two or more works by the same author in the same year have a lowercase letter added after the date: Smith 2004a, Smith 2004b, and so on. The letters are assigned by exact date of publication, earliest first. Works by an organization are alphabetized by the first significant word in the name of the organization.

- *Book Titles.* Titles of books should not be underlined, italicized, or placed in quotation marks. The first word of the book's title is capitalized, but all other words (except proper nouns) should be lowercase.

- *Publication Information.* Give the publisher's full name or consult your style guide for the preferred abbreviation. Include both the publisher's city and state or country—unless the city is well known (such as New York, Boston, or London)—in parentheses.

- *Periodical Titles.* Titles of periodicals should be abbreviated according to CSE style. The abbreviated titles should be capitalized but not underlined, italicized, or placed in quotation marks.

- *Article Titles.* Titles of articles should not be underlined, italicized, or placed in quotation marks. The first word of the article title is capitalized, but all other words (except proper nouns) should be lowercase.

- *Electronic Sources.* Include as much information as you can about electronic sources, such as author, date of publication, identifying numbers, and retrieval information. Also be sure to record the date you retrieved the information, because electronic information changes frequently.

- *Spacing.* Double-space the entire reference list. Do not add extra spacing between entries.

- *Page Numbers.* For a book entry, give the total number of pages, followed by the abbreviation *p* with no period (for example, 298 p). If you are giving a range of pages for specific articles in books and periodicals, use the abbreviation *p* and the last digit of the second number if the previous digits are identical (for example, p 151–3, *not* 151–153).

- *Dates.* Follow this format: year, month (abbreviated), day, with no periods or commas (2005 Oct 31). Use only the first three letters of each month.

- *Additional References.* A reference list includes only the sources you actually cite in your document. You may include other sources you used in researching and preparing your document in a separate alphabetical list titled "Additional References."

The models in this section show CSE's citation-sequence system. In the name-year system, the reference list would be alphabetized rather than numbered, and the publication year would immediately follow the author's name. In addition, the entries would be set with a hanging indent:

> Cunningham WS. 1980. Crisis at Three Mile Island: the aftermath of a near meltdown. New York: Madison; 342 p.

For further examples of both the citation-sequence system and the name-year system, consult *Scientific Style and Format: The CBE Manual for Authors, Editors, and Publishers* and the *National Library of Medicine Recommended Formats for Bibliographic Citation Supplement: Internet Formats.*

BOOKS

1. Book by One Author   Include the author's last name and initials (not separated by a comma), followed by the book title, the location and name of the publisher, the year of publication, and the number of pages in the book.

> 1. Gladwell M. Blink: the power of thinking without thinking. New York: Little, Brown; 2005. 288 p.

CSE: CITING A BOOK BY ONE AUTHOR

When citing a book, use the information from the title page and the copyright page (on the reverse side of the title page), not from the book's cover or a library catalog. This page gives an example of a citation in the CSE citation-sequence system.

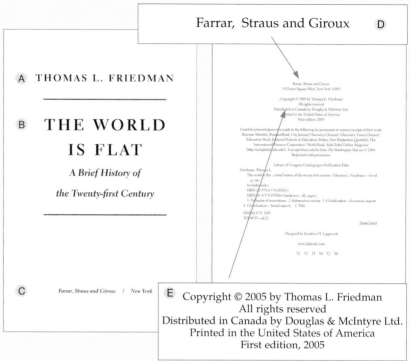

D **Farrar, Straus and Giroux**

A THOMAS L. FRIEDMAN

B **THE WORLD IS FLAT**

A Brief History of the Twenty-first Century

C *Farrar, Straus and Giroux / New York*

E Copyright © 2005 by Thomas L. Friedman
All rights reserved
Distributed in Canada by Douglas & McIntyre Ltd.
Printed in the United States of America
First edition, 2005

Record the following information:

A **The author.** Give the last name first, followed by initials for first and middle names. Separate the last name and initials with only a space, not a comma. Do not separate initials.

B **The title.** Give the full title; include the subtitle (if any), preceded by a colon. Capitalize only the first word of the title and proper nouns. Do not underline or italicize the title or subtitle. End with a period.

C **The city of publication.** If more than one city is given, use the first one listed. For a city that may be unfamiliar to your readers or confused with another city, add

an abbreviation of the state, province (if Canada), or country in parentheses: Findlay (OH). Insert a colon.

D **The publisher.** Give the publisher's name. The CBE manual includes guidelines for abbreviating publishers' names. Insert a semicolon.

E **The date of publication.** Use the publication date, if one is given; otherwise use the copyright date. If a month of publication is given, use that as well (2006 Oct). End with a period.

F **The total number of pages.** Give the total number of pages in the book, followed by *p* and a period.

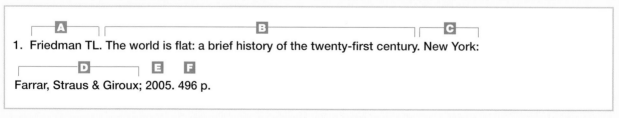

A B C
1. Friedman TL. The world is flat: a brief history of the twenty-first century. New York:

D E F
Farrar, Straus & Giroux; 2005. 496 p.

In This Book For more CSE-style models for citing other types of books, see pp. 601 and 603.

2. Book by Multiple Authors   List all the authors' names in reverse order. Do not use the word *and* between names.

> 2. Davis R, Frey R, Sarquis M, Sarquis L. Modern chemistry. New York: Holt Rinehart & Winston; 2005. 949 p.

3. Book Issued by an Organization   The organization takes the place of the author.

> 3. Planet3 Wireless. CWNA certified wireless network administrator official study guide. 3rd ed. New York: McGraw-Hill/Osborne; 2005. 578 p.

In the name-year system, an abbreviated form of the organization name may be used in both the text and the reference list. The entry should be alphabetized according to the abbreviation, not the full name of the organization.

4. Edited Book   Include the word *editor* or *editors* after the name.

> 4. Mersky P, editor. From the flight deck: an anthology of the best writing on carrier warfare. Dulles (VA): Potomac; 2005. 352 p.

5. Chapter or Section in an Edited Book   Give the author and title of the chapter or section first, followed by the word *In*, a colon, the book editor, and the book title. Then give the publication information for the book and the page numbers on which the chapter or section appears.

> 5. Morton O. Strange nuggets. In: Sobel D, editor. The best American science writing 2004. New York: Ecco; 2004. p 42–9.

6. Book in Edition Other Than First   The edition number follows the title of the book.

> 6. Kittel C. Introduction to solid state physics. 8th ed. New York: J Wiley; 2004. 704 p.

PERIODICALS

7. Journal Article   List the author's name, the article title, and the abbreviated journal title followed by the year, month, volume number, and page number(s). If the journal is paginated continuously by volume, include only the volume number after the year.

> 7. Williams JR, Gong H, Hoff N, Olubodun O. Synthesis of the shark repellent Pavoninin-4. J Org Chem 2005;70:10732–6.

If the journal is paginated by issue, include the issue number in parentheses after the volume number.

> 27. Marcus J. Students, butterflies, and cancer. J Coll Sci Teaching 2005;35(3):8–10.

8. Magazine Article   List the author's name, the article title, and the abbreviated magazine title, followed by the issue date and page number(s).

> 8. Steinberg S. Gaming 2005. Spin 2005 Dec:91–8.

CSE: CITING AN ARTICLE FROM A PERIODICAL

Periodicals include journals, magazines, and newspapers. This page gives an example of a citation for a print journal article.

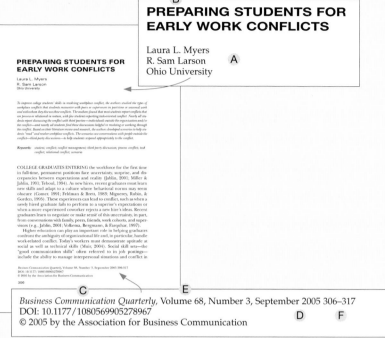

B

PREPARING STUDENTS FOR EARLY WORK CONFLICTS

Laura L. Myers
R. Sam Larson   A
Ohio University

C   E

Business Communication Quarterly, Volume 68, Number 3, September 2005 306–317
DOI: 10.1177/1080569905278967   D   F
© 2005 by the Association for Business Communication

Record the following information:

A The author. Give the last name first, followed by initials for first and middle names. Separate the last name and initials with only a space, not a comma. Do not separate initials. Separate the names of multiple authors with commas. (Carlesimo C, Thakore NR). End with a period.

B The article title. Give the full title; include the subtitle (if any), preceded by a colon. Capitalize only the first word of the title and proper nouns. Do not underline or italicize the title or subtitle. End with a period.

C The periodical title. Do not underline or italicize the periodical title; capitalize all major words. The CBE manual includes guidelines for abbreviating journal titles.

D The date of publication. For magazines and newspapers, include the month and, if available, the day (2006 Oct 16). Insert a semicolon but no space.

E The volume number and issue number. For journals, include the volume number. If each issue starts with page 1, include the issue number in parentheses. Insert a colon but no space.

F Inclusive page numbers. Give all the page numbers on which the article appears (66–9; 217–29; 1231–6).

A   B   C
2. Myers LL, Larson RS. Preparing students for early work conflicts. Business Commun Q

D E F
2005;68:306–17.

In This Book   For more CSE-style models for citing other types of periodical articles, see pp. 603 and 605.

9. Newspaper Article   List the author's name, the article title, and the newspaper name, followed by the issue date and section, page(s), and column number(s). If the newspaper does not use section numbers, use a colon between the date and the page number.

> 9. Smith S. Avian flu found in migrating geese in China. Boston Globe 2005 Jul 1; Sect A:1(col. 1).

ELECTRONIC SOURCES

10. Online Book (Monograph)   If you have to estimate the length, include it in brackets.

> 10. Graham M. The morning after earth day: practical environmental politics [monograph on the Internet]. Washington: Brookings Institution;1999 [cited 2006 Jan 18]. [about 154 p]. Available from: http://brookings.nap.edu/books/081573235X/html/ index.html

11. Article in an Online Journal or Magazine

> 11. Holy TE, Guo Z. Ultrasonic songs of male mice. PLoS Biol [serial on the Internet]. 2005 Dec [cited 2005 Dec 27];3:2177–86. Available from: http://biology.plosjournals .org/perlserv/?request=get-document&doi=10.1371/journal.pbio.0030386

12. Article in an Online Newspaper

> 12. Geraghty LN. Should you worry about the chemicals in your makeup? NY Times on the Web [Internet]. 2005 Jul 7 [cited 2005 Jul 11]:[about 20 paragraphs]. Available from: http://www.nytimes.com/2005/07/07/fashion/thursdaystyles/ 07skin.html?pagewanted=2

13. Article from a Database

> 13. Bosch X. Concerns over new EU ethics panel. The Scientist 2005 Nov 21;19(22):32. In: Expanded Academic ASAP [database on the Internet]. Farmington Hills (MI): InfoTrac; c2005- [cited 2005 Apr 13]. [about 3 paragraphs]. Available from: http://infotrac.galegroup.com; Article A139554684.

14. Web Site

> 14. Mines in Ireland [Internet]. Dublin: Mining Heritage Trust of Ireland; c2003 [updated 2005 Jan 16; cited 2005 Dec 28]. Available from: http://www.mhti.com

15. Government Site

> 15. Key facts about pandemic influenza [Internet]. Atlanta (GA): Centers for Disease Control and Prevention (US); [updated 2005 Oct 17; cited 2006 Mar 22]. Available from: http://www.cdc.gov/flu/pandemic/keyfacts.htm

CSE: CITING AN ARTICLE FROM A DATABASE

Libraries subscribe to services such as LexisNexis, ProQuest, InfoTrac, and EBSCOhost that provide access to databases of electronic texts. The databases provide publication information, abstracts, and the complete texts of documents in a specific subject area, discipline, or profession.

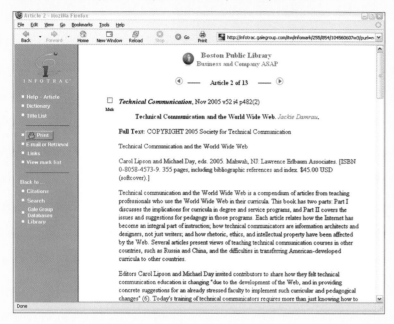

Record the following information:

A **Citation information for the article.**

B **The database title.** Include *In:* before the database name, then the words *database on the Internet* in brackets.

C **The city of publication of the database.**

D **The name of the service and the date.** Insert the name of the database provider, followed by a semicolon, then the copyright or publication date. If you use the copyright year, include a *c* (c2006).

E **The date of citation.** Include the word *cited* and the date in brackets.

F **The length of the article.** Give a length estimate (about 40 lines; about 3 screens) in brackets.

G **Retrieval information.** Include the words *Available from*, a colon, then the URL for the database. Insert a semicolon and the article number, if available.

A

3. Damrau J. Technical communication and the World Wide Web. Tech Commun

B

2005 Nov;52: 482–3. In: Business and Company ASAP [database on the Internet].

C **D** **E** **F**

Farmington Hills (MI): InfoTrac; c2005 [cited 2006 Feb 23]. [about 11 paragraphs].

G

Available from: http://infotrac.galegroup.com; Article A139215408.

In This Book   For more CSE-style models for citing other types of electronic sources, see pp. 605 and 607.

16. E-mail Message

16. Kemperman A. Recent research on primates and cognition [electronic mail on the Internet]. Message to: Parminder Shali. 2005 May 12, 4:34 pm [cited 2005 Jun 2]. [about 3 screens].

17. Online Posting

17. Murdough WJ (Krames Health and Safety. wess-murdough@krames.com). Malpractice statistics. In: MEDLIB-L [discussion list on the Internet]. [Chicago (IL): Medical Library Association]; 2005 Dec 28, 2:42 pm [cited 2005 Dec 30]. [about 8 lines]. Available from: MEDLIB-L@LISTSERV.BUFFALO.EDU

OTHER SOURCES

18. Scientific or Technical Report

18. Molina-Rivera WL. Estimated water use in Puerto Rico, 2000. Reston (VA): US Geological Survey; 2005. Report nr 2005-1201. 26 p. Available from: http://pubs.er.usgs.gov/pubs/ofr/ofr20051201

19. Paper Published in Conference Proceedings

19. Ketterle W. New frontiers with ultracold gases. In: Marcassa LG, Bagnata VS, Helmerson K, editors. Nineteenth international conference on atomic physics; 2005 Jul 25–30; Rio de Janeiro. Secaucus (NJ): Springer. p 25–9.

20. Government Document

20. Agricultural statistics 2004. Washington: US Department of Agriculture; 2004. 450 p. Available from: US GPO, Washington; ISBN 0–16–036158–3.

21. Unpublished Document   Give information about the document's availability.

21. Guidelines for OEB publications. [Publication instructions for the Department of Organismic and Evolutionary Biology at Harvard University, 2005]. Located at: office of Dr. Colleen Cavanaugh, Biological Laboratories 4083, 16 Divinity Avenue, Cambridge, MA.

22. Map or Chart   Include the type of map in brackets.

22. Africa. Average annual rainfall [climate map]. In: The new comparative world atlas. Maplewood (NJ): Hammond; 1999. p 67.

23. Other Media   Give a description of the medium in brackets.

23. A science odyssey [digital videodisk]. Friedman T, executive producer. Alexandria (VA): WGBH; 2005.

Sample CSE Reference List

Following is a sample reference list using the CSE citation-sequence system.

References

Book in edition other than first →

1. Guirdham M. Communicating across cultures at work. 2nd ed. West Lafayette (IN): Purdue Univ Pr; 2005. 360 p.

Chapter in an edited book →

2. Brinkmann J. Business ethics and intercultural communication: exploring the overlap between two academic fields. In: Samovar LA, Porter RE, McDaniel ER, editors. Intercultural communication: a reader. Boston: Wadsworth; 2006. p 430–9.

Web site →

3. Payne N. Cross culture communication across languages [Internet]. Costa Mesa (CA): Buzzle.com; 2004 Oct 10 [cited 2006 Jan 14]. Available from: http://www.buzzle.com/editorials/10-8-2004-60268.asp

Journal article, paginated by issue →

4. Jacobs G, Opdenacker L, Van Waes L. A multilanguage online writing center for professional communication: development and testing. Business Commun Q 2005;68(1):5–22.

Article in an online magazine →

5. Winters E. Communicating across cultures. Mexico Connect [serial on the Internet]. 2005 Apr [cited 2006 Jan 14];8(12):[about 10 screens]. Available from: http://www.mexconnect.com/mex_/travel/ewinters/ewcrossculture.htm

Journal article, paginated by volume →

6. Starke-Meyerring D. Meeting the challenges of globalization: a framework for global literacies in professional communication programs. J Business Tech Commun 2005;19:468–99.

On TechComm Web

For more information, see the MLA site. Click on Links Library for the Appendix on <bedfordstmartins.com/techcomm>.

MLA STYLE

MLA style consists of two elements: the citation in the text and the list of works cited at the end of the document.

MLA Textual Citations

In MLA style, the textual citation typically includes the name of the source's author and the number of the page being referred to. Textual citations vary depending on the type of information cited, the authors' names, and the context of the citation. The following models illustrate a variety of common textual citations; for additional examples, consult the *MLA Handbook for Writers of Research Papers*.

1. Entire Work   If you are referring to the whole source, not to a particular page or pages, use only the author's name.

> Parker's work provides insight into one of the world's fastest-growing economies.

2. Specific Page(s)   Immediately following the borrowed material, include a parenthetical reference with the author's name and the page number(s) being referred to. Do not use a comma between the name and the page number, and do not use the abbreviation *p.* or *pp.*

> The notion of privacy in Japanese culture is quite different from that in American culture (Feiler 1).

If your sentence already includes the author's name, include only the page number in the parenthetical notation.

> Feiler's account makes clear that the Japanese view of privacy is quite different from the American view (1).

3. Work Without Page Numbers   Give a section, paragraph, or screen number, if provided. Use *par.* or *pars.* to indicate paragraph numbers. Either spell out or use standard abbreviations for other identifying words. Use a comma after the name if it begins the citation.

> Political conservatives in Britain hold rather different views on foreign policy from conservatives in the United States (Brown, par. 5).

> Jones concludes that the city must hire a new police chief (screen 4).

4. Multiple Sources by Same Author   If you cite two or more sources by the same author, either include the full source title in the text or add a shortened title after the author's name in the parenthetical citation to prevent confusion.

> Risk is a necessary component of a successful investment strategy (Chatterjee, *Failsafe* 25).

> Chatterjee believes that diversification in investments can take many forms (*Diversification* 13).

5. Source with Multiple Authors   For a source written by two or three authors, cite all the names.

> This phenomenon was verified in the late 1970s (Grendel and Chang 281).
> Grendel and Chang assert that . . .

For a source written by four or more authors, list only the first author, followed by the abbreviation *et al.* (meaning "and others") in your parenthetical citation.

> Studies show that incidences of type 2 diabetes are widespread and rising quickly (Gianarikas et al.)

6. Source Quoted Within Another Source   Give the source of the quotation in the text. In the parenthetical citation, give the author and page number(s) of the source in which you found the quotation, preceded by *qtd. in*.

> Mukherjee challenges Southeast Asian women to imagine revised gender roles (qtd. in Spivak 256).

Only the source by Spivak will appear in the list of works cited.

7. Source Issued by an Organization   If the author is an organization rather than a person, use the name of the organization.

> The causes of narcolepsy are discussed in a recent booklet (Assn. of Sleep Disorders 2-3).

In a recent booklet, the Association of Sleep Disorders discusses the causes of narcolepsy (2-3).

8. Source with an Unknown Author   If the source does not identify an author, use a shortened form of the title in your parenthetical citation.

Multidisciplinary study in academia is becoming increasingly common ("Interdisciplinary" 23).

In a Web document, the author's name is often at the end of the document or in small print on the home page. Do some research before assuming that a Web site does not have an author. (See item 7.)

9. Multiple Sources in One Citation   To refer to two sources at the same point, separate the sources with a semicolon.

Much speculation exists about the origin of this theory (Yao 388; Brady 42).

10. Multiple Authors with Same Last Name   If two or more sources have authors with the same last name, spell out the first names of those authors in the text and use the authors' first initials in the parenthetical citation.

The economy's strength may be derived from its growing bond market (J. Martinez 87).

In contrast, Albert Martinez has a radically different explanation (29).

11. Chapter or Section in an Edited Book   Cite the author of the work, not the editor of the anthology. (See item 21 on page 615.)

Wolburg and Treise note that college binge drinkers include students with both high and low GPAs (4).

12. Multivolume Work   If you use only one volume of a multivolume work, list the volume number in the works cited list only. If you list more than one volume of a multivolume work in the works cited, indicate the specific volume you are referring to, followed by a colon and the page number, in your parenthetical citation.

Many religious organizations opposed the Revolutionary War (Hazlitt 2: 423).

13. Entry in a Reference Work   If the entry does not have an author, alphabetize it by the word or term you referenced. You do not need to cite a page number for encyclopedias and dictionaries because they are arranged alphabetically.

The term *groupism* is important to understand when preparing to communicate with Japanese business counterparts ("Groupism").

14. Electronic Source   When citing electronic sources in your document, follow the same rules as for print sources, providing author names and page numbers, if available. If an author's name is not given, use either the full title of the source in the text or a shortened version of the title in the parenthetical citation. If no page numbers are used, include any other identifying numbers. (See item 3 on page 610.) Include the URL in the works cited list but not in the text.

> Twenty million books were in print by the early sixteenth century (Rawlins, ch. 3, sec. 2).

The MLA List of Works Cited

 In This Book

For a sample MLA-style list of works cited, see p. 625.

A list of works cited provides the information your readers will need to find each source you have cited in the text. It should not include background reading. Following are some guidelines for an MLA-style list of works cited.

- *Arranging Entries.* The entries are arranged alphabetically by the author's last name. Two or more works by the same author are arranged alphabetically by title. Works by an organization are alphabetized by the first significant word in the name of the organization.
- *Book Titles.* Titles of books should follow standard capitalization rules and should be either underlined or italicized; use a consistent method throughout your document.
- *Publication Information.* Shorten the publisher's name. For cities outside the United States, include the province (if Canada) or country, abbreviated, unless the city is well known (such as Tokyo or London).
- *Periodical Titles.* Titles of periodicals should be either underlined or italicized, and all major words should be capitalized. Omit any initial article.
- *Article Titles.* Titles of articles and other short works should be placed in quotation marks, and all major words should be capitalized.
- *Electronic Sources.* Include as much information as you can about electronic sources, such as author, date of publication, identifying numbers, and retrieval information. Also be sure to record the date you retrieved the information, because electronic information changes frequently. Titles of entire Web sites should be either underlined or italicized; titles of works within Web sites, such as articles and video clips, should be treated as in print sources.
- *Indenting.* Use a hanging indent, with the second and subsequent lines of each entry indented one-half inch.
- *Spacing.* Double-space the entire works cited list. Do not add extra spacing between entries.
- *Page Numbers.* Do not use the abbreviation *p.* or *pp.* when giving page numbers. For a range of pages, give only the last two digits of the second number if the previous digits are identical (for example, 243-47, *not* 243-247 or 243-7). Use a plus sign (+) to indicate that an article continues on subsequent pages interrupted by other articles or advertisements.

- *Dates.* Follow this format: day, month, year, with no commas (20 Feb. 1999). Spell out *May, June,* and *July*; abbreviate all other months by using the first three letters (except *Sept.*) plus a period.

Following are models of works cited list entries for a variety of sources. For further examples of MLA-style citations, consult the *MLA Handbook for Writers of Research Papers.*

BOOKS

15. Book by One Author Include the author's full name, in reverse order, followed by the book title. Next give the location and name of the publisher, followed by the year of publication.

> Sachs, Jeffrey. *The End of Poverty: Economic Possibilities for Our Time.* New York: Penguin, 2005.

16. Book by Multiple Authors For a book by two or three authors, present the names in the sequence in which they appear on the title page. Only the name of the first author is presented in reverse order. A comma separates the names of the authors.

> Kim, W. Chan, and Renee Mauborgne. *Twilight in the Desert: The Coming Saudi Oil Shock and the World Economy.* Cambridge: Harvard Business School, 2005.

For a book by four or more authors, use the abbreviation *et al.* (meaning "and others") after the first author's name.

> Danesh, Arman, et al. *Mastering ColdFusion MX.* Alameda: Sybex, 2002.

17. Multiple Books by Same Author For the second and subsequent entries by the same author, use three hyphens followed by a period. Arrange the entries alphabetically by title.

> Tufte, Edward R. *Envisioning Information.* Cheshire: Graphics, 1990.
>
> ---. *Visual Explanations: Images and Quantities, Evidence and Narrative.* Cheshire: Graphics, 1997.

18. Book Issued by an Organization The organization takes the position of the author.

> WetFeet. *Careers in Investment Banking: WetFeet Insider Guide.* San Francisco: WetFeet, 2005.

19. Book by an Unknown Author If the author of the book is unknown, begin with the title.

> *Flash 5: Advanced.* Boston: Course Technology, 2001.

MLA: CITING A BOOK BY ONE AUTHOR

When citing a book, use the information from the title page and the copyright page (on the reverse side of the title page), not from the book's cover or a library catalog.

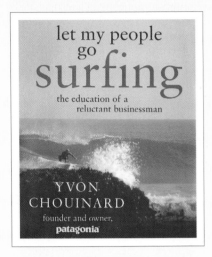

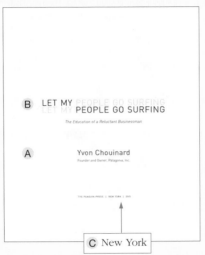

D THE PENGUIN PRESS
Published by the Penguin Group

B LET MY PEOPLE GO SURFING

A Yvon Chouinard

C New York

E Copyright © Yvon Chouinard, 2005
All rights reserved

Record the following information:

A **The author.** Give the last name first, followed by a comma, the first name, and the middle initial (if given). Don't include titles such as MD, PhD, or Sir; include suffixes after the name and a comma (Jones, Durham F., Jr.). End with a period.

B **The title.** Give the full title; include the subtitle (if any), preceded by a colon. Underline or italicize the title and subtitle, capitalizing all major words. End with a period.

C **The city of publication.** If more than one city is given, use the first one listed. For a city outside the United States that may be unfamiliar to your readers

or confused with another city, add an abbreviation of the province (if Canada) or country: Plymouth, Eng. Insert a colon.

D **The publisher.** Give a shortened version of the publisher's name (Simon for Simon and Schuster; Houghton for Houghton Mifflin; Columbia UP for Columbia University Press). Do not include the word *Press*, *Publisher*, or *Inc.* Insert a comma.

E **The date of publication.** If more than one copyright date is given, use the most recent one. Use *n.d.* if no date is given. End with a period.

A **B**

Chouinard, Yvon. *Let My People Go Surfing: The Education of a Reluctant Businessman.*

C **D** **E**

New York: Penguin, 2005.

In This Book   For more MLA-style models for citing other types of books, see pp. 613 and 615–16.

20. Edited Book   The book editor's name, followed by *ed.* (or *eds.* if more than one editor) is used in place of the author's name.

> Albelda, Randy, Susan Himmelwit, and Jane Humphries, eds. *The Dilemmas of Lone Motherhood: Essays from Feminist Economics.* London: Taylor, 2005.

21. Chapter or Section in an Edited Book   Give the author and title of the article first, followed by the book title and editor. Present the editor's name in normal order, preceded by *Ed.* (for "Edited by"). After the publication information, give the pages on which the article appears.

> Wolburg, Joyce M., and Debbie Treise. "Drinking Rituals among the Heaviest Drinkers: College Student Binge Drinkers and Alcoholics." *Contemporary Consumption Rituals: A Research Anthology.* Ed. Cele C. Otnes and Tina M. Lowrey. Mahwah: Erlbaum, 2004. 3-20.

22. Book in Edition Other Than First   The edition number follows the title of the book.

> Shiller, Robert J. *Irrational Exuberance.* 2nd ed. Princeton: Princeton UP, 2005.

23. Multivolume Work   If you use two or more of the volumes, give the total number of volumes before the place of publication (*4 vols.*). If you use only one volume, give the volume number before the place of publication. Give the total number of volumes after the publication date, if you wish.

> Lieven, Dominic, ed. *The Cambridge History of Russia: Imperial Russia, 1689-1917.* Vol. 2. Cambridge: Cambridge UP, 2006. 2 vols.

24. Book That Is Part of a Series   Include the name of the series and the series number before the publication information.

> Horngren, Charles T., Srikant M. Datar, and George M. Foster. *Cost Accounting: A Managerial Emphasis.* 12th ed. Charles T. Horngren Ser. in Accounting. Upper Saddle River: Prentice, 2005.

25. Translated Book   After the title, present the translator's name in normal order, preceded by *Trans.* (for "Translated by").

> Roth, Joseph. *Report from a Parisian Paradise: Essays from France, 1925-1939.* Trans. Michael Hoffman. New York: Norton, 2004.

26. Book in a Language Other Than English   You may give a translation of the book's title in brackets.

> Silva, Jose, and Philip Miele. *El método Silva de control mental* [*The Silva Mind Control Method*]. Mexico City: Diana, 2005.

27. Entry in a Reference Work   If the work is well known, you do not need to include the publisher or place of publication.

> "Groupism." *Dictionary of International Business Terms.* 3rd ed. Hauppauge: Barron's, 2004.

PERIODICALS

28. Journal Article   List the author's name, the article title (in quotation marks), and the journal title (underlined or italicized), followed by the volume number, year, and page number(s). If the journal is paginated continuously throughout a volume, include only the volume number after the journal title.

> Pandian, Ravi S. "The Political Economy of the Trans-Pakistan Gas Pipeline Project: Assessing the Political and Economic Risks for India." *Energy Policy* 33 (2005): 659-70.

If the journal is paginated by issue, include the issue number after the volume number and separate the two with a period.

> Barzegar, Kayhan. "Understanding the Roots of Iranian Foreign Policy in the New Iraq." *Middle East Policy* 12.2 (2005): 49-58.

29. Magazine Article   List the author's name, the article title (in quotation marks), and the magazine title (underlined or italicized), followed by the issue date and page number(s).

> Yang, Catherine. "At Stake: The Net As We Know It." *Business Week* 26 Dec. 2005: 38-39.

30. Newspaper Article   List the author's name, the article title (in quotation marks), and the newspaper name (underlined or italicized), followed by the issue date and page number(s). If the newspaper appears in more than one edition, add a comma after the date and cite the edition (for example, *late ed.*).

> Nickerson, Colin. "Europe Launches First of GPS Satellites." *Boston Globe* 29 Dec. 2005: A18.

31. Unsigned Article   If the author of an article is not indicated, begin with the title. In your list, alphabetize the work by title, ignoring any initial article.

> "The Real Lesson of BlackBerry." *Economist* 17 Dec. 2005: 12.

32. Article That Skips Pages   Give the first page on which the article appears, followed by a plus sign (+).

> Buzzell, Colby. "The Making of the 21st-Century Soldier." *Esquire* Apr. 2005: 150+.

33. Review   For a book or film review, give the author of the review and the title of the review (in quotation marks), followed by the words *Rev. of*

MLA: CITING AN ARTICLE FROM A PERIODICAL

Periodicals include journals, magazines, and newspapers. This page gives an example of a citation for a print journal article.

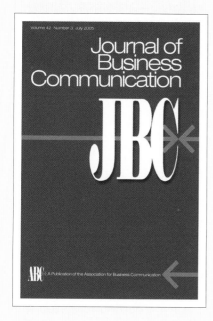

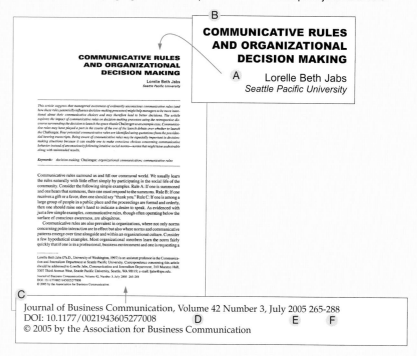

Record the following information:

A **The author.** Give the last name first, followed by a comma, the first name, and the middle initial (if given). Omit titles such as MD, PhD, or Sir; include suffixes after the name and a comma (Jones, Durham F., Jr.). End with a period.

B **The article title.** Give the title; include the subtitle (if any), preceded by a colon. Enclose the full title in quotation marks and capitalize major words. Insert a period inside the closing quotation mark.

C **The periodical title.** Underline or italicize it. Omit any initial article and capitalize major words.

D **The volume number and issue number.** For journals, give the volume number; if each issue starts

with page 1, include a period (no space) and then the issue number as well.

E **The date of publication.** For journals, give the year in parentheses, followed by a colon. For monthly magazines, don't use parentheses; give the month and year. For weekly magazines and newspapers, don't use parentheses; give the day, month, and year (in that order). Abbreviate the names of all months except May, June, and July.

F **Inclusive page numbers.** For numbers 100 and above, give only the last two digits and any other preceding digits if different from the first number (54-59, 108-09, 1172-76, 891-904). Include section letters for newspapers, if relevant. End with a period.

Jabs, Lorelle Beth. "Communicative Rules and Organizational Decision Making." *Journal of Business Communication* 42 (2005): 265-88.

In This Book For more MLA-style models for citing other types of periodical articles, see pp. 616 and 618.

and the title of the work reviewed (underlined or italicized). Insert a comma and the word *by,* then give the name of the author of the work. (Instead of *by,* you might use *ed., trans.,* or *dir.,* depending on the work.) End with the publication information for the periodical in which the review was published.

> Menand, Louis. "From the Ashes." Rev. of *Postwar: A History of Europe since 1945,* by Tony Judt. *New Yorker* 28 Nov. 2005: 168-76.

ELECTRONIC SOURCES

34. Entire Web Site   If you are citing an entire Web site, begin with the title of the site (underlined or italicized) and the editor of the site (if given). Then give the date of publication or most recent update, the name of the sponsoring institution or organization (if any), your access date, and the URL in angle brackets.

> *The Collection of Computer Science Bibliographies.* Ed. Paul Ortyl. 2005. 11 July 2005 <http://liinwww.ira.uka.de/bibliography/index.html>.

35. Short Work from a Web Site   If you are citing a portion of a Web site, begin with the author, the title of the work (in quotation marks), and the title of the site (underlined or italicized). Then include the date of publication and the site's sponsor before your retrieval information.

> Winters, Kevin E. "Ad Agency Relationship." *MarcommWise.* 2001. Klebanoff Assoc. 3 Jan. 2006 <http://www.marcommwise.com/article.phtml?id=288>.

If the URL is very long or complex, you may give the URL for the home page, followed by the word *Path* and the sequence of links you followed to find the document.

> Yamamura, Motoaki. "Wobbler Hoax." *Security Response.* 2002. Symantec. 4 Feb. 2006 <http://www.symantec.com/>. Path: Security Response; Hoaxes; Wobbler Virus.

36. Online Book   Begin with the author's name and the title of the work, along with any available information about the print source. If the book has not been published before, include the online publication date and publisher. End with your access date, followed by the URL in angle brackets.

> Rawlins, Gregory J. E. *Moths to the Flame.* Cambridge: MIT P, 1997. 10 Mar. 2006 <http://mitpress.mit.edu/e-books/Moths/>.

37. Article in an Online Periodical   Begin with the author's name and include the title of the document, the name of the periodical, and the date of publication. If the periodical is a scholarly journal, include relevant

MLA: CITING A SHORT WORK FROM A WEB SITE

You will likely need to search the Web site to find some of the citation information you need. For some sites, all of the details may not be available; find as many as you can. Remember that the citation you provide should allow readers to retrace your steps electronically to locate the source.

Record the following information:

A The author. Give the last name first, followed by a comma, the first name, and the middle initial (if given). Omit titles such as MD, PhD, or Sir; include suffixes after the name and a comma (Jones, Durham F., Jr.). End with a period.

B The document title. Give the full title; include the subtitle (if any), preceded by a colon. Enclose the title and subtitle in quotation marks and capitalize all major words. Place a period inside the closing quotation mark.

C The title of the Web site. Give the title of the Web site underlined or italicized. If there is no clear title and it is a personal home page, use *Home page* without underlining or italicizing it. End with a period.

D The date of publication or most recent update. Use the day, month, year format; abbreviate all months except May, June, and July. End with a period.

E The name of the sponsoring organization. Look for the sponsor's name at the bottom of the home page. End with a period.

F The retrieval date and URL. Give the most recent date you accessed the site. Give the complete URL, enclosed in angle brackets. If the URL is very long and complicated, however, you can give the URL of the site's search page instead. If the URL will not fit on one line, break it only after a slash, and do not add a hyphen.

Veen, Jeffrey. "Click Here, You Idiot." *Webmonkey*. 11 Jan. 2000. Lycos. 5 Mar. 2006 <http://webmonkey.wired.com/webmonkey/00/02/index1a.htm>.

In This Book   For more MLA-style models for citing other types of Web sources, see pp. 618, 620 and 622–23.

identifying numbers, such as volume, issue, and page numbers. For abstracts of articles, include the word *Abstract*, followed by a period, after the page number(s). End with your access date, followed by the URL in angle brackets.

> Manjoo, Farhad. "Another Tiny Revolution." *Salon* 8 Sept. 2005. 19 Jan. 2006
> <http://www.salon.com/tech/feature/2005/09/08/ipod_nano/
> index.html?sid=1387100>.

38. Article from a Database or Subscription Service   After giving the print article information, give the name of the database, the subscription service, the library where you retrieved the article, your access date, and a brief URL for the service in angle brackets.

> Cogan, Brian, and Gina Cogan. "Gender and Authenticity in Japanese Popular
> Music." *Popular Music and Society* 29.1 (2006): 69–90. *Academic Search
> Premier*. EBSCOhost. Emerson Coll. Lib., Boston. 3 Feb. 2006
> <http://search.epnet.com>.

39. CD-ROM   Include *CD-ROM* before the place of publication.

> Fulton-Calkins, Patsy. *Technology and Procedures for Administrative Professionals*.
> CD-ROM. Cincinnati: South-Western, 2005.

40. E-mail Message   Include the author's name and the subject line (if any), then the words *E-mail to* followed by the name of the recipient (if you, *the author*), and the date the e-mail was sent.

> Trivedi, Priya. "Data Management in Consulting." E-mail to the author. 23 May 2006.

41. Real-Time Communication   To cite a synchronous discussion, give the name of the speaker, the name and date of the discussion, the forum title (if any), the date you accessed the information, and the URL in angle brackets. If possible, cite an archived version of the communication.

> Priestly, Liza. Instant message on service learning projects. 5 Oct. 2006. Google Talk.
> 19 Nov. 2006 <http://www.google.com/talk/>.

42. Online Posting   List the author's name, the subject line (if any), the words *Online posting*, the posting date, the name of the discussion group or newsgroup, the date you accessed the posting, and the URL of the discussion group or newsgroup.

> Moogk-Soulis, Neal. "Implementing a Glossary." Online posting. 1 Nov. 2005.
> TECHWR-L. 29 Jan. 2006 <http://www.techwr-l.com/techwhirl/>.

MLA: CITING AN ARTICLE FROM A DATABASE

Libraries subscribe to services such as LexisNexis, ProQuest, InfoTrac, and EBSCOhost that provide access to databases of electronic texts.

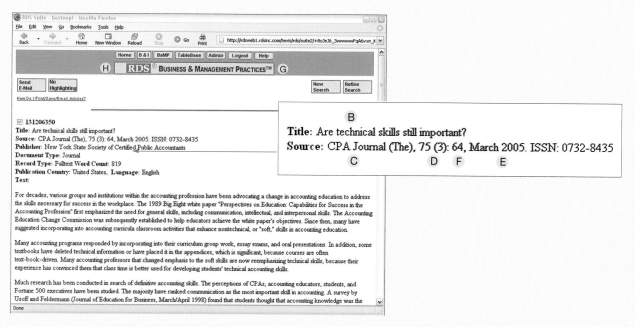

Record the following information:

A The author. Give the last name first, followed by a comma, the first name, and the middle initial.

B The article title. Give the full title; include the subtitle (if any), preceded by a colon. Enclose the title in quotation marks and capitalize all major words.

C The periodical title. Underline or italicize it. Omit any initial article and capitalize major words.

D The volume number and issue number (if appropriate).

E The date of publication. For journals, give the year in parentheses. For monthly magazines, don't use parentheses; give the month and year. For weekly magazines and newspapers, don't use parentheses; give the day, month, and year (in that order).

F Inclusive page numbers. If only the first page number is given, follow it with a hyphen, a space, and a period.

G The name of the database. Underline or italicize it.

H The name of the service, if available.

I The library at which you found it. If the location isn't clear, include the city. If the city may be unfamiliar, add the state abbreviation.

J The retrieval date and URL. Use the day, month, year format. Enclose the URL in angle brackets.

> **A** **B** **C** **D** **E**
>
> Blanthorne, Cindy. "Are Technical Skills Still Important?" *CPA Journal* 75.3 (2005):
>
> **F** **G** **H** **I**
>
> 64- . *Business and Management Practices.* RDS. Caestecker Public Lib., Green Lake,
>
> **J**
>
> WI. 20 Apr. 2006 <http://search.rdsinc.com/>.

In This Book   For more MLA-style models for citing other types of electronic sources, see pp. 618, 620, and 622–23.

43. Computer Software or Video Game   Include information about the medium by which it is distributed and the version, if applicable.

> *Microsoft Money 2006 Small Business*. CD-ROM. Redmond: Microsoft, 2005.

44. Other Online Sources   Follow the MLA guidelines, adapting them as appropriate to the electronic medium. The following examples are for a podcast and a blog.

> "Word Processing Goes Online." *Future Tense*. Podcast. Host Joe Gordon. 20 Dec. 2005. Amer. Public Media. 3 Jan. 2006 <http://www.publicradio.org/columns/futuretense/>.
>
> Baseler, Randy. "Milestones." Weblog post. *Randy's Journal*. 22 Dec. 2005. Boeing. 3 Feb. 2006 <http://www.boeing.com/randy/>.

OTHER SOURCES

45. Government Document   Give the government name and agency as the author, followed by the publication title, the edition or identifying number (if any), the place, and the date.

> United States. Dept. of Energy. *Wind Power Today: Wind Energy Program Highlights 2001*. Technical Pub. 102002-1556. Washington: GPO, 2002.

For an online government publication, begin with the name of the country and the government agency. Next give the title of the document, the author (if known, preceded by the word *By*), and the date of publication. End with your access date, followed by the URL in angle brackets.

> United States. Federal Communications Commission. *FCC Consumer Advisory: Cell Phone Fraud*. 26 Sept. 2005. 28 Jan. 2006 <http://www.fcc.gov/cgb/consumerfacts/cellphonefraud.html>.

46. Article from Conference Proceedings   List the author's name, the article title, the proceedings title, and the editor's name, followed by the publication information.

> Thomsett-Scott, Beth. "Yeah, I Found It! Performing Web Site Usability Testing to Ensure That Off-Campus Students Can Find the Information They Need." *The Eleventh Off-Campus Library Services Conference Proceedings*. Ed. Patrick B. Mahoney. Binghamton: Haworth, 2004. 471-84.

47. Dissertation Abstract   Include the abbreviation for *Dissertation Abstracts International* (*DAI*), followed by the *DAI* volume, date, and page number.

> Cooke, Lynne Marie. "Remediation and the Visual Evolution of Design." Diss. Rensselaer Polytechnic Inst., 2001. *DAI* 62 (2001): 1973.

48. Pamphlet   Cite a pamphlet as you would a book.

> *Which Medicare Prescription Drug Plan Is Right for Me?* Hartford: Aetna, 2005.

49. Report   Cite a report as you would a book.

> Najork, Mark, and Allan Heydon. *Systems Research Center Report: High-Performance Web Crawling.* Palo Alto: Compaq, 2001.

50. Interview   Begin with the name of the person interviewed. If the interview has a title, enclose it in quotation marks; otherwise use the word *Interview,* followed by a period and the bibliographic information for the work in which it was published.

> Carter, Jimmy. Interview. *Esquire* Jan. 2005: 78-79.

If it is a personal interview, give the interviewee's name, the words *Personal interview,* and the date.

> Hussan, Makarim. Personal interview. 22 Apr. 2005.

51. Letter or Memo   If the letter or memo was written to you, give the writer's name, the words *Letter/memo to the author,* and the date it was written.

> Jackson, Shaina. Letter to the author. 16 Feb. 2006.

If it was written to someone else, give his or her name in place of *the author.*

52. Lecture or Speech   Give the speaker's name, the title of the lecture or speech, and the place and date that the lecture or speech was given. If there is no title, use a descriptive label (such as *Lecture* or *Speech*), not enclosed in quotation marks.

> Lipsey, Ellen. "Preserving Boston's Landmarks." Boston Public Lib. 15 Mar. 2006.

53. Map or Chart   Cite a map or chart as you would a book. Follow the title with the word *Map* or *Chart*.

> *Calgary, Canada.* Map. Union: Hammond, 2005.

54. Photograph or Work of Art   Give the name of the artist; the title of the work; the date of completion (optional); the name of the collection, museum, or owner; and the city.

> Gursky, Andreas. *99 Cent.* 1999. Museum of Mod. Art, New York.

55. Legal Source   For a legal case, give the name of the case, the number, the name of the court, and the date of the decision.

> Antonio Dwayne Halbert v. Michigan. No. 03-10198. Supreme Ct. of the US. May 2004.

For an act, give the name of the act, the public law number, the date it was enacted, and the catalog number.

> Family Entertainment and Copyright Act of 2005. Pub. L. 109-9. 27 Apr. 2005. Stat. 119.218.

56. Radio or Television Program   Give the title of the episode or segment, if applicable, and the title of the program. Include relevant information about the host, director, or performers. Then give the network, the local station (if any), and the broadcast date.

> "Performance Review." *The Office.* NBC. WHDH-TV, Boston. 15 Nov. 2005.
>
> *Talk of the Nation.* Host Neal Conan. Natl. Public Radio. KNSR, Collegeville, MN. 13 Jan. 2006.

57. Film, Video, or DVD   Give the title of the film and the name of the director. You may also give the names of screenplay writers and major performers. Then give the distributor and the year of the original release.

> *The Informer.* Dir. Michael Mann. Perf. Russell Crowe and Al Pacino. Walt Disney Video, 1999.

58. Advertisement   Include the name of the product, organization, or service advertised; the word *Advertisement;* and the publication information.

> Bank of New York. Advertisement. *Bloomberg Markets* Jan. 2006: 47.

Sample MLA List of Works Cited

Following is a sample list of works cited using the MLA citation system.

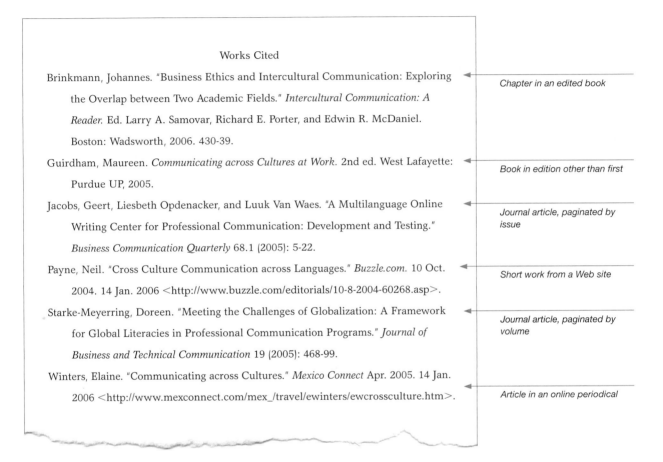

Works Cited

Brinkmann, Johannes. "Business Ethics and Intercultural Communication: Exploring the Overlap between Two Academic Fields." *Intercultural Communication: A Reader.* Ed. Larry A. Samovar, Richard E. Porter, and Edwin R. McDaniel. Boston: Wadsworth, 2006. 430-39.

Chapter in an edited book

Guirdham, Maureen. *Communicating across Cultures at Work.* 2nd ed. West Lafayette: Purdue UP, 2005.

Book in edition other than first

Jacobs, Geert, Liesbeth Opdenacker, and Luuk Van Waes. "A Multilanguage Online Writing Center for Professional Communication: Development and Testing." *Business Communication Quarterly* 68.1 (2005): 5-22.

Journal article, paginated by issue

Payne, Neil. "Cross Culture Communication across Languages." *Buzzle.com.* 10 Oct. 2004. 14 Jan. 2006 <http://www.buzzle.com/editorials/10-8-2004-60268.asp>.

Short work from a Web site

Starke-Meyerring, Doreen. "Meeting the Challenges of Globalization: A Framework for Global Literacies in Professional Communication Programs." *Journal of Business and Technical Communication* 19 (2005): 468-99.

Journal article, paginated by volume

Winters, Elaine. "Communicating across Cultures." *Mexico Connect* Apr. 2005. 14 Jan. 2006 <http://www.mexconnect.com/mex_/travel/ewinters/ewcrossculture.htm>.

Article in an online periodical

Part C: Editing and Proofreading Your Documents

This part of the handbook contains advice on editing your documents for grammar, punctuation, and mechanics.

If your organization or professional field has a style guide with different recommendations about grammar and usage, you should of course follow those guidelines.

Your instructor might use the following abbreviations to refer you to specific topics in Parts C and D of this Appendix.

Abbreviation	Topic	Page Number	Abbreviation	Topic	Page Number
abbr	abbreviation	650	ref	ambiguous pronoun reference	629
adj	adjective (ESL)	631, 665	rep	repeated word (ESL)	667
adv	adverb (ESL)	666	run	run-on sentence	629
agr p/a	pronoun-antecedent agreement	632	sent	sentence part (ESL)	655
agr s/v	subject-verb agreement (ESL)	632, 662	sub	subordinating clause (ESL)	658
art	article (a, an, the) (ESL)	664	t	verb tense	633
cap	capitalization	651	vb	verb tense (ESL)	658
comp	comparison of items	631	.	period	639
cond	conditional sentence (ESL)	663	!	exclamation point	639
coor	coordinating clause (ESL)	657	?	question mark	640
cs	comma splice	628	,	comma	634
frag	sentence fragment	627	;	semicolon	638
help	helping verb and main verb (ESL)	661	:	colon	638
inf	infinitive form of the verb (ESL)	661	—	dash	640
-ing	-ing form of the verb (ESL)	660	( )	parentheses	641
ital	italics (underlining)	645	-	hyphen	646
num	number	648	'	apostrophe	642
omit	omitted word or words (ESL)	667	" "	quotation marks	643
			. . .	ellipses	644
			< >	angle brackets	646
			[ ]	square brackets	645

GRAMMATICAL SENTENCES

frag   ## Avoid Sentence Fragments

A sentence fragment is an incomplete sentence, an error that occurs when a sentence is missing either a verb or an independent clause. To correct a sentence fragment, use one of the following two strategies:

1. **Introduce a verb.**

FRAGMENT   The pressure loss caused by a worn gasket.

This example is a fragment because it lacks a verb. (The word *caused* does not function as a verb here; rather, it introduces a phrase that describes the pressure loss.)

COMPLETE   The pressure loss was caused by a worn gasket.

Pressure loss has a verb: *was caused.*

COMPLETE   We identified the pressure loss caused by a worn gasket.

Pressure loss becomes the object in a new main clause: *We identified the pressure loss.*

FRAGMENT   A plotting program with clipboard plotting, 3-D animation, and FFTs.

COMPLETE   It is a plotting program with clipboard plotting, 3-D animation, and FFTs.

COMPLETE   A plotting program with clipboard plotting, 3-D animation, and FFTs will be released today.

2. **Link the fragment (a dependent element) to an independent clause.**

FRAGMENT   The article was rejected for publication. Because the data could not be verified.

Because the data could not be verified is a fragment because it lacks an independent clause: a clause that has a subject and a verb and could stand alone as a sentence. To be complete, it needs more information.

COMPLETE   The article was rejected for publication because the data could not be verified.

The dependent element is joined to the independent clause that precedes it.

COMPLETE   Because the data could not be verified, the article was rejected for publication.

The dependent element is followed by the independent clause.

On TechComm Web

For online exercises covering these grammar skills, click on Re:Writing, then Exercise Central on <bedfordstmartins.com/techcomm>.

FRAGMENT	Delivering over 150 horsepower. The two-passenger coupe will cost over $32,000.
COMPLETE	Delivering over 150 horsepower, the two-passenger coupe will cost over $32,000.
COMPLETE	The two-passenger coupe will deliver over 150 horsepower and cost over $32,000.

cs   Avoid Comma Splices

A comma splice is an error that occurs when two independent clauses are joined, or spliced together, by a comma. Independent clauses in a comma splice can be linked correctly in three ways:

1. **Use a comma and a coordinating conjunction (*and, or, nor, but, for, so,* or *yet*).**

SPLICE	The 909 printer is our most popular model, it offers an unequaled blend of power and versatility.
CORRECT	The 909 printer is our most popular model, for it offers an unequaled blend of power and versatility.

   The coordinating conjunction *for* explicitly states the relationship between the two clauses.

2. **Use a semicolon.**

SPLICE	The 909 printer is our most popular model, it offers an unequaled blend of power and versatility.
CORRECT	The 909 printer is our most popular model; it offers an unequaled blend of power and versatility.

   The semicolon creates a somewhat more distant relationship between the two clauses than the comma-and-coordinating-conjunction link; the link remains implicit.

3. **Use a period or another form of terminal punctuation.**

SPLICE	The 909 printer is our most popular model, it offers an unequaled blend of power and versatility.
CORRECT	The 909 printer is our most popular model. It offers an unequaled blend of power and versatility.

   The two independent clauses are separate sentences. Of the three ways to punctuate the two clauses correctly, this punctuation suggests the most distant relationship between them.

run **Avoid Run-on Sentences**

In a run-on sentence (sometimes called a *fused sentence*), two independent clauses appear together with no punctuation between them. A run-on sentence can be corrected in the same three ways as a comma splice:

1. **Use a comma and a coordinating conjunction (*and, or, nor, but, for, so, or yet*).**

   RUN-ON   The 909 printer is our most popular model it offers an unequaled blend of power and versatility.

   CORRECT   The 909 printer is our most popular model, for it offers an unequaled blend of power and versatility.

2. **Use a semicolon.**

   RUN-ON   The 909 printer is our most popular model it offers an unequaled blend of power and versatility.

   CORRECT   The 909 printer is our most popular model; it offers an unequaled blend of power and versatility.

3. **Use a period or another form of terminal punctuation.**

   RUN-ON   The 909 printer is our most popular model it offers an unequaled blend of power and versatility.

   CORRECT   The 909 printer is our most popular model. It offers an unequaled blend of power and versatility.

ref **Avoid Ambiguous Pronoun References**

Pronouns must refer clearly to their antecedents—the words or phrases they replace. To correct ambiguous pronoun references, try one of these four strategies:

1. **Clarify the pronoun's antecedent.**

   UNCLEAR   Remove the cell cluster from the medium and analyze it.

                  Analyze what: the cell cluster or the medium?

   CLEAR   Analyze the cell cluster after removing it from the medium.

   CLEAR   Analyze the medium after removing the cell cluster from it.

   CLEAR   Remove the cell cluster from the medium. Then analyze the cell cluster.

   CLEAR   Remove the cell cluster from the medium. Then analyze the medium.

2. **Clarify the relative pronoun, such as *which*, introducing a dependent clause.**

   UNCLEAR   She decided to evaluate the program, which would take five months.

                  What would take five months: the program or the evaluation?

CLEAR
She decided to evaluate the program, a process that would take five months.

By replacing *which* with *a process that,* the writer clearly indicates that it is the evaluation that will take five months.

CLEAR
She decided to evaluate the five-month program.

By using the adjective *five-month,* the writer clearly indicates that it is the program that will take five months.

3. **Clarify the subordinating conjunction, such as *where*, introducing a dependent clause.**

UNCLEAR
This procedure will increase the handling of toxic materials outside the plant, where adequate safety measures can be taken.

Where can adequate safety measures be taken: inside the plant or outside?

CLEAR
This procedure will increase the handling of toxic materials outside the plant. Because adequate safety measures can be taken only in the plant, the procedure poses risks.

CLEAR
This procedure will increase the handling of toxic materials outside the plant. Because adequate safety measures can be taken only outside the plant, the procedure will decrease safety risks.

Sometimes the best way to clarify an unclear reference is to split the sentence in two, drop the subordinating conjunction, and add clarifying information.

4. **Clarify the ambiguous pronoun that begins a sentence.**

UNCLEAR
Allophanate linkages are among the most important structural components of polyurethane elastomers. They act as cross-linking sites.

What act as cross-linking sites: allophanate linkages or polyurethane elastomers?

CLEAR
Allophanate linkages, which are among the most important structural components of polyurethane elastomers, act as cross-linking sites.

The writer has rewritten part of the first sentence to add a clear nonrestrictive modifier and has combined it with the second sentence.

If you begin a sentence with a demonstrative pronoun that might be unclear to the reader, be sure to follow it immediately with a noun that clarifies the reference.

UNCLEAR
The new parking regulations require that all employees pay for parking permits. These are on the agenda for the next senate meeting.

What are on the agenda: the regulations or the permits?

CLEAR   The new parking regulations require that all employees pay for parking permits. These regulations are on the agenda for the next senate meeting.

comp   Compare Items Clearly

When comparing or contrasting items, make sure your sentence communicates their relationship clearly. A simple comparison between two items often causes no problems: "The X3000 has more storage than the X2500." Simple comparisons, however, can sometimes result in ambiguous statements:

AMBIGUOUS   Trout eat more than minnows.

Do trout eat minnows in addition to other food, or do trout eat more than minnows eat?

CLEAR   Trout eat more than minnows do.

If you are introducing three items, make sure the reader can tell which two are being compared:

AMBIGUOUS   Trout eat more algae than minnows.

CLEAR   Trout eat more algae than they do minnows.

CLEAR   Trout eat more algae than minnows do.

Beware of comparisons in which different aspects of the two items are compared:

ILLOGICAL   The resistance of the copper wiring is lower than the tin wiring.

LOGICAL   The resistance of the copper wiring is lower than that of the tin wiring.

Resistance cannot be logically compared with *tin wiring*. In the revision, the pronoun *that* substitutes for *resistance* in the second part of the comparison.

adj   Use Adjectives Clearly

In general, adjectives are placed before the nouns that they modify: *the plastic washer*. In technical communication, however, writers often need to use clusters of adjectives. To prevent confusion in technical communication, follow two guidelines:

1. **Use commas to separate coordinate adjectives.**
   Adjectives that describe different aspects of the same noun are known as coordinate adjectives.

   portable, programmable CD player

   adjustable, removable housings

   The comma is used instead of the word *and*.

Sometimes an adjective is considered part of the noun it describes: *electric drill*. When one adjective modifies *electric drill*, no comma is required: *a reversible electric drill*. The addition of two or more adjectives, however, creates the traditional coordinate construction: *a two-speed, reversible electric drill*.

2. Use hyphens to link compound adjectives.

A compound adjective is made up of two or more words. Use hyphens to link these elements when compound adjectives precede nouns.

> a variable-angle accessory

> increased cost-of-living raises

> The hyphens prevent *increased* from being read as an adjective modifying *cost*.

A long string of compound adjectives can be confusing even if you use hyphens appropriately. To ensure clarity, turn the adjectives into a clause or a phrase following the noun.

UNCLEAR	an *operator-initiated default-prevention* technique
CLEAR	a technique *initiated by the operator to prevent default*

agr s/v   Maintain Subject-Verb Agreement

The subject and verb of a sentence must agree in number, even when a prepositional phrase comes between them. The object of the preposition may be plural in a singular sentence.

INCORRECT	The *result* of the tests *are* promising.
CORRECT	The *result* of the tests *is* promising.

The object of the preposition may be singular in a plural sentence.

INCORRECT	The *results* of the test *is* promising.
CORRECT	The *results* of the test *are* promising.

Don't be misled by the fact that the object of the preposition and the verb don't sound natural together, as in *tests is* or *test are*. Here, the noun *test(s)* precedes the verb, but it is not the subject of the verb. As long as the subject and verb agree, the sentence is correct.

agr p/a   Maintain Pronoun-Antecedent Agreement

A pronoun and its antecedent (the word or phrase being replaced by the pronoun) must agree in number. Often an error occurs when the antecedent is a collective noun—one that can be interpreted as either singular or plural, depending on its usage.

INCORRECT	The *company* is proud to announce a new stock option plan for *their* employees.
CORRECT	The *company* is proud to announce a new stock option plan for *its* employees.

Company acts as a single unit; therefore, the singular pronoun is appropriate.

When the individual members of a collective noun are emphasized, however, plural pronouns are appropriate.

CORRECT	The inspection team have prepared their reports.

The use of *their* emphasizes that the team members have prepared their own reports.

t   Use Tenses Correctly

Two verb tenses are commonly used in technical communication: the present tense and the past perfect tense. It is important to understand the specific purpose of each.

1. **The present tense is used to describe scientific principles and recurring events.**

INCORRECT	In 1992, McKay and his coauthors argued that the atmosphere of Mars *was* salmon pink.
CORRECT	In 1992, McKay and his coauthors argued that the atmosphere of Mars *is* salmon pink.

Although the argument was made in the historical past—1992—the point is expressed in the present tense, because the atmosphere of Mars continues to be salmon pink.

When the date of the argument is omitted, some writers express the entire sentence in the present tense.

CORRECT	McKay and his coauthors *argue* that the atmosphere of Mars *is* salmon pink.

2. **The past perfect tense is used to describe the earlier of two events that occurred in the past.**

CORRECT	We *had begun* excavation when the foreman *discovered* the burial remains.

Had begun is the past perfect tense. The excavation began before the burial remains were discovered.

CORRECT	The seminar *had concluded* before I *got* a chance to talk with Dr. Tran.

PUNCTUATION

, Commas

On TechComm Web

For online exercises covering punctuation, click on Re:Writing, then Exercise Central on <bedfordstmartins.com/techcomm>.

The comma is the most frequently used punctuation mark, as well as the one about whose usage writers most often disagree. Examples of common misuses of the comma are noted within the following guidelines. This section concludes with advice about editing for unnecessary commas.

1. Use a comma in a compound sentence, to separate two independent clauses linked by a coordinating conjunction (*and*, *or*, *nor*, *but*, *so*, *for*, or *yet*):

INCORRECT	The mixture was prepared from the two premixes and the remaining ingredients were then combined.
CORRECT	The mixture was prepared from the two premixes, and the remaining ingredients were then combined.

2. Use a comma to separate items in a series composed of three or more elements:

   The manager of spare parts is responsible for ordering, stocking, and disbursing all spare parts for the entire plant.

   Despite the presence of the conjunction *and*, most technical-communication style manuals require a comma after the second-to-last item. The comma clarifies the separation and prevents misreading.

CONFUSING	The report will be distributed to Operations, Research and Development and Accounting.
CLEAR	The report will be distributed to Operations, Research and Development, and Accounting.

3. Use a comma to separate introductory words, phrases, and clauses from the main clause of the sentence:

   However, we will have to calculate the effect of the wind.

   To facilitate trade, the government holds a yearly international conference.

   In the following example, the comma actually prevents misreading:

   Just as we finished eating, the rats discovered the treadmill.

   NOTE: Writers sometimes make errors by omitting commas following introductory words, phrases, or clauses. A comma is optional only if the introductory text is brief and cannot be misread.

CORRECT	First, let's take care of the introductions.

CORRECT	First let's take care of the introductions.
INCORRECT	As the researchers sat down to eat the laboratory rats awakened.
CORRECT	As the researchers sat down to eat, the laboratory rats awakened.

4. **Use a comma to separate a dependent clause from the main clause:**

> Although most of the executive council saw nothing wrong with it, the advertising campaign was canceled.

> Most PCs use green technology, even though it is relatively expensive.

5. **Use commas to separate nonrestrictive modifiers (parenthetical clarifications) from the rest of the sentence:**

> Jones, the temporary chairman, called the meeting to order.

 In This Book

For more about restrictive and nonrestrictive modifiers, see Ch. 11, p. 233.

NOTE: Writers sometimes introduce an error by dropping one of the commas around a nonrestrictive modifier.

| INCORRECT | The phone line, which was installed two weeks ago had to be disconnected. |
| CORRECT | The phone line, which was installed two weeks ago, had to be disconnected. |

6. **Use a comma to separate interjections and transitional elements from the rest of the sentence:**

> Yes, I admit that your findings are correct.

> Their plans, however, have great potential.

NOTE: Writers sometimes introduce an error by dropping one of the commas around an interjection or a transitional element.

| INCORRECT | Our new statistician, however used to work for Konaire, Inc. |
| CORRECT | Our new statistician, however, used to work for Konaire, Inc. |

7. **Use a comma to separate coordinate adjectives:**

> The finished product was a sleek, comfortable cruiser.

> The heavy, awkward trains are still being used.

The comma here takes the place of the conjunction *and*.

If the adjectives are not coordinate—that is, if one of the adjectives modifies the combined adjective and noun—do not use a comma:

> They decided to go to the first general meeting.

For more about coordinate adjectives, see page 631.

8. **Use a comma to signal that a word or phrase has been omitted from a sentence because it is implied:**

> Smithers is in charge of the accounting; Harlen, the data management; Demarest, the publicity.

> The commas after *Harlen* and *Demarest* show that the phrase *is in charge of* has not been repeated.

9. **Use a comma to separate a proper noun from the rest of the sentence in direct address:**

> John, have you seen the purchase order from United?

> What I'd like to know, Betty, is why we didn't see this problem coming.

10. **Use a comma to introduce most quotations:**

> He asked, "What time were they expected?"

11. **Use a comma to separate towns, states, and countries:**

> Bethlehem, Pennsylvania, is the home of Lehigh University.

> He attended Lehigh University in Bethlehem, Pennsylvania, and the University of California at Berkeley.

> Note that a comma precedes and follows *Pennsylvania*.

12. **Use a comma to set off the year in a date:**

> August 1, 2007, is the anticipated completion date.

> If the month separates the date and the year, you do not need to use commas because the numbers are not next to each other:

> The anticipated completion date is 1 August 2007.

13. **Use a comma to clarify numbers:**

> 12,013,104

> NOTE: European practice is to reverse the use of commas and periods in writing numbers: periods signify thousands, and commas signify decimals.

14. **Use a comma to separate names from professional or academic titles:**

> Harold Clayton, PhD
>
> Marion Fewick, CLU
>
> Joyce Carnone, PE

NOTE: The comma also follows the title in a sentence:

Harold Clayton, PhD, is the featured speaker.

UNNECESSARY COMMAS

Writers often introduce errors by using unnecessary commas. Do not insert commas in the following situations:

- Commas are not used to link two independent clauses without a coordinating conjunction (known as a "comma splice"):

INCORRECT   All the motors were cleaned and dried after the water had entered, had they not been, additional damage would have occurred.

CORRECT   All the motors were cleaned and dried after the water had entered; had they not been, additional damage would have occurred.

CORRECT   All the motors were cleaned and dried after the water had entered. Had they not been, additional damage would have occurred.

For more about comma splices, see page 628.

- Commas are not used to separate the subject from the verb in a sentence:

INCORRECT   Another of the many possibilities, is to use a "first in, first out" sequence.

CORRECT   Another of the many possibilities is to use a "first in, first out" sequence.

- Commas are not used to separate the verb from its complement:

INCORRECT   The schedules that have to be updated every month are, numbers 14, 16, 21, 22, 27, and 31.

CORRECT   The schedules that have to be updated every month are numbers 14, 16, 21, 22, 27, and 31.

- Commas are not used with a restrictive modifier:

INCORRECT   New and old employees who use the processed order form, do not completely understand the basis of the system.

   The phrase *who use the processed order form* is a restrictive modifier necessary to the meaning: it defines which employees do not understand the system.

CORRECT   New and old employees who use the processed order form do not completely understand the basis of the system.

INCORRECT   A company, that has grown so big, no longer finds an informal evaluation procedure effective.

   The clause *that has grown so big* is a restrictive modifier.

CORRECT   A company that has grown so big no longer finds an informal evaluation procedure effective.

- Commas are not used to separate two elements in a compound subject:

  | INCORRECT | Recent studies, and reports by other firms confirm our experience. |
  | CORRECT | Recent studies and reports by other firms confirm our experience. |

; Semicolons

Semicolons are used in the following instances.

1. **Use a semicolon to separate independent clauses not linked by a coordinating conjunction:**

   The second edition of the handbook is more up-to-date; however, it is also more expensive.

2. **Use a semicolon to separate items in a series that already contains commas:**

   The members elected three officers: Jack Resnick, president; Carol Wayshum, vice president; Ahmed Jamoogian, recording secretary.

   Here the semicolon acts as a "supercomma," grouping each name with the correct title.

MISUSE OF SEMICOLONS

Sometimes writers incorrectly use a semicolon when a colon is called for:

| INCORRECT | We still need one ingredient; luck. |
| CORRECT | We still need one ingredient: luck. |

: Colons

Colons are used in the following instances.

1. **Use a colon to introduce a word, phrase, or clause that amplifies, illustrates, or explains a general statement:**

   The project team lacked one crucial member: a project leader.

   Here is the client's request: we are to provide the preliminary proposal by November 13.

   We found three substances in excessive quantities: potassium, cyanide, and asbestos.

   The week was productive: 14 projects were completed and another dozen were initiated.

   NOTE: The text preceding a colon should be able to stand on its own as a sentence:

INCORRECT	We found: potassium, cyanide, and asbestos.
CORRECT	We found the following: potassium, cyanide, and asbestos.
CORRECT	We found potassium, cyanide, and asbestos.

2. Use a colon to introduce items in a vertical list if the sense of the introductory text would be incomplete without the list:

> We found the following:
>
> > potassium
> >
> > cyanide
> >
> > asbestos

In This Book

For more on constructing lists, see Ch. 11, p. 225.

3. Use a colon to introduce long or formal quotations:

> The president began: "In the last year . . ."

MISUSE OF COLONS

Writers sometimes incorrectly use a colon to separate a verb from its complement:

INCORRECT	The tools we need are: a plane, a level, and a T square.
CORRECT	The tools we need are a plane, a level, and a T square.
CORRECT	We need three tools: a plane, a level, and a T square.

◾ Periods

Periods are used in the following instances.

1. Use a period at the end of sentences that do not ask questions or express strong emotion:

> The lateral stress still needs to be calculated.

2. Use a period after some abbreviations:

> U.S.A.
>
> etc.

For more about abbreviations, see page 650.

3. Use a period with decimal fractions:

> 4.056
>
> $6.75
>
> 75.6 percent

! Exclamation Points

The exclamation point is used at the end of a sentence that expresses strong emotion, such as surprise or doubt.

The nuclear plant, which was originally expected to cost $1.6 billion, eventually cost more than $8 billion!

In technical documents, which require objectivity and a calm, understated tone, exclamation points are rarely used.

? Question Marks

The question mark is used at the end of a sentence that asks a direct question.

What did the commission say about effluents?

NOTE: When a question mark is used within quotation marks, no other end punctuation is required.

She asked, "What did the commission say about effluents?"

MISUSE OF QUESTION MARKS

Do not use a question mark at the end of a sentence that asks an indirect question.

He wanted to know whether the procedure had been approved for use.

— Dashes

To make a dash, use two uninterrupted hyphens (--). Do not add spaces before or after the dash. Some word-processing programs turn two hyphens into a dash, but with others, you have to use a special character to make a dash; there is no dash key on the keyboard.

Dashes are used in the following instances.

1. **Use a dash to set off a sudden change in thought or tone:**

   The committee found—can you believe this?—that the company bore full responsibility for the accident.

   That's what she said—if I remember correctly.

2. **Use a dash to emphasize a parenthetical element:**

   The managers' reports—all 10 of them—recommend production cutbacks for the coming year.

   Arlene Kregman—the first woman elected to the board of directors—is the next scheduled speaker.

3. **Use a dash to set off an introductory series from its explanation:**

   Wet suits, weight belts, tanks—everything will have to be shipped in.

NOTE: When a series follows the general statement, a colon replaces the dash.

> Everything will have to be shipped in: wet suits, weight belts, and tanks.

MISUSES OF DASHES

Sometimes writers incorrectly use a dash as a substitute for other punctuation marks:

INCORRECT	The regulations—which were issued yesterday—had been anticipated for months.
CORRECT	The regulations, which were issued yesterday, had been anticipated for months.
INCORRECT	Many candidates applied—however, only one was chosen.
CORRECT	Many candidates applied; however, only one was chosen.

( )   Parentheses

Parentheses are used in the following instances.

1. Use parentheses to set off incidental information:

> Please call me (x3104) when you get the information.
>
> Galileo (1546–1642) is often considered the father of modern astronomy.
>
> The cure rate for lung cancer has almost doubled in the last thirty years (Capron 1999).

2. Use parentheses to enclose numbers and letters that label items listed in a sentence:

> To transfer a call within the office, (1) place the party on HOLD, (2) press TRANSFER, (3) press the extension number, and (4) hang up.
>
> Use both a left and a right parenthesis—not just a right parenthesis—in this situation.

MISUSE OF PARENTHESES

Sometimes writers incorrectly use parentheses instead of brackets to enclose their insertion within a quotation.

INCORRECT	He said, "The new manager (Farnham) is due in next week."
CORRECT	He said, "The new manager [Farnham] is due in next week."

For more about square brackets, see page 645.

, Apostrophes

Apostrophes are used in the following instances.

1. Use an apostrophe to indicate possession:

the manager's goals   the employee's credit union

the workers' lounge   Charles's T square

For joint possession, add an apostrophe and an *s* only to the last noun or proper noun:

Watson and Crick's discovery

For separate possession, add an apostrophe and an *s* to each of the nouns or pronouns:

Newton's and Galileo's theories

NOTE: Do not add an apostrophe or an *s* to possessive pronouns: *his, hers, its, ours, yours, theirs.*

2. Use an apostrophe to indicate possession when a noun modifies a gerund:

We were all looking forward to Bill's joining the company.

The gerund *joining* is modified by the proper noun *Bill.*

3. Use an apostrophe to form contractions:

I've   shouldn't

can't   it's

The apostrophe usually indicates an omitted letter or letters:

can(no)t = can't

it (i)s = it's

NOTE: Some organizations discourage the use of contractions; others have no preference. Find out the policy your organization follows.

4. Use an apostrophe to indicate special plurals:

three 9's

two different JCL's

the why's and how's of the problem

NOTE: For plurals of numbers and abbreviations, some style guides omit the apostrophe: *9s, JCLs.* Because usage varies considerably, check with your organization.

MISUSE OF APOSTROPHES

Writers sometimes incorrectly use the contraction *it's* in place of the possessive pronoun *its*.

INCORRECT   The company does not feel that the problem is it's responsibility.

CORRECT   The company does not feel that the problem is its responsibility.

66 99   Quotation Marks

Quotation marks are used in the following instances.

1. **Use quotation marks to indicate titles of short works, such as articles, essays, or chapters:**

    Smith's essay "Solar Heating Alternatives" was short but informative.

2. **Use quotation marks to call attention to a word or phrase used in an unusual way or in an unusual context:**

    A proposal is "wired" if the sponsoring agency has already decided who will be granted the contract.

    NOTE: Do not use quotation marks to excuse poor word choice:

    INCORRECT   The new director has been a real "pain."

3. **Use quotation marks to indicate a direct quotation:**

    "In the future," he said, "check with me before authorizing any large purchases."

    As Breyer wrote, "Morale *is* productivity."

    NOTE: Quotation marks are not used with indirect quotations.

    INCORRECT   He said that "third-quarter profits will be up."

    CORRECT   He said that third-quarter profits will be up.

    CORRECT   He said, "Third-quarter profits will be up."

In This Book

For more about quoting sources, see Appendix, Part A, p. 577.

Also note that quotation marks are not used with quotations that are longer than four lines; instead, set the quotation in block format. In a word-processed manuscript, a block quotation is usually

- indented one-half inch from the left-hand margin
- typed without quotation marks
- introduced by a complete sentence followed by a colon

Different style manuals recommend variations on these basic rules; the following example illustrates APA style.

McFarland (1997) writes:

> The extent to which organisms adapt to their environment is still being charted. Many animals, we have recently learned, respond to a dry winter with an automatic birth control chemical that limits the number of young to be born that spring. This prevents mass starvation among the species in that locale. (p. 49)

Hollins (1999) concurs. She writes, "Biological adaptation will be a major research area during the next decade" (p. 2).

USING QUOTATION MARKS WITH OTHER PUNCTUATION

- If the sentence contains a *tag*—a phrase identifying the speaker or writer—a comma separates it from the quotation:

    Wilson replied, "I'll try to fly out there tomorrow."

    "I'll try to fly out there tomorrow," Wilson replied.

    Informal and brief quotations require no punctuation before a quotation mark:

    She asked herself "Why?" several times a day.

- In the United States (unlike most other English-speaking nations), commas and periods at the end of quotations are placed within the quotation marks:

    The project engineer reported, "A new factor has been added."

    "A new factor has been added," the project engineer reported.

- Question marks, dashes, and exclamation points are placed inside quotation marks when they are part of the quoted material:

    He asked, "Did the shipment come in yet?"

- When question marks, dashes, and exclamation points apply to the whole sentence, they are placed outside the quotation marks:

    Did he say, "This is the limit"?

- When a punctuation mark appears inside a quotation mark at the end of a sentence, do not add another punctuation mark.

    INCORRECT   Did she say, "What time is it?"?

    CORRECT   Did she say, "What time is it?"

▪▪▪ Ellipses

Ellipses (three spaced periods) indicate the omission of material from a direct quotation.

SOURCE	My team will need three extra months for market research and quality-assurance testing to successfully complete the job.
QUOTE	She responded, "My team will need three extra months . . . to successfully complete the job."

Insert an ellipsis after a period if you are omitting entire sentences that follow:

> Larkin refers to the project as "an attempt . . . to clarify the issue of compulsory arbitration. . . . We do not foresee an end to the legal wrangling . . . but perhaps the report can serve as a definition of the areas of contention."

The writer has omitted words from the source after *attempt* and after *wrangling*. After *arbitration*, the writer has inserted an ellipsis after a period to indicate that a sentence has been omitted.

NOTE: If the author's original statement has ellipses, MLA style recommends that you insert brackets around an ellipsis that you introduce in a quotation.

> Sexton thinks "reuse adoption offers . . . the promise to improve business [. . .] worldwide."

[ ]   Square Brackets

Square brackets are used in the following instances.

1. **Use square brackets around words added to a quotation:**

   > As noted in the minutes of the meeting, "He [Pearson] spoke out against the proposal."

   A better approach would be to shorten the quotation:

   > The minutes of the meeting note that Pearson "spoke out against the proposal."

2. **Use square brackets to indicate parenthetical information within parentheses:**

   > (For further information, see Charles Houghton's *Civil Engineering Today* [1997].)

MECHANICS

ital   Italics

Although italics are generally preferred, you may use underlining in place of italics. Whichever method you choose, be consistent throughout your document. Italics (or underlining) are used in the following instances.

 On TechComm Web

For online exercises covering mechanics, click on Re:Writing, then Exercise Central on <bedfordstmartins.com/techcomm>.

1. **Use italics for words used as words:**

   In this report, the word *operator* will refer to any individual who is in charge of the equipment, regardless of that individual's certification.

2. **Use italics to indicate titles of long works (books, manuals, and so on), periodicals and newspapers, long films, long plays, and long musical works:**

   See Houghton's *Civil Engineering Today*.

   We subscribe to the *Wall Street Journal*.

   Note that *the* is not italicized or capitalized when the title is used in a sentence.

   NOTE: The MLA style guide recommends that the names of Web sites be italicized.

   The Library of Congress maintains *Thomas*, an excellent site for legislative information.

3. **Use italics to indicate the names of ships, trains, and airplanes:**

   The shipment is expected to arrive next week on the *Penguin*.

4. **Use italics to set off foreign expressions that have not become fully assimilated into English:**

   Grace's *joie de vivre* makes her an engaging presenter.

   Check a dictionary to determine whether a foreign expression has become assimilated.

5. **Use italics to emphasize words or phrases:**

   Do not press the red button.

< > Angle Brackets

Many style guides now advocate using angle brackets around URLs in print documents to set them off from the text.

   Our survey included a close look at three online news sites: the *New York Times* <www.nytimes.com>, the *Washington Post* <www.washingtonpost.com>, and CNN <www.cnn.com>.

You may want to check with your instructor or organization before following this recommendation.

- Hyphens

Hyphens are used in the following instances.

8. Time of day is expressed in numerals if A.M. or P.M. is used; otherwise, it is written out:

> 6:10 A.M.
>
> six o'clock
>
> the nine-thirty train

9. Page numbers and titles of figures and tables are expressed in numerals:

> Figure 1
>
> Table 13
>
> page 261

10. Back-to-back numbers are written using both words and numerals:

> six 3-inch screws
>
> fourteen 12-foot ladders
>
> 3,012 five-piece starter units

In general, the technical unit should be expressed with the numeral. If the nontechnical quantity would be cumbersome in words, use the numeral for it instead.

11. Numbers in legal contracts or in documents intended for international readers should be represented in both words and numerals:

> thirty-seven thousand dollars ($37,000)
>
> five (5) relays

12. Street addresses may require both words and numerals:

> 3801 Fifteenth Street

SPECIAL CASES

- A number at the beginning of a sentence should be spelled out:

> Thirty-seven acres was the size of the lot.

> Many writers would revise the sentence to avoid this problem:

> The lot was 37 acres.

- Within a sentence, the same unit of measurement should be expressed consistently in either numerals or words:

INCORRECT	On Tuesday the attendance was 13; on Wednesday, eight.
CORRECT	On Tuesday the attendance was 13; on Wednesday, 8.
CORRECT	On Tuesday the attendance was thirteen; on Wednesday, eight.

- In general, months should not be expressed as numbers. In the United States, 3/7/06 means March 7, 2006; in many other countries, it means July 3, 2006. The following forms, in which the months are written out, are preferable:

    March 7, 2006

    7 March 2006

abbr Abbreviations

Abbreviations save time and space, but you should use them carefully because your readers may not understand them. Many companies and professional organizations provide lists of approved abbreviations.

Analyze your audience to determine whether and how to abbreviate. If your readers include a general audience unfamiliar with your field, either write out the technical terms or attach a list of abbreviations. If you are new to an organization or are publishing in a field for the first time, find out which abbreviations are commonly used. If for any reason you are unsure about a term, write it out.

The following are general guidelines about abbreviations.

1. When an unfamiliar abbreviation is introduced for the first time, the full term should be given, followed by the abbreviation in parentheses. In subsequent references, the abbreviation may be used alone. For long works, the full term and its abbreviation may be written out at the start of major units, such as chapters.

    The heart of the new system is the self-loading cartridge (SLC).

    The cathode-ray tube (CRT) is your control center.

2. To form the plural of an abbreviation, an *s* is added, either with or without an apostrophe, depending on the style of your organization:

    GNPs

    PhD's

    Most unit-of-measurement abbreviations do not take plurals:

    10 in.

    3 qt

3. Most abbreviations in scientific writing are not followed by periods:

    lb

    cos

    dc

If the abbreviation can be confused with another word, however, a period should be used:

> in.
>
> Fig.

4. **If no number is used with a measurement, an abbreviation should not be used.**

INCORRECT	How many sq meters is the site?
CORRECT	How many square meters is the site?

cap   Capitalization

For the most part, the conventions of capitalization in general writing apply in technical communication.

1. **Proper nouns, titles, trade names, places, languages, religions, and organizations should be capitalized:**

> William Rusham
>
> Director of Personnel
>
> Quick-Fix Erasers
>
> Bethesda, Maryland
>
> Italian
>
> Methodism
>
> Society for Technical Communication

In some organizations, job titles are not capitalized unless they refer to specific persons.

> Alfred Loggins, Director of Personnel, is interested in being considered for vice president of marketing.

2. **Headings and labels should be capitalized:**

> A Proposal to Implement the Wilkins Conversion System
>
> Mitosis
>
> Table 3
>
> Section One
>
> The Problem
>
> Rate of Inflation, 1995–2005
>
> Figure 6

Proofreading Symbols and Their Meanings

Mark in margin	Instructions	Mark on manuscript	Corrected type
ℓ	Delete	$10 billion dollars	$10 billion
∧	Insert	enviroment	environment
(stet)	Let stand	let it stand	let it stand
(cap)	Capitalize	the english language	the English language
(lc)	Make lowercase	the English Language	the English language
—	Italicize	Technical Communication	*Technical Communication*
(tr)	Transpose	recieve	receive
⌒	Close up space	diagnostic ultra sound	diagnostic ultrasound
(sp)	Spell out	Pres Smithers	President Smithers
#	Insert space	3amp light	3 amp light
¶	Start paragraph	. . . the results. These results	. . . the results. These results
run in	No paragraph	. . . the results. For this reason,	. . . the results. For this reason,
(sc)	Set in small capitals	Needle-nosed pliers	NEEDLE-NOSED PLIERS
(bf)	Set in boldface	Needle-nosed pliers	**Needle-nosed pliers**
⊙	Insert period	Fig 21	Fig. 21
⌄	Insert comma	the plant which was built	the plant, which was built
=	Insert hyphen	menu driven software	menu-driven software
⊙	Insert colon	Add the following	Add the following:
⌄	Insert semicolon	. . . the plan however the committee	. . . the plan; however the committee
⌄	Insert apostrophe	the users preference	the user's preference
⌄/⌄	Insert quotation marks	Furthermore, she said . . .	"Furthermore," she said . . .
(/)	Insert parentheses	Write to us at the Newark office	Write to us (at the Newark office)
[/]	Insert brackets	President John Smithers	President [John] Smithers
$\frac{1}{N}$	Insert en dash	1984 2001	1984–2001
$\frac{1}{M}$	Insert em dash	Our goal victory	Our goal—victory
⌄	Insert superscript	4,000 ft2	4,000 ft^2
⌃	Insert subscript	H2O	H_2O
//	Align	$123.05 $86.95	$123.05 $86.95
[	Move to the left	PVC piping	PVC piping
]	Move to the right	PVC piping	PVC piping
⌐	Move up	PVC piping	PVC piping
⌐	Move down	PVC piping	PVC piping

Part D: Guidelines for Multilingual Writers (ESL)

CULTURAL AND STYLISTIC COMMUNICATION ISSUES

Just as native speakers of English must learn how to communicate with non-native speakers of English in the United States and abroad, technical communicators whose first language is not English must learn how to communicate with native speakers in the United States.

In This Book

For more about communicating across cultures, see Ch. 5, p. 78.

If you want to communicate effectively with native speakers, you need to understand U.S. culture. Specifically, you need to understand how U.S. readers expect writers to select, organize, and present information and what writers expect from their readers. Beyond readers and writers, speakers and listeners in the United States also have expectations. Indeed, cultural values affect all styles of communication. Of course, no two communicators are exactly alike. Still, if you know how culture affects Western communicators in general, you can analyze your communication task and communicate effectively.

Readers, writers, speakers, and listeners in the United States value the following qualities:

- *Directness.* U.S. audiences expect writers and speakers to get to the point quickly and to communicate information clearly. So when you write a claim letter, for example, clearly state what you want the individual you are addressing to do to correct a situation. Related to directness is *task orientation.* Do not begin a letter with a comment about the weather or family. Instead, communicate immediately about business.

In This Book

For more about claim letters, see Ch. 14, p. 349.

- *Independence.* In spite of the increasingly significant role of collaborative writing, U.S. audiences still value individualism and people who can work independently. Therefore, when you write a letter to an individual in an organization, be aware that the recipient sees you as one person, too, not merely as a mouthpiece of an organization. Use the pronoun *I* rather than *we.*

In This Book

For more about writing collaboratively, see Ch. 4.

- *Time consciousness.* Try to meet deadlines and to arrive on time for appointments. U.S. audiences consider slowness in responding to issues a sign of disrespect.

To become familiar with the U.S. style of communication, study documents, talk to people, and ask for feedback from U.S. readers and listeners. Following are some specific guidelines for applying the preceding general cultural values as you listen, speak, and write to U.S. audiences.

Listening

Speakers in the United States expect you, their audience, to listen actively. They assume that you will ask questions and challenge their points—but not interrupt them unless you are invited to do so. To become a better listener, try the following strategies:

- *Look at the speaker's eyes, or at least at the speaker's face.* Lean forward or nod your head to encourage the speaker. If you avoid looking at the speaker, he or she may think that you are not interested in the message.

- *Do not interrupt the speaker.* Interrupting shows the speaker that you do not value his or her opinion. Give the speaker enough time to complete his or her presentation.

- *Do not become indignant.* Be prepared to hear speakers state clearly what they like and dislike, often without considering other people's personal feelings.

- *Assume that the speaker values your opinion.* Form responses and, at the appropriate time, express your opinions openly.

- *Ask questions.* If you have questions, ask them. If you do not ask questions, the speaker may assume that you not only understand but also agree with the message of the presentation. It is altogether appropriate to ask questions such as these: "Do you mean ...?" "Did I understand you to say ...?" "Would you repeat ...?"

Speaking

As suggested in Chapter 21, U.S. audiences expect speakers to control the situation, keep the audience interested, address listeners directly, and speak with authority. Do not apologize for problems in your content or your fluency. Doing so may diminish your credibility and make the audience think you are wasting their time. To become a better speaker, try the following strategies:

- *Start and end your presentation on time.* If you start late or speak too long, you send the message "Your time is less valuable than mine."

- *Make eye contact and smile.* If you make eye contact with people, you look friendly and confident, and you send the message "You are important."

- *Speak up.* If you speak with your head bowed or in too low a voice, audience members may become distracted or think you are hiding something.

- *Make friendly gestures.* Invite the audience to ask questions. It is appropriate to say "Please feel free to ask me questions at any time" or "If you have questions, I'd be glad to answer them at the conclusion of my talk." Also, try to break the invisible barrier between you and your audience. For example, step away from behind the podium or move toward the audience.

Writing

In the United States, technical writers generally state their claims up front and clearly. They support their claims by presenting the most important information first and by using numerical data. To become a better writer, try the following strategies:

- *State your claims directly.* In most cases, state your purpose directly in the first paragraph of a memo or letter, as well as at the start of any other document and at the start of each section within it.

- *Avoid digressions.* Focus on your task. If a piece of information is interesting but does not help you make your point, do not include it.

- *Move from one point to the next systematically.* Use an appropriate pattern of organization, and use transitions and other devices to ensure a smooth flow within a paragraph and between paragraphs.

- *Use logic and technical information rather than allusion, metaphor, or emotion.* Western readers are persuaded more by numerical data—that is, by statistics, be they raw scores, dollar amounts, or percentages—than by an argument from authority.

- *Use an appropriate level of formality.* Consider your audience, your subject, and your purpose. In the United States, e-mails and memos tend to be less formal than reports and proposals. In most cases, avoid overly formal words, such as *pursuant, aforementioned,* and *heretofore,* in favor of clear, concise writing.

In This Book

For more about claims, see Ch. 8, p. 158. For more about introductions, see Ch. 18, p. 464.

In This Book

For more about organizing information, see Ch. 7. For more about writing coherent paragraphs, see Ch. 10.

In This Book

For more about persuasion, see Ch. 8.

In This Book

For more about choosing the right words and phrases, see Ch. 11, p. 235.

SENTENCE-LEVEL ISSUES

sent   Basic Characteristics of a Sentence

A sentence has five characteristics.

1. It starts with an uppercase letter and ends with a period, a question mark, or (rarely) an exclamation point attached to the final word.

   I have a friend.

   Do you have a friend?

   I asked, "Do you have a friend?"

   The question mark is part of the quoted question.

   Did you write, "Ode to My Friend"?

   The question mark is part of the question, not part of the title in quotation marks.

   Yes! You are my best friend!

2. **It has a subject, usually a noun. The subject performs the action(s) mentioned in the sentence or exists in a certain condition according to the rest of the sentence.**

SUBJECT

My friend speaks five languages fluently.

The subject performs an action—*speaks*.

SUBJECT

My friend is fluent in five languages.

The subject exists as (*is*) a fluent person.

3. **It has a verb, which tells what the subject does or states its existence.**

VERB

My friend speaks five languages fluently.

The verb tells what the subject does.

VERB

My friend is fluent in five languages.

The verb states that the subject exists.

4. **It has a standard word order.**

The most common sequence in English is subject-verb-object:

SUBJECT   VERB   OBJECT

We hired a consulting firm.

You can add information to the start of the sentence:

Yesterday we hired a consulting firm.

or to the end of the sentence:

Yesterday we hired a consulting firm: *Sanderson & Associates*.

or in the middle:

Yesterday we hired *the city's most prestigious* consulting firm: Sanderson & Associates.

In fact, any element of a sentence can be expanded.

In This Book

For more about subordinating words and phrases, see p. 658.

5. **It has an independent clause (a subject and verb that can stand alone— that is, a clause that does not begin with a subordinating word or phrase).**

The following is a sentence:

SUBJECT VERB

The pump failed because of improper maintenance.

The following is also a sentence:

SUBJECT VERB

The pump failed.

But the following is not a sentence because it lacks a subject with a verb and because it begins with a subordinating phrase:

Because of improper maintenance.

An independent clause is required to complete this sentence:

Because of improper maintenance, the pump failed.

coor   Linking Ideas by Coordination

One way to connect ideas in a sentence is by coordination. Coordination means that ideas in the sentence are roughly equal in importance. There are three main ways to coordinate ideas.

1. Use a semicolon (;) to coordinate ideas that are independent clauses:

    The information for bid was published last week; the proposal is due in less than a month.

2. Use a comma and a coordinating conjunction (*and*, *but*, *or*, *nor*, *so*, *for*, or *yet*) to coordinate two independent clauses:

    The information for bid was published last week, but the proposal is due in less than a month.

    In this example, *but* clarifies the relationship between the two clauses: the writer hasn't been given enough time to write the proposal.

3. Use transitional words and phrases to coordinate two independent clauses. You can end the first independent clause with a semicolon or a period. If you use a period, begin the transitional word or phrase with a capital letter.

    The Pentium III chip has already been replaced; *as a result*, it is hard to find a Pentium III in a new computer.

    The Pentium III chip has already been replaced. *As a result*, it is hard to find a Pentium III in a new computer.

 In This Book

For more about transitional words and phrases, see Ch. 10, p. 214.

ESL
vb

| **sub** | **Linking Ideas by Subordination** |

Two ideas can also be linked by subordination—that is, by deemphasizing one of them. There are two basic methods of subordination.

1. **Use a subordinating word or phrase to turn one idea into a subordinate clause.**

after	because	since	until	while
although	before	so that	when	who
as	even though	that	where	whom
as if	if	unless	which	whose

Start with two independent clauses:

> The bridge was completed last year. The bridge already needs repairs.

Then choose a subordinating word and combine the clauses:

> *Although* the bridge was completed last year, it already needs repairs.

> *Although* subordinates the first clause, leaving *it already needs repairs* as the independent clause.

Note that a writer could reverse the order of the ideas:

> The bridge already needs repairs *even though* it was completed last year.

Another way to subordinate one idea is to turn it into a nonrestrictive clause using the subordinating word *which*:

In This Book

For more about restrictive and nonrestrictive modifiers, see Ch. 11, p. 233.

> The bridge, which was completed last year, already needs repairs.

> This version deemphasizes *was completed last year* by turning it into a nonrestrictive clause and emphasizes *already needs repairs* by leaving it as the independent clause.

2. **Turn one of the ideas into a phrase modifying the other.**

> Completed last year, the bridge already needs repairs.

> *Completed last year* was turned into a phrase by dropping the subject and verb from the independent clause. Here the phrase is used to modify *the bridge*.

| **vb** | **Verb Tenses** |

In This Book

For more about verb tenses, see Appendix, Part C, p. 633.

1. **SIMPLE: An action or state that was, is, or will be static or definite**

   SIMPLE PAST (*verb* + ed [or irregular past])

   > Yesterday we *subscribed* to a new ecology journal.

The action of subscribing happened at a specific time. The action of subscribing definitively happened regardless of what happens today or tomorrow.

SIMPLE PRESENT (VERB or VERB + s)

We *subscribe* to three ecology journals every year.

The action of subscribing never changes; it's regular, definite.

SIMPLE FUTURE (*will* + VERB or simple present of *be* + *going to* + VERB)

We *will subscribe* to the new ecology journal next year.

We *are going to subscribe* to the new ecology journal next year.

The action of subscribing next year (a specific time) will not change; it is definite.

2. PROGRESSIVE: An action in progress (continuing) at a known time

PAST PROGRESSIVE (simple past of *be* + VERB + *ing*)

We *were updating* our directory when the power failure occurred.

The action of updating was in progress at a known time in the past.

PRESENT PROGRESSIVE (simple present of *be* + VERB + *ing*)

We *are updating* our directory now.

The action of updating is in progress at a known time, this moment.

FUTURE PROGRESSIVE (simple future of *be* + VERB + *ing*)

We *will be updating* our directory tomorrow when you arrive.

The action of updating will be in progress at a known time in the future.

3. PERFECT: An action occurring (sometimes completed) at some indefinite time before a definite time

PAST PERFECT (simple past of *have* + VERB + *ed* [or irregular past])

We *had* already *written* the proposal when we got your call.

The action of writing began and ended at some indefinite past time before a definite past time.

PRESENT PERFECT (simple present of *have* + VERB + *ed* [or irregular past])

We *have written* the proposal and are proud to hand it to you.

The action of writing began at some indefinite past time and is being commented on in the present, a definite time.

FUTURE PERFECT (simple future of *have* + VERB + *ed* [or irregular past])

We *will have written* the proposal by the time you arrive.

The action of writing will have begun and ended at some indefinite time in the future before the definite time in the future when you arrive.

4. PERFECT PROGRESSIVE: An action in progress (continuing) until a known time

PAST PERFECT PROGRESSIVE (simple past of *have* + *been* + *verb* + *ing*)

We *had been working* on the reorganization when the news of the merger became public.

The action of working continued until a known time in the past.

PRESENT PERFECT PROGRESSIVE (simple present of *have* + *been* + *verb* + *ing*)

We *have been working* on the reorganization for over a year.

The action of working began at some indefinite past time and is continuing in the present, when it is being commented on.

FUTURE PERFECT PROGRESSIVE (simple future of *have* + *been* + *verb* + *ing*)

We *will have been working* on the reorganization for over a year by the time you become CEO.

In the future, the action of working will have been continuing before another future action.

-ing   Forming Verbs with *-ing*

English uses the *-ing* form of verbs in three major ways.

1. As part of a progressive or perfect progressive verb (see numbers 2 and 4 in the previous section):

   We are *shipping* the materials by UPS.

   We have been *waiting* for approval since January.

2. As a present participle, which functions as an adjective either by itself:

   the *leaking* pipe

   or as part of a participial phrase:

   Analyzing the sample, we discovered two anomalies.

   The sample *containing* the anomalies appears on Slide 14.

3. As a gerund, which functions as a noun either by itself:

   Writing is the best way to learn to write.

   or as part of a gerund phrase:

   The designer tried *inserting* the graphics by hand.

inf   Infinitives

Infinitives consist of the word *to* plus the base form of the verb (*to write, to understand*). An infinitive can be used in three main ways.

1. **As a noun:**

    The editor's goal for the next year is *to publish* the journal on schedule.

2. **As an adjective:**

    The company requested the right *to subcontract* the project.

3. **As an adverb:**

    We established the schedule ahead of time *to prevent* the kind of mistake we made last time.

help   Helping Verbs and Main Verbs

Instead of a one-word verb, many English sentences contain a *verb phrase*.

The system *meets* code.

This sentence has a one-word verb, *meets*.

The new system *must meet* all applicable codes.

This sentence has a two-word verb phrase, *must meet*.

The old system *must have met* all applicable codes.

This sentence has a three-word verb phrase, *must have met*.

In a verb phrase, the verb that carries the main meaning is called the *main verb*. The other words in the verb phrase are called *helping verbs*. The following discussion explains four categories of helping verbs.

1. **Modals**
    There are nine modal verbs: *can, could, may, might, must, shall, should, will,* and *would*. After a modal verb, use the base form of the verb (the form of the verb used after *to* in the infinitive).

    BASE FORM

    The system *must meet* all applicable codes.

2. **Forms of *do***
    After a helping verb that is a form of *do—do, does,* or *did*—use the base form of the verb.

BASE FORM

↓

Do we *need* to include the figures for the recovery rate?

3. Forms of *have* plus the past participle

To form one of the perfect tenses (past, present, or future), use a form of *have* as the helping verb plus the past participle of the verb (usually the *-ed* form of the verb or the irregular past).

PAST PERFECT

We *had written* the proposal before learning of the new RFP.

PRESENT PERFECT

We *have written* the proposal according to the instructions in the RFP.

FUTURE PERFECT

We *will have written* the proposal by the end of the week.

 In This Book

For more about active and passive voice, see Ch. 11, p. 236.

4. Forms of *be*

To describe an action in progress, use a form of *be* (*be, am, is, are, was, were, being, been*) as the helping verb and the present participle (the *-ing* form of the verb).

We *are testing* the new graphics tablet.

The company *is considering* flextime.

To create the passive voice, use a form of *be* and the past participle.

The piping *was installed* by the plumbing contractor.

agr s/v   Agreement of Subject and Verb

The subject and the verb in a clause or sentence must agree in number. That is, if the noun is singular, the verb must be singular.

The *valve needs* replacement.

Note the *s* that marks a singular present-tense verb.

If the noun is plural, the verb must be plural.

The *valves need* replacement.

Note the *s* that marks a plural noun.

Here are additional examples of subject-verb agreement.

The new *valve is* installed according to the manufacturer's specifications.

The new *valves are* installed according to the manufacturer's specifications.

When you edit your document for subject-verb agreement, keep in mind the following guidelines.

1. **Make sure the subject and verb agree when information comes between the subject and the verb.**

   The *result* of the tests *is* included in Appendix C.

   The *results* of the test *are* included in Appendix C.

2. **Certain pronouns and quantifiers always require singular verbs. Pronouns that end in -*body* or -*one*—such as *everyone*, *everybody*, *someone*, *somebody*, *anyone*, *anybody*, *no one*, and *nobody*—are singular. In addition, quantifiers such as *something, each*, and *every* are singular.**

   SINGULAR   *Everybody is* invited to the preproposal meeting.

   SINGULAR   *Each* of the members *is* asked to submit billable hours by the end of the month.

3. **When the clause or sentence contains a compound subject, the verb must be plural.**

   COMPOUND
   SUBJECT   *The contractor and the subcontractor want* to meet to resolve the difficulties.

4. **When a relative pronoun such as *who*, *that*, or *which* begins a clause, make sure the verb agrees in number with the noun that the relative pronoun refers to.**

   The *numbers* that *are* used in the formula do not agree with the ones we were given at the site.

   Numbers is plural, so the verb in the *that* clause (*are*) is also plural.

   The *number* that *is* used in the formula does not agree with the one we were given at the site.

   Number is singular, so the verb in the *that* clause (*is*) is also singular.

cond   Conditions

The word *if* in English can introduce four main types of conditions.

1. **Conditions of fact**
   Conditions of fact usually—but not always—call for the same verb tense in both clauses. In most cases, use a form of the present tense:

   If rats *eat* as much as they want, they *become* obese.

   If you *see* "Unrecoverable Application Error," the program *has crashed*.

2. Future prediction

For prediction, use the present tense in the *if* clause. Use a modal (*can, could, may, might, must, shall, should, will,* or *would*) plus the base form of the verb in the independent clause.

> If we *win* this contract, we *will need* to add three more engineers.

> If this weather *keeps* up, we *may postpone* the launch.

3. Present-future speculation

The present-future speculation usage suggests a condition contrary to fact. Use *were* in the *if* clause if the verb is *be*; use the simple past in the *if* clause if it contains another verb. Use a modal plus the base form of the verb in the independent clause.

> If I *were* president of the company, I *would be* much more aggressive.

> If I *took* charge of the company, I *would be* much more aggressive.

> The example sentences imply that you are not president of the company and have not taken charge of it.

The past tense in the example *if* clauses shows distance from reality, not distance in time.

4. Past speculation

Use the past perfect in the *if* clause. Use a modal plus the present perfect in the independent clause.

> If we *had won* this contract, we *would have needed* to add three engineers.

> This sentence implies that the condition is contrary to fact: the contract wasn't won, so the engineers were not needed.

art   Articles

Few aspects of English can be as frustrating to the nonnative speaker of English as the correct usage of the articles *a, an,* and *the* before nouns. Although there are a few rules that you should try to learn, remember that there are many exceptions and special cases.

Here is an outline to help you look at nouns and decide whether they may or must take an article—or not. As you will see, to make the decision about an article, you must determine

- whether a noun is proper or common
- for a common noun, whether it is countable or uncountable
- for a countable common noun, whether it is specific or nonspecific, and if it is nonspecific, whether it is singular or plural
- for an uncountable common noun, whether it is specific or nonspecific

Specific in this context means that the writer and the reader can both identify the noun—"which one" it is.

1. Proper nouns

Singular proper nouns usually take no article but occasionally do take *a* or *an*:

> James Smith, but not John Smith, contributed to the fund last year.
> *A* Smith will contribute to the fund this year.

The speaker does not know which Smith will make the contribution, so an article is necessary. Assuming that there is only one person with the name *Quitkin*, the sentence "Quitkin will contribute to the fund this year" is clear, so the proper noun takes no article.

Plural proper nouns often, but not always, take *the*:

> *The* Smiths have contributed for the past 10 years.

> There are Smiths on the class roster again this year.

2. Countable common nouns

Singular and plural specific countable common nouns take *the*:

> *The* microscope is brand-new.

> *The* microscopes are brand-new.

Singular nonspecific countable common nouns take *a* or *an*:

> *A* microscope will be available soon.

> *An* electron is missing.

Plural nonspecific countable common nouns take no article but must have a plural ending:

> Microscopes must be available for all students.

3. Uncountable common nouns

Specific uncountable common nouns take *the*:

> *The* research started by Dr. Quitkin will continue.

> The subject under discussion is specific research.

Nonspecific uncountable common nouns generally take no article:

> Research is always critical.

> The subject under discussion is nonspecific—that is, research in general.

adj Adjectives

Adjectives are modifiers. They modify—that is, describe—nouns and pronouns. Keep in mind three main points about adjectives in English.

1. Adjectives do not take a plural form.

> a *complex* project

> three *complex* projects

2. Adjectives can be placed either before the nouns they modify or after linking verbs.

> The *critical* need is to reduce the drag coefficient.
>
> The need to reduce the drag coefficient is *critical*.

3. Adjectives of one or two syllables take special endings to create the comparative and superlative forms.

Positive	Comparative	Superlative
big	bigger	biggest
heavy	heavier	heaviest

4. Adjectives of three or more syllables take the word *more* for the comparative form and the words *the most* for the superlative form.

Positive	Comparative	Superlative
qualified	more qualified	the most qualified
feasible	more feasible	the most feasible

adv   Adverbs

Like adjectives, adverbs are modifiers. They modify—that is, describe—verbs, adjectives, and other adverbs. Their placement in the sentence is somewhat more complex than the placement of adjectives. Remember five points about adverbs.

1. Adverbs can modify verbs.

> Management terminated the project *reluctantly*.

2. Adverbs can modify adjectives.

> The executive summary was *conspicuously* absent.

3. Adverbs can modify other adverbs.

> The project is going *very* well.

4. Adverbs that describe how an action takes place can appear in different locations in the sentence—at the beginning of a clause, at the end of a clause, right before a one-word verb, and between a helping verb and a main verb.

> *Carefully* the inspector examined the welds.
>
> The inspector examined the welds *carefully*.
>
> The inspector *carefully* examined the welds.
>
> The inspector was *carefully* examining the welds.

NOTE: The adverb should not be placed between the verb and the direct object.

INCORRECT   The inspector examined *carefully* the welds.

5. Adverbs that describe the whole sentence can also appear in different locations in the sentence—at the beginning of a sentence, before an adjective, and at the end of a sentence.

> *Apparently*, the inspection was successful.
>
> The inspection was *apparently* successful.
>
> The inspection was successful, *apparently*.

omit   Omitted Words

Except for imperative sentences, in which the subject *you* is understood (*Get the correct figures*), all sentences in English require a subject.

> *The company* has a policy on conflict of interest.

Do not omit the expletive *there* or *it*.

INCORRECT   Are four reasons for us to pursue this issue.

CORRECT   *There* are four reasons for us to pursue this issue.

INCORRECT   Is important that we seek his advice.

CORRECT   *It* is important that we seek his advice.

 In This Book

For more about expletives, see Ch. 11, p. 230.

rep   Repeated Words

1. Do not repeat the subject of a sentence.

INCORRECT   The company we are buying from *it* does not permit us to change our order.

CORRECT   The company we are buying from does not permit us to change our order.

2. In an adjective clause, do not repeat an object.

INCORRECT   The technical communicator does not use the same software that we were writing in *it*.

CORRECT   The technical communicator does not use the same software that we were writing in.

3. In an adjective clause, do not use a second adverb.

INCORRECT   The lab where we did the testing *there* is an excellent facility.

CORRECT   The lab where we did the testing is an excellent facility.

References

Chapter 1   Introduction to Technical Communication

Center for Plain Language. (2005). Plain language. Retrieved May 10, 2005, from http://www.centerforplainlanguage.org/plainlang.htm

Dell Inc. (2005). Dell Inc. home page. Retrieved May 10, 2005, from http://www.dell.com

Galvin, T. (2001). 2001 Industry report. Retrieved February 22, 2002, from http://www.trainingmag.com/training/images/pdf/2001_industry_report.pdf

Michaels, Bud. (2003, March 11). *Next generation customer service: Keeping up with customer demand in telecommunications* (DM Direct Special Report). Retrieved November 17, 2004, from http://www.dmreview.com/editorial/newsletter_article.cfm?nl=bireport&articleId=6455&issue=321

Plain English Network. (2002). Writing and oral communication skills: Career-boosting assets. Retrieved August 5, 2002, from http://www.plainlanguage.gov/Summit/writing.htm

Technical Communication. (1990). *37*(4), 385.

Xerox Corporation. (2000). *The document centre at a glance.* Webster, NY: Xerox Corporation.

Chapter 2   Understanding Ethical and Legal Considerations

Donaldson, T. (1991). *The ethics of international business.* New York: Oxford University Press.

Helyar, P. S. (1992). Products liability: Meeting legal standards for adequate instructions. *Journal of Technical Writing and Communication, 22*(2), 125–147.

Institute of Electrical and Electronics Engineers Inc. (2004). IEEE code of ethics. Retrieved November 19, 2004, from http://ieee.org/portal/site/mainsite/menuitem.818c0c39e85ef176fb2275875bac26c8/index.jsp?&pName=corp_level1&path=about/whatis&file=code.xml&xsl=generic.xsl

Murphy, P. (1995). Corporate ethics statements: Current status and future prospects. *Journal of Business Ethics 14*, 727–740.

Natural Science Industries Ltd. (2005). Rock Tumbler. Retrieved October 5, 2005, from http://www.amazon.com/exec/obidos/tg/detail/-/B00000ISUU/104-7612043-2382338?v=glance&s=imaginarium&me=A1PA6795UKMFR9&vi=pictures&img=14#

Texas Instruments. (2004). TI ethics quick test. Retrieved November 19, 2004, from http://www.ti.com/corp/docs/company/citizen/ethics/quicktest.shtml

Velasquez, M. G. (2002). *Business ethics: Concepts and cases* (5th ed.). Upper Saddle River, NJ: Prentice Hall.

Chapter 3 Understanding the Writing Process

Microsoft Corporation. (2004). Memo, professional theme. Retrieved November 23, 2004, from http://office.microsoft.com/en-us/templates/TC010129271033.aspx?CategoryID=CT011389821033

Chapter 4   Writing Collaboratively

ABET Inc. (2003). Criteria for accrediting engineering programs (p. 2). Retrieved November 24, 2004, from http://www.abet.org/images/Criteria/E001%202004-05%20EAC%20Criteria%2011-20-03.pdf

Aethra Inc. (2005). Video conferencing. Retrieved May 16, 2005, from http://www.aethra.com/worldwide/proddoc.asp?IDProd=74&IDT=10&M=150

Borisoff, D., & Merrill, L. (1987). Teaching the college course in gender differences as barriers to conflict resolution. In L. B. Nadler, M. K. Nadler, & W. R. Todd-Mancillas (Eds.), *Advances in gender and communication research* (pp. 351–361). Lanham, MD: University Press of America.

Chodorow, N. (1978). *The reproduction of mothering: Psychoanalysis and the sociology of gender.* Berkeley: University of California Press.

Duin, A. H., Jorn, L. A., & DeBower, M. S. (1991). Collaborative writing—Courseware and telecommunications. In M. M. Lay & W. M. Karis (Eds.), *Collaborative writing in industry: Investigations in theory and practice* (pp. 146–169). Amityville, NY: Baywood.

Lustig, M. W., & Koester, J. (1999). *Intercultural competence.* New York: HarperCollins.

Matson, R. (1996, April). The seven sins of deadly meetings. Retrieved July 22, 1999, from www.fastcompany.com/online/02/meetings.html

McMillan, J. R., Clifton, A. K., McGrath, D., & Gale, W. S. (1977). Women's language: Uncertainty or interpersonal sensitivity and emotionality? *Sex Roles, 3,* 545–549.

Tannen, D. (1990). *You just don't understand.* New York: William Morrow.

Chapter 5   Analyzing Your Audience and Purpose

Anderson School, UCLA. (2002). Japanese communication styles. Retrieved January 22, 2002, from http://www.anderson.ucla.edu/research/japan/mainfrm.htm

Bathon, G. (1999, May). Eat the way your mama taught you. *Intercom,* 22–24.

Bell, A. H. (1992). *Business communication: Toward 2000.* Cincinnati, OH: South-Western.

Bosley, D. S. (1999). Visual elements in cross-cultural technical communication: Recognition and comprehension as a function of cultural conventions. In C. R. Lovitt & D. Goswami (Eds.), *Exploring the rhetoric of international professional communication: An agenda for teachers and researchers* (pp. 253–276). Amityville, NY: Baywood.

Enäjärvi, M. (2004). The Director General's report. *National Board of Patents and Registration of Finland annual report 2003.* Retrieved November 29, 2004, from http://www.prh.fi/stc/attachments/prh_vk2003_en.pdf

Ferraro, G. P. (1990). *The cultural dimensions of international business.* Englewood Cliffs, NJ: Prentice Hall.

Heilemann, J. (2001, December 2). Reinventing the wheel [Electronic version]. *Time.* Retrieved January 22, 2002, from http://www.time.com/time/business/article/0,8599,186660,00.html

Hoft, N. L. (1995). *International technical communication: How to export information about high technology.* New York: Wiley.

Jain, S. J. S. (2002). Disaster management during super cyclone 1999 in Orissa—A case study of railways. South Eastern Railway (India). Retrieved January 22, 2002, from http://ce_ser.tripod.com/orissa.html

Kamen, D., Ambrogi, R. R., Duggan, R. J., Heinzmann, R. K., Key, B. R., Skoskiewicz, A., et al. (1999). United States Patent 5,971,091. Retrieved January 22, 2002, from http://www.uspto.gov

Limaye, M. R., & Victor, D. A. (1991). Cross-cultural business communication research: State of the art and hypotheses for the 1990s. *Journal of Business Communication, 28*(3), 277–299.

Lovitt, C. R. (1999). Introduction: Rethinking the role of culture in international professional communication. In C. R. Lovitt & D. Goswami (Eds.), *Exploring the rhetoric of international professional communication: An agenda for teachers and researchers* (pp. 1–13). Amityville, NY: Baywood.

Lustig, M. W., & Koester, J. (2006). *Intercultural competence* (5th ed.). New York: HarperCollins.

Norton, J. (2002, January 14). Tampa post office to test Segway™ human transporter. Retrieved January 22, 2002, from http://www.segway.com/consumer/team/press_releases/pr_011402.html

Segway LLC. (2005). Segway LLC introduces 2005 product line with more power, more attitude and more options. Retrieved May 18, 2005, from http://www.segway.com/aboutus/press_releases/pr_030105c.html

Stetson, E. (2005, March 3). Segway rolling out three new models. Retrieved May 18, 2005, from http://abcnews.go.com/Technology/wireStory?id=547289

Sugimoto, Toshiharu. (2004). Message from the president. FDK Corporation. Retrieved November 29, 2004, from http://www.fdk.co.jp/company_e/message-e.html

Tebeaux, E., & L. Driskill. (1999). Culture and the shape of rhetoric: Protocols of international document design. In C. R. Lovitt & D. Goswami (Eds.), *Exploring the rhetoric of international professional communication: An agenda for teachers and researchers* (pp. 211–251). Amityville, NY: Baywood.

U.S. Census Bureau. (2004). *Statistical abstract of the United States: 2004–2005.* Washington, DC: U.S. Government Printing Office.

Chapter 6   Researching Your Subject

Bowman, J. P. (1999). Human relations: Conversations and interviews. *Business communication: Managing information and relationships.* Retrieved July 22, 1999, from http://spider.hcob.wmich.edu/bis/faculty/bowman/dyads.html

Cohen, L. (2002). Conducting research on the Internet. Retrieved February 13, 2002, from http://library.albany.edu/internet/research.html

CSA Illumina. (2005). *Linguistics and language behavior abstracts.* Retrieved July 13, 2005, from http://www.iiisci.org/Journal/sci/Abstract.asp?var=&id=P394107

Insurance Institute for Highway Safety, Highway Loss Data Institute. (2005). Q&A: Teenagers: General. Retrieved July 13, 2005, from http://www.hwysafety.org/safety_facts/qanda/teens.htm

Lovgren, J. (2000). Achieving performance-centered design. Reisman Consulting Group. Retrieved February 21, 2002, from http://www.reisman-consulting.com/pages/a-Perform.html

McComb, G. (1991). *Troubleshooting and repairing VCRs* (2nd ed.). Blue Ridge Summit, PA: TAB/McGraw-Hill.

Zakon, R. H. (2002). Hobbes' Internet timeline 5.5. Retrieved February 18, 2002, from http://www.zakon.org/robert/internet/timeline/

Chapter 7   Organizing Your Information

Alred, G. J., Brusaw, C. T., & Oliu, W. E. (2006). *Handbook of technical writing* (8th ed.). Boston: Bedford/St. Martin's.

Bergman, Michael K. (2004). The deep Web: White paper. BrightPlanet Corporation. Retrieved November 30, 2004, from http://www.brightplanet.com/technology/deepweb.asp

Canon U.S.A. Inc. (2005). PowerShot A310 kit contents. Retrieved June 13, 2005, from http://consumer.usa.canon.com/ir/controller?act=BoxContentsAct&fcategoryid=145&modelid=9829

Invisalign. (2005). Is Invisalign right for me? Retrieved June 13, 2005, from http://www.invisalign.com/generalapp/us/en/for/compare.jsp

Metropolitan Museum of Art. (2005). Timeline of art history. Retrieved June 13, 2005, from http://www.metmuseum.org/toah/hm/09/hm09.htm

National Transportation Safety Board. (2000). Putting children first. Retrieved June 25, 2001, from http://www.ntsb.gov/Publictn/2000/SR0002.pdf

United Kingdom Department of Trade and Industry. (2003). Our energy future: Creating a low carbon economy. Retrieved December 9, 2004, from http://www.dti.gov.uk/energy/whitepaper/wp_text.pdf

Chapter 8   Communicating Persuasively

AT&T Foundation. (2004). AT&T Foundation programs. Retrieved November 30, 2004, from http://www.att.com/foundation/programs/community.html

Bowman, J. P. (1999). Understanding persuasion. *Business communication: Managing information and relationships.* Retrieved July 22, 1999, from http://spider.hcob.wmich.edu/bis/faculty/bowman/persuade.html

Dell Inc. (2005). New DJ 20 and Pocket DJ from Dell. Retrieved June 14, 2005, from http://www1.us.dell.com/content/products/category.aspx/dj?c=us&cs=19&l=en&s=dhs&~ck=mn

Hewlett Packard Development Company LP. (2004). Use color to grow your business (p. 4). Retrieved November 30, 2004, from http://h71028.www7.hp.com/ERC/downloads/HP%20SMB%20WP%20final%20print.pdf

Honeywell International Inc. (2005). What makes A-410A a better refrigerant. Retrieved June 14, 2005, from http://www.410a.com/about/index.html

Insurance Institute for Highway Safety. (2005). Chevrolet Cobalt tested with optional side airbags. Retrieved June 14, 2005, from http://www.hwysafety.org/vehicle_ratings/ce/html/side/s0501.htm

KentuckyFriedCruelty.com. (2005). Emmylou Harris steers motorists away from KFC. Retrieved June 13, 2005, from http://www.kentuckyfriedcruelty.com/EmmyLouHarris.asp

Mayberry, K. J. (2002). *For argument's sake: A guide to writing effective arguments* (4th ed.). New York: Longman.

Microsoft Corporation. (2005). Employee profile: Jayendran. Retrieved June 14, 2005, from http://members.microsoft.com/careers/epdb/profileDetailPage.aspx?profileID=41

O'Reilly, T. (2002). Piracy is progressive taxation, and other thoughts on the evolution of online distribution. Retrieved July 20, 2005, from http://www.openp2p.com/lpt/a/3015

Princess Cruises. (2004). *South America 2004/2005* (p. 25). Santa Clarita, CA: Author.

Chapter 9   Drafting and Revising Definitions and Descriptions

Brain, M. (2005). How computer viruses work. Retrieved June 20, 2005, from http://computer.howstuffworks.com/virus1.htm

Ford Motor Company. (2004a). Ford Escape Hybrid. Retrieved December 17, 2004, from http://www.fordvehicles.com/escapehybrid/technology/

Ford Motor Company. (2004b). Ford Escape Hybrid. Retrieved December 17, 2004, from http://www.fordvehicles.com/suvs/escapehybrid/features/specs/

Fraternity Insurance and Purchasing Group. (2003). Risk management manual (p. 45). Retrieved June 20, 2005, from http://www.fipg.org/media/FIPGRiskMgmtManual.pdf

Hewlett Packard Company. (2002). HP digital projectors xb31 & sb21 (p. 9). Retrieved September 3, 2002, from http://h200004.www2.hp.com/bc/docs/support/SupportManual/bpia6001/bpia6001.pdf

Masterson, U. O. (2001, November 20). Biometrics and the new security age. Retrieved March 11, 2002, from http://www.msnbc.com/news/654788.asp?cp1=1

Microsoft Corporation. (2005). Criminal law. Retrieved June 16, 2005, from http://encarta.msn.com/encnet/refpages/RefArticle.aspx?refid=761557653&pn=10

Petzl. (2005). *Petzl sport catalog 2005* (p. 120). Paris: Author.

Sweetman, B. (2002). Spy in the sky. *Popular Science.* Retrieved March 12, 2002, from http://www.popsci.com/popsci/aviation/article/0,12543,194509-4,00.html

University of Guelph Department of Physics. (2005). What is torque? Retrieved June 16, 2005, from http://www.physics.uoguelph.ca/tutorials/torque/Q.torque.intro108.html

U.S. Congress, Office of Technology Assessment. (1995). *Renewing our energy future* (OTA-ETI-614). Washington, DC: U.S. Government Printing Office.

U.S. Department of Agriculture. (2000). Irradiation of raw meat and poultry: Questions & answers. Retrieved September 3, 2002, from http://www.fsis.usda.gov/oa/pubs/qa_irrad.htm

U.S. Department of Energy. (2001). The Nevada 1-MW Solar Dish-Engine Project. Retrieved March 8, 2002, from http://www.energylan.sandia.gov/sunlab/PDFs/nevada.pdf

U.S. Environmental Protection Agency. (2001). Global warming. Retrieved June 25, 2001, from http://www.epa.gov/globalwarming/climate/index.html

U.S. Transportation Security Administration. (2004). Business opportunities. Retrieved December 17, 2004, from http://www.tsa.gov/public/interapp/editorial/editorial_0149.xml

Chapter 10   Writing Coherent Documents

Benson, P. (1985). Writing visually: Design considerations in technical publications. *Technical Communication, 32,* 35–39.

Cohen, S., & Grace, D. (1994). Engineers and social responsibility: An obligation to do good. *IEEE Technology and Society, 13,* 12–19.

Darling, C. (2002). Coherence: Transitions between ideas. *Guide to grammar and writing.* Retrieved March 12, 2002, from http://ccc.commnet.edu/grammar/transitions.htm

Snyder, J. D. (1993). Off-the-shelf bugs hungrily gobble our nastiest pollutants. *Smithsonian, 24,* 66+.

U.S. Agency for International Development. FY 2004 performance and accountability report. Retrieved June 21, 2005, from http://www.usaid.gov/policy/par04/performance.pdf

Chapter 11   Writing Effective Sentences

Freedman, V. A., Martin, L. G., & Schoeni, R. F. (2004). Disability in America (p. 3). Population Research Bureau. Retrieved December 22, 2004, from http://www.prb.org/Template.cfm?Section=Population_Bulletin1&template=/ContentManagement/ContentDisplay.cfm&ContentID=11671

Fuchsberg, G. (1990, December 7). Well, at least "terminated with extreme prejudice" wasn't cited. *Wall Street Journal,* p. B1.

National Science Foundation. (2002). Announcement of Fall 2002 target date for proposal submissions, Division of Physics. Retrieved July 8, 2002, from http://www.nsf.gov/pubs/2002/nsf02139/ nsf02139.txt

Snow, K. (2001). People First language. Retrieved March 19, 2002, from http://www.disabilityisnatural .com/peoplefirstlanguage.htm

Strunk, W. (1918). *The elements of style* [Electronic version]. Ithaca, NY: Privately printed. Retrieved November 1, 1999, from http://www.bartleby.com/ 141/strunk.html#13

Userlab Inc. (2004). Simplified English. Retrieved December 22, 2004, from http://www.userlab.com/ SE.html

Williams, J. (2003). *Style: Ten lessons in clarity and grace* (7th ed.). New York: Addison-Wesley Educational Publishers.

Chapter 12 Designing the Document

Biggs, J. R. (1980). *Basic typography.* New York: Watson-Guptill.

Carnegie Science Center. (n.d.). Brochure. Pittsburgh, PA: Author.

Carr, B. J., & Giddings, S. B. (2005, May). Quantum black holes. *Scientific American*, 48–55.

Clark, G., & Bower, J. L. (2002, May). Disruptive change: When trying harder is the problem. *Harvard Business Review*, 95–101.

Dell Home Systems Company (2005, October). Sales brochure. Dallas, TX: Author.

Discover (2005, February). [Letters]. *Discover*, 6.

Doyle, R. (2005, May). Measuring beauty: Life with sun, water and other natural amenities. *Scientific American*, 32.

Felker, D. B., Pickering, F., Charrow, V. R., Holland, V. M., & Redish, J. C. (1981). *Guidelines for document designers.* Washington, DC: American Institutes for Research.

General Electric. (2001). GE annual report 2000. Retrieved April 2, 2002, http://www.ge.com/ annual00/download/images/GEannual00.pdf

Gibaldi, J. (1999). *MLA handbook for writers of research papers* (5th ed.). New York: MLA.

Gilbert, C., & Bower, J. L. (2002, May). Disruptive change: When trying harder is part of the problem. *Harvard Business Review*, 95–101.

Gruber, J. (2005). *Public finance and public policy.* New York: Worth.

Haley, A. (1991). All caps: A typographic oxymoron. *U&lc, 18*(3), 14–15.

Horton, W. (1993). The almost universal language: Graphics for international documents. *Technical Communication, 40*, 682–693.

Ichimura, M. (2001). Intercultural research in page design and layout for Asian/Pacific audiences. *Proceedings of the STC's 48th Annual Conference*. Retrieved April 9, 2002, from http://www.stc.org/ proceedings/ConfProceed/2001/PDFs/STC48- 000122.pdf

Institute of Scientific and Technical Communicators. (2005, Spring). Industry news. *Communicator*, 43.

Kerman, J., & Tomlinson, G. (2004). *Listen* (brief 5th ed.). Boston: Bedford/St. Martin's.

Keyes, E. (1993). Typography, color, and information structure. *Technical Communication, 40*, 638–654.

Kittery Outlets. (2005). *Maine Kittery outlets & Kittery Trading Post.* Kittery, ME: Author.

Kostelnick, C., & Roberts, D. D. (1998). *Designing visual language: Strategies for professional communicators.* Needham Heights, MA: Allyn & Bacon.

Kuo, C. J. (2004). Free anti-virus tips and techniques. Retrieved December 24, 2004, from http://www .nai.com/common/media/vil/pdf/free_AV_tips _techniques.pdf

Micron Technology Inc. (2005). Q-flash memory: MT28F128J3, MT28F640J3, MT28F320J3 data sheet. Retrieved July 11, 2005, from http://download. micron.com/pdf/datasheets/flash/qflash/ mt28f640j.pdf

Microsoft Corporation. (2001). *Discovering Microsoft Office XP Standard and Professional Version 2002.* Redmond, WA: Author.

Museum of Contemporary Art. (2003). Brochure. Chicago: Author.

Myers, D. G. (2003). *Exploring psychology* (5th ed. in modules). New York: Worth.

National Plant Board. (1999). Safeguarding American plant resources. Retrieved November 23, 2005, from http://www.aphis.usda.gov/ppq/safeguarding/ MainReport.PDF

National Science Foundation. (2002). National Science Foundation guide to programs: FY 2001 NSF funding opportunities (p. 20). Retrieved October 18, 2002, from http://www.nsf.gov/pubs/2001/ nsf013/nsf013.pdf

Nissan North America Inc. (2004). *Nissan Murano selection guide* (p. 3).

Norman Rockwell Museum. (n.d.). Brochure. Stockbridge, MA: Author.

Poulton, E. (1968). Rate of comprehension of an existing teleprinter output and of possible alternatives. *Journal of Applied Psychology, 52*, 16–21.

Purves, W. K., Sadava, D., Orians, G. H., & Heller, H. C. (2004). *Life: The science of biology* (7th ed.). Sunderland, MA: Sinauer.

Roark, J. L., Johnson, M. P., Cohen, P. C., Stage, S., Lawson, A., & Hartmann, S. M. (2005). *The American promise: A history of the United States: Vol. 1. To 1877*. Boston: Bedford/St. Martin's.

U.S. Department of Agriculture. (2002, March 5). Thermometer usage messages and delivery mechanisms for parents of young children. Retrieved April 4, 2002, from http://www.fsis.usda.gov/oa/research/rti_thermy.pdf

U.S. Federal Reserve Board. (2002). Industrial production and capacity utilization: The 2001 annual revision. Retrieved April 4, 2002, from http://www.federalreserve.gov/pubs/bulletin/2002/0302_2nd.pdf

Valley, J. W. (2005, October). A cool early earth? *Scientific American*, 58–65.

White, J. V. (1990). *Great pages: A common-sense approach to effective desktop design*. El Segundo, CA: Serif Publishing.

Williams, G. A., & Miller, R. B. (2002, May). Change the way you persuade. *Harvard Business Review*, 65–73.

Williams, T., & Spyridakis, J. (1992). Visual discriminability of headings in text. *IEEE Transactions on Professional Communication, 35*, 64–70.

Chapter 13 Creating Graphics

Barnum, C. M., & Carliner, S. (1993). *Techniques for technical communicators*. New York: Macmillan.

Brockmann, R. J. (1990). *Writing better computer user documentation: From paper to hypertext*. New York: Wiley.

Corante. (2005, June 21). Going global: Translation. Retrieved July 5, 2005, from http://www.corante.com/goingglobal/archives/cat_translation.php

Dean, R. S., & Kulhavy, R. W. (1981). Influence of spatial organization in prose learning. *Journal of Educational Psychology, 73*, 57–64.

Dell Home Systems Company. (2005, February). Sales brochure. Dallas, TX: Author.

Gatlin, P. L. (1988). Visuals and prose in manuals: The effective combination. In *Proceedings of the 35th International Technical Communication Conference* (pp. RET 113–115). Arlington, VA: Society for Technical Communication.

Grimstead, D. (1987). Quality graphics: Writers draw the line. In *Proceedings of the 34th International Technical Communication Conference* (pp. VC 66–69). Arlington, VA: Society for Technical Communication.

Gruber, J. (2005). *Public finance and public policy*. New York: Worth.

Holmes, N., & Bagby, M. (2002). USA: An annual report. Retrieved July 11, 2002, from http://www.understandingusa.com/chaptercc=2&cs=18.html

Horton, W. (1991). *Illustrating computer documentation: The art of presenting information graphically on paper and online*. New York: Wiley.

Horton, W. (1993). The almost universal language: Graphics for international documents. *Technical Communication, 40*, 682–693.

Illinois State Board of Education. (2005). Flowchart: Making AYP in Illinois. Retrieved January 28, 2005, from http://www.isbe.net/ayp/making_ayp.htm

Levie, W. H., & Lentz, R. (1982). Effects of text illustrations: A review of research. *Journal of Educational Psychology, 73*, 195–232.

Morrison, C., & Jimmerson, W. (1989, July). Business presentations for the 1990s. *Video Manager, 4*, 18.

Myers, D. G. (2003). *Exploring psychology* (5th ed. in modules). New York: Worth.

National Aeronautics and Space Administration. (2004). International Space Station imagery. Retrieved December 28, 2004, from http://spaceflight.nasa.gov/gallery/images/station/crew=9/html/iss009e05034.html

Purves, W. K., Sadava, D., Orians, G. H., & Heller, H. C. (2004). *Life: The science of biology* (7th ed.). Sunderland, MA: Sinauer.

Software602 Inc. (2005). 602 PC Suite 4.1 user manual (p. 10). Retrieved January 21, 2005, from http://download.software602.com/pdf/pcs/4/pcs4_manual.pdf

Tufte, E. R. (1983). *The visual display of quantitative information*. Cheshire, CT: Graphics Press.

Tufte, E. R. (1999). *The visual display of quantitative information*. Adapted by Saul Greenberg. Retrieved August 2, 1999, from http://www.cpsc.ucalgary.ca/projects/grouplab/699/vis_display.html

U.S. Census Bureau. (2004). *Statistical abstract of the United States: 2004–2005* (p. 119). Retrieved

December 28, 2004, from http://www.census.gov/prod/2004pubs/04statab/health.pdf

U.S. Consumer Product Safety Commission. (1999). Your used crib could be deadly. Retrieved August 3, 1999, from http://www.cpsc.gov/cpscpub/pubs/usedcrib.pdf

White, J. V. (1984). *Using charts and graphs: 1000 ideas for visual persuasion.* New York: R. R. Bowker.

White, J. V. (1990). *Color for the electronic age.* New York: Watson-Guptill.

Zimmer, C. (2005, February). Testing Darwin. *Discover,* 29–35.

Chapter 14   Writing Letters, Memos, and E-mails

American Management Association and ePolicy Institute Research. (2005). 2004 workplace e-mail and instant messaging survey. Retrieved October 26, 2005, from http://www.epolicyinstitute.com/survey/index.html

Chapter 15   Preparing Job-Application Materials

Bowman, J. P. (2004). Selling yourself. *Business communication: Managing information and relationships.* Retrieved December 31, 2004, from http://homepages.wmich.edu/~bowman/c7bframe.html

College Entrance Examination Board National Commission on Writing. (2004). Writing skills necessary for employment, says big business. Retrieved January 18, 2005, from http://www.writingcommission.org/pr/writing_for_employ.html

Dumas, M. (2001). Résumé consultation & writing. Retrieved July 9, 2001, from http://www.distinctiveweb.com/writing.htm

Florida State University. (2004). Sample career portfolio. Retrieved December 31, 2004, from http://www.career-recruit.fsu.edu/careerportfolio/enter/output/main.html

Harcourt, J., Krizan, A. C., & Merrier, P. (1991). Teaching résumé content: Hiring officials' preferences versus college recruiters' preferences. *Business Education Forum, 45*(7), 13–17.

Isaacs, K. (2004). How to decide on résumé length. Retrieved December 30, 2004, from http://resume.monster.com/components/length/

JobWeb.com (2004). Job outlook 2005. Retrieved December 30, 2004, from http://www.jobweb.com/joboutlook/2005outlook/3a.htm

Lorenz, K. (2005). 10 new resume secrets. Retrieved July 20, 2005, from http://www.careerbuilder.com/jobseeker/careerbytes/0205resumesecrets.htm

Sahadi, J. (2004, December 9). Top 5 resume lies. CNNMoney.com. Retrieved July 20, 2005, from http://money.cnn.com/2004/11/22/pf/resume%5Flies/index.htm

Thompson, M. A. (2002). Writing your international résumé. Retrieved July 24, 2002, from http://www.jobweb.com/Resources/Library/International/Writing_Your_185_01.htm

U.S. Department of Labor. (2004, August 25). News. Document 04-1678 (p. 1). Retrieved July 20, 2005, from http://www.bls.gov/news.release/pdf/nlsoy.pdf

Vaas, L. (2002, April 29). It pays to be outstanding. *eWEEK.* Retrieved May 3, 2002, from http://www.eweek.com/article/0,3658,s=25210&a=26116,00.asp

Wait, P., & Dizard, W. P., III. (2003, July 21). False credentials, real problems [Electronic version]. *Washington Technology, 18,* 8. Retrieved July 20, 2005, from http://www.washingtontechnology.com/news/18_8/federal/21210-1.html

Chapter 16   Writing Proposals

Bethke, D., Cowles, S., Frachiseur, A., & Stoffel, J. (2004). Proposal for feasibility study on table-saw capability. Unpublished document.

CBD/FBO Online. (2004). Spring 2005 Hoedad tree planting. Retrieved January 11, 2005, from http://www.cbdweb.com/index.php/search/show/730240

Miner, L. E. (2002). A guide to proposal planning and writing. University of Vermont Office of Sponsored Projects. Retrieved July 24, 2002, from http://www.oryxpress.com/miner.htm

National Research Foundation. (2002). Innovation Fund Trust call for pre-proposals: Round 6. Retrieved July 24, 2002, from http://www.nrf.ac.za/innovationfund/

Reid, A. N. T. (2001). A practical guide for writing proposals. Retrieved April 29, 2002, from http://members.dca.net/areid/proposal.htm

SmartDraw.com. (2004). Gantt chart & timeline center. Retrieved April 30, 2005, from http://www.smartdraw.com/tutorials/gantt/tutorial1.htm#what

Thrush, E. (2000, January 20). Writing for an international audience: Part I. Communication skills. Retrieved November 5, 2002, from http://www.suite101.com/article.cfm/5381/32233

U.S. Census Bureau. (2004). *Statistical abstract of the United States: 2004–2005* (p. 310). Retrieved January 11, 2005, from http://www.census.gov/prod/2004pubs/04statab/fedgov.pdf

Chapter 17   Writing Informal Reports

Alred, G. J., Brusaw, C. T., & Oliu, W. E. (2006). *Handbook of technical writing* (8th ed.). Boston: Bedford/St. Martin's.

Bethke, D., Cowles, S., Frachiseur, A., & Stoffel, J. (2004). Progress report for feasibility study on table-saw capability. Unpublished document.

Finkelstein, L., Jr. (2000). *Pocket book of technical writing for engineers and scientists.* New York: McGraw-Hill.

Robert, S. C., Evans, W. J., Honemann, D. H., & Balch, T. J. (Eds.). (2000). *Robert's rules of order: Newly revised* (10th ed.). Cambridge, MA: Perseus Books.

Sabin, W. (1999). *Gregg reference manual* (7th ed.). Lake Forest, IL: Glencoe/McGraw-Hill.

U.S. Chemical Safety and Hazard Investigation Board. (2004). Investigation report: Dust explosion (6 killed, 38 injured). West Pharmaceutical Services, Inc., Kinston, North Carolina, January 29, 2003. Retrieved January 17, 2005, from http://www.csb.gov/completed_investigations/docs/CSB_WestReport.pdf

Walsham, G. (2001). Globalization and ICTs: Working across cultures. Judge Institute of Management Studies Research Studies in Management Studies. Retrieved November 6, 2002, from http://www.jims.cam.ac.uk/research/working_papers/abstract_01/0108.html

Chapter 18   Writing Formal Reports

Abraham, S., Evans, D. L., Veneman, A. L., & Whitman, C. T. (2002, July 8). Letter to George W. Bush, President of the United States. U.S. Department of Energy. Retrieved August 1, 2002, from http://www.energy.gov/HQPress/releases02/julpr/GreenhouseGasRegistryLetter.pdf.

Bethke, D., Cowles, S., Frachiseur, A., & Stoffel, J. (2004). Completion report for the feasibility study regarding table-saw replacement. Unpublished document.

Centers for Disease Control. (2002). Assessing health risk behaviors among young people: Youth Risk Behavior Surveillance System, at a glance 2002. Retrieved August 1, 2002, from http://www.cdc.gov/nccdphp/dash/yrbs/yrbsaag.htm

Honold, P. (1999). Learning how to use a cellular phone: Comparison between German and Chinese users. *Technical Communication 46,* 2 (195–205).

Chapter 19   Writing Instructions and Manuals

Agilent Technologies. (2002). Agilent E2929A Opt. 200 PCI-X Performance Optimizer user's guide (p. 26). Retrieved November 18, 2002, from http://cp.literature.agilent.com/litweb/pdf/5988-4907EN.pdf

Anthro Corporation. (2005a). Anthro IdeaCart assembly instructions (p. 1). Retrieved October 3, 2005, from http://www.anthro.com/assemblyinstructions/300-5055-00.pdf

Anthro Corporation. (2005b). Anthro Space Pal assembly instructions (p. 2). Retrieved September 29, 2005, from http://www.anthro.com/assemblyinstructions/300-5237-00.pdf

Apple Computer Inc. (2005). iPod Nano features guide (p. 51). Retrieved October 3, 2005, from http://manuals.info.apple.com/en/iPod_nano_Features_Guide.pdf

Canon U.S.A. Inc. (2002). MultiPASS C755 quick start guide. Retrieved November 18, 2002, from http://www.usa.canon.com/cpr/pdf/Manuals/C755_Setup.pdf

Casio Computer Company Ltd. (2005). Celvian AP-24 user's guide. Retrieved September 30, 2005, from http://ftp.casio.co.jp/pub/world_manual/emi/en/ap_24/01_e.pdf

CEMA (Conveyor Equipment Manufacturers Association). (2004). CEMA safety labels placement guidelines: Palletizers. Retrieved January 28, 2005, from http://www.cemanet.org/safety/pl1.pdf

Cormier, R. A. (1997). One last look: The final quality control review. *The Editorial Eye.* Retrieved July 21, 1997, from http://www.eeicom.com/eye/qc-lead.html

Delio, M. (2002, June 4). Read the f***ing story, then RTFM. *Wired News.* Retrieved June 6, 2002, from http://www.wired.com/news/culture/0,1284,52901,00.html

Dell Computer Corporation. (2001). *Dell™ Dimension™ L Series systems reference and troubleshooting guide.* Round Rock, TX: Author.

Dumas, J. S., & Redish, J. C. (1993). *A practical guide to usability testing.* Norwood, NJ: Ablex.

General Electric. (2003a). Installation instructions: Above the cooktop oven, JVM1600 Series (Manual 164D3370P335 49-40409 10-03 JR) (p. 6).

General Electric. (2003b). Installation instructions: Free-standing electric ranges (Manual 229C4053P545-1 31-10556-1 04-03 JR) (p. 2).

Greiner, L. (2004, August 6). Installation not always a snap. *Computer Dealer News, 20*(11), 12.

HCS LLC. (2005). HCS 2004 safety label catalog. Retrieved January 28, 2005, from http://www .safetylabel.com/catalogs/view.php?page =0&catalog=1&category=25

Jandy. (2005). Replacement kit instructions: Jandy® Never-Lube® backwash valve replacement kits. Retrieved October 3, 2005, from http://www.jandy-downloads.com/pdfs/NL_BWV_Replacement_Kit.pdf

Kantner, L. (1994). The art of managing usability tests. *IEEE Transactions on Professional Communication 37,* 143–148.

McDATA Corporation. (2004). SANavigator® topology layout customization user manual (P/N 621-000029-020 Rev A). Retrieved February 15, 2005, from http://www.mcdata.com/downloads/ tpub/umanual/layout_sanav42.pdf

Mead, J. (1998). Measuring the value added by technical documentation: A review of research and practice. *Technical Communication 45,* 353–379.

Nintendo of America Inc. (2005). Nintendo GameCube health & safety precautions manual— English. Retrieved February 15, 2005, from http://www.nintendo.com/consumer/manuals/ precautions_gcn_english.jsp

Rubin, J. (1994). *Handbook of usability testing: How to plan, design, and conduct effective tests.* New York: Wiley.

Slide-Lok Garage and Storage Cabinets. (2005). P2468 pantry cabinet assembly instructions (p. 2). Retrieved September 29, 2005, from http://www .slide-lok.com/assembly/P2468/P2468.pdf

Sun Microsystems Inc. (2005). Sun usability labs and service. Retrieved October 3, 2005, from http://www.sun.com/usability/

Toshiba America Consumer Products Inc. (2005). Toshiba owner's manual 3LCD data projector (p. 33). Retrieved February 15, 2005, from http://tacpservice .toshiba.com/ConsumerProductSupport/Manuals/ projectors/650ee.pdf

U.S. Department of Labor, Occupational Safety and Health Administration. (2000). OSHA regulations (Standards—29 CFR). Retrieved February 20, 2000, from http://www.osha-slc.gov/OshStd_toc/ OSHA_Std_toc.html

Chapter 20   Designing Web Sites

Corel Corporation. (2005). Corel Corporation Web page. Retrieved February 18, 2005, from http://www.corel.com/servlet/Satellite?pagename =Corel2/Home

Global Reach. (2004). Global Internet statistics (by language). Retrieved October 5, 2005, from http://global-reach.biz/globstats/index.php3

Google Inc. (2005a). Google Inc. fact sheet. Retrieved February 17, 2005, from http://www.google.com/ press/facts.html

Google Inc. (2005b). Google site map. Retrieved February 18, 2005, from http://www.google.com/ sitemap.html

J. Paul Getty Trust. (2005). Visit the Getty. Retrieved February 18, 2005, from http://www.getty .edu/visit/

Lynch, P. J., & Horton, S. (1997). Web style guide. Yale University. Retrieved September 12, 1999, from http://info.med.yale.edu/caim/manual/ contents.html

National Marine Fisheries Service. (2005). Home page. Retrieved September 3, 2005, from the NOAA Web site: http://www.nmfs.noaa.gov/

O'Mahoney, B. (2005). Web design issues. Retrieved February 18, 2005, from http://www.benedict .com/digital/Web/WebDesign.aspx. Website linking issues. Retrieved February 18, 2005, from http:// www.benedict.com/digital/Web/WebLinks.aspx

Palm, Inc. (2005). PalmSource home page. Retrieved February 18, 2005, from http://www.palmsource.com/

Silver Council. (2005). About us. Retrieved on February 18, 2005, from http://www.silvercouncil .org/html/default.htm

Sun Microsystems. (1999). Guide to Web style. Retrieved September 10, 1999, from http://www .sun.com/styleguide/

U.S. Copyright Office. (2005). Frequently asked questions about copyright. Retrieved February 18, 2005, from http://www.copyright.gov/help/faq/

U.S. Department of Energy, Human Genome Program. (2005). Science behind the Human

Genome Project: Presentation resources. Retrieved November 7, 2005, from http://www.ornl.gov/ sci/techresources/Human_Genome/graphics/slides/ genetalk.shtml

W3 Schools. (2005). W3 Schools home page. Retrieved October 5, 2005, from http://www.w3schools.com/

Chapter 21   Making Oral Presentations

Smith, T. C. (1991). *Making successful presentations: A self-teaching guide* (2nd ed.). New York: Wiley.

Selected Bibliography

Technical Communication

Alred, G. J., Brusaw, C. T., & Oliu, W. E. (2006). *Handbook of technical writing* (8th ed.). Boston: Bedford/St. Martin's.

Beer, D. F. (Ed.). (2003). *Writing and speaking in the technology professions: A practical guide* (2nd ed.). New York: IEEE.

Blicq, R. S., & Moretto, L. A. (2004). *Technically— Write!* (6th ed.). Upper Saddle River, NJ: IEEE.

Day, R. A., & Gastel, B. (2006). *How to write and publish a scientific paper* (6th ed.). Westport, CT: Greenwood.

Gurak, L., & Lay, M. M. (2002). *Research in technical communication.* Westport, CT: Greenwood.

Hoft, N. L. (1995). *International technical communication: How to export information about high technology.* New York: Wiley.

Pickett, N. A. (2001). *Technical English: Writing, reading, and speaking* (8th ed.). New York: Longman.

Sides, C. H. (1999). *How to write and present technical information* (3rd ed.). Phoenix, AZ: Oryx.

Ethics

Beauchamp, T. L., & Bowie, N. E. (2004). *Ethical theory and business* (7th ed.). New York: Pearson Education.

Markel, M. (2000). *Ethics and technical communication: A synthesis and critique.* Westport, CT: Greenwood.

Velasquez, M. G. (2006). *Business ethics: Concepts and cases* (6th ed.). Upper Saddle River, NJ: Prentice Hall.

Collaborative Writing

Cross, G. A. (1993). *Collaboration and conflict: A contextual exploration of group writing and positive emphasis.* Cresskill, NJ: Hampton.

Ede, L., & Lunsford, A. (1990). *Singular texts/plural authors: Perspectives on collaborative writing.* Carbondale, IL: Southern Illinois University.

Forman, J. (Ed.). (1992). *New visions of collaborative writing.* Portsmouth, NH: Boynton/Cook.

Research Techniques

Berkman, R. I. (2000). *Find it fast: How to uncover expert information on any subject* (5th ed.). New York: HarperInformation.

Gray, D. E. (2004). *Doing research in the real world.* London: Sage.

Harnack, A., & Kleppinger, E. (2000). *Online!: A reference guide to using Internet sources* (3rd ed.). Boston: Bedford/St. Martin's.

Schlein, A. M. (2002). *Find it online: The complete guide to online research* (3rd ed.). Tempe, AZ: Facts on Demand Press.

Usage and General Writing

Burchfield, R. W., & Fowler, H. W. (Eds.). (1996). *The new Fowler's dictionary of modern English usage* (3rd ed.). New York: Oxford University Press.

Maggio, R. (1997). *Talking about people: A guide to fair and accurate language.* Phoenix, AZ: Oryx.

Partridge, E. (1997). *Usage and abusage: A guide to good English.* New York: W. W. Norton.

Strunk, W., & White, E. B. (1999). *The elements of style* (4th ed.). Boston: Allyn & Bacon.

Weiss, E. H. (2005). *The elements of international English style: A guide to writing correspondence, reports, technical documents, and Internet pages for a global audience.* Armonk, NY: M. E. Sharpe.

Williams, J. (2003). *Style: Ten lessons in clarity and grace* (7th ed.). New York: Addison-Wesley Educational Publishers.

Handbooks for Grammar and Style

Hacker, D. (2005). *The Bedford handbook* (7th ed.). Boston: Bedford/St. Martin's.

Lunsford, A. A. (2003). *The St. Martin's handbook* (5th ed.). Boston: Bedford/St. Martin's.

Style Manuals

The Chicago manual of style. (2003). (15th ed.). Chicago: University of Chicago Press.

Dodd, J. S. (Ed.). (1997). *The ACS style guide: A manual for authors and editors* (2nd ed.). Washington, DC: American Chemical Society.

Gibaldi, J. (2003). *MLA handbook for writers of research papers* (6th ed.). New York: Modern Language Association of America.

Microsoft Corporation. (2004). *Microsoft manual of style for technical publications* (3rd ed.). Redmond, WA: Author.

Publication manual of the American Psychological Association. (2001). (5th ed.). Washington, DC: American Psychological Association.

Rubens, P. (2001). *Science and technical writing: A manual of style* (2nd ed.). New York: Routledge.

Style Manual Committee, Council of Biology Editors. (1994). *Scientific style and format: The CBE manual for authors, editors, and publishers* (6th ed.). Chicago: Cambridge University Press.

U.S. Government Printing Office style manual 2000. (2000). Washington, DC: U.S. Government Printing Office. http://www.access.gpo.gov/styleman/2000/browse-sm-00.html

Graphics, Design, and Web Pages

Campbell, K. S. (1995). *Coherence, continuity, and cohesion: Theoretical foundations for document design.* Hillsdale, NJ: Erlbaum.

Eccher, C. (2005). *Professional Web design: Techniques and templates* (2nd ed.). Hingham, MA: Charles River Media.

Farkas, D. K., & Farkas, J. (2002). *Principles of Web design.* New York: Longman.

Horton, W. (1991). *The icon book: Visual symbols for computer systems and documentation.* New York: Wiley.

Kosslyn, S. M. (1994). *Elements of graph design.* New York: W. H. Freeman.

Kostelnick, C., & Roberts, D. D. (1998). *Designing visual language: Strategies for professional communicators.* Needham Heights, MA: Allyn & Bacon.

Lipton, R. (2004). *Information graphics and visual clues: Communicating information through graphic design.* Gloucester, MA: Rockport Publishers.

Lupton, E. (2004). *Thinking with type: A critical guide for designers, writers, editors, and students.* New York: Princeton Architectural Press.

Nielsen, J. (2000). *Designing Web usability: The practice of simplicity.* Indianapolis, IN: New Riders.

Parker, R. C., & Berry, P. (2003). *Looking good in print* (5th ed.). Sebastopol, CA: Paraglyph.

Robbins, N. B. (2005). *Creating more effective graphs.* Hoboken, NJ: Wiley-Interscience.

Sutherland, R., & Karg, B. (2004). *Graphic designer's color handbook: Choosing and using color from concept to final output.* Gloucester, MA: Rockport Publishers.

Tufte, E. R. (1983). *The visual display of quantitative information.* Cheshire, CT: Graphics Press.

Tufte, E. R. (1990). *Envisioning information.* Cheshire, CT: Graphics Press.

Tufte, E. R. (1997). *Visualizing explanations.* Cheshire, CT: Graphics Press.

Vaughan, T. (2004). *Multimedia: Making it work* (6th ed.). New York: McGraw-Hill Technology Education.

White, J. V. (1990). *Color for the electronic age.* New York: Watson-Guptill.

Williams, R. (2004). *The non-designer's design book: Design and typographic principles for the visual novice* (2nd ed.). Berkeley, CA: Peachpit.

Williams, R., & Tollett, J. (2000). *The non-designer's Web book: An easy guide to creating, designing, and posting your own Web site* (2nd ed.). Berkeley, CA: Peachpit.

Job-Application Materials

Baron, C. L. (2004). *Designing a digital portfolio.* Indianapolis, IN: New Riders.

Bolles, R. N. (2005). *What color is your parachute 2006.* Berkeley, CA: Ten Speed Press.

Greene, D. (2005). *Get the interview every time: Fortune 500 hiring professionals' tips for writing winning résumés and cover letters.* Chicago: Dearborn Trade.

Yate, M. (2005). *Knock 'em dead 2005: The ultimate job seekers guide.* Cincinnati, OH: Adams Media.

Technical Manuals

Barker, T. (2003). *Writing software documentation: A task-oriented approach* (2nd ed.). New York: Longman.

Barnum, C. (2001). *Usability testing and research.* Boston: Allyn & Bacon.

Courage, C., & Baxter, K. (2005). *Understanding your users: A practical guide to user requirements, methods, tools, and techniques.* San Francisco: Morgan Kaufman.

Dumas, J. S., & Redish, J. C. (1993). *A practical guide to usability testing.* Norwood, NJ: Ablex.

Hackos, J. T. (1994). *Managing your documentation projects.* New York: Wiley.

Horton, W. (1994). *Designing and writing online documentation: Hypermedia for self-supporting products* (2nd ed.). New York: Wiley.

Nielsen, J., & Mack, R. L. (Eds.). (1994). *Usability inspection methods.* New York: Wiley.

Price, J., & Korman, H. (1993). *How to communicate technical information: A handbook of software and hardware documentation.* Redwood City, CA: Benjamin/Cummings.

Rubin, J. (1994). *Handbook of usability testing: How to plan, design, and conduct effective tests.* New York: Wiley.

Velotta, C. (1995). *Practical approaches to usability testing for technical documentation.* Arlington, VA: Society for Technical Communication.

Wieringa, D., Moore, C., & Barnes, V. (1998). *Procedure writing: Principles and practices* (2nd ed.). Columbus, OH: Battelle.

Woolever, K. R., & Loeb, H. M. (1998). *Writing for the computer industry.* Upper Saddle River, NJ: Prentice Hall.

Oral Presentations

D'Arcy, J. (1998). *Technically speaking: A guide for communicating complex information.* Columbus, OH: Battelle.

Gurak, L. J. (2000). *Oral presentations for technical communication.* Boston: Allyn & Bacon.

Hill, M., & Storey, A. (2000). *SpeakEasy!: Oral presentation skills in English for academic and professional use.* Hong Kong: Hong Kong University Press.

Smith, T. C. (1991). *Making successful presentations: A self-teaching guide* (2nd ed.). New York: Wiley.

Proposals

Bowman, J. P., & Branchaw, B. P. (1992). *How to write proposals that produce.* Phoenix, AZ: Oryx.

Freed, R. C., Freed, S., & Romano, J. (2003). *Writing winning business proposals: Your guide to landing the client, making the sale, persuading the boss.* New York: McGraw-Hill.

Hill, J. W., & Whalen, T. (1993). *How to create and present successful government proposals.* New York: IEEE.

Johnson-Sheehan, R. (2001). *Writing proposals: Rhetoric for managing change.* New York: Longman.

Miner, L. E., & Miner, J. T. (2003). *Proposal planning and writing* (3rd ed.). Westport, CT: Greenwood.

Pugh, D. G., & Bacon, T. R. (2005). *Powerful proposals: How to give your business the winning edge.* New York: American Management Association.

Acknowledgments (continued from page ii):

Figure 4.6: Used by permission of Aethra, Inc.

Figure 5.3: Excerpt from "Tampa Post Office Completes Limited Feasibility Test of Segway™ Human Transporter." Used by permission of Segway Inc.

Figure 5.4: Excerpt from John Heilemann, "Reinventing the Wheel" (December 2, 2001), www.time.com/time/business/article/0,8599,186660,00.html. Copyright © 2001 by Time, Inc. Reprinted by permission.

Figure 5.5: FDK Corporation, "Message from the President," www.fdk.co.jp/company_e/message-e.html. Reprinted by permission.

Figure 5.5: Excerpt from Web site of the National Board of Patents and Registration of Finland, www.prh.fi. Reprinted by permission.

Figure 5.7: Excerpt from "Segway LLC Introduces 2005 Product Line with More Power, More Attitude and More Options" (March 2005). Reprinted with the permission of Segway Inc.

Figure 5.8: Eric Stetson, "Segway Rolling Out Three New Models" (Associated Press, March 3, 2005). Copyright © 2005 by The Associated Press. Reprinted with permission.

Figure 5.8, screenshot: Reprinted with the permission of Walt Disney Internet Group.

Figure 6.4: Reprinted with the permission of CSA Illumina.

Page 111: Reprinted with the permission of the Insurance Institute for Highway Safety.

Figure 7.3: Reprinted with the permission of The Metropolitan Museum of Art, New York.

Figure 7.6: Copyright © 2005 by BrightPlanet Corp., 3510 South First Avenue Circle, Sioux Falls, SD 57105. All rights reserved.

Page 141: Reprinted with the permission of Align Technology, Inc.

Figure 7.8: Copyright © 2005 Canon U.S.A., Inc. All rights reserved.

Page 161: Reprinted with the permission of O'Reilly Media.

Figure 8.2: Reprinted with the permission of People for the Ethical Treatment of Animals (PETA).

Figure 8.3: Copyright © 2005 by Dell, Inc. All Rights Reserved.

Figure 8.4: Reprinted by permission of Princess Cruises.

Figure 8.5: Reprinted with the permission of the Insurance Institute for Highway Safety.

Figure 8.7: Reprinted with the permission of AT&T Corp.

Figure 8.8: Reprinted with the permission of Hewlett-Packard Company.

Figure 8.9: Reprinted with the permission of Honeywell International Inc.

Page 182: Marshall Brain, excerpt from "Types of Infection" from http://computer.howstuffworks.com/virus1.htm. Reprinted by permission.

Figure 9.2: Reprinted with the permission of Petzl America.

Figure 9.3: From John Brogan and S. Venkateswaran, "Diverse Choices for Hybrid and Electric Motor Vehicles," *Proceedings of the International Conference on Urban EVs* (Stockholm: Organization for Economic Cooperation and Development, May 1992). Copyright © 1992 by the Organization for Economic Cooperation and Development. Reprinted by permission.

Figure 9.5: Used by permission of Ford Motor Company.

Figure 9.6: Used by permission of Ford Motor Company.

Figure 9.7: Reprinted by permission of the Victorian Institute of Forensic Medicine.

Figure 12.1: Used by permission of Nissan North America, Inc.

Figure 12.2: Used by permission of the Carnegie Science Center, Pittsburgh, PA.

Figure 12.3: From David Myers, "Module 5: The Nature and Nurture of Behavior" in *Exploring Psychology, Fifth Edition in Modules.* Copyright © 2003. Reprinted with the permission of Worth Publishers, Inc.

Figure 12.4: From C. Gilbert and J. L. Bower, "Disruptive Change: When Trying Harder Is Part of the Problem" from *Harvard Business Review* (May 2002): 95–101. Copyright © 2002 by the Harvard Business School Publishing Corporation. Reprinted with the permission of *Harvard Business Review.* All rights reserved.

Table 12.2: Reprinted with the permission of *Discover.*

Figures 12.6 and 12.7: From J. Gruber, *Public Finance and Public Policy.* Copyright © 2005. Reprinted with the permission of Worth Publishers, Inc.

Figure 12.9: J. Kerman and G. Tomlinson, *Listen, Brief Fifth Edition.* Copyright © 2004 by Bedford/St. Martin's. Reprinted with the permission of Bedford/St. Martin's.

Figure 12.10a: From G. A. Williams and R. B. Miller, "Change the Way You Persuade" from *Harvard Business Review* (May 2002). Copyright © 2002 by the Harvard Business School Publishing Corporation. Reprinted with the permission of *Harvard Business Review.* All rights reserved.

Figure 12.10b: From David Myers, "Module 1: The History and Scope of Psychology" in *Exploring Psychology, Fifth Edition in Modules.* Copyright © 2003. Reprinted with the permission of Worth Publishers, Inc.

Figure 12.10c: Reprinted with the permission of The Norman Rockwell Museum at Stockbridge.

Figure 12.17: From W. K. Purves, D. Sadava, G. H. Orians, and H. C. Heller, *Life: The Science of Biology, Seventh Edition.* Copyright © 2004. Reprinted with the permission of Sinauer Associates, Inc., Publishers.

Table 12.3: From Institute of Scientific and Technical Communicators, "Industry News" from *Communicator* (Spring 2005). Reprinted with the permission of the Institute of Scientific and Technical Communicators.

Table 12.3: From J. W. Valley, "A Cool Early Earth?" from *Scientific American* (October 2005): 58–65. Copyright © 2005 by Scientific American, Inc. All rights reserved. This figure includes all illustration by Lucy Reading-Ikkanda, which is reprinted with the permission of the illustrator.

Table 12.3: From W. K. Purves, D. Sadava, G. H. Orians, and H. C. Heller, *Life: The Science of Biology, Seventh Edition.* Copyright © 2004. Reprinted with the permission of Sinauer Associates, Inc., Publishers.

Table 12.3: From David Myers, *Exploring Psychology, Fifth Edition in Modules.* Copyright © 2003. Reprinted with the permission of Worth Publishers, Inc.

Table 12.3: From J. L. Roark, M. P. Johnson, P. C. Cohen, S. Stage, A. Lawson, and S. M. Hartman, *The American Promise: A History of the United States, Volume I: To 1877.* Copyright © 2005 by Bedford/St. Martin's. Reprinted with the permission of Bedford/St. Martin's.

Index

Note: f indicates a figure and t indicates a table.

INDEX OF FEATURES